THE ECONOMICS OF ADAM SMITH

STUDIES IN CLASSICAL POLITICAL ECONOMY / I

SAMUEL HOLLANDER

The economics
of Adam Smith

UNIVERSITY OF TORONTO PRESS
Toronto and Buffalo

© University of Toronto Press 1973
Toronto and Buffalo
Reprinted in paperback edition 1976
Printed in USA
ISBN 0-8020-1811-4 (cloth)
ISBN 0-8020-6302-0 (paper)
LC 72-185717

TO VINCENT BLADEN

CONTENTS

PREFACE   ix

INTRODUCTION   3
The neo-classical approach   3
to productive organization
Aspects of the 'marginal   7
revolution'
'Progress' in economics   11
Smithian economics: some   17
problems of interpretation
Plan of work   22

1/Aspects of the   25
pre-Smithian literature

I

AUTOMATIC EQUILIBRATING   27
PROCESSES
The scholastic tradition   27
Seventeenth-century   33
pamphlet literature
Some major eighteenth-   37
century contributions
The Physiocrats   44

2

ECONOMIC DEVELOPMENT   52
The mercantilist literature   52

Population size   59
Technical progress   65
The role of agriculture   68
The rate of interest   70
International adjustment   73
mechanisms
The physiocratic literature   78

II/The economics   93
of Adam Smith

3
THE INDUSTRY STRUCTURE   95
The agricultural sector   95
The manufacturing sector   98
Industrial organization   103
Manufacturing inputs   106
Mining and metallurgy   108
Summary and conclusion   109

4
THE THEORY OF VALUE   114
Price determination   114
The concept of competition   125
The role of utility and   133
demand

5

THE THEORY OF   144
DISTRIBUTION
The national income accounts   144
The distributive shares   147
Factor productivity   148
Factor supply   160
The theory as-a-whole   171
The declining rate of profit   179

6

CAPITAL ACCUMULATION   188
The savings process   188
The structure of capital   193
Wages as net income   199
The place of money in   205
accumulation

7

TECHNICAL CHANGE   208
The division of labour   209
Sources of technology   210
internal to the firm
Sources of technology external   213
to the firm
Constancy of materials-   217
output ratio
Wage-rate variations as a   219
motive for labour-saving
processes?
Technological displacement   223
of labour
Capital-saving technical   225
change and labour
displacement
Agricultural progress   227
Summary and conclusion: 236
Smith and the industrial
revolution

8

THE APPROACH TO ECONOMIC   242
DEVELOPMENT
The state of employment and   242
real wages

The desirability of economic   246
development
Government intervention in   256
economic development
Government and the labour   258
market
Alternative policy objectives   264
Summary and conclusion   266

9

FOREIGN TRADE: THEORY AND   268
POLICY
Vent-for-surplus theory   268
The analysis of colonial trade   270
policy
Efficiency advantage of trade   273

10

THE ANALYSIS OF   277
INVESTMENT PRIORITIES
Agriculture and manufactures   280
Industrial development   281
Some implications of Smithian   283
international trade theory
An agricultural bias?   286
Agricultural development   292
The trading sector   293
Direct foreign investment   300
A 'case-study'   302
Conclusion   304

CONCLUSION   305

Appendix A Eighteenth-   323
century population and
national income data
Appendix B The national   325
product of England and
Wales, c.1770
Appendix C Some growth   326
rates

BIBLIOGRAPHY OF WORKS CITED   328

INDEX   339

PREFACE

This book is intended to be the first of a series devoted to the major classical economists (Smith, Malthus, Ricardo, J.S. Mill, and Marx); accordingly, I have prepared a more detailed introduction than might otherwise be appropriate, and have borne in mind throughout the work the relationship between Smith and his intellectual successors. It is not one of my purposes to trace Smith's sources in precise detail, but since it is essential to place his contribution in broad perspective I have devoted two chapters to the pre-Smithian literature. It will be apparent that I do not eschew use of the term 'mercantilism,' despite a certain current hostility thereto. I also believe that the (cautious) treatment of Smith's economics apart from other branches of endeavour is a justified procedure, but due attention is paid to broader issues when the interpretation touches upon the desirability of economic development. And if there is a characteristic feature of the study it lies in its attempt to relate Smith's analysis to contemporary historical circumstances.

It is my hope that this study will prove of value to students; some of the materials have been adopted from lectures which I have given at the University of Toronto in undergraduate and graduate courses. My experience has been that secondary commentaries on the great economists – while essential as guides through the massive literature – leave no lasting impression unless considerable use is made of *direct* quotation, although it is, of course, a matter of personal taste where the line should be drawn. Close textual exegesis is also an efficient, though labour-intensive, means of eliminating at source a variety of Smith 'problems' and 'mysteries.'

Thanks are due to the editors of the *Southern Economic Journal* and *History of Political Economy* and to Hakkert Ltd. (Toronto) for permission to draw upon some already published work. I am most grateful to the John Simon Guggenheim Memorial Foundation for the grant of a fellowship during the academic year 1968–9, and to the Canada Council for grants in aid of research during the period 1969–71. Both sources of support were indispensable. This book has been published with the help of a grant from the Social Science Research Council of Canada, using funds provided by the Canada Council. I am happy also to express my appreciation to Lord Robbins, Joseph Dorfman, Karl Helleiner, William Jaffé, J.I. McDonald, J.C. McManus, George Slasor, and Donald Winch for their advice and critical observations. My greatest debt is to Professor V.W. Bladen, to whom this book is dedicated.

SAMUEL HOLLANDER
Toronto, February 1972

I have taken the opportunity of the issue of this paperback reprint to correct a number of minor errors and misprints. A more substantive correction which I would make in the event of a new edition relates to the extent of Smith's recognition of the Hume specie-flow mechanism. The impression given by my account (p. 305) is that Smith appreciated the operation of the mechanism in the context of his discussion of paper money issues. This view I now believe cannot be justified. However, I stand by the position that Smith placed great emphasis upon the mechanism in his analysis of a metallic currency.

On various occasions throughout the work, in the course of comparing Smith and Ricardo, reference is made to the central role in Ricardian analysis of the subsistence wage theory (e.g., p. 186). Further research on the economics of David Ricardo suggests that this allusion is erroneous. For analytical convenience Ricardo frequently assumed a *constant* real wage rate (as for example in his discussions of wage taxation) but not necessarily or usually at subsistence; moreover, his theory of growth presumes a *declining* secular real wage. This latter issue is taken up in Sir John Hicks and Samuel Hollander, 'Mr. Ricardo and the Moderns,' *Quarterly Journal of Economics*, 91 (1977).

There is little in the present work on the 'historical dimension' of the *Wealth of Nations* – including the notions of a materialist conception of history and developmental stages (the 'four stages theory') – which has recently attracted so much attention amongst scholars. In my view, these matters are best considered a digression as far as concerns the principal themes of the *Wealth of Nations* and may be set aside without endangering the accuracy of interpretation. This position is further developed in my forthcoming paper, '*The Wealth of Nations*: Foundation of Classical (Ricardian) Economics,' *Transactions of the Royal Society of Canada 1976*.

S.H.
Toronto, May 1976

THE ECONOMICS OF ADAM SMITH

INTRODUCTION

The neo-classical textbook approach to productive organization in conditions
of pure competition comprises a theory of distribution, or service pricing; for
the allocation process – itself accomplished by means of the price mechanism –
determines simultaneously the general level of each resource price by assuring
an equalization of returns among alternative uses. In the model, the demand
prices of productive resources in each branch of activity are derived through
the 'imputation' among them of the value of final products – the demand
prices of the latter depending upon the 'marginal' significance to consumers;
it is assumed that 'marginal' variations in the proportions in which services
can be combined are technically possible, so that the contribution of a
resource to the joint product can be isolated. Conversely, resource prices play
a role in the determination of product prices. This approach to productive
organization is one of general equilibrium (involving two systems of markets
and prices, one for products and one for resources) in which the meaning of
'economy' lies in the maximizing of a value return by each participating
individual.

It is with the foregoing standard of reference in mind that Professor Knight's
celebrated critique of the Ricardian theory of production and distribution
was written: 'Economic theory is nothing, or is significant only as an intellectual curiosity, unless it shows how, in a price economy, the price system works
out: (a) in the assignment of productive capacity in society to different
uses or industries; (b) in the technical organization of productive agents
within each industry; and (c) in the sharing of the joint product among the
co-operating individual owners of productive capacity. What is called "distribution theory" has to do with the pricing of productive services. These prices
are significant in connection with the division of the product, but their prior
and even more fundamental function is the dual one of apportioning produc-

tive capacity in the various forms among industries and among financial and technical productive units within each industry.'[1]

The Ricardian approach, by contrast, was to consider distribution in terms of three aggregative income shares, proceeding by way of a 'double dichotomy' – between land and labour-and-capital, and between labour and capital – whereby that part of the national product constituting the return to land-owners is explained by the theory of differential rent; and that part constituting the return to labour is explained by the subsistence theory of wages; while the residual constitutes profits. According to the critique Ricardo failed to recognize that the problem of distribution is a problem of 'valuation' in the sense that returns to factors represent competitively-determined prices of productive services.

This 'deficiency' is ascribed to a complete ignorance of the 'principles of analysis' which involve 'a conception of causality in the mechanistic or "positive" sense of function and variable; or, in less technical language, the relation between a continuously varying cause and its effect varying (quantitatively) in some corresponding way.' More specifically, what was required was at least 'an elementary grasp of the notion of increments, if not of the refinement of this in the theory of rates of change' since the 'effect of any cause must be measured as a variation in a total effect associated with a small variation in that cause, other elements of which it is part being held constant.'[2] It must be noted that what was involved in classical theory, according to Knight's view, is not merely the absence of a statement of a quantitative nature which constitutes the starting-off point for the derivation of a particular proposition *within* a given institutional framework and social organization. It is rather the absence of a basic analytical principle making it impossible to deal at all with the institutional framework described as an 'exchange economy.'

Furthermore, while the development of economic analysis is viewed, in the critique, as a matter of intellectual 'progression from error to truth,'[3] the Ricardian 'error,' in Knight's view, was *inexcusable* since the valid approach to productive organization was potentially within his grasp. Physical scientists had long understood that causes and effects must be brought into relation through various applications of 'the principle of small increments or rates of change.' Indeed it is one of the 'mysteries' of economic theory that the correct view of production and distribution was delayed since 'most of the essentials

1 Frank H. Knight, 'The Ricardian Theory of Production and Distribution,' *Canadian Journal of Economics and Political Science*, I (1935) 171–96; reprinted in Knight, *On the History and Method of Economics* (Chicago, 1956), 42. Cf: 'The 'correct' approach to the theory of distribution in economics is by way of a theory of productive organization; in fact, a sound distribution theory is hardly more than a corollary or footnote to an exposition of the mechanism by which resources are apportioned among different uses, and organized in each use, under the force of price competition' (*ibid.*, 61).

2 *Ibid.*, 40.

3 A definition of the 'absolutist' approach to historiography by Werner Stark, *History of Economics in Its Relation to Social Development* (London, 1944), 1.

are things of which no fairly intelligent adult living in a world where exchange relations are at all developed could possibly be ignorant.'[4]

With regard to Smith, the verdict is less severe. For in the analysis of 'Natural and Market Price' (*Wealth of Nations*, I, vii) Smith 'explicitly places the three types of productive agencies – land, labour and capital – in the same position and role in the process of economic readjustment and treats them all as productive capacity, not as "pain." Smith makes it fairly clear that the process of adjustment is one of transferring resources of any of the three kinds (individually) from less to more remunerative uses until the remuneration in all competing fields is equalized.'[5]

Much the same view of the 'valid' approach to production and distribution is taken in the commentary by J.A. Schumpeter: 'Production in the economic sense of the term is nothing but a combination, by purchase, of requisite and scarce services. In this process, each of the requisite and scarce services secures a price, and the determination of these prices is all that distribution or income formation fundamentally consists in. Thus the process effects, in one and the same series of steps, production in the economic sense, and through the evaluation of productive services incident to production, also distribution or the formation of incomes.'[6] And while 'Professor Knight went perhaps too far if he accused Ricardo of not having seen the problem of distribution as a problem of valuation *at all* ... it is true that Ricardo failed to see the explanatory principle offered by the valuation aspect.'[7] Similarly, the fundamental source of the Ricardian failure is reduced to an inability 'to understand substitution (both of factors and of products) in its full importance.'[8] Indeed the absence

---

4 Knight, 'The Ricardian Theory,' 42. Cf. 'Practically all the fundamentals of economic analysis are too obvious to be really overlooked by any observer who thinks about the problems at all' (*ibid.*, 74).

5 *Ibid.*, 64.

6 J.A. Schumpeter, *History of Economic Analysis* (New York, 1954), 567.

7 *Ibid.*, 568. Cf. 543n.: 'The full implications of the fact that capitalist distribution is a value phenomenon were not clearly seen even by Ricardo.' In fact, Knight was careful to allow for exceptions to the rule, conceding the interpretive problems thus raised: 'General negative statements are to be taken subject to interpretation. They mean that the system expounded by the writers does not take account of the facts in question. To say that they absolutely failed to see anything essential to a sound theory is generally too strong ... Such general negative statements are in no wise disproved by citing particular passages in which the fact or principle in question is, or seems to be, recognized. But it is sometimes a matter of interpretation whether they are taken into account where they need to be' (Knight, 'The Ricardian Theory,' 41–2n). Indeed the 'problem of interpreting the classical works in their treatment of distribution is more obscure than it would be if all theory of organization were absent' (*ibid.*, 63). Thus an exception is seen in the Ricardian theory of rent which 'involves a rudimentary recognition of the notion of increments and of imputation' (*ibid.*, 40n). The same view held by Schumpeter, *History of Economic Analysis*, 590; *Economic Doctrine and Method* (1912; London, 1954), 131.

8 Schumpeter, *History of Economic Analysis*, 680n. The reference to *substitution of products*, in addition to factor substitution, should be noted carefully. It is of particular significance in the discussion below of general equilibrium mechanisms.

of a principle of substitution 'constitutes one of the most serious shortcomings of [the classical] analytical apparatus.'[9] It may be noted here that insofar as a degree of insight into the 'correct' view of productive organization is to be found upon occasion in Adam Smith's *Wealth of Nations* (and in the work of J.B. Say, Lauderdale, Malthus, and Senior), Schumpeter regards the Ricardian approach as a 'detour,' an aberration, in the general progress of economic analysis.[10]

The approach to the history of economics adopted in the above accounts implies belief in a process of what is sometimes called 'development-by-accumulation' towards the present state of knowledge. The function of the historian is to provide an account of the successive increments, and of the 'errors' which inhibited a more rapid accumulation of the modern truth. We shall consider the validity of this approach, within the context of the present issue.[11] It is worthwhile, at the outset, to place the neo-classical critique in

9 Schumpeter, *History of Economic Analysis*, 590. Cf. *ibid.*, 568: 'It is nothing short of pathetic that, owing to a complete lack of understanding on the part of opponents and owing to a complete ignorance of even the most elementary mathematical tools on the part of exponents, this promising start [towards an appreciation of the production-distribution process of capitalist society as a web of exchanges, by J.B. Say, Lauderdale, Malthus and Senior] not only was left to hibernate for decades but also acquired a reputation for superficiality and sterility.' In Schumpeter, *Economic Doctrine and Method*, 114, the failure to develop the so-called 'productivity theory of distribution' is attributed to 'the lamentable incompetence of some of its representatives.'

10 Schumpeter, *History of Economic Analysis*, 568, 1010. We may recall Schumpeter's unbounded admiration for Léon Walras, who it is said, was the first to realize all the advantages of ascending to a high level of ' "generalizing abstraction" on which we construct a composite instrument or engine or organon of economic analysis ... which functions *formally* in the same way, whatever the economic problem to which we may turn it' (*ibid.*, 16). Schumpeter (either explicitly or implicitly) frequently utilized proximity to the Walrasian ideal – namely the mathematical formulation of the general equilibrium system – as a standard of reference in his evaluations of past performance. There seems to be some truth to the suggestion that Schumpeter's admiration for the Walrasian model may be accounted for partially in terms of the *sentiment de rationalité* which it generates. (Cf. W. Stark, 'The "Classical Situation" in Political Economy,' *Kyklos*, XII (1959), 58.)

   The well-known account of the classical theory of production and distribution by Edwin Cannan (*A History of the Theories of Production and Distribution From 1776 to 1848*, 3rd ed. (London, 1917; New York, 1966) utilizes no such standard of reference in terms of a general equilibrium approach to productive organization based upon the principle of substitution. In this case the criteria are simply that a meaningful theory of production must deal with the determinants of *per capita* annual produce – with economic development in effect – while the subject-matter of a theory of distribution must be the division of the aggregate produce (preferably between income from labour and income from property) *ibid.*, 299–301.

11 A splendid account of the 'absolutist' historical method in the physical sciences – which emphasizes scientific progress as a continuous accumulation of present truth – is given in T.S. Kuhn, *The Structure of Scientific Revolutions*, 2nd ed. (Chicago, 1970) especially pp. 1f., 95–6, 137–43, Kuhn attempts to demonstrate the invalidity of the approach, and provides evidence in support of the view that in fact science develops by way of revolutionary and discontinuous reformulations of the preceding scientific tradition. (See below, 12f.)

perspective by a brief consideration of some of the post-1870 'marginalist' developments.

ASPECTS OF THE 'MARGINAL REVOLUTION'

Considerable dissatisfaction on empirical grounds was expressed with the concept of a *short-period* marginal product – the additional product due to a small increase in the quantity of labour when the quantity of co-operating capital is unchanged – almost from its inception. The fundamental requirement of the theory *at the level of the enterprise* is that technical methods should be freely variable. It is only then possible to reorganize the business by reducing the number of units of a factor used together with given amounts of other factors without rendering a part of the supply of the fixed factors *completely useless*, or to increase the variable factor and derive some positive product.[12] In the event that these alterations are technically ruled out, the reduction in output in the first case would far exceed the amount that can be attributed to that factor; and in the second, the contribution to output would be zero. Such a range evidently renders the theory useless in explaining wage and employment decisions by the firm.

One argument which was offered in defence by J.B. Clark is that the theory presumes the possibility of alterations in the 'forms' taken by capital, implying a degree of flexibility which permits the nature of capital equipment to be altered without any alteration in its aggregate amount.[13] But Clark's concession that such changes in form are only relevant in the long run left the main objection intact.[14] Moreover, there remained considerable scepticism regarding the manner in which, and the degree to which, a modern large-scale, fully-utilized enterprise might employ additional labour unless *in fact* it expanded capacity.[15]

Marshall (and Edgeworth) gave lessons in partial differentiation in reply to the celebrated rejection of marginal productivity by J.A. Hobson. What is

12 Even in the case of variability the reduction of one input will entail the less advantageous use of those inputs held constant. But that part of their supply becomes completely useless is another matter.

13 J.B. Clark, *Distribution of Wealth* (New York, 1899), 159. Cf. D. Robertson's famous example of the absorption of a tenth man into the ditch-digging crew by providing each with ten smaller or cheaper spades than were the original nine, in 'Wage Grumbles,' *Economic Fragments* (London, 1931), reprinted in William Fellner and Bernard F. Haley, eds., *Readings in the Theory of Income Distribution* (Philadelphia, 1951), 225.

14 Cf. J.R. Hicks, *Theory of Wages* (London, 1932), 20–1. 'Since the whole conception of marginal productivity depends upon the variability of industrial methods, little advantage seems to be gained from the attempt which is sometimes made to define a 'short period marginal product' – the additional production due to a small increase in the quantity of labour, when not only the quantity, but also the form, of the co-operating capital is unchanged. It is very doubtful if this conception can be given any precise meaning which is capable of useful application.'

15 'For if the capitalist is to be allowed time and facilities for turning his spades into a steam plough, it seems unreasonable not to allow him time and facilities for turning them into beer. The notion that, with a defined quantity of capital and a defined quantity of labour, there is, in a certain defined sense, a definite marginal produc-

involved it was pointed out, is not a *finite* product at the margin but a rate of change of total product relative to the variable input. The units are infinitesimal so that the objection that variations in output cannot be attributed to the variable input alone is unfounded.[16] Evidently this is quite unsatisfactory as a defence of the marginal productivity theory. It is an argument which presumes a differentiable production function and it is precisely this form of the production function which Hobson questioned.

The fact that Marshall himself gave an alternative answer in terms of joint demand for inputs suggests that he may have realized this. The case of the marginal shepherd who requires the support of co-operating factors will be recalled. The problem as expressed by Marshall is that 'the net product of such shepherds cannot be ascertained simply; but it is a case of derived demand, and requires us to take account of the prices which have to be paid for the aid of all these other agents of production.'[17] But the theory of derived demand[18] deals with the *joint use* of inputs. In fact Marshall is quite explicit that this problem entails severe delimitation of the marginal productivity theory of distribution: 'This doctrine has sometimes been put forward as a theory of wages. But there is no valid ground for any such pretension. The doctrine that the earnings of a worker tend to be equal to the net product of his work has by itself no real meaning; since in order to estimate net product we have to take for granted all the expenses of production of the commodity on which he works, other than his own wages.'[19] Thus Marshall's suggestion does not avoid the assumption of *fixed proportions*; and even in this case we can proceed to derive demand prices of one input only with prior knowledge of the prices of complementary inputs.

However, it *may* be possible to avoid the latter weakness if we interpret

tivity of labour, does not lose its validity; but it seems to become, under certain conditions, less interesting as a guide to conduct, than some expositions of the theory would lead us to hope ... For instance, the tendency to industrial rationalization is, in one of its aspects, a tendency to install such elaborate and expensive and durable plant, and to devise such a close and intimate co-ordination between it and the labour force required to work it, as to leave as little room as possible for the operation of the Principle of Variation. Under such conditions the position and shape of the true or Clarkian curve of marginal productivity may well become a matter of somewhat remote interest.' Robertson, 'Wage Grumbles,' 228–9. Cf. Hans Neisser, ' "Permanent" Technological Unemployment,' *American Economic Review*, XXXII (March 1942), 67.

16 Alfred Marshall, in C.W. Guillebaud, ed., *Principles of Economics*, 9th (*variorum*) ed. (London, 1961), I, 409–10n; F.Y. Edgeworth, *Papers Relating to Political Economy*, II (London, 1925), 19–20n.

17 *Ibid.*, II, 586, in 3rd to 5th editions only. The notion of net product is defined at one point in the following manner (*ibid.*, I, 406): 'He estimates as best he can how much *net product* (i.e. net addition to the value of his total product) will be caused by a certain extra use of any one agent; *net*, that is, after deducting for any extra expenses that may be indirectly caused by the change, and adding for any incidental savings.'

18 *Ibid.*, I, 383.

19 *Ibid.*, I, 518.

Marshall here as offering a general – rather than a partial – equilibrium solution. For, even when factor proportions are fixed, it is not necessarily the case that the returns to factors are indeterminate causing the mechanism of competitive adjustment to collapse. If the ratios in which factors must be combined differ from sector to sector the competitive process may yet assure a determinate solution.[20] Interestingly enough the process of inter-industry adjustment is sometimes regarded as applicable in the short-run period during which the 'principle of variation' may not be fully operative.[21] If we allow both for the inter-industry process and for the principle of variation, then in full long-run equilibrium the net product and the marginal product must be equal since there can be no advantageous opportunities *either* of transferring the resources between industries, *or* of altering the proportions between factors – the 'process' in effect – in the establishment.

Even if the possibility of 'internal' factor substitutability is conceded, the relative importance thereof compared with inter-industry commodity substitution as an equilibrating mechanism cannot be evaluated *a priori*. It may be added that *in practice* both mechanisms might be overshadowed by the absorption effects of changes in the actual size of plants, since there is no reason to expect that the period of time during which it is possible to vary the 'form' taken by capital is any shorter than that needed to vary its aggregate quantity. In brief, formal recognition of internal factor substitutability tells us nothing about the practical significance of this particular equilibrating mechanism compared with others.[22]

Of greater theoretical significance, the mechanism of commodity substitu-

20 On this mechanism, see Fritz Machlup, 'On the Meaning of the Marginal Product,' in *Explorations in Economics: Essays in Honor of F.W. Taussig* (1936), reprinted in *Readings in the Theory of Income Distribution*, 172; Hicks, *Theory of Wages*, 13–14.

21 Machlup, 'Marginal Product,' 173. 'The principle of variation and the [Marshallan] principle of net productivity yield the same results, if enough time is allowed for the former to come into full play. But also in the short run one may consider the strict marginality principle as fully satisfied by the net productivity principle. For it secures, for the economy as a whole, through factor transfers between different establishments, the perfect variability of proportions which is postulated by the clause that "additional units of one factor are used with a given (unchanged) amount of other factors".' Cf. Hicks, *Theory of Wages*, 14.

22 For the most part, the 'empirical' arguments – both of a critical and defensive nature – were of the armchair variety, at least until quite recently. The difficulties of observation even at the purely technological level are outlined in a well-known paper by E.H. Phelps Brown. The problems are least severe in agriculture where it is frequently possible to vary one factor by small amounts while changes in product-quality or kind are small enough to allow the expression in a common physical unit of different outputs. Thus all the data of the Econometric Committee on Source Materials for Quantitative Production Studies (established in 1932), as well as Marshall's evidence, related to the effects on yields of different amounts of ploughing and harrowing. But even in agriculture a wide range of conditions escape control. See E.H. Phelps Brown, 'The Marginal Efficacy of a Productive Factor – First Report of the *Econometrica* Committee on Source Materials for Quantitative Production Studies,' *Econometrica*, IV (1936), 123–37.

tion (by itself) may not permit the absorption of any amount of a factor, even though the mechanism may be highly relevant in explaining the *stability* of the system (assuming that it possesses an equilibrium solution in the first place). Similarly, a system of equations in which the coefficients of production are variable, but in which the production functions are similar from sector to sector, need not possess a meaningful solution; the relevant consideration is the degree of elasticity of technical substitutability. It may be shown that unemployment of some factors may result from restraints imposed by the pattern of resource endowment, technology, and the structure of demand – despite formal price flexibility – which precludes the absorption of all factors at positive prices.[23]

The possibility that a determinate solution might not exist in the pricing of factors was not raised by Marshall[24] or by the Austrians. And the problem is neatly avoided by Léon Walras. The data of the basic Walrasian system include consumers' tastes and the quantities of productive services, the technical coefficients, and *the propensities of service owners to consume them or part with them.*[25] It is on this basis that Walras set out to show that a consistent set of quantities and prices exists, and concluded that a (stable) solution in fact is yielded. In the model, the possibility of an indeterminate solution is not apparent since 'excess factors' can always be absorbed into non-industrial uses.[26]

Those who are confident in the determinacy of the general equilibrium model tend to minimize the problem outlined above on the grounds that the principle of variation will ultimately come into its own and contribute, *along with* commodity substitution, to the clearing of factor markets. Of course, it is true that the likelihood of indeterminacy diminishes when both mechanisms are operative, but even in this case there is no *guarantee* of determinacy unless we allow for the absorption of factors into non-industrial uses.

We have seen that in defending the theory of marginal productivity,[27] the marginalists conceded much, admitting that little confidence could be placed

---

23 For full discussions see Neisser, ' "Permanent" Technological Unemployment'; Masao Fukuoka, 'Full Employment and Constant Coefficients of Production,' *Quarterly Journal of Economics*, LXIX (Feb. 1955), 23–44; and Richard S. Eckaus, 'The Factor Proportions Problem in Underdeveloped Areas,' *American Economic Review* (Sept. 1955), 539–65.

24 See the formulation of general equilibrium in Note XXI of Mathematical Appendix, *Principles of Economics*, I, 855.

25 *Elements of Pure Economics*, 1st ed. (1874); 4th (definitive) ed. (1926); ed. W. Jaffé (London, 1954), 237f.

26 See Kenneth J. Arrow and Gerard Debreu, 'Existence of Equilibrium for a Competitive Economy,' *Econometrica*, XXII (July 1954), 265–90, especially the historical note, 287–9, relating to the discussions centred on that version of the Walrasian fixed coefficient system which did not allow for the possibility of direct use by service owners, by Gustav Cassel, *Theory of Social Economy* (New York, 1924).

27 That is, the version which assumes general substitutability between factors to apply rather than that utilizing constant coefficients of production and relying upon substitution between products, or inter-industry substitution.

in the notion of a 'short-run' marginal product. The modern version of the theory makes these concessions explicitly; in the final resort the theory, as utilized in the analysis of the behaviour of the competitive 'firm,' simply defines the conditions that must be satisfied for the assurance of profit maximization. Unless the price of each factor equals the value of its marginal product opportunities exist to alter advantageously the methods used.[28] This interpretation suggests that the production function incorporating substitutability between factors 'is valid only at a high level of abstraction, for planned and not for existing plants ...; as we approach the patterns of real business life we lose that pure logic more and more from sight. ... The fundamental analytical schema that uses nothing but the substitutional relation needs to be supplemented if we wish to approach reality more closely, but remains valid within its proper sphere.'[29] It is clear that the range and importance of the conclusions which can be derived from the theory at the level of the firm are considerably constrained.[30]

Moreover, our discussion indicates that the conception of incremental change applied to factor relations at the level of the enterprise constitutes neither a necessary nor a sufficient condition for the achievement of general equilibrium. From this point of view as well, the significance of factor substitutability is much reduced.[31]

'PROGRESS' IN ECONOMICS

It is clear from the above account that there has been an advance in our appreciation of the operation of the price mechanism, in the sense that we are

28 Cf. Hicks, *Theory of Wages*, 21: 'it is not true to say that a man's wage must always (or even normally) equal his marginal product ... If wages are above the marginal productivity of labour, entrepreneurs have an incentive to contract employment; they will contract their output, and contract it in such a way as to use less labour proportionally to other factors than they have previously been doing. This may not be feasible at once; it may have to wait until machinery comes to be replaced; however, an incentive to the dismissal of labour exists, and the employment of a certain number of labourers is so far precarious.'

29 Schumpeter, *History of Economic Analysis*, 1038–9. A similar view is adopted by F. Machlup, 'Marginal Analysis and Empirical Research,' *American Economic Review*, XXXVI (Sept. 1946), 519–54, to the effect that the marginal net value product curves of modern theory must be understood as curves *imagined* by the entrepreneur but having no objective significance.

30 Cf. M.W. Reder, 'A Reconsideration of the Marginal Productivity Theory,' *Journal of Political Economy*, LV (Oct. 1947), 450.

31 Cf. P.A. Samuelson, in D. McCord Wright, ed., *The Impact of the Labor Union* (1951; New York, 1966), 327 regarding the marginal productivity theory: 'Its recognition and assertion of substitutability among inputs within the firm does provide one extra reason for elasticity in the sloping demand curve for labor. But except for this I cannot see that this theory is particularly relevant to the question of whether competition will result in low or high wages, or of whether collective bargaining can hope to raise wages. Within the realm of economic theory itself, marginal productivity relations are one subset of the conditions of general equilibrium; and if the existence of the partial derivative postulated by this theory contradicted technological fact, the status of labor economics would be in no significant sense altered.'

now aware to a degree hitherto unsurpassed of the necessary and sufficient conditions for general equilibrium. The modern economist who, for example, incorporates fixed factor proportions into his model does so consciously and with awareness of the consequences. We therefore take the view that it is meaningful to talk of 'progress' *within the present context*.[32]

On the other hand, the rather extreme 'absolutist' approach to the history of economics discussed in the first section of this chapter is, in light of the preceding discussion, clearly unsatisfactory insofar as it takes for granted that the 'neo-classical' approach to productive organization is an obvious one, clear to any 'fairly intelligent adult.' The severe conceptual difficulties presented by the notion of marginal productivity and the subsequent debate regarding the scope of the marginal-productivity theory suggest that this is not the case. Moreover, the legitimacy of the emphasis in the critique by Professor Knight upon the role of variable proportions in the general equilibrium solution may be questioned. The more recent approaches tend to accord the mechanism less weight insofar as the application of incremental analysis to factor combinations is not a necessary condition of equilibrium.

Neither is it legitimate, in our view, to suggest that the neo-classical model, wherein distribution and value theory are inextricably combined, is in some sense the 'correct' one. The conceptions of 'paradigm' and of 'normal science' developed by T.S. Kuhn are of relevance here. Paradigms are defined as

32 It was the view of Professor Schumpeter that it is meaningful to talk of 'progress' in *analytical* economics, since it is within the competence of professionals in the field (at any given time) to recognize 'unambiguously' the differential qualities of alternative technical apparatuses. (*History of Economic Analysis*, 7.) But the fact is that Schumpeter, rather inconsistently, conceded that 'Although it is possible ... to speak for every epoch of established professional opinion *on scientific topics* ... we cannot speak with as much confidence about it as can physicists and mathematicians.' Our own standards are not 'absolutely valid' because our rules of procedure are always 'subject to controversy and in a state of flux' (*ibid.*, 6–8). Thus in an evaluation of the analytical quality of mercantilist writing – the separation of 'substandard chaff from valuable wheat' – he asks: 'what, beyond a rather small number of performances on which we may all agree, is the wheat? Here, every one of us must rely on his personal evaluation of analytic quality – the only kind of value judgments that are both permissible and unavoidable in a history of scientific economics – a matter in which often the only agreement attainable will be the agreement to differ' (*ibid.*, 348). Not surprisingly Schumpeter's various accounts of the 'quality' of mercantilist analysis were not consistent. Cf. William R. Allen, 'Modern Defenders of Mercantilist Theory,' *History of Political Economy*, II (fall 1970), 384–5.

A more pertinent example of the contradictions into which Schumpeter was drawn is his treatment of Smithian economics. For, in presenting his methodological position he conceded that the Smithian system of political economy – the policy program – was but the 'cloak of a great analytic achievement' (*ibid.*, 38). Yet subsequently he wrote: 'The fact is that the *Wealth of Nations* does not contain a single *analytic* idea, principle, or method that was entirely new in 1776.' Smith's function was merely that of co-ordinator: 'His mental stature was up to mastering the unwieldy material that flowed from many sources and to subjecting it, with a strong hand, to the rule of a small number of coherent principles' (*Ibid.*, 184–5).

'universally recognized scientific achievements that for a time provide model problems and solutions to a community of practitioners.'[33] Scientists engaged in 'normal science' are concerned with the solution to 'puzzles' following the rules of the game established by the paradigm.[34] Concern with these rules – paradigm-testing as distinct from puzzle-solving – occurs only during periods of crisis and is generated by the appearance of anomalous puzzles not amenable to solution within the established frame of reference.[35] An alternative structure *may* in turn replace the original. What is of particular interest is the proposition that to a degree alternative paradigms are 'incommensurable.' It is true that the newly successful one can apparently deal with the anomaly, but it answers only one question in the first instance; there is no assurance that it can deal equally well with others which arise.[36] Moreover, something is lost as well as gained in the transfer insofar as previously standard procedures and questions are discarded; paradigm changes typically are 'destructive as well as constructive,'[37] so that 'the normal-scientific tradition that emerges from a scientific revolution is not only incompatible but often actually incommensurable with that which has gone before.'[38] The choice between paradigms is not, therefore, made on purely 'objective' grounds.

We do not intend to suggest that the concept of a 'paradigm' can be applied unambiguously to economics.[39] But there is an inherent attraction in the implication that the concept of 'progress' (and the comparability of technical performances) is more meaningful once we are assured that a past writer is dealing with the same 'basic theory' as our own.[40] Accordingly, we adopt the position that the use of modern analytical tools, concepts, and procedures may be of considerable aid in an analysis of the work of an early writer, *provided that he was operating within the general frame of reference for which these devices are appropriate*. In particular, we believe that there is justification for the utilization of the current state of knowledge regarding the general equilibrium process in a study of the economics of Adam Smith insofar as he adopted the position that the price mechanism can be relied upon to clear product and factor markets. We may therefore seek for the variety of equilibrating

33 *The Structure of Scientific Revolutions*, viii; cf. also 10f., 23f.
34 *Ibid.*, 35f.
35 *Ibid.*, 52f.
36 *Ibid.*, 153.
37 *Ibid.*, 66
38 *Ibid.*, 103.
39 Cf. discussions of the issue by D.F. Gordon, 'The Role of the History of Economic Thought in the Understanding of Modern Economic Theory,' *American Economic Review*, LV (May 1965), 119–27; G.J. Stigler, 'Does Economics Have a Useful Past?' *History of Political Economy*, I (fall 1969), 217–30; A.W. Coats, 'Is there a "Structure of Scientific Revolutions" in Economics?' *Kyklos*, XXII (1969), 289–96.
40 It may be noted that despite Professor Kuhn's emphasis upon the element of incommensurability of paradigms he nonetheless appears to believe that there is some sense in which, at least in the physical sciences, it is still possible to weigh their merits (cf. *The Structure of Scientific Revolutions*, 8, 66, 140f., 148f., 160f.).

mechanisms which he assumed to bring about the result, utilizing in the process the categories of modern theory. Professor Samuelson has justifiably noted that 'there is a worse sin than the anthropomorphic one of reading modern analysis into older writers' works. There is in addition the sophisticated-anthropomorphic sin of not recognizing the equivalent content in older writers because they do not use the terminology and symbols of the present.'[41] Moreover, whether or not an early writer himself recognized a legitimate role for model-building, a case may be made for the formalization of his theoretical arguments. The main objective of such an exercise is to isolate not only the explicit assumptions but also the implicit assumptions of which he himself was perhaps unaware, and might not even have found acceptable.[42] The historian must, however, be alive to the danger that, in following this procedure, he will end up with an account of 'Smithian' or 'Ricardian' economics rather than the economics of Adam Smith or David Ricardo; it cannot be too strongly emphasized that it is with the latter that we are concerned.

The current approach to productive organization – with its basic postulate of the maximizing individual in a free market – might, however, in some cases be an invalid frame of reference. This is so, for example, in a discussion of a writer within the historical or institutionalist tradition. Here the rules of the game are not the same and the different traditions are in a real sense incommensurable. Even in the case of a work such as that of Smith there may be *particular* theoretical concepts which cannot be discussed in terms of the current theory of allocation. For these concepts had other purposes in mind and their logical and empirical validity can only be appreciated in light of these objectives.

The issue may also be illustrated from the work of Ricardo. The classification of Ricardian economics as a 'detour' in the general advance of economic analysis might be valid if it can be demonstrated that the characteristically 'Ricardian' features lie within the tradition of allocation economics. That this is so is by no means certain. To the extent that Ricardo was in fact developing an alternative 'basic theory' – whereby distribution and value are treated *separately* – the view of Knight and Schumpeter according to which his approach is 'non-scientific' and in error is seriously misleading. In this regard we may take note of recent work by Piero Sraffa which can be interpreted as a modern attack in Ricardian terms upon the foundations of orthodox doctrine.[43] His discovery of a number of 'paradoxes' in neo-classical capital theory regarding the choice of techniques is one of the most serious specific challenges ever directed at the neo-classical structure.[44] An even more potent challenge lies in the proposition that a 'quantity of capital' is meaningless

41 Review of Hla Myint, *Theories of Welfare Economics* (London, 1948), in *Economica*, XV (Nov. 1949), 373.

42 Cf. J.J. Spengler, 'Adam Smith's Theory of Economic Growth – Part II,' *Southern Economic Journal*, XXVI (July 1951), 5f.

43 *Production of Commodities by Means of Commodities: Prelude to a Critique of Economic Theory* (Cambridge, 1963).

44 Cf. the concession by Professor Paul Samuelson, 'Paradoxes in Capital Theory,' *Quarterly Journal of Economics*, LXXX (Nov. 1966), 579.

apart from the rate of profit, so that the explanation of the rate of profit in terms of the 'marginal product of capital' breaks down.

The extent to which Marxian economics falls within the tradition of economic equilibrium via the price mechanism is a particularly interesting issue. It may well be the case that the 'debate' between Marxist and orthodox economists regarding the validity of the marginalist developments of the 1870s cannot by its nature be resolved by logical or empirical testing.

The problem is complicated when a writer unwittingly adopts simultaneously two inconsistent basic theories. It is, for example, an open issue whether Ricardo, while attempting to introduce a new model, nonetheless retained parts of Smith's allocative framework which in certain key respects was inconsistent with it. Similarly the question arises with regard to Smith himself insofar as certain theoretical structures relating to the process of economic growth, it has been suggested, conflict with the basic theory of economic equilibrium via the price mechanism. This particular issue will be taken up in some detail presently.

Yet another qualification is in order. Even when we are assured of a common 'basic theory' the present state of the science is an unsatisfactory yardstick for the *evaluation* of a past performance; although as already maintained, it may provide a helpful catalogue of questions to ask about the work. Professor Kuhn has referred to the potential effects of external conditions upon the development of the physical sciences, particularly in transforming anomalies which cannot be resolved by a particular 'paradigm' into acute crises, and in influencing the range of alternative revolutionary reforms.[45] There can be no question that in a study of the economics of Adam Smith, great attention must be paid to external influences, for although it is true that he was not the *first* to formulate the general theory of economic equilibrium by way of the price mechanism he was an early exponent. While environmental influences may be particularly significant during times of *exceptional* intellectual unrest, it would be premature for the historian of economics to rule them out at other times too. Our expectation regarding their potential significance will depend upon the extent to which we may talk in the first place of a well established 'basic theory' and the cohesiveness of the scientific community adhering to it. In the case of the basic theory of economic equilibrium both the formulation itself and the relevant 'community' are so loosely defined − at least for substantial parts of a lengthy timespan − that it would be foolhardy to neglect consideration of the potential influence of external circumstances, particularly in a study dealing with a period prior to the professionalization of economics as a science.[46]

It is precisely because of the need to make allowance for historical conditions

45 *The Structure of Scientific Revolutions*, x.
46 Cf. J.J. Spengler, 'Exogenous and Endogenous Influences in the Formation of Post-1870 Economic Thought,' in R.V. Eagly, ed., *Events, Ideology and Economic Theory* (Detroit, 1968), 159f., and discussion by Eagly (*ibid.*, 188f); G.J. Stigler. 'The Influence of Events and Politics on Economic Theory,' in Stigler, *Essays in the History of Economics* (Chicago, 1965), 16f.

that attribution of meaning to 'progress' in economics does not lead us to the conclusion that the present state of knowledge is the relevant standard for evaluation.[47] Moreover, even when we are able to assert that an early con-

47 Although Schumpeter's 'main purpose' in the *History of Economic Analysis* was 'to describe what may be called the process of Filiation of Scientific Ideas – the process by which men's efforts to understand economic phenomena produce, improve, and pull down analytical structures in an unending sequence' (*ibid.*, 6), he none-theless allowed for the influence of external events, recognizing a variety of obstacles in the way of the 'progressive' development of economic analysis: 'Scientific analysis is not simply a logically consistent process that starts with some primitive notions and then adds to the stock in a straight-line fashion. It is not simply progressive discovery of an objective reality – as is, for example, discovery in the basin of the Congo. *Rather it is an incessant struggle with creations of our own and our predecessors' minds and it 'progresses,' if at all, in a criss-cross fashion, not as logic, but as the impact of new ideas or observations or needs, and also as the bents and temperaments of new men dictate*' (*ibid.*, 4, author's emphasis). These impediments derive essentially from two related facts. First, the subject matter of economics is a 'unique process in historic time' to the extent that the source of the materials used are derived from specific historical experiences. Since it is impossible for an economist to use more material than is actually available, theoretical results which are achieved at any time may not be justified in the light of further experience. Moreover the institutional frameworks which are subsumed in theoretical models have application to specific historical conditions. It follows that the scope and validity of 'economic laws' work out differently in different institutional circumstances (*ibid.*, 12–3; 20–1). (These conditions provide the rationale for the role accorded by Schumpeter to economic history of *primus inter pares* amongst the fundamental fields of economic analysis, namely economic history, statistics, economic theory and economic sociology.) Historical relativity intrudes also *via* a second route. The economist himself 'is the product of a given social environment – and of his particular location in this environment – that condition him to see certain things rather than others, and to see them in a certain light. And even this is not all: environmental factors may even endow the observer with a subconscious craving to see things in a certain light' (*ibid.*, 34; cf. *ibid.*, 13). Here Schumpeter touches upon the question of ideological bias.
    It is still possible, he maintained, to isolate the points at which ideological and general environmental influences are most likely to appear. New analytical effort is preceded by a 'vision' of a set of loosely related phenomena calling for investigation. The vision – 'a preanalytic cognitive act' – is almost definitionally ideological in the above sense; but *in principle* these subjective elements can be eradicated. The precise formulation of the constituent elements of the initial vision, the subsequent application of statistical and theoretical methods derived from the analyst's tool box, the use of rules of logic, and the incorporation of new facts will verify or destroy all or parts of the initial vision. In brief, the use of 'neutral' procedures is capable of assuring the eradication of ideologically vitiated elements (*ibid.*, 41–3; cf. *ibid.*, 15).
    The view of progress in 'criss-cross' fashion seems to be a potentially helpful one if we apply it to the development of the basic theory of general equilibrium via the price mechanism (particularly prior to 1870). But whether we can be confident in the operation of processes whereby ideological bias is eradicated is an open question. For an alternative view to that of Schumpeter see, in particular, Gunnar Myrdal, *The Political Element in the Development of Economic Theory* (London, 1953); R.L. Meek, 'Economics and Ideology,' *Scottish Journal of Political*

tribution is faulty according to our lights – making full allowance for the particular historical conditions of the time – we may nevertheless consider it to be of the highest scientific quality when evaluated according to the 'professional' standards of the time. And it would be the latter index which is more meaningful than the current state of knowledge.[48] Judgment of performance should not, however, be defined simply in terms of how a theory stands up, compared with that of the writer's predecessors, when formulated mathematically. The qualifications, and the precise *emphasis* placed upon the crucial elements are, in our view, as significant as any degree of novelty.

SMITHIAN ECONOMICS: SOME PROBLEMS OF INTERPRETATION

In this book we are concerned more with interpretation than with ranking according to 'originality,' or any other index. It is our view that it is impossible to understand the underlying intention of the *Wealth of Nations* without ascertaining not only the nature of the British economy of Smith's day but equally, or even more important, Smith's vision thereof. Furthermore, since this is a critical study we are interested in the *accuracy* of the picture portrayed, that is in Smith's qualities as an observer. We shall also examine the procedures utilized by Smith in his attempts to explain and understand the contemporary economy. For this purpose we adopt a working definition of scientific method suggested by Professor Letwin: 'One of the chief elements of the scientific method is a taste for economy in analysis, an abhorence of *ad hoc* explanations, a determination to explain as wide as possible a range of phenomena in terms of a few simple principles.'[49] Can it be said that Smith adopted the 'scientific method' in this sense? What were the range of phenomena to be accounted for? What were the 'simple principles' adopted in the process? And how much light was cast by the theoretical devices utilized?

We can only hope to provide convincing answers to the latter questions if

Economy (Feb. 1957), IV, reprinted in Meek, *Economics and Ideology and Other Essays* (London, 1967), 196–224; and Joan Robinson, *Economic Philosophy* (London, 1962).

48 Cf. Schumpeter, *History of Economic Analysis*, 8–9. We may refer to an interesting Schumpeterian *obiter dictum* which also implies that the relevant criterion of quality is the contemporary and not the present standard: 'At all times, including the present, in judging from the standpoint of the requirements of each period (not judging the state of the theory as it was at any time by standards of a later time) the performance of economic theory has been below reasonable expectation and open to valid criticism' (*ibid.*, 18–19). What the criteria are for a 'normal' rate of progress is not made clear.

Schumpeterian methodology is sometimes regarded as illustrating *par excellence* the 'absolutist' procedure. (Cf. Alfred F. Chalk, 'Relativist and Absolutist Approaches to the History of Economic Theory,' *Southwestern Social Science Quarterly*, 48 (June 1967), 5–12; Lawrence Nabers, 'The Positive and Genetic Approaches,' in S.R. Krupp, ed., *The structure of Economic Science* (Englewood Cliffs, 1966), 68f.) But it should be clear that his approach was a somewhat ambiguous one.

49 William Letwin, *The Origins of Scientific Economics* (London, 1963), 143.

our first task is satisfactorily accomplished. For Smith did not always – or even usually – provide a careful formulation either of his theoretical models or of their intended scope, so that it is in practice often difficult *without reference to the state of the contemporary economy* to ascertain the nature of the model, or its appropriateness in terms of the accuracy of its assumptions and the range of problems for which it was designed. We may illustrate the problem by a brief reference to the so-called 'corn model' which, it is sometimes said, represented Smith's fundamental method of abstraction for analysis of the growth process.

The main characteristics of the model are that the only form of capital is circulating or working capital advanced from past produce; that there is only one kind of circulating capital good, namely 'corn'; and that the period of its circulation is the agricultural year. Labour is the sole variable factor, currently producing either corn – in which case it is defined as 'productive' – or luxury services when it is defined as 'unproductive.' This model casts light on the forces determining the growth rate of the economy – where the national dividend is defined in terms of physical product (corn output) – under various conditions of productivity, labour supply, and allocation of employment between the two categories of labour.[50] The point which we wish to emphasize at this stage is that the view according to which the corn model represents an accurate statement of Smithian growth economics is at least in part based

---

50 See for example Myint, *Theories of Welfare Economics,* 1f., and John Hicks, *Capital and Growth* (Oxford, 1965), 36f.

In the case that all the corn output is employed in the support of productive labour we can state the size of this year's corn output as
$$X_t = (p/w) \cdot X_{t-1},$$
where X_{t-1} represents last year's corn, w the corn wage, p the productivity of labour (that is corn per man), and X_{t-1}/w the number of men employed. The growth rate of the economy will be
$$(X_t - X_{t-1})/X_{t-1} = p/w - 1.$$
If some of last year's harvest is diverted to non-labourers (landlords and capitalists) or to non-corn producers ('unproductive' labourers) then this year's corn output becomes
$$X_t = k(p/w) \cdot X_{t-1}$$
where k is the fraction of the harvest which is paid to corn producers. Here the capital used in corn production equals kX_{t-1}; the number of corn producers equals $(kX_{t-1})/w$, and the growth rate reduces to
$$k(p/w) - 1.$$
Material wealth can be increased, either by raising the physical productivity (p), or the supply, of productive labour. The corn model need not actually be interpreted as a model of a regularly progressive economy with p, w, and k constant from year to year. But frequently certain of the key variables – particularly the average wage rate – are presumed to be constant.

See also a rather more detailed model of the Smithian growth process developed by A. Lowe, 'The Classical Theory of Economic Growth,' *Social Research*, XXI (1954), 132–41, and W.O. Thweatt, 'A Diagramatic Presentation of Adam Smith's Growth Model,' *ibid.*, XXIV (1957), 227–30. Here too the essential emphasis is upon productivity increase (particularly by way of division of labour) and the growth of labour and capital.

upon evidence drawn from the nature of the eighteenth-century economy. There can be no doubt that this is the model that was in Smith's mind, it has been suggested, since 'at the time when he wrote agriculture was still (in all countries) far and away the most important of activities; to fit the case of agriculture naturally seemed to be the prime necessity.'[51] Similarly:

In the light of the economic conditions existing at that time, there is much to be said for such a method of abstraction. In those days, wage goods in fact consisted of a few primary products that could be lumped together under the head of a single commodity, 'corn' ... At the subsistence level of real wages ... a given output of 'corn' could maintain a determinate quantity of labour. Labour, being a versatile factor, could then be turned to the production of all sorts of articles, both 'necessaries' and 'luxuries,' particularly so, when the bulk of the luxury consumption was in the form of direct personal services. The concept of labour as the single variable factor is again a justified assumption [since] fixed capital played a relatively unimportant part in the economic life of that time and investment was mainly in the form of 'advances to labour.' Since land was assumed to be fixed in supply, social output could then be treated as the function of a single major variable, the quantity of labour.[52]

A fundamental characteristic of the corn model should be noted. The model neglects both the role of factor endowments and relative factor prices, and that of technology, as determinants of the pattern of activity, insofar as allowance is made for only one productive factor and one product, and the analysis confined to the physical level. It casts no light at all upon either the manufacturing or the commercial sectors, and accordingly upon the determination of the pattern of activity between these branches, between agriculture, manufacturing and commerce, and within each. How useful the model is will indeed depend upon the nature of the economy to which it was applied and it will be one of our tasks to consider the accuracy of the evaluation offered above.

Smith's basic concern, according to the preceding view, is with the increasing of material wealth rather than the efficient allocation of scarce resources among alternative uses. (The subjective level of analysis, runs the argument, is pushed into the background by the implicit assumption that consumers' satisfaction is roughly proportional to physical product.) But we must refer at this point to an alternative well-known view according to which the very *essence* of Smithian economics lies precisely in the statement of the role of relative product and factor prices in assuring an optimum allocation of scarce resources. We illustrate the argument from the work of Lord Robbins:

although Adam Smith's great work professed to deal with the causes of the wealth of nations, and did in fact make many remarks on the general question of the conditions of opulence which are of great importance in any history of applied Economics, yet from the point of view of theoretical Economics, the central achievement of

51 Hicks, *Capital and Growth*, 38.
52 Myint, *Theories of Welfare Economics*, 8. It may be remarked that the 'realism' of the model is said to apply not only to Smith's day, but to the first part of the nineteenth century too.

his book was his demonstration of the mode in which the division of labour tended to be kept in equilibrium by the mechanism of relative prices – a demonstration which ... is in harmony with the most refined apparatus of the modern School of Lausanne. The theory of value and distribution was really the central core of the analysis of the Classics, try as they might to conceal their objects under other names.[53]

A similar emphasis on the 'general equilibrium' aspect of the *Wealth of Nations* is made by Marian Bowley: 'Adam Smith's adoption of the consumers' concept of wealth – "the necessaries and conveniences of life" – together with the theory of the "hidden hand," finally turned economic speculation towards the discovery of the mechanism connecting production with consumers' demand.'[54] It will be our primary aim to define the scope envisaged by Smith for the respective structures relating to growth and to general equilibrium, and the affinity, if any, between them.

It will be a further objective of this study to evaluate the Smithian theory of policy, in particular the consistency of his alternative proposals, and the manner in which, and the extent to which, they were supported by reference to some analytical apparatus. In this regard too we may again refer to the apparent conflict between the assumptions implicit in the corn model of growth and those implicit in the general equilibrium approach. The difference would not be serious if it amounted simply to alternative evaluations of the relative emphasis placed in the *Wealth of Nations* on various issues. In fact, the attribution to Smith of a strictly growth-oriented outlook – a concern with the technical efficiency of the economy and the maximization of employment and gross produce in some physical sense – has implications of the greatest relevance to matters of policy. Indeed, the textual evidence suggests to some

53 Lord Robbins, *An Essay on the Nature and Significance of Economic Science* (London, 1935), 68–9. For a similar statement of this view see his *Robert Torrens and the Evolution of Classical Economics* (London, 1958), 234; and a review of Frank H. Knight, *On the History and Method of Economics* (Chicago, 1956), in *American Economic Review*, XLVII (1957), 398. 'I cannot believe that it is even approximately correct to argue, as Knight argues, that the "Classical economists give no picture of a system of prices and practically no hint of a system of economic organization worked out and directed by price forces" ... Surely it was just such a picture – a picture of the division of labour in relation to the market – which was the great achievement of the classical system.'

A more recent statement by Lord Robbins of the main purpose of the *Wealth of Nations* suggests a change in emphasis. See *The Theory of Economic Development in the History of Economic Thought*, (London, 1968), 9: 'The main credit for putting economic development on the map as a subject for general analysis belongs undoubtedly to Adam Smith ... [As] political economy its coverage [of the *Wealth of Nations*] is wide, ranging from an exhibition of the essential structural relationships of an exchange economy practising division of labour, to the economic functions of the state and the canons of taxation. But, as the title itself implies, the central focus is on development – what makes the wealth of nations greater or less.'

54 *Nassau Senior and Classical Economics* (London, 1937), 67.

The interpretation by Myint has been strongly criticized in the review by P.A. Samuelson (*Economica*, XV (Nov. 1949), 373–4) on grounds of the ubiquity of the relative-price mechanism in Smithian, and classical, economics.

that the price mechanism may even have been seen by Smith as a hindrance to the growth process. We should not rule out inconsistency but it seems improbable that Smith would have remained unaware of a conflict between his theories of growth and allocation which is as serious as that which has been suggested. We shall, accordingly, examine the hypothesis that the objectives of equilibrium allocation and growth were not in conflict but rather that the price mechanism played a positive role in the achievement of the growth program.

Our concern, therefore, is both with the degree of success achieved by Smith in his attempt to explain 'scientifically' contemporary economic conditions, and with the quality of his policy program in terms of its internal consistency and its logical relationship with an underlying theoretical structure. We have already made clear, in general terms, the extent to which we believe it is justified to make use of modern analytical concepts and procedures in attempting to understand and interpret an earlier writer. We may add that while particular caution is called for in the case of the *Wealth of Nations* – where the intermingling of descriptive, statistical, historical and purely theoretical arguments makes it difficult in the extreme to isolate and formalize the precise functional relationships intended – it is nonetheless the case that Smith himself recognized a legitimate place for 'model building.'[55] But the results require the most careful interpretation; above all it is unjustified to presume that Smith was *aware* of all the logical implications of a particular construct. A study of Smith's economics must concern itself also with logical error and poorly related, and even contradictory, relationships, and attention must be paid to arguments which do *not* fit into a neat and logical framework.

One final word regarding the methodology of this study. Our investigation draws upon evidence provided by economic historians. But the rules of procedure and the nature of the evidence in that discipline are as much prone to constant revision as are those of pure economic theory. And whether we can talk of an 'unambiguous' standard amongst professionals at any time is a question which also arises.[56] Of particular relevance is the fact that some of the indexes of quickening activity characterizing the 'industrial revolution,' once generally dated from the closing decades of the eighteenth century, are in the light of new procedures and evidence now said to be apparent earlier

---

55 'It gives us a pleasure to see the phenomena which we reckoned the most unaccountable, all deduced from some principle (commonly a well-known one) and all united in one chain, far superior to what we feel from the unconnected method, where everything is accounted for by itself, without reference to the others.'
Lectures on Rhetoric and Belles Lettres, ed. J.M. Lothian (London, 1963) 140. On Smith's scientific methodology see Herbert F. Thomson, 'Adam Smith's Philosophy of Science,' *Quarterly Journal of Economics*, LXXIX (May 1965), esp. 221-3, 232.

56 More precisely perhaps – as Schumpeter has pointed out (*History of Economic Analysis*, 13) – 'we have to face the fact that, economic history being part of economics, the historian's techniques are passengers in the big bus that we call economic analysis.'

in the century. Clearly this change in outlook may have deep implications for any evaluation of Smithian economics. For this reason it is all the more important to ascertain Smith's own vision of the mid-eighteenth-century economy.

PLAN OF WORK

In Part I we examine in very broad terms certain essential aspects of the economic literature prior to the *Wealth of Nations,* in order to provide a suitable framework within which to place Smith's contribution. Particular attention will be paid to physiocratic doctrine.

Smith's own work is studied in Part II. In Chapter 3 we consider the industry structure in Smith's time. It will be argued that although in *absolute* terms the economy of his day was still predominantly agricultural, the absolute data are misleading. Structural changes within the broad sectors were under way and, what is particularly relevant, are clearly discernible in Smith's account. Moreover, the trend from domestic to factory organization was noted by Smith, and the greatest potential for future growth was seen to lie in the manufacturing sector. Our conclusion is that it is misleading to regard the nature of the economy – and Smith's 'vision' thereof – as basically 'agricultural.' The analysis of the *Wealth of Nations,* we argue, was not founded upon the observation of a non-industrial economy.

In Chapter 4 Smith's theory of exchange value is discussed within a general-equilibrium framework. Particular attention is paid to a number of restrictive assumptions regarding the properties of the production function implicit in the formal treatment of 'market and natural price.' But it will be made clear that the formal analysis does not represent Smith's entire contribution, since allowance is made for 'substitution' relationships of various kinds in actual applications of the analysis. Similarly, the crucial role played by demand in allocation theory is illustrated within a broad context where the strict assumptions of the formal analysis are relaxed.

Chapter 5 deals with the closely related theory of distribution. The vexed question of the productivity of land and capital is taken up with an eye upon the applicability of a model which regards labour as the sole productive factor. Smith's statements representing rent and profits as deductions from the contribution by labour to the national income reflect, we shall argue, his negative evaluation of the 'moral' legitimacy of property income, but do not constitute a denial of the value productivity of either land or capital. Smith's 'model' of value and distribution as-a-whole is then outlined with particular emphasis upon the unique role played by the price of corn. The secular tendency of the profit rate to decline is examined in the final section.

Chapter 6 considers Smith's discussion 'Of the Accumulation of Capital' with particular reference to the nature of the savings process, and the structure of capital. The 'corn model of growth,' it is argued, does not throw light upon numerous issues of interest to Smith within the growth context, neglecting in particular the basic characteristic of Smith's theory of production which allows for raw materials and machinery. Smith's emphasis upon wages as net income in the first two chapters of Book II, which is in apparent contrast to the approach of his third chapter, is then explained. The final section of the chapter deals with the place of money in accumulation.

Chapter 7 treats the nature and scope of the 'division of labour' including the determinants of plant and industry organization; the function of fixed capital and its maintenance in the context of technical change; the role of economic pressures in determining the particular factor-saving direction of new processes; and the sources of new technology. We conclude that Smith dealt with many of the important technical developments of his day, and accordingly cannot be charged with having failed to anticipate the 'industrial revolution.'

Smith's position on the fundamental questions regarding the 'desirability' of economic development (in the sense of rising *per capita* income) and the role of government in the achievement of development is discussed in Chapter 8.

In Chapters 9 and 10 we show that while Smith was fundamentally concerned with the analysis of the growth process (and accordingly with capital accumulation), he considered the function of the price mechanism in assuring the maximization (at any time) of the surplus constituting the source of savings. In particular, Smith did not lose sight of factor endowments and relative prices in dealing with economic development, and there is no conflict, such as has frequently been attributed to his arguments, between the imperatives of growth and those indicated by the price mechanism. Attention is paid in these chapters to the discussion of foreign trade and development policy; while there are apparent contradictions in Smith's formal exposition it is shown that when allowance is made for the 'propaganda' effect of the arguments, a far greater degree of consistency may be detected.

In the conclusion we draw upon the preceding materials to define the characteristic features of Smith's economics and to draw some relationships with predecessors, contemporaries, and successors.

I / ASPECTS OF THE PRE-SMITHIAN LITERATURE

ONE

Automatic equilibrating processes

In this chapter we are not concerned with the interrelationship between economic analysis and environmental influences. Our object is to provide a summary account of the state of economic science in the mid-eighteenth-century with particular reference to the operation of automatic equilibrating processes, in order to facilitate evaluation of Smith's relationship with his predecessors and contemporaries, and place his contribution in suitable perspective.

THE SCHOLASTIC TRADITION

The attribution to early Scholastic writers of discovery of the condition of long-run competitive equilibrium is frequently made in the secondary litera-ture.[1] This view appears to be unjustified. In the case of St Thomas Aquinas, support of the competitively determined market price of a commodity as an index of commutative justice appears to have been given reluctantly. Sale at a market price which permitted a 'gain' – in the sense of an excess over the price initially paid by the seller for the product (or the raw materials thereof) – was regarded as morally satisfactory provided that costs were reflected thereby; in brief, that the 'surplus' in fact represented a return to effort of some kind such as labour, risk-taking, or transportation (although there were acceptable claims to a 'moderate' excess of sales price over the original pur-chase price based upon the use to which the excess was put). The case where one is justified in earning the excess simply 'because the price of a thing has

1 J.A. Schumpeter, *History of Economic Analysis* (New York, 1954), 93; Raymond de Roover, 'La doctrine scolastic en matière de monopole et son application à la politique économique des communes italiennes,' in *Studi in Onore di Amintore Fanfani* (Milan, 1962), 154; and Raymond de Roover 'The Concept of the Just Price: Theory and Economic Policy,' *Journal of Economic History*, XVIII (Dec. 1958), 418–34.

changed with the change of place or time,' occurs in a restricted context, namely where the individual had not originally purchased the commodity in question with the intention of reselling it, that is where he is not strictly a trader at all. Such qualifications suggest that Aquinas accepted the market price as 'just' most hesitantly and would not have recommended its adoption as a general rule.[2]

Conversely, a market price which failed to cover 'legitimate' expenses was not obligatory, so that a trader might with justice charge a price higher than that ruling in the market should an opportunity to do so present itself.[3]

This result, which reflects both an absence of pure profit and of loss, will be attained in the long run by the classical or neo-classical competitive process. But Aquinas did not reach these conclusions by means of analytical reasoning. He did not explain how the market price could come to reflect normal costs by tracing through the consequence of a failure to cover supply price, or indicate the manner in which resources will move between occupations in response to relative profitability. This problem in fact did not concern him. He was prescribing certain 'just' courses of action according to which the market price was a satisfactory criterion provided that it did not permit pure profit on the one hand, and did not lead to losses on the other; while preoccupation with the ethics of pricing might lead to the analysis of economic phenomena, it does not seem to be the case that St Thomas took the step from ethics to analysis. A similar conclusion may be applied to Duns Scotus (d.1308); to identify the just price with the competitive common price and also with the 'normal' cost of the good may at most be said to 'imply' the law of cost but cannot be regarded as an analytical statement thereof.[4]

Later Scholastic writers (particularly the Jesuits) formally took issue with the apparent willingness of their predecessors to legitimize charges in excess of the 'common estimation' by individual sellers who had undergone – through no 'fault' of their own – abnormally high costs. Reliance upon the common evaluation was to be the rule henceforth whether or not losses, or on the other hand pure profits, resulted. This becomes clear, for example, in a rejection by Molina (1536–1600) of the position taken by Duns Scotus: 'The price of goods is not to be gauged by the gains of the merchants or their losses but from the common appraisal of them in the place where they are sold, in view

---

2 See S. Hollander, 'On the Interpretation of the Just Price,' *Kyklos*, XVIII (1965), 627.

3 This interpretation is based on a condemnation of the recovery of *usurious* payments by charging in excess of the general market price. The ruling by St Thomas is in terms which imply that the recovery of legitimate costs (those not incurred carelessly or imprudently) – even if it necessitated a price exceeding the going market price – would be justified (*ibid.*, 630–1). See n.5 below regarding later Scholastic criticism of this view.

4 Duns Scotus' just price corresponded to costs including actual expenses and opportunity costs, a risk compensation, and a normal profit. See Raymond de Roover, 'J.A. Schumpeter and Scholastic Economics,' *Kyklos* (1957), 115–46.

of all the current circumstances. And this is true whether through ill-luck or lack of skillful dealing they gain little or even suffer loss, or with good luck and energetic trading they make a great gain.'[5] The just price of commodities in particular exchanges will accordingly be the same as the prices which would be determined 'at a public valuation if they were openly displayed in the market place with the whole town coming together at the voice of the town crier.'[6]

A formal emphasis upon 'utility' as the cause or source of value is also to be noted. For example, in Molina's formulation: 'the value of things is not considered as resident in their entity but in their utilities and advantages.'[7] But such formal statements occur repeatedly in the work of Aquinas (and indeed of Aristotle) and should not be exaggerated. Utility was regarded as a necessary condition of exchange value but not as a sufficient condition or the determinant of exchange value.[8]

Yet despite their criticism of Duns Scotus it would not be true to say that the later Schoolmen divorced the 'common evaluation' from production costs. An individual in a random case may indeed be permitted to enjoy profits or be obliged to suffer losses by reliance upon the going competitive price, but on the other hand it was their view that this price will in fact 'tend' to reflect normal costs. Thus Lugo rejected the argument that professional merchants should be allowed to sell at a higher price than someone finding an object by

---

5 Quoted in Bernard Dempsey, *Interest and Usury* (Washington, 1943), 151. The statement is preceded by a summary of the earlier position: 'One must compute (they say) all the expenses which they incur in buying, transporting, or preserving such goods, and then the just compensation for the industry and labor expended and the risks to which they have exposed themselves, just as if having been hired for a wage, they served the commonwealth in this affair. If the article is sold at the price corresponding to this, more or less, this will be the just price for all; and if it notably exceeds it, it will be unjust to the extent of this excess. From this they infer that if a merchant's boat is sunk by some accident or the goods are taken by thieves or the building is burned in which the goods are stored, he may compensate himself by selling dearer in the commonwealth the rest of his goods.'

See also a critique of Duns Scotus by Lugo (1593–1660) who argued that a shipwreck or theft cannot justify the charging of a price in excess of the ruling price, and conversely, that a high market price may be relied upon even if a pure surplus should result (*ibid.*, 152).

6 Quoted in *ibid.*, 150, from Lugo. Cf. also the view of Molina: The common price is based upon the 'common valuation, made in good faith, entered into without conspiracy or trickery, in view of the supply or scarcity of goods, buyers and sellers, and other circumstances.' The factors affecting price are summarized by Lessius (1554–1623) as 'the circumstances with which the common evaluation of things rises and falls. Some concern the goods themselves as abundance, scarcity, or their necessity and utility; some concern the sellers, as their labor, expenses, risks, and losses in obtaining, assembling, and storing the goods, and also, the manner of selling, namely, whether they are willingly offered or sold on request; some concern the buyers, whether they be few or many, and whether there be an abundance or shortage of money' (*ibid.*, 151).

7 *Ibid.*, 149.

8 Cf. Hollander, 'The Interpretation of the Just Price,' 622.

chance on the grounds that they have undertaken expenses of various types (including alternative earnings foregone). The reason Lugo offered for his position is that 'in evaluating the common price of goods, attention is paid to these costs and profits of merchants and the common and natural price arises for all of these ... Recall ... that a merchant cannot compensate himself for expenses he has incurred when other merchants who have incurred smaller expenses commonly sell the same goods at a lower price. He must reckon it his bad luck that he has brought goods at a great outlay to a place where their common price was less.'[9]

A particularly comprehensive statement to the same effect was made by Lessius (1554–1623). In the following passage three cases are distinguished, one where there exists no established price at all for the product, a second where prices are fixed by authority, and thirdly – and of particular relevance – where a competitively-determined price exists. It is clearly his view in the latter case that – while an individual merchant may rely upon the market price even if a large net profit results, and must rely upon it, even if he suffers a loss in consequence – the common price takes into account normal costs:

One may charge a higher price by reason of labor and expense which one has undergone in getting, transporting, and storing goods; that is, if goods have not a price set for them. If they have, then the merchant can take account of extraordinary expenses in the setting of the price at the time when it is first fixed, as we see in the case of goods brought through dangerous places where there is need of military escort against freebooters. But this is not to be understood of expenses incurred by reason of misfortune or imprudence. The case is different if goods already have their own price at which they are generally sold; then the merchant is bound to sell at that price or to keep the goods ... But in arriving at a price of this kind account has already been taken of the expenses which are ordinarily and usually incurred. But if the merchant's expenses have been greater, that is hard luck, and the common price may not be increased for that reason, just as it need not be decreased even if he had no expenses at all. This is the merchant's situation: just as he can make a profit if he has small expenses, so he can lose if his expenses are very large or extraordinary.[10]

Thus despite formal criticism in later Scholastic writings of the cost orientation of their predecessors, costs nonetheless appeared as a crucial – perhaps the predominant – factor in the 'common estimation.'[11] But the *analytical* implications of this fact must not be exaggerated. The distinction between normal and abnormal costs, and the argument that it is the former which contribute to the determination of the common estimation suggests perhaps a degree of appreciation of the notion of supply price, but there is nonetheless inadequate investigation of the *process* of long-run cost-determination of

9 Dempsey, *Interest and Usury*, 153.
10 *Ibid.*
11 In this regard we differ from the view of Schumpeter that the later Scholastics tended to divorce the competitive price from costs of production. Cf. Schumpeter, *History of Economic Analysis*, 98–9.

price, and little to suggest an appreciation of the function of prices in the general allocation of resources. For it is not at all made clear how the price reflecting the 'common appraisal' – which takes into account expenses which are ordinarily and usually incurred – is in fact arrived at. (Indeed certain formulations are sufficiently ambiguous to allow even for a common evaluation achieved by 'experts.') Moreover, the Scholastics did not apply the supply-demand apparatus to the problem of income formation and developed no integrated theory of distribution.[12]

Above all, it must be emphasized that the fundamental concern of the Scholastic authorities was to assure the avoidance of monopsonistic and monopolistic exploitation. If this end could be achieved by means of the market, then well and good. But upon occasion there existed preferable criteria such as the price determined by the civil authority in unusual circumstances. There is no evidence that the Scholastics were market enthusiasts because of a belief in 'economic freedom' or because they recognized the function of the competitive price mechanism in the organization of general economic activity.[13]

Much the same *analytical lacunae* may be discerned in the writings of the seventeenth-century natural-law philosopher Samuel Pufendorf which were well known to Adam Smith.[14] In the first place the formal references to utility are made. 'Ordinary Price' is said to be 'found in things and actions or labours, which enter into exchange, in so far as they afford service and pleasure to men.' The 'foundation' of ordinary price 'is the aptitude of a thing or action, by which it can either mediately or immediately contribute something to the necessity of human life, or to making it more advantageous and pleasant.' But the actual determinant of exchange value depends not only upon 'the need of the article'; rather the 'chief factor in high price is scarcity, the maintenance of which is considered by some to be one of the secrets of business.' To this he adds further the comment that 'the price of manufactured articles is usually raised not only by their rareness but because of their workmanship ... Considerable store is set upon some objects by reason of the reputation of the workman.' In addition, he refers to the price-enhancing effects of 'the difficulty of the work, the abundance or scarcity of workmen, and the like.'[15]

12 Cf. Marian Bowley, 'Some Seventeenth-Century Contributions to the Theory of Value,' *Economica*, XXX (May 1963), 122–39.
13 Cf. Jacob Viner, 'The Intellectual History of Laissez-Faire,' *Journal of Law and Economics*, III (Oct. 1960), 53.
14 *De Jure Naturae et Gentium (On the Law of Nature and of Nations)* (1672); *The Classics of International Law*, no. 17, vol. II (Oxford, 1934), Book V, chap. 1: 'On Price.' Schumpeter, *History of Economic Analysis*, 116, refers with justification to the natural-law writers as 'Protestant or Laical Scholastics' on grounds of methodological similarity (and includes also Hobbes and Locke within the designation).
15 Pufendorf, *De Jure Natural*, 676–84. With regard to the prices of *services*, Pufendorf stated that they are affected by 'their difficulty, the dexterity required in them, their usefulness, necessity, the scarcity of workers, their reknown or position, their freedom to work when they choose, and similar considerations' (684).

Thus far Pufendorf has dealt with *general* causes of high and low prices in the state of 'natural liberty' or of 'nature' where the actual prices of commodities and services will be 'fixed by agreement between the parties concerned.' In organized states prices will be determined in practice either by authority ('legal' price), or 'by the general valuation and judgment of men, with the further consent of those who are the parties to the bargain' ('common' or 'natural' price). The natural price is defined more specifically 'as a just price which is commonly set by those who are sufficiently acquainted with both the merchandise and the market.'[16] The factors taken into account in the establishment thereof are then listed; the costs allowed for include labour and expense 'commonly' incurred and a moderate 'profit':

Now in fixing common price consideration is to be given to the labour and expense which merchants undergo in importing and handling their wares, for this is the principal reason why a merchant is allowed to sell his goods for more than the purchase price. But this consideration must be understood only of those expenses as are commonly to be met, since unusual conditions are considered as of no concern in the matter. Therefore, a tradesman will receive no attention if he tries to place a higher price upon his merchandise because he broke his leg, or became seriously ill while bringing them into the country, or because he lost a part of them by shipwreck or at the hands of thieves; provided, of course, such accidents did not contribute to the scarcity of the wares ... But merchants can include in their estimation the time they have spent, the plans they have formed, and the troubles they have met in acquiring, preserving, or distributing their merchandise, as well as all necessary expenses for the labour of their servants. And it would surely be inhuman, and likely to destroy the industry of men, to try to allow a man for his business, or any other sort of occupation, no more profit than barely allows him to meet his necessities by frugality and hardships.[17]

What is to be noted particularly is the apparent possibility that the 'common' cost price may be determined not by the market process at all but by *experts* 'acquainted with both the merchandise and the market.' On this matter, however, Pufendorf appears to be ambiguous.

At the same time a temporary price determined in the market is recognized: 'But it is also well known how subject a market is to sudden and frequent changes from the plenty or scarcity of purchasers, money, and commodities. For a scarcity of purchasers and money, due to some particular reason, with an abundance of commodities decreases the price.'[18] Yet as in the case of the later Scholastics no account at all is given of the precise relationship envisaged between the cost and the temporary market prices.

Francis Hutcheson used Pufendorf as a text in his lectures on moral phi-

16 *Ibid.*, 685–7.
17 *Ibid.*, 687–8. Pufendorf includes also *damnum emergens* and *lucrum cessans*:
'There can be included in the common price any loss ensuing, or foregoing of profit, which befalls the seller by virtue of the sale' (689).
18 *Ibid.*, 688.

losophy at Glasgow which were attended by Adam Smith as a student. The published version of Hutcheson's lectures contains a chapter dealing with price, but the subject is carried no further than it had been by Pufendorf.[19] It is clear that the fundamental *hiatus* in the analysis of price determination by the scholastic writers and the ethical jurists remained to be filled.

SEVENTEENTH-CENTURY PAMPHLET LITERATURE

We are concerned in this section with the treatment of the price mechanism in the seventeenth-century 'pamphlet' literature. As for the bulk of the contributions it is probably a justified view that they reflect little appreciation of the role of relative prices in the organization of economic activity.[20] To adopt this position is not, however, to deny some advance in economic analysis

19 A version of Hutcheson's lectures was published in Latin in 1745 and a translation appeared in 1747 as 'A Short Introduction to Moral Philosophy,' in *Collected Works of Francis Hutcheson*, IV (Hildesheim, 1969). The following passage from Book II, chap. 12, 'Concerning the Values or Prices of Goods' (*ibid.*, 209–10) appears to be drawn from Pufendorf: 'The ground for all price must be some fitness in the things to yield some use or pleasure in life; without this, they can be no value. But this being presupposed, the prices of things will be in a compound proportion of the *demand* for them, and the *difficulty* of acquiring them. The *demand* will be in proportion to the numbers who are wanting them, or their necessity to life. The *difficulty* may be occasioned many ways; if the quantities of them in the world be small; if any accidents make the quantity less than ordinary; if much toil is required in producing them, or much ingenuity, or a more elegant genius in the artists; if the persons employed about them according to the custom of the country are men in high account, and live in a more splendid manner; for the expence of this must be defrayed by the higher profits of their labours, and few can be thus maintained.

Some goods [are] of the highest use, yet have either no price or but a small one. If there's such plenty in nature that they are acquired almost without any labour, they have no price; if they may be acquired by easy common labour, they are of small price. Such is the goodness of God to us, that the most useful and necessary things are generally very plentiful and easily acquired.'

See also on Hutcheson's theory of value, the discussion by Edwin Cannan in his Introduction to the *Wealth of Nations*, Modern Library ed. (New York, 1937), xlv-xlvi; and by H.M. Robertson and W.L. Taylor, 'Adam Smith's Approach to the Theory of Value,' *Economic Journal*, LXVII (June, 1957), 181–98.

20 Cf. William R. Allen, 'The Position of Mercantilism and the Early Development of International Trade Theory,' in R.V. Eagly, ed., *Events, Ideology and Economic Theory* (Detroit, 1968), 73–5; Allen, 'Modern Defenders of Mercantilist Theory,' *History of Political Economy*, II (fall 1970), 381–97; J.J. Spengler, 'Mercantilist and Physiocratic Growth Theory,' in B.F. Hoselitz, ed., *Theories of Economic Growth* (New York, 1960), 23; and Bowley, 'Some Seventeenth Century Contributions to the Theory of Value,' 132–4.

This is not the view, however, of William D. Grampp, 'The Liberal Elements in English Mercantilism,' *Quarterly Journal of Economics*, LXVI (Nov. 1952); reprinted in Grampp, *Economic Liberalism*, I (New York, 1965), 48–97. Grampp draws attention to a very early appreciation of the role of the price mechanism in resource allocation by John Hales, *Discourses of the Common Weal of This Realm of England* (1549). Hales emphasized the profit motive; he recognized that the imposition of maximum wheat prices by reducing the relative profitability of wheat production was responsible for its scarcity. Freeing the price of wheat would stimu-

and its application. Thus while the determination of the market prices of commodities by simple demand and supply ('utility and scarcity') analysis was already received doctrine, a new degree of sophistication was achieved in the use made of the concept of exchange value as a purely relative magnitude in the investigation of policy problems, particularly those relating to the foreign exchanges, the precious metals, and the rate of interest.[21]

In treating these issues the 'mercantilist' writers scarcely touched upon the *general* problem of resource allocation. Moreover, as in the traditional treatments by the moralists, factor returns were on the whole not dealt with as prices to be analysed in terms of the general theory of exchange value. But there were some striking contributions in the seventeenth-century literature to which we shall turn.

As a brief preliminary we note that recognition of the desire for 'profit' as a controlling motive in economic behaviour is of ancient vintage; indeed in its traditional formulations the 'economic man' was taken to be a matter of fact rather than an abstraction.[22] Moreover, as Professor Heckscher has emphasized, the recognition of a certain causality in social organization was quite typical in mercantilist literature. But to say this is not to imply necessarily that the outcome of freely operating 'natural' forces was considered desirable. In fact the mercantilists combined a view of society determined by inexorable

late wheat production at the expense of wool: 'Yet that price would provoke every man to set plough in the ground to husband waste grounds, yes to turn the lands which be enclosed from pasture to arable land; for every man will gladder follow that wherein they see the more profit and gains. And thereby must needs ensue both great plenty of corn, and also much treasure must should be brought into this realm by occasion thereof ...' (quoted in Grampp, *Economic Liberalism*, 78. See also the view of Schumpeter, *History of Economic Analysis*, 166–7.) Yet Hales did not endorse the unrestricted operation of the price mechanism.

21 The literature is discussed fully by Bowley, 'Some Seventeenth Century Contributions to the Theory of Value,' and W. Letwin, *The Origins of Scientific Economics* (London, 1964). In the argument between Malynes and Mun regarding the foreign exchanges, it was accepted by both sides that the exchange value of goods was determined by supply and demand; the question related to the relevance of this analysis to the foreign exchanges (Bowley, 'Some Seventeenth Century Contributions to the Theory of Value,' 124–6). It is here, it may be added, that Mun's most significant contribution to analysis lies, namely in the recognition that the foreign exchange rate depends upon the trade balance as a whole and not upon the machinations of individual exchange dealers (*England's Treasure by Forraign Trade* (1664, written c. 1630; Oxford, 1959), chap. XIV, 'The admirable feats supposed to be done by Bankers and the Merchants Exchange'). Although there is some recognition in Mun's work of the functional nature of demand and supply and the process of equilibration, welfare implications are not drawn regarding the advantages or disadvantages to society of the competitive market mechanism.

The relativity of exchange value was applied also, for example, by Nicholas Barbon, *A Discourse of Trade* (1690), to the precious metals leading him, upon occasion, to denigrate the contemporary concern with the accumulation of specie (Bowley, 'Some Seventeenth Century Contributions to the Theory of Value,' 128–9; Letwin, *The Origins of Scientific Economics*, 63–4).

22 Cf. Jacob Viner, *Studies in the Theory of International Trade* (New York, 1937), 91f.

laws with support for state interference.[23] Either, as in the typical view, the profit motive was deplored and considered to be potentially ruinous for the nation unless subjected to controls;[24] or positive social advantages were attributed to it provided it were directed along suitable channels.[25]

It was, however, argued by a small but growing body of opponents that regulations in the public interest might be a greater evil than unregulated trade insofar as they emanated from pressure groups, or because the regulators might be incompetent. Some even took a more positive view and formulated the proposition that *unregulated* trade actually served the public interest on the grounds that the profit motive did not lead to a chaotic outcome but on the contrary could be relied upon to organize economic activity in a satisfactory manner. It must be emphasized at once that the mere assertion of such harmony of interest between the individual and society is not the issue; our concern is with the reasoning used in support of the proposition.[26]

23 Eli F. Heckscher, *Mercantilism*, 2nd ed., II (London, 1955), 308–24. Accordingly great care is needed in considering formal statements apparently of a 'liberal' nature such as the celebrated proposition by Mun to the effect that devices designed to check a bullion outflow – such as enhancement or debasement of the coinage; the Statute of Employment; and exchange control – are useless: 'all these actions can work no other effects in the course of trade than is declared in this discourse. For so much Treasure only will be brought in or carried out of a Commonwealth, as the Forraign Trade doth over or under ballance in value. And this must come to pass by a Necessity beyond all resistance. So that all other courses (which tend not to this end) howsoever they may seem to force mony into a Kingdom for a time, yet are they (in the end) not only fruitless but also hurtful: they are like to violent flouds which bear down their banks, and suddenly remain dry again for want of waters.' (Mun, *England's Treasure by Forraign Trade*, 87–8). Here we see clearly the recognition of social causality; but what is called for, as we discuss presently (see below, 53f., is a *suitable* direction thereof, that is, one which deals with causes and not symptoms.

24 See Viner, *Studies in the Theory of International Trade*, 93.

25 Viner (*ibid.*, 98n) refers to casual statements to this effect by Sir William Petty, *Treatise of Taxes* (1662) and subsequently by Josiah Tucker, *Elements of Commerce* (1755). But he emphasizes in particular the exposition by Nathanial Forster, *An Enquiry into the Causes of the Present High Price of Provisions* (1767). Bernard Mandeville should be added as a particularly significant instance (see below).

26 Loose statements by Edward Misselden, *The Circle of Commerce* (1623); Sir Josiah Child, *The Humble Answer of the Governor ... of the East-India Company* (1692); Charles Davenant, *An Essay on the East-India Trade* (1697); Josiah Tucker, *Instructions for Travelers* (1757); and a more specific statement by George Whatley (under physiocratic influence), *Principles of Trade* (1774), are referred to by Viner, *Studies in the Theory of International Trade*, 98–100. Nicholas Barbon is sometimes regarded as falling within the present category. Cf. Schumpeter, *History of Economic Analysis*, 368.

William Letwin has warned against the careless identification of early writers as advocates of *laissez-faire*. In particular Child, in his view, cannot be regarded – despite formal statements which seem unambiguous – as a forerunner of Smith, for he wrote with a superior principle – the balance of trade – in mind, dictating exceptions. Similarly Letwin shows that in matters of analysis, particularly the recognition of economic interdependence, Child cannot be said to have made any substantial contributions (*The Origins of Scientific Economics*, 41–7).

The argument is stated in general terms in the preface to Dudley North's celebrated *Discourses Upon Trade* (1691): 'There can be no Trade unprofitable to the Publick; for if any prove so, men leave it off; and wherever the Traders thrive, the Publick, of which they are a part, thrive also ... All favour to one Trade or Interest against another, is an Abuse, and cuts so much Profit from the Publick.'[27] The automatic process is explicitly outlined in North's recommendation that the interest rate be freed from all controls: 'I averr, that high Interest will bring Money out from Hoards, Plate, &c. into Trade, when low Interest will keep it back.'[28] Even in the absence of regulation therefore the relative stability of the interest rate is assured.

An equally striking illustration occurs in North's critique of the sumptuary laws regulating the use of plate on the grounds that money is required for trade. Such constraints, North insisted, impeded the process of equilibration, which assured that suitable variations in the money supply will be forthcoming in response to changes in requirements:

There is required for carrying on the Trade of the Nation, a determinate Sum of Specifick Money, which varies, and is sometimes more, sometimes less, as the Circumstances we are in require ... This ebbing and flowing of Money supplies and accommodates itself, without any aid of Politicians. For when Money grows scarce, and begins to be hoarded, then forthwith the Mint works till the occasion be filled up again. And on the other side, when Peace brings out the Hoards, and Money abounds, the Mint not only ceaseth, but the overplus of Money will be presently melted down, either to supply the Home Trade, or for Transportation.[29]

A particularly brilliant statement of the socially beneficial effects of the profit motive appears in the tract entitled *A Vindication of a Regulated Inclosure* (1656) by Joseph Lee, a Protestant clergyman. This brief work constitutes a sophisticated application of some tools of economic analysis – particularly the concepts of efficiency and relative prices – to a matter of public policy, and, what is particularly relevant, states clearly a basic presumption that the case made in favour of free enterprise presumes the existence of a suitable legal framework.[30]

27 *Discourses Upon Trade* (1691), in J.R. McCulloch, ed., *Early English Tracts on Commerce* (1856; Cambridge, 1952), 513–14. (The preface is by Roger North, Dudley North's brother.) For the contribution by John Locke to the theory of market price and its utilization in an argument against legal regulation of the rate of interest see *Some Considerations of the Consequences of the Lowering of Interest, and Raising the Value of Money* (1691; New York, 1968), 1–6. Letwin, *The Origins of Scientific Economics*, 181, has justly observed that (unlike North) Locke failed to carry his analysis one step further to explain how the self-stabilizing process worked. The main force of the argument is simply that the pressure of excess demand would render ineffectual any legal maximum set below the market rate.
28 McCulloch, *Early English Tracts*, 519. Wage regulation is not discussed. But North, with substantial insight comparing interest to rent, does ask why rent should not be treated in precisely the same way as interest (*ibid.*, 522).
29 *Ibid.*, 538–9.
30 See R.H. Tawney, *Religion and the Rise of Capitalism* (London, 1926), 258–9; and Heckscher, *Mercantilism*, II, 129, 322–3.

'The advancement of private persons,' Lee wrote, 'will be the advantage of the publick ... whatsoever benefit we make to ourselves, tends to the publick good.'[31] In reply to the argument that enclosure would displace labour Lee stated that no one was bound to retain more employees than was necessary; on the contrary, to prevent the change implied support for a program of technical retrogression (comparable to the replacement of ploughs by men). Moreover, he objected to any obligation imposed on cultivators to produce a particular product (corn) when a greater profit is yielded by another (sheep), for if the market should require increased supplies of the former they would be forthcoming, farmers finding such a change in the pattern of activity profitable.

The statement of the benefits to society from non-interference was not, as already indicated, unqualified. Certain pre-conditions, Lee insisted, had to be satisfied. In the first place, in conditions of unemployment a sound argument might be made against enclosure; but in the case at hand, it was claimed, an excess demand for labour existed so that displaced workers would be easily reabsorbed elsewhere. Moreover, if under freedom of enterprise shortages of corn appeared as a result of monopolistic impediments (such as, for example, withholding in times of scarcity) the law might legitimately intervene. Finally, the cottages of peasants should be protected by contract; and the law of the land should assure that those who were forced to leave were rehoused.[32]

Thus a legitimate field for regulation existed in those instances where a conflict arose between normally coincidental private and public interests. Given this degree of regulation – implied indeed in the title of the tract – enclosures would be profitable for *all* and not merely for property owners.

Yet these instances of a recognition of social interdependencies which ought not to be disturbed were still atypical. The view that the profit motive organizes activity in a socially desirable fashion belonged to a later period.

SOME MAJOR EIGHTEENTH-CENTURY CONTRIBUTIONS
It may again be relevant to repeat that our concern here is not with the policy recommendations of a particular author regarding the desirable extent of government intervention but rather with the technical arguments utilized in support of a program. Bernard Mandeville is frequently said to have played a large part in the development of the proposition that (unregulated) self-interest works for the public benefit.[33] But it should be clear that reference

Mandeville

31 *A Vindication of a Regulated Inclosure*, 22–3.
32 *Ibid.*, 6–11.
33 *The Fable of the Bees; or Private Vices, Publick Benefits,* 1st ed. (1714); 6th ed., ed. F.B. Kaye (1732); (Oxford, 1924). See Schumpeter, *History of Economic Analysis*, 184n who suggests that Smith learned more than he was prepared to admit from the anticipation of his 'own pure Natural Liberty'; and Jacob Viner, *Studies in the Theory of International Trade*, 99 who argued that Mandeville's 'elaborate reasoning in support of individualism and laissez faire' was more relevant than the seventeenth-century economic literature 'in preparing the way for Adam Smith.' (Subsequently, Viner changed his position in this regard, see below.) Edwin

to the potential benefits arising from self-interest has no necessary implications for a policy of laissez faire. In fact, while Mandeville indeed emphasized the importance of self-interest as a governing motive ('man never exerts himself but when roused by his desires') and stated further that 'private vices' are 'publick benefits' he insisted that the social benefits follow only when the system is under the 'dexterous management of the clever politician.'[34] Government, he recommended, should touch the passions of its citizens in various ways to stimulate efforts; it should encourage agriculture, industry, trade, the arts, and the handicrafts to assure full employment; it should put the poor to work; it should relieve wants although not totally alleviate them; and so forth in mercantilist fashion.[35]

It is the case that Mandeville rejected certain instances of sumptuary legislation, but only because there were better ways of accomplishing the same objective. It is also true that he attacked the charity schools of the Anglican church on the grounds that they over-educated the children of the poor and distorted the allocation of resources: The required 'Proportion as to Numbers in every Trade finds it self, and is never better kept than when no body meddles or interferes with it.'[36] This argument is not, however, stated as a general rule against intervention in the labour market as is sometimes implied, but is formulated for the specific circumstances of contemporary Britain which in his view was adequately supplied with skilled labour. The fact is that he praised the government support of vocational training introduced by Peter the Great.[37]

There is more to be learned from Richard Cantillon than from any other eighteenth-century predecessor of Smith regarding the self-adjusting and autonomous character of the competitive process.[38] The working of the price system is portrayed by Cantillon with such clarity that scientific economics, it is sometimes claimed with considerable justification, makes its appearance with his demonstration of the essential interdependencies of the system of

Cannan, 'Introduction' to Wealth of Nations, li, argued similarly that it was from Mandeville that Smith probably obtained the belief that 'self-interest works for the benefit of the whole economic community.' Cannan's argument is accepted by J.J. Spengler 'The Problem of Order in Economic Affairs,' Southern Economic Journal, XV (July 1948), reprinted in J.J. Spengler and W.R. Allen, eds., Essays in Economic Thought: Aristotle to Marshall (Chicago, 1960), 31, n.40.

34 Jacob Viner, 'Introduction to Bernard Mandeville, A Letter to Dion (1732),' in Viner, The Long View and the Short (Glencoe, 1958), 339–42.

35 Mandeville, Fable of the Bees, I, questions Q, 181–98; Y, 247–51.

36 'An Essay on Charity Schools,' ibid., 299–300. On charity schools see Jacob Viner, 'Man's Economic Status,' in James L. Clifford, ed., Man versus Society in 18th-Century Britain (Cambridge, 1968), 33–4.

37 'In proportion to the Extent of his Dominions and the Multitudes he commands, he had not that Number or Variety of Tradesmen and Artificers which the true Improvement of the Country required, and therefore was in the right in leaving no Stone unturn'd to procure them' ('An Essay on Charity Schools,' 322).

38 Essai Sur la Nature du Commerce en Général (1755), ed. H. Higgs (London, 1931). Written between 1730 and 1734.

production and exchange. What is as striking as the particular technical apparatus utilized is the methodology, involving a conscious separation of pure theory from normative policy declarations and value judgments, a meticulous statement of the assumptions (including the *ceteris paribus* conditions) upon which the analysis is constructed, and the complication by stages of simple models into those of greater complexity.[39]

A few words are in order regarding Cantillon's price theory. The cost price ('intrinsic value') of a commodity was assumed to be constant with respect to output[40] and was defined formally as 'the measure of the quantity of Land and of Labour entering into its production, having regard to the fertility or produce of the Land, and to the quality of the labour.'[41] While the notion of fertility remained ambiguous, allowance was made for the market determination of a wage scale reflecting superior skill.[42] The possibility of combining the average technical coefficients to arrive at real unit costs by means of a reduction of the labour input to land was subsequently developed; since 'those who labour must subsist on the produce of the Land it seems that some relation might be found between the value of Labour and that of the produce of the Land.'[43] The labour input, it is suggested, can be reduced to the 'quantity of Land of which the produce is allotted to those who have worked upon it.'[44]

39 Cf. W.S. Jevons, 'Richard Cantillon and the Nationality of Political Economy,' *Contemporary Review* (Jan. 1881), reprinted in Jevons, *Principles of Economics* (London, 1905) and in Cantillon, *Essai*, ed. Higgs, 333–60; Henry Higgs, 'Life and Work of Richard Cantillon,' in *ibid.*, 363–89; J.J. Spengler, 'Richard Cantillon: First of the Moderns,' *Journal of Political Economy*, LXII (Aug.–Oct. 1954), in Spengler and Allen, eds. *Essays in Economic Thought*, 105–40; and Letwin, *The Origins of Scientific Economics*, 220–1.

40 Cantillon, *Essai*, ed. Higgs, 31.

41 *Ibid.*, 29.

42 *Ibid.*, 21–3: 'Some Handicrafts-men earn more, others less, according to the different Cases and Circumstances,' which include – apart from 'Ingenuity and Industry' (skill) – differential returns reflecting 'time in training'; 'risks and dangers'; and 'Capacity and trustworthiness.' (Although Cantillon states that 'it is easily seen that the difference of price paid for daily work is based upon natural and obvious reasons' he did not at this point provide a formal account of the causal mechanisms at work.)

  A problem arises insofar as the productiveness of land and of labour is already included within the quantity of the respective inputs used per unit of output. This apparently superfluous qualification may, however, be intended as a reference to the relevant factor prices to be used in the calculation of average cost.

43 *Ibid.*, 31. The general idea was suggested by Sir William Petty's attempt to establish a 'par' between land and labour. *Political Anatomy of Ireland* (1691), chap. IX, in C.H. Hull, ed., *Economic Writings of Sir William Petty* (Cambridge, 1899) I, 176f.

44 Cantillon, *Essai*, ed. Higgs, 41. The calculation assumes the payment of subsistence wages, that is, enough to maintain the labourers and also to rear the children required to replace them in the labour market, allowance being made for differential infant mortality rates. Cantillon calculated the subsistence wage (of the 'meanest Peasant' or journeyman) as double the produce of the land needed for an individual worker's direct maintenance.

The treatment of 'profits' by Cantillon is, in some key respects, thoroughly novel and of particular relevance in the present context of price theory. A sharp distinction was drawn between 'undertakers' ('entrepreneurs') and 'hired people,' according to which the former are 'as it were on unfixed wages and the others on wages fixed so long as they receive them though their functions and ranks may be very unequal.' The class of 'undertakers' thus comprises all those who purchase inputs at a 'certain' price but sell at an 'uncertain' price, including the self-employed and farmers and master manufacturers who were typically employers.[45] 'Profits' in brief represents a generic term for any uncertain income and not simply for the income of employers. Moreover, while farmers and master manufacturers received their earnings in the form of profits – as a kind of residual – Cantillon nonetheless suggested that these returns, in the case of the *majority*, may be valued at three times the produce of the land needed for any individual (standard) labourer's direct maintenance.[46] The general impression is thus that a kind of normal profit was included within long-run (cost) price. But the essential point is that this return did not represent merely the 'wages of management.' Cantillon subsequently made it clear that there existed a distinct (net) return out of which, in certain circumstances, interest is paid. This surplus, it must also be emphasized, is recognized not only in the case of agriculture – as was to be the subsequent physiocratic practice – but in manufacturing as well.[47]

We perceive, therefore, an interest in Cantillon's work in the nature and measurement of the factors directly involved in the production process, reflecting a departure from a traditional concern with the *merchant* – in contrast with the employer (master-manufacturer or farmer) – as the recipient of 'profits' or the bearer of 'loss.' But the 'net' return to the master-manufacturer or farmer to which Cantillon refers is not *formally* related to their function's as capitalist-employers; for all recipients of uncertain incomes were profit-earning entrepreneurs 'whether they set up with a capital to conduct their enterprise' or direct their own labour 'without capital.'[48] Moreover, the precise 'source' of the net return was not considered; that in the last resort at least, net

45 *Ibid.*, 39–41, 51–5. (The category also included beggars and robbers.)
46 *Ibid.*, 41. While it was possible to talk of a 'wage' (of 'superintendence' or management) per time unit, Cantillon seemed to be troubled by the fact that management costs per unit of output declined with size of operation.
47 *Ibid.*, 121, 201f.
48 *Ibid.*, 55. It may also be remarked that profits and wages were said to have a common source in, or to be dependent upon, the property of landowners: 'except the Prince and the Proprietors of Land, all the Inhabitants of a State are dependent ...[and] derive their living and their advantages from the property of the Land-owners.' Taken literally, profits and wages are thus in the nature of transfer payments. The possession of 'saved capital,' it is argued – in a reference to merchant's 'stores of corn, wool, copper, gold, silver or some produce or merchandise' – does not alter the conclusion, for 'however one may have gained or saved them they are always derived from the land of actual Proprietors either by gain or by saving of the wages destined for one's subsistence' (*ibid.*, 57).

profits may have been regarded as the consequence of 'buying cheap and selling dear' in the traditional fashion is suggested by Cantillon's aside that 'it may perhaps be urged that Undertakers seek to snatch all they can in their calling and to get the better of their customers.'[49]

The determination of market prices of commodities was treated by Cantillon in more sophisticated fashion than by earlier writers.[50] The possibility of divergencies between the market and cost price was discussed, although little formal attention was paid to the precise process by which the normal price emerges.[51] Yet the view that the process was merely taken for granted without examination[52] is not justified since it is implied in applications of the theory, as we shall now see.

Cantillon considered the effects of an exogenous change in tastes (on the part of landlords) upon the pattern of agricultural activity. The general prediction is that farmers 'will not fail to change from year to year the use of the land till they arrive at proportioning their production pretty well to the consumption of the Inhabitants,' referring probably to consumption at the cost price.[53] This result is achieved by the price mechanism: 'When a Landowner has dismissed a great number of Domestic Servants, and increased the number of his Horses, there will be too much Corn for the needs of the Inhabitants, and so the Corn will be cheap and the Hay dear. In consequence the Farmers will increase their grass land and diminish their Corn to proportion it to the demand. In this way the Fancies or Fashions of Landowners determine the use of the Land and bring about the variations of demand which cause the variations of Market prices. If all the Landowners of a State cultivated their own estates they would use them to produce what they want; and as the varia-

---

49 *Ibid.*, 55. From the viewpoint of method it is of significance that he refuses to be diverted by this issue on the grounds that it is 'outside my subject.'

50 'Of Market Price,' *ibid.*, 117-21.

51 *Ibid.*, 30-1. The main weakness lies in the tendency to talk of a *particular* quantity of corn needed for the year's consumption implying zero price elasticity. This is not, however, the case in the chapter, 'Of Market Price,' and if we understand him as referring to consumption at the (given) cost price then the argument fits into place: 'If the Farmers in a State sow more corn than usual, much more than is needed for the year's consumption, the real and intrinsic value of the corn will correspond to the Land and Labour which enter into its production; but as there is too great an abundance of it and there are more sellers than buyers the Market Price of the Corn will necessary fall below the intrinsic price or Value. If on the contrary the Farmers sow less corn than is needed for consumption there will be more buyers than sellers and the Market Price of corn will rise above its intrinsic value.'

52 Schumpeter, *History of Economic Analysis*, 220.

53 Landlords as a whole were assumed to have quantitatively great purchasing power, to be leaders in matters of taste and style, and to be volatile in their spending habits. Cantillon was attempting to show that these characteristics assured a pattern of agricultural activity roughly equivalent to that which would exist if landowners cultivated their own estates rather than rented out their land and relied upon the market process.

tions of demand are chiefly caused by their mode of living the prices which they offer in the Market decide the Farmers to all the changes which they make in the employment and use of the land.'[54]

The great concern with method and organization of work which characterizes the writings of Cantillon appears too in the Inquiry of Sir James Steuart. A balanced use of the inductive and deductive methods was recommended, whereby induction from statistical data was to establish the hypotheses and deduction to derive logical 'principles' therefrom. At the same time Steuart was concerned with the potential misuse of deductive method in applications to practical issues, referring to 'the habit of running into what the French call *Systèmes*' which represent 'a chain of contingent consequences, drawn from a few fundamental maxims, adopted, perhaps, rashly' and applied by the author 'far beyond the limits of the ideas present to his understanding, when he made his definition.'[55] General principles might indicate general directions but the complexity of verification had to be continually allowed for. As with Cantillon, the procedure emphasized the *ceteris paribus* conditions and built up step-by-step from simple to more complicated models.

In the case of Steuart we find further a fascinating instance of a (partial) comprehension of the process of expansion and contraction of industry in response to profit and loss on the part of one who called for government control of the mechanism. Formally much emphasis is placed on the characteristic interdependencies of an exchange economy,[56] and in discussion of industry and trade Steuart explicitly stated that it is 'the combination of every private interest which forms the public good.'[57] But (as with Mandeville) self-interest, of immense potency as a regulatory force, was to be supervised. This will be illustrated in terms of the theory of competitive price.

In a significant chapter devoted to the issue 'How the Prices of Goods are determined by Trade' a distinction is drawn between the 'real value' of the commodity – covering labour costs (where wages are at subsistence), and costs relating to materials and equipment – and the so-called 'profit upon alienation' received by the manufacturer which will be 'in proportion to demand, and

54 Cantillon, *Essai*, ed. Higgs, 63–5. We can further illustrate the operation of automatic equilibrating forces by reference to Cantillon's demographic applications of the 'market price-cost price' relationship (see below).
55 Sir James Steuart, *An Inquiry into the Principles of Political Economy* (1767), ed. Andrew S. Skinner (Chicago, 1966), 8. See 'Analytical Introduction' by Skinner, lx–lxii; Douglas Vickers, *Studies in the Theory of Money* (London, 1960), 244–6; and S.R. Sen, *The Economics of Sir James Steuart* (London, 1957), 26–31, on Steuart's methodology.
56 The use of inter-sectoral analysis is adopted to explain the interdependencies although the specific method is less powerful than that of the Physiocrats. Cf. Skinner, 'Analytical Introduction,' lxix.
57 Steuart, *Inquiry*, 143. The consequences to an economy whose inhabitants are 'disinterested' are said to be disastrous: 'were a rich merchant to begin and sell his goods without profit, what would become of trade? ... were people to feed all who would ask charity, what would become of industry?'

therefore will fluctuate according to circumstances.'[58] According to this version, apparently, profits do *not* appear in supply price. Yet subsequently, in an account of long-run equilibrium, it seems to be the view of Steuart that 'a small addition for Profit' must be allowed for: 'When we say that the balance between work and demand is to be sustained in equilibrio, as far as possible, we mean that the quantity supplied should be in proportion to the quantity *demanded*, that is, *wanted*. While the balance stands justly poised, prices are found in the adequate proportion of the real expence of making the goods, with a small addition for profit to the manufacturer and merchant.'[59] It may also be noted that by (normal) profits Steuart really referred to a return to a particular category of labour.[60]

Alterations in either demand or supply were seen to generate divergencies between the market price and the cost price. But the 'automatic' process of correction was not to be given free reign. Thus in the case of an excess supply, 'it should be inquired, whether the quantity furnished has really swelled, in all respects, beyond the proportion of the consumption, (in which case the statesman should diminish the number of hands, by throwing a part of them into a new channel).'[61] It was to be the *responsibility of government* to reallocate resources. The competitive process itself was not to be relied on, for the excess supply 'diminishes the reasonable profits, or perhaps, indeed, obliges the workmen to sell below prime cost. The effect of this is, that the workmen fall into distress, and that industry suffers a discouragement.'[62] It seems, therefore, that Steuart recognized the existence of automatic mechanisms which assure the contraction of unprofitable industries but did not wish to rely upon them.

The case of an excess demand was also considered. In the absence of regulation, price would rise, allowing excess profits. But in this event Steuart did not envisage consequential expansion of the industry. On the contrary, he feared that the profits would become 'consolidated,' that is, would come to be regarded as the norm, with the consequence that prices would become inflexible downwards. In the case of excess demand, accordingly, 'the statesman should be still more upon his guard, to provide a proportional supply.' Unfortunately, the implied constraints, whereby in the absence of intervention price would permanently exceed the original cost level, are not considered.

It is of some importance to recognize that Steuart's support for extensive

58 *Ibid.*, 160–1.
59 *Ibid.*, 189. We are abstracting from the weak points of his argument which derive in part from a failure to distinguish shifts of, and movements along, the demand curve.
60 See, e.g., *ibid.*, 193n. Indeed the entire emphasis in Steuart's discussion of the equilibrating process is placed upon the movement of labour.
61 *Ibid.*, 191. He allows for an excess due to a miscalculation by sellers, 'in which case proper information and even assistance should be given them to prevent merchants from taking advantage of their want of experience: but these last precautions are necessary in the infancy of industry only.'
62 *Ibid.*, 192.

intervention was in part designed to *correct* distortions in the market process. Thus it was his view that competition between labourers should be encouraged (particularly in the export sector) at least until wages were reduced to the subsistence level, and accordingly monopolistic impediments (such as labourers' 'fraternities'), which 'prevent competition, and raise profits beyond the standard of the *physical-necessary*,' discouraged. In this context Steuart addressed himself to explain observed wage-rate differentials. Amongst the restrictions on supply he included peculiar location; 'extraordinary dexterity' which 'set a celebrated artist in a manner above a possibility of rivalship, and make him the master of his price'; 'the difficulty of acquiring the dexterity requisite,' that is to say the cost of apprenticeship; and the cost of the complementary inputs which may be required.[63]

THE PHYSIOCRATS

This entire work is in essence concerned with the relationship between Smith's analyses of economic development and 'general equilibrium.' A similar problem exists in the understanding of Physiocracy. It is not appropriate to deal extensively with the issue here, but we shall consider briefly the organizational function of the price mechanism in physiocratic economics, bearing in mind that the ultimate concern of the economists might have been with issues for which the mechanism in question is not 'appropriate.'

Certainly Quesnay recognized the phenomenon of general economic interdependence which characterizes the 'exchange economy.' The problem of explaining the nature of this interdependence – 'the general system of expenditures, work, gain, and consumption' – was dealt with in terms of 'tableaux économiques,' representing a circular-flow process.[64] The broad conception of an interdependent economic system subject to regular laws (although perhaps not 'original,' as we have seen) and the particular mode of treatment in terms of a conception of circular flow represent together an outstanding intellectual achievement. None of the earlier writers can be said to have conceptualized economic life, to a comparable degree and with such formal elegance, in terms of component streams of goods and money moving in opposite directions.[65]

What concerns us here, however, is the precise analysis of the co-ordinating, harmonizing, and organizing function of the price mechanism in free competition.[66] It is clear that Quesnay formally accorded to 'self-interest' – the

---

63 *Ibid.*, 273–5. Cf. the analysis of the wage structure by Cantillon, above. Demographic applications are discussed below. We may also refer to a suggestion of a self-regulating mechanism in the context of monetary theory. Steuart explained the movement of money into and out of hoards in terms of the response to interest-rate movements. (See Viner, *Studies in the Theory of International Trade*, 86–7.)

For a discussion by David Hume of the coincidence of private and social returns in the labour market, explicitly utilized by Smith, see below 263.

64 R.L. Meek, *The Economics of Physiocracy* (London, 1962), 374.

65 On the probable influence of Cantillon, see *ibid.*, 266f.

66 We are therefore deliberately abstracting from the blend of philosophical, religious, and political doctrine upon which the Physiocrats drew in arriving at their laissez-

objective of the economic unit in maximum receipts and minimum outlays – the role of fundamental motive force governing the operation of the market-exchange system. Under certain conditions this governing motive was said to assure a (desirable) order in economic affairs. Was this consequence in any way 'demonstrated' in terms of a theory of resource allocation?

The process whereby competition assures that prices in the long run will tend to reflect production costs is described for the manufacturing sector by Quesnay. The characteristic physiocratic distinction between manufacturing and agriculture according to which only the latter generates any net return over costs will be noted:

the wealth which constitutes the costs of agriculture differs greatly, as regards its employment, from industrial wealth. It is the former which causes revenue to be generated, whereas the product of industrial wealth is confined to goods which are worth only the expenses which they entail. The worker who makes a piece of cloth purchases the raw material and incurs expenses for his needs while he is making it. The payment he receives when he sells it returns to him the purchase price and his expenses; the gain which his labour procures for him is confined to the restitution of the expenses he has incurred ... The competition of workers who are trying to procure for themselves a similar gain in order to get a living restricts the price of manufactured goods to the level of this gain itself. *Thus this gain, or restitution of expenses, is not, like the revenue of landed property, an original form of wealth representing a pure profit.*[67]

Evidently manufacturing prices tend to equal long-run costs which, it would appear, include raw material and subsistence expenses with no special allowance for 'normal' profits.[68]

It is the operation of the competitive mechanism in agriculture which is problematic. For Quesnay emphasized that in a closed economy, because of the extreme volatility of supply in the face of high inelasticity of demand, there was no regular process by which the market price of corn tended to coincide with production costs: 'The revenue of a kingdom is regulated by the price of its produce; and the price of produce is maintained and regulated by foreign trade. For in a state which has no external trade at all, either of export or of

faire position, in order to focus upon their economic analysis of the co-ordinating function of free competition. On the broader issues see *ibid.*, 370–4; Spengler, 'The Problem of Order in Economic Affairs,' 17–8; J.J. Spengler, 'Quesnay: Philosophe, Empiriste, Economiste,' in A. Sauvy, ed., *François Quesnay et la Physiocratie* (Institut National d'Etudes Démographiques, Paris, 1958; hereafter cited as INED), 70–1; and Viner, 'The Intellectual History of Laissez-Faire,' 59.

67 F. Quesnay, 'Impôts,' in *L'Encyclopédie* (1757) (author's emphasis). See INED, 583; translated in Meek, *The Economics of Physiocracy* (hereafter cited as Meek when referring to a translation from the French), 105.

68 Wages were generally assumed to be at subsistence. This is clear from the analysis of the effects of taxation on wages; any such tax would lead to an increase in the wage rate as a consequence of reduced population. See F. Quesnay, 'Second problème économique,' *Physiocratie* (1767). INED, 984; Meek, 194.

import, the price of produce cannot be subject to any rule or any order. It necessarily follows the variations of scarcity and abundance in the country, and the state has to put up with excessively low or excessively high prices [*des valeurs et des chertés*], both of which are equally disastrous and inevitable.'[69] Such fluctuations would be avoided in an open economy where the price would be determined by world market conditions: 'On the assumption of freedom of external trade the price will always be regulated by the competition of neighbouring nations in the produce trade.'[70]

But Quesnay developed further for the case of agriculture the concept of *cost* price in a manner which clouds the nature of long-run competitive equilibrium. The (domestic) 'fundamental price' is defined 'by the expenses or costs which have to be incurred in their production or preparation.' If commodities sell at a price 'which is high enough to yield a gain sufficient to encourage people to maintain or increase their production, they are at their proper level [*elles sont à bon prix*].'[71] If, however, as a result of scarcity their price rises to a level 'which is burdensome to the people, then this price is excessively high [*cherté*].' A *bon prix* is thus apparently any price *above costs* yielding a 'gain' by a margin which is not 'excessive.' Such a price could, it was believed, be determined by the world market to the great advantage of the state. Quesnay made the further remark that while a *bon prix* might be advantageous, a price below costs could never be so: 'A low price which constantly failed to exceed the fundamental price would be a different matter; for there is no case in which such a price would not be ruinous, and in which it would not necessitate the abandonment of the production of the produce whose price was constantly limited to such a low level.'[72]

The vague definition of long-run cost price will be noted. On the one hand production may apparently be 'maintained' at a constant level even where a 'gain' over costs is forthcoming, while a price which just equals the 'fundamental' cost level leads to contraction. Clearly, while agricultural profits were *formally* excluded from the ordinary costs of cultivation, the argument implies that they were *in fact* regarded as a necessary compensation, so that prices covering only 'paid out' costs would fail to assure the maintenance of the current level of activity. Indeed, Quesnay formally warned against the taxation of agricultural profits on the grounds that they constituted a necessary return (and in this regard had to be distinguished from rent):

The profits of the farmers and the gains of the men whom the farmers employ in cultivation ought to be distinguished from the revenue which this same cultivation

69 Quesnay, 'Hommes,' in *L'Encyclopédie* (1757). INED, 529; Meek, 93.
70 From 'Grains,' in *L'Encyclopédie* (1757). INED, 509; Meek, 87. Cf. a statement implying perhaps a coincidental price floor and ceiling: 'When trade is free, the dearness of produce has necessary limits which are determined by the prices of the produce of other nations which have extended their trade to all parts of the world. The same cannot be said of the valuelessness or dearness of produce caused by the absence of free trade. These follow one another in turn and irregularly' (Meek, 86).
71 INED, 529; Meek, 93.
72 Meek, 94.

brings in every year for the proprietors; for it is the costs and profits of the husband-men which assure cultivation and the revenue ...

Thus it is not on the productive wealth of the husbandmen that taxes should be assessed, since this would mean the destruction of the means necessary to produce the annual wealth of the nation.

The richer the husbandman is, and *the more he is spurred on by profit*, the more will cultivation be assured.[73]

We may summarize the above argument by saying that for Quesnay the competitive process in the case of manufacturing will assure that market prices tend to equal the natural price which includes paid-out expenses (largely raw materials and subsistence). In the case of agriculture an *additional* element representing normal profits will have to be yielded for the achievement of equilibrium. Yet the impression is that in a closed economy the process of equi-libration in agriculture is defective; it is in the open economy that an equilibrium might be achieved.

The analysis has serious implications for the physiocratic approach to rent which was viewed as a surplus income yielded uniquely by agricultural activity. The immediate source of rent – a net value product – lies in the excess of price over paid-out costs. It was taken for granted that, in the long run, the excess – presumably with the exception of that part constituting normal profits – would be transferred by farmers to the landlords upon the renewal of the lease:

First, the farmers of landed property profit up to the renewal of their leases from the constant increase in the prices of products which occurs during the terms of these leases ... And these profits, which increase the number of wealthy farmers, promote at the time of the renewal of the leases a greater degree of competition between them, which then assures to the proprietors and the sovereign the full return of the net product – not only that which results directly from the increase in prices, but also that additional amount which is generated by the more ample means of the farmers; for we know that wealth is the great and principal implement of cultivation, and that a wealthy farmer can often profitably rent land at a rate one-third or one-half above that which a poor farmer could pay only with difficulty and at the risk of ruining himself.[74]

But the outcome of our discussion above is that with the exception of the artificial device of a price floor determined in the world market, Quesnay provided no logical explanation for a surplus of revenue over costs. In a closed economy there appears to be no reason for the existence of a rental income, for it might legitimately be expected that competition would assure that prices

73 'Impôts,' INED, 594–5; Meek, 106 (author's emphasis). Professor Meek's conclusion is that apart from the profits yielded by short-run price fluctuation or by improved methods, Quesnay adopted the view that the profit of agricultural entrepreneurs was envisaged as a superior wage to be included within costs of cultivation (Meek, 304–5). (Manufactures were seen to be under the control of 'workers on their own account' and the long-run price covered the cost of raw materials and of subsistence goods consumed.) But cf. our discussion below.

74 'Premier problème économique,' *Journal d'agriculture* (1766). INED, 870–1; Meek, 180–1.

must *fall* to the level of costs (including normal profits): 'Quesnay ne relie pas sa théorie du prix de longue période (coût de production) à sa théorie de la valeur puisqu'il s'agit d'une valeur nette.'[75] The analytical weakness of the physiocratic argument has particular relevance in light of its support for free trade in corn. The policy was championed not merely as a means of guaranteeing a stable corn price; it was clearly the *sine qua non* of the entire rental income, given the assumption that corn would be exported.[76]

The Physiocrats were much concerned with mercantilist regulations which had diverted resources away from the agricultural sector. Particular attention was paid to encouragements of the domestic manufacture (for export) of luxury goods (utilizing imported raw materials) – 'dont la fabrication ne restitue à nos ouvriers et à l'Etat que les frais de leur subsistance' – and the discouragement of agriculture by export constraints placed upon agricultural produce. Similarly, depopulation of the countryside was attributed to the poverty therein compared with the superior conditions in the artificially created towns; Quesnay was much concerned with the 'mauvaise distribution des hommes.'[77]

Yet no clear mechanism was outlined to explain how, in the absence of intervention, resources would be allocated. It is true that continual reference is made to France as 'une nation agricole,' or a nation 'si riche en biens-fonds,' and it may be implied thereby that the high land endowment would assure, in the absence of intervention, an expansion of agriculture at the expense of manufacturing. The argument is perhaps implicit in the following passage dealing with international trade (and referring to *absolute* cost differentials):

A nation ought to carry on the production only of those manufactured commodities for which it possesses the raw materials; and it should purchase from abroad such manufactured commodities as can be bought at a price lower than the cost which would be involved if the nation made them itself. Through these purchases mutual trade is stimulated; for if nations tried to buy nothing and sell everything, this would do away with external trade and the advantages of the export of raw produce, which is infinitely more profitable than that of manufactured commodities. An agricultural nation should facilitate an active external trade in raw produce, by means of a passive external trade in manufactured commodities which it can profitably buy from abroad.[78]

75 J.F. Faure-Soulet, *Economie Politique et Progrès au Siècle des Lumières* (Paris, 1964), 121.
76 'Hommes,' INED, 558.
77 'Fermiers,' *ibid.*, 455. Actually he here refers to the trend towards the towns as inevitable but as going too far in consequence of governmental pressures. Cf. *ibid.*, 459: 'on y a employé une multitude d'hommes, dans le temps que le royaume se dépeuplait et que les campagnes devenaient désertes. On a fait baisser le prix de nos blés, afin que la fabrication et la main-d'œuvre fussent moins chères que chez l'étranger: les hommes et les richesses se sont accumulées dans les villes; l'agriculture, la plus féconde et la plus noble partie de notre commerce, la source des revenus du royaume n'a pas été envisagée comme le fond de nos richesses.'
78 'Maximes Générales,' *Physiocratie* (1767). INED, 964; Meek, 247.

But the argument is carried no further; Quesnay, in general, merely expressed the optimistic view that if agriculture is well looked after, activity in other sectors will be automatically undertaken in satisfactory fashion.[79] Moreover, it is sometimes suggested tangentially that intervention *in favour* of agriculture would be desirable in an agricultural state: 'Thus the political administration of agriculture and of trade in its produce is the foundation of the department of finance, and of all the other branches of administration in an agricultural nation.'[80] Indeed, at times Quesnay was perfectly explicit: '*That the government's economic policy should be concerned only with encouraging productive expenditure and trade in raw produce, and that it should refrain from interfering with sterile expenditure.*'[81]

Although we must not rule out the possibility that Quesnay intended to recommend intervention in favour of agriculture (by subsidies and the like), but only until economic reform had been achieved,[82] it would seem more likely that free trade was recommended in the case of corn on the assumption that the world price exceeded the price attainable in a closed economy. We can deduce that the policy might well have been qualified in different circumstances:

On ne doit jamais perdre de vue dans le gouvernement que la valeur des produits des biens-fonds et celle des gains des hommes ne peuvent s'estimer que par leur prix, que l'État n'est riche qu'à raison de ce prix; que les revenus du Roi doivent être réglés aussi sur ce prix, et qu'il n'a de réalité dans un État commerçant qu'autant qu'il a cours chez l'étranger. Ainsi toute l'attention du gouvernement dans la dimunition des richesses annuelles du royaume doit tendre continuellement à ne point laisser tomber les denrées au-dessous du prix ordinaire qui a cours chez l'étranger, et il ne peut y réussir qu'en facilitant le plus qu'il est possible le commerce extérieur. L'état des richesses d'une nation dépend entièrement de cette conduite. Tous droits de sortie et d'entrée, toutes prohibitions et tous règlements qui contraignent le commerce extérieur et intérieur diminuent le fond des richesses de l'État et les revenus du souverain; toute imposition de droits préjudiciables au commerce et à la purduction des denrées est imposition destructive.[83]

In fact, occasionally Quesnay was quite explicit that free trade might be undesirable: '*That the prices of produce and commodities in the kingdom*

79 'Hommes,' INED, 559: 'Ne nous amusons donc point, nous qui sommes si riches en biens-fonds, à un petit commerce de luxe, qui ne rend que les frais de main-d'œuvre; fertilisons nos terres, vendons des grains, des vins, des chanvres, des étoffes de nos laines, le plus qu'il est possible. Le produit multipliera réellement les richesses; et ces richesses annuelles toujours renaissantes nous assureront des manufactures et des ouvrages d'industrie en tout genre. Car l'opulence est la mère des arts et du luxe.'

80 'Maximes Générales.' INED, 975; Meek, 260.

81 *Ibid.*, 951; Meek, 233.

82 Cf. 'Impots,' INED, 602.

83 *Ibid.* See also Norman J. Ware, 'The Physiocrats: A Study in Economic Rationalization,' *American Economic Review*, XXI (Dec. 1931), 607; Arthur I. Bloomfield, 'The Foreign-Trade Doctrines of the Physiocrats,' *ibid.* (Dec. 1938), reprinted in Spengler and Allen, *Essays in Economic Thought*, 228; and Spengler, 'Quesnay,' (INED), 62, on the potential limitation upon the doctrine of free trade.

should never be made to fall; for then mutual foreign trade would become disadvantageous to the nation.'[84]

The *Tableau Economique*, it may also be noted, is a portrayal of a flow of goods for payment in conditions of sectoral equilibrium, and is thus not strictly concerned with resource allocation. Moreover, in some respects the portrayal of perpetual (inter-class) static equilibrium may be fatal to analysis; a stress on regularity in process is valuable if it should lead to a view of economic phenomena as *causally* inter-dependent. In fact the actual system portrayed has only regular internal motion. To the extent that these comments are justified it seems to be the case that the 'analytical' support for the physiocratic programme of laissez-faire and free trade was deficient.

In the work of A.R.J. Turgot, who perhaps should not be regarded as an 'orthodox' member of the physiocratic school, we do find some dazzling demonstrations of the organizing function of the competitive price mechanism. This is above all the case in the analysis of the return to capital. The rates of return to various employments of capital – including rental earnings on investments in the purchase of land; the return to loanable funds; and the earnings on capital invested in agriculture, manufacturing and commerce – are maintained in 'a sort of equilibrium' by competitive pressures, the differentials reflecting non-monetary advantages or disadvantages of the various investments:

The different employments of capitals produce, therefore, very unequal products; but this inequality does not prevent the exercise of a reciprocal influence one upon the other, or the establishment between them of a sort of equilibrium, as between two liquids of unequal gravity which communicate with one another at the bottom of a reversed syphon of which they occupy the two branches; they will not be on a level, but the height of one cannot increase without the other also rising in the opposite branch.[85]

A similar treatment involving 'a kind of equilibrium' occurs in the analysis of the effects of taxation of wages contained in an explanatory letter to David Hume. Turgot ascribed to the general physiocratic view that wages would tend to be at subsistence,[86] or more specifically that the long-run return to

84 'Maximes Générales,' INED, 954; Meek, 235.
85 A.R.J. Turgot, *Reflections on the Formation and Distribution of Riches* (1766, published 1769–70; New York, 1963), 83–4. The return to entrepreneurship includes profit viewed as an opportunity cost equal to the interest earned if money is lent out. Elsewhere (53) the alternative referred to is the purchase of an estate. Thus the return to capital invested in agriculture, manufacturing and commerce must *exceed* that invested in the purchase of land or loaned out to assure a compensation to 'the undertaker' for 'his care, his labour, his talents and his risks, and to furnish him in addition with that wherewith he may replace the annual wear and tear of his advances' (*ibid.*, 83).

See the discussion by P.D. Groenewegen, 'Turgot and Adam Smith,' *Scottish Journal of Political Economy*, XVI (Nov. 1969), 280–2, comparing Smith's analysis of the various employments of capital with that of Turgot.
86 *Ibid.*, 8.

labour will include subsistence and an allowance 'to provide for accidents' and 'to bring up families.' A tax on wages must accordingly lead to a rise in wages:

In a nation where trade and industry are free and vigorous, competition fixes this profit at the lowest possible rate. A kind of equilibrium establishes itself between the value of all the productions of the land, the consumption of the different kinds of commodities, the different sorts of works, the number of men employed at them, and the price of their wages.

Wages can be fixed and remain constantly at a definite point only in virtue of this equilibrium, and of the influence which all the parts of the society, all the branches of production and commerce, exercise upon one another. This granted, if you change one of the weights, a movement cannot but result from it in the whole of the machine which tends to restore the old equilibrium. The proportion which the current value of wages bears to their fundamental value was established by the laws of this equilibrium and by the combination of all the circumstances under which all the parts of the society are placed.

You augment the fundamental value [by a tax on wages or on wage goods]: the circumstances which have before fixed the proportion which the current value bears to this fundamental value cannot but cause the current value to rise until the proportion is re-established. I am aware that this result will not be sudden; and that in every complicated machine there are frictions which delay the results most infallibly demonstrated by theory.[87]

It is relevant to remark in this note regarding equilibrating mechanisms that Turgot provided what is probably the first explicit recognition of incremental analysis in a full discussion of diminishing returns (based upon variability of proportions rather than scale) distinguishing between total, average and marginal product, and defining the mathematical relationship betwen them.[88] The argument was not, however, incorporated into his basic theoretical structures.[89]

87 Letter to Hume dated March 25, 1767, *ibid.*, 108–9. Hume had argued that 'the price of labour will always depend on the quantity of offers of labour and the quantity of the demand, and not upon the taxes' (*ibid.*, 104–5).

88 'Observations sur le mémoire de M. de Saint-Péravy' (1767), in E. Daire and H. Dussard, eds. *Œuvres de Turgot* I (Paris, 1844), 420–2.

89 In a comment in the 'Observation sur le mémoire de M. Graslin' (1767), *ibid.*, 436, Turgot suggests that the range of increasing returns was still relevant in the case of French agriculture: 'Comme la fertilité de la terre est bornée, il y a sans doute un point où l'augmentation des avances n'augmenterait pas la production à proportion de l'augmentation des frais; mais jusqu'à présent on est bien loin d'avoir atteint cette limite, et l'expérience prouve que là où les avances sont les plus fortes, c'est-à-dire là où les cultivateurs sont les plus riches, là est non-seulement la plus grande production totale, mais là sont les plus grands *produits nets.*'

The discovery of the law of diminishing returns has been ascribed, by J.A. Schumpeter, to Steuart regarding the 'extensive' margin, and to Turgot regarding the 'intensive' margin. Turgot's contribution, Schumpeter comments, 'cannot be commended too highly. It embodies an achievement that is nothing short of brilliant and suffices in itself to place Turgot as a theorist high above A. Smith.' *History of Economic Analysis*, 260.

TWO

Economic development

THE MERCANTILIST LITERATURE

The basic rationalizations offered for the characteristic mercantilist preoccupation with a long-run national accumulation of precious metals are still matters of contention. But it is probably broadly accepted, following the extensive researches of Professor Viner in particular, that Smith exaggerated when he ascribed to his predecessors an unambiguous identification of wealth and the precious metals. More important than any absolute identification was the attribution to the metals of special functions leading the pamphleteers to draw an excessively close relationship between national wealth and the stock of hard currency.

In particular, the commonly-held doctrine favouring thrift on moral or religious or class grounds entailed an emphasis upon saved wealth in the form of stored-up goods, implying thereby a failure to appreciate the true nature of productive investment. Saved wealth was in turn identified with commodities of a kind physically most suitable for accumulation, namely the precious metals which could be acquired normally only by way of a favourable foreign-trade balance.[1] Some writers were concerned with 'genuine' capital accumulation, but tended to talk of capital employed by its owner or lent out in monetary terms, identifying it with the monetary metals and accordingly attaching to the latter peculiar significance.[2]

1 The view of savings referred to in the text is found, for example, in the work of Sir William Petty, *Political Arithmetic* (1690), and Charles Davenant, *An Essay on the East-India Trade* (1696). The attribution to the precious metals of characteristics rendering them particularly suitable to function as stores of wealth is also made by Petty amongst many others. See Jacob Viner, *Studies in the Theory of International Trade* (New York, 1937), 26–30.

2 See Viner, *Studies in the Theory of International Trade*, 31–2, who draws evidence from various monetary theories of the rate of interest according to which interest was paid for the use of money or depended upon the quantity of money.

Since inflows of precious metals depended upon the foreign-trade balance, overwhelming emphasis was placed upon the social desirability of output expansions (without reference to real income per head) able either directly or indirectly to generate such inflows. Thus in the case of Thomas Mun – who appears to have been concerned with the accumulation of the precious metals because they are most suitable as a 'store of wealth' – production is emphasized in order to provide goods for export and to replace imports; for example, although England was 'already exceeding rich by nature,' its riches might be increased 'by laying the waste grounds (which are infinite) into such employments as should no way hinder the present revenues of other manured lands, but hereby to supply our selves and prevent the importations of Hemp, Flax, Cordage, Tobacco, and divers other things which now we fetch from strangers to our great impoverishing.'[3] At the same time the use of British shipping in trading should be encouraged in order to include in the export price the various freight and insurance charges,[4] implying thereby that shipping is a costless service or – what is closer to Mun's intention – implying the irrelevance of the productive factors absorbed in undertaking a project provided that a positive effect upon the balance of trade is assured. With the objective of reducing imports, 'excessive consumption of forraign wares' should be discouraged 'by commanding their own manufactures to be used;'[5] consumption of luxury goods – even if domestically produced – should be minimized in order to release commodities for export;[6] and the authorities should encourage re-exportation by the establishment of staple towns,[7] and by preferential customs treatment for those goods produced for export but utilizing imported raw materials.[8]

Throughout his argument Mun makes reference to the desirability of high employment. In one passage he argued that if, despite all discouragement, the wealthy insisted upon prodigal behaviour it was preferable that they consume commodities produced at home with domestic materials such that 'the excess of the rich may be the employment of the poor, whose labours notwithstanding of this kind, *would be more profitable for the commonwealth, if they were done for the use of strangers.*'[9] Clearly, employment in the *export* sector is the most desirable. Similarly, reference is made to the desirability of investment in the colonial fishing grounds which would afford 'much wealth and employments to maintain a great number of poor, and to encrease our

3 *England's Treasure by Forraign Trade* (1664; Oxford 1959), 7.
4 *Ibid.*, 8–9. Accordingly, trade with distant countries was said to be particularly desirable (*ibid.*, 10–11).
5 *Ibid.*, 7. This is partly justified on the grounds that foreign countries also carried out such internal regulation.
6 *Ibid.*, 9.
7 *Ibid.*, 10.
8 *Ibid.*, 11. In addition great attention should be paid by merchants to the maximizing of the value returns of exports by taking into consideration foreign demand elasticities in their pricing policies (*ibid.*, 8).
9 *Ibid.*, 9 (author's emphasis).

decaying trade.'[10] As a further instance, Mun called for the removal of charges upon exported goods utilizing imported raw materials (although not the import duties upon the materials themselves) in order to stimulate production and employment as well as government revenues derived from import duties: 'it would employ very many poor people, and *much encrease the value of our stock yearly issued into other Countreys*, and it would (for this purpose) cause the more forraign Materials to be brought in, to the improvement of His Majesties Customes.'[11] We may also refer to Mun's recommendation that the community fully utilize its 'Natural' and 'Artificial' resources but particularly the latter, 'forasmuch as the people which live by the Arts are far more in number than they who are masters of the fruits, we ought the more carefully to maintain those endeavours of the multitude, in whom doth consist the greatest strength and riches both of King and Kingdom: for where the people are many, and the arts good, there the traffique must be great, and the Countrey rich. The *Italians* employ a greater number of people, and get more money by their industry and manufactures of the raw Silks of the Kingdom of *Cicilia*, than the King of *Spain* and his Subjects have by the revenue of this rich commodity. But what need we fetch the example so far, when we know that our own natural wares doe not yield us so much profit as our industry?'[12]

Subsequently, Mun recognized the danger that reductions in imports might ultimately have an adverse effect upon exports and accordingly employment. He called, therefore, for moderation in the approach to luxury consumption: 'if we should become so frugal, that we would use few or no Forraign wares, how shall we then vent our own commodities? what will become of our Ships, Mariners, Munitions, our Poor Artificers, and many others? doe we hope that other Countreys will afford us money for All our wares without buying or bartering for Some of theirs?; ... it is more safe and sure to run a middle course by spending moderately, which will purchase treasure plentifully.' Here he implied a danger of unemployment if export markets fail. Moreover, luxury consumption involving purely domestic materials and labour 'cannot impoverish the Kingdome,' but rather 'will maintain the poor with the purse of the rich, which is the best distribution of the Commonwealth.' But immediately he qualified his concession: '*if any man say, that when the people want work, then the Fishing-trade would be a better employment, and far more profitable; I subscribe willingly.*'[13]

A qualification was also introduced regarding the advantages of manufac-

10 *Ibid.*, 10. It is revealing that the development of the fishing industry would, Mun states, 'cost nothing but labour.'

11 *Ibid.*, 11 (author's emphasis). Duties on imported raw materials ultimately to be re-exported in manufactured form should not be too high, it is suggested, because of the depressing effects on exports. But high duties on imports for domestic use should be 'more charged' both for the effect upon the trade balance and for revenue purposes (*ibid.*, 12).

12 *Ibid.*, 12–13 (author's emphasis).

13 *Ibid.*, 60 (author's emphasis). A relevant comment occurs in the context of public finance (*ibid.*, 62). As one of the consequences of excise taxes, Mun noted the higher price of wage-goods. Since money wages are assumed to rise proportionately it is

turing. Mun recommended some diversification as an assurance against serious unemployment in the event of dislocations during war:

I will deliver my opinion concerning our *Clothing*, which although it is the greatest Wealth and best Employment of the Poor of this Kingdome, yet neverthelesse we may peradventure employ ourselves with better Safety, Plenty, and Profit in using more Tillage and Fishing, than to trust so wholly to the making of Cloth; for in times of War, or by other occasions, if some forraign Princes should prohibit the use thereof in their dominions, it might suddenly cause much poverty and dangerous uproars, especially by our poor people, when they should be deprived of their ordinary maintenance, which cannot so easily fail them when their labours should be divided into the said diversity of employment, whereby also many thousands would be better enabled to do the Kingdom good service in occasion of war, especially by Sea.[14]

From the preceding account we conclude that Mun took for granted the desirability of a fully employed work force, in some degree because of the dangers to social stability of severe unemployment, but fundamentally because of the beneficial effects upon the trade balance. High employment as an end in itself or as a means to high consumption played no part. Moreover, high output *per head* was not formally mentioned as an objective of policy although it is implied in increased employment *given* the population. What is more relevant is the assumption that wages were and, apparently it is taken for granted, would be (and should be) at subsistence. Little is said of the maintenance of the workless, but in the event that some were living at below subsistence standards, improved employment opportunities would raise them to the subsistence level. This would however occur merely as a by-product of the desirable program. Indeed since the ultimate end was the accumulation of the precious metals it was *essential* that real wages do not rise above subsistence thus absorbing goods otherwise available for export.

Mun's approach to high employment – as a means towards a favourable balance of trade – is representative of the dominant doctrine. But there were those who reversed the argument and who emphasized a favourable trade balance as the *means* of assuring high employment. In some instances increased employment was seen to be the desirable consequence of a favourable balance by way of the stimulatory effects of the monetary inflow. This was so in the case of Malynes (1601) : 'the more ready money ... that our merchants should make their return by, ... the more employment would they make upon our home commodities, advancing the price thereof, which price would aug-

claimed that the workers will not suffer: 'as the food and rayment of the poor is made dear by Excise, so doth the price of their labour rise in proportion, whereby the burden (if any be) is still upon the rich.' A potential effect upon employment is then touched upon: The wealthy may respond by attempting 'to advance their endeavours' (implying a positively-sloped effort curve) or perhaps by reducing 'their sinful excess and idle retainers.' In this manner it is claimed 'vertue, plenty and arts' all advance at the same time, although it is not made clear how the released menial servants are re-employed.

14 *Ibid.*, 73.

ment the quantity by setting more people on work.'[15] An abundance of the circulating medium as a means to stimulate trade and employment does not, however, require increased metallic currency, but could equally well be assured by paper money. Indeed, this fact came to be recognized by a number of exponents who, if they continued to emphasize the desirability of a favourable balance, did so for other reasons.[16] But the *direct* effect of a favourable trade balance upon employment – the emphasis placed upon exports as the produce of domestic labour, and upon imports (of finished products or those competitive with home products as distinct from raw materials) as involving the displacement thereof – received more emphasis. This argument was formally unrelated to bullion inflows and appears in the literature long after concern with the desirability of specie had faded.[17] It has been argued that the primary policy objective from this point of view finally became the importation of a surplus of food and raw materials (to be worked up) and the exportation of a surplus of 'work' in the form of manufactured goods.[18]

Within this framework Nicholas Barbon (1690) formulated a measure of the social benefits of alternative exports in terms of the employment generated directly and of alternative imports in terms of the employment generated in their further manufacture, according high rank to raw materials and basic subsistence goods. Later exponents, such as Arthur Young in 1772, approached the position of comparing the amount of English labour in exports with that of foreign labour embodied in imports in arriving at the English 'balance of labour.' And we may refer to Cantillon's resounding rendition of the theme:

It is by examining the results of each branch of commerce singly that Foreign trade can be usefully regulated. It cannot be distinctly apprehended by abstract reasons. It will always be found by examining particular cases that the exportation of all Manufactured articles is advantageous to the State, because in this case the Foreigner always pays and supports Workmen useful to the State: that the best returns or payments are specie, and in default of specie the produce of Foreign land into which there enters the least labour.[19]

15 Quoted in Viner, *Studies in the Theory of International Trade*, 54n. See also Petyt's argument below.
16 For example, by William Potter, *The Key to Wealth* (1650) and John Law, *Money and Trade Considered* (1705). Cf. Viner, *Studies in the Theory of International Trade*, 38–9.
17 On the 'disintegration' of the balance of trade doctrine see below, 73f. On the labour doctrine see Viner, *Studies in the Theory of International Trade*, 51f.; N.G. Pauling, 'The Employment Problem in Pre-Classical English Economic Thought,' *Economic Record*, XXVII (June 1951), 53. Professor Viner demonstrates that the employment argument is not of late seventeenth-century origin, as sometimes thought, but appears in sixteenth-century literature and persists throughout the seventeenth and eighteenth centuries.
18 Cf. J.J. Spengler, 'Mercantilist and Physiocratic Growth Theory,' in B.F. Hoselitz, ed., *Theories of Economic Growth* (New York, 1960), 39.
19 'Of Foreign Trade,' in *Essai sur la Nature du Commerce en Général* (1755), ed. H. Higgs (London, 1931), part III, chap. 1, 233. Trade between two countries, in one example, is regarded as disadvantageous to that partner whose exports absorb the greater acreage in spite of the fact that there is no bullion outflow. Of this

The question of the mercantilists' attitude to employment generated by the production of goods for *domestic* consumption may now be briefly considered. The doctrine of 'thrift' – the desirability of *saved* wealth – which represents a fundamental rationale for the concern with bullion inflows, served originally also as a basis for the employment case in favour of a favourable trade balance. For from this viewpoint, not only the consumption of imported luxury goods was frowned upon, but the consumption of domestically-produced luxury goods was also unwelcome, thus endangering employment unless production occurred for foreign markets. The objective of a favourable balance of trade accordingly reflected, for some, both the dislike of (luxury) imports and the 'necessity' of exports to assure against unemployment.[20]

But the doctrine of thrift tended to be qualified. We have already noted the equivocation on the part of Mun who, while insisting that it was preferable to employ labour in the 'fishing trade,' conceded that the consumption of domestically produced luxuries 'cannot impoverish the kingdome' and was, in fact, desirable, since it would 'maintain the poor at the expense of the rich.' Similarly, Samuel Fortrey gave qualified assent to luxury consumption on three conditions: first 'that the vanity of the expence do not depend on such commodities, as have too much of the substance of gold, silver, or silk; whereby the publick treasure is wasted and lost'; secondly, 'that we impoverish not ourselves to enrich strangers, by that unnatural vanity, in preferring foreign commodities though worse, before our own, that are better'; and thirdly, 'that the excess of this expense consist chiefly in the art, manufacture and workmanship of the commodity made in our own countrey; whereby ingenuity would be encouraged, the people employed, and our treasure kept at home.'[21] And Davenant too while maintaining that 'thrift does proportionately enrich a whole people, as it betters the condition of a private man' nonetheless conceded reluctantly that 'perhaps it is not impossible but that our industry would be less active if it were not awakened and incited by some irregular appetites which are more easily found fault with than avowed.'[22] A striking statement by Daniel Defoe of the advantages of high domestic expenditure,

---

example Cantillon writes: 'I have chosen it to shew more strikingly how one State may be the dupe of another Trade, and the method of judging the advantages and disadvantages of Foreign trade' (*ibid.*). Yet it is also argued that a state which possesses raw produce in excess of its own needs should import bullion rather than manufactures which 'would be to weaken and diminish the inhabitants and the strength of the State at both ends' (*ibid.*, 235).

See also Sir James Steuart, *An Inquiry into the Principles of Political Economy* (1767), ed. Andrew Skinner (Chicago, 1966), 'A sagacious statesman will, at all times, keep a watchful eye upon every branch of foreign commerce ...

If the value of the matter [raw produce] imported be greater than the value of what is exported, the country gains. If a greater value of labour be imported, than exported, the country loses.'

20 Viner, *Studies in the Theory of International Trade*, 30.

21 *England's Interest and Improvement* (1673), in J.R. McCulloch, ed., *Early English Tracts on Commerce* (1856); Cambridge, 1952), 235.

22 *Discourses on publick revenues* (1698), quoted in T.E. Gregory, 'The Economics of Employment in England, 1660–1713,' *Economica*, I (1921–2), 39n.

similar to the celebrated formulation by Mandeville, noted earlier, to the effect that 'private vices are publick benefits,' may also be referred to: 'Trade is propagated by our crimes, the people support one another by their extravagance and luxury, their Gaiety and Pride: gluttony and drunkenness assist to maintain the Nation, the people grow rich by the people, they support one another.'[23] It is, however, noteworthy that Mandeville's recommendations relating to high luxury spending in the interest of employment were categorically rejected by Francis Hutcheson on the grounds, in effect, that money is never permitted to remain idle: 'Unless therefore a nation can be found where all men are already provided with all the necessaries and conveniencies of life abundantly, men may, without any luxury, make the very greatest consumption, by plentiful provision for their children, by generosity and liberality to kinsmen and indigent men of worth, and by compassion to the distresses of the poor.'[24]

The fact is that there was much confusion as to what was and what was not beneficial consumption. Apart from the necessity of avoiding the consumption of foreign luxury goods, or of diverting resources away from the export sector, there was a difference with implications for the role of *working-class* consumption, between those who, because of fear of disturbing the social structure, or the perhaps not unrelated belief in a backward-bending supply curve of labour, or the need to reduce the money costs of home products in foreign markets, maintained the dominant doctrine of low wages, and the smaller but growing group of dissenters (including Defoe) who opposed the doctrine.[25] Moreover, even those who attributed some advantages to domestic consumption did not escape from the fundamental conception that one man gained at another's expense in internal trade.[26] On the whole, the continued preoccupation with the foreign-trade sector suggests that it was generally presumed that full employment was unlikely unless production, supported by the importation of raw materials, was also undertaken for export.[27]

What must also be emphasized is the fact that socially desirable patterns of trade would not be achieved 'automatically' by way of a self-operating causal mechanism. The export of labour-intensive manufactures in exchange for land-intensive raw materials would have to be brought about, apparently, by direction. The implications of the loose recognition by some writers – to be

23 *The Compleat English Tradesman* (1725). Further references are also given in Pauling, 'The Employment Problem,' 56. In some instances the argument served as the basis for an ordering of the relative social advantages of alternative expenditure patterns. Cf. *ibid.*, 57–8, regarding George Berkeley (1736).

24 *A System of Moral Philosophy*, vol. II (1755), in *Collected Works of Francis Hutcheson* (Hildesheim, 1969) VI, 321.

25 See Viner, *Studies in the Theory of International Trade*, 57, and Pauling, 'The Employment Problem,' 60.

26 Gregory, 'Economics of Employment,' 39–40.

27 D.C. Coleman, ed., *Revisions in Mercantilism* (London, 1969), 14–15 has emphasized (at least with regard to the seventeenth century) the extreme difficulty of expansions in aggregate domestic consumption.

presently discussed – that foreign trade permitted international specialization were not drawn upon, perhaps because in conditions of unemployment the efficiency aspect of trade loses much of its relevance. Moreover, support for protection on grounds of the infant-industry case although occasionally utilized – as by Tucker (1757) and Steuart (1767) – was not widespread.[28] The mercantilist policies, in brief, had implications for economic growth but were scarcely adequately supported by a theory of growth.

Much the same conclusion may be applied to the internal distribution of resources. Thus we find that the author of *Britannia Languens*, while denying any intention of questioning the usefulness of a variety of categories of service labour (including the clergy, doctors, retailers, lawyers), was concerned with the expansion of the service sector at the expense of the manufacturing sector, on the grounds that it did not contribute to the balance of trade: 'as far as they are *Imployments*, and intended for *private gain*, 'tis plain they add no Treasure to the Nation, but only enable the persons so imployed to share and heap up the Treasures already Imported.'[29] But the criterion of desirable allocation was not supported by any mechanism which would assure its achievement, and the necessity for government regulations was usually taken for granted.[30]

POPULATION SIZE

Without doubt the mercantilist preoccupation with a money inflow and with employment must be understood in a context of unemployment and under-employment. Yet what is striking is the support in such circumstances by late seventeenth-century and eighteenth-century writers of a larger population:[31] 'A vague, though tenaciously held, idea that England's population was too small for its territory possessed the minds of these later Mercantilist writers. How such a notion could have survived in the midst of prevailing poverty and pauperism, and retained its hold upon the minds of men continually wrestling with the problem of lightening the burden of poor relief, it is difficult to comprehend.'[32]

This paradoxical state of affairs was in fact recognized in the literature. Thus Samuel Fortrey, in calling for increased population by way of immigra-

28 Cf. Viner, *Studies in the Theory of International Trade*, 70–1; Lord Robbins, *The Theory of Economic Development in the History of Economic Thought* (London, 1968), 6, 112f.

29 William Petyt[?] *Britannia Languens* (1680), in McCulloch, ed., *Early English Tracts*, 378.

30 Cf. E.A.J. Johnson, *Predecessors of Adam Smith* (New York, 1937), 244.

31 Scattered data imply that population in fact was increasing more rapidly during the sixteenth century than subsequently. See D.C. Coleman, 'Labour in the English Economy of the Seventeenth Century,' in E.M. Carus-Wilson, ed., *Essays in Economic History*, II (London, 1962), 305–6.

   Edgar S. Furniss, *The Position of the Laborer in a System of Nationalism* (1920; New York, 1965), 28–9, points out that while population increase was applauded during Tudor times the motive was military and not economic.

32 *Ibid.*, 29.

tion, raised the issue 'that it doth not appear that people are wanting, but rather that we have already too many, if we consider the number of poor people that are found in every place.' His answer was simply that although 'we already have more people than are well employed' nonetheless 'if the manufactures and other profitable employments of this nation, were rightly improved and encouraged, there is no doubt but the people, and riches of the kingdom might be greatly increased and multiplied, both to the profit, and honour of the Prince.'[33]

The desirability of a large population was supported by a variety of arguments by no means always consistent or logical. In some instances – more satisfactory in the case of that minority which opposed the dominant low-wage doctrine – emphasis was placed on the higher consumption power of a large population (although what would be strictly relevant are the *increasing* expenditures relating to a *growing* population) upon the optimistic assumption that the work force would be fully employed. An instance can be drawn from Defoe: 'Multitude of people, if they can be put into a condition to maintain themselves, must increase trade; they must have food, that employs land; they must have clothes, that employs the manufacturer; they must have houses, that employs the handicrafts; they must have household stuff, that employs a long variety of trades.'[34] A particularly interesting example is that of Petyt, who regarded a large population – or in his case specifically a large population in the trading sector – as a function of the trade balance:

a Forraign Trade (if managed to the best advantage) will yet further advance the values of Lands, by necessitating a vast *increase of people*, since it must maintain great multitudes of people in the very business of Trade, which could not otherwise be supported ...: All which having the Rewards of their Labours in their hands, will still enlarge the choice of Chapman to the Sellers, and there being so many more persons to be fed and cloathed, there must be a far greater home Consumption of all the products of Land.[35]

Nonetheless, the confusion regarding the role of *domestic* consumption emanating largely from preoccupation with the trade balance, was scarcely conducive to a clear statement of the advantages of a large population from

33 *England's Interest and Improvement*, in McCulloch, ed., *Early English Tracts*, 224–5.
34 *A Plan of English Commerce* (1728), quoted by Pauling, 'The Employment Problem', 61. See also references to Davenant (and his support for immigrants who *even though poor* 'would consume our home products'), Roger North, and Cary.
35 *Britannia Languens*, 291. An increase in demand for agricultural products would, he argued, ultimately be reflected in increased rents and consequently in land improvements.
    This argument is independent of a further case in favour of an export surplus, namely the positive effect upon demand of an increased bullion inflow: 'the people having universally more money than before, the *Seller* will not be so *necessitous* for money as before, and will have a greater *choice of Chapmen*, who will be more able and ready to buy' (*ibid.*, 290).

the viewpoint of consumption. And in fact it has been convincingly argued that 'population was looked upon mainly as a factor of production, only incidentally as a factor in consumption, owing to a theory of foreign trade which threw suspicion upon home consumption.'[36]

A different argument encountered occasionally ascribes a variety of advantages to a *dense* population. Thus, for example, Petty – in one of the few passages in the early literature which implies increasing average, as distinct from total, incomes as a consequence of growing population – referred to scale economies relating to the activities of government: 'Fewness of people, is real poverty; and a Nation wherein are Eight Millions of people, are more than twice as rich as the same scope of Land wherein are but Four; For the same Governours which are the great charge, may serve near as well, for the greater, as the lesser number.'[37] Similarly, Davenant approached the notion of increasing average returns to increasing population in a statement to the effect that 'when great numbers are confined to a narrow compass of ground, necessity puts them into invention, frugality and industry.'[38]

But the 'characteristic' mercantilist preoccupation with the trade balance constituted the fundamental rationale for a large population (oddly enough even by those – such as Davenant and Petyt – who in some contexts rejected the low-wage doctrine).[39] The necessity from this viewpoint of a large popula-

---

36 Gregory, 'Economics of Employment,' 40.

37 *Treatise of Taxes* (1662) in C.H. Hull, ed., *Economic Writings of Sir William Petty* (Cambridge, 1899), I, 34. See also a discussion of scale economies in *Political Arithmetic of the City of London* (1682), *ibid.*, II, 473–4. An oblique reference to *decreasing* average returns is made by Cantillon in a passage (*Essai*, ed. Higgs, 85) of some methodological importance: 'It is also a question outside of my subject whether it is better to have a great multitude of Inhabitants, poor and badly provided, than a smaller number, much more at their ease: a million who consume the produce of 6 acres per head or 4 millions who live on the produce of an Acre and a half.'

38 Quoted in E.A.J. Johnson, *Predecessors of Adam Smith*, 266.

The anonymous author of the pamphlet *Considerations on the East-India Trade* (1701) in calling for the establishment of a 'free-port' peopled to a large degree by surplus labour based his case upon the assumption that 'the poor People collected thus together, wou'd find more variety of Imployments, fit for Persons of all conditions, in a place exceeding Populous, abounding with variety of Business and full of Manufactures, than as now, dispers'd over all the Kingdom, confin'd to Parishes, in which they are of little use, disabled to go where proper business calls for them. The Blind and Lame, Young and Old, Women and Children, by their united Labours might be serviceable to one another, they are now dispers'd; they are neither useful to the Publick nor Themselves. Collected together, the Poor wou'd be more likely to provide their own Maintenance, to ease the Publick of this Charge.' (McCulloch, ed., *Early English Tracts on Commerce*, 627. The work is discussed in detail by Markus Arkin, 'A Neglected Forerunner of Adam Smith,' *South African Journal of Economics*, XXIII (1955), 299–314.)

39 Cf. the view of Furniss, *Position of the Laborer*, 30–1; and Gregory, 'Economics of Employment,' 42 and 50 emphasizing the key influence of the doctrines regarding international trade. Other cases were based upon the need for a large tax revenue, for 'power' and for a high colonization capacity.

tion and the need to *encourage* population growth to furnish the labour factor of production is expressed clearly in the following passages by Davenant:

The people being the first matter of power and wealth, by whose labor and industry the nation must be the gainers in the balance, their increase or decrease must be carefully observed by the government that designs to thrive; that is, their increase must be promoted by good conduct and wholesome laws, and if they have been decreased by war or by any other accident, the breach is to be made up as soon as possible, for it is a maim to the body politic affecting all its parts ...

In order to have hands to carry on labor and manufactures, which make us gainers in the balance of trade, we ought not to deter but rather invite men to marry, which is to be done by privileges and exemptions, for such a number of children, and by denying certain offices and dignities to all unmarried persons ...

A country that makes provision to increase its inhabitants, whose situation is good, and whose people have a genius adapted to trade, will never fail to be gainers in the balance, provided the labor and industry of their people be well managed and carefully directed.[40]

A large population was not only desirable as the source of the basic productive factor. The presumption that increased population would raise Britain's competitiveness by exerting a depressing effect on the wage rate also played some part. This is made explicit, for example, by Petyt (although it must be noted that it is population increase in a particular sector that he had in mind):

The *odds in Populacy* must also produce the like odds in Manufacture; plenty of people must also cause *cheapnesse of wages*: which will cause the cheapness of the Manufacture; in a scarcity of people wages must be dearer, which must cause the dearnesse of the Manufacture ...; the populacy I intend and which only can be serviceable to Manufacture, are those exuberant numbers which cannot find Imployment in husbandry, nor otherwise but in Trade ...[41]

Thirdly, we find numerous references to the increased effort on the part of labour expected in response to reduced living standards. Thus, for example, Sir William Temple in 1673:

40 *Essay on the Probable Methods of Making a People Gainers in the Balance of Trade* (London, 1699; 2nd ed., 1700), quoted by Furniss, *Position of the Laborer*, 30n. A similar approach was taken by Sir Josiah Child, *New Discourses of Trade* (1693) discussed by W. Letwin, *The Origins of Scientific Economics* (London, 1964), 42.

41 *Britannia Languens*, 349. This *desideratum* of low wages is in turn related explicitly to the ultimate objective of a bullion inflow (*ibid.*, 457–8): 'From what hath been said, it is evident that National power is not Chimerical, but is founded on *People and Treasures*; and that, according to the different condition of these its true Pillars, it immediately grows more vigorous or languid; that sufficient stores of Treasure cannot otherwise be gotten, than by the industry of the people; and, That till they have it, they cannot pay.'

If increased labour supplies were expected to reduce the average wage rate it would appear that wages were dependent upon the market forces of demand and supply, unrelated to the cost of subsistence although the view that money wages fluctuated with food prices played a considerable role in mercantilist discussions.

I conceive the true and original ground of trade to be great numbers of people crowded into small compass of land, whereby all things necessary to life become dear, and all men who have possessions are induced to parsimony; but those who have none are forced to industry and labor, or else to want. Bodies that are vigorous fall to labor; such as are not, supply that defect by some sort of inventions of ingenuity. These customs arise first from necessity and grow in time to be habitual in a country. And wherever they are so if it lies upon the sea, they naturally break into trade ...[42]

Steuart who ascribed, as we have seen, to the 'balance of labour' doctrine, also provided a strong statement of the social desirability of reducing (real) wages to subsistence by intervention – in order to stimulate effort and assure low prices in foreign markets. The objective, if the market price of labour exceeded the subsistence level, might be achieved by government stimulus of population:

Let him [the statesman] inquire what are the prices abroad; what are the prices at home; how those who work in exportable commodities live; what superfluities they enjoy; and what days of idleness they indulge in.

If he finds that goods are not exported, because of high prices, while manufacturers are enjoying superfluity, and indulging themselves in idleness, let him multiply hands, and he will reduce them all to their physical-necessary; and by thus augmenting the supply, he will also reduce the prices of his markets at home.[43]

Alternatively, he recommended lowering real wages by imposing taxes on subsistence goods or a combination of the two policies.[44]

In general, therefore, it was with the object in mind of raising the labour supply, lowering wage rates and increasing effort per man, that Mercantilists recommended a larger population. Some consequences of this approach can be illustrated by reference to the question of poverty.[45] While there was much concern in the literature to reduce the burden of poor relief, a *fall* in popula-

(See Furniss, *Position of the Laborer*, 157f.) Gregory has argued: 'whether the theories were reconciled or not, there is no doubt about the practical anxiety displayed as to the necessity of low wages' ('Economics of Employment,' 44).

It may be noted that some writers denied explicitly that money wages moved with the price of food. This is true of Petty and also of Steuart (*Inquiry*, II, 400–1, 689f). But both Petty and Steuart were in favour of steps which would assure that in practice real wages do not exceed the subsistence level.

42 *Observations on the United Colonies* (1673), quoted by Furniss, *Position of the Laborer*, 139.

43 *Inquiry*, 693. Cf.: 'idleness will not be totally rooted out, until people be forced, in one way or another, to give up both superfluity and days of recreation' (*ibid.*, 691). Petty relied on direct intervention by the state in wage regulation, and refers to a satisfactory law as one which allows 'the Labourer but just wherewithall to live.' Anything more will mean that the labourer works less than he might 'which is a loss to the Publick of the fruit of so much Labour' (*Treatise of Taxes*, I, 87).

44 Steuart, *Inquiry*, 695.

45 Furniss, *Position of the Laborer*, 36–7, 196. See also Gregory, 'Economics of Employment,' 44–6, who considers exceptions such as Defoe.

Furniss has argued that earlier workhouse proposals (of the late seventeenth

tion was to be avoided. The existing poor law and the Settlement Acts, for example, were challenged on the grounds that parish officers tended to discourage marriage among the poor. A further principal complaint was that the contemporary system withdrew excess labour from the work force thus preventing a fall in the wage rate. These disadvantages could be avoided by setting the poor to work on a variety of projects in competition with free labour. Proponents of a large population on condition that 'full employment' could be assured thus were referring frequently to the artificial creation of employment opportunities in workhouses, by which device aggregate output would be increased and at the same time the wages of *independent* handicraftsmen lowered to the advantage of Britain's competitive position in foreign markets. Thus it was possible for a nation's 'wealth' to be increased by *increasing* its pauper population.

It is the emphasis upon the desirability of a large population which above all makes it difficult to accept as adequate those rationalizations of Mercantilism (such as by Keynes)[46] which regard the characteristic concern with bullion inflows simply in terms of the stimulatory effect upon employment. The expansion of aggregate output was, indeed, to be achieved by full use of resources – particularly labour – if necessary by government intervention. And, as we have seen, there is evidence that some writers desired a favourable balance of trade to this end, although it is clear that the object of full employment was unrelated to high income per head and high working-class consumption. But the general desire for a large population amongst writers preoccupied with the problem of achieving full employment can only be fully understood if we bear in mind – apart from a concern with defence and tax revenues, and particular class sympathies – a preoccupation with the foreign trade sector and the evaluation of policy in terms of the effects thereupon.

There is, however, evidence which suggests a growing trend, particularly after 1750, by economists and others in favour of labour's well-being.[47] Of particular interest is the statement by Hume that while high wages reduced Britain's competitiveness in foreign markets this 'is not to be put in competition with the happiness of so many millions.'[48] The change in attitude, it has been

century) were formulated to provide work for the involuntarily unemployed. Subsequently (towards the mid-eighteenth century) the tone changed and the workhouse proposals were envisaged as a means of dealing with the voluntarily unemployed by imposing discipline and enforcing labour (*Position of the Laborer,* 85f).

Other burning policy issues examined from the viewpoint of population were the colonies and naturalization.

46 The General Theory of Employment, Interest and Money (London, 1936), 333f.
47 Cf. Viner, *Studies in the Theory of International Trade,* 57; A.W. Coats, 'Changing Attitudes to Labour in the Mid-Eighteenth Century,' *Economic History Review,* XI, 1 (1958), 35–51; and A.W. Coats, 'Economic Thought and Poor Law Policy in the Eighteenth Century,' *ibid.,* XIII, 1 (1960), 39–51.
48 'Of Commerce,' in E. Rotwein, ed., *David Hume: Writings on Economics* (London, 1955), 16. For a discussion of Hume's approval of certain categories of luxury consumption as a stimulus to *all* classes, including labour, see Coats, 'Changing Attitudes to Labour,' 48–9.

convincingly argued by Professor Coats, may be attributed, *inter alia*, to a changing economic structure, reflected in a growing importance of mechanical devices which entailed a corresponding realization that high wages do not necessarily preclude low unit costs; and to a variety of broader intellectual trends – to which the Scottish psychological writers made the outstanding contribution – which emphasized the fundamental similarity between individuals in native ability and character suggesting that workers too were to be envisaged as human beings responding to economic incentives.

TECHNICAL PROGRESS

We devote this section to a brief discussion of the approach towards technical progress in mercantilist literature. We have seen that there was much said in favour of a large population despite the contemporary problem of unemployment. Support for an increase even in pauper labour was not uncommon given the relevant preconceptions. Logically, therefore, the Mercantilists could scarcely avoid supporting labour-displacing technical progress. And while there were exceptions,[49] the predominant sentiment was indeed in favour.

Thus Petty viewed labour-saving technical progress as an alternative to raising the labour supply: 'introducing the Compendium, and Facilitations of Art ... is equivalent to what men vainly hoped from *Polygamy*. For as much as he that can do the Work of five men by one, effects the same as the begetting four adult Workmen.'[50] Similarly, Steuart devoted an entire chapter to the question 'Is the Introduction of Machines into Manufactures prejudicial to the Interest of a State, or hurtful to Population?'[51] defining the issue so that the release of labour as an alternative to population growth appeared as the essential *desideratum*. He recognized the likelihood of *temporary* unemployment – insisting upon the duty of government to intervene if necessary on behalf of the displaced – but ascribed it to the 'suddenness' of a change: 'If therefore the machine proves hurtful, it can only be because it presents the state with an additional number of hands bred to labour; consequently, if these are afterwards found without bread, it must proceed from a want of attention in the statesmen: for an industrious man, made idle, may constantly be employed to advantage, and with profit to him who employs him.'[52] Steuart's optimism regarding long-run employment capacity in large part stemmed from his observation that available subsistence was unaffected in aggregate by the introduction of machinery or, in terms of the classical school, that 'fixed' capital did not displace 'circulating' capital. (Furthermore, he considered it unlikely that imitation by foreigners would 'over-stock' industry 'in any well-governed state.')[53]

Subsequently, Steuart defined the advantages of machinery in terms of its

49 Cf. Defoe, referred to in Gregory, 'Economics of Employment,' 48.
50 *Verbum Sapienti* (1691; probably written 1665) in Hull, ed., *Sir William Petty*, I, 118. Cf. an important reference to division of labour in watchmaking as a function of industry size, in *Political Arithmetic of the City of London, ibid.*, II, 473.
51 *Inquiry*, I., 121–5.
52 *Ibid.*, 124.
53 *Ibid.*

price-reducing effect with particular reference to the export sector.[54] From this point of view, however, it was not only the 'orthodox' Mercantilist who on the whole favoured labour-saving technical progress. For example, Cary – one of the minority who opposed the ruling low-wage doctrine – considered the introduction of machinery as the means whereby the cost disadvantage of high wages could be avoided in foreign competition.[55] And Postlethwayt denied that machinery would be beneficial at all in a closed economy.[56]

Of outstanding analytical significance is the recognition in the pre-Smithian literature of the function of stored-up goods as a necessary precondition for specialization and exchange. The phenomenon is discussed by Francis Hutcheson in his *System of Moral Philosophy* (1755), where it is noted that in the absence of such stores 'each one would be obliged to practise all sorts of mechanick arts by turns, without attaining dexterity in any; which would be a publick detriment.'[57] Similarly, Josiah Tucker emphasized the time-consuming aspect of advanced technology which precluded its adoption by poor countries and thus assured perpetuation of the superiority of advanced economies: 'The inhabitants of a poor country, who ... generally live from hand to mouth, dare not make such costly experiments or embark on such expensive or long-winded undertakings as the inhabitants of a rich country can attempt and execute with ease.'[58] Detailed analysis is made of division of labour, in Birmingham button-making plants, which permits the allocation of tasks between men, women and children according to physical strength and ability and avoids the wasting of time.[59] Tucker addressed himself specifically to the issues of the ultimate reabsorption of labour displaced by, and the ultimate benefits of, technical change:

What is the Consequence of this Abridgment of Labour, both regarding the Price of the Goods, and the Number of Persons employed? The Answer is very short and full, *viz*. That the Price of Goods is thereby prodigiously lowered from what otherwise it must have been; and that a much greater Number of Hands are employed. The first

54 *Ibid.*, 255–6.
55 *An Essay on the State of England* (1695), quoted in Furniss, *Position of the Laborer*, 176n.
56 *Universal Dictionary of Trade and Commerce* (2nd ed., 1757), cited in Alexander Gourvitch, *Survey of Economic Theory on Technological Change and Employment* (1940; New York, 1966), 25.
57 *Collected Works of Francis Hutcheson*, V, 328–9.
58 *Four Tracts Together with Two Sermons on Political and Commercial Subjects* (written 1758; Gloucester, 1774), 24. A growing awareness of the distinction between the efficiency and the money wages of labour is isolated as the most significant reason why, increasingly after 1750, economists were less concerned than their predecessors with high money wages, in Coats, 'Changing Attitudes to Labour,' 46–7.
  For further references to the division of labour in the pre-Smithian literature see Ronald Hamowy, 'Adam Smith, Adam Ferguson, and the Division of Labour,' *Economica*, XXXV (Aug. 1968), 249–59. Hamowy demonstrates that Ferguson (*Essay on the History of Civil Society*, 1767) has 'priority' over Smith for the recognition of the psychological costs of increasing specialization (*ibid.*, 257–9).
59 *Instructions for Travellers* (1757), in R.L. Schuyler, ed., *Josiah Tucker: A Selection of his Economic and Political Writings* (New York, 1931), 242–3.

of these is a Position universally assented to; but the other, though nothing more than a Corollary of the former, is looked upon by the Majority of Mankind, and even by some Persons of great Name and Character, as a monstrous Paradox. We must therefore endeavour to clear away these Prejudices Step by Step. And the first Step is, that Cheapness, *caeteris paribus*, is an Inducement to buy, – and that many Buyers cause great Demand, – and that a great Demand brings on a great Consumption; – which great Consumption must necessarily employ a vast Variety of Hands, whether the original Material is considered, or the Number and Repair of Machines, or the Materials out of which those Machines are made, or the Persons necessarily employed in tending upon and conducting them: Not to mention those Branches of the Manufacture, Package, Porterage, Stationary Articles, and Book-keeping, &c. &c. which must inevitably be performed by human Labour ... surely enough has been said, to convince any reasonable Man, though even the great Author of *L'Esprit des Loix* should once be of a different mind, that that System of Machines, which so greatly reduces the Price of Labour [labour costs], as to enable the Generality of a People to become Purchasers of Goods, will in the End, though not immediately, employ more Hands in the Manufacture, than could possibly have found Employment, had no such Machines been invented.[60]

Nonetheless, Tucker criticized factory organization on grounds of the degrading moral effects upon those who 'work together in the same shop,' the greater probability of forming associations against the employer, and the hostility created by the sharp division between employer and labourers who have little hope of advancing in rank.[61]

It may be noted finally that the anonymous author of *Considerations on the East India Trade* (1701) emphasized, in general terms, the advantage to *labour* of advanced processes in modern societies which, despite the unfavourable income distribution, assured a higher standard than could be conceivably attained in primitive societies: 'Among the wild *Indians of America*, almost every thing is the Labourer's, ninety nine parts of an hundred are to be put upon the account of Labour: In *England*, perhaps the Labourer has not two thirds of all the conveniences of Life, but then the plenty of these things is so much greater here, that a King of *India* is not so well lodg'd, and fed, and cloath'd, as a Day-labourer of *England*.'[62] A number of examples are given of the productivity advantages of specialization, and the necessary precondition of an adequate market is recognized: 'if the Demand of Watches shou'd become so very great as to find constant imployment for as many Persons as there are Parts in a Watch, if to every one shall be assign'd his proper and

60 *Ibid.*, 241–2. Particular emphasis is placed upon machinery in mining, and metallurgy; and in metal making at Birmingham, Sheffield, and Wolverhampton. The lack of progress in the woollen industry is ascribed to violent opposition by labour to machinery. But reference is made to the Derby silk-throwing mill and to some improvements in the cotton and linen manufactures (*ibid.*, 240–1).
61 *Ibid.*, 244–5.
62 McCulloch, ed., *Early English Tracts*, 593–4. Cf. John Locke, *Two Treatises of Government* (1698), II. § 41, ed. P. Laslett (Cambridge, 1967), 314–15.

constant work ... this Man must needs be more skilful and expeditious in the composition of these several Parts, than the same Man cou'd be if he were also to be imploy'd in the Manufacture of all these Parts.'[63] The process by which the first introduction of a new technique is imitated by competitors is also discussed;[64] a specific assumption is that by reducing the price of the final product the expansion of output is made possible and thus to some extent, presumably, the re-employment of those originally displaced at the original level.[65]

THE ROLE OF AGRICULTURE

While it is difficult to discern a clear 'mercantilist' position on the role of the agricultural sector in development, the issue was considered by eighteenth-century writers with an eye upon the fundamental relationship emphasized, for example, by both Cantillon and Steuart between agricultural output and population.[66] Steuart, in a tightly-argued analysis involving a two-sector economy, envisaged output in the agricultural sector exceeding internal requirements as a necessary though not sufficient condition for non-agricultural activity, for the production of a surplus will only occur if farmers receive in exchange desirable commodities. Steuart considered it essential for the state (at least in the initial stages of development) to create 'reciprocal wants' and to 'contrive different employments' for those outside the agricultural sector who would produce 'equivalents' for the surplus and justify its production. On the basis of this argument Steuart distinguished two groups within the total population, namely 'farmers' and 'free hands,' who 'procure themselves subsistence out of the superfluity of the farmers.' Any increase in the surplus, continues the argument, tends to generate an increased population of 'free hands': 'A people ... who have an industrious turn, will multiply in proportion to the superfluity produced by their farmers; because the labour of the necessitous will prove an equivalent for it.'[67]

The (automatic) determinants of population size and change therein are defined in a graphic passage:

Thus the generative faculty resembles a spring loaded with a weight, which always exerts itself in proportion to the diminution of resistance: when food has remained some time without augmentation or diminution, generation will carry numbers as high as possible; if then food come to be diminished, the spring is overpowered; the force of it becomes less than nothing. Inhabitants will diminish, at least, in proportion to

63 *Ibid.*, 591–2.
64 *Ibid.*, 590.
65 *Ibid.*, 594.
66 On the issue in general, see S.J. Brandenburg, 'The Place of Agriculture in British National Economy Prior to Adam Smith,' *Journal of Political Economy*, XXXIX (June 1931) 281–320.
67 *Inquiry*, 40. In Hume's view, by contrast, the most important force stimulating the production of a disposable surplus over the traditional requirements of a self-supporting family is the introduction of external trade and the creation thereby of new wants ('Of Commerce,' 13).

the overcharge. If, upon the other hand, food be increased, the spring which stood at 0, will begin to exert itself in proportion as the resistance diminishes; people will begin to be better fed; they will multiply, and, in proportion as they increase in numbers, the food will become scarce again.[68]

Yet, as in the case of industry price, the process was not to be given full opportunity to operate. What concerned Steuart was the competition of the single labourer who could subsist upon rations inadequate for the support of a married man, thus threatening population contraction.[69] After emphasizing the desirability of possessing extensive demographic data by occupation and location, Steuart formulated plans for maintaining the children of the poor designed to generate 'a multiplication proportioned to the possibility of our providing nourishment and employment':

I have therefore proposed, that a statesman, well informed of the situation of his people, the state of every class, the number of marriages found in each, should say, let a particular encouragement be given to so many marriages among the lower classes and let these be distributed in a certain proportion for every parish, city, borough, &c. in the country; let rules be laid down to direct a preference, in case of a competition, between different couples; and let the consequence of this approbation be, to relieve the parents of all children above what they can maintain, as has been said ... I therefore would strongly recommend hospitals for foundlings over all the country; and still more strongly the frugal maintenance of children in such hospitals, and their being bred up early to fill and recruit the lowest classes of the people.[70]

But there existed a fundamental constraint on expansion, in Steuart's view emanating ultimately from the inability of the economy to increase adequately its food supplies, that is from diminishing returns.[71] Clearly, further population growth might be assured by imports but if, as he expected, high production costs in the expanding economy reduced the competitiveness of export industries, there would be limits to this expedient.[72] The general phenomenon of rising real costs of agricultural produce was ultimately to be the dominating characteristic of classical economics.

Similarly Cantillon emphasized the proposition that 'the Number of Labourers, Handicraftsmen and others, who work in a State is naturally proportioned to the Demand for them.'[73] An excess labour supply at the subsistence wage will entail unemployment or underemployment or a wage rate depressed below subsistence. In consequence, labour will either leave the particular geographical or occupational sector in question or the labour supply will ultimately decline as a result of a fall in the marriage and birth rates, and an increase in the death rate. Conversely, an increase in the wage rate above subsistence will

68 Steuart, *Inquiry*, 32–3.
69 *Ibid.*, 77. 'The unmarried ... force the others to starve.' Cf. *ibid.*, 273.
70 *Ibid.*, 80.
71 *Ibid.*, 116.
72 *Ibid.*, 294.
73 *Essai*, ed. Higgs., 23.

ultimately generate an increased labour supply. The practical conclusion drawn was that intervention in the labour market by the State designed to increase the labour supply, without reference to the demand for labour, was useless.[74] Subsequently, Cantillon clarified the nature of the demand for labour as consisting fundamentally in the wage goods made available for the support of labour; for 'we can multiply all sorts of Animals in such numbers as we wish to maintain them even to infinity if we could find lands to infinity to nourish them; and the multiplication of Animals has no other bounds than the greater or less means allotted for their subsistence. It is not to be doubted that if all Land were devoted to the simple sustenance of Man the race would increase up to the number that the Land would support ...'[75] Cantillon's analysis represents a particularly significant preview of subsequent Smithian and Malthusian doctrine insofar as the element of interventionism is far less evident than in the formulation by Steuart.

THE RATE OF INTEREST

There is evidence during the late seventeenth century of an improved understanding of the determination and the behaviour of the 'rate of interest,' representing a significant break from scholastic usury analysis, by identifying the yield from 'stock' – understood as material goods utilized for deriving an income – and the yield from land, and from standard mercantilist practise, by avoiding the assumption that the savings process consists in the accumulation of a stock of money. An outstanding illustration of the 'new' position appears in Dudley North's discussion of the 'Abatement of Interest' designed to refute the recommendation that the legal maximum rate be reduced as a stimulus to trade. Lending and borrowing are related by North to a skewed wealth distribution (due in the last resort to differential degrees of 'industry and ingenuity') and to differential skills and preferences:

74 *Ibid.*, 25: 'From this it is easy to understand that the Charity-Schools in England and the proposals in France to increase the number of Handicraftsmen are useless. If the King of France set 100,000 of his Subjects at his expense into Holland to learn Seafaring, they would be of no use on their return if no more Vessels were sent to Sea than before.'

Yet Cantillon insisted that his result applied only to a closed economy, concluding in late-mercantilist fashion: 'It is true that it would be a great advantage to a State to teach its Subjects to produce the Manufactures which are customarily drawn from abroad, and all the other articles bought there, but I am considering only at present a State in relation to itself.'

75 *Ibid.*, 67. Since the pattern of land-use was, in Cantillon's view, largely determined by the expenditure habits of landlords it followed that the determination of population size depended upon 'the Tastes, the Fashions, and Modes of Living of the Proprietors of Land' (*ibid.*, 65).

An equally striking application of the cost price-market price nexus is made in the context of monetary theory. Cf. J.J. Spengler, 'Richard Cantillon: First of the Moderns,' *Journal of Political Economy*, LXII (Aug.–Oct. 1954), reprinted in J.J. Spengler and W.R. Allen, eds., *Essays in Economic Thought: Aristotle to Marshall* (Chicago, 1960), 122f.

Now as there are more Men to Till the Ground than have Land to Till, so also there will be many who want Stock to manage; and also (when a Nation is grown rich) there will be Stock for Trade in many hands, who either have not the skill, or care not for the trouble of managing it in Trade ...

Thus to be a Landlord, or a Stock-Lord is the same thing; the Landlord hath the advantage in this: That his Tenant cannot carry away the Land, as the Tenant of the other may the Stock; and therefore Land ought to yield less profit than Stock, which is let out at greater hazard.[76]

While in the preceding passage the demand for funds derives from traders, it was in fact North's view that the majority of borrowers demanded funds not for trading purposes but for luxury consumption; and while a negative demand function seems to be taken for granted any responsiveness to a lowering of the interest rate was attributed largely to the category of consumer-borrowers: 'the Moneys imployed at Interest in this Nation, are not near the Tenth part, disposed to Trading People, wherewith to manage their Trades; but are for the most part lent for the supplying of Luxury ... So that in truth an Ease to Interest, will rather be a support to Luxury than to Trade.' In North's analysis a positive slope is explicitly attributed to the loanable-fund supply curve: 'I averr, that high Interest will bring Money out from Hoards, Plate, &c. into Trade, when low Interest will keep it back.' The general position is that the equilibrium rate of interest will tend to fall with an increase in the supply of loanable funds relative to the demand, 'wherefore it is not low Interest makes Trade, but Trade increasing, the Stock of the Nation makes Interest low.'[77]

During the subsequent decades these general ideas were further elaborated, particularly by Cantillon and Hume. The view of Locke and others that the rate of interest tended to be inversely related with the supply of circulating money was largely rejected,[78] the emphasis being placed more firmly upon the consumption and savings habits of different classes and the productivity of investment.[79]

76 *Discourse Upon Trade* (1691), in McCulloch, ed., *Early English Tracts*, 517–8.
77 *Ibid.*, 518f. A similar position was adopted by John Locke, *Some Considerations of the Lowering of Interest, and Raising the Value of Money* (1691), 11f., regarding the inadvisability of attempting to reduce the rate artificially. The profitability of investment as an underlying determinant of the demand for loanable funds is emphasized by Locke.

   The notion of an interest-rate structure reflecting differential risk is also developed by North (*ibid.*, 518–19); although the concept was discussed earlier in detail by Petty, *Treatise of Taxes*, I, 48.
78 In point of fact, Locke believed that interest was a function of the demand and supply of loanable funds. But an increase in the money supply, it was assumed, would lower the rate of interest by increasing the supply relative to the demand. *Some Considerations of the Lowering of Interest*, 10–11.
79 On the other hand, Steuart's treatment in the *Inquiry* represents a 'synthesis' viewing the rate of interest as a monetary phenomenon rather than as a consequence of decisions relating to the sources and uses of investible funds. Cf. a full discussion by J.M. Low, 'The Rate of Interest: British Opinion in the Eighteenth Century,'

In Cantillon's formulation,[80] interest is discussed in the case of a primitive society as a function of the 'needs of borrowers' (time preference of consumers) governing the demand for funds and the 'fear and avarice' of lenders governing the supply price. In an advanced society the productivity of capital is introduced (in addition to the time preference of consumers) ; interest is paid from this point of view because of the profits that can be derived from investment of borrowed funds – with particular reference to small-scale entrepreneurs and workmen wishing to establish themselves in business. In this context the emphasis is upon *pure* profits as the source of interest and as the motive for borrowing, that is, upon an excess over the cost of the upkeep of entrepreneurs quite distinct from the wages of superintendence. In terms of this analysis Cantillon demonstrated that changes in expectations regarding profits might alter the interest rate even if the money supply is constant; conversely an increase in the money supply has no unambiguous effect upon the interest rate. Cantillon's examination – in micro-economic rather than aggregative terms – of the precise processes by which an increase in the money supply might affect the interest rate represents a pioneering achievement of the first order. Unlike North (and Barbon) who denied any relation between the money supply and the interest rate, or Locke who defined an unambiguous inverse relation, Cantillon emphasized alternative patterns depending upon the particular point of injection of the increased money supply.

Similarly, Hume's analysis of interest[81] represents an advance in terms of 'relevance' rather than 'rigour' insofar as it is recognized that differential effects on interest will follow an increase in the money supply depending on the hands through which it is introduced. In Hume's scheme, interest is a function of the 'demand for borrowing'; the supply of funds; and the 'profits from commerce.' The availability of high commercial profits, however, is not related to the *demand* for funds, but rather to the *supply*, in sharp contrast with Cantillon's approach with its emphasis upon borrowing for business purposes. The demand for loanable funds derived largely, it is presumed, from the consumption requirements of 'prodigal' landlords in particular. Hume, nonetheless, envisaged an inverse relationship between the extent of capital accumulation (specifically by merchants) and the rate of profit on (commercial) capital. Great stocks, it is contended, imply heavy competition – 'rivalships among the merchants' – so that profits are likely to decline with accumulation; but a low yield will entail a greater willingness to *lend* so that the interest rate is *ceteris paribus* likely to be reduced too. With the extension of commerce 'there must arise rivalships among the merchants, which diminish the profits

The Manchester School of Economic and Social Studies, XXII (May, 1954), 127f. It is here suggested that Steuart's approach may be better appreciated if we keep in mind a concern 'with the economics of an under-developed country in which it was plausible to assume secular-underemployment' (*ibid.*, 133).

80 *Essai*, ed. Higgs, 199f.

81 "Of Interest," in Rotwein, ed., *Writings on Economics*, 47–59.

of trade, at the same time that they encrease the trade itself. The low profits of merchanize induce merchants to accept more willingly of a low interest, when they leave off business, and begin to indulge themselves in ease and indolence. It is needless, therefore, to enquire which of these circumstances, to wit, *low interest or low profits*, is the cause, and which the effect. They both arise from an extensive commerce, and mutually forward each other.'[82] (Conversely if commerce is not well developed, the yield on commercial capital will be high and the supply of loanable funds will be adversely affected.)

While the relationship between the rate of profit on capital and the rate of interest is envisaged by Hume in a rather idiosyncratic manner, the notion of a secular decline in the profit rate with capital accumulation – and an expected consequential decline in the interest rate – is of supreme importance.[83] It may be noted, in addition, that in Hume's view not only does a low interest rate result from expansion, but a converse relationship is defined according to which a low interest is likely to stimulate industry insofar as cost prices of goods decline and the quantity demanded of products rises.[84]

In conclusion, we emphasize a fundamental characteristic of the literature discussed above, namely, the absence of any clearly defined relationship between the interest rate and saving. It was taken for granted that the total available supply of investible funds – as distinct from the supply of loanable funds – was determined by sociological and institutional factors and thus did not vary with the interest rate.[85]

INTERNATIONAL ADJUSTMENT MECHANISMS

If we turn to consider international adjustment mechanisms we are faced with the early piece-meal development of propositions – such as the quantity theory of money – potentially inconsistent with the basic mercantilist policy

82 *Ibid.*, 55.
83 While a low profit rate in Hume's model tends to generate a low interest rate by affecting favourably the supply of funds, it is also noted that a low interest rate is likely to encourage the owners of funds to invest them personally in order to avoid the sense of risk attached to lending.

Joseph Massie in his empirical treatment also refers to the phenomenon of a declining profit rate in terms of the increased competition among traders. Cf. *An Essay on the Governing Causes of the Natural Rate of Interest* (1750), ed. J.H. Hollander (Baltimore, 1912), 48–52. Francis Hutcheson similarly referred to the phenomenon, although without adequate explanation: 'When many hands and much wealth are employed in trade, as men can be supported by smaller gains in proportion upon their larger stocks, the profit made upon any given sum employed is smaller, and the interest the trader can afford must be less." *Collected Works of Francis Hutcheson*, vol. VI, *System of Moral Philosophy*, II, 72. Reference may also be made to Josiah Tucker, *Four Tracts*, 26–7.
84 'Of Public Credit,' in Rotwein, ed., *Writings on Economics*, 93–4.
85 Low, 'The Rate of Interest,' 137, refers to the 'refusal' to relate the rate of real saving and the rate of interest as the 'outstanding feature' of eighteenth century interest theory.

desideratum of a net (long-run) bullion inflow, maintained by writers who frequently were not, or did not show themselves to be, fully aware of the far-reaching implications of their arguments.[86] Changes of this nature helped clear the ground for the sophisticated statements of eighteenth-century authors of the self-regulating mechanism of specie distribution.[87]

Particular reference must be made in this regard to Isaac Gervaise's *The System or Theory of the Trade of the World* (1720) – discovered by Professor Viner – which describes the self-regulating mechanism, according a central role not only to relative *price* levels at home and abroad but also to relative *income* levels; and recognizing the function of wage-rate and exchange-rate movements in the adjustment process following an initial disturbance in equilibrium.[88] But the clearest, if not the fullest, of eighteenth-century accounts

86 The case of Mun is of particular interest. Mun insisted that an increase in the supply of money by way of a favourable trade balance must be prevented from raising the domestic price level and thereby unfavourably affecting exports: 'If wee were once poor, and now having gained some store of mony by trade with resolutions to keep it still in the Realm; shall this cause other Nations to spend more of our commodities than formerly they have done, whereby we might say that our trade is Quickened and Enlarged? no verily, it will produce no such good effect ...; for all men do consent that plenty of mony in a Kingdom doth make the native commodities dearer, which as it is to the profit of some private men in their revenues, so it is directly against the benefit of the Publique in the quantity of the trade' (*England's Treasure by Forraign Trade*, 17). He accordingly recommended that the money inflow be used in 'trading,' thereby justifying the exportation of specie by the East India Company drawing a parallel in the course of the argument with the 'husbandman in the seed-time' (*ibid.*, 19). At the same time – quite inconsistently – Mun noted, and approved of, the effects of an increased supply of money upon land values; agricultural prices are likely to rise, he argued, as merchants' export earnings and consequently their demand for additional commodities rise, thereby affecting rental earnings and also the price of land (*ibid.*, 20–2). And in fact, Mun failed to incorporate the quantity theory of price in his brief and inadequate discussion of the distribution of the precious metals among trading nations in his chapter entitled 'The Spanish Treasure cannot be kept from other Kingdomes by any prohibition made by Spain,' (*ibid.*, 22–4).

87 Viner, *Studies in the Theory of International Trade*, 75 has listed four 'stages' in the appreciation of the self-regulating mechanism: recognition that net international balances of payment must be paid in specie, that the quantity of money is a determinant of the level of prices, and that the volume of exports and the volume of imports depend on the *relative* levels of prices at home and abroad, and the integration of these propositions into a coherent theory of a self-regulating inter-national distribution of specie. As a further stage Viner refers to the realization of the inconsistency of this result with the national policy of long-run accumulation of specie. Malynes (1601) is considered by Viner as an early author who can legiti-mately be said to have recognized substantial aspects of the mechanism (although certainly not the entire mechanism or the logical deductions to be drawn) – as distinct from others who merely made 'vague statements.' Professor Schumpeter is more lavish in his attributions (*History of Economic Analysis*, (New York, 1954), 365).

88 Viner, *Studies in the Theory of International Trade*, 79f. For a detailed analysis see J.M. Letiche, 'Isaac Gervaise on the International Mechanism of Adjustment,' *Journal of Political Economy*, LX (Feb. 1952), 34–43.

is that by David Hume in 1752.[89] Hume forcefully condemned those trade controls designed to amass the precious metals or to prevent their loss, on the grounds that money cannot be 'heaped up' above its 'proper level' – defined (rather loosely) for each country in terms of its 'art and industry' or its 'commodities, labour, industry and skill' – relative to that of its trading partners.[90]

According to the analysis, an increase in the money supply in any one state will ultimately be corrected by the change in relative price levels: 'suppose, that all the money of Great Britain were multiplied fivefold in a night ... Must not all labour and commodities rise to such an exorbitant height, that no neighbouring nations could afford to buy from us; while their commodities, on the other hand, became comparatively so cheap, that, in spite of all the laws which could be formed, they would be run in upon us, and our money flow out; till we fall to a level with foreigners, and lose that great superiority of riches, which laid us under such disadvantages?'[91] The same process would operate not only in the event of a presumed exogenous expansion of the money supply, but also in the 'common course of nature, and must for ever, in all neighbouring nations, preserve money nearly proportionable to the art and industry of each nation.' The process of equalization is described as 'a moral attraction, arising from the interests and passions of men,' reacting to price differentials.[92]

Yet Hume did not follow through by rejecting all concern with the precious metals. Thus he referred to the advantages of metallic money to the state in foreign negotiations,[93] and emphasized the stimulating effect upon industry of an increase in the money supply during the *interval* between its injection and the subsequent rise in the price level. The latter concession occurs in an argument in the essay 'Of Money,' and led Hume to conclude that 'the good policy of the magistrate consists only in keeping [the quantity of money], if possible, still encreasing; because, by that means, he keeps alive a spirit of industry in the nation, and encreases the stock of labour, in which consists all real power and riches.'[94] It is worth noting that the latter argument presumed an initial state of unemployment:

89 'Of the Balance of Trade,' in Rotwein, ed., *Writings on Economics*, 60–77. See also letter to Montesquieu (April 10, 1749), *ibid.*, 188. It is important to note that Hume formally applied his analysis to intra-national as well as international trading relations.

90 *Ibid.*, 63–6. Subsequently Hume makes clear that in fact he is dealing with the automatic regulation of money *in circulation*. See *ibid.*, 72 regarding 'the gathering of large sumes into a public treasure, locking them up, and absolutely preventing their circulation.'

91 *Ibid.*, 63. Hume does not make it clear that an exogenous increase in the money supply in any one country would, after international equilibrium is restored, entail a higher *world* price level.

92 A second, and less significant corrective mechanism allowed for is the variation of the exchange rate within the specie points (*ibid.*, 64n).

93 *Ibid.*, 35, 68.

94 *Ibid.*, 39–40. While the same effects could be assured by an increase of paper money, Hume warned (in 'Of the Balance of Trade') that 'it is dangerous to precipitate

When any quantity of money is imported into a nation, it is not at first dispersed into many hands, but is confined to the coffers of a few persons, who immediately seek to employ it to advantage. Here are a set of manufacturers or merchants, we shall suppose, who have received returns of gold and silver for goods which they sent to *Cadiz*. They are thereby enabled to employ more workmen than formerly, who never dream of demanding higher wages, but are glad of employment from such good paymasters.[95]

Brief reference may be made to the contribution in Richard Cantillon's *Essai* earlier in the century. A distinction was drawn by Cantillon between the effects of an increase in the money supply emanating from domestic mines and an increase resulting from a balance of trade surplus.[96] In either case the initial effect would be upon expenditures and prices. As a consequence of resultant changes in the relative prices of domestic and foreign goods increased imports become profitable. These imports were, however, regarded as ruinous to trade and employment. The basic difference between the two cases is that in the event of an initial bullion inflow due to a trade surplus, industry is by assumption particularly competitive to start with and can hold its own longer than when the increase derives from the mines. In any event, the explanation is in terms of a catastrophic process rather than a smooth mechanism of adjustment; and in fact Cantillon provides no account of the ultimate equilibrium, if any, achieved.[97]

A number of early writers formulated economic arguments which might be incorporated into a general case for unrestricted trade, although they themselves did not necessarily do so.[98] Thus Nicholas Barbon claimed that restric-

matters, at the risk of losing all by the failing of that credit, as must happen upon any violent shock in public affairs' (*ibid.*, 68n). Apart from the case against credit based upon the jeopardy to solvency, Hume objected to the paper money on the grounds that it tended to drive up prices and cause an outflow of the precious metals to the disadvantage of the state in light of their potential role in negotiations (*ibid.*, 67–9; 71–2). (Inconsistently, an argument is made against paper in the essay 'Of Credit' according to which an injection thereof leads to inflationary price changes which *fail* to be corrected by a bullion outflow (*ibid.*, 95n).)

95 *Ibid.*, 38. Subsequently, Hume appears to assume a state of full employment although it is not clear whether this is dependent upon foreign demand or whether Hume was optimistic even with regard to a closed economy. See 'Of the Jealousy of Trade,' (1758) *ibid.*, 80 where Hume emphasizes the ease of resource diversion between various branches of manufacturing. See also reference below, 77, to 'Of the Balance of Trade' regarding protection as a stimulus to employment, which introduces a further complexity.

96 *Essai*, ed. Higgs, 163f.

97 We cannot, therefore agree with Professor Schumpeter, *History of Economic Analysis*, 367, who regards Cantillon (along with Hume) as providing a particularly eminent formulation of the automatic mechanism of specie distribution.

98 Professor Viner's finding (*Studies in the Theory of International Trade*, 92) are that the only contributors to the English economic literature prior to Smith who can be regarded as free traders are in fact Dudley North (1691), William Paterson (1701), the unknown author of *Considerations on the East-India Trade* (1701), Gervaise (1720), and Whatly, *Principles of Trade*, 2nd ed. (1774).

tions on imports would correspondingly restrict exports; moreover there was no assurance that consumers would be satisfied with the domestic production of import substitutes: 'the prohibition of foreign wares does not necessarily cause a greater consumption of the like sort of English.'[99] But he concluded by favouring high protective duties as distinct from outright prohibition or prohibitive duties.

Several others wrote of the advantages of international specialization, although none formally stated the law of comparative advantage. Reference may be made to Davenant's argument (in 1697) that the artificial stimulus of goods unsuited for the resources of the community is unwise; to the unknown author of *Considerations on the East-India Trade* (1701) who recognized that the fundamental advantage of acquiring cheap imports lies in the saving of domestic resources; and to the account by Gervaise (1720) of a 'natural' distribution of resources according to the community's productive capacities and geographic situation which renders disadvantageous the artificial extension of output by protection.[100]

It was similarly argued by Hume that interference with the distribution of specie would tend to diminish wealth by impeding international specialization,[101] the advantages of which derive from *qualitative* differentials in resource endowments:

From these principles we may learn what judgment we ought to form of those numberless bars, obstructions, and imposts, which all nations of Europe, and none more than England, have put upon trade ... Could any thing scatter our riches, it would be such impolitic contrivances. But this general ill effect, however, results from them, that they deprive neighbouring nations of that free communication and exchange which the Author of the world has intended, by giving them soils, climates, and geniuses, so different from each other.[102]

It may be noted, however, that Hume in the essay 'Of the Balance of Trade' did not reject all state interference. Import duties designed to amass the precious metals are condemned but not those introduced for revenue purposes or for the stimulation of employment.[103]

In the essay 'Of Money' Hume described a general law of growth and decay with regard to nations, based on the view that rising money wages and prices

99 *Discourses of Trade* (1690), quoted in Letwin, *The Origins of Scientific Economics*, 60.

100 See Viner, *Studies in the Theory of International Trade*, 103f; Arkin, 'A Neglected Forerunner of Adam Smith,' 303–7; and Letiche, 'Isaac Gervaise on the International Mechanism of Adjustment,' 42.

101 'Of the Balance of Trade,' in Rotwein, ed., *Writings on Economics*, 65–7.

102 *Ibid.*, 75. Cf. 'Of the Jealousy of Trade,' (1758), 79: 'Nature, by giving a diversity of geniuses, climates, and soils, to different nations, has secured their mutual intercourse and commerce, as long as they all remain industrious and civilized.'

103 'Of the Balance of Trade,' 76. Thus 'a tax on German linen encourages home manufactures, and thereby multiplies our people and industry. A tax on brandy encreases the sale of rum, and supports our southern colonies.'

must ruin the initial cost advantages of a relatively developed economy – one with 'superior industry and skill' and 'greater stocks of which its merchants are possessed, and which enable them to trade on so much smaller profits.' Consequently, industries 'gradually shift their places, leaving those countries and provinces which they have already enriched, and flying to others, whither they are allured by the cheapness of provisions and labour; till they have enriched these also, and are again banished by the same causes.'[104] This position, which suggests a possible rationale for protection, was subsequently abandoned and in the essay 'Of the Jealousy of Trade' (which appeared, in 1758, six years after the other economic essays) Hume presented a full-fledged defence of free trade utilizing the notion of differential (qualitative) resource endowment, mentioned above, to conclude that no industrious country need fear 'that their neighbours will improve to such a degree in every art and manufacture as to have no demand for them.' The modification in approach appears to have been influenced by the criticism of Josiah Tucker.[105]

THE PHYSIOCRATIC LITERATURE

A fundamental concern of the Physiocrats was with economic growth, and particularly with the modernization of the argicultural sector. Formally the *tableau économique* was used to explain the mechanism of aggregative

---

104 'Of Money,' in Rotwein, ed., *Writings on Economics*, 34–5. There is something of a 'mercantilist residue' in an argument which emphasizes the disadvantageous effects of high money wages neglecting low money wage costs which are quite consistent if efficiency is high.

105 'Of the Jealousy of Trade,' 79. (See commentary by Rotwein, *Writings on Economics*, lxxvii.) Tucker had refused to accept the concept of a finite limit to economic expansion: 'I apprehend no man can mark out the limits, or reasonably affirm, "*Hitherto* shall an industrious and moral nation increase in the quantity of their manufactures, the numbers of their people, and stock of wealth, and *no farther*".' (Letter to Lord Kames, dated July 6, 1758, Rotwein, *Writings on Economics*, 203). While maintaining the view that the rich country would not lose its advantages of high capital and skill (and ability to undersell) he suggested that the poor country might prevent its complete ruination by prohibiting the exportation of any essential raw materials it possessed and by imposing protective import duties 'to turn the scale in favour of their own manufactures' (*ibid.*).
Hume's argument that it would be the poor country with cheaper labour and raw materials that attracts industry at the expense of the latter was rejected by Tucker on the grounds that any such advantages will continually diminish with rising prices as development proceeds: 'In short, though both countries may still go on in their respective improvements, the poor country ... can never overtake the rich, unless it be through the fault and mismanagement of the latter' (*ibid.*, 205). See also Tucker, *Four Tracts*, 40f.
    The position that an advanced economy would not only *not* lose its relative advantage but on the contrary would find its advantage actually increasing was put forward by James Oswald of Dunnikier, a friend of both Hume and Smith. (See Low, 'An Eighteenth Century Controversy in the Theory of Economic Progress,' 319.) Oswald, it must be emphasized, rejected the quantity theory, emphasizing the increase in the level of activity rather than that of prices upon an expansion of the money supply.

contraction and expansion according to the extent to which their policy recommendations were accepted.[106] But the analysis is no stronger than the basic assumptions put into the model and for our purposes we can consider some of the key characteristics of physiocratic growth theory apart from the *tableau* structure.

The problem of growth was viewed from a fundamentally different perspective than that of the Mercantilists who had little appreciation of the process of genuine productive investment. In physiocratic expositions, the key to growth lay in accumulation where capital was envisaged as consisting of 'advances' and the source of new capital identified in the community's 'disposable surplus.'[107] Quesnay categorically denied the need for concern with an increased supply of money by way of the external balance as a means of achieving faster growth: 'Les avances nécessaires pour tirer le plus grand produit possible du territoire ne dépendent point de la quantité du pécule. Parcourez les fermes et les ateliers, et voyez quels sont les fonds de ces avances si précieuses. Vous trouverez des bâtiments, des bestiaux, des semences, des matières premières, des meubles et des instruments de toute espèce. Tout cela vaut de l'argent sans doute, mais rien de cela n'est de l'argent.'[108] And he insisted that the greatest care should be taken to avoid any governmental measures – particularly taxation – which might impinge upon capital: 'the advances of a kingdom's agriculture ought to be regarded as if they were fixed property requiring to be preserved with great care in order to ensure the production of taxes, revenue, and subsistence for all classes of citizens.'[109]

The work of Turgot requires particular emphasis in this context. His thor-

---

106 R.L. Meek, 'Problems of the "Tableau Economique",' *Economica* (Nov. 1960), reprinted in Meek, *The Economics of Physiocracy* (London, 1962; hereafter cited as Meek when referring to a translation from the French), especially 287–96. There is a fundamental difficulty inherent in the basic *tableau* as a device for the analysis of growth, namely the fact that while the system described is conceived to be in equilibrium so that the process is repeated year by year in precisely the same dimensions, no explanation is given of *why* – in light of the surplus available for net investment – the system was thus stationary (cf. J.J. Spengler, 'Quesnay: Philosophe, Empiriste, Economiste,' in A. Sauvy, ed., *François Quesnay et la Physiocratie* (Institut National d'Etudes Démographiques, Paris, 1958; hereafter cited as INED), I, 70n; B.F. Hoselitz, 'The Early History of Entrepreneurial Theory,' *Explorations in Entrepreneurial History*, III (1951), reprinted in Spengler and Allen, eds., *Essays in Economic Thought*, 245).

107 See R.L. Meek, 'Physiocracy and the Early Theories of Under-Consumption,' *Economica* (Aug. 1951), reprinted in Meek, *The Economics of Physiocracy*, 314f.; R.L. Meek, 'Physiocracy and Classicism in Britain,' *Economic Journal* (March 1951), *ibid.*, 345f.; J.J. Spengler, 'Mercantilist and Physiocratic Growth Theory,' in B.F. Hoselitz, ed., *Theories of Economic Growth* (New York, 1960), 58–61; Schumpeter, *History of Economic Analysis*, 236–7; and Robert V. Eagly, 'A Physiocratic Model of Dynamic Equilibrium,' *Journal of Political Economy*, LXXVII (Jan.–Feb. 1969), 66–84.

108 F. Quesnay, 'Dialogue sur le commerce,' in *Journal d'Agriculture* (1766), INED, II, 846.

109 'Maximes Générales' (1767), *ibid.*, 951; Meek, 232.

oughly non-mercantilist view of wealth includes land, movable riches or the sum of capitals employed in industry, agriculture and commerce, and durable personal goods. Specie is included in the totality of movable riches but constitutes only a minor fraction therof; and ready money in misers' hoards is included within the third category. A warning is given that *loan capital* must be excluded to avoid double counting.[110] The interest rate is said to be determined as a function of the demand by borrowers and the offers of lenders in a statement denying its dependence upon the supply of money. The offers of lenders in turn depend upon the supply of capital or of movable riches 'accumulated, saved bit by bit out of the revenues and profits ... It is these acumulated savings that are offered to borrowers, and the more there are of them the lower is the rate of interest, at least if the number of borrowers is not augmented in proportion.'[111] In the account of the *process* of capital accumulation Turgot emphasized that savings are converted into capital *without lag*, a proposition of immeasurable significance in the history of economic thought:

We have seen that money plays scarcely any part in the sum total of existing capitals; but it plays a great part in the formation of capitals. In fact, almost all savings are made in nothing but money; it is in money that the revenues come to the proprietors, that advances and the profits return to undertakers of every kind; it is, therefore, from money that they save, and the annual increase of capitals takes place in money: but none of the undertakers make any other use of it than to convert it *immediately* into the different kinds of effects upon which their undertaking depends; and thus this money returns to circulation, and the greater part of capitals exists only in effects of different kinds, as we have already explained above.[112]

The conception of capital as 'advances' in physiocratic literature placed the emphasis squarely upon the time-consuming nature of 'capitalistic' activity. Lands, for example, Quesnay recognized, have to be prepared for successful cultivation: 'And is it not also clear that the land never makes any advances, that on the contrary it makes us wait a long time for the harvest?'[113] And working capital (*avances annuelles*) is in fact defined specifically to include subsistence goods made available for the support of labour during the production period.[114] The nature of capital in its function of spanning the time-interval involved in production is even more clearly expressed by Turgot:

110 A.R.J. Turgot, *Reflections on the Formation and Distribution of Riches* (1776; New York, 1963), 86–90. Land values are calculated as the product of the net revenue of the estate and the rate at which land is sold.

111 *Ibid.*, 78–9.

112 *Ibid.*, 98–9. (See also a similar conception expressed by Quesnay himself, below 83.) Du Pont de Nemours objected to Turgot's formulations on the grounds that 'the formation of capitals arises much less from saving out of the expenditure of revenues than from the wise employment of the expenditure' (*ibid.*, ix).

113 'Grains,' *L'Encyclopédie* (1757), INED, 505; Meek, 82.

114 Cf. *Explication du Tableau Economique* (1759), INED, 675; Meek, 128. The contrast between 'annual' advances or working capital, and 'original' advances

All the various kinds of labours, whether in the cultivation of the land, in industry, or in Commerce, require advances ... The more perfect and energetic the cultivation of the land becomes, the more considerable are these advances. There is need of cattle, of implements of husbandry, of buildings ...; it is necessary to pay a number of persons proportioned to the extent of the undertaking, and to enable them to subsist until the harvest. It is only by means of considerable advances that we obtain a large return, and that the lands produce a good deal of revenue. In every craft, whatever it may be, it is necessary that the Workman should have tools in advance, that he should have a sufficient quantity of the materials upon which he has to labour; it is necessary that he should subsist while waiting for the sale of his finished goods.[115]

A severe constraint was, however, imposed upon the general applicability of physiocratic doctrine by a conception of wealth-creating activity which envisaged manufacturing and commerce as representing no more than a 'change of form' of already existing wealth generated in the agricultural sector, a view which accorded significance to biological creativity: 'Façonner et produire sont deux : on ne façonne les matières brutes, qu'après qu'elles ont été produites; rien n'est plus évident.'[116] The fundamental distinction appears too with Quesnay himself; wages earned in manufacturing are essentially a transfer payment:

La fabrication d'ouvrages de main-d'œuvre n'est pas, comme la culture, une source primitive de richesses; elle ne produit pas de revenus, elle ne rend que le prix du travail de la main-d'œuvre, elle ne se soutient que par les revenus de l'agriculture, car ce sont des revenus qui payent les ouvrages de main-d'œuvre; les fabricants, les artisans, les marchands, les ouvriers ne se rassemblent et ne subsistent dans le royaume qu'à proportion des revenus des bien-fonds.[117]

which consist largely of fixed capital is, for example, brought out in this document; in the *Philosophie Rurale* (1764) by de Mirabeau (with the collaboration of Quesnay), Meek, 138f.; and in the *Analyse de la Formule Arithmétique du Tableau Economique* (1766), INED, 795n.; Meek, 151n.

See also a statement by L'abbé Baudeau, 'Explication sur le vrai sens du mot *stérile*,' *Ephémérides*, vol. VIII (1767), in E. Daire, ed., *Physiocrates* (Paris, 1846), 871: 'La valeur de toutes ces dépenses annuelles, avec l'intérêt des avances primitives, sont des portions sacrées et privilégiées; qu'il faut les prélever sur la récolte, pour faire les frais préparatoires de la production future en 1768, frais qui commencent à présent.'

115 *Reflections*, 45.

116 Baudeau, 'Explication,' 868.

117 'Impôts,' INED, 603. Le Trosne addressed himself to an argument by L'abbé de Condillac according to which 'tous les travaux concourent à augmenter la masse des richesses; que l'industrie des marchands et des artisans est un fonds de richesses autant que l'industrie des colons.' Condillac's error, wrote Le Trosne, lay in his failure to note that 'façonner une chose produite, ou la produire sont des choses essentiellement différentes; que l'industrie ne fait qu'ajouter des formes à la matière première, au lieu que la terre donne des substances qui, de non existantes, deviennent existantes.' *De l'intérêt social* (1777) in Daire, ed., *Physiocrates*, 936-7. (The reference is to Condillac's *Du Commerce et du gouvernement considérés*

In this sense, therefore, agriculture alone could be called 'productive' while other activities were to be designated 'sterile' despite their usefulness from the viewpoint of final consumption. As Baudeau put it: 'rien n'est plus utiles que les façons et le négoce, mais c'est aux jouissances des hommes, à la consommation qu'ils servent.'[118]

But of greater significance for us is the parallel classification of 'productive' activity which turns on the ability to generate a 'net product.' It was only agricultural activity which possessed this ability. A severe ambiguity surrounds this aspect of physiocratic thought due to a failure to distinguish adequately between value and physical product and between alternative possible senses of 'net (value) product,' which may refer to a surplus over paid-out costs, or a surplus over the 'necessary' costs required to assure the maintenance of activity at a particular level, or a 'disposable' income available for net capital accumulation. It is quite conceivable, for example, that the reduction of an income item – as by taxation – leads to a contraction in the supply of the relevant productive service, while at the same time the income contains a disposable surplus potentially available for accumulation. It is possible to develop a theoretical argument to account for each category of surplus, even for a unique value surplus in any one sector. But this was not in fact achieved; on the whole the economists took for granted a *physical* surplus generated by labour on land – ascribing it to 'le bienfait de la nature' – and assumed it to have a value counterpart.

The argument of the Physiocrats in part hinges on the notion that competition will reduce *manufacturing* prices to the level of costs where it is clearly presumed that costs reflect some 'indispensable' minimum. This presumption effectively rules out the possibility that even though costs are precisely covered a disposable element may yet be present. We may illustrate from a striking statement by Le Trosne:

L'industrie diffère donc essentiellement de la culture, dont les productions ont une valeur à elle et un prix supérieur au montant des frais qu'il a fallu faire pour les tirer de la terre. Outre ses dépenses que la culture restitue sans qu'il en coûte rien à personne, et par le bienfait de la nature, elle donne par-delà ses frais une quantité plus ou moins grande de production *qui est disponible*, et qui constitue *le produit net* dont la somme est la mesure de la puissance d'une nation.

On ne trouve rien de semblable dans la prétendue production de l'industrie; les ouvrages *ne valent que leurs frais indispensables*, et ils ne les restituent qu'autant

relativement l'un à l'autre (1776).) Accordingly 'income' earned in manufacturing is not an original source: 'Ce n'est donc pas l'industrie qui fait naître la faculté de payer ses services; elle la trouve existante, et elle en profite pour tirer sa part de la reproduction. Si elle consomme, c'est parce que la première classe en a fait naître pour elle les moyens; lorsqu'elle achète, elle ne fait que rapporter l'argent qu'on lui a donné.' (Le Trosne, *De l'intérêt social*, 943.)

118 'Explication,' 870.

qu'un autre paye cette dépense. A plus forte raison, ne donne-t-elle jamais de produit net.[119]

Not unexpectedly there were problems which derived from the recognition that in fact some workers earned a return exceeding the subsistence minimum. But there was an already prepared line of defence to which we have referred above, namely the conception of all manufacturing incomes as transfer payments:

S'il est des artistes qui se font payes *au-dela des frais indispensables*, c'est qu' à raison de leur talent et des études qu'ils ont faites, ils ont droit à une plus forte consommation que les ouvriers ordinaires, et ils exigent d'autant plus qu'ils ont moins de concurrents. Mais, s'ils semblent obtenir une sorte de produit net, *ils ne le produisent pas, ils le gagnent*; et cette plus-valeur, qui est pour eux un bénéfice, est une dépense de plus pour les acheteurs.[120]

The economists were, of course, caught in serious circularity of reasoning by adopting this solution.

We have noted in our earlier discussion of physiocratic price theory that agricultural profits were viewed by Quesnay as a necessary payment. What remains to be considered is whether profits were nonetheless envisaged as containing a disposable surplus or whether rent was the only income available for accumulation.

Professor Meek[121] has emphasized one passage wherein Quesnay implies that the interest upon the farmer's 'original advances' contains a disposal element:

I am also saying that a fund which is as advantageous to the nation as that of the advances of its cultivation ought in itself to bring in net to the farmers, who combine their work and the use of their intelligence with it, an annual interest at least as high as that which is paid to idle rentiers.

The total amount of this interest is spent annually, because cultivators never allow it to remain inactive; for in the intervals when they are not obliged to use it for repairs, they do not fail to put it to profit in order to increase and improve their cultivation, without which they would be unable to provide for serious accidents. That is why interest is included in the total of annual expenditure.[122]

But there are other statements with a similar implication. Thus we also read in

119 *De l'intérêt social*, 944–5 (author's emphasis).
120 *Ibid.* (author's emphasis). Cf. Quesnay, INED, 583; Meek, 105: This gain [the return to manufacturing labour], even when it exceeds the restitution of the expenses, can exist only through the original and ever-renascent wealth which pays for the work of manufacture.'
121 *The Economics of Physiocracy*, 308.
122 'Analyse,' INED, 799; Meek, 155–6. Professor Meek has brought textual evidence

Quesnay's 'Analysis' that 'the interest of the cultivator is the mainspring of all economic operations and all agricultural progress.'[123] This formulation may be read in conjunction with an emphasis frequently placed on the desirable role of the landowner as *consumer* (rather than as saver): 'The proprietors are useful to the state only through their consumption; their revenue exempts them from labour; they produce nothing; and if their revenue was not circulated among those in the remunerative occupations, the state would be depopulated through the greed of these unjust and treacherous proprietors.'[124] Similarly, in a note in 'Hommes,' Quesnay insisted that 'les richesses du fermier soient consacrées, et que les revenus du propriétaire soient dépensés. Celles-là produisent des revenus, et ceux-ci soutiennent la population.'[125] This passage too implies that it was the farmer's function to invest, and by implication that his return contained a surplus available for accumulation.

It thus appears from the above references that, for Quesnay, while the net product *in the sense of surplus over necessary costs* includes the rental income only, yet profits – or part of profits – as well as rent are *disposable* for capital accumulation. Moreover, it is largely the farmers who, in fact, were envisaged as providing the funds for investment while the landlords consumed their income.[126]

Yet it was by no means universally or consistently maintained that the return to the landowner represented a pure surplus over cost. In reply to critics who regarded the emphasis upon unearned income to be amoral some of the Physiocrats included a long-run return to investment in the rental payment. This is true of Baudeau, for example: 'C'est que, dans le produit net ou revenu, il y a deux portions privilégiées encore, savoir: 1. le juste intérêt des sommes que le propriétaire a dépensées ci-devant, pour mettre la terre

to the effect that generally the interest earned by the farmer on his advances was conceived as compensation for cost incurred (including risk). Cf. *The Economics of Physiocracy*, 302–3.

123 'Analyse,' INED, 807n; Meek, 164n. The passage continues in the same tone: 'the more that products constantly sell at high prices, the more assured are the annual returns of the farmers, the more cultivation is extended, and the more revenue the land brings in, as much through the proper price of the products as through the increase in the annual reproduction. And the more reproduction increases, the more the wealth of the nation is expanded, and the more the power of the state is augmented.'

124 'Impôts,' INED, 582; Meek, 104.

125 'Hommes,' INED, 571.

126 It is essential to distinguish these forms of surplus. To refer to the net product as a 'disposable surplus over necessary costs' may lead to a minimization of the role of the farmer – in contrast with the landlord – in saving. See R.L. Meek, 'Ideas, Events and Environment: the Case of the French Physiocrats,' in R.V. Eagly, ed., *Events, Ideology and Economic Theory* (Detroit, 1968), 51; and Meek, 'The Physiocratic Concept of Profit,' *Economica* (1959), reprinted in *The Economics of Physiocracy*, 297–8. Elsewhere Meek refers to the surplus over paid-out costs (e.g.: *ibid.*, 314).

en valeur ou pour l'acquérir telle; 2. un fonds pour celles qu'il dépense habituellement en entretien et réparations, pour faire face aux accidents, aux pertes, aux ruines.'[127] But it is also true of Quesnay himself, who – despite apparently unambiguous statements that landlords undertake no productive functions – attempted upon occasion to define the rental income – at least in part – as a genuine 'return.' Indeed he made a strong case against the absentee landlord and in favour of the improving landlord, interestingly enough drawing for illustration upon contemporary English practice: 'En Angleterre, les grands propriétaires habitent leurs terres une partie de l'année, et ils ont porté fort loin l'amélioration de leurs biens; parce que dans ce royaume l'agriculture est la source de leurs richesses.'[128]

With the further development of physiocratic thought, writers, as Meek has shown, tended increasingly to emphasize a net element available for accumulation in the farmer's return; and more significantly, the distinction between agriculture and manufacturing became blurred. This is certainly true of Turgot as is suggested by his analysis of the competitive process of profit-rate equalization between farming, commerce and industry.[129]

It is quite clear from the *Reflections* that savings are made not only by landowners out of their 'revenues' but also by entrepreneurs out of their 'profits.' Some attention is paid to ploughed-back profits in an example drawn, in fact, from *manufacturing*: 'As fast as this capital comes back to him by the sale of his products, he uses it for new purchases in order to supply and maintain his Manufactory by this continual circulation: on his profits he lives, and he places on one side what he can spare to increase his capital and put into his business, adding to the amount of his advances in order to add still more to his profits.'[130] And the empirical observations regarding the tendency of landlords to use the surplus largely for consumption, and of both wage earners and capitalists to save do not coexist easily with the continued formal insistence that the latter 'have no revenue properly so called':

This economizing has doubtless taken place not only out of the revenues of the proprietors, but also out of the profits of all the members of the working classes. It is even

127 'Explication,' 871. These returns were, in addition to the interest on the 'dépenses primitive de la cultivation,' undertaken by the farmer.
   For Turgot, on the other hand, the rental income was a pure surplus over necessary costs. See *Reflections*, 95–6.
128 'Hommes,' INED, 560. Reference is also made to (undefined) governmental activities (financed by the net product) which contribute to growth (*ibid.*, 559; Meek, 98).
129 Cf. Meek, *The Economics of Physiocracy*, 308f; Meek, 'Adam Smith and the Classical Theory of Profit,' *Scottish Journal of Political Economy* (June 1954), reprinted in Meek, *Economics and Ideology and Other Essays* (London, 1967), 31–2; and P.D. Groenewegen, 'Turgot and Adam Smith,' *Scottish Journal of Political Economy*, XVI (Nov. 1969), 284–6 regarding Turgot's more general view of profits on capital, wherever invested, as a distinct distributive category.
130 Turgot, *Reflections*, 54.

generally true that, although the proprietors have a greater superfluity, they save less because as they have more leisure, they have more desires and more passions ... The wage-receivers, and especially the undertakers of the other classes, who receive profits proportionate to their advances, to their talent and to their activity, although they have no revenue properly so called, have yet a superfluity beyond their subsistence; and almost all of them ... save all their superfluity to invest it again in their business and so increase it.[131]

Great emphasis was placed in physiocratic writing upon the need for 'efficiency.' The object of economic activity in the first instance should be the maximization of the net value product, for other desirable social objectives would follow automatically. Inefficiency had the effect of reducing the net product and therefore had to be rejected: 'Thus it is obvious that the costs which one could avoid adding on to the price of produce, and which create gains for a number of men whose labour is not worth the rewards which are paid to them, reduce the revenue or the wealth of consumers, and also reduce the sales, the consumption, and the production of this produce.'[132] The view frequently encountered in mercantilist literature that domestic production should be stimulated irrespective of cost in the interest of population, or employment was rejected outright. What mattered was the minimization of labour cost:

In considering the employment of men, the government ought to estimate their utility not only with reference to the work which they actually do, but also, and to a greater extent, with reference to the considerable utility which the kingdom could derive from them, according to the state of the population, through other more advantageous work, or through economizing on the men who are employed in too great a number on work which could be carried out with less men and at less cost. The men who are unnecessarily employed in such work are stolen from other work in which they would be profitable to the state.[133]

Consistently with their concern with efficiency, the Physiocrats spoke in

---

131 *Ibid.*, 97. Cf. *ibid.*, 44, where the likelihood is clearly expressed that not only the
profits on capital, but wages also, contain a surplus available for accumulation:
'Although the profits of industry are not, like the revenues of the earth, a gift
of nature, and the man engaged in industry gets from his work nothing but the
price given him for it by the person who pays his wages; although this latter
economises as much as possible in this payment of wages, and competition obliges
the man engaged in industry to content himself with a price less than he would like,
it is nevertheless certain that this competition has never been numerous enough
or keen enough in all the different kinds of labours to prevent at any time a man
who was more expert, more active, and, above all, more economical than others
in his personal consumption, from gaining a little more than was necessary for the
subsistence of himself and his family and from saving this surplus to create therewith
a little store.'
132 Quesnay, 'Hommes,' INED, 563; Meek, 100.
133 *Ibid.*, 562; Meek, 100.

favour of technical progress (although not only in agriculture but quite generally). The question of the displacement of labour by new techniques was raised by Quesnay. He argued that a cost-reducing technical change would be desirable even in the event that displaced workers were permanently unemployed and would have to be maintained for life. However, he recommended that changes be introduced slowly, and in the cases he had in mind denied the likelihood of permanent unemployment.[134] As we pointed out earlier, no explanation was provided for the presumption that in the case of agriculture, as distinct from other sectors, increased profitability due to technical progress would in the long run be reflected in higher rents rather than in lower prices in consequence of competition by producers.

It is in this context that the physiocratic approach to population can best be appreciated. If the net product is increased upon the introduction of large-scale, capital-intensive farming methods a population increase would follow *in consequence*. There was no need, therefore, to pay particular attention to the size of population, for it automatically responds to the magnitude of the net product. And on the other hand, there can be no problem of excess:

the population of a state is always proportionate to the annual product and revenue of the nation. Thus men who contribute only to increase the cost of produce or commodities are detrimental equally to the increase of wealth and the increase of population. Thus all machines which can contribute to reduce the cost of men's labour, and all canals or rivers which avoid the costs which are paid to carriers, bring about a price which is favourable to the proper value of produce or commodities; they encourage sales and production, which increases wealth and consequently population, for the increase in wealth produces an increase in expenditure, which yields an increase in the gains of all the remunerative occupations and which attracts to them a greater number of men. Thus it is not true that population can expand to the detriment of the annual production of wealth: a population which consumes more than it ought to produce does not become as great as it would be possible for it to become.[135]

A particularly revealing index of the physiocratic approach may be noted in the attitude taken towards the colonies. The potentially damaging effect

134 *Ibid.*, 563n; Meek, 101. Reference is made to taffeta-making machinery; water pipes; and canals.
135 *Ibid.*, 563; Meek, 100–1. A similar case in favour of large-scale agricultural enterprises is given in the 'Maximes Générales,' *ibid.*, 953; Meek, 235: 'A multiplicity of small farmers is detrimental to the population. The population whose position is most assured ... is that maintained by the net product. All economies profitably made use of in work which can be done with the aid of animals, machines, rivers, etc., bring benefit to the population and the state, because a greater net product procures men a greater reward for other services or other kinds of work.'
See also *ibid.*, 571: 'C'est donc par le progrès des richesses, qu'une nation peut parvenir à de plus grands progrès de richesses, de population et de puissance; c'est donc en vain qu'elle tendrait à multiplier les hommes sans s'attacher préalablement à multiplier les richesses.'

thereof upon population was played down by Quesnay and attention was directed to the effect on the national product: 'On demande si les colonies ne dépeuplent pas le royaume qui les fournit; ne faudrait-il pas plutôt demander, si elles n'en diminuent pas les richesses par les dépenses et par les guerres qu'elles occasionnent?'[136]

An equally sharp distinction exists between physiocratic and mercantilist attitudes to labour. For example, Quesnay attacked those who opposed the education of peasants (on the grounds that it caused the depopulation of the countryside), conceiving the objection to reflect an approach encouraging the use of inefficient processes to provide support for labour. It was, in fact, in those provinces utilizing advanced (capital-intensive) methods under the direction of 'les riches fermiers' that the peasants were most favourably circumstanced rather than where the *métayer* system operated.[137] To assure that the agricultural population could read and write, moreover, permitted the spread of new methods and practices.

Similarly hostile to mercantilist doctrine is Quesnay's insistence that poverty – deliberately fostered – had ruinous effects in generating habits of idleness ('fainéantise') which were particularly unfortunate when acquired by the young: '*Voilà les succès des maximes de ces hommes féroces, qui prétendent qu'il faut réduire le bas-peuple à la misère, pour les forcer de travailler.*' In fact, high wages *stimulated* effort: '*C'est l'état d'aisance qui provoque le travail* parce que les hommes jouissent du bien-être qu'il leur procure ...' Moreover, high (average) incomes assured high expenditures: 'Les succès des travaux des hommes ne se bornent pas aux productions qui en naissent, mais ils procurent la consommation et les dépenses, qui sont elles-même une autre source de richesses. *Tout ce qu'un homme dépense de ses gains, ou de ses revenus profite à d'autres hommes, et retourne à la source qui l'a produit et qui le renouvelle.*'[138]

Brief consideration of the physiocratic approach to consumption is in order. We have met above with a formal statement by Quesnay which condemns

136 Quesnay, *Questions intérressantes sur la population, l'agriculture et le commerce* (1758), INED, 663. de Mirabeau, in his *Ami des Hommes*, had appeared to adopt the view of Cantillon regarding the desirability of a large population as a prerequisite of increased wealth. In July 1757 Quesnay converted him to the alternative position. Cf. Adolphe Landry, 'Les Idées de Quesnay sur la Population,' in Sauvy, ed., I, 16. Landry makes it clear that Quesnay is not suggesting that contraction or expansion of population is irrelevant. He maintained in fact that a population reduction was detrimental and an expansion had desirable consequences (both from the viewpoint of the labourer as producer and consumer). The point, however, is that population growth would occur *in consequence* of a preceding increase in revenue and need not therefore itself be a matter for policy consideration.
137 'Fermiers' (1756), INED, 453.
138 'Hommes,' INED, 541. Cf. *ibid.*, 973; Meek, 258, regarding the proposition that high wages will stimulate effort: 'In order to justify the harassment of the inhabitants of the countryside, the extortioners have put forward as a maxim that it is necessary that the *peasants should be poor, so as to prevent them from*

hoarding by the proprietors who are said to be useful to the state only through their consumption. This apparent emphasis upon the necessity for consumption in the interest of productive activity must, however, be understood in light of the requirement in physiocratic thought that it is *agricultural* products which should constantly sell at high prices in the interest of the net (value) product. There can be no doubt that the ultimate concern of the Physiocrats was with the latter variable, which represented the source for future growth. It was, moreover, presumed that where the agricultural net revenue was satisfactorily maintained there would be no need for protection of manufacturing industries which would flourish in consequence of high spending therefrom. In brief, an adequate (internal) demand for manufactures was generally taken for granted.[139] The physiocratic outlook certainly condemned the deliberate favouring of inefficient processes and unprofitable products as a device for stimulating high spending.[140]

A second general theme of relevance to the attitude towards consumption recurs in physiocratic literature, namely the distinction between consumption by those who do and those who do not make some contribution to the national product. This theme further suggests that consumption *as such* was not regarded as problematic:

Every man who shares in the wealth of the kingdom, but who does not contribute to it in any way, is useless to the state. But, it will be asked, is not every man profitable to the state by virtue of his consumption? Yes, when he makes restitution of this consumption through his work, or through his utility in contributing directly or indirectly to the production of what he consumes or appropriates for himself; for if

being idle. The contemptuous bourgeois have readily adopted this cruel maxim because they pay less heed to other more peremptory maxims – namely that the man *who is unable to save anything does only just as much work as is necessary to earn him his food; and that in general all men who can save are industrious, because all men are greedy for wealth.*

The ultimate cause of the low effort of peasants is said to be their low earnings and, interestingly, the low corn price caused by governmental interferences (*ibid.*): 'The real cause of the idleness of the oppressed peasant is that wages and employment are at too low a level in countries where restrictions on trade render produce valueless, and where other causes have ruined agriculture. Harassment, a low price of produce, and a gain which is insufficient to stimulate them to work, render them idle men, poachers, vagabonds, and robbers. Thus enforced poverty is not the way to render the peasants industrious: it is only a guarantee of the ownership and enjoyment of their gains which can put heart into them and make them diligent.'

Quesnay frequently insisted that high corn prices were *beneficial* for the labouring classes ('Maximes Générales,' INED, 954; Meek, 236) and denied that an increase involved merely benefits to some at the expense of others ('Hommes,' INED, 510; Meek, 87). Not surprisingly, he was not always consistent with regard to his approach to labour; the high price of grain took precedence. Cf. N.J. Ware, 'The Physiocrats: A Study in Economic Rationalization,' *American Economic Review*, XXI (Dec. 1931), 617–8 and references there cited.

139 Quesnay, 'Hommes,' INED, 603–4.
140 Quesnay, 'Réponse au mémoire de M.H. sur les avantages de l'industrie et du commerce ...'' (1766), INED, 756.

he does not return to the stock of wealth the value of what he takes out of it, the stock must necessarily diminish.[141]

It is of some importance that in this particular context Quesnay included not only farmers in the productive category. Contributions to the national product could be 'indirect' as well as direct, thus allowing for the activities of members of the government, church, and army as well as the (improving) landlords. Quesnay's essential concern in fact was with those – such as the idle rentiers ('les rentiers oisifs') – who, in his estimation, made no contribution which by any stretch of the imagination could be designated even indirectly productive, and who accordingly simply reduced 'la masse des richesses' by their consumption. But it is clear that Quesnay found himself on the horns of a dilemma. For he also recognized the dangers to the level of activity if the 'idle' were to hoard.[142] Accordingly, he conceded that while from this latter viewpoint their consumption was after all necessary it would be preferable if their incomes were transferred – presumably by loan – to those who were in the work force ('les hommes laborieux').[143]

Of great historical significance is the further allowance that consumption by children not yet in the work force must be considered productive or in other words that parental expenditures on their behalf are in the nature of investment outlays: 'Children ought not to be regarded as an expense of the state, because man should be considered in relation to the whole duration of his utility. Then it is seen that the years of his infancy and his old age are compensated by the period of his utility.'[144] This particular argument suggests that one aspect of the categories laid down was the distinction between consumption essential for the maintenance and growth of capacity, and consumption which had no such effect.

It is in this light that the frequent condemnation of the *artificial* stimuli given to the manufacture of luxury goods may be appreciated: '*That no encouragement at all should be given to luxury in the way of ornamentation* to the detriment of the expenditure involved in the operations and improvement of agriculture, and of expenditure on the consumption of subsistence goods, which sustains the market for raw produce, its proper price, and the reproduction of the nation's revenue.'[145] The consequence of government

---

141 'Hommes,' INED, 561; Meek, 98. It is in this context that Quesnay wrote: 'les richesses ne renaissent et ne se perpetuent que par les travaux des hommes.'
142 The problem of hoarding was seen to arise when large fortunes accumulated. (Cf. 'Maximes Générales,' INED, 951.) The implication of the physiocratic discussion is that there should be no outflows at all into hoards rather than an 'optimal' outflow.
143 'Hommes,' INED, 562; Meek, 99. Interestingly enough, Quesnay denied that this group was numerically very large: 'Happily such men are not very numerous, for there are few among the great who do not devote themselves to some essential employment, whether in high office, or in the clergy, in the military world, in the administration of the kingdom, in the judiciary, etc.'
144 *Ibid.*, 561; Meek, 99.
145 Quesnay, 'Maximes Générales,' INED, 954–5; Meek, 236.

intervention had been to encourage *excessive* production and consumption: 'L'espèce de luxe de décoration ... n'est-il pas devenu un luxe préjudiciable en dérangeant l'ordre des dépenses convenables et utiles dans les différentes classes de citoyens.'[146] To the artificially generated disorders Quesnay added the effects of an altered mode of living by landlords – in Paris, away from their estates – who tended to consume at the expense of necessary maintenance outlays upon their estates.[147]

We may summarize the preceding discussion in the proposition that while the Physiocrats recognized the dangers of hoarding, their position cannot be appreciated apart from an overriding concern with the price of agricultural produce and with investment in the agricultural sector. Their approach to consumption, although by no means clear and consistent, reflects this concern.[148] Moreover, the fundamental weakness of the physiocratic structure may be recalled. While foreign demand did not play a key role in the maintenance of an adequate level of aggregate expenditure – in contrast to mercantilist belief – it is nonetheless true that the case supporting a long-run net value product in agriculture utilized the notion of a price floor determined in the world market. A gaping hole thus remained in their entire doctrinal structure. In fact, at one juncture Quesnay actually maintained that in a closed economy the value of agricultural produce might fall disastrously, eradicating the net value product and with it the fundamental key to economic progress:

Les États qui n'ont pas l'avantage de la navigation pour se procurer un grand commerce des denrées de leur crû ne peuvent presque point accroître leurs richesses ni leur population; car, faute de commerce extérieur, elles ne peuvent pas même étendre leur agriculture, de crainte que l'abondance ne fasse tomber les productions en non valeur, n'anéantisse les revenus des propriétaires et du souverain; cette abondance, qui ferait tomber les denrées en non valeur, ne favorise pas non plus la population, car la pauvreté ne retient point, ni n'attire point les hommes; en effet, s'il y avait à proportion plus d'hommes que de richesses, surabondance d'homme ne servirait qu'à appauvrir l'État de plus en plus; car leur salaire diminuerait à pro-

146 'Questions intéressantes sur la population, l'agriculture et le commerce,' INED, 664.
147 A greater rigour was introduced by Baudeau who reserved the term 'luxury' for detrimental outlays, that is those at the expense of the desirable rate of investment in agriculture. This criterion in turn depended upon the actual state of agriculture, for a higher rate would be called for when depressed than when flourishing. Secondly, Baudeau laid down that conspicuous consumption on agricultural produce was preferable to that on manufactures although indirectly agriculture would benefit even from the latter. See the detailed references in R.L. Meek, 'Early Theories of Under-Consumption,' in Meek, *The Economics of Physiocracy*, 316–8.
148 Later (under-consumptionist) writers who emphasized the danger of *over-investment*, or the desirability of expenditures upon *manufactures* in particular have little to draw upon in this position. Cf. Meek, *The Economics of Physiocracy*, 318. Meek examines the relationship between Physiocracy and certain subsequent under-consumptionist themes in some detail. *Ibid.*, 341f.

portion de leur nombre ... ce qui les réduirait à un état de misère qui les forcerait de déserter le pays. Il en serait de même de la diminution des revenus des bien-fonds; car les propriétaires diminuant leurs dépenses, les gains de toutes les professions lucratives diminueraient aussi, et la population dépérirait.[149]

149 'Hommes,' INED, 571.

II / THE ECONOMICS OF ADAM SMITH

THREE

The industry structure

We are concerned in the present chapter with Smith's vision of the industry structure, particularly the distribution of activity between agriculture and manufacturing, the relative significance of factory as distinct from domestic forms of organization, and the nature of the inputs typical in agriculture, manufacturing and mining and metallurgy.[1]

THE AGRICULTURAL SECTOR

Data regarding eighteenth-century economic growth are notoriously difficult to interpret. The paucity of available statistics upon which Smith could rely is clear from a comparison of figures presented in the *Lectures* (1763) and in

1 There is to be found in the secondary literature the widely-held view that Smith's preoccupation in discussing the industrial sector was with domestic handicrafts, where workers were often self-employd, and in any event not maintained by a master from another *class* but rather from another generation. This frame of reference is said to account for an emphasis upon labour as the main productive factor, and the lack of emphasis upon fixed capital. Cf. E. von Bohm-Bawerk, *Capital and Interest* (London, 1890), 75f., who claimed that opposition between capital and labour, and the whole issue of the 'justice' of profits, only arose when machinery came to be empirically a significant part of capital, namely in the post-Smithian period. See also the statement by A.W. Coats, 'Adam Smith: the Modern Reappraisal,' *Renaissance and Modern Studies* (Nottingham, 1962), VI, 47, to the effect that Smith was 'the most influential economist of the stage of capitalist development that is termed the domestic system, but while he helped to lay the foundations of modern economics he was, at the same time, the last writer of the pre-Smithian age of economics.' Werner Stark, *History of Economics in Its Relation to Economic Development* (London, 1944), 31, argued further that produced means of production (tools and machines) were often ignored by Smith when considering 'stock' advanced to workers, because at the time such capital belonged to the worker himself. M.R. Goetz-Girey, 'Refléxions sur la Théorie du Capital d'Adam Smith,' *Revue d'Histoire Economique et Sociale*, XXIII (1936–7), 323, has taken a similar position regarding the primitiveness of the economic organization:

the *Wealth of Nations*.[2] In the *Lectures* income originating in agriculture is stated formally to account for 72 per cent of a total 'national income' amounting to £100 million:

Agriculture is of all other arts the most beneficent to society, and whatever tends to retard its improvement is extremely prejudicial to the public interest. The produce of agriculture is much greater than that of any other manufacture. The rents of the whole lands in England amount to about 24 millions, and as the rent is generally about a third of the produce, the whole annual produce of the lands must be about 72 millions. This is much more than the produce of either the linen or woollen manufactures, for, as the annual consumption is computed to be about 100 millions, if you deduce from this the 72 millions, the produce of agriculture, there will remain only 28 millions for all the other manufactures of the nation. Whatever measures therefore discourage the improvement of this art are extremely prejudicial to the progress of opulence.[3]

But shortly before in the *Lectures* it was said that 'the annual consumption amounts to much more than a hundred millions'; the true percentage attributable to agriculture is evidently lower by an undisclosed amount.[4]

There is clear indication in the *Wealth of Nations* of continued industrial and agricultural progress between 1763 and 1775:

At the conclusion of the late war [1763], the most expensive that Great Britain ever waged, her agriculture was as flourishing, her manufactures as numerous and as fully employed, and her commerce as extensive, as they had ever been before. The capital, therefore, which supported all those different branches of industry, must have been equal to what it had ever been before. Since the peace, agriculture has been still further improved, the rents of houses have risen in every town and village of the

'C'est une production artisanale, organisée, dans des entreprises de petites dimensions; le nombre des ouvriers est un élément prédominant de la vie économique. Ce sont les qualités d'observateur de Smith qui lui ont imposée sa conception du capital.' We note too an important comment by Thorstein Veblen, *The Place of Science in Modern Civilization* (New York, 1919), 126: 'Adam Smith owes his preconception in favor of labor to a community in which the obstrusive economic feature of the immediate past was handicraft and agriculture, with commerce as a secondary phenomenon.' (Veblen, nonetheless, ascribed a productivity theory of distribution to Smith.) We add finally a recent comment by John C.H. Fei and Gustav Ranis, 'Economic Development in Historical Perspective,' *American Economic Review* (Papers and Proceedings), LIX (May 1969), 393: 'We believe that the Smithian body of thought (and the old classical system in general) was directed precisely to a description of this mercantile agrarian society. His "capital" was basically a synthesis of a wages fund and commercial capital, with the common purpose of expanding the division of labor through trade.'

2 With few exceptions, the edition cited throughout this book is *Wealth of Nations* (1776), ed. E. Cannan, Modern Library ed. (New York 1937).

3 Adam Smith, *Lectures on Police, Justice, Revenue and Arms* (1763), ed. E. Cannan (New York, 1964), 224.

4 *Ibid.*, 199. The calculation of £100m is based on a presumed British population of some 10 million, and an average annual income of £10 per head. (See Appendix A.)

country, a proof of the increasing wealth and revenue of the people; and the annual amount of the greater part of the old taxes, of the principal branches of the excise and customs in particular, has been continually increasing, an equally clear proof of an increasing consumption, and consequently of an increasing produce, which could alone support that consumption (881–2).

Yet while agriculture – in addition to industry and trade – is said to have expanded since 1763, Smith puts the value of total agricultural revenue at only £60m annually.[5] We may take this to imply a major downward correction of the figure given in the *Lectures*. The aggregate annual income is, unfortunately, nowhere given in the *Wealth of Nations* although by the mid-seventies it clearly exceeded £100m on Smith's own terms. It is not unreasonable to put the implied upper limit of the agricultural contribution to national product in the mid-seventies at 50 rather than 60 per cent.[6]

The only other data provided by Smith relate to the distribution of the work force. In the following passage the agricultural labour force is said to constitute not more than 50 per cent of the total population: 'The most numerous class of artificers will seldom, in a large country, make more than one in fifty or one in a hundred of the whole number of families contained in it. But in such large countries as France and England, the number of people employed in agriculture has by some authors been computed at a half, by others at a third, and by no author that I know of, at less than a fifth of the whole inhabitants of the country' (646).[7] It must be emphasized that agricultural employment included not only labour directly employed by the capitalist farmer and 'improving' landlord but also service labour (menials) employed by the landlord; we read, for example, of 'landlords and farmers' who represent 'two of the largest classes of masters.'[8] We conclude from this that a comparison between France and England, and Holland and Hamburg, in which the former are said to 'consist in a great measure of proprietors and cultivators,' and the latter 'chiefly of merchants, artificers, and manufacturers,'[9] should be understood in a *comparative* rather than an absolute sense. It must, therefore, be recognized that while, according to Smith and contemporary sources, agri-

5 *Wealth of Nations*, 775. Aggregate rent is put at £20m yielding an annual agricultural produce of £60m on the assumption of a rental share equal to approximately one-third. Cf. 'In the present state of Europe, the share of the landlord seldom exceeds a third, sometimes not a fourth part of the whole produce of the land' (*ibid.*, 318).

6 The general expansion of industry and trade underway from 1745 is discussed in detail by P. Deane and W.A. Cole, *British Economic Growth 1688–1959: Trends and Structure*, 2nd ed. (Cambridge, 1967), chaps. I and II (see Appendix C) and by Charles Wilson, *England's Apprenticeship 1603–1763* (London, 1965), chap. 14.

7 In this passage Smith formally compares workers in agriculture with the total population. Presumably his *intention* is to compare either agricultural workers with the aggregate work force, or the total agricultural population with the aggregate population. Deane and Cole (*British Economic Growth*, 137) point out that it is almost impossible to give meaningful estimates because of the overlapping of occupations.

8 *Wealth of Nations*, 83.

9 *Ibid.*, 634.

culture was quantitatively the most important sector, it did not, in their estimation, account for more than 50 per cent of the annual produce.[10]

A few words may be in order regarding the main productive factors used in
agriculture. The 'principal instruments of agriculture'[11] are said to be labouring cattle, which may suggest a rather primitive technology. But considerable
attention is paid to land improvements as a category of fixed capital. These
forms of expenditure are listed by Smith (together with those relevant to mines
and iron foundries) in his recommendation that bankers should avoid long-
term financing; they include outlays in 'clearing, draining, enclosing, manuring and ploughing waste and uncultivated fields, in building farm-houses, with
all their necessary appendages of stables, granaries, &c.'[12] Agriculture was one
of the *most*, not the least, capital-intensive sectors.[13]

THE MANUFACTURING SECTOR

Smith emphasized frequently the temporal priority of agriculture as a general
historical phenomenon, and explained it in terms of the ultimate dependence
of all sectors upon subsistence.[14] In all communities which are endowed with
suitable natural resources – whether open or closed – and in the absence of

10 This should be borne in mind in considering Smith's remarks – apparently applied
to both England and France – that in terms of capital stock 'the land constitutes by
far the greatest, the most important, and the most durable part of the wealth of
every extensive country' (*ibid.*, 241); and that the most important single product
'in every civilized country' in quantitative terms, is corn (*ibid.*, 492). It is noteworthy that the contemporary national-income estimates of Arthur Young suggest
that agriculture accounted for only 45 per cent of national income *circa* 1770, which,
it has been recently argued, represents an over-estimate of agricultural output.
Cf. Deane and Cole, *British Economic Growth*, 75, 156–7, 279, 290. Their own
conclusion is that between the late seventeenth century and 1770 agriculture
accounted for a steady 40–45 per cent of national product. The authors reject the
results of a comparison of the national income data of Gregory King (1688) and
Young (1770) which suggests that the share of agriculture actually *increased*. (It
may be noted that of a national income calculated in c.1770 by Young to be just
over £130m, agricultural output was estimated at £58.2m which is very close to
Smith's rough calculation of £60m.)
11 *Wealth of Nations*, 187.
12 *Ibid.*, 291.
13 We may add also the contribution of the merchant marine. Smith refers in his
discussion of the effects of free trade on employment to the release in 1764 from the
armed forces of more than 100,000 men. The sailors were, he believed, ultimately
absorbed into the merchant marine although they may have found work temporarily
in other occupations. The only long-term effect was a reduction in the wages paid
in the merchant service. Soldiers were absorbed 'in the great mass of the people,
and employed in a great variety of occupations' (*ibid.*, 436). But the importance
in quantitative terms of the merchant marine is difficult to estimate on Smith's
data.
14 *Ibid.*, 357. Smith admitted that in practice there existed no clear relationship since
'the town ... may not always derive its whole subsistence from the country in its
neighbourhood, or even from the territory to which it belongs, but from very distant
countries' (*ibid.*). In a closed economy without agricultural resources economic
expansion would evidently be impossible; but in an open economy the problem of
poor agricultural resources might be overcome.

institutional interferences, the expectation is that towns could not increase 'beyond what the improvement and the cultivation of the territory in which they were situated could support; till such time, at least, as the whole of that territory was completely cultivated and improved.'[15] The towns which Smith has in mind here are the local market communities which to all intents and purposes are appendages of the countryside and scarcely distinguishable from it. The progressive development of such towns would be 'consequential, and in proportion to the improvement and cultivation of the territory or country' and in ordinary circumstances there would be no attempt to invest in what Smith calls manufactures designed for 'distant sale' as long as agricultural resources remained uncultivated.[16]

The intimate relation between the local communities and the countryside – reflected in the exchange of subsistence and materials for manufactured goods – has the basic advantage of allowing specialization by trade, permitting the farmer to engage in full-time farm work:[17]

The inhabitants of the town and those of the country are mutually the servants of one another. The town is a continual fair or market, to which the inhabitants of the country resort, in order to exchange their rude for manufactured produce. It is this commerce which supplies the inhabitants of the town both with the materials of their work, and the means of their subsistence. The quantity of the finished work which they sell to the inhabitants of the country, necessarily regulates the quantity of the materials and provisions which they buy. Neither their employment nor subsistence, therefore, can augment, but in proportion to the augmentation of the demand from the country for finshed work; and this demand can augment only in proportion to the extension of improvement and cultivation (358–9).[18]

And it is a relationship common to some extent to almost all communities, although of overwhelming significance in relatively primitive economies. Thus in the North American colonies, 'no manufactures for distant sale have ever yet been established in any of their towns,[19] since American industry was confined 'to such coarse and household manufactures, as a private family commonly makes for its own use, or for that of some of its neighbours in the same province.'[20]

15 *Ibid.*
16 *Ibid.*, 359. The reason for this – which implies a crucial relationship – will be discussed presently.
17 *Ibid.*, 356f.
18 Cf. also *ibid.*, 649–50.
19 *Ibid.*, 359.
20 *Ibid.*, 548–9. Cf. also 575. We shall see that this pattern – seemingly due to British regulations regarding the type of commodities the colonies might produce – in fact reflected the 'normal' pattern. Cf. the case of Poland, *ibid.*, 7, quoted below.
  It may be worthwhile to emphasize the distinction between various categories of manufacturing envisaged by reference to the following passage: 'No large country, it must be observed, ever did or could subsist without some sort of manufactures being carried on in it; and when it is said of any such country that it has no manufactures, it must always be understood of the finer and more improved, or of

By contrast, Smith's basic concern in treating manufacturing in Britain and other western European countries is not predominantly with the local centres serving the farm community – although without doubt these activities would be included in the manufacturing category. It is rather with manufacturing 'for distant sale,' for the British economy was incomparably more advanced than that of the North American colonies. Smith is concerned less with the smith, the wheelwright, and the carpenter, than with the major categories of manufacturing for distant sale. In fact much of British agricultural activity was devoted to the production of materials for the 'finer' and 'more improved' categories of manufacturing (although the manufacturing sector also drew very substantially on imported materials). And the location of manufacturing was determined by different forces than those relevant to the simpler economies.

The most important manufacturing industries were, we are told, silk, linen, wool, tanned-leather goods and hardware. But of these, wool, tanned leather and hardware are said to 'employ the greatest number of hands.'[21]

Of particular importance is the absence of any references to the cotton industry in the enumeration of significant manufacturing sectors.[22] In an added chapter of 1784, however, Smith refers to a liberalization (in 1766) of import restrictions in the case of raw cotton and to export restrictions imposed (in 1774) upon machinery used in the cotton as well as in the linen, wool and silk industries.[23]

such as are fit for distant sale. In every large country, both the clothing and household furniture of the far greater part of the people, are the produce of their own industry. This is even more universally the case in those poor countries which are commonly said to have no manufactures, than in those rich ones that are said to abound in them. In the latter, you will generally find, both in the clothes and household furniture of the lowest rank of people, a much greater proportion of foreign productions than in the former' (ibid., 381).

21 Ibid., 436. Linen, silk, and wool *weaving* are referred to at one stage as 'capital manufactures' (ibid., 135). That linen weaving should be emphasized is odd, since subsequently he refers to the spinners as making up some eighty per cent of employment in the linen industry (ibid., 608–9). On p.436 the emphasis is on the 'different branches' of woollen manufacture, tanned leather, and hardware as well as silk and linen. (The 'hardware' industry – cuttlers, locksmiths, etc. – is sometimes referred to as 'Birmingham and Sheffield ware,' cf. ibid., 243.)

Smith's statement (ibid., 135) that linen was 'not much cultivated through the greater part of the country' may refer to its localization rather than its significance by other indexes.

22 A comment, ibid., 527–8, was merely of historical relevance. Cotton was in fact a minor industry during the period 1700–75, with sales value amounting to only £600,000 in the 1760s. (Cf. Deane and Cole, *British Economic Growth*, 183.)

23 *Wealth of Nations*, 608, 624 respectively. The absence of any treatment of the cotton industry by Smith was noted by J.R. McCulloch in a reference to Smith's discussion of historical improvements in manufacturing: 'Dr Smith has not made any allusion, either here or in any other part of his work, to the cotton manufacture. At the time he wrote, it was, indeed, carried on only to a small extent and none could have anticipated the wonderful progress it has since made. It is now of vast and indeed

A very rough indication of Smith's calculation of the total size of the main branches of manufacturing can be deduced from his statement to the effect that the number 'employed in the greatest manufactures' amounted to some one hundred thousand workers.[24] The main branches as a whole in this case would amount at most to half a million workers, but since the various industries were not of equal significance, a figure closer to 400,000 might better reflect the size of the work force in the main manufacturing industries on Smith's data.[25] The contemporary estimate by Young (for 1770) of the proportion of the national income accounted for by the main branches of manufacturing (excluding hardware production) is 10 per cent; a further 11 per cent is attributed to hardware, building, mining and metallurgy.[26]

One important difference between wool, tanned leather, and hardware on the one hand, and silk and linen on the other, is that the former flourished without the need of protection, while the latter had grown only as a result of government intervention. Thus it was that 'a great part of all the different branches of our woollen manufacture, of our tanned leather, and of our hardware, are annually exported to other European countries without any bounty, and *these are the manufactures which employ the greatest number of hands.*'[27]

The recommended removal of all import restrictions on manufactured goods in the first category would have no adverse effects since these industries were certainly producing 'cheaper at home' than any European firm could manage.[28] On the other hand, there existed quantitatively important cases where, as a result of protection, 'particular manufactures ... have been so far extended as to *employ a great multitude of hands.*'[29] 'The silk, perhaps, is the manufacture which would suffer the most by this freedom of trade, and after it the

paramount importance, and it may be truly affirmed that its progress in Great Britain since 1770 and present magnitude, form, beyond all question, the most extraordinary phenomenon in the history of industry.' *Wealth of Nations*, ed. McCulloch (Edinburgh, 1872), 114n.

24 *Wealth of Nations*, 436. The calculation compares the size of the 'greatest manufactures' with the number of demobilized servicemen upon the peace of 1763, namely 100,000 men. This latter figure accords with official data. *Number of men in the armed forces*: 1763, 159,000; 1764, 52,000. Source: T.S. Ashton, *Economic Fluctuations in England, 1700–1800* (Oxford, 1959), 187; from *British Parliamentary Papers*, vol. XXXV (1863–9), 2, 693f.

25 In their study of British economic growth, Deane and Cole (*British Economic Growth*, 136f.) have confined their attention, when dealing with the industrial distribution of the labour force, to the nineteenth and twentieth centuries because of the difficulties in the way of reaching meaningful estimates for the eighteenth century. (Even the distribution between agricultural and manufacturing labour is too blurred to allow accurate statements.)

26 See Appendix B.

27 *Wealth of Nations*, 436. Author's emphasis.

28 The implied 'absolute cost' argument is to be noted. Cf. *ibid.*, 7, for further reference to the efficiency of the British hardware and coarse linen manufactures.

29 *Ibid.*, 435. Author's emphasis.

linen, though the latter much less than the former.'[30] The removal of trade barriers should, Smith concluded, be accomplished slowly in such cases. Yet the non-competitiveness with European producers of domestic silk manufactures was attributed in large part to the high cost of raw silk imports. Free trade extended to the importation of raw materials would, he believed, have given home producers a net cost advantage over Europeans not only in the domestic, but also in foreign markets: 'If raw silk could be imported from China and Indostan duty-free, the silk manufacturers in England could greatly undersell those of both France and Italy. There would be no occasion to prohibit the importation of foreign silks and velvets. The cheapness of their goods would secure to our own workmen, not only the possession of the home, but a very great command of the foreign market' (837).[31]

The significance to Smith of manufacturing is implied particularly clearly in the fact that it is this sector, and not agriculture, in which he envisaged the greatest prospects for technical improvements. Thus we read at the outset of the *Wealth of Nations* that productivity differentials between advanced and backward countries are minimal in the case of agriculture, since seasonal characteristics tend to preclude the application of specialized processes; and very great in the case of manufacturing, where technical improvements can be more readily applied (so long as the raw materials used are easily obtainable) :

But though the poor country, notwithstanding the inferiority of its cultivation, can, in some measure, rival the rich in the cheapness and goodness of its corn, it can pretend to no such competition in its manufactures; at least if those manufactures suit the soil, climate, and situation of the rich country. The silks of France are better and cheaper than those of England, because the silk manufacture, at least under the present high duties upon the importation of raw silk, does not so well suit the climate of England as that of France. But the hard-ware and the coarse woollens of England are beyond all comparison superior to those of France and much cheaper too in the same degree of goodness. In Poland there are said to be scarce any manufactures of any kind, a few of those coarser household manufactures excepted, without which no country can well subsist (6–7).

Furthermore, technical improvement is said to be in large part determined by the nature of the raw material used in production, implying a particularly significant potential in specific branches of manufacturing. It is in these terms

30 *Ibid.*, 436. Cf. 426: 'several of the home manufactures would probably suffer, and some of them perhaps, go to ruin altogether, and a considerable part of the stock and industry at present employed in them, would be forced to find out some other employment.'

31 Smith is even more explicit at the outset of the work (*ibid.*, 7), where he notes that 'the silks of France are better and cheaper than those of England, because the silk manufacture, at least under the present high duties upon the importation of raw silk, does not so well suit the climate of England as that of France.' Note too that subsequently (*ibid.*, 836) Smith argues that the free importation of 'the necessaries of life' as well as 'all the materials of manufacture' would much help Britain's competitive position.

that Smith explains the particularly rapid advance of the hardware compared with the clothing industries.[32] And it was in the manufacturing sector (and in trade) that England had relatively great natural advantages in the form of good means of transport and cheap supplies of raw materials: 'England, on account of the natural fertility of the soil, of the great extent of the sea-coast in proportion to that of the whole country, and of the many navigable rivers which run through it, and afford the conveniency of water carriage to some of the most inland parts of it, is perhaps as well fitted by nature as any large country in Europe, to be the seat of foreign commerce, and manufactures for distant sale, and of all the improvements which these can occasion' (393).

INDUSTRIAL ORGANIZATION

A few words are in order at this point regarding the distribution of production in manufacturing between the factory and the domestic unit. It must first be emphasized that the implications of organizational change from cottage to factory should not be exaggerated, for it *may* involve no more than the congregation into one place of units hitherto scattered, rather than the complete integration of a work force into an independent unit designed to take advantage of a common source of power and direction. Conversely, domestic workers are not necessarily to be identified with self-employed handicraftsmen; capitalistic forms of organization – involving the dependence of wage labour upon the capitalist for inputs and subsistence – are quite consistent with domestic work.[33]

But Smith is in fact explicit that self-employment was the *exception* in the economy as a whole: 'in every part of Europe, twenty workmen serve under a master for one that is independent; and the wages of labour are every where understood to be, what they usually are, when the labourer is one person, and the owner of the stock which employs him another' (66).[34] It should also be

32 *Ibid.*, 243. (Discussed further in chapter 7.) Cf. *Lectures*, 164: 'But our toys, which have no dependence on the climate, and in which labour can be divided, are far superior to those of France.'

33 Cf. H.L. Beales, *The Industrial Revolution: 1750–1850* (London, 1967), 37–8 regarding industrial organization prior to the 'industrial revolution': 'The factory was not yet the usual industrial unit; nor, on the other hand, was the independent producer or the part-time manufacturer the representative figure of English industry. Relationships essentially capitalistic characterized English industry before the industrial revolution developed ... Considerable variation in manufacturing arrangements was possible, but the field of industry was no longer, if it ever had been, occupied by independent producers to any large extent. The wage relationship was well-nigh universal.'

   See also A. Redford, *The Economic History of England, 1760–1860*, 2nd ed. (London, 1960), 9f.; and P. Mantoux, *The Industrial Revolution in the Eighteenth Century* (London, 1961), 250.

34 As examples of the 'independent workman' (as distinct from the journeyman, the journeyman-artificer, or the common day labourer) Smith refers often to the weaver, or the shoemaker (cf. *Wealth of Nations*, 69). Despite the insignificant proportion of independent workmen, Smith pays some attention to this group. The independent

noted that in the bulk of activities – both domestic and factory – workers are said to be largely specialists by occupation: 'In opulent countries the market is generally so extensive that any one trade is sufficient to employ the whole labour and stock of those who occupy it.'[35]

Particular attention is paid to the domestic spinning of linen yarn which is said to constitute 80 per cent of the entire linen industry in terms of employment.[36] We know that the woollen industry was also largely domestically organized.[37] Silk, however, is a somewhat more complex case empirically; by 1760 the factory system and even the use of power-driven machines was well established, and we shall note presently that Smith probably recognized the relatively large-scale factory in the silk industry.[38] In the case of the hardware group of manufactures, that is the metal-manufacturing trades, the organization was typically domestic.[39] But while Smith makes much of the simple separation of employments the bulk of his attention in dealing with details of specialization is upon sub-division of labour within the plant. For

worker is likely to hire himself out as journeyman in bad years (*ibid.*, 83); he is said to be more industrious than the journeyman (who is paid piece wages) because he does not share his income with a master, and because he is not hindered by bad company common to large manufactories (*ibid.*, 83–4). In fact the advantages of retail trades are illustrated by reference to the effect on the independent worker: 'If a poor workman was obliged to purchase a month's or six months' provisions at a time, a great part of the stock which he employs as a capital in the instruments of his trade, or in the furniture of his shop, and which yields him a revenue, he would be forced to place in that part of his stock which is reserved for immediate consumption, and which yields him no revenue' (*ibid.*, 342).

35 *Ibid.*, 117, cf. 246–7. It was no longer true that English coarse wool manufacturing was carried on by household workers who were engaged also in other activities. It is, however, admitted that the 'greater part' of manufacturing workers are 'occasionally employed in country labour' (*ibid.*, 437). Smith pinpoints Scottish linen spinning and Shetland knitting – apparently both domestic operations – where it was still common for workers to be engaged therein part-time while largely earning their living elsewhere (*ibid.*, 116–7).

36 *Ibid.*, 608–9, 116–7.

37 Discussed above. Cf. Phyllis Deane, *The First Industrial Revolution* (Cambridge, 1967), 85. The cotton industry was also largely a domestic industry.

38 A mill for the manufacture of silk was started at Stockport in 1732 after parliament had bought Lombe's silk-throwing machinery – upon the expiry of his patent – for the purpose of stimulating the widespread adoption of the process. The machines could only be used in factory work. (The Stockport venture has been termed by G. Unwin 'an epoch in the rise of the Factory System,' see Beales, *The Industrial Revolution*, 38.) Cf. Redford, *Economic History of England*, 18, for an account of the wide establishment of the factory-system, and the use of power-driven machinery, in silk-throwing by 1760; and T.S. Ashton, *Economic Fluctuations in England*, 74–5 for an account of the expansionary effects of reduced duties on raw silk imports during the period 1748–1751.

39 Cf. Redford, *The Industrial Revolution*, 32 and W.H.B. Court, *A Concise Economic History of Britain* (Cambridge, 1958), 56. It has been argued (John Lord, *Capital and Steam Power, 1750–1800*, 2nd ed. (London, 1966), 41–2) that the hardware sector – particularly the Birmingham gun trade – was much stimulated by the Jacobite rebellion of 1745.

both invention and innovation are said to be dependent upon scale; and although, in principle, any size of work force might be scattered in domestic units, Smith seems to have in mind increase in scale of plant when dealing specifically with the major preconditions for technical advance.[40] Although his specific illustrations of specialized process are from the hardware industry[41] wherein the *typical* organization was on domestic lines, his overriding concern was with those 'firms' organized in factories. Moreover, while his best known example was drawn from the account of pin making in the *Encyclopédie* (1755) there is no doubt that he was fully aware of the metal-working activities of the Midlands explaining the relatively high wages earned in Birmingham by the fact that many of the local trades were not long established.[42] It need only be added that while Smith's illustrations of division of labour were derived from relatively small-scale nail-making and pin-making plants he was aware of the large-scale iron works at Carron where there had 'lately been a considerable rise in the demand for labour.'[43] Indeed, as we shall see, Smith entered into a highly sophisticated analysis of the effect of scale of *industry* upon the degree of division of labour practised at the plant.[44] This in itself is eloquent testimonial to the fact that factory organization was to Smith's mind well established and calling for detailed analysis.

Further evidence that Smith's analytical structure was largely designed for factory, rather than domestic, organization may be drawn from the discussion

40 *Wealth of Nations*, 86, 260, discussed further in chapter 7.

41 *Ibid.*, 4f., *Lectures*, 164, 255.

42 *Wealth of Nations*, 114–5. See Lord, *Capital and Steam Power*, 93–4 for a discussion of Boulton's celebrated hardware plant at Soho (Birmingham), established 1762, which manufactured buttons, watch chains, sword hilts, etc. James Watt, a friend of Smith, in 1767 described the processes used at Soho before leaving Glasgow to join Boulton. Lord concludes from his account: 'It is evident that Boulton was fully aware of the value of the division of labour, and that his works, even with the limited power at his disposal, were beginning to be largely machine operated. In the organization of his business, Boulton consciously practised a thorough division of labour, and ... taught all his workpeople some special department, and made every one a skilled hand.' Lord Shelburne also commented upon the machinery and specialization practised at the plant in button making on a visit of 1766, and James Boswell remarked upon the equipment in use (see Wilson, *England's Apprenticeship*, 302–3). It may be noted, however, that a recent investigation insists that even firms such as Soho achieved their output expansion largely by 'order and organization' rather than by costly mechanical devices. Cf. Sidney Pollard, 'Fixed Capital in the Industrial Revolution in Britain,' *Journal of Economic History*, XXIV (Sept. 1964), 301.

A tendency, around mid-century, towards the 'concentration' of activity in relatively large 'factory' units may be noted also in the silk industry (discussed below); in the Staffordshire potteries (notably Wedgewood's plant at Burslam, established 1759, taking full advantage of the division of labour); in Midland glass-making; in the metal works of Sheffield and Newcastle; in brewing (particularly the new 'porter') as well as in primary iron smelting. Cf., Wilson, *England's Apprenticeship*, 299–312; 359–360.

43 *Wealth of Nations*, 76.

44 See chapter 7.

of 'profits.' For much is made of the element representing a return to the 'labour of inspection and direction' which in fact is said to vary little with the size of the establishment so that even 'in many great works, almost the whole labour of this kind is committed to some principal clerk.'[45]

MANUFACTURING INPUTS

Throughout the book great emphasis is placed on the various forms of government interference with foreign trade. But of particular relevance is a chapter added in 1784, wherein Smith refers to reduced import duties or exemptions newly introduced in the case of sheep's wool, cotton wool, undressed flax, dying drugs, undressed hides, seal skins, and pig and bar iron. This entire list is attributed to pressure exerted on the government by Britain's manufacturers and merchants, and it covers the material requirements of nearly all the major manufacturing industries listed above.[46] The pressure towards liberalizing material imports was coupled, Smith informs us, with similarly successful efforts by manufacturers to assure the continued discouragement of exports both of materials and equipment. Thus export duties on all manufactured goods were removed; but there follows a list of items upon which export duties were retained. As Smith noted: 'If you except horses, all these are either materials of manufacture, or incomplete manufactures (which may be considered as materials for still further manufacture), or instruments of trade.'[47] A complete export prohibition was retained in the case of wool,[48] raw hides,[49] the 'frames or engines for knitting gloves or stockings'[50] and what Smith calls the various 'utensils' used in cotton, linen, wool, and silk manufactures.[51]

This account confirms the vital significance of circulating capital in the main manufacturing sectors, particularly organic raw materials, much of it imported into the country. It is rather more difficult to evaluate the importance of fixed capital in the manufacturing sector from Smith's account. Smith conceded the posibility that free trade in manufactured goods might endanger the fixed capital investments of manufacturers, and accordingly recommended a gradual reduction of duties with ample warning:

The undertaker of a great manufacture, who, by the home markets being suddenly laid open to the competition of foreigners, should be obliged to abandon his trade, would no doubt suffer very considerably. That part of his capital which had usually been employed in purchasing materials and in paying his workmen, might, without much difficulty, perhaps, find another employment. But that part of it which was fixed

45 *Wealth of Nations*, 49.
46 *Ibid.*, 608f.
47 *Ibid.*, 621. The list includes alum, lead, lead ore, tin, tanned leather, copperas, coals, wool cards, white woollen cloths, lapis calaminaris, skins, glue, coney hair or wool, hares' wool, hair, horses, litharge of lead.
48 *Ibid.*, 612.
49 *Ibid.*, 233. For details on regulations regarding skins cf. 231f.
50 *Ibid.*, 623.
51 *Ibid.*, 624.

in workhouses, and in the instruments of trade, could scarce be disposed of without considerable loss (438).[52]

But it is possible that Smith did not intend this to be generally applicable; he probably had in mind here the silk industry, for it was precisely the growth of this industry which, he emphasized, took place under a protective umbrella as we have seen.[53]

Apart from the possible case of silk, Smith does not seem to consider manufacturing to be a capital-intensive sector. In a reference to weaving Smith writes that although much more fixed capital is required than in shoe-making and tailoring yet 'the far greater part of the capital of all such master artificers ... is circulated, either in the wages of their workmen, or in the price of their materials.'[54] Whether the other important manufacturing branches – namely leather tanning and hardware – were also regarded as falling in the same category is not so clear. (It is true that organization into factories is particularly emphasized in the case of hardware; but we should avoid jumping to conclusions regarding the capital intensity of the industry.) But since Smith specifies mining and metallurgy as the heavily capital-intensive sectors, as we shall see, it may be concluded that the quantitative significance of fixed capital was taken to be limited throughout most of the manufacturing sector, at least relatively to mining and metallurgy.

In the chapter added in 1784 Smith makes one new reference to machine-making, although some ambiguity attaches to it. His point is that the encouragement by manufacturers of the removal, or lowering, of import duties on materials was not extended to equipment since this might have damaged the machine-builders' investments: 'I do not observe, at least in our Statute Book, any encouragement given to the importation of the instruments of trade. When manufactures have advanced to a certain pitch of greatness, the fabrication of the instruments of trade becomes itself the object of a great number of very important manufactures. To give any particular encouragement to the importation of such instruments would interfere too much with the interest of those manufactures' (607). Of itself, this passage might suggest some regard to a growing importance of fixed capital in manufacturing and a consequent expansion of domestic equipment making. But he then illustrates the argument by reference to a prohibition against the importation of wool cards going back

---

52 In the present context Smith is dealing with manufacturing generally and not with any specific branch such as mining and metallurgy which, as we shall see, he recognized as being particularly capital-intensive.

53 T.S. Ashton, *Economic Fluctuations in England*, 151–2, has shown that with the peace of 1763, and the ending of war-time protection to the silk trade, there occurred some destruction of machinery by labour.

   C. Wilson, *England's Apprenticeship*, 308, has also commented upon the particular capital-intensity of the *brewing* industry, drawing upon the researches of Peter Mathias, *The Brewing Industry in England: 1700–1830* (Cambridge, 1959).

54 *Wealth of Nations*, 263. It will be recalled that the three 'capital industries' were linen, silk, and wool weaving.

to Edward IV, and it is by no means certain that he has in mind recent developments.[55]

It is of the greatest importance to note that Smith emphasized on several occasions great similarity between the technologies utilized in at least three of the main branches of manufacturing, namely linen, silk and wool weaving. On these grounds he argued that the introduction of free trade would not be dangerous since displaced labourers might easily transfer between sectors.[56]

MINING AND METALLURGY

Other branches of industrial activity which receive particular attention by Smith are 'iron works' and 'coal works and other mines.' In contrast to the situation in manufacturing, much fixed capital is required: 'In other works a much greater fixed capital is required. In a great iron-work, for example, the furnace for melting the ore, the forge, the slitt-mill, are instruments of trade which cannot be erected without a very great expence. In coal-works, and mines of every kind, the machinery necessary both for drawing out the water and for other purposes, is frequently still more expensive' (263).[57] In fact, in his warning to bankers not to extend loans for the finance of fixed capital construction, Smith refers specifically in his examples to the case of mining and metallurgy:

Still less could a bank afford to advance him any considerable part of his fixed capital; of the capital which the undertaker of an iron forge, for example, employs in erecting his forge and smelting house, his work-houses and warehouses, the dwelling-houses of his workmen, &c.; of the capital which the undertaker of a mine employs in sinking his shafts, in erecting engines for drawing out the water, in making roads and waggon-ways, &c.; ... The returns of the fixed capital are in almost all cases much slower than those of the circulating capital; and such expences, even when laid out with the greatest prudence and judgment, very seldom return to the undertaker till after a period of many years, a period by far too distant to suit the conveniency of a bank (291).[58]

Unfortunately, no statement is given of the relative importance – in terms of employment, capital stock, or production – of this sector compared with manufacturing. But Young's estimate of 1770 for mining, metallurgy, building and hardware combined is some 11 per cent of national income.[59]

The coal industry was seen to have wide ramifications. For example: 'The coal trade from Newcastle to London ... employs more shipping than all the

55 Nor is it clear exactly what Smith intended by 'the great number of very important manufactures' engaged in the production of equipment. The *engineering* works recently established at Soho by Boulton and Watt (1775) may be his concern.

56 *Ibid.*, 134–5, 437. (Discussed further in chapter 9.)

57 Cf. *ibid.*, 548. For some details regarding the high fixed capital requirement see T.S. Ashton, *Iron and Steel in the Industrial Revolution* (Manchester, 1963), 162f.

58 The only other formal examples in the *Wealth of Nations* of heavy fixed capital investment are drawn from the agricultural sector.

59 See above, 101.

carrying trade of England, though the ports are at no great distance.'[60] Smith recognized the use of coal as a producer good – 'coals may be considered both as a material of manufacture and as an instrument of trade.'[61] As we shall see, Newcomen's invention of the 'atmospheric engine,' and subsequent improvement thereupon, were noted too.[62] The use of coal in production was limited largely to metallurgy, glass-making, and iron, and was not nearly as relevant in either the woollen, cotton, silk, linen or leather industries: 'In some manufactures ... coal is a necessary instrument of trade; as in those of glass, iron, and all other metals.'[63] Smith's emphasis upon the use of coal in iron-making is highly revealing. For widespread use of coal in place of charcoal occurred only after mid-century, as at the Carron Company which pioneered the Darby process in Scotland.[64]

Coal as a consumer good is also emphasized. In the context of fuel used for home heating Smith wrote, in a passage of outstanding relevance: 'The price of fuel has so important an influence on that of labour, that all over Great Britain manufactures have confined themselves principally to the coal countries; other parts of the country, on account of the high price of this necessary article, not being able to work as cheap' (825).[65] Thus it is that a fundamentally significant change in industry location is explained partly in terms of the significance of coal in *consumption*.[66]

SUMMARY AND CONCLUSION

The data used by Smith indicate that perhaps as much as 50 per cent of the national product was accounted for by agriculture although this is an extreme upper limit; 40–45 per cent reflects a more accurate estimate. By contrast, the contribution of manufacturing, mining and metallurgy amounted to some

60 *Wealth of Nations*, 352.
61 *Ibid.*, 623.
62 *Ibid.*, 9.
63 *Ibid.*, 825–6.
64 R.H. Campbell, *Carron Company* (Edinburgh, 1961), 5–6. Problems relating to the use of coal as an industrial fuel in copper, tin and lead smelting – as well as in soap and sugar boiling, in malting, brewing and glass-making and in salt-refining – had been overcome much earlier, in some cases prior to 1700. It was in iron-making that the technological problem proved more intractable. (Cf., Wilson, *England's Apprenticeship*, 198f.) It may be added that the wool cleansing, fulling and dyeing operations in cloth manufacture also required heating and utilized coal. (Cf. Ashton, *An Economic History of England*, 92–3.)
65 Cf. also *Wealth of Nations*, 166–7, where Smith discusses the relative prices of coal and wood for heating, raising the issue of substitution in consumption, and *ibid.*, 104 where the relative high *money* wages of colliers and London coal heavers are explained by bad working conditions.
66 A general alteration in the location of activity in the case of the woollen industry from the West Country to Yorkshire (which specialized increasingly in the lighter worsteds rather than the heavier woollens), commencing early in the century, is one of the notable features of British industrial experience. Similarly the development of cotton manufacture in Lancashire and near Glasgow can be explained in part by proximity to local coal. See Wilson, *England's Apprenticeship*, 292f.

20 per cent only. Smith's own account of the contemporary British economy shows that certain of the characteristics of the 'industrial revolution' were not yet evident. We may recall the absence of the cotton industry among the primary branches of manufacturing; the emphasis upon coal largely in the metallurgical and glass-making industries rather than in the textile branches of manufacturing; and the explanation of industry location by the need for coal as a consumer good, rather than a producer good.

We shall have more to say about these matters in a later discussion of technical progress; but it should be emphasized here that, on the whole, we cannot find fault in Smith's characterization of the main lines of British industry before the last quarter of the eighteenth century. Modern scholarship suggests that during the eighteenth century, prior to the seventies, there is little evidence of any marked changes in structure between agriculture and 'industry.'[67] And in fact Smith nowhere suggests that any significant changes had occurred, although he certainly emphasized a general across-the-board expansion of the economy.[68]

But the absolute figures of the agricultural and industrial contributions to national income or employment are misleading. Structural changes within the broad categories were taking place prior to the 'industrial revolution': whereas in 1688 the wool industry accounted for over 30 per cent of manufacturing (including building, mining and metallurgy), and no other industry approached it in significance, by 1770, according to Young, the contribution

67 Deane and Cole, *British Economic Growth*, 157f. According to the King (1688)-Young (1770) data, manufacturing, mining and building increased only from 21 to 24 per cent of national income. But Young appears to have overestimated the share of agriculture (at the expense of trade and transport). Accordingly, the authors reject the accuracy of an apparent increase in the agricultural contribution, 1700–70.

68 See above the comments of Smith regarding a general expansion since 1763. Cf. also: 'But though the profusion of government must, undoubtedly, have retarded the natural progress of England towards wealth and improvement, it has not been able to stop it. The annual produce of its land and labour is, undoubtedly, much greater at present than it was either at the restoration or at the revolution' (*Wealth of Nations*, 328). In discussing the effects of the 'substitution' of paper for metallic money Smith points to the recent rapid growth of the Scottish economy: 'I have heard it asserted, that the trade of the city of Glasgow, doubled in about fifteen years after the first erection of the banks there; and that the trade of Scotland has more than quadrupled since the first erection of the two public banks at Edinburgh [1695 and 1727] ... Whether the trade, either of Scotland in general, or of the city of Glasgow in particular, has really increased in so great a proportion, during so short a period, I do not pretend to know. If either of them has increased in this proportion, it seems to be an effect too great to be accounted for by the sole operation of this cause. That the trade and industry of Scotland, however, have increased very considerably during this period, and that the banks have contributed a good deal to this increase, cannot be doubted' (*ibid.*, 281). Cf. too: 'The manufacture of linen in Scotland, and that of coarse woollens in the west riding of Yorkshire, are growing manufactures' (*ibid.*, 84).

See Appendix C for a number of relevant statistical facts regarding contemporary growth rates.

in terms of value of the woollen and worsted manufactures to the total had fallen to some 23 per cent while the metal manufactures had risen to achieve an equal significance.[69]

This greater diversification within industry, particularly the growing relative significance of the metal-using and making sectors, is clearly discernible in Smith's account. It was in the manufacturing sector, rather than agriculture, that Smith found the greatest potential for technical and organizational advances, and in manufacturing that he envisaged Britain's principal advantages to lie. Accordingly, he forecast much of what was about to occur: 'England ... is perhaps as well fitted by nature as any large country in Europe, to be the seat of foreign commerce, and manufactures for distant sale, and of all the improvements which these can occasion.'[70] Smith's attention is upon the metal-using sectors above all as the most amenable to technological progress. And the trend away from domestic towards factory organization is particularly emphasized in this branch.

The traditional textile branches – wool, linen, silk – receive less attention as potential 'growth' sectors. Smith's celebrated observation that 'in the clothing manufacture, the division of labour is nearly the same now as it was a century ago, and the machinery employed is not very different'[71] may be seen as an *appreciation* – not an unawareness – of contemporary technological progress, for as we shall see presently there were in fact relatively few advances, *specifically relevant to factory operations*, in the traditional sectors during the seventies.

While the *aggregate* shares of national income due to 'agriculture' and 'industry' are typical of a pre-industrial structure,[72] the greatest of differences was seen by Smith to exist between the agricultural communities of North America (where 'no manufactures for distant sale have ever yet been established') or of Poland, and the economy of Britain (and other west European states). A substantial export trade in manufactured produce was recognized in the case of Britain. And much of domestic agricultural activity was devoted to the provision of materials for manufacturing rather than for re-use in agriculture. Indeed, the advantages Britain possessed in manufacturing were ascribed in part to its excellent domestic sources of materials. It will also be recalled that the use of coal as an important item in workers' consumption was seen by Smith to explain the pattern of location of manufacturing centres.

It is a fact that fixed capital was not emphasized in Smith's discussion of manufacturing technology except in the case of silk. The emphasis is upon working capital including the raw materials used, the latter playing a large role in determining the applicability of improved equipment and organization. But the empirical fact is that manufacturing industries – indeed even such advanced hardware firms as at Soho, or the early cotton industry into which

69 Deane and Cole, *British Economic Growth*, 157f.
70 *Wealth of Nations*, 393.
71 *Ibid.*, 244.
72 Deane and Cole, *British Economic Growth*, 280.

many of the principal changes were to be introduced – were not 'capital in-tensive' compared with mining and iron-making.[73] Prior to the industrial revolution mining and metallurgy required relatively substantial fixed capital investment and these are precisely the sectors – apart from agriculture[74] – which Smith emphasized in his discussion of the use of fixed capital. Yet, as we shall see, much attention was paid in generally applicable discussions to theoretical issues relating to fixed capital and its depreciation, and in particu-lar to the phenomenon of 'embodied' technical change.[75]

We conclude that it is as misleading to regard Britain in Smith's day, or Smith's view thereof, as basically 'agricultural' as to ascribe to it the features of a highly industrialized capital-intensive economy. In the words of a modern commentator 'the midland coal and metal-fashioning industries were expand-ing at a rate unique for the times. Already by the 1760s we may see the shape

73 Pollard, 'Fixed Capital in Britain,' 301; Beales, *The Industrial Revolution*, 50.

74 Deane and Cole, *British Economic Growth*, 261, argue that 'the rate of capital formation advanced and steadied, perhaps reaching a long-term average of 5 or 6 per cent before the American War depressed the economy.' Particularly significant in this regard were the agricultural enclosures, roads and bridges, canals, public and private buildings, mills and spinning machinery (*ibid.*, 261 and 304). We should note the heavy investment required in dams, ponds, culverts, troughs, water-wheels which were required to provide the power needed by the mills that ground corn and malt, fulled cloth, slit iron, or ground rags to make paper. Cf. T.S. Ashton, *An Economic History of England: The 18th Century* (London, 1966), 109.

75 The issue at hand is a particularly difficult one. Even if the *predominant* form of organization was in fact 'agricultural' and of a 'primitive' kind, a keen observer might well note indications – perhaps localized – of ensuing and general change. Thus it has been argued that Smith's division of society into classes for distribution purposes, itself presupposes 'quite a considerable infiltration of capital and capitalistic methods of organization into agriculture and manufacture.' (R.L. Meek, 'Adam Smith and the Classical Theory of Profit,' *Scottish Journal of Political Economy*, I (June 1954), reprinted in Meek, *Economics and Ideology and Other Essays* (London, 1967), 23.

While this might not have been a *general* phenomenon there were certain districts where the picture is accurate. Capitalist methods of agricultural organization – in which, for example, improving tenants were the rule – was common in the East Lothians. But particularly significant were industrial developments in and around Glasgow: 'In "manufacture" the great potentialities of the capitalist form of productive organization, and in particular the considerable extent to which this form allowed the division of labour to be carried, were most readily apparent. Adam Smith was evidently greatly impressed with the large manufactories of his time. The typical master manufacturer of the *Wealth of Nations* is one who has invested a fairly large proportion of his capital in machines and the "instruments of his trade" ... It is this investment in fixed capital which constitutes, as it were, the undertaker's stake in the manufacture, and broadly speaking it is this investment in fixed capital which marks him off as a manufacturer rather than as a merchant.' (Meek, 'Adam Smith,' 25–6.)

Meek's argument fails to make the distinction between manufacturing and mining and metallurgy clear, for the references to fixed capital are presumed to apply to 'the typical master manufacturer of the *Wealth of Nations*.' But it does seem to be the case that fixed capital had caught Smith's eye as an issue requiring detailed investigation even in manufacturing.

of things to come ... The portents of large-scale industrial capitalism were visible in [the] Birmingham industries ...'[76] The structural changes which had occurred or were about to occur cannot be neglected, and were not neglected in the *Wealth of Nations*. The 'corn model' is not an adequate tool with which to treat the issues raised by economic growth in an economy such as that described by Smith, despite the undoubted quantitative importance of the agricultural sector and of the product, corn. It does not explain the mechanism of *capital allocation* between the various sectors and industries, saying nothing about the nature of the production function relevant to each sector, failing, for example, to take into account the particular role played by raw materials in manufacturing. In any event, it implies that agriculture was a 'primitive,' labour-intensive sector, whereas in fact, particularly in light of the process of 'improvement' under way, it was regarded by Smith as a capital-intensive sector.

76 Wilson, *England's Apprenticeship*, 301–2.

The theory of value

PRICE DETERMINATION

Smith's formal treatment of value theory may best be appreciated if envisaged as an attempt to achieve a conception of long-run *general* equilibrium.[1] This is clear from the emphasis upon 'alternative opportunity' apparent even in the treatment of price determination as recorded in the early *Lectures*, which attempted to define the conditions inducing men 'to a certain species of industry, rather than any other.'[2] While labour is the sole factor allowed for, the analysis utilizes the principle which is elaborated upon in the *Wealth of Nations* and requires attention.

Long-run prices are determined, according to the analysis, by *labour cost* rather than *labour quantity* since allowance is made for a money-wage structure (reflecting differential characteristics of employment). Thus non-monetary rewards such as the prestige derived from 'the eminence of the profession' will be allowed for in a relatively lower monetary return. And 'the time and pains' exerted in acquiring the relevant skills (actual training costs), and the risks involved in undertaking training must be covered: 'A man then has the natural price of his labour, when it is sufficient to maintain him during the time of labour, to defray the expence of education, and to compensate the risk of not living long enough, and of not succeeding in business. When a man has this, there is sufficient encouragement to the labourer, and the commodity will be cultivated in proportion to the demand.'[3] Smith evidently had in mind in the preceding comment an allocation of labour which assures satisfaction of demand for each commodity *at its cost price*.

---

1 However, Mark Blaug, *Economic Theory in Retrospect*, 2nd ed. (Homewood, 1968), 42, draws attention to a 'partial equilibrium' penchant in the key chapter *Wealth of Nations*, I. vii.

2 Adam Smith, *Lectures on Justice, Police, Revenue and Arms* (1763), ed. E. Cannan (New York, 1964), 173–4.

3 *Ibid.*, 175–6.

It must be noted carefully that at the level of discourse undertaken in the *Lectures*, there is no place for a *labour market* as such. The return to labour is obtained directly in the price of the commodity. The argument is appropriate for an economy of independent specialist handicraftsmen (possibly utilizing barter exchange, although the existence of a common medium of exchange is nowhere ruled out). Moreover, the definition of the long-run return as a sum 'sufficient to maintain' the labourer should not perhaps be strictly interpreted as reflecting a subsistence 'theory' of wages since Smith throughout presumed the labour force to be a *datum*, as we shall see, and addressed himself to its allocation. In brief, no mechanism of long-run wage determination is provided and doubtless Smith had in mind a customary norm.

The report of Smith's position on the determination of 'market price' is opaque. As in traditional formulations, there is a reference to 'the demand, or need of the commodity' and 'the abundance or scarcity of the commodity in proportion to the need of it.'[4] The income of the purchasers appears to be treated formally as an *independent* factor.[5] It is, however, observed that as price rises successive groups – defined by income – are excluded from the market. Thus, 'when the quantity of corn falls short, as in a sea-voyage, it always occasions a famine, and then the price becomes enormous. Corn then becomes the purchase of a higher set of people, and the lower must live on turnips and potatoes.'[6] The magnitude of income, according to this observation, determines the responsiveness of quantity demanded to price variations.[7] It is thus clear that Smith attempted to provide some rationale for a negatively-sloping demand curve.

An excess of market over cost price implies – and it is this which constitutes the essence of the process analysis – that 'labour is very highly rewarded' and, in consequence, that there will be an inflow of labour into this trade, an expansion of output and a fall in price to the equilibrium (cost) level. In the opposite case where the market price is below the natural price and 'there is not enough got for the labour of the manufacture,' there follows a consequent outflow from the trade and market price will rise.[8] The introduction of restraints or stimuli into any industry tends to break the so-called 'natural balance.' A subsidy, for example, causes not merely the artificial expansion of the output of a particular commodity but does so by drawing labour 'from

4 *Ibid.*, 176. A qualifying comment to the effect that 'there is no demand for a thing of little use; it is not a rational object of desire' is rather difficult to understand, and is probably a garbled version of Smith's intention. For Smith immediately refers to iron as being 'much more useful' than 'diamonds and other precious stones,' while it is clear to him that there *is* a demand for the latter.

5 *Ibid.*, 177.

6 *Ibid.*, 177–8.

7 The same conception reappears in the *Wealth of Nations*, as we shall see.

8 *Ibid.*, 178. The contention by H.M. Robertson and W.L. Taylor, 'Adam Smith's Approach to The Theory of Value,' *Economic Journal,* LXVII (June 1957), 192, that the relationship between the market and normal price in the *Lectures* is nothing but an 'assertion' may therefore be questioned.

other productions which are less encouraged.'⁹ That Smith took for granted full employment of a given work force in this analysis of allocation via the price mechanism seems to be a justified interpretation.

While the entire discussion thus far presumes the presence of only one scarce factor there does occur a passage – suggestive of the approach which subsequently took on particular importance – wherein reference is made to the fact that when manufactures were introduced – after the pastoral age 'in which provisions were the immediate produce' of labour – 'nothing could be produced without a great deal of time.' Accordingly, each industry requires a preliminary stock of wages goods. The aggregate stock is specifically taken to be a constant and is said to act as a constraint upon the total number employed: 'Suppose then, as is really the case in every country, that there is in store a stock of food, clothes, and lodging, the number of people that are employed must be in proportion to it.' Accordingly expansion due to a subsidy in one trade must mean that 'you take away the stock from the rest.'¹⁰ A reallocation of activity thus involves both the transfer of labour *and* capital between industries. Yet this extension is not allowed to complicate the main body of analysis for no return to capital is defined.¹¹

The treatment of the allocation process in the *Wealth of Nations* represents a vast improvement in terms of rigour over that reported in the *Lectures*. The analysis involves the deliberate complication stage-by-stage of simple models into those of greater complexity, and meets the high standard of method already set, for example, by Steuart and Cantillon.

The 'pure' labour theory of exchange value is initially formulated in the celebrated passage relating to the deer-beaver case. The argument here – in contrast with the *Lectures* – is restricted explicitly to the 'state of society which precedes both the accumulation of stock and the appropriation of land.'¹² But a significant qualification is immediately introduced which effectively allows for a *labour cost* explanation of price even in the simple state. Allowance will be made in the wage-rate structure, it is recognized, for the varying 'hardship' and varying 'dexterity and ingenuity' attached to labour in different occupa-

---

9 *Lectures*, 182. Throughout the discussion of equilibration it is implicitly presumed that the 'natural price' of each commodity remains unchanged and does not, in particular, vary with output.

10 *Ibid.*, 181. Needless to say, the capital constraint is meaningful only if the average wage rate is a *datum* which evidently Smith took for granted.

11 Even if capital is presumed to be owned by each individual labourer, a return on capital paid out of sales proceeds may be required (for example, as a compensation for abstaining from present consumption). No such reward is introduced.

   Casual reference is also made to the *rent of land* (*ibid.*, 181–2) but the implications are simply neglected.

12 Adam Smith, *Wealth of Nations*, 47. Whether or not the simple state is a barter economy is not the important issue; a common medium of exchange might be utilized.

tions.[13] The second differential is in turn interpreted as a 'compensation for the time and labour' devoted to acquiring the relevant skills.

Smith did not attempt to provide a formal justification of the 'labour cost' theory of exchange value by analysing the equilibration process set in motion by a disturbance. Less than a page is devoted to the case at hand; what in the *Lectures* represented the central issue is now no more than a summary statement clearly designed as an introduction to the main case. The great attention paid to the labour quantity and labour cost theories of value in commentaries upon the Smithian treatment is, in our view, unjustified. The basic argument – and the only one which Smith regarded as of any practical relevance – relates to the complex case where returns to capital and land are allowed for in the price of each commodity. It is true nevertheless that the decision to work from the simplest case of one factor to a greater degree of complexity tended to generate problems of interpretation.[14]

Process analysis relevant to the complex case is undertaken in the remarkable chapter 'Of the Natural and Market Price of Commodities' (I.vii). At the outset 'natural' rates are defined for wages, profit, and rent. These rates refer simply to the *average* return to the three factors labour, capital and land respectively pertaining at any time, and are *data* of the particular analysis at hand: 'These ordinary or average rates may be called the natural rates of wages, profit, and rent, at the time and place in which they commonly prevail.'[15] The 'natural price' is then simply the long-run cost price where factors receive the natural rate:

> When the price of any commodity is neither more nor less than is sufficient to pay the rent of the land, the wages of the labour, and the profits of the stock employed in raising, preparing, and bringing it to market, according to their natural rates, the commodity is then sold for what may be called its natural price ... When the quantity brought to market is just sufficient to supply the effectual demand and no more, the market price naturally comes to be either exactly, or as nearly as can be judged of, the same with the natural price.[16]

The 'market price' of a commodity is said to be 'regulated by the proportion between the quantity which is actually brought to market, and the demand

13 The higher returns attained in occupations involving labour of particular dexterity and ingenuity are formally ascribed to 'the esteem which men have for such talents' (*ibid.*).

14 Particularly the question whether profits and rent are a *deduction* from the produce of labour or an *additional* contribution.

15 *Wealth of Nations*, 55. The natural price of labour is not the subsistence rate except in a special case. But see Blaug, *Economic Theory in Retrospect*, 46, for the contrary view.

16 *Wealth of Nations*, 55–7. It has been suggested that Smith may have been at least in part indebted to James Oswald for the distribution of price between the component elements of rent, wages, and profits. Cf. W.R. Scott, *Adam Smith as Student and Professor* (Glasgow, 1937), 117–8; 124–5; 319–20. See also R.L. Meek, 'Adam Smith and the Classical Concept of Profit,' *Economics and Ideology and Other*

of those who are willing to pay the natural price' or the 'effectual' demand for the commodity.[17] Supply and demand are thus formally defined as specific quantities. But the argument which follows to substantiate the preceding proposition makes it clear that Smith had in mind the concept of a negatively-sloped demand schedule; the 'effectual demand' was, in other words, understood as a quantity demanded at a particular price, namely at the long-run cost price. That a positively-sloped supply curve applicable to the market period was similarly envisaged may also be demonstrated.

The degree of any increase in price above the long-run cost level depends in part, Smith argued, upon the magnitude of excess demand at the latter level; but given the excess demand, other forces will determine the extent of price increase. In effect this argument amounts to an attempt to explain the degree of demand elasticity.[18] Smith makes reference in this regard to consumers' 'wealth and wanton luxury,' and it is suggested that the higher the consumers' incomes the greater the price rise, or the more *inelastic* the demand. It is likely that Smith had in mind the proposition (already noted in

Essays (London, 1967), 30f.; and J.M. Low, 'An Eighteenth Century Controversy in The Theory of Economic Progress,' *Manchester School of Economic and Social Studies*, XX (Sept. 1952), 312n. Professor Meek ('Adam Smith,' 29) has also drawn attention to an anticipation of the natural-price doctrine by William Temple in 1758: 'I can most clearly perceive that the value of all commodities, or the price, is a compound of the value of the land necessary to raise them, the value of the labour exerted in producing and manufacturing them, and of the value of the brokerage which provides and circulates them.' David Hume, on the other hand, reacted critically, to Smith's representation of rent as a component part of price on a par with the returns to capital and labour: 'I cannot think, that the Rent of Farms makes any part of the Price of the Produce, but that the Price is determined altogether by the Quantity and the Demand.' (Letter to Smith, dated 1 April, 1776, *The Letters of David Hume*, II, ed. J.Y.T. Greig (Oxford, 1932), 311.)

In the following extract from a letter by Hume to Turgot (1766) dealing with the *aggregative* shares there is emphasis not only upon the function of capital in the support of labour in all activities but also upon the return to capital, from an aggregate view, as a class income on a par with the rent of land and the wages of labour: 'I beg you also to consider, that, besides the Proprietors of Land and the labouring Poor, there is in every civilized Community a very large and a very opulent Body who employ their Stocks in Commerce and who enjoy a great Revenue from their giving Labour to the poorer sort. I am perswaded that in France and England the Revenue of this kind is much greater that that which arises from Land: For besides Merchants, properly speaking, I comprehend in this Class all Shop-keepers and Master-Tradesmen of every Species.' *David Hume: Writings on Economics*, ed. E. Rotwein (London, 1955), 209. For Turgot's own contribution in the *Reflections* see above, 85–6. It is argued convincingly by P.D. Groenewegen, 'Turgot and Adam Smith,' *Scottish Journal of Political Economy*, XVI (Nov. 1969), 286–7, that similarities between Turgot and Smith regarding the distributive shares provide no substantive evidence of a 'debt' by the latter to the former.

17 *Wealth of Nations*, 56.

18 Instead of asking, as is current practice, what is the change in quantity demanded for a given change in price (starting from a base price and quantity), Smith phrases the issue in terms of the change in price corresponding to a given change in quantity starting from some initial base.

the *Lectures*) that a certain 'carelessness' in budget allocation, resulting in insensitiveness to price increases, characterizes high-income consumers, while low-income consumers tend to be more price conscious. Within any particular income group, it is further pointed out, 'necessaries' – apparently commodities for which there are few alternatives – will have more inelastic demands. The above interpretation is based on the following key passage in the chapter:

When the quantity of any commodity which is brought to market falls short of the effectual demand, all those who are willing to pay the whole value of the rent, wages, and profit, which must be paid in order to bring it thither, cannot be supplied with the quantity which they want. Rather than want it altogether, some of them will be willing to give more. A competition will immediately begin among them, and the market price will rise more or less above the natural price, according as either the greatness of the deficiency, or the wealth and wanton luxury of the competitors, happen to animate more or less the eagerness of the competition. Among competitors of equal wealth and luxury the same deficiency will generally occasion a more or less eager competition, according as the acquisition of the commodity happens to be of more or less importance to them. Hence the exorbitant price of the necessaries of life during the blockade of a town or in a famine (56).[19]

In the case of an excess supply at cost price, two mechanisms are said to operate. In the first place, there is competition on the part of consumers. In the following passage the conception of *marginal* demand price is quite clear: 'When the quantity brought to market exceeds the effectual demand, it cannot all be sold to those who are willing to pay the whole value of the rent, wages and profit, which must be paid in order to bring it thither. Some part must be sold to those who are willing to pay less, and the low price which they give for it must reduce the price of the whole' (57). In addition Smith remarks that in the case at hand market price will fall 'according as the greatness of the excess increases more or less the competition of the sellers, or according as it happens to be more or less important to them to get immediately rid of the commodity. The same excess in the importation of perishable, will occasion a much greater competition than in that of durable commodities; in the importation of oranges, for example, than in that of old iron.'[20] Here the emphasis is upon the responsiveness of supply. In effect an attempt is made to determine supply elasticity.[21] Given the excess supply at cost price the extent of price reduction will depend on the possibility of withdrawal of supplies from the market.

It follows from the above account that the 'quantity which is actually brought to market' was not in fact regarded as decisive by Smith, because of the necessity of allowing for possible withdrawal of supplies. That Smith did

19 The low price (and income) elasticity for food is noted also, *ibid.*, 164: 'The desire of food is limited in every man by the narrow capacity of the human stomach.'
20 *Ibid.*, 57.
21 The question posed relates to the change in price given a change in supply from some base position.

not recognize the equivalent complication in the case of an excess demand where the drawing down of inventories would be a relevant consideration, but placed the entire burden of response on demand, seems to be merely the accidental consequence of the particular formulation adopted rather than a matter of principle. Accordingly we may say that some justification is provided both for a negatively-sloped demand curve and also for a positively-sloped supply curve – throughout their respective lengths – relating to the market period.[22]

The crucial mechanism in the process of adjustment which assures that the prices of commodities will in fact be 'continually gravitating' or 'constantly tending towards' their respective cost prices is the tendency towards an equality of the returns to labour, capital and land respectively in different activities. The harshest critics of Smithian value theory concede that his treatment in this regard represents a substantial achievement.[23] For Smith explicitly recognized that resources are transferred individually from less to more remunerative uses until an equality across the board is assured, in each case; the conception of alternative opportunity is clear in the following passage:

If at any time [the quantity supplied] exceeds the effectual demand, some of the component parts of its price must be paid below their natural rate. If it is rent, the interests of the landlords will immediately prompt them to withdraw a part of their land; and if it is wages or profit, the interest of the labourers in the one case, and of their employers in the other, will prompt them to withdraw a part of their labour or stock from this employment. The quantity brought to market would soon be no more than sufficient to supply the effectual demand. All the different parts of its price will rise to their natural rate, and the whole price to its natural price.

If, on the contrary, the quantity brought to market should at any time fall short of the effectual demand, some of the component parts of its price must rise above their natural rate. If it is rent, the interest of all other landlords will naturally prompt them to prepare more land for the raising of this commodity; if it is wages or profit, the interest of all other labourers and dealers will soon prompt them to employ more labour and stock in preparing and bringing it to market. The quantity brought thither will soon be sufficient to supply the effectual demand. All the different parts of its

22 A good account of Smith's approach, emphasizing his recognition of the vital distinction between a shift in the demand curve and a movement along a given demand curve, will be found in Victor E. Smith, 'The Classicists' Use of Demand,' *Journal of Political Economy*, LIX (June 1951), 242–57. By limiting his discussion to the *Wealth of Nations*, I.vii, V.E. Smith is, however, led to conclude (*ibid.*, 243) that 'the demand for a particular commodity entered directly into Smith's value theory only when the actual or market price was to be explained.' This is also the view of Blaug, *Economic Theory in Retrospect*, 43 and seems now to represent the received doctrine. We shall show presently that this is an inaccurate representation of Smith's *general* position.

23 Cf. Frank H. Knight, 'The Ricardian Theory of Production and Distribution,' *Canadian Journal of Economics and Political Science*, I (Feb. 1935); reprinted in Knight, *On the History and Method of Economics* (Chicago, 1956), 64; and J.A. Schumpeter, *History of Economic Analysis* (New York, 1954), 568.

"All prices gravitate toward natural price"

equilibrium

price will soon sink to their natural rate, and the whole price to its natural price (57–8).

A variety of issues regarding this mechanism of adjustment require consideration.

Professor Joan Robinson has recently emphasized that 'in a market economy, either there may be a tendency towards uniformity of wages and the rate of profit in different lines of production, or prices may be governed by supply and demand, but not both. Where supply and demand rule, there is no room for uniform levels of wages and the rate of profits. The Walrasian system makes sense if we interpret it in terms of an artisan economy, where each producer is committed to a particular product, so that his income depends on his output and its price. Each can have a prospective rate of return on investment in his own line, but there is no mechanism to equalize profits between one line and another.'[24] The observation is based (apparently) on the supposition that among the *data* of the system are included the quantities of each and every specific kind of labour, capital good, and land.

Now it is certain that Smith presumed constant *aggregate* amounts of each of the three factors throughout the analysis of Book I, vii; the issue which concerned him was specifically the distribution of the factors between alternative uses. But it is also evident that the amounts of the particular kinds of each factor were *not* given. Indeed the object of the analysis was precisely to explain how alterations in the particular forms taken by the factors will be brought about; it was Smith's contention that a change in the pattern of demand would lead to a reallocation of factors, involving not merely a transfer from one use to another made possible by a presumed versatility, but more significantly by a change in form such as by retraining in the case of labour.[25] It is in fact made quite explicit that the processes involved are *not* instantaneous, but take time: 'The natural price, therefore, is, as it were, the central price, to which the prices of all commodities are continually gravitating. Different accidents may sometimes keep them suspended a good deal above it, and may sometimes force them down even somewhat below it. But whatever may be the obstacles which hinder them from settling in this center of repose and continuance, they are constantly tending towards it' (58). The existence of a tendency towards a uniform level of wages, of profits and of rents does not seem to be ruled out in such a system which is intended to apply to a 'long-run' situation. (While Smith, of course, allowed elsewhere for alterations in the aggregate amounts of the factors, in Chapter vii he was enquiring into the processes of equilibration in a state of artificially presumed stationariness.)

all prices gravitate to natural price

Yet the issue raised by Professor Robinson is of some significance in any

24 Joan Robinson, 'Prelude to a Critique of Economic Theory,' *Oxford Economic Papers*, XIII (Feb. 1961), 57.
25 See the discussion below regarding the determination of the competitive wage-rate structure.

attempt to evaluate the actual as well as the intended scope of the *Wealth of Nations*. For while Smith was, on the whole, concerned with the analysis of an economy characterized by 'capitalist' institutional arrangements involving the dependence of labour upon others for the provision of capital goods, there yet remain arguments which seem more suitable for a 'mixed' system wherein skilled labourers – or at least some of them – owned their own tools and plant (while merchant-capitalists provided only working capital) and which has accordingly an artisanal character. In such a system, transfer of capital and labour between sectors in response to profit opportunities will clearly be limited.[26]

The analysis of general equilibrium outlined above is constrained in various respects. The average rates of return are not themselves determined in the adjustment process; the mechanism whereby productive factors are directed into or repelled from an industry affects the product price and the price of the factor in that particular industry (although only in the immediate and short run) but the average returns remain throughout constant. Secondly, there is no recognition of variability of factor proportions in any productive unit. It is thus implied both that factor proportions are identical from industry to industry – only then will the average rates of return remain constant following a change in the structure of industry in response, for example, to a changed pattern of demand – and that factor proportions in each productive unit are constant.[27]

26 Smith's celebrated illustration (*Wealth of Nations*, 59, cf. also 116) of the effects of a change in the pattern of demand for cloth of various kinds permitted him to by-pass some of the fundamental issues requiring attention. In the first instance the profits of merchants holding stocks of black cloth will be increased; the change will also involve an excess demand at the original wage rate for the labour of journeymen taylors engaged upon black cloth and a consequent increase in their wage rate. The profits of merchants holding stocks of coloured cloth will fall, as will the wages of labourers involved in the production of coloured cloth. Unfortunately the case chosen of a temporary change in the pattern of demand ruled out a full analysis of the readjustment mechanism when we assume the initiating changes to be permanent, so that in the final resort the prices of both categories of goods (and of labour) would return to their original levels by way of output variation and the necessary movement of all factors. His attention was almost entirely upon variations in *rents* – in the modern sense of the term – to the holders of inventories.

Moreover, Smith's formal discussion of the competitive profit-rate structure (see below) implies frequently an emphasis upon the merchant rather than the capitalist-employer who provides fixed as well as working capital.

27 Cf. Knight, 'The Ricardian Theory of Production and Distribution,' 65. One of the most serious charges directed by David Ricardo against the Smithian analysis of price was in fact precisely that it failed to recognize differences between the capital structures of various industries. Ricardo objected not to the fact that in the Smithian analysis value is based upon production costs rather than upon labour quantity, since he himself maintained a cost-of-production theory of price determination. His charge was rather that Smith had failed to recognize the true effects of the payment of profit on relative value because of a complete neglect of the differential degrees of capital durability in different goods or any other technological characteristic not common to all products. According to Ricardo, changes in factor prices would

The formal analysis of the effect of changing wage rates in manufacturing also implies strongly that factor proportions were taken to be constant and identical across the board. Of the effects on price of a general upward trend in wages – which is expected to coincide with economic expansion – Smith wrote: 'The increase in the wages of labour necessarily increases the price of many commodities, by increasing that part of it which resolves itself into wages, and so far tends to diminish their consumption both at home and abroad.'[28] Consistently, a wage reduction – which Smith expected to follow from the removal of import duties upon subsistence goods – would lower the prices of manufactured goods 'in proportion': 'The reduction in the money price of labour would necessarily be attended with a proportionable one in that all home-manufactures, which would thereby gain some advantage in all foreign markets.'[29] Similarly, the effect of rising materials' prices according to Smith is to cause unit (materials) costs to rise in proportion.[30]

influence exchange values, the exact manner and extent depending upon the factor ratios relevant to the particular commodities. The argument is most clearly stated in a letter to James Mill dated 28 December 1818 quoted by Piero Sraffa in 'Introduction' to *Principles of Political Economy, The Works and Correspondence of David Ricardo*, I (Cambridge, 1951), xxxvi–xxxvii:

'He [Torrens] makes it appear that Smith says that after capital accumulates and industrious people are set to work the quantity of labour employed is not the only circumstance that determines the value of commodities, and that I oppose this opinion. Now I want to shew that I do not oppose this opinion in the way that he represents me to do so, but Adam Smith thought, that as in the early stages of society, all the produce of labour belonged to the labourer, and as after stock was accumulated, a part went to profits, that accumulation, necessarily, without any regard to the different degrees of durability of capital, or any other circumstance whatever, *raised* the prices or exchangeable value of commodities, and consequently that their value was no longer regulated by the quantity of labour necessary to their production. In opposition to him, I maintain that it is not because of this division into profits and wages – it is not because capital accumulates, that exchangeable value varies, but it is in all stages of society, owing only to two causes: one, the more or less quantity of labour required, the other the greater or less durability of capital: – that the former is never superseded by the latter, but is only modified by it.'

See also letter to Mill dated 14 October 1816, *ibid.*, xxxv; and Ricardo's comment in his first two editions (1817, 1819): Smith 'has no where analysed the effects of the accumulation of capital, and the appropriation of land on relative value' (quoted in Sraffa, *ibid.*, 22–3n.).

28 *Wealth of Nations*, 86. The context implies that the discussion relates to manufacturing. The import of this restriction will be investigated presently.

29 *Ibid.*, 836–7. Presumably Smith means in proportion to the fraction of costs attributable to the labour input.

Elsewhere it is made clear that prices will vary more than 'in proportion' to any wage-cost variation because of the necessary correction for profits charged on wage advances (*ibid.*, 816).

In considering the effects of the contemporary Corporation Laws Smith also seems explicitly to make the assumption of fixed proportions between capital and labour. The context suggests that Smith's concern was with manufacturing, although the assumption might have general relevance: 'Whatever obstructs the free circulation of labour from one employment to another, obstructs that of stock likewise; the

Now, while in Book I.vii Smith, as we have seen, assumed constant aggregate supplies of the factors, the theoretical question arises how, upon alterations in the relative amounts of the factors the equilibration process would operate under the restrictive conditions in question. It is, of course, possible that the assumptions of the formal account of the general equilibrium process were introduced as a deliberate first approximation. But whether this is so or whether, as is more likely, Smith was simply unaware of all the assumptions implicit in his analysis, the fact is that he did allow in practical applications, for certain substitution relationships. Differential factor ratios, for example, between broad categories of products play a vital role in the chapter 'Of Different Employment of Capitals' (II.v).[31] If, moreover, full allowance is made for the adoption of processes applicable at large scale in manufacturing, a further mechanism relating to changes in the capital-labour ratio within a productive unit becomes relevant.[32] Thus, while it is true that he did not formally introduce the substitution relation into his analysis as a general phenomenon, certain specific aspects thereof were recognized in the treatment of particular problems within the economics of allocation.[33]

quantity of stock which can be employed in any branch of business depending very much upon that of the labour which can be employed in it' (*ibid.*, 135).

Explicit statements of a fixed materials coefficient are rare in classical literature. Nassau Senior, however, makes the assumption explicitly – even in the case where technological improvements are allowed for – of zero, or almost zero substitutability between materials and other inputs:

'The difference between the efficiency of agricultural and of manufacturing industry ... consists in the power which agricultural industry possesses, and manufacturing industry does not possess, of obtaining an additional product from the same materials. We have seen that the use of implements and the division of labour assist the exertions of man to an extent quite incalculable at present, and apparently capable of indefinite increase. But manufacturing improvements ... cannot enable the same amount of labour, or even increased labour, employed on the same quantity of *materials*, to produce a much larger amount of finished work of the same quality, than could have been produced before. If the labour and the skill now employed throughout England on the manufacture of cotton were doubled, but the quantity of raw materials remained the same, the quantity of manufactured produce could not be sensibly increased ... its quantity could be increased only by the saving which might be made of that small portion of the raw material which now is wasted.' (*An Outline of the Science of Political Economy* (London, 1836), 82.)

30 See below, 118–9.
31 The issue is discussed below, 139f.   32. See below, Chapter 7.
33 The nature of the agricultural production function envisaged by Smith is difficult to discern. On the one hand there is an explicit statement defining fixed proportions between land and capital: 'Each farmer occupies a certain quantity of land for which he pays rent. For the proper cultivation of this land a certain quantity of stock is necessary.' (*Wealth of Nations*, 807.) On the other hand, there are general statements implying the possibility of varying the ratio between land and labour or capital. Thus, for example, we read that 'The produce of land, mines, and fisheries, when their natural fertility is equal, is in proportion to the extent and proper application of the capitals employed about them. When the capitals are equal and equally well applied, it is in proportion to their natural fertility' (*ibid.*, 268). And at the outset of the *Wealth of Nations* in his comparison

THE CONCEPT OF COMPETITION

Before treating the Smithian conception of competition a few words are in order, by way of contrast, regarding monopoly price. A celebrated observation – which has given rise to considerable merriment – that monopoly price 'is upon every occasion the highest which can be ... squeezed from the buyers, or which, it is supposed, they will consent to give'[34] should be read in conjunction with a more specific discussion relating to the determination of the price of coal, wherein Smith defined a *range* of possible prices between a minimum determined by long-run costs, and a maximum determined by the price of wood (corrected for the costs of transporting coal from the mine to the market), from which the seller (or group of colluding sellers) might choose: 'Coals, in the coal country, are every where much below this highest price. If they were not, they could not bear the expence of a distant carriage, either by land or by water. A small quantity only could be sold, and the coal masters and coal proprietors find it more for their interest to sell a great quantity at a price somewhat above the lowest, than a small quantity at the highest' (166–7). The conception of an artificial reduction of output to force up price is expressed in Smith's discussion of the corn trade: 'were it possible, indeed, for one great company of merchants to possess themselves of the whole crop of an extensive country, it might, perhaps, be in their interests ... to destroy or throw away a considerable part of it, in order to keep up the price of the rest.'[35] Evidently, Smith was unable to specify the actual 'monopoly price.' *only for necessities* But it is quite clear that the 'maximum which can be squeezed from the buyers' is subject to the seller's interest.

The specific conditions assuring a *competitive* structure are clarified by Smith at various stages. The requirements for large numbers and for the absence of collusion are formulated in the following passage relating to tradesmen (as distinct from producers):

The prejudices of some political writers against shopkeepers and tradesmen, are altogether without foundation. So far is it from being necessary, either to tax them, or to restrict their numbers, that they can never be multiplied so as to hurt the

---

between agriculture in rich and poor countries, Smith wrote of the former: 'Their lands are in general better cultivated, and having more labour and expence bestowed upon them, produce more in proportion to the extent and natural fertility of the ground, but this superiority of produce is seldom much more than in proportion to the superiority of labour and expence' (*ibid.*, 6). In these passages, which allow apparently for variable factor proportions, there is little evidence of diminishing returns at the 'intensive margin' of cultivation. Diminishing returns at the 'extensive margin' is, however, recognized. (See below, 183–4n.)

34 *Ibid.*, 61.
35 *Ibid.*, 491. Smith had earlier commented: 'I have known the different undertakers of some particular works agree privately among themselves to give a bounty out of their own pockets upon the exportation of a certain proportion of the goods which they dealt in. This expedient succeeded so well, that it more than doubled the price of their goods in the home market, notwithstanding a very considerable increase in the produce' (484).

publick, though they may so as to hurt one another. The quantity of grocery goods, for example, which can be sold in a particular town, is limited by the demand of that town and its neighbourhood. The capital, therefore, which can be employed in the grocery trade cannot exceed what is sufficient to purchase that quantity. If this capital is divided between two different grocers, their competition will tend to make both of them sell cheaper, than if it were in the hands of one only; and if it were divided among twenty, their competition would be just so much the greater, and the chance of their combining together, in order to raise the price, just so much the less (342).

It has been observed that Smith's notion of competition entails 'rivalry in a race – a race to get limited supplies or a race to be rid of excess supplies. Competition is a process of responding to a new force and a method of reaching a new equilibrium.'[36] There is much truth to this observation. Thus we have seen that in conditions of excess demand at cost price some purchasers 'rather than want it altogether ... will be willing to give more' and similarly in conditions of excess supply. Accordingly, the Smithian conception of competition must be carefully distinguished from the modern conception which envisages sellers (and consumers) as 'price takers' rather than 'price makers.'

A specific example of a competitive structure of particular historical significance is provided by the internal corn trade which, Smith contended, was 'the least liable to be engrossed or monopolized by the force of a few large capitals.'[37] The impediment to engrossment of corn by professional dealers derived not only from the great disproportion between the annual output and the ability of 'a few private men' to purchase it, but also from the existence of many independent producers who can each take on the function of dealer:

When it first comes from the ground too, it is necessarily divided among a greater number of owners than any other commodity; and these owners can never be collected into one place like a number of independent manufacturers, but are necessarily scattered through all the different corners of the country ... The inland dealers in corn, therefore, including both the farmer and the baker, are necessarily more numerous than the dealers in any other commodity, and their dispersed situation renders it altogether impossible for them to enter into any general combination (492).

The consequence of large numbers is the price competition which is characteristic of Smithian theory; the reference which follows to the seller's 'rivals and competitors' illustrates admirably the principle at hand:

If in a year of scarcity therefore, any of them should find that he had a good deal more corn upon hand than, at the current price, he could hope to dispose of before the end of the season, he would never think of keeping up this price to his own loss, and to the sole benefit of his rivals and competitors, but would immediately lower it,

36 George J. Stigler, 'Perfect Competition, Historically Considered,' *Journal of Political Economy*, LXV (Feb. 1957), reprinted in Stigler, *Essays in the History of Economics* (Chicago, 1965), 235. See also Paul J. McNulty, 'A Note on the History of Perfect Competition,' *Journal of Political Economy*, LXXV (Aug. 1967), 397.
37 *Wealth of Nations*, 491–2.

in order to get rid of his corn before the new crop began to come in. The same motives, the same interests, which would thus regulate the conduct of any one dealer, would regulate that of every other, and oblige them all in general to sell their corn at a price, which, according to the best of their judgment, was most suitable to the scarcity or plenty of the season (492).

The satisfaction of the fundamental condition of large numbers of independently operating buyers and sellers guarantees the eradication of excess demands or excess supplies. But it is clear that competition meant much more to Smith. The processes whereby market prices tend in the long run towards cost prices entail the satisfaction of further conditions, namely knowledge of profit opportunities available to resource owners; and freedom of movement between industries. In what follows we shall consider Smith's analysis of the wage-rate and profit-rate structures with an eye upon the assumptions made in this regard. But it should be recognized that Smith's treatment of the competitive wage-rate structure served also to justify his use of 'labour commanded' as a measure of what is referred to in the *Wealth of Nations* as 'real' value, and this too must be kept in mind if we are to do justice to Smith's account.

The 'real value' of a commodity, or of commodities in general, is defined formally as their 'price in labour' as distinct from their nominal value or their 'price in money.'[38] The issue at hand, it is now generally recognized, corresponds to the modern 'index number' problem of estimating changes in 'real income' over space and time.[39] But the particular choice of numéraire also has a normative significance.[40] It has been correctly emphasized that from this point of view we are not dealing with the *logical* derivation of values in a model with empirical relevance, so that no theory of 'exchange value' is involved. Yet it should at the same time be recognized that it does make sense to inquire how well a particular index serves the precise purpose for which it is designed.

Smith makes it clear that the well-being of an individual is ultimately a function of his command over consumer goods: 'Every man is rich or poor according to the degree in which he can afford to enjoy the necessaries, conveniencies, and amusements of human life.' The introduction of specialization, however, means that the bulk of the goods consumed by an individual are produced by the labour of others. Accordingly, the labour commanded by a commodity provides an index of its general purchasing power: 'The value

38 *Ibid.*, 30.

39 Cf. Donald F. Gordon, 'What Was the Labour Theory of Value,' *American Economic Review* (Supplement), XLIX (May 1959), 462–72; V.W. Bladen, 'Adam Smith on Value,' *Essays in Political Economy in Honor of E.J. Urwick*, ed. H.A. Innis (Toronto, 1938), 27–43; Blaug, *Economic Theory in Retrospect*, 51–4.

40 It has been suggested that Smith might have expressed nominal prices of particular goods in terms of a general level of prices, had he been aware of the index-number technique. (Schumpeter, *History of Economic Analysis*, 188.) This is true, but the observation neglects to take account of the particular normative implications of labour as social accounting unit.

of any commodity ... to the person who possesses it, and who means not to use or consume it himself, but to exchange it for other commodities, is equal to the quantity of labour which it enables him to purchase or command. Labour, therefore, is the real measure of the exchangeable value of all commodities.'[41] The term 'real value' thus applies to purchasing power over consumer goods, while command over labour serves as the indirect means thereto. The generality of the applications made by Smith throughout the *Wealth of Nations*[42] makes it clear that the index was not merely designed for the simple state; but clearly it operates less satisfactorily in the complex economy where command over labour is an inadequate assurance of purchasing power over commodities (because of the contribution to output of other factors). Its initial introduction within the discussion of early society, where the labour *embodied* in a commodity then happens to coincide with its *command* over labour, did much to assure that a labour theory of price would be mistakenly attributed to Smith.[43] It is also implied that in Smith's evaluation secularly rising labour productivity would not render the chosen index of real purchasing power totally inadequate.

There is, in addition, a second implication of the term real value, namely labour commanded in the sense of the effort cost of production: 'The real price of everything, what every thing really costs to the man who wants to acquire it, is the toil and trouble of acquiring it. What every thing is really worth to the man who has acquired it, and who wants to dispose of it or exchange it for something else, is the toil and trouble which it can save to himself, and which it can dispose upon other people' (30). Smith is led to an even clearer statement according to which 'what is dear' is, by definition, said to correspond to 'what is difficult to come by,' in terms of the disutility engendered by effort, rather than mere time units.[44] It is from this point of view that the issue involved takes on particular relevance within the general analysis of allocation.

An hour of work could not be regarded as an unambiguous measure of disutility – the 'time and trouble' involved – since allowance must be made for 'the different degrees of hardship endured, and of ingenuity exercised ... There may be more labour in an hour's hard work than in two hours easy business; or in an hour's application to a trade which it cost ten years labour

41 *Wealth of Nations*, 30.
42 The index is applied, for example, to estimate the well-being of landlords under various circumstances and it is clear that by 'real value' Smith is referring to purchasing power over commodities: 'Whatever was the rate at which labour was commonly maintained in that country, this greater surplus could always maintain a greater quantity of it, and consequently enable the landlord to purchase or command a greater quantity of it. The real value of his rent, his real power and authority, his command of the necessaries and conveniencies of life with which the labour of other people could supply him, would necessarily be much greater' (*ibid.*, 159).
43 See on this issue Paul H. Douglas, 'Smith's Theory of Value and Distribution,' in J.M. Clark, *et al.*, *Adam Smith, 1776–1926* (Chicago, 1928), 88f.
44 *Wealth of Nations*, 33.

to learn, than in a month's industry at an ordinary and obvious employment.' A rough resolution of the difficulty is provided in practise 'by the higgling and bargaining of the market' whereby relative degrees of hardship and ingenuity come to be reflected roughly in the wage structure.[45]

It seems therefore to be Smith's view that the value of output in terms of wage units – utilizing perhaps the rate applicable to unskilled labour – would provide an *adequate*, if not perfect, measure of 'labour commanded' in the required sense of the term, namely in the sense of 'toil and trouble.' Smith makes explicit an underlying assumption that the ultimate psychic cost corresponding to a unit of labour in this sense is a constant from place to place and from time to time: 'Equal quantities of labour, at all times and places, may be said to be of equal value to the labourer. In his ordinary state of health, strength and spirits; in the ordinary degree of his skill and dexterity, he must always lay down the same portion of his ease, his liberty, and his happiness.' Formally the proposition is maintained in the case of a single labourer; but in practice it is extended to labour as a whole implying thereby not only the cardinal measurement of disutility, but also the possibility of inter-personal comparisons and more strongly the presumption of identical labour disutility functions between individuals: 'Labour alone, therefore, never varying in its own value, is alone the ultimate and real standard by which the value of *all* commodities can at *all* times and places be estimated and compared.'[46]

45 *Ibid.*, 31.
46 *Ibid.*, 33. Smith's discussions of the statistical difficulties involved are of particular interest: 'But the current prices of labour at distant times and places can scarce ever be known with any degree of exactness. Those of corn, though they have in few places been regularly recorded, are in general better known and have been frequently taken notice of by historians and other writers. We must generally, therefore, content ourselves with them, not as being always exactly in the same proportion as the current price of labour, but as being the nearest approximation which can commonly be had to that proportion' (38; cf. 482).

The fact that *corn* was a second-best choice in light of secular movements in the corn wage is expressed clearly by Smith in the following passage: 'Equal quantities of labour will at distant times be purchased more nearly with equal quantities of corn, the subsistence of the labourer than with equal quantities of gold and silver, or perhaps of any other commodity. Equal quantities of corn, therefore, will, at distant times, be more nearly the same real value, or enable the possessor to purchase or command more nearly the same quantity of the labour of other people. They will do so, I say, more nearly than equal quantities of almost any other commodity; for even equal quantities of corn will not do it exactly. The subsistence of the labourer, or the real price of labour ... is very different upon different occasions ... Every other commodity, however, will at any particular time purchase a greater or smaller quantity of labour in proportion to the quantity of subsistence which it can purchase at that time. A rent therefore reserved in corn is liable only to the variations in the quantity of labour which a certain quantity of corn can purchase. But a rent reserved in any other commodity is liable, not only to the variations in the quantity of labour which any particular quantity of corn can purchase, but to the variations in the quantity of corn which can be purchased by any particular quantity of that commodity' (35–6).

The choice of corn is further justified on the grounds that it is produced at roughly

It is clear from the preceding argument that an hour of skilled work is assumed to incorporate a fraction of the accumulated toil and trouble involved in training.[47] This permits Smith to reduce differential degrees of 'ingenuity' to equivalent differential degrees of disutility. But a more complete account of the determination of the wage structure is given subsequently (*Wealth of Nations*, I.x), wherein *five* main characteristics which compensate for monetary differentials are distinguished in a well-known discussion:

The five following are the principal circumstances which, so far as I have been able to observe, make up for a small pecuniary gain in some employments, and counterbalance a great one in others: first, the agreeableness or disagreeableness of the employments themselves; secondly, the easiness and cheapness, or the difficulty and expence of learning them; thirdly the constancy or inconstancy of employment in them; fourthly, the small or great trust which must be reposed in those who exercise them; and fifthly, the probability or improbability of success in them (100).

The argument is based on the assumptions that the movement of labour between occupations is unimpeded by institutional constraints;[48] that the different occupations are 'well known and long established' assuring knowledge of available opportunities; and that the occupations are 'the sole or principal employments of those who occupy them,' since workers operating on a part-time basis are likely to accept particularly low monetary returns.[49]

In this full analysis training costs are treated as a form of investment in human capital formation which requires a return as does any other investment: 'The work which he learns to perform, it must be expected, over and above the usual wages of common labour, will replace to him the whole expense of his education, with at least the ordinary profits of an equally valuable capital.'[50] The costs taken into consideration include foregone earning op-

constant costs (*ibid.*, 187). But this argument is difficult to appreciate since the corn wage depends solely on demand and supply conditions in the labour market.

The issue of an index of 'real value' had already been raised by Francis Hutcheson and corn prices suggested as the required series: 'but the real value of these mettals [bars of gold, silver] and of money too, like that of all other goods, is lessened as they are more plentiful; and increase when they grow scarcer, tho' the pieces keep the same names. The common necessaries of life have a more stable natural price, tho' they are some little changes of their values according to the fruitfulness of the several seasons. Were one to settle perpetual salaries to certain offices, which should support men perpetually in the same station in respect to their neighbours, these salaries should be constituted in certain quantities of such necessary goods as depend upon the plain inartificial labours of men, such as grain, or other necessaries in a plain simple way of living.' (*A Short Introduction to Moral Philosophy* (1747), *Collected Works of Francis Hutcheson* (Hildesheim, 1969), IV, 201-2.)

Hutcheson's position has much in common with that of Pufendorf, *De Jure Naturae et Gentium* (*On the Law of Nature and of Nations*) (1672), the Classics of International Law, no. 17, vol. II (Oxford, 1934), 696-8.

47 The same issue is discussed within the context of the simple state (above, 116-7).
48 *Wealth of Nations*, 99, 118f.
49 *Ibid.*, 114.
50 *Ibid.*, 101.

portunities;[51] maintenance undertaken on behalf of the trainee by his parents; and direct outlays for training paid to the employer. But the point is that over a working lifetime there must yet be a *net* differential paid to the skilled to assure that adequate supplies of the skill in question will be forthcoming. This net return is interpreted as a form of interest payment and represents an important amplification of the initial discussion of a differential compensation for 'superior skill' or 'ingenuity' which accounted only for the psychic costs relating to the 'toil and trouble' of training.

It has been suggested that the interest return may be legitimately interpreted as a compensation for the psychic cost involved in postponing consumption during the period of training.[52] But, as we shall see presently, there is nothing in Smith's general approach to interest which suggests recognition of a need for special inducement to assure the postponement of present consumption, and it is accordingly not apparent that the interpretation is legitimate. It appears to be the case that Smith's analysis is incomplete; taking the existence of an interest rate for granted, he argued that any investment in a given direction (such as on training) must earn 'at least the ordinary rate' available in other directions. But in taking this short cut he failed to demonstrate that money-wage differentials, insofar as they reflect a return to investment in training, are reduced by the market to equal monetary returns per unit of *disutility*.

The remaining amplifications – apart from the basic 'agreeableness or disagreeableness of the employment themselves' – may now be considered. While the differences in the 'regularity of employment' envisaged by Smith are seasonal, it is nonetheless recognized that in equilibrium a net compensatory payment will appear even in the *annual* return to workers in unsteady employments to compensate for 'those anxious and desponding moments which the thought of so precarious a situation must sometimes occasion.'[53]

The differential accounted for in terms of the degree of 'trust' is more difficult to appreciate. Only to the extent that the adoption of responsibility entails a psychic burden is the argument consistent with the view of wage differentials as compensatory payments. This element appears to be present in the argument; but in addition Smith suggests[54] that the superior earnings of professionals – doctors, lawyers etc. – are necessary to assure them 'that rank in the society which so important a trust requires,' which can scarcely be interpreted as a disutility compensation.[55]

By the fifth feature whereby in equilibrium the monetary return must allow for the differing degrees of chance of success, Smith (apparently) had in mind

51 'During the continuance of the apprenticeship,' for example, 'the whole labour of the apprentice belongs to his master' (*ibid.*, 102).
52 Douglas, 'Smith's Theory of Value and Distribution,' 83.
53 *Wealth of Nations*, 103.
54 *Ibid.*, 105.
55 J.S. Mill understood this return to be a kind of monopoly payment. Cf. J.M. Robson, ed., *Collected Works of John Stuart Mill*, vol. II, *Principles of Political Economy* (Toronto, 1965), 385.

high returns as a compensation not only for the 'tedious and expensive education' involved – the direct disutility of training – but also for that of those who failed in the race. As in the preceeding case, it may be noted that only if the adoption of risk is a disutility can the argument be easily fitted into the general framework. In point of fact, the observed tendency for people to over-estimate their chance of *outstanding* success and to crowd into professions promising a *small* likelihood of very great profits – a tendency which in practice is said to impede full achievement of an equilibrium wage structure – would suggest that the adoption of risk is not a psychic burden.

The discussion of the wage structure should, however, be evaluated in its own right, as an essential part of the basic model of resource allocation, and not only as the foundation for the measure of the 'real value' of national income defined in terms of labour disutility. And from this broader view it must be acknowledged to be a remarkable achievement.[56]

56 It is, of course, true that substantial work had already been done on the concept of a competitive wage structure, particularly by Richard Cantillon, and Sir James Steuart. And the subsequent criticisms of Smith's analysis by J.S. Mill are very well made.

Smith recognized that monetary returns in any occupation must in equilibrium suffice to indemnify education costs, but failed to consider the possibility that returns might persist which exceed the amount required, apart from instances of excessive returns due to institutional constraints upon entry into skilled trades. In fact, Mill argued, both financial and social obstacles prevented the attainment of skills by sufficiently large numbers to assure the eradication of monopoly returns in skilled trades even in the absence of institutional constraints. In the *Wealth of Nations* the analysis of the wage structure referred essentially to the earnings of the 'working class'; professional men were a non-competing group. The recognition by Mill that *within* the working class there were non-competing groups was the essence of the change. Cf. *Principles of Political Economy*, 386–7.

But Mill's objections went further. According to Smith it was to be expected that the least pleasant occupations would be, *ceteris paribus*, the highest paid. It was pointed out by Mill that at best – that is apart from the presence of impediments to mobility which hamper the process of net equalization – the result envisaged presumes that the aggregate labour market is in equilibrium. Should unemployment exist in the labour force as a whole, it is likely that the least agreeable (and unskilled) trades would be the worst paid since the excess supply would tend to be relatively greater in such trades (*ibid.*, 383) : 'If the labourers in the aggregate, instead of exceeding, fell short of the amount of employment, work which was generally disliked would not be undertaken, except for more than ordinary wages. But when the supply of labour so far exceeds the demand that to find employment at all is an uncertainty, and to be offered it on any terms a favour, the case is totally the reverse. Desirable labourers, those whom every one is anxious to have, can still exercise a choice. The undesirable must take what they can get. The more revolting the occupation, the more certain it is to receive the minimum of remuneration, because it devolves on the most helpless and degraded, on those who from squalid poverty, or from want of skill and education, are rejected from all other employments. Partly from this cause, and partly from the natural and artificial monopolies ... the inequalities of wages are generally in an opposite direction to the equitable principle of compensation erroneously represented by Adam Smith as the general law of the remuneration of labour.' It is a striking phenomenon to find in the work of a

By contrast, the discussion of the competitive profit-rate structure in *Wealth of Nations*, I.x is rather disappointing. Smith rejected as a possible cause of profit-rate differentials the 'constancy or inconstancy of employment' on the grounds that 'whether the stock is or is not constantly employed depends, not upon the trade, but the trader.'[57] The argument is quite extraordinary in light of his acceptance of variations in the regularity of employment between occupations as a basis for wage-rate differentials. If capital is understood in the sense of capital goods – whether fixed capital, materials or wage goods – it is evident that any irregularity peculiar to an occupation which affects labour must also affect capital. It is most likely, therefore, that Smith had uniquely in mind *trading* capital or inventories; the reference throughout to the 'trader' in the present context must be taken seriously. Much the same comment is applicable to Smith's denial that the profit rate structure is unaffected by the differential 'degrees of trust reposed in the traders.'[58] And the discussion relating to differential risk as a determinant of the structure of profit rates turns on the capitalist *qua trader*.[59]

But it is essential to realize that this does not represent the full picture. Even in the chapter at hand Smith shows some concern with the capitalist employer of labour; new manufactures, and new agricultural practices – as well as new branches of trade – yield rates of profit temporarily out of line with the average.[60] And in the earlier discussion of cost-price determination it is clear that the necessary conditions include full knowledge of profit opportunity deriving not only from changes in the pattern of demand but also from those which lower costs, such as the discovery of new types of inputs.[61] Above all (largely in Books II and III) Smith made an extensive and sophisticated application of the principles of profit-rate equalization – within a development context – to the issue of 'investment priorities' between manufacturing, agriculture, and commerce.[62]

THE ROLE OF UTILITY AND DEMAND

The interpretation offered by Paul H. Douglas in 1928 refers to Smith's rejection of utility as a 'determinant of value,' and attributes to Smith the

leading classical economist, an objection to the Smithian principles of relative wage-rate determination based on the presumption that typically unemployment existed in the labour market as a whole. Excessive or monopoly returns were thus regarded by Mill to be the *rule*, and to result both from relatively great excess labour supply in unskilled trades, and to various impediments to mobility.

57 *Wealth of Nations*, 105.   58 *Ibid.*
59 *Ibid.*, 110–11.   60 *Ibid.*, 114f.
61 *Ibid.*, 60.
62 See below, Chapter 10.

The profit-rate structure developed in Book II.v ('Of the Different Employment of Capitals'), when supplementd by the additional opportunities relating to investment in the purchase of land in loanable funds discussed at the close of the preceding chapter (*Wealth of Nations*, 340), has much in common with A.R.J. Turgot's analysis in his *Reflections on the Formation and Distribution of Riches* (1766, publ. 1769–70); see above, 50.

view that utility 'is not even a necessary prerequisite of exchange value.' The reason for the abandonment of utility as a determinant of value by Smith (and his successors) lies, it is suggested by Douglas, in the comparison of the total utilities yielded by varying types of objects rather than their marginal utilities. Smith's emphasis upon water as a *class* and diamonds as a *class* was the source of the error and represented a real challenge for the development of marginal analysis.[63]

In their well-known account, Professors Robertson and Taylor do not contend that Smith actually rejected utility as a determinant of value. But they seek to *explain* what they believe is the novel orientation of the *Wealth of Nations*. For while Francis Hutcheson – whose position is traced via Gershom Carmichael to Pufendorf and ultimately to the Scholastics and Aristotle – had placed the emphasis firmly 'on the two basic elements of use-fulness and scarcity,' Smith makes only the briefest *explicit* reference to utility (in the paragraph dealing with 'value-in-use and value-in-exchange') con-cluding the discussion of value with an analysis in terms of production costs and the introduction of a labour standard, 'utility or "value-in-use" having been dismissed from the scene.' And scarcity – both the term and the concept – is accorded little attention at the 'critical point' in the analysis.[64] In point of fact, a similar contrast is drawn between the *Wealth of Nations* and the *Lectures* with their 'perceptive connection and lucid linking together in a basic and fundamental explanation of utility, scarcity and demand.'[65] These contrasts indicate, it is suggested, 'a major turning point in the history of economic thought.'[66] For those who adopt the approach to economics which emphasizes the essential roles of scarcity and utility 'there can be only regret' for Smith's emphasis in the *Wealth of Nations*, 'which led on to at least a serious under-emphasis on, and, at times, to the almost complete eclipse of these ideas in British political economy for nearly a hundred years.'[67] In their own view Smith's position may be accounted for in terms of a concern with the long-run causes of variation in (per capita) real national income for which issue deep analysis of the nature of demand and its utility underpinning had little purpose.[68]

In our view these commentaries do not do justice to Smith's position. In the first place, while it is indeed essential to take into account the orientation of his predecessors, the general picture is *not* one of such overwhelming emphasis upon utility and scarcity as has been suggested, and accordingly it seems inappropriate to perceive as a 'problem' requiring a 'solution' Smith's deliberations regarding costs even if they were markedly 'one sided' in their

63 Douglas, 'Smith's Theory of Value and Distribution,' 78.
64 Robertson and Taylor, 'Adam Smith's Approach to the Theory of Value,' 181–4.
65 *Ibid.*, 187.
66 *Ibid.*, 185.
67 *Ibid.*, 188. E. Kauder, 'Genesis of the Marginal Utility Theory,' *Economic Journal*, LXIII (Sept. 1953), 650, takes the position that Smith 'made waste and rubbish out of the thinking of two thousand years.'
68 Robertson and Taylor, 'Adam Smith's Approach to the Theory of Value,' 191–3.

emphasis. We have seen[69] that Aristotle, Aquinas and subsequently the later Scholastics (such as Molina, Lugo, and Lessius) when considering the *determination* of price placed greater emphasis upon costs than upon utility and demand, although it is true that utility was frequently envisaged as a necessary *condition*, or even as the 'cause' or 'source,' of value. But it is Pufendorf's contribution that must be noted with great care. He defined the 'foundation' of price as the 'aptitude of a thing or action, by which it can either mediately or immediately contribute something to the necessity of human life, or to making it more advantageous and pleasant.' And the actual *determinant* of price is said to depend not only on 'the need for the article but also on its scarcity.'[70] But this discussion pertains to the state of 'nature' where exchange occurs between the parties by way of a bargaining process. In organized states the so-called 'natural price' is relevant, defined as a price set by those 'who are sufficiently acquainted with both the merchandise and the market' in light of the labour, the expenses 'commonly' incurred, with an allowance for a moderate 'profit.' A temporary market price was also recognized determined by relative scarcity. But no adequate account was provided of the precise relationship envisaged between the market and cost prices, an observation which may be applied equally to the Scholastic literature. A fundamental hiatus thus remained and Hutcheson did not contribute to further elucidation of the issue. Finally, it must be added that in the discussions by the leading eighteenth century 'lay' contributors, particularly Cantillon and Steuart (and previously Petty), the orientation is without question towards cost price, the means of reducing all cost elements to a common unit, and the nature of profit. And once again the precise process by which the long-run ('normal') cost price emerges left much to be desired.

It is, therefore, scarcely surprising that Smith showed great concern with the nature of cost price, and the processes whereby a tendency of price towards costs is assured in the long run. As for Smith's approach in the *Lectures*, there is at least as much concern with production costs and long-run price as there is with the market price. And we have noted the preliminary attempt to combine the conceptions into a theory of allocation. But there is also no convincing evidence to indicate an unconcern with utility and demand in the *Wealth of Nations* relative to that reported in the *Lectures*. The source of the view to the contrary appears to lie in Smith's adoption of a labour commanded index of 'real value'; his comments on 'value-in-use'; and the restriction of the analysis of long-run price in Book I.vii to constant-cost industries.

The choice of a labour-command index of 'real value,' it will be recalled, had a two-fold objective. On the one hand, it was intended to provide a measure of the *disutility* represented by the effort counterpart of the national income; on the other, it was intended as an indirect measure of purchasing power over commodities since 'every man is rich or poor according to the degree in which he can afford to enjoy the necessaries, conveniencies and

69 See Chapter 1.
70 Above, 31.

amusements of human life.' There can thus be no question of the ultimate 'subjective' orientation of Smith's argument and the choice of index is evidence thereof rather than evidence to the contrary.

In Smith's unhappy contrast between 'value-in-use' and 'value-in-exchange,' according to which 'the things which have the greatest value in use have frequently little or no value in exchange' while 'those which have the greatest value in exchange have frequently little or no value in use,'[71] the term 'value-in-use' must be understood in the narrow sense of biological significance and not in the economist's broad sense of desirability. The proposition amounts to an insistence that physical properties of commodities are quite irrelevant in the determination of exchange value. It is solely this category of utility which Smith rejected as a value determinant and, indeed, as a necessary condition of exchange value. From his observations in this regard we can learn nothing of his position regarding the relationship between price and utility in the sense of desirability.[72]

There is, in fact, no evidence that Smith rejected utility in the latter sense as a necessary condition of exchange value. The contrary is without any question true as is clear, for example, from the following extract (from Book II.v; 'Of the Different Employment of Capitals') which is quite unambiguous: 'Unless a capital was employed in manufacturing that part of the rude produce which requires a good deal of preparation before it can be fit for use and consumption, it either would never be produced, because there could be no demand for it; or if it was produced spontaneously, it would be of no value in exchange, and could add nothing to the wealth of the society' (341). Similarly, we may refer to Smith's discussion of the causes of price variations over time in the case of the 'materials of cloathing and lodging,' which evidently constitute a class possessing high 'value-in-use' (in a biological sense), yet whose 'usefulness' (per unit) in the sense of desirability varies with quantity: 'In the one state [an early state of development] ... there is always a super-abundance of those materials, which are frequently, upon that account,

---

71 *Wealth of Nations*, 28.
72 Professor Douglas, 'Smith's Theory of Value and Distribution,' 80, goes to some lengths to account for Smith's so-called rejection of utility 'as a possible cause of value' in terms of his 'moralistic sense.' 'Of course,' Douglas remarks, 'as the moralists from Ruskin on have pointed out, economic values are not necessarily moral values.' But according to our understanding of the discussion in the *Wealth of Nations*, this is precisely the point which *Smith* was making.

It may also be noted that, in Smith's view, a commodity might be of high use value because of its cultural properties, and not merely by dint of biology: 'By necessaries I understand, not only the commodities which are indispensably necessary for the support of life, but whatever the custom of the country renders it indecent for creditable people, even of the lowest order, to be without ... Under necessaries therefore, I comprehend, not only those things which nature, but those things which the established rules of decency have rendered necessary to the lowest rank of people. All other things I call luxuries; without meaning by this appelation, to throw the smallest degree of reproach upon the temperate use of them.' (*Wealth of Nations*, 821–2.)

of little or no value. In the other there is often a scarcity, which necessarily augments their value. In the one state a great part of them is thrown away as useless ... In the other they are all made use of, and there is frequently a demand for more than can be had ...' (161–2). The role actually accorded utility in the broad sense is equally clear in the following discussion of the demand for precious metals, which is based on a wide variety of desirable characteristics, which happens to include their 'value in use.' Thus 'the demand for those metals arises partly from their utility, and partly from their beauty'; in fact, their '*principal merit* ... arises from their beauty, which renders them peculiarly fit for the ornaments of dress and furniture.' In addition some reference is made to the phenomenon of conspicuous consumption: 'The merit of their beauty is greatly enhanced by their scarcity. With the greater part of rich people, the chief enjoyment of riches consists in the parade of riches, which in their eye is never so complete as when they appear to possess those decisive marks of opulence which nobody can possess but themselves.' To these determinants of general desirability Smith adds finally the *utilitarian* demand for the metals arising from their monetary function: 'That employment ... by occasioning a new demand, and by diminishing the quantity which could be employed in any other way, may have ... contributed to keep up or increase its value.'[73]

We may now draw together the elements which constitute Smith's position. The 'paradox of value' was not formulated as a *problem* requiring a *solution*; it was rather a statement of fact regarding the irrelevance for exchange value of the physical (biological or cultural) properties of commodities. Smith did not reject utility in the economist's sense of the term as a necessary condition of exchange value; on the contrary he accounted for the latter in terms of utility and scarcity in the traditional manner. Needless to say, the latter approach was not water-tight because of the absence of an explicit incremental conception, but this 'deficiency' did not *preclude* an explanation of price in terms of relative scarcity.[74] Moreover, the explanation was not considered to be in conflict with the theory of price which runs in terms of production costs.[75] The subsequent development of marginal utility certainly

73 *Ibid.*,172.

74 It was the view of Professor Schumpeter that while the paradox of value had long been resolved in terms of the concept of relative scarcity Smith (by 'dismissing' value-in-use) barred 'for the next two or three generations, the door so auspiciously opened by his French and Italian predecessors' (*History of Economic Analysis*, 309). It is clear from our account that we cannot accept this view. But what must be noted is the following observation regarding Galiani, who is said to be the most proficient of Smith's predecessors: 'What separates Galiani from Jevons and Menger is, first, that he lacked the concept of marginal utility – though the concept of relative scarcity comes pretty near it – and, second, that he failed to apply his analysis to the problems of cost and distribution' (301). In our view the first observation applies equally to Smith who made full use of the concept of relative scarcity and, in addition, made considerable progress towards the resolution of the second set of problems.

75 Thus with regard to the preceding extract relating to conspicuous consumption

improved the treatment of price in terms of relative scarcity. We must, how-ever, try to avoid an outlook narrowly constrained by the marginalist principles of 1871. There is a strong element of truth in the observation that the history of demand theory is not to be identified with the history of utility.[76] Despite the absence of a formal notion of marginal utility – the lack of which, from a modern perspective, may not be a deficiency at all – Smith made extensive use, in a variety of applied economic problems of a theory of *choice*.

Where a hierarchy of basic wants exists there is little scope for a theory of choice; the significance of demand theory is much diminished in the event that substitution in consumption is 'technically' precluded. The presumption that at the time Smith wrote wage goods consisted of a few primary products has done much to establish the supposed negligability of the role of demand in the *Wealth of Nations*. In point of fact Smith was thoroughly aware of the complexity even of the working-class budget, and the role of relative commodity prices in the choice of the basket is given great attention.

That the working-class budget was envisaged to be sophisticated is clear from Smith's analysis of changes in the 'cost-of-living.' While technical pro-gress was reducing the prices of a number of consumer goods (potatoes, carrots, turnips, cabbages, apples, onions, coarser woollens and linens, coarser metals, furniture), increased taxes were having the opposite effect in other cases (soap, candles, salt, leather, liquor).[77] Now it is conceded by Smith that if certain prices rise and others fall 'it becomes a matter of more nicety to judge how far the rise in the one may be compensated by the fall in the other.' But it was his belief that in contemporary circumstances real labour incomes were rising, for the quantity of those relatively more expensive items 'which the labouring poor are under any necessity of consuming, is so very small, that the increase in their price does not compensate the diminution in that of so many other things.'[78] This particular observation may refer only to the small weight attached to certain items in an actual basket. But elsewhere Smith understood that consumers might be in a position to *substitute* relatively cheap

Smith refers to the 'enhancement' of the 'merit' of a commodity 'by its scarcity, or by the great labour which it requires to collect any considerable quantity of it' *Wealth of Nations*, 172). See also below (140–1) for a further illustration.

For a similar view, see also Andrew Skinner, 'Introduction,' *Wealth of Nations* (Penguin Books, 1970), 48–9.

76 G.J. Stigler, 'The Development of Utility Theory,' *Journal of Political Economy*, LVIII (Aug./Oct. 1950), reprinted in Stigler, *Essays in the History of Economics*, 70.

77 *Wealth of Nations*, 78. Smith also points out that the contemporary upward trend in the prices of a number of animal foods (poultry, fish, wild fowl, venison) was less important than the fall in the price of potatoes and maize for the working class. (Butcher's meat generally was no longer rising; and the current rise in corn prices although significant was abnormal and merely due to bad harvests.): 'They suffer more, perhaps, by the artificial rise which has been occasioned by taxes in the price of some manufactured commodities; as of salt, soap, leather, candles, malt, beer, and ale, &c.' (*ibid.*, 242). We should also recall Smith's discussion of the choice in terms of relative price between coal and wood for domestic heating (*ibid.*, 165–7).

78 *Ibid.*, 242, and 78 respectively.

for relatively expensive items. The implications of the recognition of substitutability in consumption are of considerable importance. For it was Smith's view, which we shall presently discuss in some detail, that only to the extent that workers devote their rising command over commodities towards specific categories would a population response be set in motion. In principle, the government might, by the judicious imposition of excise taxes, *direct* consumption away from 'luxuries' and towards these categories: 'The high price of such commodities ["luxuries"] does not necessarily diminish the ability of the inferior ranks of people to bring up families. Upon the sober and industrious poor, taxes upon such commodities act as sumptuary laws, and *dispose them either to moderate, or to refrain altogether from the use of superfluities which they can no longer easily afford.*'[79]

It is, at the same time, noted that substitution is much limited in the case of certain lower-class consumers – 'the dissolute and disorderly' – who 'might continue to indulge themselves in the use of such commodities after this rise in price in the same manner as before.' In effect, demand elasticity is here analysed in terms of the extent of substitutability in consumption; and alternative patterns of tastes are recognized for the 'typical' consumer in different social groupings. (It will also be recalled that Smith elsewhere gave a second rationalization for the degree of elasticity which turned on the fraction of the budget absorbed by the commodity in question; the smaller the fraction, the less the price-consciousness of the consumer.)

As a second illustration of the role of substitution in consumption we note Smith's observation, already considered above, that the price of wood imposes a ceiling upon the price of coal, or in other words, that the demand for coal becomes perfectly elastic at a specific level because of the availability of an excellent alternative. (The observation, at the same time, illustrates admirably the significance of utility in the broad sense of 'desirability') : 'Coals are a less agreeable fewel than wood; they are said too to be less wholesome. The expence of coals, therefore, at the place where they are consumed, must generally be somewhat less than that of wood.'[80]

The analysis of rationing over time provides a further significant illustration of the role accorded demand by Smith. The function of the corn dealer (or speculator) is to assure that corn stocks last from harvest to harvest:

It is the interest of the people that their daily, weekly, and monthly consumption, should be proportioned as exactly as possible to the supply of the season. The interest of the inland corn dealer is the same. By supplying them, as nearly as he can judge, in this proportion, he is likely to sell all his corn for the highest price, and with the greatest profit; and his knowledge of the state of the crop, and of his daily, weekly, and monthly sales, enable him to judge, with more or less accuracy, how far they really are supplied in this manner (491).

It is by the judicious use of prices that the rationing process is undertaken by the dealer:

79 *Ibid.*, 823 (author's emphasis). See discussion below, 161–2.　　　80 *Ibid.*, 165.

It is his interest to raise the price of his corn as high as the real scarcity of the season requires, and it can never be his interest to raise it higher. By raising the price he discourages the consumption, and puts every body more or less, but particularly the inferior ranks of people, upon thrift and good management. If, by raising it too high, he discourages the consumption so much that the supply of the season is likely to go beyond the consumption of the season, and to last for some time after the next crop begins to come in, he runs the hazard, not only of losing a considerable part of his corn by natural causes, but of being obliged to sell what remains of it for much less than what he might have had for it several months before. If by not raising the price high enough he discourages the consumption so little, that the supply of the season is likely to fall short of the consumption of the season, he not only loses a part of the profit which he might otherwise have made, but he exposes the people to suffer before the end of the season, instead of the hardships of a dearth, the dreadful horrors of a famine (490–1).

It is Smith's conclusion that government intervention in the corn trade was ruinous precisely because of its neglect of the effects of low price upon the rate of consumption.[81]

The tradition that Smith 'played down' demand analysis derives as well from almost exclusive concentration upon the chapter 'Of the Natural and Market Price of Commodities' (I.vii) which utilizes the assumption that industries are characterized by constant cost conditions. But this chapter was designed for a specific purpose, namely to elucidate the fundamental propositions regarding resource allocation. For this purpose the assumption of constant costs was adequate. It is quite clear, however, that it did not represent Smith's typical position regarding cost conditions. The issue can best be appreciated as an aspect of the 'dynamics of consumption.'

Smith categorized agricultural produce (other than corn)[82] into broad classes according to the secular pattern of price movement. The first category includes all those items which are more-or-less fixed in supply – for example, rare birds, fishes, and game – and which face a demand which is continually increasing as (real) incomes rise: 'The quantity of such commodities, therefore, remaining the same, or nearly the same, while the competition to purchase them is continually increasing, their price may rise to any degree of extravagance, and seems not to be limited by any certain boundary.'[83] By contrast are instances of products amenable to increase in response to secularly rising demand. The analysis of these latter cases is eloquent testimony to Smith's full recognition of the economic significance of scarcity and at the same time illustrates the fact that the 'explanation' of price in terms of 'supply and demand' or 'relative scarcity' was not regarded as an 'alternative' to that in terms of costs. The scarcity approach was not, to rephrase our contention, restricted to the analysis of 'market price.' We refer to Smith's observation

---

81 *Ibid.*, 493–4.
82 The implications of this exception are considered in Chapter 5.
83 *Wealth of Nations*, 218.

that in the course of economic development the extensions of tillage on the one hand, and consequent reductions in the supply of cattle hitherto available on the wilds as free goods (that is at zero cost), and rising demand on the other – related both to increasing population and real purchasing power per head – tend to force up cattle prices ultimately rendering the production of butcher's meat profitable, at which time some land areas, initially prepared for cereals, will be utilized for commercial cattle raising. A (long-run) price ceiling is, therefore, ultimately imposed as demand for butcher's meat continues to rise. (A similar analysis is made of cattle rearing for dairy products) :

The second sort of rude produce of which the price rises in the progress of improvement, is that which human industry can multiply in proportion to the demand. It consists in those useful plants and animals, which, in uncultivated countries, nature produces with such profuse abundance, that they are of little or no value, and which, as cultivation advances are therefore forced to give place to some more profitable produce. During a long period in the progress of improvement, the quantity of these is continually diminishing, while at the same time the demand for them is continually increasing. Their real value, therefore, the real quantity of labour which they will purchase or command, gradually rises, till at last it gets so high as to render them as profitable a produce as any thing else which human industry can raise upon the most fertile and best cultivated land. When it has got so high it cannot well go higher. If it did, more land and more industry would soon be employed to increase their quantity (219–20).[84]

The third category includes all those cases where output variation in response to expanding demand is 'either limited or uncertain.' The category covers wool and hides (which are treated as joint products with the carcass). Even in an underdeveloped economy there is sufficient demand, emanating from the world market if not domestically, for wool and hides to assure commercial preparation. The secular increase in domestic real incomes, therefore, has a much smaller (relative) effect upon the total demand for such products than in the case of butcher's meat. But the supply of wool and hides will be affected along with that of butcher's meat as the latter is increased in response to expanding demand.[85]

The category also includes commodities produced at increasing cost. The following statement relating to the fisheries contains a clear formulation of diminishing *average* returns as output increases in response to secularly rising demand:

But it will generally be impossible to supply the great and extended market without employing a quantity of labour greater than in proportion to what had been requisite for supplying the narrow and confined one. A market which, from requiring only one thousand, comes to require annually ten thousand ton of fish, can seldom be supplied

84 Cf. also *ibid.*, 148–9, 239–40. The issue will be taken up again in our discussion of distribution.
85 *Ibid.*, 228f.

without employing more than ten times the quantity of labour which had before been sufficient to supply it. The fish must generally be sought for at a greater distance, larger vessels must be employed, and more expensive machinery of every kind made use of. The real price of this commodity, therefore, naturally rises in the progress of improvement (235).[86]

Contrasting with agricultural cost conditions[87] are those of manufacturing industry. Smith predicted in the case of manufactured goods a *downward* secular trend in (real) costs. In light of the role accorded scale economies in the *Wealth of Nations* these instances take on particular importance. It follows that an increase in demand from an initial state of full industry equilibrium will cause an increase in price in the short run only, while the new long-run equilibrium price is below the initial level. This conclusion is clearly stated by Smith as follows: 'The increase of demand, besides, though in the beginning it may sometimes raise the price of goods, never fails to lower it in the long run. It encourages production, and thereby increases the competition of producers, who, in order to undersell one another, have recourse to new divisions of labour and new improvements of art, which might never otherwise have been thought of.'[88]

Little purpose is served by *strict* conceptualization of the preceding observations in terms of the modern distinction between a change in the production function and a movement along a given production function to hitherto inappropriate areas. It would appear that Smith had in mind a combination of the two notions. For while he refers to the adoption of *newly* generated technology, the requisite development clearly is undertaken by large firms only and is visualized as an almost automatic consequence of size.[89] A second charac-

---

86 Smith refers elsewhere to different processes available in the white-herring fishing industry. Fishing can be undertaken by relatively large size 'busses or decked vessels' or by smaller boats. (A tonnage subsidy granted to the industry had in fact encouraged the use of the former method in Scotland.) But the economic choice, in the absence of the subsidy, between the processes, is explained in terms of the nature of the fisheries, or the scale at which it is undertaken, rather than the factor-price structure: 'the mode of fishing for which this tonnage bounty in the white herring fishery has been given (by busses or decked vessels from twenty to eighty tons burthen), seems not so well adapted to the situation of Scotland as to that of Holland; ... Holland lies at a great distance from the seas to which herrings are known principally to resort; and can, therefore, carry on that fishery only in decked vessels, which can carry water and provisions sufficient for a voyage to a distant sea. But [the Scottish coastlines] are everywhere intersected by arms of the sea ... A boat fishery, therefore, seems to be the mode of fishing best adapted to the peculiar situation of Scotland: the fishers carrying the herrings on shore, as fast as they are taken, to be either cured or consumed fresh' (*ibid.*, 486–7). It is clear that Smith had in mind the resort to more expensive methods at large scale involving the use of busses.

87 It will be made clear presently that rising cost conditions are not attributed to the production of *corn* itself.

88 *Wealth of Nations*, 706.

89 The view that cost-reducing methods – utilizing machinery for their embodiment – would be introduced by large firms appears to be an extension of the view that the

teristic of the Smithian treatment is the absence of a true theory of the firm, and thus of the limits to the output of the firm. Smith simply takes for granted – without formal justification – that the size of the average productive unit will rise along with the expansion of the industry. Thirdly, the predictions regarding unit costs take into account alterations in input prices. It is Smith's contention, for which no analytical support is provided, that unit labour requirements will fall sufficiently to outweigh the effects of rising wage rates.

Yet whatever the conceptual difficulties involved in Smith's account there can be no question of the general principle, namely that 'the increase of demand' in manufacturing 'never fails to lower price in the long run.' It is apparent that the analysis of chapter I.vii ('Of the Natural and Market Price of Commodities'), which is strictly limited to the case of constant long-run costs, is not representative of Smith's general position according to which demand plays a fundamental role in the long run as well as in the short run. Moreover, while Smith's conception of competition as entailing *rivalry* in a race to obtain or to discard supplies appears more appropriate from the viewpoint of traders or dealers, the same notion also appears in the present treatment of cost-price determination which involves decisions regarding production on the part of resource owners; thus an increase in demand in the long run 'encourages production, and thereby increases the competition of producers, who, in order to undersell one another, have recourse to new divisions of labour and new improvements of art.' Smith's concept was an all-embracing one.

---

use of machinery is dependent upon prior subdivision of labour, which in turn is dependent upon large-scale operations: 'As the operations of each workman are gradually reduced to a greater degree of simplicity, a variety of new machines come to be invented for facilitating and abridging those operations' (*ibid.*, 260).

The theory of distribution

Smith's predominant concern in those chapters of the *Wealth of Nations* which deal with the returns to the three factors of production was, in Cannan's terminology, with 'pseudo-distribution' or wages per man, profit per cent and rent per acre, as distinct from 'distribution proper' or aggregate wages, profits and rent as shares in the total national product.[1] But Smith did comment upon the latter issue and we shall first consider briefly his position within the context of national-income accounting as developed in the *Wealth of Nations*.

THE NATIONAL INCOME ACCOUNTS

At certain junctures Smith took the position that *all* payments by the individual firm during the annual period can be reduced to those made to the factors land, labour, and capital. In the following passage, for example, the case for treatment of depreciation as a separate cost category is rejected:

In every society the price of every commodity finally resolves itself into some one or other, or all of those three parts [wages, profits, rent]; and in every improved society, all the three enter more or less, as component parts, into the price of the far greater part of commodities ... These three parts seem either immediately or ultimately to make up the whole price of corn. A fourth part, it may perhaps be thought, is neces-

---

1 Edwin Cannan, *A History of the Theories of Production and Distribution From 1776 to 1848*, 3rd ed. (1917; New York, 1967), 180–1.

It is important to keep in mind that throughout his analysis of the *average* returns to the factors, and their movement over time, Smith takes for granted that the wage structure will be largely unchanged. This assumption is not merely a simplifying device – such as that subsequently adopted by Ricardo – but reflects an empirical belief that the structure 'seems not to be much affected by the riches or poverty, the advancing, stationary, or declining state of the society. Such revolutions in the public welfare, though they affect the general rates both of wages and profit, must in the end affect them equally in all different employments' (*Wealth of Nations*, 143; cf. 63).

sary for replacing the stock of the farmer, or for compensating the wear and tear of his labouring cattle, and other instruments of husbandry. But it must be considered that the price of any instrument ... is itself made up of the three parts (50).

A formal extension of the proposition to the national income is then made:

As the price or exchangeable value of every particular commodity, taken separately, resolves itself into some one or other, or all of those three parts; so that of all the commodities which compose the whole annual produce of the labour of every country, taken complexly, must resolve itself into the same three parts, and be parcelled out among different inhabitants of the country, either as the wages of their labour, the profits of their stock, or the rent of their land. The whole of what is annually either collected or produced by the labour of every society, or what comes to the same thing, the whole price of it, is in this manner originally distributed among some of its different members. Wages, profit, and rent, are the three original sources of all revenue as well as of all exchangeable value, all other revenue is ultimately derived from some one or other of these (52).[2]

Yet on the matter of the national accounts we may also discern an approach distinguishing *net* national income, made up of wages, rent and profits, from *gross* national income, which also allows for depreciation. In light of the great attention paid throughout the *Wealth of Nations* to the depreciation of fixed capital this latter approach may well reflect Smith's considered opinion. Three features common both to the stock of money and fixed capital are emphasized by Smith. In the first place, money is compared with fixed capital insofar as 'those machines and instruments of trade, &c., require a certain expence, first to erect them, and afterwards to support them, both which expences, though they make a part of the gross, are deductions from the neat revenue of the society.'[3] It will in fact be noted that not only is the maintenance of fixed capital to be deducted from gross revenue to arrive at net revenue but also the *additions* in any year made to the fixed capital stock. This, of course, differs from our accounting practice. But it may be suggested that to neglect to include in net national product the additions to fixed capital does not mean that such additions were believed not to occur. The reason given for the exclusion appears to be the belief that the counterpart of the net revenue of the society is the production of *consumer goods*, that is to say 'the stock reserved for immediate consumption, the subsistence, conveniencies, and amusements of individuals.'[4]

Secondly, money is similar to fixed capital insofar as 'the machines and instruments of trade, &c., which compose the fixed capital either of an individual or of a society, make no part either of the gross or of the neat revenue of either.'[5] Thus the actual stock of equipment is excluded – in conformity with

2 Similar statements are made in Book II. Cf. *Wealth of Nations*, 248, where Smith refers to 'the three great, original and constituent orders of every civilized society, from whose revenue that of every other order is ultimately derived.' Also *ibid.*, 270.

3 *Ibid.*, 273.

4 *Ibid.*   5 *Ibid.*

present-day accounting – from the gross national product. But the argument which is used to support this approach is again one which conflicts with modern practice. It is real goods not money, Smith argues, which represent 'the community's periodical income'; but these real goods are restricted to consumption goods once more, and exclude capital goods: 'Their real riches ... the real weekly or yearly revenue ... must always be great or small in proportion to the quantity of consumable goods which they can all of them purchase.'[6]

Thirdly, Smith argues that all technical improvements which allow simplifications in equipment and consequent reductions in annual maintenance (replacement) costs tend to add to the net national product. In this respect, too, money can be compared with fixed capital. Thus 'every saving in the expence of erecting and supporting those machines, which does not diminish the productive powers of labour, is an improvement of the neat revenue of the society.'[7] But it is not clear if it is only the maintenance of, or both maintenance of and additions to, fixed capital that Smith has in mind here.

It would thus appear that the Smithian accounts after all make special allowance for depreciation. The distinction in particular between the 'gross rent,' or the total payment to the landlord, and 'the neat rent,' or 'what remains free to the landlord,' after deducting not only 'the expence of management' but also the cost of repairs,[8] suggests that Smith, while insisting that the entire national income is a compound of wages, profit and rent, may have *included* within rent and profit an amount representing depreciation.[9]

Two characteristics of the accounting scheme are of particular relevance. In the first place it should be carefully noted that Smith, unlike Ricardo,[10] included within the net income not only profits and rent but also wages. The 'maintenance' or replacement of that part of 'capital' representing wage payments is *not* deducted from gross revenue to arrive at the net national income. The replacement costs of fixed capital are the only deductions.[11] On the other hand, the only category of wage payments which is included is that paid to

6 *Ibid.*, 275.
7 *Ibid.*, 276.
8 *Ibid.*, 270.
9 On Smith's formal resolution of the *total* national income into 'revenue' and the subsequent statements which allow for depreciation of fixed capital, see the unflattering comments by Karl Marx, *Theories of Surplus Value*, Part I (Moscow, n.d.), 95–100.
10 *Principles of Political Economy, The Works and Correspondence of David Ricardo*, ed. P. Sraffa, I (Cambridge, 1951), 347–51. It may be noted, however, that Ricardo here presumed wages to be at subsistence and defined net revenue as that part of national income available for taxation and savings. He himself conceded (*ibid.*, 348n.): 'Perhaps this is expressed too strongly, as more is generally allotted to the labourer under the name of wages, than the absolutely necessary expenses of production. In that case a part of the net revenue of the country is received by the labourer, and may be saved or expended by him; or it may enable him to contribute to the defence of the country.'
11 *Wealth of Nations*, 272. The issue is discussed at length, below, 199f.

'productive' labour – or labour supported by capital – as distinct from 'unproductive' labour which is hired for direct satisfaction out of income or 'revenue.' The wages of such labour, it must be emphasized, represent a transfer payment and not an *original* income: 'a great part of the revenue arising from both the rent of land and the profits of stock, is annually distributed ... in the wages and maintenance of menial servants, and other unproductive labourers.'[12] It is indeed precisely the view that only labour bestowed on the production of material goods was capable of 'adding value,' as distinct from service labour 'which adds to the value of nothing,' which constitutes the rationale for the unfortunate choice of terminology.[13] The fact that all eighteenth-century investigators of national income considered services in this light[14] reflects, it may be suggested, a conceptual difficulty in according like treatment (in neo-classical fashion) to valuable material goods and valuable services, and the labour yielding them. (It is true that the term 'productive' is also sometimes used to designate specifically labour in the *capital-goods* sector, but in general the term includes labour in the *capitalist* sector, whether it produces capital-goods or consumer-goods.)[15]

THE DISTRIBUTIVE SHARES

We may now turn to Smith's brief observations regarding aggregate income shares. At the close of the chapter 'Of the Rent of Land' it is contended that rent, not only in total but as a proportion of national income, tends to rise secularly with 'the extension of improvement and cultivation': 'The real value of the landlord's share, his real command of the labour of other people, not

---

12 *Wealth of Nations*, 838–9.

13 *Ibid.*, 314.

14 Cf. Phyllis Deane and W.A. Cole, *British Economic Growth: 1688–1959*, 2nd ed. (Cambridge, 1967), 279n.

15 The sense of Smith's distinction is well expressed in modern terms by W.A. Lewis, 'Economic Development with Unlimited Supplies of Labour,' *Manchester School of Social and Economic Studies*, XXII (May 1954), 146–7: 'The capitalist sector is that part of the economy which uses reproducible capital and pays capitalists for the use thereof. (This coincides with Smith's definition of productive workers ...) ... The distinction between productive and unproductive workers had nothing to do with whether the work yielded utility, as some neo-classicists have scornfully but erroneously asserted.'

It has been suggested that Smith's interest in the growth of the 'productive' (capitalist) sector at the expense of the service sector was due to the expected expansion of annual produce resulting from the higher productivity and average wages potentially available in the former only. (V.W. Bladen, 'Adam Smith on Productive and Unproductive Labour,' *Canadian Journal of Economics and Political Science*, XXVI (Nov. 1960), 628–9.) But according to our understanding of Smith, while he indeed recognized a wage differential between sectors, it must be borne in mind that since service income, in his view, was 'derivative' and not 'original,' the national income would accordingly rise by the increased earnings generated in the productive sector and it is not necessary to correct for the reduced earnings in the service sector.

only rises with the real value of the produce, but the proportion of his share of the whole produce rises with it.'[16] But in the second book precisely the opposite position is adopted, namely that while rent per acre and aggregate rents had historically tended to rise, the rental share had declined:

In the present state of Europe, the share of the landlord seldom exceeds a third, sometimes not a fourth part of the whole produce of the land. The rent of land, however, in all the improved parts of the society, has been tripled and quadrupled since those ancient times; and this third or fourth part of the annual produce is, it seems, three or four times greater than the whole had been before. In the progress of improvement, rent, though it increases in proportion to the extent, diminishes in proportion to the produce of the land (318).

In the same context it is also contended that aggregate wages tend to rise at a more rapid rate than aggregate rent and profits. Whether the profit share considered alone rises or falls is not clarified; it is merely observed that total profits rise in consequence of an increase in the capital stock which more than compensates for the tendency of the rate of profit on capital to fall.[17]

The contradictory predictions regarding the rental share and the failure to clarify the behaviour of the profit share reflect the absence of a sufficiently rigorous model whereby the issue might be treated. Furthermore, the recognition of rising *total profits* does not fit well with the celebrated observation to the effect that, because of the declining *rate of profit*, the interests 'of those who live by profits' are opposed to those of society as a whole.[18] But the latter proposition is of some historical importance insofar as it constitutes a sharp divergence from an emphasis upon class *harmony* found in physiocratic literature.

FACTOR PRODUCTIVITY

It is sometimes said that in Smith's view labour was the sole productive factor. This attribution is largely based upon passages in the *Wealth of Nations* which regard labour as producing all wealth or as adding all value but as suffering deductions at the hands of capitalists and landowners.[19] For example, we read frequently that in the 'early and rude state of society which precedes both the accumulation of stock and the appropriation of land ... the whole produce of labour belongs to the labourer.'[20] This idyllic state came to be transformed:

As soon as stock has accumulated in the hands of particular persons, some of them will naturally employ it in setting to work industrious people, whom they will supply

16 *Wealth of Nations*, 247. Landlords enjoy an additional advantage deriving from increasingly favourable terms of trade in the exchange between agricultural and manufacturing products, in consequence of technical progress largely affecting the latter.

17 *Ibid.*, 318–9.   18 *Ibid.*, 249–50.

19 Paul H. Douglas, 'Smith's Theory of Value and Distribution,' in J.M. Clark, *et al.*, *Adam Smith, 1776–1926* (Chicago, 1928), 96.

20 *Wealth of Nations*, 47. Cf. 49; 64–5; 79.

with materials and subsistence, in order to make a profit by the sale of their work, or by what their labour adds to the value of the materials. In exchanging the complete manufacture ... something must be given for the profits of the undertaker of the work who hazards his stock in this adventure. The value which the workmen add to the materials, therefore, resolves itself in this case into two parts, of which the one pays their wages, the other the profits of their employer upon the whole stock of materials and wages which he advanced (48).

The capitalist appears simply as a 'grub-staker' who, by his possession of working capital, is able to induce the workers because of their immediate needs to surrender a part of their final product.[21] According to this view, profits represent an income associated with the use of capital in the employment of wage labour, derived as a forced 'deduction' from the value added by labour to the advances. Variations in the profit rate, accordingly, are explained by variations in either or both the demand – in terms of wage advances – and supply of labour.

Similarly with regard to rent Smith stated: 'As soon as the land of any country has all become private property, the landlords, like all other men, like to reap where they never sowed, and demand a rent even for its natural produce.'[22] Here too, rent represents, it is said, a deduction from produce which is entirely due to labour. Let us consider the evidence.

The demand for land services

It must first be noted that Smith is quite emphatic that land is productive when he is not considering the imaginary original society and the imaginary transfer to the modern state; indeed, it is the 'additional' contribution of land to national income which he considers to be one of the main arguments in favour of agricultural investment. Thus we read that in agriculture

nature labours along with man; and though her labour costs no expence, its produce has its value, as well as that of the most expensive workman ... Over and above the capital of the farmer and all its profits, they [labourers and cattle] regularly occasion the reproduction of the rent of the landlord. *This rent may be considered as the produce of those powers of nature, the use of which the landlord lends to the farmer.* It is greater or smaller according to the supposed extent of those powers, or in other words, according to the supposed natural or improved fertility of the land. It is the work of nature which remains after deducting or compensating every thing which can be regarded as the work of man ... No equal quantity of productive labour employed in manufactures can ever occasion so great a reproduction. In them nature does nothing; man does all; and the reproduction must always be in proportion to the strength of the agents that occasion it (344–5; author's emphasis).

Similarly he wrote subsequently: 'The rent of land is paid for the use of a productive subject. The land which pays it produces it.'[23]

21 Douglas, 'Smith's Theory of Value and Distribution,' 104.
22 *Wealth of Nations*, 49. Cf. *ibid.*, 65.
23 *Ibid.*, 794.

It is accordingly more likely that the references to the deduction made by rent from the contribution of the labourer were intended to reflect a change in conditions of scarcity which was envisaged as occurring along with a change in property relationships, rather than a denial of the productivity of land.[24] Land was originally held 'in common' so that there was no distinction between a labouring and land-owning class; the rationing device utilized in such circumstances is nowhere clarified and it is probably taken for granted that land scarcity was not yet apparent. Private property in land, subsequently established, does not of itself entail rent as Smith was perfectly well aware.[25] It is the metamorphosis in property relations which is presumed to have occurred along with manifestations of scarcity which generated a rental income; and the view that 'landlords like to reap where they never sowed and demand a rent even for [the] natural produce' cannot be understood as a denial of the productive contribution of *land*. Neither should the numerous references to the 'produce of the labourer' be understood as an affirmation of the view that only the labourer contributes to production. After all, in that very passage which ascribes to land a productive capacity,[26] we have also read that 'over and above the capital of the farmer and all its profits, they [the productive labourers in agriculture][27] regularly occasion the reproduction of the rent of the landlord.'

The demand for capital services

Should the formal statements attributing output to labour – usually made in the context of the transfer to the modern state – be taken as a denial of the contribution of 'capital' to production? It will be noted that in the key passage referred to earlier which describes the transfer from a simple to a modern economy the strong implication is that such stock existed in the simple economy.[28] That stock comes to be accumulated 'in the hands of particular persons' may then mean that capital was originally utilized in production but was not in the hands of a special class of capitalists distinct from the worker. In brief, the economy, originally, was made up of independent workmen using stock owned by themselves and the return to these artisans included both profits and wages. (What is certain is that the income shares of Smith's day *were* related to separate classes: 'Such cases [of independent workmen], how-

24 Douglas, 'Smith's Theory of Value and Distribution,' 114, touches upon this 'solution,' but contends that Smith made no use of it.
25 See below, 166.
26 Rent is the 'work of nature which remains after deducting or compensating everything which can be regarded as the work of man.'
27 And labouring cattle.
28 'As soon as stock has accumulated *in the hands of particular persons* some of them will naturally employ it in setting to work industrious people.' Similarly, we read further: 'In that original state of things, which precedes both the appropriation of land and the accumulation of stock, the whole produce of labour belongs to the labourer. He has neither landlord nor master to share with him' (*Wealth of Nations*, 64).

ever, are not very frequent, and in every part of Europe, twenty workmen serve under a master for one that is independent; and the wages of labour are everywhere understood to be, what they usually are, when the labourer is one person, and the owner of the stock which employs him another.'[29] Similarly, in discussing the increase in wealth which allows an independent workman to become an employer the emphasis is entirely on the profits earned in setting others to work and not on the implicit profits he may have earned hitherto.[30]) This interpretation allows for the possibility that stock was privately owned even in the simple economy. More likely, capital was not originally used at all, or if used was completely free, while in the modern economy it comes both to be scarce and owned by a separate class of capitalists. In any event, the statements defining profits as 'deductions from the produce of labour' do not seem to bear upon the issue of the productivity of capital.[31] We shall deal in what follows with working and fixed capital respectively.

In the relevant analyses of Book I ('Of the Component Parts of Price'; 'Of Wages'; 'Of Profits') capital or 'stock' is understood largely to refer to materials and subsistence, which are *advanced* to labour by capitalists, and which permit time-consuming processes to be undertaken by specialist labour. But the clearest statement is to be found in the Introduction to Book II:

In that rude state of society in which there is no division of labour, in which exchanges are seldom made, and in which every man provides everything for himself, it is not necessary that any stock should be accumulated or stored up beforehand, in order to carry on the business of the society. Every man endeavours to supply by his own industry his own occasional wants as they occur ...

But when the division of labour has once been thoroughly introduced, the produce of a man's own labour can supply but a very small part of his occasional wants. The far greater part of them are supplied by the produce of other mens labour, which he purchases with the produce, or what is the same thing, with the price of the produce of his own. But this purchase cannot be made till such time as the produce of his own labour has not only been completed, but sold. A stock of goods of different kinds, therefore, must be stored up somewhere sufficient to maintain him, and to supply him with the materials and tools of his work, till such time, at least, as both these events can be brought about. A weaver cannot apply himself entirely to his peculiar business, unless there is beforehand stored up somewhere, either in his own possession or in that of some other person, a stock sufficient to maintain him, and to supply him with the materials and tools of his work, till he has not only completed, but sold his web. This accumulation must, evidently, be previous to his applying his industry for so long a time to such a peculiar business (259).[32]

29 *Ibid.*, 66. 30 *Ibid.*, 69.
31 But see the strictures of Lord Lauderdale, *The Nature and Origin of Public Wealth* (1804; New York, 1962), 117–9; 155–6; 169–70, which taking for granted that in Smith's view land and labour are the only productive factors finds contradictory all statements regarding profits as an original income.
32 Cf. *Lectures on Justice, Police, Revenue and Arms* (1763), ed. E. Cannan (New York, 1964), 181.

We do not intend to enter into a detailed treatment of Smithian conjectural history. But it can be said that Smith was not consistent regarding the proposition that it is only in the 'modern' economy that the division of labour is applied, necessitating wage advances. Certainly at times – as in the passage just cited – Smith did carefully limit the need for accumulations of working capital to the moden economy where alone specialization was undertaken. But sometimes it is implied that the advantages of specialization – and evidently the necessary accumulations – were at least potentially available in the simple economy: 'Had this [simple] state continued, the wages of labour would have augmented with all those improvements in its productive powers, to which the division of labour gives occasion.'[33] That he believed this latter account is doubtful, since he further argued that 'this original state of things, in which the labourer enjoyed the whole produce of his own labour ... was at an end ... long before the most considerable improvements were made in the productive powers of labour, and it would be to no purpose to trace further what might have been its effects upon the recompense or wages of labour.'[34] Moreover, Smith recognized the abysmally *low* living standards which characterized actual primitive societies of his time and this too suggests that we should not take seriously his comment that large productivity increases were potentially available even in the simple economy. Such assertions, however, confirm that the statements referring to profits as deductions from the produce of labour do not refer to the non-productivity of capital, but reflect rather the 'injustice' of profits as a separate class income.

In a broad sense Smith can be said to have recognized the essence of 'capitalistic' production, namely the use of methods involving roundabout processes which yield a higher product than more direct methods, but which require a period of waiting and accordingly 'capital' in the form of wages goods.[35] This of itself is a vital contribution. In a more precise sense he even recognized that refinements in the degree of specialization involves extensions

The passage quoted from Book II does not emphasize the characteristic of profits as representing a deduction from labour's contribution. The following extract from Book I, on the other hand does: 'It seldom happens that the person who tills the ground has wherewithal to maintain himself till he reaps the harvest. His maintenance is generally advanced to him from the stock of a master, the farmer who employs him, and who would have no interest to employ him, unless he was to share in the produce of his labour, or unless his stock was to be replaced to him with a profit ... The produce of almost all other labour is liable to the like deduction of profit. In all arts and manufactures the greater part of the workmen stand in need of a master to advance them the materials of their work, and their wages and maintenance till it is compleated' (65). Smith's analysis both in the *Lectures* and the *Wealth of Nations* is incomplete in that it is limited to the case of the individual. Capital is no longer needed, according to Smith, once the weaver's web is sold; but in fact the function of capital is that it enables *society as a whole* to carry on complicated operations involving lengthy intervals from the beginning of production to the time of enjoyment. (Cf. F.W. Taussig, *Wages and Capital* (1896; New York, 1968), 138.)

33 *Wealth of Nations*, 64.   34 *Ibid.*, 65.

35 Strictly it is the high *value* product which is the truly relevant phenomenon of capitalistic production, and which Smith had in mind, as we shall see. The fuller

in the period of production: this is clear from the fact that the invention of machines is seen to be the result of the division of labour and, in principle, the use of machinery increases the 'roundaboutness' of the process with resultant increases in the productivity of the 'original factors':

As the accumulation of stock must, in the nature of things, be previous to the division of labour, so labour can be more and more subdivided in proportion only as stock is previously more and more accumulated. The quantity of materials which the same number of people can work up, increases in a great proportion as labour comes to be more and more subdivided; and as the operations of each workman are gradually reduced to a greater degree of simplicity, a variety of new machines come to be invented for facilitating and abridging those operations. As the division of labour advances, therefore, in order to give constant employment to an equal number of workmen an equal stock of provisions, and a greater stock of materials and tools than would have been necessary in a ruder state of things, must be accumulated before-hand. But the number of workmen in every branch of business generally increases with the division of labour in that branch, or rather it is the increase of their number which enables them to class and subdivide themselves in this manner (260).

The necessity for stored-up wages goods as a prerequisite for employment is formally stated in the *Lectures* as we have seen. But in the *Wealth of Nations* employment capacity is defined in a more sophisticated fashion to allow for the presence of items in the capital structure apart from wages goods. This is implied in the Introduction itself: 'The number of useful and productive labourers ... is every where in proportion to the quantity of capital stock which is employed in setting them to work, and to the particular way in which it is so employed.'[36] It is also of historical significance that in the passage repro-duced above the emphasis is in one vital respect diverted from wage advances. It is only to the extent that the work force is actually increased – and this is indeed frequently a prerequisite for increased specialization – that added sub-sistence is absolutely required (unless real per capital wages are to fall). Extensions of the period of production (including the use of machines) in the case of a given work force do not necessarily require additional subsistence (although presumably Smith would agree that – to use a Jevonsian term – 'the amount of investment of capital' does increase, the given wage fund remaining invested for an increased length of time).[37] In other words, it is recognized by Smith that capital, at least in principle, may increase in the case of a given

recognition in the English literature of the nature of 'capitalistic' production came only in the neo-classical period of course. Cf. for example, W.S. Jevons, *The Theory of Political Economy*, 1st ed. (London, 1871).

36 *Wealth of Nations*, lviii.

37 See Jevons, *The Theory of Political Economy*, 4th ed. (London, 1911), 229f. The distinction is made between 'the amount of capital invested' which is a stock concept having a quantity dimension only, and the 'amount of investment of capital' which takes into account the time period over which the capital is invested. It should be added that in the event of an increase in subsistence with no change in the period of investment, presumably all that occurs is an increase in the wage rate rather than an increase in productivity.

work force in such a manner as to leave average wages unchanged. In all cases, however – whether or not the labour force is constant – the increased productivity of the 'original' productive factors (land and labour) potentially available from extensions of the period of production can only be accomplished if additional *raw materials* are made available.

Fixed capital, in industry, includes machinery and structures; and in agriculture, it includes land improvements, structures and labouring cattle. More specifically, the community's 'fixed capital' comprises those physical items which yield 'a revenue' or profit without changing masters, namely 'useful machines,' and 'profitable buildings' (which are the means of 'procuring a revenue, not only to their proprietor who lets them for a rent, but to the person who possesses them and pays that rent for them' and are 'a sort of instruments of trade') ; 'improvements in land' and 'acquired and useful abilities' or the 'improved dexterity of [the] workman.'[38] Fixed capital is only introduced by the firm if it is expected that revenue will cover depreciation and yield at least the normal rate of return: 'When any expensive machine is erected, the extraordinary work to be performed by it before it is worn out, it must be expected, will replace the capital laid out upon it, with at least the ordinary profits.'[39] Similarly, 'the expence which is properly laid out upon a fixed capital of any kind, is always repaid with great profit, and increases the annual produce by a much greater value than that of the support which such improvements require.'[40] Moreover, 'wear and tear' as an annual expense is also allowed for.[41]

The basic function of fixed capital is to 'facilitate and abridge labour'; thus, by means of fixed capital 'an equal circulating capital can afford a much greater revenue to its employer.'[42] Similarly, we read that 'the intention of

38 *Wealth of Nations*, 263–6. (It may be noted that Smith here identifies structures and equipment with regard to their effect on labour productivity. This he does not consistently do.)

   In the present context, farm improvements are said to be 'equally advantageous and more durable' than industrial fixed capital, 'frequently requiring no other repairs than the most profitable application of the farmer's capital employed in cultivating it' (265). It should also be remarked that whereas in Book I the return to 'improved dexterity' is included in wages, it is here regarded implicitly as interest. Finally, it is to be noted that Smith is by no means crystal clear whether in fact he intends to distinguish *physical* items as 'fixed' or 'circulating' capital, or whether it is a categorization of *financial funds* according to use. For in the opening pages of the chapter under discussion he in fact seems to have in mind the latter.

39 *Ibid.*, 101.

40 *Ibid.*, 271. Cf. also 344: 'The labourers and labouring cattle, therefore, employed in agriculture, not only occasion, like the workmen in manufactures, the reproduction of a value equal to their own consumption, or of the capital which employs them, together with its owners profits ...'

41 For examples, see *ibid.*, 18; the analysis of repair or maintenance labour, 266–7; and the chapter on Physiocracy where 'original expences' refer to the initial outlay on cattle and instruments by farmers, while 'annual expences' include depreciation (629).

42 *Ibid.*, 265–6.

fixed capital is to increase the productive powers of labour, or to enable the same number of labourers to perform a much greater quantity of work.'[43] In fact, investment in fixed capital is *defined* as 'the purchase of useful machines and instruments of trade, or in such like things as yield a revenue or profit without changing masters, or circulating any further.'[44] The only other means of raising labour productivity apart from the use of fixed capital is an improved 'distribution of employment': the 'productive powers of the same number of labourers cannot be increased, but in consequence either of some addition and improvement to those machines and instruments which facilitate and abridge labour; or of a more proper division and distribution of employment.'[45] It may therefore be accurate to attribute to Smith the view that capital is *primarily* subsistence goods whereas machinery, tools, raw materials (and skill) are 'simply more complicated forms.'[46] (And increases in productivity due proximately to the support of new or improved machinery can be regarded as due, indirectly, to extensions of the time period of production for which additions in the amount of investment of subsistence capital, and actual increases in the amount of working capital, are required.) But it would be illegitimate to conclude that the subsidiary role of capital goods from this point of view implies that the Smithian theory of production can be appreciated without taking the role of machinery into account, since it is through the use of machinery that the effects of the extensions of the time period of production are enjoyed.[47] And from the point of view of distribution it would appear that Smith was attempting to formulate a relationship between the productivity

43 *Ibid.*, 271.
44 *Ibid.*, 263. Although the distinction between what is fixed and what is circulating capital is here drawn in terms of the irrelevant issue of whether or not the item 'stays' with the owner or is 'circulated' by him, there is a parallel definition too which Smith sometimes refers to. Thus in his discussion of banking policy, Smith makes it quite clear that the durability of fixed capital is much greater than that of circulating capital, and on these grounds particular care should be taken to avoid financing of mining and metallurgical projects or agricultural improvements: 'Still less could a bank afford to advance him any considerable part of his fixed capital; ... The returns of the fixed capital are in almost all cases much slower than those of the circulating capital; and such expences ... very seldom return to the undertaker till after a period of many years' (291).
45 *Ibid.*, 326. Cf. 641.
46 Marian Bowley, *Nassau Senior and Classical Economics* (London, 1937), 138.
47 Cf. H. Barkai, 'A Formal Outline of a Smithian Growth Model,' *Quarterly Journal of Economics*, LXXXIII (August 1969), 396–414. It is nevertheless true that Smith warned his reader not to be 'carried away' by the productivity of machinery or of land, however improved. Fixed capital (or land) would be useless without the labour which works and maintains it (*Wealth of Nations*, 266–7).

The tendency to play down the role of fixed capital in discussions of Smithian economics may partly be explained by a failure to consider in context the numerous statements which formally relate the employment capacity of the community to its 'circulating capital.' Many of these statements are made to emphasize the fact that in discussing the employment potential of the economy we must exclude money and focus attention on real capital goods. But money is classified – on the grounds that it 'circulates' – with circulating capital. Thus in emphasizing the role in production of circulating capital, Smith intends not a statement of the irrelevance of fixed

of capital goods and the rate of return on capital comparable to that between the productivity of land and the rental income. Differences between capital and land are to be found in their respective conditions of *supply* as we shall see.

The demand for labour services

Smith's inclusion within 'working capital' of subsistence goods advanced to labour implies the rudiments of the wages-fund theory (although there is no justification for drawing the further conclusion that accordingly the significance of fixed capital was played down). In fact, the only more-or-less full treatment of the *competitive* labour market which Smith provided runs in terms of a variant of the wages-fund theory as we shall see.[48] And the distinctive feature of *advance*s specifically in the case of wage payments is emphasized: 'The workman must always have been fed in some way or other while he was about the work; but the landlord may not always have been paid.'[49]

capital in the production process, but the irrelevance of money. For example, we read:

'When we compute the quantity of industry which the circulating capital of any country can employ, we must always have regard to those parts of it only, which consist in provisions, materials, and finished work: the other, which consists in money, and which serves only to circulate those three, must always be deducted. In order to put industry into motion, three things are requisite; materials to work upon, tools to work with, and the wages or recompence for the sake of which the work is done. Money is neither a material to work upon, nor a tool to work with; and though the wages of the workman are commonly paid to him in money, his real revenue, like that of other men, consists, not in the money, but in the money's worth; not in the metal pieces, but in what can be got for them' (279–80). But there is nothing in these statements which denies the contribution to output of real capital goods.

It should also be added that for certain economic issues it is perfectly legitimate, and indeed helpful, to focus attention on man-hours as representing the 'resources' of the community and exclude the services of land and of existing capital goods. This is illegitimate in dealing with the determination of prices or the distribution of income, but not when the issue is the 'source of wealth.' In this context, it has been suggested, we may regard 'man-time as an original, homogeneous resource, and to introduce the factors which co-operate with man in the guise of "coefficients of transformation" of man-time into products (consumption goods).' (K. Boulding, 'Equilibrium and Wealth,' *Canadian Journal of Economics and Political Science*, V (Feb. 1939), 10.) The coefficient will be high if labour co-operates with large amounts of good land and equipment, or when labour's skill is high, and conversely. But if this does explain Smith's emphasis on *labour* in production, the roles of capital goods and land are still of the greatest significance for the production function, albeit at 'one remove'; and cannot be neglected.

48 The analysis of *imperfections* in the labour market is taken up below, 185f.

49 *Wealth of Nations*, 97. Very frequently Smith speaks of the 'stock' from which wages are derived in money terms – as in his reference to the 'funds destined for the payment of wages' – and introduces thereby a serious source of confusion. It is, nonetheless, clear that Smith's objective was to account for the average *real* wage rate. Taussig, *Wages and Capital*, 145f., has noted that when dealing specifically with wages, Smith tends to use money terms, but when treating capital he comes nearer to the truth in emphasizing the more relevant *real* counterpart (as in II.1).

The characteristic feature of Smith's analysis is the role accorded to the rate of capital accumulation as an 'independent' variable governing the demand for labour, upon which depends the (long-run or secular) real wage rate and the growth rate of population; to each growth rate of labour demand there corresponds a long-run real wage rate which assures an equivalent rate of growth of population, and therefore in the work force.[50] But as was the case with his successors, Smith failed to account adequately for the allocation of total capital between working and fixed capital, and frequently took for granted that a change in the total would be accompanied by a proportionate change in each constituent element. For the present we shall follow this practice.[51]

Smith relied upon competitive market pressures to assure that a wage rate diverging from the long-run 'equilibrium' trend will be corrected; for example, a relatively low wage rate will be forced upwards by a kind of 'Walrasian' competitive process with a subsequent effect upon the growth rate of population:

Every species of animals naturally multiplies in proportion to the means of their subsistence, and no species can ever multiply beyond it. But in civilized society it is only among the inferior ranks of people that the scantiness of subsistence can set limits to the further multiplication of the human species; and it can do so in no other way than by destroying a great part of the children which their fruitful marriages produce.

The liberal reward of labour, by enabling them to provide better for their children, and consequently to bring up a greater number, naturally tends to widen and extend those limits. It deserves to be remarked too, that it necessarily does this as nearly as possible in the proportion which the demand for labour requires. If this demand is continually increasing, the reward of labour must necessarily encourage in such a manner the marriage and multiplication of labourers, as may enable them to supply that continually increasing demand by a continually increasing population. If the reward should at any time be less than what was requisite for this purpose, the deficiency of hands would soon raise it; and if it should at any time be more, their excessive multiplication would soon lower it to this necessary rate. The market would be so much under-stocked with labour in the one case, and so much over-stocked with labour in the other, as would soon force back its price to that proper rate which the circumstances of the society required (79–80).

It is, however, Smith's usual practice to 'short-circuit' the full process, and state simply a relationship between the rate of capital accumulation and the

50 The demand for service labour must also be taken into account. Cf., *Wealth of Nations*, 69.

51 The discussion of extensions in the time-period of production does, at least in principle, allow for the theoretical possibility that net investment may take the form entirely of fixed rather than wage-goods capital with consequent direct effects upon productivity rather than the wage rate.

  A full discussion of the *differential* labour-supporting capacities of equal capitals invested in different sectors of the economy will be found in Chapter 6.

real wage, taking for granted the operation of market processes which assure a corresponding long-run rate of growth in labour supply.[52]

According to the Smithian position, it should be emphasized, an increase in the (long-run) wage rate will occur in consequence of a *change* in the rate of capital accumulation. A steady rate of increase of capital will not alter (long-run) *per capita* wages: 'It is not ... in the richest countries, but in the most thriving, or in those which are growing rich the fastest, that the wages of labour are highest.'[53] But it is not uncommon for Smith to slip into misleading statements according to which a wage increase is related simply to increasing labour demand,[54] although it is true that a 'high' level of wages corresponds to a steady but high growth rate of capital.

Smith also took note of fluctuations in both the demand for, and supply of, labour about the secular path. Thus in 'years of plenty' the demand for labour tends to rise relatively to the supply and conversely in 'years of scarcity.' The operation of 'Walrasian' market processes in such cases should be carefully noted:

It is because the demand for labour increases in years of sudden and extraordinary plenty, and diminishes in those of sudden and extraordinary scarcity, that the money price of labour sometimes rises in the one, and sinks in the other.

In a year of sudden and extraordinary plenty, there are funds in the hands of many of the employers of industry, sufficient to maintain and employ a greater number of industrious people than had been employed the year before; and this extraordinary number cannot always be had. Those masters, therefore, who want more workmen, bid against one another, in order to get them, which sometimes raises both the real and the money price of their labour.

The contrary of this happens in a year of sudden and extraordinary scarcity. The funds destined for employing industry are less than they had been the year before. A considerable number of people are thrown out of employment, who bid against one another, in order to get it, which sometimes lowers both the real and the money price of labour (85–6).[55]

52 In Smith's account a change in the wage rate leaves the secular pattern of demand for labour unaffected. Yet it will be shown presently that this was not invariably the assumption made. On a number of occasions it is conceded that the secular pattern of labour demand may in fact be influenced by wage costs, an allowance which introduces an element of indeterminacy into the analysis. (See below, 180, n.114.)

53 *Wealth of Nations*, 69.

54 For example: 'It is not the actual greatness of national wealth, but its continual increase, which occasions a rise in the wages of labour' (*ibid.*, 69).

55 Cf. *ibid.*, 83, where changes in demand and changes in supply in the opposite direction are said to occur periodically: 'In years of plenty, servants frequently leave their masters, and trust their subsistence to what they can make by their own industry. But the same cheapness of provisions, by increasing the fund which is destined for the maintenance of servants, encourages masters, farmers especially, to employ a greater number. Farmers upon such occasions expect more profit from their corn by maintaining a few more labouring servants, than by selling it at a low price in the market. The demand for servants increases, while the number of those

From this account it appears that (short-run) labour demand is elastic with respect to price, so that the wage rate acts as a rationing device.[56] The emphasis throughout is upon the direction of change in the wage rate rather than the level of wages, which is to be expected in light of the temporary nature of the presumed disturbance.[57]

The foregoing discussion of labour demand should not be understood as implying the absence in the *Wealth of Nations* of any other accounts. Smith talks, at one point, of wages regulated by the 'quantity and supposed value of the work.'[58] And, at another, he relates the demand for labour to the demand for final output; thus a reduction in taxes upon subsistence or raw materials would allow workers 'to work cheaper, and to send their goods cheaper to market. The cheapness of their goods would increase the demand for them, and consequently for the labour of those who produced them. This increase in the demand for labour, would both increase the numbers and improve the circumstances of the labouring poor.'[59] These statements suggest that the wages-fund analysis does not constitute a true 'theory' of wage-rate determination, precisely because Smith failed to explain the allocation of total capital between wages-goods and other items; any genuine theory would require a precise account of the determinants of the magnitude of the wage advances which capitalists choose to make and his loose references to labour productivity in the context of labour demand represent, at most, only a first step in this direction.[60]

who offer to supply that demand diminishes. The price of labour, therefore, frequently rises in cheap years.

In years of scarcity, the difficulty and uncertainty of subsistence makes all such people eager to return to service. But the high price of provisions, by diminishing the funds destined for the maintenance of servants, disposes masters rather to diminish than to increase the number of those they have. In dear years too, poor independent workmen frequently consume the little stocks with which they had used to supply themselves with the materials of their work, and are obliged to become journeymen for subsistence. More people want employment than can easily get it; many are willing to take it upon lower terms than ordinary, and the wages of both servants and journeymen frequently sink in dear years.'

56 But nowhere does Smith formally state, in the manner of some later classical writers, that the wages bill is in some sense *fixed* at the outset of the production period.

57 In any event, it is made clear by G. Rosenbluth, 'A Note on Labour, Wages, and Rent in Smith's Theory of Value,' *Canadian Journal of Economics*, II (May, 1969), 311f., that the equilibrium path itself is not affected by the precise assumptions made regarding the short-run labour demand and the adjustment mechanism. The argument takes for granted the maintenance throughout of a competitive structure.

58 *Wealth of Nations*, 74.

59 *Ibid.*, 890–1.

60 The average wage rate and changes therein depends also upon the demand for and supply of labour in the service sector. It has been suggested that Smith distinguished between wages per head in the two sectors: the productive work force, supported by fixed capital and operating under intelligent management, runs the argument, would have a higher productivity and accordingly higher wages than labour in the service sector where primitive technology reigned. The failure of service workers to move – or to attempt to move – to the better-paying sector and thus equalize

FACTOR SUPPLY

It is clear that Smith's concern was not merely with the physical productivity of factors but with their value productivity. We turn now to consider the precise factor supply conditions which Smith envisaged as defining the 'scarcity' of labour, land, and capital.

Labour supply conditions

A few words are in order at the outset regarding the Smithian approach to contemporary population change. The principal theoretical check to population is said to be infant mortality.[61] The role of the level of subsistence is applied specifically to the 'inferior ranks of people,' such that when wages are at subsistence, working-class population will be constant. But poverty only discourages marriage a little and is even accompanied by a higher birth rate – 'it seems even to be favourable to generation.' It is by way of an increase in the *infantile death rate* that poverty exerts its influence:

But poverty, though it does not prevent the generation, is extremely unfavourable to the rearing of children ... This great mortality, however, will every where be found chiefly among the children of the common people, who cannot afford to tend them with the same care as those of better station. Though their marriages are generally more fruitful than those of people of fashion, a smaller proportion of their children arrive at maturity. In foundling hospitals, and among the children brought up by parish charities, the mortality is still greater than among those of the common people (79).[62]

The upward trend in labour demand and the increased living standards made possible were seen to be stimulating population expansion in Britain largely by way of reductions in the infantile death rate, although a fall in the

marginal products and wages may be explained by immobility, and the need to allow for non-monetary advantages which exist in the traditional sector. (Bladen, 'Adam Smith on Productive and Unproductive Labour,' 625f.) There appears to be some justification for this view insofar as Smith indeed refers to better wages earned in the capitalist sector and the relative poverty of those in the service sector (*Wealth of Nations*, 319). Yet it would perhaps be going too far to accord to Smith any *full* appreciation of a relationship between the wage rate and productivity. Any differential which he perceived might well have been explained in terms of the distinct personal characteristics of labour in the two sectors, that is in terms of the supply side of the market.

61 Although there are some references to a *general* increase in the death rate with poor living standards. Cf. *ibid.*, 83.

62 For further references to population response to changes in the food supply cf. *ibid.*, 164f., 429, 476, 533.

It had earlier been asserted by Hume – in a discussion of equality of income distribution – that improved living standards would assure population expansion: 'The prolific virtue of men, were it to act in its full extent, without that restraint which poverty and necessity imposes on it, would double the number every generation,' *Of the Populousness of Ancient Nations* (1752), in E. Rotwein, ed., *David Hume: Writings on Economics* (London, 1955), 128–9.

general death rate is also noted.[63] It is true that in a celebrated statement Smith compares the slow growth of European population – which scarcely doubles in 500 years – with that of North America – which doubles in some 25 years only. In North America the high earnings available render the 'value of children ... the greatest of all encouragements to marriage,' so that in addition to low infant mortality there is an extremely high birth rate:

The most decisive mark of the prosperity of any country is the increase of the number of its inhabitants. In Great Britain, and most other European countries, they are not supposed to double in less than five hundred years. In the British colonies in North America, it has been found, that they double in twenty or five-and-twenty years. Nor in the present times is this increase principally owing to the continual importation of new inhabitants, but to the great multiplication of the species ... Labour is there so well rewarded that a numerous family of children, instead of being a burthen is a source of opulence and prosperity to the parents ... Notwithstanding the great increase occasioned by such early marriages, there is a continual complaint of the scarcity of hands in North America. The demand for labourers, the funds destined for maintaining them, increase, it seems, still faster than they can find labourers to employ (70–1).[64]

But there is no question, at least in the British case, that Smith was aware of significant population expansion in response to rising labour demand – although certainly at a slower rate than in the colonies.

It is revealing, in the present context regarding long-run labour supply, to examine Smith's recognition of an element of 'surplus' even in wage income. The population mechanism was normally defined in terms of subsistence goods; and was confined specifically to the productive (or capitalist) sector. Moreover, in this sector high *per capita* wages were envisaged as generating population growth to the extent only that expenditures were devoted to the consumption of 'necessaries' towards which indeed the 'sober and industrious' might be attracted by selective excise taxes which raise the relative price of 'luxury' goods.[65] The argument thus defines certain fundamental demographic implications of the differential behaviour pattern of productive as distinct from unproductive labour:

The high price of such commodities does not necessarily diminish the ability of the inferior ranks of people to bring up families. Upon the sober and industrious poor, taxes upon such commodities act as sumptuary laws, and dispose them either to moderate, or to refrain altogether from the use of superfluities which they can no

63 *Wealth of Nations*, 80f.
64 A number of commentators have interpreted Smith to deny a significant contemporary increase in population. Cf. *Wealth of Nations*, ed. J.R. McCulloch (Edinburgh, 1863), 32n. corresponding to *Wealth of Nations*, mod. lib. ed., 70. In fact population was rising markedly after the mid-forties. See Deane and Cole, *British Economic Growth*, 94.
65 Smith is quite explicit elsewhere (*Wealth of Nations*, 79) that riches are unfavourable to population because of a characteristically low birth rate among the opulent.

longer easily afford. Their ability to bring up families, in consequence of this forced frugality, instead of being diminished, is frequently, perhaps, increased by the tax. It is the sober and industrious poor who generally bring up the most numerous families, and who principally supply the demand for useful labour. All the poor indeed are not sober and industrious, and the dissolute and disorderly might continue to indulge themselves in the use of such commodities after this rise of price in the same manner as before; without regarding the distress which this indulgence might bring upon their families. Such disorderly persons, however, seldom rear up numerous families; their children generally perishing from neglect, mismanagement, and the scantiness or unwholsomeness of their food. If by the strength of their constitution they survive the hardships to which the bad conduct of their parents exposes them; yet the example of that bad conduct commonly corrupts their morals; so that, instead of being useful to society by their industry, they become public nuisances by their vices and disorders. Though the advanced price of the luxuries of the poor, therefore, might increase somewhat the distress of such disorderly families, and thereby diminish somewhat their ability to bring up children; it would not probably diminish much the useful population of the country (823–4).[66]

But the foregoing extract does not merely restrict the population mechanism to the productive sector. Smith's allowance that productive workers might choose to enjoy above-subsistence wages in the form of 'luxury' goods plays havoc, potentially, with the automatic population response usually envisaged.[67] For it is characteristic of Smith's analysis that even when real wages

66 The precise classification of 'luxuries' as distinct from 'necessaries' certainly dilutes considerably the mercantilist flavour of parts of the passage: 'By necessaries I understand, not only the commodities which are indispensably necessary for the support of life, but whatever the custom of the country renders it indecent for creditable people, even of the lowest order, to be without ... All other things I call luxuries; without meaning by this appellation, to throw the smallest degree of reproach upon the temperate use of them. Beer and ale, for example, in Great Britain, and wine, even in the wine countries, I call luxuries. A man of any rank may, without any reproach, abstain totally from tasting such liquors. Nature does not render them necessary for the support of life; and custom nowhere renders it indecent to live without them' (ibid., 821–2). Cf. Smith's criticism of Mandeville referred to below, 249.

67 J.J. Spengler, 'Adam Smith's Theory of Economic Growth – Part II,' Southern Economic Journal, XXV (July 1959), 7, has argued that the Smithian population mechanism is not clearcut precisely because Smith has recognized the phenomenon of rising working-class tastes: 'For, though food is described as the principal population-limiting factor, the argument that there is no limit to the rate at which one may consume housing, dress, equipage, etc., [Wealth of Nations, 164] suggests the possibility that desire for these items might come to check population as incomes rose in countries where land was scarce.' We may add too the fact that Smith recognized the dependence of the terms 'luxury' and 'necessity' upon custom, implying that the subsistence minimum was not envisaged as biologically determined (see n.66). Moreover, since the 'subsistence' wage must be such as to allow labourers to 'bring up a family' (ibid., 67–8) it would appear, in principle, that the long-run minimum might vary with alterations in the infantile death rate itself.

are in excess of 'subsistence' any increase in the corn price, given the growth rate of the capital stock and accordingly of labour demand, will be compensated by a proportionate money-wage rise and the adequate population response thus assured. But this prediction implies that the distribution of expenditure is steady despite income variation.[68] Smith's allowance to the contrary suggests that the argument may be justified only if we presume government intervention, a conclusion which, obviously, has momentous implications.

We turn briefly to consider the short-run supply of labour. While some writers of the eighteenth century, in particular prior to 1750 – in fact Smith himself in the *Lectures*[69] – tended to relate a fall in average wages to increased effort, Smith in 1776 positively rejected the notion. There is therefore little evidence of 'voluntary unemployment' as a common phenomenon in the *Wealth of Nations*. On the contrary, a problem of *excessive* exertion is noted:

The liberal reward of labour, as it encourages the propagation, so it increases the industry of the common people ... Some workmen, indeed, when they can earn in four days what will maintain them through the week, will be idle the other three. This, however, is by no means the case with the greater part. Workmen, on the contrary, when they are liberally paid by the piece, are very apt to over-work themselves, and to ruin their health and constitution in a few years (81–2).[70]

The sharp distinction between Smith's approach to the nature of the labour supply function in the *Lectures* and the *Wealth of Nations* is striking: it suggests, perhaps, a metamorphosis in attitudes from those typical of a 'pre-industrial' to those of a 'proletarian' labour force with a rising taste for manufactures and 'luxuries'. But the aproach scarcely accords with the assumption of constant disutility per hour encountered elsewhere.

Land supply conditions

Smith opened his formal discussion 'Of Rent' with the resounding theme that 'rent, considered as the price paid for the use of land, is naturally the highest which the tenant can afford to pay in the actual circumstances of the land'; it is 'naturally a monopoly price.'[71] This formulation has given rise to criticism on the grounds that the market in agricultural land satisfied all the conditions

68 *Ibid.*, 85.
69 There it was stated that because of lack of education and discipline labourers tended in fact to have primitive standards such that they were satisfied once they managed to achieve some 'target income.' (*Lectures*, 257): 'We find that in the commercial parts of England, the tradesmen are for the most part in this despicable condition; their work through half the week is sufficient to maintain them, and through want of education, they have no amusement for the other, but riot and debauchery.'
70 Cf. *Wealth of Nations*, 122: 'An apprentice is likely to be idle, and almost always is so, because he has no immediate interest to be otherwise. In the inferior employments, the sweets of labour consist altogether in the recompence of labour.'
71 *Wealth of Nations*, 144–5.

of competition.[72] But Smith intended simply to insist upon the distinction between a payment made for 'unimproved' land by dint of its scarcity and that which represents a return upon land improvements undertaken by the landlord.[73] It was Ricardo who recognized subsequently that the principles of rent – envisaged as a payment 'for the use of the original and indestructible powers of the soil' – applied equally to capital investments which are perpetually sunk in the land.[74]

The rent which tenants will pay for the use of land (per acre), Smith continued, 'depends upon the demand' for the product. Conceivably, rent may be reduced to zero with no withdrawal of land services, for there is no minimum supply price. The following celebrated passage formulates this characteristic of rent:

Rent it is to be observed, therefore, enters into the composition of the price of commodities in a different way from wages and profit. High or low wages and profits, are the causes of high or low price; high or low rent is the effect of it. It is because high or low wages and profit must be paid, in order to bring a particular commodity to market, that its price is high or low. But it is because its price is high or low; a great deal more, or very little more, or no more, than what is sufficient to pay those wages and profit, that it affords a high rent, or a low rent, or no rent at all (145–6).

Now, in the discussion of food-producing land Smith makes reference to a physical surplus over the food absorbed in production on 'land, in almost any situation': 'Land, in almost any situation, produces a greater quantity of food than what is sufficient to maintain all the labour necessary for bringing it to market, in the most liberal way in which that labour is ever maintained. The surplus too is always more than sufficient to replace the stock which employed that labour, together with its profits. Something, therefore, always remains for a rent to the landlord' (146). For this contention regarding the ubiquity of a physical surplus, little empirical evidence is provided. But it is nonetheless true that Smith considered the existence of a physical surplus merely as a *necessary* and not a *sufficient* condition for the appearance of rent; there can be no doubt that he took for granted the scarcity of land services relative to demand which derives in turn from the demand for food. The contrast with land suitable only for materials, which does not always yield rent is not merely based on supposed *historical* experience whereby the level of demand for food products – in contrast to that for raw materials – had at all times proven to be so high as to assure a return to land suitable for their production. Theoretical underpinning is provided for the distinction, in the proposition – which does not fit well with Smith's more sophisticated approach to working-class consumption noted above – that any increase in food supplies *generates its*

72 G.J. Stigler, 'Perfect Competition, Historically Considered,' *Journal of Political Economy*, LXV (Feb. 1957), reprinted in Stigler, *Essays in the History of Economics* (Chicago, 1965), 237.

73 For a detailed account of 'improving' landlords see *Wealth of Nations*, 784; 796.

74 *Principles of Political Economy*, 67; 266–7n.

own demand: 'as men, like all other animals, naturally multiply in proportion to the means of their subsistence, food is always, more or less in demand.'[75]

Attention is also paid in the present context to the conception of differential rent: 'The rent of land not only varies with its fertility, whatever be its produce, but with its situation, whatever be its fertility.' Thus on good land a given area 'not only maintains a greater number of cattle, but as they are brought within a smaller compass, less labour becomes requisite to tend them, and to collect their produce,' and the cost differential is eradicated by a rent payment. On the same principle, rent on land near the towns will exceed that on land at a distance: 'Though it may cost no more labour to cultivate the one than the other, it must always cost more to bring the produce of the distant land to market.'[76]

The import of Smith's analysis of those agricultural commodities produced on land which *'sometimes does and sometimes does not, afford Rent'* lies in

75 *Wealth of Nations*, 146. Cf. 164: 'The poor in order to obtain food exert themselves to gratify [the] fancies of the rich.'

A sharp distinction is drawn between the effects of the discovery of new and efficient mines and new food-producing areas. In the former event, the price of the output may fall and force the original, poorer mines out of business; in this case the demand for output is a *datum*. But in the case of 'estates above the ground' the increase in supply generates a shift in the demand curve, and accordingly 'the value of the most barren lands is not diminished by the neighbourhood of the most fertile' (*ibid.*, 173–4).

An application of the general principle is made in Smith's analysis of the corn-export subsidy. The argument in its favour, according to Smith, was based on the view that in consequence 'our merchants and manufacturers ... will be enabled to sell their goods as cheap or cheaper than their rivals in the foreign market. A greater quantity, it is said, will thus be exported, and the balance of trade consequently turned more in favour of our own country' (*ibid.*, 472). Now it is agreed by those who championed the policy that given the 'extent of tillage' the bounty must withdraw output from the home market thus leading to a short-run price rise; but it is claimed that the extent of tillage would be expanded in consequence of the larger foreign market and in response to the higher price obtainable in the short run. In the long run the domestic price will in fact be reduced: 'This double encouragement must, they imagine, in a long period of years, occasion such an increase in the production of corn, as may lower its price in the home market, much more than the bounty can raise it, in the actual state which tillage may, at the end of that period, happen to be in' (*ibid.*, 474). The argument is rejected by Smith. In the short run every additional bushel exported is drawn from the home market; its domestic sale would have served 'to increase the consumption, and to lower the price of that commodity' (*ibid.*, 475). But in addition the policy brings about an actual fall in demand (and not merely a fall in the quantity demanded) – or perhaps rather a smaller increase than otherwise would occur – because in the case at hand there is likely to result a check to the growth rate of population: 'The extraordinary exportation of corn, therefore, occasioned by the bounty, not only, in every particular year, diminishes the home, just as much as it extends the foreign market and consumption, but by restraining the population and industry of the country, its final tendency is to stunt and restrain the gradual extension of the home market, and thereby in the long run, rather to diminish, than to augment, the whole market and consumption of corn' (*ibid.*, 476).

76 *Ibid.*, 147

the implicit rejection of physiocratic doctrine.[77] The argument refers to an empirical observation that at early stages of development, *despite the expropriation of land into private hands*, the owners of forest land, or of quarries and mines cannot obtain a rent for the services of their properties. Competitive bidding for the abundant supplies is too weak to generate a positive return. An example is given from wood-land: 'When the materials of lodging are so super-abundant, the part made use of is worth only the labour and expense of fitting it for that use. It affords no rent to the landlord, who generally grants the use of it to whoever takes the trouble of asking it' (163). An increase in the level of purchasing power, however, entails a rising demand for wood and minerals and accordingly for the use of forests and mines, so that a rent comes to be generated. But even in a developed economy 'the demand for [such products] is not always such as to afford a greater price than is sufficient to pay the labour, and replace, together with its ordinary profits, the stock which must be employed in bringing them to market.' Marginal mines, for example – in terms of low productivity or poor location – may yield no rent.[78] The emphasis upon circumstances in which rent will not be generated sets Smith's position apart from that of the Physiocrats. At the same time, his attempt to define the circumstances under which rent *will* be generated, in terms of the productivity and scarcity of land, is an equally significant contribution. For the physiocratic analysis was extremely fragile; Quesnay provided no sound explanation for the existence of a surplus revenue representing rent over the 'costs' of agricultural produce (corn), except for the artificial device of a price floor determined by world market conditions. For a closed economy, he provided no convincing reason to account for a long-run rental income.

There are also distinct differences between the Smithian and Ricardian approaches, even when attention is restricted to food-producing land con-

---

77 Reference is also made by Smith to ground rent in cities which vary with situation (*ibid.*, 792); and to the absence of a minimum supply price in this case (*ibid.*, 793, 795) rendering urban land suitable for taxation (*ibid.*, 791).

78 *Ibid.*, 164–5. In this regard attention must be paid to Smith's contention, which encountered strong criticism from Ricardo, that 'the most fertile coal-mine ... regulates the price of coals at all the other mines of the neighbourhood' (*ibid.*, 167). Ricardo's insistence (*Principles of Political Economy*, 331) that price is determined by the costs of the marginal mine appears to be misdirected. Although Smith formulated his assumptions with inadequate care, it is evident that he had in mind the *monopolistic* determination of price in the present case. For the context involves a choice of price between a maximum level at which demand falls off pricipitously and the cost price; in fact, according to Smith, 'the coal masters and coal proprietors find it more for their interest to sell a great quantity at a price *somewhat above the lowest* ...' (See above, 125.) Monopoly power is manifested – and exerts itself – in the undercutting of less productive mines: 'Both the proprietor and the undertaker of the work find, that the one can get a greater rent, the other that he can get a greater profit, by somewhat underselling all their neighbours. Their neighbours are soon obliged to sell at the same price, though they cannot so well afford it, and though it always diminishes, and sometimes takes away altogether both their rent and their profit. Some works are abandoned altogether; others can afford no rent, and can be wrought only by the proprietor.' (*Wealth of Nations*, 167.)

sidered as-a-whole rather than in a single use. In the first place, for Smith rent was *not* envisaged merely as a 'transfer' payment.[79] This is clear from our earlier account of the productivity of land, but it is also apparent within the chapter 'Of Rent' now under discussion where the notion of a price-determined surplus is emphasized. In actuality, Smith did not regard the approach in terms of the productivity of land and that in terms of a demand-determined surplus as being in conflict; they were envisaged rather as different aspects of the same phenomenon, the former representing the conditions underlying the demand for the factor, and the latter representing the supply conditions.[80] Secondly, Smith did not envisage marginal land as necessarily rent free in the Ricardian manner. *Even the least well situated or the least fertile* 'always' yields rent because of the typically high demand for the product. Thus land scarcity manifests itself in a more general manner than in the Ricardian theory; and differential productivity appears rather as a detail of the analysis than as the characteristic feature.[81]

Capital supply conditions

The basic 'dilemma of interest' is to explain how there comes to be in competitive long-run general equilibrium any net return to produced productive factors. There ought, in principle, to be no surplus value over the values of the land and labour contained in the product; and the value of capital goods should, at least in the long run, equal that of the factors used up to produce them.[82] Merely to postulate the existence at any time of a given complex of capital goods does not overcome the problem which is formulated for the *long*

79 See Ricardo, *Principles of Political Economy*, 65f.; 398f.
80 But see Schumpeter, *History of Economic Analysis* (New York, 1954), 191; and Douglas, 'Smith's Theory of Value and Distribution,' 113–14.
81 The Smithian conception is utilized, for example, in a discussion of the effects upon rent (per acre) emanating from a change in the basic food crop of a nation: 'If in any country the common and favourite vegetable food of the people should be drawn from a plant of which the most common land, with the same or nearly the same culture, produced a much greater quantity than the most fertile does of corn, the rent of the landlord, or the surplus quantity of food which would remain to him, after paying the labour and replacing the stock of the farmer together with its ordinary profits, would necessarily be much greater. Whatever was the rate at which labour was commonly maintained in that country, this greater surplus could always maintain a greater quantity of it, and consequently enable the landlord to purchase or command a greater quantity of it. The real value of his rent, his real power and authority, his command of the necessaries and conveniencies of life with which the labour of other people could supply him, would necessarily be much greater' (*Wealth of Nations*, 159). This argument is only partially satisfactory, for it does not make explicit the revenue patterns relevant in the alternative cases; but it may perhaps legitimately be presumed that Smith had in mind a higher demand function in the new case in light of the effects of food supplies upon population. (In principle, the analysis applies equally to an innovation raising the productivity of land in a given use, and not only to the adoption of a new source of food which can be produced at lower cost.)
82 J.A. Schumpeter, *The Theory of Economic Development* (Cambridge, Mass., 1934), 29–30.

run. The 'classical' solution was, of course, to conceive of a third 'ultimate' productive factor in addition to labour and land, namely 'abstinence,' whereby a permanent scarcity of capital goods may be accounted for. It is, accordingly, essential to discover Smith's position on the matter, particularly the extent to which a reward for abstinence is recognized.

Close examination of the Smithian account of profits reveals that profits on capital include a return to uncertainty, or a premium on risk apparently borne by the user of capital and a 'surplus' over the risk premium: 'The lowest ordinary rate of profit must always be something more than what is sufficient to compensate the occasional losses to which every employment of stock is exposed.'[83] The so-called 'neat surplus' is, however, broken down further. Part represents interest – 'the interest which the borrower can afford to pay is in proportion to the clear profit only';[84] the remainder constitutes what in effect is a return for *entrepreneurship* covering the risk of insuring borrowed funds to the lender, and 'a recompence for the trouble of employing the stock.'[85]

If a *true* net return exists in profits it can only appear in the interest rate since all other items have been accounted for. But the interest rate is also broken down: 'The lowest ordinary rate of interest must, in the same manner, be something more than sufficient to compensate the occasional losses to which lending, even with tolerable prudence, is exposed. Were it not more, charity or friendship could be the only motives for lending.'[86] There is, therefore, a minimum supply price of *loanable funds*. It is, however, clear that a failure to cover the necessary return for lending does not imply that the rate of *savings* must be adversely affected. It simply means that – as in Holland – 'all people of small or middling fortunes would be obliged to superintend themselves the employment of their own stocks.'[87] A fall in the rate of return on capital, thus does *not* reduce savings; indeed, the contrary is true: 'The demand for labour increases with the increase of stock whatever be its profits; and after these are diminished, stock may not only continue to increase, but to increase much faster than before ... A great stock, though with small profits, generally increases faster than a small stock with great profits. Money, says the proverb, makes money' (93).[88] We conclude that interest was not regarded by Smith as a 'necessary' payment; in particular there is little to suggest a

83 *Wealth of Nations*, 96. (This latter differs from industry to industry: 'the ordinary rate of profit varies more or less with the certainty or uncertainty of the returns' (*ibid.*, 110).)

84 *Ibid.*, 96.

85 *Ibid.*, 97. This latter is *not* identified with the 'labour of inspection and direction' of the operation, which Smith excluded from 'profits' (*ibid.*, 48), but represents a special element.

86 *Ibid.*, 96.

87 *Ibid.*

88 Cf. *ibid.*, 578: 'The high rate of profit seems every where to destroy that parsimony which in other circumstances is natural to the character of the merchant.'
  In this regard, Smith differs from A.R.J. Turgot, *Reflections on the Formation and Distribution of Riches* (1766; New York, 1963), 92f. who denied that interest is 'disposable'; taxation thereof would reduce savings.

conception of interest as a reward for abstinence from present consumption.[89] Indeed, we find a statement within the *Wealth of Nations* to the effect that the disposition to save is of itself as powerful, or more so, than that to consume, which represents a position closer to that of Marx than Senior:

With regard to profusion, the principle which prompts to expence, is the passion for present enjoyment; which, though sometimes violent and very difficult to be restrained, is in general only momentary and occasional. But the principle which prompts to save, is the desire of bettering our condition, a desire which, though generally calm and dispassionate, comes with us from the womb, and never leaves us till we go in to the grave ... Though the principle of expence, therefore, prevails in almost all men upon some occasions, and in some men upon almost all occasions, yet in the greater part of men, taking the whole course of their life at an average, the principle of frugality seems not only to predominate, but to predominate very greatly (324–5).[90]

Smith formally drew the fundamental conclusion that – at least in a closed economy – interest might be taxed with no repercussions on the supply of capital. The similarity in this respect between interest and rent is clarified, and a sharp distinction is drawn between that part of the return on capital representing interest and that part representing entrepreneural compensation:

The revenue or profit arising from stock naturally divides itself into two parts; that which pays the interest, and which belongs to the owner of the stock; and that surplus part which is over and above what is necessary for paying the interest.

This latter part of profit is evidently not taxable directly. It is the compensation, and in most cases it is no more than a very moderate compensation, for the risk and trouble of employing the stock ...

The interest of money seems at first sight a subject equally capable of being taxed directly as the rent of land. Like the rent of land, it is a neat produce which remains after completely compensating the whole risk and trouble of employing the stock. As a tax upon the rent of land cannot raise rents; because the neat produce which remains after replacing the stock of the former, together with his reasonable profit, cannot be greater after the tax than before it: so, for the same reason, a tax upon the interest of money could not raise the rate of interest, the quantity of stock or money

89 A similar position is adopted by Bowley, *Nassau Senior and Classical Economics,* 139; Nathan Rosenberg, 'Some Institutional Aspects of the *Wealth of Nations,*' *Journal of Political Economy,* LXVIII (Dec. 1960), 558; and G.S.L. Tucker, *Progress and Profits in British Economic Thought* (Cambridge, 1960), 72–3. But cf. Schumpeter, *History of Economic Analysis,* 639; and J.J. Spengler, 'Adam Smith's Theory of Economic Growth – II,' 7.

90 The emphasis in the *Theory of Moral Sentiments* (1759; New York, 1966) is somewhat different. Attention is there paid to the psychic pressures towards present consumption. But it is 'the sense of propriety' which is relied upon – not the interest rate – to achieve a postponement thereof: 'The pleasure which we are to enjoy ten years hence interests us little in comparison with that which we may enjoy to-day; the passion which the first excites is naturally so weak in comparison with that violent emotion which the second is apt to give occasion to, that the one could never be any balance to the other, unless it was supported by the sense of propriety, by the consciousness that we merited the esteem and approbation of every body by acting in the one way, and that we became the proper objects of their contempt and derision by behaving in the other' (*ibid.,* 273).

in the country, like the quantity of land, being supposed to remain the same after the tax as before it (798–800).

A well-known statement referring to landlords as 'the only one of the three orders whose revenue costs them neither labour nor care, but comes to them, as it were, of its own accord, and independent of any plan or project of their own'[91] must, therefore, be qualified. This proposition distinguishes the return to *labour* and to *entrepreneurship* from that to *land*, but neglects to take into account interest payments, which in principle should be classified together with rent.

A number of difficult issues relating to Smith's over-all position regarding the theory of distribution can be better appreciated in light of the foregoing analysis. The distinction, sometimes attributed to J.B. Say,[92] between the reward of the entrepreneur as 'organiser,' from that of the capitalist is apparent in the *Wealth of Nations*. But it is the case that the 'source' of the return to the entrepreneur as such is formally traced (together with the return to the capitalist proper) to the use of capital goods in production, a practice which camouflages 'entrepreneurship' as a separate factor. Moreover, the precise functions of the entrepreneur are not adequately explained.[93] In particular, references to risk are normally unrelated to risky innovation, although Smith does occasionally recognize a *short-run* return to innovation[94]; he had in mind, evidently, 'measurable' risk consistent with long-run competitive equilibrium.

Secondly, there is clearly much evidence to support the view that Smith was attempting to formulate a productivity theory of distribution. This view has been forcefully stated by Thorstein Veblen, according to whom each of the three components of price at their 'natural' levels represented for Smith 'the measure of the productive effect of the factor to which it pertains. The further discussion of these shares in distribution aims to account for the facts of distribution on the grounds of the productivity of the factors which are held to share the product between them ... Adam Smith's discussion of distribution as a function of productivity might be traced in detail through his handling of Wages, Profits, and Rent.'[95] This view must certainly be qualified in light of the fact that Smith lacked any clear conception of a means of isolating the marginal factor products; moreover, the analysis of wages within a wages-fund structure precludes any *direct* connection between the wage rate and

91 *Wealth of Nations*, 249.
92 See Lord Robbins, *The Theory of Economic Development in the History of Economic Thought* (London, 1968), 103–4.
93 The development of the conception by Say is fully discussed by G. Koolman, 'Say's Conception of The Role of the Entrepreneur,' *Economica*, XXXVIII (Aug. 1971), 269–86.
94 *Wealth of Nations*, 115. But see the references to the risky experiments undertaken by improving landlords (*ibid.*, 784).
95 *The Place of Science in Modern Civilization* (New York, 1919), 121–2. A similar position is adopted by Overton H. Taylor, *A History of Economic Thought* (New York, 1960), 116–17.

productivity. If we ascribe a productivity theory to him, it is therefore as a general conception only. Within this conceptual framework, the return on capital was not regarded as an 'exploitation' income, for capital goods make a net contribution to the national income. But when allowance is also made for the absence of a long-run supply price of capital, it may be expected that the interest element in the return will ultimately be eradicated and the total national income divided between landowners and workers and, it must be emphasized, 'entrepreneurs.' Thus from the point of view of the long-run stationary state there is no net return to capital and capital goods themselves will be reducible to land and labour with the necessary allowance for 'entrepreneurship.'[96] (We return to this issue in the final section of the chapter.)

THE THEORY AS-A-WHOLE

We are now in a position to consider the theories of value and distribution as a whole, particularly their consistency. It will be the contention of this section that Smith's position is considerably more coherent than is generally believed.

The essence of the Smithian position is reflected in the two approaches taken to rent. According to one, rent appears as a cost item on a par with wages and profits; according to the second, it appears as a residual.[97] The resolution of this apparent inconsistency lies simply in the fact that *the theory of cost price was not applied to corn*. The corn price is determined in the *Wealth of Nations* by other principles – a practice noted by Buchanan, Malthus, and Ricardo – and the rent per acre thereby generated appears as a *datum* in the analysis of the economic system as a whole.[98] This is the import, for example, of Smith's observation that the rent of corn land *governs* that of other food-producing land: 'In Europe corn is the principal produce of land which serves immediately for human food. Except in particular situations, therefore, the rent of corn land regulates in Europe that of all other cultivated

---

96 Smith's statement that 'all useful machines and instruments of trade are originally derived from a circulating capital, which furnishes the materials of which they are made, and the maintenance of the workmen who make them' (*Wealth of Nations*, 266); or 'land and capital stock are the two original sources of all revenue' because 'capital stock pays the wages of productive labour' (*ibid.*, 897), may be appreciated as reflecting the ultimate absence of a net return to capital in the long run.

97 For Ricardo's criticisms, see his *Principles of Political Economy*, 67f.

98 When Smith does make reference to labour productivity in the case of corn, it is to emphasize its *long-run constancy*: 'In every state of society, in every stage of improvement, corn is the production of human industry. But the average produce of every sort of industry is always suited, more or less exactly, to the average consumption, the average supply to the average demand. In every different stage of improvement, besides, the raising of equal quantities of corn in the same soil and climate, will at an average, require nearly equal quantities of labour; or what comes to the same thing, the price of nearly equal quantities; the continual increase in the productive powers of labour in an improving state of cultivation being more or less counterbalanced by the continually increasing price of cattle, the principal instrument of agriculture. Upon all these accounts, therefore, we may rest assured, that equal quantities of corn will, in every state of society, in every

land.'[99] Indeed, the full meaning of Smith's discussion of food-producing land is only revealed when allowance is made for alternative uses, particularly the distribution of (cultivated) land between arable and pasture or forage. A sharp distinction is drawn in this context between *physical* surplus and *value* surplus; thus a corn field 'of moderate fertility' is said to be physically more productive than 'the best pasture of equal extent,' and 'the surplus which remains after replacing the seed and maintaining all the labour, is likewise much greater'; but the revenue yielded by the sale of butchers' meat relative to that yielded by corn may yet be such as to justify the use of land for pasture.[100] It is the prices of other agricultural products which must be accommodated to that of corn.[101]

stage of improvement, more nearly represent, or be equivalent to, equal quantities of labour, than equal quantities of any other part of the rude produce of land. Corn, accordingly ... is, in all the different stages of wealth and improvement, a more accurate measure of value than any other commodity or set of commodities' (*Wealth of Nations*, 186–7). Similarly: 'If you except corn and such other vegetables as are raised altogether by human industry, that all other sorts of rude produce, cattle, poultry, game of all kinds, the useful fossils and minerals of the earth, &c. naturally grow dearer as the society advances in wealth and improvement, I have endeavoured to show already' (*ibid.*, 217).

On this issue see the comments by David Buchanan, *Observations on the Subjects Treated of in Dr Smith's ... Wealth of Nations* (1817; New York, 1966) 36–8; Malthus, *Principles of Political Economy*, 2nd ed. (1836; New York, 1964), 184f. (discussed below); and, in particular, Ricardo, *Principles of Political Economy*, 374. Ricardo insisted that a cost of production theory was applicable to corn as to any other commodity: 'Why should corn and vegetables alone be excepted? Dr Smith's error throughout his whole work, lies in supposing that the value of corn is constant; that though the value of other things may, the value of corn never can be raised. Corn, according to him, is always of the same value because it will always feed the same number of people. In the same manner it might be said, that cloth is always of the same value, because it will always make the same number of coats. What can value have to do with the power of feeding and clothing?'

For a recent account which recognizes clearly that the cost-of-production theory of price was not applied to corn see Rosenbluth, 'A Note on Labour, Wages and Rent in Smith's Theory of Value,' 308–11.

99 *Wealth of Nations*, 159. Cf. *ibid.*, 149: 'It is thus in the progress of improvement that rent and profit of unimproved pasture come to be regulated in some measure by the rent and profit of what is improved, and these again by the rent and profit of corn'; and *ibid.*, 228: '... the price of each particular produce must be sufficient, first, to pay the rent of good corn land, as it is that which regulates the rent of the greater part of other cultivated land ...'

100 *Ibid.*, 148. It is observed in the course of the analysis that the same cattle prices which assure the transfer of cultivated land from arable to pasture (or forage) will apply to cattle raised on 'uncultivated moors' which clearly have no alternative use. Consequently their owners will enjoy windfall gains since the supply price of such land services is zero: 'The cattle bred upon the most uncultivated moors, when brought to the same market, are ... sold at the same price as those which are reared upon the most improved land. The proprietors of those moors profit by it, and raise the rent of their land in proportion to the price of their cattle' (*ibid.*, 149).

101 Daniel H. Buchanan, 'The Historical Approach to Rent and Price Theory,'

We must now deal with the crucial question: if the price of corn is not determined by production costs in the manner of all other commodities, by what process is it determined? It was Malthus who noted that while Smith had provided a sound account of secular movements in the prices of animal-food and raw materials relative to that of corn, 'he had not entered into the explanation of the natural causes which tend to determine the price of corn,' but 'left the reader indeed to conclude that he considers the price as deter-mined only by the state of the mines, which at the time supply the circulating

Economica, IX (June 1929), reprinted in W. Fellner and B.F. Haley, eds., *Readings in the Theory of Income Distribution* (Philadelphia, 1951), 603f. distinguishes between rent on land-as-a-whole which has the characteristic of a demand-determined surplus, and rent on land in particular uses, which has the characteristic of a cost. But his argument does not recognize the particular features attributed by Smith to the price of corn and the rent of corn land.

Smith's position represents the rejection of a mutual relationship between the rent which must be paid per acre of land in various uses, and is strengthened by reference to the *quantitative* significance of corn, and the *historical* fact that the relative price of cattle to that of corn was only recently high enough to justify the transfer of land from corn production. The reverse case of a return of land from forage crops to corn was (as yet) of less practical relevance. Moreover, the historical sequence whereby the commercial production of vegetables precedes that of other foods and materials is not accidental, as Smith makes clear in the proposition that 'There are some parts of the produce of land for which the demand must always be such as to afford a greater price than what is sufficient to bring them to market; and there are others for which it either may or may not be such as to afford this greater price' (*Wealth of Nations*, 145).

Nonetheless, a conception of mutuality intruded from time to time into the argument as, for example, in the following insistance that the (potential) existence of a physical surplus in any one use is no assurance that land will be devoted to that purpose; the value return must be such as to meet the competition arising from alternative uses: 'As an acre of land, therefore, will produce a much smaller quantity of the one species of food than of the other, the inferiority of the quantity must be compensated by the superiority of the price. If it was more than com-pensated, more corn land would be turned into pasture; and if it was not compen-sated, part of what was in pasture would be brought back into corn' (*ibid.*, 149). Smith in fact slips occasionally into considering the rent on corn land *and* pasture land as determining the rent which must be yielded by other products.

It is also to be noted that while in any one use rent represents a cost of production determined by the alternative opportunity available in corn (or corn and pasture) full attention is paid to price-determined surpluses generated wherever transfer between use is somehow impeded: 'It sometimes happens, indeed, that the quantity of land which can be fitted for some particular produce, is too small to supply the effectual demand. The whole produce can be disposed of to those who are willing to give somewhat more than what is sufficient to pay the whole rent, wages and profit necessary for raising and bringing it to market, according to their natural rates, or according to the rates at which they are paid in the greater part of other cultivated land. The surplus part of the price which remains after defraying the whole expence of improvement and cultivation may commonly, in this case, and in this case only, bear no regular proportion to the like surplus in corn or pasture, but may exceed it in almost any degree; and the greater part of this excess naturally goes to the rent of the landlord' (*ibid.*, 155; cf. 149–50). Precisely the same principle appears also in the earlier chapter on long-run price

medium of the commercial world.'[102] Malthus makes reference to the following extract as evidence: 'The average or ordinary price of corn again is regulated ... by the value of silver, by the richness or barrenness of the mines which supply the market with that metal, or by the quantity of labour which must be employed, and consequently of corn which must be consumed, in order to bring any particular quantity of silver from the mine to market' (36).[103] This approach is considerably amplified in the 'Digression on Silver' attached to the chapter on rent, where it is made clear that it is not only changes in the productivity of the silver mines, governing the supply of silver, but also changes in the domestic demand for silver which influence the corn-silver exchange rate. The entire 'Digression on Silver' in fact represents an attempt to distinguish between these two categories in the analysis of several centuries of corn prices, and above all to avoid a simple-minded relationship between the money supply and corn prices. It was Smith's contention that, starting from a state of general international equilibrium – in terms of a common silver price of corn – an increase in the aggregate level of activity in any country will generate a fall in the silver price of corn, as a necessary precondition for the inflow of the metal. The inflow itself, of course, raises the corn price (and, correspondingly, the outflow will lower it in metal-losing countries) until a new equilibrium is achieved where the metal price of corn is again everywhere equal:

> determination where failure to satisfy the conditions of mobility is illustrated by reference not only to *institutional or monopolistic* obstacles impeding the movement of capital and labour, but also to *natural* scarcities which rule out the transfer of land between uses. Thus 'the rent of land which affords such singular and esteemed productions, like the rent of some vineyards in France of a particularly happy soil and situation, bears no regular proportion to the rent of other equally fertile and equally well-cultivated land in its neighbourhood' (*ibid.*, 61). The conception of rent as a surplus is recognized also in the chapter relating to profits: 'The highest ordinary rate of profit may be such as, in the price of the greater part of commodities, eats up the whole of what should go to the rent of the land, and leaves only what is sufficient to pay the labour of preparing and bringing them to market, according to the lowest rate at which labour can anywhere be paid, the bare subsistence of the labourer. The workman must always have been fed in some way or other while he was about his work; but the landlord may not always have been paid' (*ibid.*, 97).

102 *Principles of Political Economy*, 184–5.

103 It must be emphasized that it is not the relative labour costs of corn and silver which are here said to determine the silver price of corn. In another context, Smith accounts in *general* terms for the silver 'price level' in terms of relative costs but a specific reference to corn is conspicuously absent: 'The proportion between the value of gold and silver and that of goods of any other kind depends in all cases, not upon the nature or quantity of any particular paper money ... but upon the richness or poverty of the mines, which happen at any particular time to supply the great market of the commercial world with those metals. It depends upon the proportion between the quantity of labour which is necessary in order to bring a certain quantity of gold and silver to market, and that which is necessary in order to bring thither a certain quantity of any other sort of goods' (*Wealth of Nations*, 312–13).

The quantity of the precious metals may increase in any country from two different causes: either, first from the increased abundance of the mines which supply it; or secondly, from the increased wealth of the people, from the increased produce of their annual labour. The first of these causes is no doubt necessarily connected with the diminution of the value of the precious metals; but the second is not.

When more abundant mines are discovered, a greater quantity of the precious metals is brought to market, and the quantity of the necessaries and conveniencies of life for which they must be exchanged being the same as before, equal quantities of the metals must be exchanged for smaller quantities of commodities. So far, therefore, as the increase of the quantity of the precious metals in any country arises from the increased abundance of the mines, it is necessarily connected with some diminution of their value.

When on the contrary, the wealth of any country increases, when the annual produce of its labour becomes gradually greater and greater, a greater quantity of coin becomes necessary in order to circulate a greater quantity of commodities ... The quantity of their coin will increase from necessity ... [But] gold and silver are not likely to be worse paid for ... *gold and silver will naturally exchange for a greater quantity of subsistence in a rich than in a poor country, in a country which abounds with subsistence, than in one which is but indifferently supplied with it* (188–9; author's emphasis).[104]

The re-establishment of international equilibrium following a disturbance is noted in the following passage:

104 An increase in the supply of silver due to the first cause implies a rise in the money price of corn, and given the corn wage, a rise in the money wage rate. The 'value' of silver, in terms either of corn or labour, therefore 'necessarily' falls. In the second situation, by contrast, the inflow is induced by a falling price of corn and, given the corn wage, a falling money wage rate. Even in the new equilibrium the price of corn will be lower than it had been originally.

While Smith sometimes refers to the silver price of 'necessaries and conveniencies,' as a whole, the entire 'digression,' in fact, revolves around the silver price of *corn*. It will become clear presently that it is the money price of corn which is envisaged as determining or at least constituting the predominant influence on the prices of manufactured commodities.

In his discussion of the downward trend in corn prices 1350–1500, Smith strictly defined the alternative causes: 'This rise in the value of silver, in proportion to that of corn may either have been owing altogether to the increase of the demand for that metal, in consequence of increasing improvement and cultivation, the supply in the mean time continuing the same as before: Or, the demand continuing the same as before, it may have been owing altogether to the gradual diminution of supply; the greater part of the mines which were then known in the world, being much exhausted, and consequently the expence of working them much increased. Or it may have been owing partly to the one and partly to the other of those two circumstances' (*ibid.*, 180–1).

The upward movement of corn prices, 1570–1640, is attributed 'to the discovery of abundant mines of America' which outweighed the effects of increasing demand for silver due to advances 'in industry and improvement' (191); while the falling level of corn prices 1700–64 is explained largely in terms of rising demand for silver (198).

That that increase in the quantity of the precious metals which arises in any country from the increase of wealth, has no tendency to diminish their value, I have endeavoured to show already. Gold and silver naturally resort to a rich country, for the same reason that all sorts of luxuries and curiosities resort to it; not because they are cheaper there than in poorer countries, but because they are dearer, or because a better price is given for them. It is the superiority of price which attracts them, and *as soon as that superiority ceases they necessarily cease to go thither* (216–17; author's emphasis).

It is worth making explicit that the analysis of the distribution of the metals does not relate to the relative purchasing power of silver over labour. For Smith was well aware that the money wage rate in a 'rich' country (such as England compared with Scotland) may be relatively *high* in consequence of a rapid rate of growth in the demand for labour; if the mechanism revolved around purchasing power over labour there would be an outflow from England to Scotland rather than the reverse movement.[105]

The next step of the argument relates to the determination of money wages. The silver price of corn, determined by the principles of specie distribution, together with the 'demand for labour' will jointly determine the money-wage rate; or *given* labour demand conditions, the money-wage rate will vary directly with the corn price:

Though the variations in the price of labour, not only do not always correspond with those in the price of provisions, but are frequently quite opposite, we must not, upon this account, imagine that the price of provisions has no influence upon that of labour. The money price of labour is necessarily regulated by two circumstances; the demand for labour, and the price of the necessaries and conveniencies of life. The demand for labour, according as it happens to be increasing, stationary, or declining, or to require an increasing, stationary, or declining population, determines the quantity of the necessaries and conveniencies of life which must be given to the labourer; and the money price of labour is determined by what is requisite for purchasing this quantity. Though the money price of labour, therefore, is sometimes high where the price of provisions is low, it would be still higher, the demand continuing the same, if the price of provisions was high (85).[106]

105 Thus, the downward movement in corn prices, 1700–1764, is said to represent a *rise* in the 'real value' of silver in the European, including the British, market. (*Ibid.*, 198) But during the same period corn wages in England were rising sharply, and money wages also tended upwards despite the fall in corn prices. (*Ibid.*, 189) In brief, the value of silver in terms of *labour* was actually falling.

It is only when Smith is able to assume a constant corn wage that the 'value' of silver may refer to either corn or labour. In all other cases he remains with corn as the ultimate 'standard'. This characteristic is noted by Malthus, *The Measure of Value* (1823; New York, 1957), iii: 'In [Smith's] elaborate inquiry into the value of silver during the four last centuries, he uses corn as the measure, not labour; and arrives at conclusions entirely different from those which would have been the consequence of his using labour.'

106 It will be noted that in this passage Smith inserts a reference to the prices of the 'conveniencies of life,' in addition to the 'necessaries.' But in other almost identical

It is thus the purpose of the chapter 'Of Wages' to account for both the nominal and the corn price of labour.[107] And <u>it is the essence of the argument that changes in the price of corn will influence the money wage rate *even though the real wage is above the subsistence level.*</u> But it should again be noted that to the extent workers choose to alter their pattern of consumption as real wages rise in favour of 'luxuries' – a possibility of which Smith himself was well aware – the preceding relationships are rendered quite imprecise.[108]

Finally, the circle is closed when we utilize the money price of labour in the analysis of the determination of cost price in manufacturing. This final relationship holds good, it must again be carefully noted, *given* the conditions of demand for labour, and is expressed most clearly in the following extract drawn from the chapter 'Of Bounties,' in Book IV, which also summarizes much of the preceding argument:

[The] money price of corn regulates that of all other home-made commodities.

It regulates the money price of labour, which must always be such as to enable the labourer to purchase a quantity of corn sufficient to maintain him and his family either in the liberal, moderate, or scanty manner in which the advancing, stationary or declining circumstances of the society oblige his employers to maintain him.

It regulates the money price of all the other parts of the rude produce of the land, which, in every period of improvement, must bear a certain proportion to that of corn, though this proportion is different in different periods. It regulates, for example, the money price of grass and hay, of butcher's meat, of horses, and the maintenance of horses, of land carriage consequently, or the greater part of the inland commerce of the country.

By regulating the money price of all the other parts of the rude produce of land, it

    statements (*Wealth of Nations*, 815, 824) he is more explicit that it is the price of 'necessaries' or 'provisions' which is the predominant regulator of money wages (given labour demand conditions), basing himself doubtless upon the view that 'corn ... or whatever else is the common and favorite vegetable food of the people, constitutes, in every civilized country, the principal part of the subsistence of the labourer ... The money price of labour, therefore depends much more upon the average money price of corn, the subsistence of the labourer, than upon that of butcher's meat, or of any other part of the rude produce of land' (*ibid.*, 187).

107 According to the account of Rosenbluth, 'A Note on Labour, Wages and Rent in Smith's Theory of Value,' 308f., the object of the chapter on wages was to determine the price of corn in terms of *labour*. In our view this is formally correct, but because we believe that Smith did *not in practice* use labour as numéraire, it is more accurate to say that the object was to account for the price of labour in terms of corn, and also in terms of *silver*.

108 Ricardo was evidently troubled by this problem. He took the position that an increase in corn prices need not lead to an increase in money wages in the event that initial real wages exceeded subsistence, 'as the labourer may be contented with fewer enjoyments.' But he emphasized the limited possibility of continued price rises and unchanged money wages and concluded that 'under ordinary circumstances, no permanent rise takes place in the price of necessaries, without occasioning, or having been preceded by a rise in wages.' (*Principles of Political Economy*, 118.)

regulates that of the materials of almost all manufactures. By regulating the money price of labour, it regulates that of manufacturing art and industry. And by regulating both, it regulates that of the complete manufacture. The money price of labour, and of every thing that is the produce either of land or labour, must necessarily either rise or fall in proportion to the money price of corn (476–7).[109]

Further light is cast on the Smithian 'model' by his discussion of corn prices in the years 1764–76. While variations in input prices leave the silver price of corn unaffected according to the basic analysis, poor harvest conditions during this period and the contemporary corn export subsidy were said to have exerted a powerful influence on the domestic level of corn prices. But governmental intervention by export subsidies (or by import duties), as a means of raising agricultural profitability, Smith insisted, generated merely a *nominal* variation in corn price (in sharp contrast to the *real* effects which similar intervention would generate if applied to manufactured commodities) precisely because of the effects upon the money wage and therefore prices in general. The entire argument, it must be noted, is based upon the assumption of given labour demand conditions:

[Our country gentlemen] did not perhaps attend to the great and essential difference which nature has established between corn and almost every other sorts of goods ... The nature of things has stamped upon corn a real value which cannot be altered by merely altering its money price. No bounty upon exportation, no monopoly of the home market can raise that value. The freest competition cannot lower it. Through the world in general that value is equal to the quantity of labour which it can maintain ... in the way, whether liberal, moderate, or scanty, in which labour is commonly maintained in that place. Woollen or linen cloth are not the regulating commodities by which the real value of all other commodities must be finally measured and determined; corn is. The real value of every other commodity is finally measured and determined by the proportion which its average money price bears to the average money price of corn. The real value of corn does not vary with those variations in its average money price, which sometimes occur from century to century. It is the real value of silver which varies with them (482).[110]

The case of an *increase in imports* is attended to subsequently in the 'Digression on the Corn Trade.' Here a reverse sequence is defined whereby a fall in the corn price will, given labour demand conditions, entail a reduced money wage and therefore reduced money prices generally:

109 See also Smith's discussion of taxes imposed upon wage goods: 'Taxes upon necessaries, by raising the wages of labour, necessarily tend to raise the price of all manufactures, and consequently to diminish the extent of their sale and consumption' (Below, 180).
110 Cf. *ibid.*, 476: 'The real effect of the bounty is not so much to raise the real value of corn, as to degrade the real value of silver; or to make an equal quantity of it exchange for a smaller quantity, not only of corn, but of all other home-made commodities; for the money price of corn regulates that of all other home-made commodities.'

It tends, indeed, to lower somewhat the average money price of corn, but not to diminish its real value, or the quantity of labour which it is capable of maintaining. If importation were at all times free, our farmers and country gentlemen would, probably, one year with another, get less money for their corn than they do at present ...; but the money which they got would be of more value, would buy more goods of all kinds, and would employ more labour. Their real wealth, their real revenue, therefore, would be the same as at present, though it might be expressed by a smaller quantity of silver ... (502).[111]

It is clear that Smith's observations relating to value and distribution constitute a more-or-less consistent whole. To summarize briefly, given labour market conditions the money or silver price of corn (governed by the principle of specie distribution) determines the money wage rate and thus labour costs throughout the economy and – taking for granted nominal profits – the silver price of all commodities produced without land. And given the conditions of scarcity and productivity relating to land, the same silver price of corn together with the money wage rate (and profit rate), will govern the rent per acre of corn land and thus the alternative cost that must be met by all other land-using products.[112]

THE DECLINING RATE OF PROFIT

In the foregoing discussion, we have taken for granted a particular rate of growth of the capital stock and therefore a particular (long-run) real wage rate. The rate of profit was also taken for granted. In this section we consider the proposition that in the course of economic expansion the profit rate will tend downwards, while because of the rising rate of capital accumulation[113] the real wage rate tends to rise. It must be borne in mind that the argument refers to variations in the real or corn rate of profit, and not merely to the nominal or silver rate.

In any attempt to discern the necessary and sufficient conditions for the declining rate of return on capital attention must be paid to Smith's formal proposition that increased wage costs will, in the long run, be passed on by capitalists to the consumer in the form of higher industrial prices and to the landlord in lower rents. This fundamental proposition is formulated clearly in an analysis of taxes imposed upon wages which, it may be added, confirms the differential treatment accorded the determination of price in the manufacturing and agricultural sectors:

111 According to the argument which follows, the fall in prices generally would stimulate the *export* industries, and actually lead to an increase in the demand for corn, on the part of those in the export sector enjoying increased revenues. The fall in corn prices thus will be accompanied by an *increase* in the domestic market for corn and encourage agricultural production.

112 Frequently Smith's treatment of mines and quarries implies the absence of an altenative use in the production of food. The prices of their products in this case are not accounted for adequately within the foregoing 'model.'

113 See above, 168.

A direct tax upon the wages of labour ... though the labourer might perhaps pay it out of hand, could not properly be said to be even advanced by him; at least if the demand for labour and the average price of provisions remained the same after the tax as before it. In all such cases, not only the tax, but something more than the tax, would in reality be advanced by the person who immediately employed him. The final payment would in different cases fall upon different persons. The rise which such a tax might occasion in the wages of manufacturing labour would be advanced by the master manufacturer, who would both be entitled and obliged to charge it, with a profit, upon the price of his goods. *The final payment of this rise of wages, therefore, together with the additional profit of the master manufacturer, would fall upon the consumer.* The rise which such a tax might occasion in the wages of country labour would be advanced by the farmer, who, in order to maintain the same number of labourers as before, would be obliged to employ a greater capital. In order to get back this greater capital, together with the ordinary profits of stock, it would be necessary that he should retain a larger portion, or what comes to the same thing, the price of a larger portion of the produce of the land, and consequently that he should pay less rent to the landlord. *The final payment of this rise of wages, therefore, would in this case fall upon the landlord, together with the additional profit of the farmer who had advanced it* (816; author's emphasis).[114]

More generally, any tax upon wage goods has a similar incidence, and is borne ultimately by the consumers of manufactured goods, and by landlords: 'Taxes upon necessaries, by raising the wages of labour, necessarily tend to raise the price of all manufactures, and consequently to diminish the extent of their sale and consumption ... Taxes upon necessaries, so far as they affect the labouring poor, are finally paid, partly by landlords in the diminished rent of their lands, and partly by rich consumers, whether landlords or others, in the advanced price of manufactured goods; and always with a considerable over-charge.'[115] There is no reason to believe that the secular rise in *per capita*

114 It is conceded that workers may suffer a decline in real wages in the event that the demand for labour is adversely affected by taxation: 'If direct taxes upon the wages of labour have not always occasioned a proportionable rise in those wages, it is because they have generally occasioned a considerable fall in the demand for labour ... In consequence of them, however, the price of labour must always be higher than it otherwise would have been in the actual state of the demand: and this enhancement of price, together with the profit of those who advance it, must always be finally paid by the landlords and consumers' (*Wealth of Nations*, 816–17). See also *ibid.*, 475–6, 839 on this issue.

115 *Ibid.*, 824. Moreover, any such increase in the prices of *manufactured* wage goods implies a further rise in the money wage rate with a further sequence of inflationary effects.

Even a tax imposed directly upon profits can, according to Smith, also be passed on, either to the consumer or to the landlard or, in this case, to the rentier: 'If he employed [his capital] as a farming stock in the cultivation of land, he could raise the rate of his profit [to cover the tax] only by retaining a greater portion, or, what comes to the same thing, the price of a greater portion of the produce of the land; and as this could be done only by a reduction of rent, *the final payment of the tax would fall upon the landlord.* If he employed it as a mercantile or manufacturing

wages in consequence of an increasing rate of capital accumulation was treated differently than a tax on wages or on wage goods. The increase in wage costs in this case too would be passed on in the form of higher prices and reduced rents.[116]

It is precisely this argument which attracted Ricardo's attention and severe criticism. It was his objective to demonstrate that wage-rate variations leave the general level of prices unchanged; and his fundamental theorem on distribution – defining a strict inverse relation between wages and profits – was developed in direct opposition to Smith's analysis.

The Ricardian critique clarifies considerably Smith's position. Ricardo used a variety of arguments to prove Smith's error according to which it is apparently possible for an increase in wages to leave capitalists 'no worse off' than

stock, he could raise the rate of his profit only by raising the price of his goods; in which case *the final payment of the tax would fall altogether upon the consumers of those goods*. If he did not raise the rate of his profit, he would be obliged to charge the whole tax upon that part of it which was allotted for the interest of money. He could afford less interest for whatever stock he borrowed, and *the whole weight of the tax would in this case fall ultimately upon the interest of money'* (*ibid.*, 799; author's emphasis).

It will, however, be noted that in the second edition of 1778 Smith slightly altered the propositions, and allowed perhaps for *some* increase in agricultural prices: 'A tax upon the wages of country labour does not raise the price of the rude produce of land *in proportion to the tax*; for the same reason that a tax upon the farmer's profit does not raise that price *in that proportion*' (*ibid.*, 817; italicized phrases added in second edition).

The sharp distinction between the effects of wage-cost increases upon the prices of manufactured goods and of agricultural products obviously flows from the different accounts of price determination in the two sectors discussed above. But during an account of taxes upon the profits of particular products Smith is more explicit and refers to the actual process whereby prices of manufactured goods rise to cover increased costs, namely by a reduction in output and sales; by contrast, in the case of the farmer, it is presumed that supply elasticity is *zero*: 'But when a tax is imposed upon the profits of stock employed in agriculture, it is not the interest of the farmers to withdraw any part of their stock from that employment. Each farmer occupies a certain quantity of land for which he pays rent. For the proper cultivation of this land a certain quantity of stock is necessary; and by withdrawing any part of this necessary quantity, the farmer is not likely to be able to be more able to pay either the rent or the tax. In order to pay the tax, it can never be his interest to diminish the quantity of his produce, nor consequently to supply the market more sparingly than before. The tax, therefore will never enable him to raise the price of his produce, so as to reimburse himself by throwing the final payment upon the consumer. The farmer, however, must have his reasonable profit as well as every other dealer ... A tax of this kind imposed during the currency of a lease may, no doubt, distress of ruin the farmer. Upon the renewal of the lease it must always fall on the landlord' (*ibid.*, 807).

116 John Barton, *Observations on the Circumstances which Influence the Condition of the Labouring Classes of Society* (London, 1817), 20, reprinted in G. Sotiroff, ed., *Economic Writings of John Barton*, I (Regina, 1962), 44, explains the neglect of a causal relationship between wage-rate changes and the adoption of capital-intensive processes by Smith's contention that wage increases are simply passed on to the consumer. In this case no motive is created for change.

originally. One argument is based upon the inability of envisaging an increase in the level of prices without an inflow of the precious metals or an increase in domestic mining, neither of which would be forthcoming under the given circumstances. Of greater relevance for our present purposes is Ricardo's observation that even if the price level is (somehow) increased 'the proposition would not be less true, which asserts that high wages invariably affect the employers of labour, by depriving them of a portion of their real profits,' for the *purchasing power* of the unchanged nominal profits would be reduced.[117] Smith's formal argument, however, went even further; as we have seen, his contention was that manufacturers and farmers advanced the higher wages and recompensed themselves 'together with the additional profit' on the advances. This, as Ricardo observed, suggests that even the loss in purchasing power is somehow avoided and the entire 'real' burden borne in the last resort by *landowners*.[118]

The ultimate source of the differences between himself and Smith was traced by Ricardo to the absence in the work of his predecessor of the conception of rent-free land at the margin of cultivation.[119] And it is true that in the Smithian structure the burden of an increase in wage costs might, in principle, be borne entirely by landlords.[120] Yet it is doubtful whether if faced by this extraordinary implication Smith would not have modified his formal position.

With the foregoing problem in mind, we turn to Smith's account of the declining secular rate of return on capital. While rising wages are a probable concomitant of the process of expansion it is clear that they do not represent a necessary condition for the decline in profits; and those secondary accounts which explain Smith's position on profit-rate variation simply in terms of the supply and demand for wage advances are misleading. (On the other hand, Smith's loose formulations leave open the possibility that increasing wages constitute one of the operative pressures.) The most general statement relates the declining profit rate to 'increased competition' between capitalists in *commodity* markets: 'The increase of stock, which raises wages, tends to lower profit. When the stocks of many rich merchants are turned into the same trade, their mutual competition naturally tends to lower its profit; and when there is a like increase of stock in all the different trades carried on in the same society,

117 *Principles of Political Economy*, 126–7.
118 *Ibid.*, 223–4. Ricardo objected equally strongly to the implication – actually noted by Smith – that an increase in the prices of manufactured wage goods in consequence of the initial disturbance would lead to a further money wage increase without apparent limit to the upward spiral (*ibid.*, 225).

  Smith's observations (*Wealth of Nations*, 97–8; 565–6) regarding the effects of high profits on prices are examined by Ricardo, *Principles*, 345–6.
119 *Ibid.*, 225–6.
120 Although the argument would be tortuous; for, unless we assume that workers consume agricultural produce only, there is no limit to the upward movement in money wages and the prices of manufactured wage goods, once the process is set in motion.

the same competition must produce the same effect in them all' (87).[121] This formulation has much in common with the traditional view of the matter already expressed, for example, by Hume, Massie, and Hutcheson. A fuller and more satisfactory account of the phenomenon in terms of an increasing paucity of available investment opportunities, which is consistent with Smith's general proposition that 'the ordinary rate of profit ... is every where regulated by the quantity of stock to be employed in proportion to the quantity of the employment, or the business which must be done with it,'[122] appears in Book II:

As capitals increase in any country, the profits which can be made by employing them necessarily diminish. It becomes gradually more and more difficult to find within the country a profitable method of employing any new capital. There arises in consequence a competition between different capitals, the owner of one endeavouring to get possession of that employment which is occupied by another. But upon most occasions he can hope to justle that other out of this employment, by no other means but by dealing upon more reasonable terms. He must not only sell what he deals in somewhat cheaper, but in order to get it to sell, he must sometimes too buy it dearer. The demand for productive labour, by the increase of the funds which are destined for maintaining it, grows every day greater and greater. Labourers easily find employment, but the owners of capitals find it difficult to get labourers to employ. Their competition raises the wages of labour, and sinks the profits of stock (336).[123]

A fuller understanding of the mechanisms involved may be achieved by consideration of disturbances which check or even reverse the trend. Smith had in mind the acquisition of 'new branches of trade' (as well as of 'new

---

121 Conversely, diminution of the capital stock raises the profit rate; for wages decline while at the same time capitalists remaining are enabled to sell at a higher price because of reduced competition: 'Their goods cost them less, and they get more for them' (*ibid.*, 94).

122 *Ibid.*, 799.

123 The only *specific* illustration of diminished investment opportunity – actually within agriculture itself – is given in conjunction with the initial statement. The cause of the downward trend is here related to the necessity of having recourse to land of increasingly inferior quality, namely to diminishing returns at the extensive margin in the special case of new colonies: 'High wages of labour and high profits of stock, however, are things, perhaps, which scarce ever go together, except in the pecular circumstances of new colonies. A new colony must always for some time be more under-stocked in proportion to the extent of its territory, and more under-peopled in proportion to the extent of its stock, than the greater part of other countries. They have more land than they have stock to cultivate. What they have, therefore, is applied to the cultivation only of what is more fertile and most favourably situated, the land near the sea shore, and along the banks of navigable rivers. Such land too is frequently purchased at a price below the value even of its natural produce. Stock employed in the purchase and improvement of such lands must yield a very large profit ... Its rapid accumulation in so profitable an employment enables the planter to increase the number of his hands faster than he can find them in a new settlement. Those whom he can find, therefore, are very liberally rewarded. As the colony increases, the profits of stock gradually diminish.

territory'). It must be emphasized that the argument does not relate to new opportunities which permit the profitable use of hitherto *idle* capital; but rather involves the possibility of diverting hitherto *fully utilized* capital away from low yielding branches of activity:

The acquisition of new territory, or of new branches of trade, may sometimes raise the profits of stock, and with them the interest of money, even in a country which is fast advancing in the acquisition of riches. The stock of the country not being sufficient for the whole accession of business, which such acquisitions present to the different people among whom it is divided, is applied to those particular branches only which afford the greatest profit. Part of what had before been employed in other trades, is necessarily withdrawn from them, and turned into some of the new and more profitable ones. In all those old trades, therefore, the competition comes to be less than before. The market comes to be less fully supplied with many different sorts of goods. Their price necessarily rises more or less, and yields a greater profit to those who deal in them, who can, therefore, afford to borrow at a higher interest (93).[124]

The analysis is, incidentally, applied to explain an upward movement in interest rates in London after the peace of 1763. 'New business' was provided by the British 'acquisitions' in North America and the West Indies, and capital was diverted away from the Mediterranean and European branches of trade.[125] The provision of the new markets by itself would not in fact raise the profit rate unless such diversions took place, and in the event that spare capital were available no such increase would have occurred: 'So great an accession of new business to be carried on by the old stock, must necessarily have diminished the quantity employed in a great number of particular branches, in which the competition being less, the profits must have been greater.'[126]

At this stage of the argument we note that when, in the course of development, the minimum rate of return has been reached and net investment reduced to zero, there then exists no pressure either to raise the wage rate or even to maintain it constant. It is certainly the case that Smith was concerned by the possibility that a cessation of accumulation would ultimately entail a

When the most fertile and best situated lands have been all occupied, less profit can be made by the cultivation of what is inferior both in soil and situation ... [But] the wages of labour do not sink with the profits of stock. The demand for labour increases with the increase of stock whatever be its profits; and after these are diminished, stock may not only continue to increase, but to increase much faster than before (*ibid.*, 92–3).

124 But Smith failed to consider profit opportunities regenerated by *technical progress*. (On this matter, see L.C. Robbins, 'On a Certain Ambiguity in the Conception of Stationary Equilibrium,' *Economic Journal*, XL (June 1930), 198n.: 'It is not until we come to Marshall and Clark that the technical presuppositions of Static analysis are thoroughly and clearly stated'.)

125 *Wealth of Nations*, 93–4; 562f.

126 *Ibid.*, 93–4. While the emphasis is on the profit rate on mercantile capital, in principle the average profit rate on all investments is affected.

wage rate actually reduced to the minimum of subsistence as a consequence of population expansion:

In a country which had acquired that full complement of riches which the nature of its soil and climate, and its situation with respect to other countries, allowed it to acquire; which could, therefore, advance no further, and which was not going backwards, both the wages of labour and the profits of stock would probably be very low. In a country fully peopled in proportion to what either its territory could maintain or its stock employ, the competition for employment would necessarily be so great as to reduce the wages of labour to what was barely sufficient to keep up the number of labourers, and, the country being already fully peopled, that number could never be augmented. In a country fully stocked in proportion to all the business it had to transact, as great a quantity of stock would be employed in every particular branch as the nature and extent of the trade would admit. The competition, therefore, would every-where be as great, and consequently the ordinary profit as low as possible (94-5).

But the reduction of wages to the level of subsistence did not, in Smith's view, *necessarily* require an actual expansion of population. For in static conditions the competitive determination of the wage-rate is likely to be irrelevant; employers' associations – difficult to maintain in circumstances of rising labour demand, as masters 'voluntarily break through the natural combination ... not to raise wages' – take on renewed vigour in conditions of stagnation and are able to impose low wages (although no amount of bargaining strength could for long force real wages *below* the subsistence level if the work force is to be maintained).[127] Wages are thus prevented by way of monopsonistic pressures from swallowing up profits. This evidently is the situation Smith had in mind when he observed that in old-established and slowly expanding or stagnant countries 'rent and profit eat up wages, and the two superior orders of people oppress the inferior one.'[128] Where profits too are at a minimum the designation 'oppressive' attached to capitalists would scarcely be appropriate.

Any situation wherein wages are *artificially* reduced to subsistence would not, in strict logic, be a permanent one. The stationariness initially postulated would be temporary only, insofar as accumulation out of artificially maintained profits recommences. If the stationary state is indeed to be 'permanent' then it will set in only in circumstances which preclude the further effective exer-

127 *Ibid.*, 67-8. In this context, it is to 'common humanity' that Smith has recourse to explain why wages will not be reduced below subsistence (*ibid.*, 71) confirming that it is the arbitrary decision of the monopsonistically-organized employers – rather than the population mechanism – which assures a floor to the real wage rate.

F.H. Knight, 'The Ricardian Theory of Production and Distribution,' *Canadian Journal of Economics and Political Science*, I (Feb. 1935), reprinted in Knight, *On the History and Method of Economics* (Chicago, 1956), 80f.; and L.C. Robbins, 'On a Certain Ambiguity in the Conception of Stationary Equilibrium,' 196-7, provide valuable accounts of Smith's position but do not clarify adequately the circumstances under which the alternative approaches were said to apply.

128 *Wealth of Nations*, 532.

tion of monopsony power, that is when population size is such that wages are at subsistence in consequence of the preceding phase of operation of the competitive mechanism in the labour market. Here there is no further scope for the artificial regeneration of profits.[129]

Smith's position may be briefly compared with those adopted subsequently by Ricardo and Marx. Central to the Ricardian analysis are, of course, the assumptions of 'long-run' competitively-determined subsistence wages, and falling productivity of labour in the production of agricultural wage goods. But Ricardo took for granted, without adequate justification, the *stability* of the (competitively-determined) 'short-run' wage rate which characterizes the stage prior to population expansion and missed the import of Smith's discussion of unequal bargaining power in certain circumstances. Indeed he took a cavalier approach to the population mechanism as a whole, failing, for example, to recognize the significance of Smith's concern with the precise choice of commodities purchased by labour out of their (initially) high *per capita* wages.[130] His methodological technique diverted attention from the practical issues which so much concerned Smith.

The breakdown of competitive processes in the labour market which Smith takes into account – and the allowance that wages might be depressed artificially – has the further implication that the practice of 'moral restraint' would be a less effective means of maintaining (or raising) working-class living standards than is the case according to orthodox classical analysis. Smith's vision was actually one of rapid expansion and rising living standards, in which circumstances population increase was not considered undesirable, but the conceptual relationships which we have outlined take on particular relevance in any attempt to define Smith's place within classical economic thought. And from this viewpoint we note an interesting parallel between Smithian and Marxian doctrine. The tendency for the rate of profit to fall, of

129 The account provided of contemporary China, *ibid.*, 71, apparently illustrates such a situation.

Cannan, *Theories of Production and Distribution*, 218, remarks that Smith's proposition regarding the small likelihood of high wages and high profits scarcely fits in well with his contention that the stationary state is characterized by both low wages and low profits. It follows from our account, however, that the former situation is typical of a 'temporary' degree of stationariness, while the latter characterizes the 'permanent' state – in the absence of exogenous disturbances – where although wages are at subsistence there is no possibility of artificially raising the profit rate.

130 In the Ricardian analysis, an increase in savings – in the case of a given population – entails a transfer of purchasing power from capitalists to labour. The aggregate level of expenditure remains constant since workers are in a position to purchase *luxury goods*. It is taken for granted that population would ultimately expand, and little attention is paid to the precise demographic processes involved. Cf. *Principles of Political Economy*, 289: 'If the funds for the maintenance of labour were doubled, trebled, or quadrupled, there would not long be any difficulty in procuring the requisite number of hands, to be employed by those funds.' In fact, by the 'demand for labour' Ricardo commonly meant the *employment capacity* of the economy when wages are at subsistence.

course, plays a key role in Marx's predictions. In this case, however, the mechanism which assures that profits are not in fact swallowed up by wages is the introduction of labour-saving technical change which regenerates a 'permanent' excess labour supply and assures the depression of wages to the subsistence minimum.[131] This mechanism is independent of any population response and thus plays precisely the same role as does monopsonistic pressure in the Smithian argument.

131 *Capital*, I, Modern Library ed. (New York, 1906), 681–703.

SIX

Capital accumulation

THE SAVINGS PROCESS

Smith's formulation of the savings process – to the effect that 'what is annually saved is as regularly consumed as what is annually spent, and nearly in the same time too; but it is consumed by a different set of people'[1] – has created chaos in the secondary literature. It suggests, it is said, that saving never leads to any *actual* change in the real stock of capital goods, since it is not apparently the machinery and structures created by capital-goods labour which is 'saved' but rather the food, clothing and lodging – the wages goods – consumed by them: ' "What is annually saved," is thus made to signify, not the annual additions to the stock of the community, the surplus of production over consumption, but the **wages of productive labourers**. Whether it means the wages of all productive labourers or only the wages of those who are employed in producing the additions to the capital, it is not necessary to decide. In either case, it is plain that Adam Smith does not mean by "saving" what we mean by it. His "savings," instead of being accumulations or stores of the produce of past labour, are a part of the annual produce and annual consumption.'[2]

1 Adam Smith, *Wealth of Nations*, 321.
2 Edwin Cannan, *A History of the Theories of Production and Distribution in English Political Economy From 1776 to 1848*, 3rd ed. (London, 1917; New York, 1967), 58.
  Cannan (*ibid.*, 51f.) has made the point that Smith in his analysis of II.3 failed to appreciate that capital should be understood as a *stock* concept, for in this chapter he apparently envisages capital *as part of the annual produce*. For example, he calculated the current profit rate on a part of the annual produce or expenditure (instead of on the true capital), that is, as a rate on 'capital' considered as that portion of the annual produce which is neither rent nor profit. In brief 'capital *annually employed*' seems to be the relevant concept in II.3. The only way a particular part of the annual produce can be identical with a particular part of the accumulated stock is if 'the whole stock of provisions, materials and finished goods is turned over or circulated once a year, so that the annual produce of them and the stock of them [when at maximum] are equal' (*ibid.*, 62).

It is, however, very unlikely that this was Smith's position in view of the attention paid to fixed capital and its maintenance in the two immediately preceding chapters, and while there is little formal attention paid to fixed capital in Book II, Chapter 3 there can be no doubt that Smith would insist upon an allowance for depreciation when calculating net profits and rent. The formulation of the savings process leaves much to be desired but it is apparent that Smith was not attempting to define the actual *outcome* thereof as we shall now show.[3]

We need not repeat here Smith's numerous references to real capital goods. We note, however, that immediately before the above formulation of the savings process, Smith had been careful to refer to an actual expansion of the capital stock: 'But whatever industry might acquire, if parsimony did not save and *store up*, the capital would never be the greater.'[4]

This conception is developed further in Smith's elaboration of the fundamental index of national 'prosperity or decay' which runs in terms of the 'balance of the annual produce and consumption.' The ambiguity is not resolved, it may still be insisted, insofar as the process of *expansion* is concerned, since Smith might by 'consumption' be excluding that by capital-goods workers. But it becomes clear from the account of the process of *decline* that Smith can only have in mind changes in the actual stock of accumulated goods:

If a nation consume more than it produces, poverty is inevitable; if its annual produce be ninety millions and its annual consumption an hundred, then it spends, eats, and drinks, tears, wears, ten millions more than it produces, and its stock of opulence must gradually [go] to nothing.[5]

There is another balance, indeed, which has already been explained [*Wealth of Nations*, 321], very different from the balance of trade, and which, according as it happens to be either favourable or unfavourable, necessarily occasions the prosperity or decay of every nation. This is the balance of the annual produce and consumption. If the exchangeable value of the annual produce, it has already been observed, exceeds that of the annual consumption, the capital of the society must annually increase in proportion to this excess. The society in this case lives within its revenue, and what is

Our approach, however, suggests that in II.3 the emphasis is on capital as part of the annual produce because the special context makes this procedure suitable.
It does not necessarily mean that, in principle, or as a rule, long-lived fixed capital is ruled out.

Karl Marx, *Capital*, vol. I, Modern Library ed. (New York, 1906), 647, has directed a similar criticism against Smith. All that apparently is involved in capital accumulation is the support of labour: 'Adam Smith, by a fundamentally perverted analysis, arrives at the absurd conclusion, that even though each individual capital is divided into a constant and a variable part, the capital of society resolves itself only into variable capital, *i.e.*, is laid out exclusively in payment of wages.'

3 For this view see also Lord Robbins, *The Theory of Economic Development in the History of Economic Thought* (London, 1968), 49.

4 *Wealth of Nations*, 321 (author's emphasis).

5 Adam Smith, *Lectures on Police, Justice, Revenue and Arms* (1763), ed. E. Cannan (1896; New York, 1964), 207.

annually saved out of its revenue, is naturally added to its capital, and employed so as to increase still further the annual produce. If the exchangeable value of the annual produce, on the contrary, fall short of the annual consumption, the capital of the society must annually decay in proportion to this deficiency. The expence of the society in this case exceeds its revenue, and necessarily encroaches upon its capital. Its capital, therefore, must necessarily decay, and, together with it, the exchangeable value of the annual produce of its industry (464).

Moreover, in a discussion of contemporary British economic experience, within the present context of 'Accumulation of Capital,' Smith in fact deals directly with changes in the real capital stock:

So great a share of the annual produce of the land and labour of the country, has, since the revolution, been employed upon different occasions, in maintaining an extraordinary number of unproductive hands. But had not those wars given this particular direction to so large a capital, the greater part of it would naturally have been employed in maintaining productive hands, whose labour would have replaced, with a profit, the whole value of their consumption. The value of the annual produce of the land and labour of the country, would have been considerably increased by it every year, and every year's increase would have augmented still more that of the following year. *More houses would have been built, more lands would have been improved, and those which had been improved before would have been better cultivated, more manufactures would have been established, and those which had been established before would have been more extended* ... (328; author's emphasis).

Finally we note Smith's distinction within consumption expenditure between two different categories, namely non-durables (including services) and durables. The process of 'accumulation' of durable consumer goods is here quite clear:

durable
goods

The revenue of an individual may be spent, either in things which are consumed immediately, and in which one day's expence can neither alleviate nor support that of another; or it may be spent in things more durable, which can therefore be accumulated, and in which every day's expence may, as he chuses, either alleviate or support and heighten the effect of that of the following day ... Were two men of equal fortune to spend their revenue, the one chiefly in the one way, the other in the other, the magnificence of the person whose expence had been chiefly in durable commodities, would be continually increasing ... that of the other on the contrary, would be no greater at the end of the period than at the beginning ...

As the one mode of expence is more favourable than the other to the opulence of an individual, so is it likewise to that of a nation. The houses, the furniture, the clothing of the rich, in a little time, become useful to the inferior and middling ranks of people (329–30).

But the initial outlay is stated to involve, in the one case, the employment of 'a great number of menial servants' and, in the other, 'the setting to work masons, carpenters, upholsterers, mechanics, &c.'[6] In essence we can draw a parallel between this latter process whereby durable consumer goods are produced, and a process of true savings where labour is currently maintained with the objective of making additions to the stock of capital goods.

We conclude, therefore, that while the savings process involves the *maintenance* of capital-goods workers, the outcome of the process is an addition to the real capital stock including both fixed and circulating capital.[7] In the chapter on accumulation it was the process which Smith had in mind – particularly the proposition that no leakage from the income stream, no gap between planned savings and investment is involved – and for this purpose it was not strictly essential to emphasize the outcome itself.[8] Unfortunately he failed to explain precisely how, in the end result, the capital stock will be allocated between alternative categories of capital, particularly the fixed and circulating elements thereof.

The basic assumptions of the corn model outlined above – that capital is all circulating capital and that there is a single capital good – may be recalled at this juncture. These assumptions make it possible to regard the annual period as completely 'self-contained,' insofar as we exclude (by the first) long-lived capital goods and the problem that the value of such capital goods – both old and currently produced – depends on their *expected* lifetime earnings; and (by the second) the problem of explaining the distribution of the final capital stock which also would depend upon the conditions *expected* to prevail in the future. A growth model of this kind, it is argued – one which uses the 'static method' in that in each single period equilibrium is determined by current parameters – was the only one within Smith's vision or technical capability.[9]

6 *Wealth of Nations*, 329, 331.
7 Smith also recognized that additional capital goods may be obtained by importation following changes in the supply of paper money. See below, 207.
8 David Ricardo's clarification of the proposition that 'savings are consumed' is helpful. It is made quite clear that what he has in mind by the proposition is not the *outcome* of a 'completed' savings process but the use to which saved income is put: 'When we say that revenue is saved, what we mean is, that the portion of revenue, so said to be added to capital, is consumed by productive instead of unproductive labourers. There can be no greater error than in supposing the capital is increased by non-consumption.' (*On the Principles of Political Economy and Taxation*, in Piero Sraffa, ed., *The Works and Correspondence of David Ricardo*, I (Cambridge, 1951), 151n.) By 'productive' labour Ricardo means workers engaged in the capital-goods industries and by 'unproductive workers' he refers to consumer-goods workers: 'If I have a revenue of £2,000 – in the expenditure of which I necessarily employ labour. If I turn this revenue into capital, I at first employ the same labour as before, but productively instead of unproductively. This labour may be employed in making a machine ... Or the labour may be employed on the land [in producing wages goods].' (*Notes on Malthus' Principles*, in Sraffa, ed., *Works*, II, 234–5.) We need not enter here into an analysis of the precise form taken by additions to the capital stock in the Ricardian analysis. The main point, however, stands out. While the saving process involves the *maintenance* of the capital-goods workers, the *completed outcome* of the process is an addition to the capital stock.
9 J.R. Hicks, *Capital and Growth* (Oxford, 1965), 33, 40–1.

It may be true that the incorporation into the growth model of fixed capital could not have been treated correctly with the available analytical tools. But this fact does not mean that Smith was necessarily *aware* of the limitation. We cannot rule out the possibility that his system was more complex than that suggested by the corn model, even if this necessitates the conclusion that it suffered from logical error, for example, in a neglect of expectations. Reversing the argument, although the neglect of expectations, and interrelations between periods, may imply the assumption of homogeneous circulating capital, we cannot conclude that Smith was necessarily conscious of this implication. The model does not appear to be an accurate representation of Smith's intention.

It must also be noted that Smith failed to clarify the fact that, in strict logic, an increase in the capital stock can be achieved only by means of a transfer of labour from the consumer-goods sector rather than the service sector since we must be assured of the availability of complementary inputs required to support the new capital-goods workers. Such inputs we may suppose might be released along with a reduction in the output of consumer goods only since services are produced by labour alone in the Smithian system.[10] It is in the subsequent period, after additions to the capital stock have been generated, that it will be possible to absorb increased numbers of men from the service sector.[11]

We must also recognize certain conceptual difficulties in the way of an adequate account of the process. The distinction between *stock* and *flow* was not clearly drawn and consistently maintained in the *Wealth of Nations*. As one obvious example, the very title of the work refers to a stock concept whereas Smith's concern, as defined in the initial paragraph of the introduction and as is clear throughout, is annual income. As a second instance, the wages-fund theory itself involves dealing with a flow in terms of the fund which determines it. The failure to make a clear-cut distinction is not, perhaps, surprising, for the mercantilist writers never emphasized *income* (and the Physiocrats never emphasized labour as the source of income); the problem was a new one. The conceptual difficulty of distinguishing between stock and flow concepts doubtless contributes to an explanation of Smith's peculiar formulation of the savings process. It is unlikely, had the distinction been clear to him, that he would have coined the paradoxical phrase – 'what is annually saved is as regularly consumed as what is annually spent' – which indeed formally implies a confusion between the consumption by capital-goods workers and the additions to capital goods themselves.[12] It is noteworthy too

---

10 In fact in the formal analysis of the savings process it is presumed that saving involves both a reduction in the employment of servants and a reduction in direct consumption (*Wealth of Nations*, 321–2).

11 Alternatively the productive work force might be recruited from natural population growth.

12 *Wealth of Nations*, 321. The problem of interpretation arises throughout the *Wealth of Nations*, e.g.: 318–19; 326; 456–7; 877f. Note for example the ambiguity of the following statement: 'When the public expence is defrayed by funding, it is defrayed by the annual destruction of some capital which had before existed in

that in Smithian national-income accounting practice not only depreciation, but even *additions* to fixed capital are formally excluded from the definition of net national product. It is possible that this practice clouded the issue further. To say this is not, however, to attribute to Smith a neglect of 'genuine' capital accumulation.

THE STRUCTURE OF CAPITAL

In the final chapter of Book II ('Of Different Employment of Capitals'), Smith distinguishes between the employment-supporting capacities of alternative investments. The main proposition of the chapter is in fact that 'Though all capitals are destined for the maintenance of productive labour only, yet the quantity of that labour, which equal capitals are capable of putting into motion, varies extremely according to the diversity of their employment; as does likewise the value which that employment adds to the annual produce of the land and labour of the country' (341).[13]

It is worthwhile recalling briefly at this point Smith's formal statement of the functions of different categories of capital. Technical improvements, to be effective, must be embodied in *fixed* capital. It is *circulating* capital which is said to have the function of 'putting industry into motion' by the provision of materials and wages; this function refers to the support of both 'maintenance' and 'operating' labour.[14] As Cannan has pointed out, however, Smith sometimes relates the employment capacity of the economy to its *total* (rather than merely its circulating) capital.[15] This must presumably be taken subject to the assumption that the *distribution* of capital between agriculture, manufacturing, and trade, is constant.

Yet, significantly, the actual treatment of the employment capacities of each sector in II.v does *not* turn upon the fixed-circulating capital ratio. For the

the country; by the perversion of some portion of the annual produce which had before been destined for the maintenance of productive labour, towards that of unproductive labour' (*ibid.*, 878).

13 *Ibid.*, 341. Cf. almost identical statements, *ibid.*, 343 and 348.

14 Smith is careful to emphasize the role of *maintenance* labour. Thus to some extent circulating capital is used in the maintenance of fixed capital, and technical changes which simplify equipment allow a transfer of such circulating capital to operating functions. See in particular, *ibid.*, 266–7 (II.i) regarding the need for circulating capital to support maintenance men; *ibid.*, 272, 276 (II.ii) regarding technical change lowering the maintenance costs of fixed capital and thus releasing circulating capital and labour for current operations; and *ibid.*, 266–7 (II.i), 279–80 (II.ii) regarding the dependence of employment capacity on circulating capital.

E. Cannan, *Theories of Production and Distribution*, 66, has complained of a certain confusion insofar as circulating capital is said to have the *same* function as fixed capital, while at the same time it is also said 'to put industry in motion.' This is scarcely a serious criticism: both maintenance and operating labour are supported by materials and wage goods and their total number depends on circulating capital.

15 *Ibid.*, 67.

categorization is based simply on the fraction of the capital outlay which is devoted within each of the three broad sectors to wages capital as distinct from expenditure on *any* produced input, whether fixed capital or raw materials. The 'very different proportions between the fixed [capital structures and equipment] and circulating capitals [materials and wages] employed in [different occupations]'[16] plays no part, and the relevance of this distinction for employment is simply neglected. Thus, for example, according to II.v, trade is regarded as *more* capital-intensive than manufactures despite the fact that the fixed capital required – as emphasized in II.i – is quite negligible.[17]

The *retailer* will per $100 invested (immediately) employ very little productive labour. Indeed he alone represents the 'productive labour' employed and his profits are all that is added to the annual produce.[18] The bulk of his investment outlay merely replaces the capital of wholesale merchants from whom he purchases inventory (with the merchants' profits). Per $100, the *wholesale merchant* employs (immediately) more productive labour. His capital employs – apart from himself – sailors and carriers, and only indirectly contributes to employment by replacing the capitals of farmers and manufacturers with their profits. The value added in this case to the price of commodities amounts to the wages of transportation workers and the wholesaler's own profits. In the case of the *manufacturer* an investment of $100 will be allocated partly in 'a fixed capital in the instruments of his trade' and replace with its profits the capitals of the machine makers; and part of the 'circulating capital' investment is 'in purchasing materials' and replaces with profit the capital of farmers. But in contrast to wholesale and retail trade

a great part of it is always, either annually, or in a much shorter period, distributed among the different workmen whom he employs. It augments the value of those materials by their wages, and by their masters profits upon the whole stock of wages, materials, and instruments of trade employed in the business. It puts immediately into motion, therefore, a much greater quantity of productive labour, and adds a much greater value to the annual produce of the land and labour of the society, than an equal capital in the hands of any wholesale merchant (344).

16 *Wealth of Nations*, 263.
17 'Different occupations require very different proportions between the fixed and circulating capitals employed in them.
    The capital of a merchant, for example, is altogether a circulating capital. He has occasion for no machines or instruments of trade, unless his shop, or warehouse, be considered as such.
    Some part of the capital of every master artificer or manufacturer must be fixed in the instruments of his trade. This part, however, is very small in some, and very great in others ...' (*Wealth of Nations*, 263). The definition of 'fixed' and 'circulating' capital is in terms of whether a particular item remains with or leaves the owner; but it will be recalled that a parallel and more meaningful definition in terms of durability is sometimes given.
18 *Ibid.*, 343. Note that 'the persons whose capital are employed in any of those four ways are themselves productive labourers.' Smith consistently classifies employers in the present chapter as productive labourers and their profits as the return to labour. A similar approach is made in his analysis of Physiocracy.

But the employment generating capacity of *agriculture* heads the list. The following passage contains several extraordinary propositions:

No equal capital puts into motion a greater quantity of productive labour than that of the farmer. Not only his labouring servants, but his labouring cattle, are productive labourers. In agriculture too nature labours along with man; and though her labour costs no expence, its produce has its value, as well as that of the most expensive workman ... The labourers and labouring cattle, therefore, employed in agriculture, not only occasion, like the workmen in manufactures, the reproduction of a value equal to their own consumption, or the capital which employs them, together with its owners profits; but of a much greater value ... the reproduction of the rent of the landlord (344).

If it is possible to accept the definition of labouring cattle as 'productive labour,' the propositions here are that, per $100, more labour is (immediately) employed than in any other sector, and that the value added by the investment is greater than in any other sector because of the utilization of land in the agricultural production function: 'The capital employed in agriculture, therefore, not only puts into motion a greater quantity of productive labour than any equal capital employed in manufactures, but in proportion too to the quantity of productive labour which it employs, it adds a much greater value to the annual produce of the land and labour ...'[19] Accordingly, Smith concluded that 'of all the ways in which a capital can be employed, it is by far the most advantageous to the society.'[20]

19 *Ibid.*, 345.
20 *Ibid.* The issues involved here are unsound. In the first place, Smith had elsewhere – more correctly – categorized labouring cattle as an item in 'fixed capital' (e.g. *ibid.*, 263). Secondly, he assumes that the phenomenon of rent is solely limited to agricultural activity. And thirdly, he looks upon land as an efficient machine which – being relevant solely in agriculture – raises the physical and value productivity in that sector and in that sector only. Apart from the impossibility of comparing the physical productivities of different sectors at the same point in time, the minimal applicability of specialized processes in the agricultural sector is completely neglected in the present context. Finally, land scarcity as a necessary condition for the appearance of rent is also neglected.

Cannan, *Theories of Production and Distribution*, 69, condemns Smith of basing his argument entirely on the number of employees which the retailer, merchant, manufacturer, and farmer respectively employ, rather than the number employed by a *given outlay*. However, the fact is that Smith is extremely careful to say that it is 'equal capitals' which are involved in the comparison. It should be allowed that he was led nonetheless to make the error by reasoning along the lines suggested by Cannan. In other words, despite Smith's statements regarding the employment-generating capacity of given sums invested in different sectors, he has failed to prove his point and it may be that he was misled into making the statements by arguing too widely from the observation that fewer men are employed in a shop, than in a workhouse or a farm (where in fact cattle are classified with men).

Cannan also argues that in the individual firm employment may be constrained by capital because the firm has to conform with the going technique, while this is not so for the total economy (*ibid.*, 70). A similar criticism is directed against J.S. Mill

The neglect in the present context, of the distribution of the capitalist's outlays between fixed capital and materials means in fact that all *industrial* activities are taken to be identical with regard to their employment-generating potentials.[21] Two instances of this general neglect of the capital structure within industry may be noted here. An argument that the weaver needs 'more capital' than the spinner implies the almost complete neglect of the capital structures involved in the production of different goods, or, more specifically in the present instance, in the different 'stages' in the production of a particular good. For the weaver is said to require more capital than the spinner[22] simply

(*ibid.*, 92f.) : 'It is perfectly obvious that industry or labour can never be brought to a stand by the inaccessibility of materials or the instruments of production so long as food, drink and, in some situations, clothing are obtainable.' Now, while Cannan is correct in noting that as long as the means of feeding and clothing are available men can be set to work producing *something*, the important question, which he neglects, is whether it is thereby possible to satisfy the actual pattern of expenditure by consumers and others. Cf. discussion by the present writer, 'Technology and Aggregate Demand in J.S. Mill's Economic System,' *Canadian Journal of Economics and Political Science*, XXX (May 1964), 176.

21 Marx attributes to 'variable' capital (the classical wages-fund) only – the counterpart of the labour input – the ability to generate surplus value. Constant capital (including both fixed capital and materials) is merely replaced in the process of production. Consequently, it will be that sector with the highest variable-constant capital ratio which will generate (per $100) the greatest surplus value. In essence Smith's classifications of Book II.v also emphasize *constant* and *variable* capital (rather than fixed and circulating capital), and it is his contention in this chapter that the value added per dollar of investment will be the greatest in those sectors with the highest labour-capital ratios.

How far the analogy with Marx should be taken is a matter of judgment. By 'surplus value' Marx means rent as well as profit, whereas Smith attributes rent to the contribution of *land* in the production process. If, however, we ignore these latter occasions – that is, we consider only industry and trade where in Smith's own view rent is inapplicable – it does indeed appear that at least a *formal* analogy may be made. But it must then be noted that the Marxian problem of profit-rate equalization makes an appearance. Smith does not neglect interest or profit on the value of the fixed capital (the 'manufactory' and the machinery), although he fails to account adequately for it; profits are generated 'upon the whole stock of wages, materials, and instruments of trade employed in the business' (*Wealth of Nations*, 344). Moreover, profits are proportional to value added: 'The produce of industry is what it adds to the subject or materials upon which it is employed. In proportion as the value of this produce is great or small, so will likewise be the profits of the employer' (*ibid.*, 423). We must then explain the process whereby profit rates are equalized across the board when different constant-variable capital ratios exist between industries. Those sectors with a relatively high fraction of wages in a given capital should, in principle, have a relatively high profit rate. (The problem only arises, it must be emphasized, in consequence of the classifications utilized in Book II.v which are not typical.)

22 *Ibid.*, 51. There is considerable ambiguity here regarding the units of measurement of output, but it seems clear that Smith has in mind a comparison which relates to the same level of output. Thus if the basic unit for the spinner is 1000 pounds weight of raw flax, the 'equivalent' unit for the weaver will be that amount of spun yarn which has been manufactured therefrom.

on the grounds that he has in his outlays to 'replace the capital' of the spinner – in the present instance the 'periodical expenditure of the earlier manufacturer' – and also pays the wages of his immediate employees.[23] A consideration of the capital structures in weaving and spinning, however, would inquire into the fixed capital structures required, and there is no evidence that weaving technology calls for a heavier fixed capital complex than does spinning. Moreover, there is no good purpose served in comparing capital outlays for the 'same' level of output, since the most efficient output may be quite different in the two cases.[24]

A similar criticism may be made of the analysis by Smith according to which 'high profits tend much more to raise the price of work than high wages.'[25] Here too, as Cannan has pointed out, the capital structure of different stages is neglected: 'It is assumed either that profits means profit on turn-over and not on capital per annum, or else that the employers each have their capital turned over once a year.'[26] Smith may be assuming the existence of fixed capital, although in this case it is ignored in the sense that the profit calculation is on circulating capital (materials and wages) only; or it may be that the capitalist is assumed to have no fixed capital.

Smith extends the argument of II.v in dealing with 'wholesale trade.' A variety of different employment potentials are distinguished depending upon whether capital is invested in the 'home trade' (purchase of commodities and their sale domestically), in the 'foreign trade of consumption' (purchase abroad for sale at home or conversely), or in the 'carrying trade' (exchange between the commodities of foreign countries). There are two criteria involved here. In the first place, Smith argues that investment in the home trade replaces 'two distinct capitals' and 'thereby enables them to continue that employment,' whereas the foreign trade of consumption replaces only one home capital, and the carrying trade none at all.[27] The second criterion relates to the more rapid 'turnover rate' in the home trade compared with the foreign trade of consumption, and of the latter compared with the carrying trade: 'A capital ... employed in the home trade will sometimes make twelve operations, or be sent out and returned twelve times, before a capital employed in the foreign trade of consumption has made one. If the capitals are equal, therefore, the one will give four and twenty times more encouragement and support to the industry of the country than the other' (349).[28]

But the first of the two considerations added in the discussion of the wholesale trade is in fact in direct conflict with the basic criterion developed earlier, which, it will be recalled, dealt with the 'immediate' employment-generating

23 Cannan, *ibid.*, 51n.
24 Essentially Smith traces the passage of a particular weight of flax through the process of manufacture, noting correctly that the cost thereof rises with its passage up the vertical ladder. No one can deny this, but it is economically and technically immaterial.
25 *Wealth of Nations*, 97.   26 *Ibid.*, 98n.
27 *Ibid.*, 349.   28 Cf. also *ibid.*, 457f.; 462.

capacity of different investments and *not* with the question of expenditures which 'replace capitals.' The second consideration is also problematic: Smith applies it formally *solely to wholesale trade* although in principle the issue of alternative 'turnover rates' is highly relevant in all sectors including manufacturing and agriculture, as Ricardo recognized.[29]

We conclude that in the formal treatment of the employment-generating capacity of alternative investments, Smith neglects to make use of his recognition of empirical differences between the fixed-circulating capital ratios from product to product within industry or of differences in factor proportions generally within agriculture. (This neglect is all the more extraordinary in the light of his analysis of improvements in equipment which allows a transfer of expenditure by the firm from fixed to circulating capital and hence increased employment.[30])

Smith's failure to make use of his empirical recognition of different fixed-circulating capital ratios within the broad sectors seems to result partly from his classification of fixed and circulating capital according to whether or not the physical item in question remained with its owner. This classification is indeed quite immaterial from the viewpoint of employment (or value) theory.

A second consideration relates to the *empirical* observation that there were no significant differences in the technology utilized in at least three of the main manufacturing industries, namely silk, linen, and wool.[31] The heavy fixed capital requirement in mining and metallurgy was not taken into account in this context and it may be the case similarly that mining and metallurgy were ignored in the analysis of II.v. (It is, moreover, possibly the case that Smith's treatment of the effects of changing wage rates upon prices which implied identical coefficients between sectors was also limited to a treatment of the principal branches of manufacturing.)

Differences in the input structures which are emphasized in the fundamental chapter 'Of Different Employment of Capitals' are of three kinds. First, there are variations in the 'constant-variable' capital ratios between agriculture, manufacturing, wholesale trade, and retail trade.[32] Secondly, there is the

29 That it is in principle limited to trade is confirmed, *ibid.*, 566–7. Had he applied the concept generally however – as Cannan has remarked – 'it would have made havoc of the argument as to the superiority of agriculture' (*ibid.*, 349n) with its annual turnover period. Cf. Hla Myint, *Theories of Welfare Economics* (London, 1948), 77; J.J. Spengler, 'Adam Smith's Theory of Economic Growth – Part II,' *Southern Economic Journal*, XXVI (July 1959), 2n.

30 See below, 226–7.

31 Above, Chapter 3.

32 With regard to the ratio between capital and labour in agriculture the analysis is seriously vitiated by the classification of cattle as labour. This makes little sense. If we ignore it then the main feature distinguishing agriculture from other sectors is the use of land only. There may be no difference between the capital-labour ratio in agriculture and manufacturing when we reclassify cattle as fixed capital.

recognition within wholesale trade of a variety of differing 'turnover' rates. Thirdly, the use of land specifically in agriculture is given the greatest emphasis: here it is perhaps implied that land is irrelevant in any other branch of activity or that its relevance is quantitatively very slight.

Whether or not Smith consistently followed the outline developed in his chapter 'Of Different Employments of Capital' is, however, a further matter. We shall indeed show that differential factor proportions between agriculture and manufacturing were said to exert a pervasive influence upon the pattern of foreign trade.[33]

WAGES AS NET INCOME

At this point we turn to consider the Smithian approach to wages adopted in the first two chapters of the Second Book. These chapters in fact appear to deny the wages-fund approach; for in them very little emphasis is placed on capital as *advances* of subsistence, and its function in permitting time-consuming processes – the bridging of the interval between the commencement and the termination of a project. The emphasis is almost entirely upon items of the physical-capital structure which *co-operate* with labour in production. And wages are treated on a par with rent and profits as part of *net* revenue.[34]

33 The recognition of differing employment-supporting capacities by equal investments in alternative sectors plays havoc with the wages-fund theory strictly defined. For the logic of the theory requires that factor proportions are both constant and everywhere identical. If these conditions are not satisfied it follows that variations in the wage rate will affect the size of the aggregate wages bill by inducing some alteration in the technique adopted within each establishment and in the pattern of activity between industries. The wages bill then becomes an unknown and cannot be used together with the given population to determine the wage rate. The basic criticism directed against their predecessors by late nineteenth-century economists relates precisely to the issue of the 'pre-allocation' of the total stock of capital between the major sub-categories when allowance is made for the 'substitution' effects engendered by alterations in the factor returns. (See George J. Stigler, *Production and Distribution Theories* (New York, 1941), 283–5, and his comments on the critique by Knut Wicksell.)

The discussion of the present section is confined to technical relationships in various branches of the 'productive' sector. Very little formal analysis is to be found in the *Wealth of Nations* regarding the service or 'unproductive' sector. But it seems clear that in Smith's view wage goods *alone* are required for the employment of service workers. The necessity of providing *capital goods*, strictly defined, is specifically stated to apply only in the productive sector: 'In order to put industry into motion, three things are requisite; materials to work upon, tools to work with, and the wages or recompence for the sake of which the work is done' *Wealth of Nations*, 279–80. See also *ibid.*, 314: 'the labour of the manufacturer adds, generally, to the value of the materials which he works upon, that of his own maintenance, and of his master's profit. The labour of a menial servant, on the contrary, adds to the value of nothing.' This characteristic is potentially of some theoretic importance in light of the fact that the materials-output ratio was regarded as a *datum*. There are no such technical constraints in the service sector.

34 It has been pointed out by F.W. Taussig (*Wages and Capital* (New York, 1896), 147f.) that Smith failed to develop adequately the idea of capital as the source of *real* wages. For we might expect him 'to look for the capital which is the immediate

Part of the inventory of goods in the economy at any time (its 'stock') is 'reserved for immediate consumption' and is made up of the food, clothing, furniture and housing in the hands of the final consumer. The rest is 'capital,' both fixed and circulating.[35]

In the aggregative view of the economy, circulating capital was envisaged by Smith as an 'inventory' into which flows the current produce from farms and factories in the first instance, and from which flows consumers' goods and the means of maintaining fixed capital. All goods, in the business sector, including final consumption goods not yet sold, are included in the category of circulating capital.

The items constituting the community's 'circulating capital' include 'the stock of provisions in the possession of the butcher, grazier, farmer, the corn merchant, the brewer &c. and from the sale of which they expect to derive a profit'; the materials – raw and semi-manufactured – 'of clothes, furniture and buildings, which are not yet made up into any of these three shapes, but which remain in the hands of the growers, the manufacturers, the mercers'; and 'work which is made up and completed, but which is still in the hands of the merchant or manufacturer, and not yet disposed of or distributed to the proper consumers; such as the finished work ... ready made in the shops of the smith, the cabinet-maker, the goldsmith, the jeweller, the china merchant, &c.' Money is also an item in circulating capital although subsequently it is treated, in effect, as a category apart. In brief: the circulating capital consists 'of the provisions, materials, and finished work of all kinds that are in the hands of their respective dealers, and of the money that is necessary for circulating and distributing them to those who are finally to use, or to consume them.'[36]

Items of circulating capital (with the exception of money) 'are, either annually, or in a longer or shorter period, regularly withdrawn from it, and placed either in the fixed capital or in the stock reserved for immediate consumption.'[37] These are the *two* 'outlets' into which 'flows' the circulating

real source of wages, as of all other income' in the category relating to the consumables in dealers' hands ready for purchase by labourers. Yet Smith fails to do so illustrating his notion of 'circulating capital' by reference to luxury goods, namely 'the finished work which we frequently find ready-made in the shops of the smith, the cabinet-maker, the goldsmith, the jeweller, the china-merchant, &c.' He thus fails to explain adequately the connection between money and real wages or 'the nature and determination of the flow of consumable commodities whence real wages must come.'

J.A. Schumpeter, *History of Economic Analysis* (New York, 1954), 192, has also noted that while 'circulating capital' is said, in II.i, to include money, it does *not* include the means of labourers' subsistence although Smith's argument implies and calls for their inclusion.

M. Bowley (*Nassau Senior and Classical Economics* (London, 1937), 138–9) argues similarly that in these early chapters of Book II 'the time aspect of capital became more and more buried under the enumeration of the different forms of capital, and appeared to be flatly contradicted by the exclusion of subsistence in the hands of the labourer from capital.'

35 *Wealth of Nations*, 264.

36 *Ibid.*, 266.   37 *Ibid.*

capital of the community. The objective of circulating and fixed capital together is to 'maximize' the supply of consumer goods, which, it must be emphasized, includes goods purchased by labour: 'To maintain and augment the stock which may be reserved for immediate consumption, is the sole end and purpose both of the fixed and circulating capitals. It is this stock which feeds, clothes, and lodges the people. Their riches or poverty depends upon the abundant or sparing supplies which those two capitals can afford to the stock reserved for immediate consumption' (267).[38] In this formulation, workers purchase consumer goods along with, and from the same source, as capitalists and landlords.[39] There are no *special* characteristics attached to the source of real wages. In fact, the definition of 'circulating capital,' we have just seen, included the finished work 'in the shops of the smith, the cabinet-maker, the goldsmith, the jeweller, the china-merchant, &c.' items which are certainly not wage goods. The inclusion of such items in the same category as 'provisions' (and in fact that of raw materials as such) is an indication that Smith is simply defining as circulating capital the entire inventory of goods *of all kinds* wherever they may be in the business sector. These goods are circulating capital because their owners expect to sell them at a profit.[40] But if the immediate source of real wages is to be found in this category, so too is that of real profits and rent. There is absolutely no differentiation between wages and other incomes in this regard.

A full appreciation of this fact requires consideration of Smith's refusal, in the present context, to exclude wages from the *net* income of the community.

38 Cf. *ibid.*,273 where the objective is to augment the community's 'stock reserved for immediate consumption, the subsistence, conveniencies, and amusements of individuals.'

Circulating capital – envisaged as an inventory of completed and semi-completed goods in the business sector – is thus said to be the proximate source both for the maintenance of fixed capital and for the provision of consumer goods to the final purchaser. Yet it is important to note that fixed capital is required both in agriculture and mining, that is, in those sectors which provide raw materials and subsistence goods which, in the first instance, enter into the community's business inventory:

'So great a part of the circulating capital being continually withdrawn from it, in order to be placed in the other two branches of the general stock of the society, it must in its turn require continual supplies, without which it would soon cease to exist. These supplies are principally drawn from three sources, the produce of the land, of mines, and of fisheries. These afford continual supplies of provisions and materials, of which part is afterwards wrought up into finished work, and by which are replaced the provisions, materials and finished work continually withdrawn from the circulating capital ...

Land, mines, and fisheries, require all both a fixed and a circulating capital to cultivate them: and their produce replaces with a profit, not only those capitals, but all the others in the society. Thus the farmer annually replaces to the manufacturer the provisions which he had consumed and the materials which he had wrought up the year before; and the manufacturer replaces to the farmer the finished work which he had wasted and worn out in the same time' (267).

39 Cf. *Wealth of Nations*, 459, where there is evidently no 'simple minded' notion of advances to workers.

40 To be consistent, Smith should also have included machinery and buildings not yet sold to their final users.

Annual national income ('the whole price or exchange value of that annual produce') resolves itself into wages, profits and rents.[41] This annual revenue however must be further distinguished: 'The gross revenue ... comprehends the whole annual produce of their land and labour; the neat revenue, what remains free to them after deducting the expence of maintaining; first, their fixed; and, secondly, their circulating capital; or what, without encroaching upon their capital, they can place in their stock reserved for immediate consumption' (271). All expenses relating to the maintenance of fixed capital must be deducted to arrive at the net revenue. As Smith puts it: 'Neither the materials necessary for supporting their useful machines and instruments of trade, their profitable buildings, &c. nor the produce of the labour necessary for fashioning those materials into the proper form, can ever make any part of it' (271). Thus part of the labour exerted in any year and part of the stock of available materials is being used for maintenance operations, or what amounts to the same thing, to the 'production' of capital equipment and structures which replace those used up during the period.[42] Yet the wages of maintenance labour – labour involved in maintaining fixed capital intact – are still part of the net national income: 'The price of that labour may indeed make a part of it; as the workmen so employed may place the whole value of their wages in their stock reserved for immediate consumption.'[43] The point is that 'in other sorts of labour, both the price and the produce go to this stock, the price to that of the workmen, the produce to that of other people, whose subsistence, conveniencies, and amusements, are augmented by the labour of those workmen.'[44]

The distinction is illustrated by consideration of the effects on net income of a technical improvement, the advantage of which lies in the simplification of equipment thereby reducing annual maintenance charges.[45] On the assumption that the capitalists' total expenses are not reduced, so that any savings made on maintenance will be diverted to operating costs,[46] Smith points out

41 *Wealth of Nations,* 270.
42 In modern national income practice we deduct from GNP the accumulated depreciation allowances of all firms to arrive at an estimate of NNP. In essence, this amounts to the view that part of current annual production is being used to replace capital goods which have been worn out currently.
43 *Wealth of Nations,* 271.   44 *Ibid.*
45 *Ibid.,* 272. A repetition of the example (276) makes it explicit that the productivity of labour is presumed unchanged: 'every saving in the expence of supporting the fixed capital is an improvement of the neat revenue of the society. The whole capital of the undertaker of every work is necessarily divided between his fixed and his circulating capital. While his whole capital remains the same, the smaller the one part, the greater must necessarily be the other. It is the circulating capital which furnishes the materials and wages of labour, and puts industry into motion.
Every saving, therefore, in the expence of maintaining the fixed capital, which does not diminish the productive powers of labour, must increase the fund which puts industry into motion, and consequently the annual produce of land and labour, the real revenue of every society.'
46 Edwin Cannan, in an editorial comment (*ibid.,* 272n), points out that there is no reason for supposing that this transfer is at all 'necessary.'

that whereas wage costs remain unchanged – there being merely a diversion of labour from maintenance to operating functions – there is a reduction in depreciation charges and a consequent increase in profits.[47] In the case of maintenance operations, therefore, while wages do constitute part of the net national income, 'the produce' thereof does not, representing replacement items for the fixed capital stock, that is, 'depreciation.' But in the case of operating labour, both the wages earned and 'the produce' constitute part of the net income, the produce representing net profits or net rent.[48]

Thus far, Smith has been discussing the maintenance of fixed capital. That of circulating capital is treated quite differently:

But though the whole expence of maintaining the fixed capital is thus necessarily excluded from the neat revenue of the society, it is not the same case with that of maintaining the circulating capital. Of the four parts of which this latter capital is composed, money, provisions, materials and finished work, the three last, it has already been observed, are regularly withdrawn from it, and placed either in the fixed capital of the society, or in their stock reserved for immediate consumption. Whatever portion of those consumable goods is not employed in maintaining the former, goes all to the latter, and makes a part of the neat revenue of the society. The maintenance of those three parts of the circulating capital, therefore, withdraws no portion of the annual produce from the neat revenue of the society, besides what is necessary for maintaining the fixed capital (272).

At the aggregate level, therefore, production which 'replaces' goods consumed by workers, capitalists, and landlords represents net revenue.[49]

47 Thus suppose machine A requires $10.00 annually to be maintained intact and B requires only $9.00. Here in the second case $1 less is spent on maintenance and $1 more is available for operating the equipment. In both cases wage income is the same but there is $1 less depreciation charges in the case of B and accordingly $1 more profit on the assumption that the capitalists' total outlays are constant.

48 In this context, Smith draws the analogy discussed in Chapter 5 between the community's metallic money stock and its stock of fixed capital.

49 From the firm's viewpoint wages do appear as a 'cost' item (along with materials), even though from the aggregate point of view they are seen as part of 'net income' by Smith (*Wealth of Nations*, 266–7; author's emphasis): 'Every fixed capital is both originally derived from, and requires to be continually supported by a circulating capital. All useful machines and instruments of trade are originally derived from a circulating capital, which furnishes the materials of which they are made, *and the maintenance of the workmen who make them*. They require too a capital of the same kind to keep them in constant repair.

No fixed capital can yield any revenue but by means of a circulating capital. The most useful machines and instruments of trade will produce nothing without the circulating capital which affords the materials they are employed upon, *and the maintenance of the workmen who employ them*. Land, however improved, will yield no revenue without a circulating capital, *which maintains the labourers who cultivate and collect its produce*.'

It will be noted that Smith specifically insisted upon a distinction between circulating capital from the viewpoint of the firm and from that of the economy: 'That of an individual is totally excluded from making any part of his neat revenue, which must consist altogether in his profits. But though the circulating capital of every individual makes a part of that of the society to which he belongs, it is not

It appears from the analysis of the first two chapters of the second book that Smith *does not emphasize capital in its capacity of advances to labour*. (Indeed the entire treatment plays down advances altogether and emphasizes the regular flow of input and product, or what has come to be called synchronized activity.) Were it Smith's intention' to emphasize advances out of capital to labour specifically he would have found it necessary to represent circulating capital as flowing not only into the maintenance of fixed capital and into the provision of final consumption goods, but to the support of labour – as a separate category – as well.

This apparent contrast with the notion of wages as advances from capital can only be understood if Smith's objectives are made explicit. From the point of view of 'growth' Smith's emphasis is upon 'net income' in the sense of profits and rent only. Wages are excluded to the extent that the wherewithal for savings out of wage income is limited. From this viewpoint wages appear as a 'social cost' (comparable to depreciation of fixed capital) which must be met first before the potential means for further expansion is calculated.[50] The notion of *subsistence advances out of capital* comes into its own almost automatically as a useful tool in this context.

But the first two chapters do not have the specific treatment of growth or 'accumulation' in mind. Smith is writing *qua national income statistician*; and his classification of gross and net revenue is consistent with a general 'welfare' outlook according to which wages may be identified with rent and profit as part of 'net income.' (It was in fact precisely this approach to which Ricardo objected; for he took the position that a large aggregate wage income, representing a large population, was no advantage to society.[51]) From this viewpoint the only relevant deduction from gross national product which must be made to obtain net national income is the depreciation of fixed capital and not wage costs.

Furthermore, since Smith was dealing with the issue of national income from a welfare point of view, his attention was not focused specifically upon the notion of the production function. Accordingly, the role of capital in production, *narrowly defined* to include only activities in agriculture and industry, is played down: merchant stocks of all kinds appear as capital instead of the more specific categories of subsistence wages and raw materials.[52]

upon that account totally excluded from making a part likewise of their neat revenue' (*ibid.*, 273).

50 This version of net income is also used by Smith in estimating taxation capacity although he is careful to note that allowance should be made not only for rent and profits but also for wages above subsistence: 'It must always be remembered, however, that it is the luxurious and not the necessary expence of the inferior ranks of people that ought ever to be taxed' (*ibid.*, 839). See William J. Barber, *A History of Economic Thought* (London, 1967), 46–7 for a lucid account of this issue.

51 *Principles of Political Economy*, in Sraffa, ed., *Works*, vol. I, chap. XXVI, 'On Gross and Net Revenue,' 347f.

52 It will become clear below that such a distinction is of the greatest importance in the *Wealth of Nations* insofar as profits in agriculture and manufacturing are related to the employment of labour in production, whereas the profits of the merchants are the result of a process of 'buying cheap and selling dear.' In short, the traditional

THE PLACE OF MONEY IN ACCUMULATION

Smith in the *Wealth of Nations*, as in the earlier *Lectures*, made full use of Hume's specie-flow mechanism.[53] In his formal discussion of an exogenous increase in the supply of paper money Smith, it is true, merely states without specific reference to the relative price level that when more currency is issued (by way of bank loans) than is required to circulate internal trade – an amount presumed to be equal to the metallic currency originally circulating – the surplus would be exported 'to seek that profitable employment which it cannot find at home.'[54] But in this context Smith's object was essentially to contrast two alternative systems, namely a purely metallic currency and a mixed currency (including convertible paper) with the object of demonstrating that the aggregate money supply in both cases will be the same in the long run. For this purpose a full account of the precise effects emanating from an increase in the money supply by way of note issues was not perhaps deemed essential. However, in the context of a presumed injection into an economy of increased supplies of the monetary metals, in excess of the 'effectual demand,' it is made crystal clear that what must follow is an initial increase in the price level and a subsequent exportation of specie. Indeed, the point which Smith insists upon is that the process of equilibration is likely to be a very rapid one so that the initial disequilibrium will be speedily corrected, with little opportunity for relative price levels to remain long out of line:

The quantity of every commodity which human industry can either purchase or produce, naturally regulates itself in every country according to the effectual demand, or according to the demand of those who are willing to pay the whole rent, labour and profits which must be paid in order to prepare and bring it to market. But no commodities regulate themselves more easily or more exactly according to this effectual demand than gold and silver; because, on account of the small bulk and great value of those metals, no commodities can be more easily transported from one place to another, from the places where they are cheap, to those where they are dear, from the places where they exceed, to those where they fall short of this effectual demand ...

When the quantity of gold and silver imported into any country exceeds the effec-

way of considering profits was apparently retained in the case of the trader.

In this regard the view of Marx is particularly relevant. Cf. *Capital*, vol. II, (C.H. Kerr, Chicago, 1919), 243–4. Here Marx distinguishes between 'productive,' 'commodity,' and 'money capital.' The stocks of finished goods in the hands of producers or final sellers are no longer part of productive capital, but a special category apart from the production nexus, namely 'commodity capital.' Accordingly, Marx rejected the inclusion of wages goods within 'circulating capital' – in Smith's sense of the term.

53 A tradition has grown up in the secondary literature to the contrary. Cf. Jacob Viner, *Studies in the Theory of International Trade* (New York, 1937), 87; J.M. Low, 'An Eighteenth Century Controversy in the Theory of Economic Progress,' *The Manchester School of Economic and Social Studies*, XX, (Sept. 1952), 329; Frank Petrella, 'Adam Smith's Rejection of Hume's Price-Specie-Flow Mechanism: A Minor Mystery Resolved,' *Southern Economic Journal*, XXXIV (Jan. 1968), 365–74.

54 *Wealth of Nations*, 278. Specifically, since paper money is unacceptable abroad, it is the metallic currency that flows out.

tual demand, no vigilance of government can prevent its exportation. All the sanguinary laws of Spain and Portugal are not able to keep their gold and silver at home. The continual importations from Peru and Brazil exceed the effectual demand of those countries, and sink the price of those metals there below that in the neighbouring countries. If, on the contrary, in any particular country their quantity fell short of the effectual demand, so as to raise their price above that of the neighbouring countries, the government would have no occasion to take any pains to import them (404).[55]

Smith thus gave due attention in making his case against mercantilist preoccupations to the international distribution of specie with specific reference to the relative price level.[56]

Where Smith differed from Hume was, rather, with regard to certain more specific propositions relating to the place of money in the development process. In the first place, it was Hume's position in the essay 'Of Money' that a developing country would find its initial cost advantages continually diminishing in consequence of a rising level of money wages and prices. Smith in the *Wealth of Nations*, on the other hand, categorically rejected the view that the price level is likely to rise with growth; on the contrary, he insisted it was more likely to decline: 'Gold and silver will naturally exchange for a greater quantity of subsistence in a rich than in a poor country, in a country which abounds with subsistence, than in one which is but indifferently supplied with it.'[57] There were thus no necessary 'monetary' tendencies likely to check an ongoing process of development.

55 Cf. *Ibid.*, 479, regarding attempts to retain excessive supplies of the metals: 'The cheapness of gold and silver, or what is the same, the dearness of all commodities, which is the necessary effect of this redundancy of the precious metals, discourages both the agriculture and manufactures of Spain and Portugal, and enables foreign nations to supply them with many sorts of rude, and with almost all sorts of manufactured produce, for a smaller quantity of gold and silver than what they themselves can either raise or make them for at home.' The various prohibitions 'not only lower very much the value of the precious metals in Spain and Portugal, but by detaining there a certain quantity of those metals which would otherwise flow over other countries, they keep up their value in those other countries somewhat above what it otherwise would be, and thereby give those countries a double advantage in their commerce with Spain and Portugal. Open the flood-gates, and there will presently be less water above, and more below, the dam-head, and it will soon come to a level in both places.' (See also *Lectures*, 197.)
   The role of exchange-rate variation in the process of international adjustment is referred to, *Wealth of Nations*, 402.
56 For a full account see Robert V. Eagly, 'Adam Smith and the Specie-Flow Mechanism,' *Scottish Journal of Political Economy*, XVII (1970), 61–8. It is correct to emphasize, as does Eagly, the fact that Smith failed to recognize possible impediments to the specie-flow mechanism which a mixed currency might entail, as for example, when the initial disturbance relates to an *inadequate* money supply due to an expansion of the national product.
57 *Wealth of Nations*, 189. Cf. *ibid.*, 323–4. The position differs from that recorded in the *Lectures*, 198.

Of equal significance, Smith did not accept Hume's contention that, while the absolute quantity of money is immaterial, certain advantages may pertain to an economy while its money supply is actually increasing. These initial advantages – of higher employment without increased wages and higher output – presume initial unemployment. Since, as we shall see, Smith assumed as a rule full employment we may deduce that the stimuli envisaged by Hume would not pertain in the Smithian structure.[58]

Nonetheless, Smith himself in fact noted a specific relationship between the money supply and 'real' growth. In discussing the probable outcome of a relaxation by Spain and Portugal of their restrictions against the exportation of metals Smith argued that a large proportion of the metal exports would be exchanged abroad for *capital goods* rather than consumer goods, since in the first instance, real income and therefore consumption, will be little affected:

The gold and silver which would go abroad would not go abroad for nothing, but would bring back an equal value of goods of some kind or another. Those goods too would not be all matters of mere luxury and expence, to be consumed by idle people who produce nothing in return for their consumption. As the real wealth and revenue of idle people would not be augmented by this extraordinary exportation of gold and silver, so neither would their consumption be much augmented by it. Those goods would, probably, the greater part of them, and certainly some part of them, consist in materials, tools, and provisions, for the employment and maintenance of industrious people, who would reproduce, with a profit, the full value of their consumption. A part of the dead stock of the society would thus be turned into active stock, and would put into motion a greater quantity of industry than had been employed before (480).

Precisely the same argument appears in Smith's account of the probable effects of increased paper money by way of bank discounts, insofar as specie is exported in consequence partly for the purchase of 'an additional stock of materials, tools, and provisions, in order to maintain and employ an additional number of industrious people.'[59]

Yet, the positions of Hume and Smith are fundamentally dissimilar. In the first place, only for Smith is an expansion of capacity a necessary precondition for increased output and employment (in the productive sector). Equally significant is the obvious limit to any deliberate program of inflationary note issue designed to expand capacity in the Smithian structure, as outlined above, for Smith's entire case in favour of paper money as an efficient means of circulation is subject to a guarantee of ultimate convertibility. Hume, on the other hand, was able to recommend a policy of keeping the money supply continually rising, for the advantageous results expected therefrom did not depend specifically upon the issue of paper currency.

58 Smith in fact noted critically in the *Lectures* (197) that Hume seemed 'to have gone a little into the notion that public opulence consists in money.'
59 *Wealth of Nations*, 278.

Technical change

THE DIVISION OF LABOUR

As a necessary preliminary to a discussion of technical change strictly defined, we shall first consider Smith's treatment of 'division of labour.' The general analysis is well known although the sophistication of the argument and its implications are perhaps not adequately appreciated.

Smith's illustrations are drawn from nail-making and pin- and button-making. In the case of nail-making, specialization is merely by trade; while in that of buttons and pins each plant worker concentrates upon a single operation of the process. It is the advantages of *sub-division* of labour which Smith emphasizes.[1] The difference may be explained along the lines developed at greater length in a subsequent chapter, namely by the principle that 'the division of labour is limited by the extent of the market'[2]: demand for the output of the plant was sufficiently large in the case of pins and buttons to justify a labour force adequate for sub-division.

Smith's specific choice of an illustration from what was nonetheless a small-scale industry – a 'trifling manufacture' – is frequently noted. We may appreciate the choice to some extent from our earlier discussion of industry structure. Both the wool and linen industries, for example (two of the largest) were still organized in domestic units rather than in factories, while Smith's concern was clearly with specialization by factory labour where sub-division is relevant. The reason formally given by Smith – that he was choosing a case where all the stages involved could be observed within four walls – takes for granted workhouse as distinct from domestic organization: 'In those great manufactures ... which are destined to supply the great wants of the great body of the people, every different branch of the work employs so great a number of workmen,

1 Namely improved dexterity, saving of time, and the application of machinery invented by workmen. Adam Smith, *Wealth of Nations*, 7f.
2 *Ibid.*, 17.

that it is impossible to collect them into the same workhouse. We can seldom see more, at one time, than those employed in one single branch.'[3] The size of industry is thus seen to exert an influence upon the organization of activity, specifically the dispersion of processes between plants; this will help explain Smith's failure to illustrate specialization from the substantial iron-works at Carron with which he was familiar,[4] and where doubtless sub-division of labour was also practised.[5] It is the account of dependence of *sub-division* of labour upon size of plant; and of *dispersion of processes* between plants in large industries which represents Smith's original contribution.[6] It should be remarked that Smith's account is, in principle, quite applicable to the Soho hardware works.[7]

Although Smith did not, of course, introduce the notion of division of labour into the literature, his approach was novel insofar as he related subdivision of labour to size of plant and industry as shown above; but also in that it was seen to represent a crucial factor in economic progress. Technical progress and invention were to a considerable extent said to be *induced* by it. We shall discuss this matter in the next section. It is necessary, however, to bear in mind the fact that as far as the *application of new technology* – as distinct from organizational change – is concerned Smith's emphasis is almost entirely upon innovatory investment: technical change, apart from that of an organizational kind, must be 'embodied' in the capital structure.

The role of division of labour is emphasized specifically in the manufacturing sector: 'The perfection of *manufacturing* industry, it must be remembered, depends altogether upon the division of labour; and the degree to which the division of labour can be introduced into any manufacture, is necessarily regulated ... by the extent of the market.'[8] Seasonal characteristics limited

3 *Ibid.*, 4.

R.L. Meek ('Adam Smith and the Classical Theory of Profit,' in Meek, *Economics and Ideology and Other Essays* (London, 1967) 26n.) understands Smith's comment to be a reference to the domestic work in wool and linen manufacture. However, it seems that Smith is dealing here specifically with factory-organized activities, and intended to explain his neglect of other instances of plant operation.

4 *Wealth of Nations*, 76.

5 This view differs from that given by the present writer in his 'Some Technological Relationships in the *Wealth of Nations* and Ricardo's *Principles*,' *Canadian Journal of Economics and Political Science*, XXXII (May 1966), 192, where it is implied that the Carron works did not practise sub-division of labour.

Cannan has added a further reason for reference to the pin-factory: it allowed 'the exhibiting of division of labour in statistical form' (*Wealth of Nations*, 4n). Another suggestion offered for the neglect, in the present context, of any reference to Carron is that Smith wished to isolate the results of the application of division of labour from those of the use of machinery and power. Pin-making was ideal insofar as only simple appliances were used. Cf. T.S. Ashton, *An Economic History of England: The 18th Century* (London, 1966), 103.

6 See Jacob Viner, *Guide to John Rae's Life of Adam Smith* (New York, 1965), 103–9 who adopts this view in a discussion of some eighteenth-century literature on the division of labour.

7 See Chapter 3.   8 *Wealth of Nations*, 645. Author's emphasis.

specialization in agriculture. Accordingly, there is relatively little to chose between agricultural production costs in 'advanced' and 'under-developed' countries:

The nature of agriculture, indeed, does not admit of so many subdivisions of labour, nor of so complete a separation of one business from another, as manufactures. It is impossible to separate so entirely, the business of the grazier from that of the corn-farmer, as the trade of the carpenter is commonly separated from that of the smith. The spinner is almost always a distinct person from the weaver; but the plough-man, the harrower, the sower of the seed, and the reaper of the corn, are often the same. The occasions for those different sorts of labour returning with the different seasons of the year, it is impossible that one man should be constantly employed in any one of them (6).

Since large scale is of lesser relevance in agriculture, relatively little damage had been done historically by governmental restrictions of the market.[9] However it was a matter of degree only as we shall have occasion to see.

A considerable distinction was envisaged between the technological progress possible in different branches of manufacturing. A key determinant of the rate of change was said to be the nature of the raw materials used. Thus while, during the process of economic advance, rising wages and raw material prices tended to be counterbalanced by reduced labour costs due to 'better machinery,' 'greater dexterity,' and improved organization, there is no regular pattern. In 'carpenters and joiners work' there had in fact been no net cost reduction. In the case of clothing, we are told, there had occurred no large price reductions since about 1600; and – in the case of superfine cloth – there had even occurred a rise during the previous quarter century, because of 'the considerable rise in the price of the material, which consists altogether of Spanish wool.' Generally in fact 'in the clothing manufacture, the division of labour is nearly the same now as it was a century ago, and the machinery employed is not very different.' By contrast, there had occurred very extensive improvements in hardware manufacturing during the previous century. Thus in watch-making especially, but also in the work of cutlers and lock-smiths and in the production of 'Birmingham and Sheffield ware,' there had occurred very large price reductions: 'There are perhaps no manufactures in which the division of labour can be carried further, or in which the machinery employed admits of a greater variety of improvements, than those of which the materials are the coarser metals.'[10]

SOURCES OF TECHNOLOGY INTERNAL TO THE FIRM

Economic growth in the *Wealth of Nations* is characterized in part by the introduction of improved organization and new techniques, representing the

9 In discussing ancient states which 'had an aversion to the sea' so that trading outlets were restricted, Smith points out that greater damage was done to manufactures than to agriculture: 'Manufactures require a much more extensive market than the most important parts of the rude produce of the land' (*ibid.*, 646).

10 *Ibid.*, 243–4.

application by the firm of newly-developed knowledge; and in part by the introduction of techniques or organizational methods only profitable, or financially possible, at a larger scale of operation.

A number of characteristic features of the Smithian analysis may be noted. In the first place, we cannot always attribute to Smith a clear-cut distinction between technical change strictly defined and scale economies, either internal or external, for the development of new technology is itself often envisaged as a phenomenon of large size. The incentive for entrepreneurs to devote activity to invention (and innovation) is said to be a rising function of *total* employment, insofar as the probability of success in the effort to generate new technology increases with the size of plant:

The person who employs his stock in maintaining labour, necessarily wishes to employ it in such a manner as to produce as great a quantity of work as possible. He endeavours, therefore, both to make among his workmen the most proper distribution of employment, and to furnish them with the best machines which he can either *invent* or afford to purchase. *His abilities in both these respects are generally in proportion to the extent of his stock, or to the number of people whom it can employ* (260; author's emphasis).

The owner of the stock which employs a great number of labourers, necessarily endeavours, for his own advantage, to make such a proper division and distribution of employment, that they may be enabled to produce the greatest quantity of work possible. For the same reason, he endeavours to supply them with the best machinery which either he or they can think of (86).

To the formal efforts of the entrepreneur, emphasized in the above passages, we must add the informal and apparently costless inventive effort originating on the floor of the plant. New inventions were frequently the outcome of observations by specialist operators, so that until processes had become finely *subdivided* – also a result of large scale – an important source of new knowledge was unavailable: 'the invention of all those machines by which labour is so much facilitated and abridged, seems to have been originally owing to the division of labour ... A great part of the machines made use of in those manufactures in which labour is most subdivided, were originally the inventions of common workmen, who, being each of them employed in some very simple operation, naturally turned their thoughts towards finding out easier and readier methods of performing it' (9).[11]

11 This source was regarded by Smith as an important not a minor one as is clear from his demonstration of the inefficiency of slavery: 'Slaves, however, are very seldom inventive; and all the most important improvements, either in machinery, or in the arrangement and distribution of work, which facilitate and abridge labour, have been the discoveries of freemen. Should a slave propose any improvement of this kind, his master would be very apt to consider the proposal as the suggestion of laziness, and of a desire to save his own labour at the master's expence. The poor slave, instead of reward, would probably meet with much abuse, perhaps with some punishment' (*ibid.*, 648). In this regard he compares mining costs of the free Hungarians and the enslaved Turks to the disadvantage of the latter: 'The Hungarian mines are wrought by freemen, who employ a great deal of machinery, by which they facilitate and abridge their own labour' (*ibid.*).

Secondly, the flow of improvements, in the above accounts, is taken for granted in almost the same way that one may forecast, in particular industries, cost reductions due simply to the overcoming of indivisibilities at large scale. To this extent the element of risk is scarcely discernible at either the inventive or the innovative stages. This is confirmed also by Smith's subsequent comment to the effect that 'the intention of fixed capital is to increase the productive powers of labour ... The expence which is properly laid out upon a fixed capital of any kind, is always repaid with great profit.'[12]

Thirdly, the distinction between innovation and invention is much clouded. The development of new knowledge is not carefully distinguished above from its actual application; there is no recognition, for example, of the 'inventive genius' as distinct from the 'entrepreneurial' spirit.[13]

Smithian 'innovation' as described above should not, therefore, be identified with the Schumpeterian variety which is sharply distinguished from invention and which involves radical changes in process characterized by a substantial degree of riskiness.[14] The characteristics of the Smithian process of improvement are summarized in a discussion of the effects of demand expansion upon costs, where technical progress was seen to be an almost automatic and assured process engendered by competition: 'The increase of demand, besides, though in the beginning it may sometimes raise the price of goods, never fails to lower it in the long run. It encourages production, and thereby increases the competition of the producers, who, in order to undersell one another, have recourse to new divisions of labour and new improvements of art, which might never otherwise have been thought of' (706).[15] We note also in the *Wealth of Nations* the attention paid by Smith to 'small savings and small gains':

12 *Ibid.*, 271.
13 This is scarcely surprising in light of Smith's general view that innate differences in ability are of little importance.
14 For this view see A. Lowe, 'The Classical Theory of Economic Growth,' *Social Research*, XXI (Summer 1954), 135–6; and J.J. Spengler, 'Adam Smith's Theory of Economic Growth – Part I,' *Southern Economic Journal*, XXV (April 1959), 407. Spengler suggests that the emphasis upon circulating capital may have contributed to the underestimation of the role of invention and innovation which is often associated with fixed capital. (Cf. J.J. Spengler, 'Adam Smith's Theory of Economic Growth – Part II,' *Southern Economic Journal*, XXVI (July 1959), 11–12.) R. Koebner, 'Adam Smith and the Industrial Revolution,' *Economic History Review*, XI, 1959, 381–91, argues the case strongly: the whole topic of novel ventures was not given its proper due by Smith, it is contended; he did not turn his attention to the phenomenon of 'inventive genius' and had no appreciation of the 'business spirit' and the joint enterprise of engineer and capitalist. See also A.L. Macfie, 'The Scottish Tradition in Economic Thought,' *Scottish Journal of Political Economy*, II, reprinted in Macfie, *The Individual in Society: Papers on Adam Smith* (London, 1967), 35n. regarding Smith's failure to emphasize 'know-how.'
15 This approach to the generation and application of new technology can also be discerned from a highly significant reference in the *Lectures* which emphasized the cumulative effect of *minor* changes generated by machine users. Major technological changes were played down because of their initially imperfect nature: 'We have

To improve land with profit, like all other commercial projects, requires an exact attention to small savings and small gains, of which a man born to a great fortune, even though naturally frugal, is very seldom capable (364).

The habits, besides, of order, oeconomy and attention, to which mercantile business naturally forms a merchant, render him much fitter [than the traditional landowner] to execute, with profit and success, any project of improvement (385).[16]

Our discussion tends to confirm Spengler's view that in the Smithian system the undertaker is 'a prudent, cautious, not overly imaginative fellow, who adjusts to circumstances rather than brings about their modification.' Technical progress is 'primarily the product of a vast number of minor changes introduced by a multitude of comparatively small undertakers. It is not essentially the result of activity on the part of a minority of creative leaders.'[17] Yet we shall show presently that the evidence is by no means as one-sided as it thus far appears.

SOURCES OF TECHNOLOGY EXTERNAL TO THE FIRM

We have referred above to a functional relation between improved techniques and scale of *plant*. The extension of the relationship from the level of the firm to that of the economy is outlined in the conclusion to one of the above-quoted passages:

What takes place among the labourers in a particular workhouse, takes place, for the same reason, among those of a great society. The greater their number, the more they naturally divide themselves into different classes and subdivisions of employment. More heads are occupied in inventing the most proper machinery for executing the work of each, and it is, therefore, more likely to be invented. There are many commodities ... which, in consequence of these improvements, come to be produced by so much less labour than before ... (86).

Similarly at the outset of the book:

All the improvements in machinery, however, have by no means been the inventions of those who had occasion to use the machines. Many improvements have been made by the ingenuity of the makers of the machines, when to make them became the business of a peculiar trade; and some by that of those who are called philosophers

not, nor cannot have, any complete history of the invention of machines because most of them are at first imperfect, and receive gradual improvements and increase of powers from those who use them.' Adam Smith, *Lectures on Police, Justice, Revenue and Arms* (1763), ed. E. Cannan (1896; New York, 1964), 167. See too a similar argument (quoted below, n.51) by Smith from his *Principles Which Lead and Direct Philosophical Enquiries, Illustrated by the History of Astronomy* (publ. posth. 1795), in J. Ralph Lindgren, ed., *The Early Writings of Adam Smith* (New York, 1967), 66.

16 It will be noted that Smith does here recognize differences in ability between different individuals. It may be the case that such differences are acquired rather than innate.

17 Spengler, 'Smith's Theory of Economic Growth – Part II,' 8–9.

or men of speculation, whose trade it is not to do any thing, but to observe every thing; and who, upon that account, are often capable of combining together the powers of the most distant and dissimilar objects (10).

Here Smith notes that *from the viewpoint of the firm*, novel techniques may derive from developments occurring in other industries, particularly with suppliers of equipment and with full-time inventors.[18] Both sources are ultimately the result of growing opportunities for specialization created by expansion of the industry and of the economy as a whole.

It is of the first importance that the initial development of the steam engine was said by Smith to be due to independent inventors, while a subsequent labour-saving improvement followed from the observations of a machine user.[19] The reference without doubt is to the Newcomen invention.[20]

The recognition by Smith of a wide variety of sources of new technology

18 Smith may have had specifically in mind the co-operative efforts to improve the Newcomen engine undertaken by James Watt and Joseph Black at Glasgow University during the 1760s.

19 *Wealth of Nations*, 10. In the *Lectures* (168, 171) both the water-wheel and the steam engine are attributed to independent inventors.

   Foreign sources of new technology are said to be relevant for China: if the economy were opened up to foreign contact the Chinese could learn 'the art of using and constructing themselves all the different machines' of Europe (*Wealth of Nations*, 645). And land-saving technical changes introduced in Britain are said to have derived from foreign sources (*ibid.*, 241-2).

20 John Lord, *Capital and Steam Power, 1750–1800*, 2nd ed. (London, 1966), 37: Paul Mantoux, *The Industrial Revolution in the Eighteenth Century* (London, 1961), 317.

   The Newcomen machine is better called an 'atmospheric engine' than a 'steam engine' since it did not utilize the *expansion* of steam; it only used steam to create, through condensation, a vacuum in the tank. In principle, if connected with a transmitting apparatus, it could have been made into a driving engine. But in practice, it was used in the generation of power to pump up water into a reservoir and then to drive the hammers required for turning the water-wheel. An important development of the early eighteenth-century, was the substitution of an improved 'overshot' for the 'undershot' wheel to allow a great increase in energy from a given volume of water. When combined with the 'atmospheric engine' the savings made possible (particularly of horse power) were very substantial.

   About mid-century the combined 'fire engine' and 'water wheel' was to be found in general use. The great defects of the process were very high fuel consumption, and very high maintenance costs relating to the necessary dams, ponds, culverts, troughs, water wheels etc. It is in this context that we can appreciate the significance of Watt's steam engine. Watt's invention permitted significant savings in fuel consumption. Its subsequent improvement permitted the generation of power independently of water and allowed substantial reductions in maintenance costs relating to hydraulic works.

   (See Mantoux, *The Industrial Revolution*, 317–8; T.S. Ashton, *The Industrial Revolution* (London,1966), 68–9; Ashton, *An Economic History of England: The 18th Century*, 109–11.)

   The Newcomen device was also utilized in the pumping out of mines. In this case it was often economical for a considerable period after Watt's invention had displaced it in the generation of power insofar as advantage could be taken of cheap or free coal from slag heaps.

is of the greatest significance. It suggests that it would be an error to regard the contribution of specialist plant operators as almost the sole source of new technology.[21] The fact is that Smith recognized certain limits to what can be expected from simple subdivision of labour arising from the deadening effects on initiative and intelligence of too close specialization:

In the progress of the division of labour, the employment of the far greater part of those who live by labour, that is, of the great body of the people, comes to be confined to a few very simple operations, frequently to one or two. But the understandings of the greater part of men are necessarily formed by their ordinary employments. The man whose whole life is spent in performing a few simple operations, of which the effects too are, perhaps, always the same, or very nearly the same, has no occasion to exert his understanding, or to exercise his invention in finding out expedients for removing difficulties which never occur. He naturally loses, therefore, the habit of such exertion, and generally becomes as stupid and ignorant as it is possible for a human creature to become (734).

Yet he did not express fear that the sources of new technology would be exhausted. In part the nefarious effects of specialization might be countered by (government supported) elementary education. But it has been convincingly argued that the role of simple subdivision of labour must be seen in proper perspective: while there might be limits to the potential contribution by the plant operator, specialization in its broadest sense – encompassing inventor and machine-maker – would continue to play a vital, in fact an increasing, role in the production of knowledge.[22]

The fact that Smith opposed bank-financing of long-term (capital-inten-

21 Cf. the view of Karl Marx, *Capital*, vol. I, Modern Library ed. (New York, 1906), 382n.: 'Adam Smith has not established a single new proposition relating to division of labour. What, however, characterises him as the political economist par excellence of the period of Manufacture, is the stress he lays on division of labour. The subordinate part which he assigns to machinery gave occasion in the early days of modern mechanical industry to the polemic of Lauderdale, and, at a later period, to that of Ure'; J.A. Schumpeter, *History of Economic Analysis* (New York, 1954), 187: the division of labour was 'practically the only factor in economic progress'; and W.C. Mitchell, *Types of Economic Theory*, vol. I (New York, 1967), 40: 'he finds that division of labour is the great agency for raising the efficiency of labour. A modern theorist might be more *inclined* to say that the great agency for increasing man-hour output is the application of science through engineering technique – but of course, Adam Smith belongs in the pre-factory age. He follows through the analysis on the lines suggested by division of labour.'
22 For this view see N. Rosenberg, 'Adam Smith on the Division of Labour: Two Views or One?' *Economica*, XXXII (May 1965), 127f. The conflicting treatments by Smith in Books I and V are emphasized in E.G. West, 'Adam Smith's Two Views of the Division of Labour,' *Economica*, XXXI (Feb. 1964), 23–32.
   It is difficult to accept Marx's view that Smith 'confounds differentiation of the instruments of labour, in which the detail labourers themselves took an active part, with the invention of machinery; in this latter, it is not the workmen in manufactories, but learned men, handicraftsmen, and even peasants (Brindley), who play a part' (*Capital*, 383n.). As we have seen, Smith makes much of the distinction.

sive) industrial and agricultural projects cannot be regarded as sufficient evidence that such projects were neglected or were regarded as of small significance.[23] For Smith by no means neglected the phenomena of *risk attached to innovation*; or of innovative activity unrelated to scale as such. Costly innovatory investment undertaken with the prospect of extraordinary returns in the face of risk is discussed upon occasion:

The establishment of any new manufacture, of any new branch of commerce, or of any new practice in agriculture, is always a speculation, from which the projector promises himself extraordinary profits. These profits sometimes are very great, and sometimes, more frequently, perhaps, they are quite otherwise; but in general they bear no regular proportion to those of other old trades in the neighbourhood. If the project succeeds, they are commonly at first very high. When the trade or practice becomes thoroughly established and well known, the competition reduces them to the level of other trades (115).[24]

Smith seems to have had in mind, it appears from the text, particularly the new Birmingham trades. Indeed, despite his well-known minimization of the potentialities – as a profit-making organization – of the joint-stock company, on grounds of the typical negligence of management divorced from control by the owners, Smith was prepared to make qualifications.[25] Thus if the undertaking required particularly heavy conscription of capital there might be a legitimate argument for the establishment of a joint-stock organization.[26] (Such was the case with banks, insurance companies, canals, and waterworks.) But it is also conceded that a joint stock trading company might with justification be formed in the case of a new, risky, and expensive venture

---

23 Contemporary banking failures are discussed by Smith in detail to illustrate the dangers of long-term financing (*Wealth of Nations*, 297f.). As already noted in Chapter 3, illustrations were drawn from iron-making. In point of fact, the Carron Company was severely hit during the financial crisis. On 27 June 1772 David Hume wrote to Smith at Kirkaldy: 'the Carron Company is reeling, which is one of the greatest Calamities of the whole [financial crisis]; as they gave Employment to near 10,000 People. Do these Events any-wise affect your Theory? Or will it occasion the Revisal of any Chapters?' Hume's pessimistic forecast did not, however, materialize. Cf. J.Y.T. Greig, ed., *The Letters of David Hume*, vol. II (Oxford, 1932), 263; and R.H. Campbell, *Carron Company* (Edinburgh, 1961), 133.

24 There are in the *Wealth of Nations*, largely in the context of the equilibrium profit-rate structure, numerous references to 'risk.' However, these references are not related to innovation as such. (For example, 'the stock is at the risk of the borrower,' so that the equilibrium profit rate must include a return 'upon the risk of this insurance' (*ibid.*, 97); secondly, 'the lowest ordinary rate of profit must always be something more than what is sufficient to compensate the occasional losses to which every employment of stock is exposed' (*ibid.*, 96) so that 'in all the different employments of stock, the ordinary rate of profit varies more or less with the certainty or uncertainty of the returns' (*ibid.*, 110); thirdly, 'the lowest ordinary rate of interest must, in the same manner be something more than sufficient to compensate the occasional losses to which lending, even with tolerable prudence, is exposed. Were it not more, charity or friendship could be the only motives for lending' (*ibid.*, 96).)

25 *Ibid.*, 699f.   26 *Ibid.*, 714.

which, if successful, might even be accorded a (temporary) monopoly: 'It is the easiest and most natural way in which the state can recompense them for hazarding a dangerous and expensive experiment, of which the public is afterwards to reap the benefit.'[27] Moreover, it is of significance that these same grounds are offered in justification of patent and copyright protection.[28]

Finally, we note that in his analysis of agricultural development Smith also recognized (implicitly) expense and risk attached to *inventive* activity, and spoke of the new commercial landowner as a 'bold undertaker' (in contrast with the traditional great lords) willing to make large innovatory expenditures.[29]

We conclude that in Smith's view a certain range of inventive and innovative activity did in fact require costly investment and did entail a significant element of risk. There is also some attention given to the qualities peculiarly conducive to successful 'improvement.' These elements should not, perhaps, be over-emphasized. In dealing with the causes for the check to the profit-rate decline after 1763, Smith after all made no reference to the effects of technical change. Yet it must be recognized that the economy at the time was in flux, and no single account was used in the *Wealth of Nations* of the state of technology.

CONSTANCY OF MATERIALS-OUTPUT RATIO

We consider at this point an apparent assumption of the *Wealth of Nations* that the materials required per unit of output is constant even when allowance is made for changes in technology. It is clear from the following passage that new techniques are directed specifically at the *labour* input (although the prices of both materials and labour tend to rise during the process of expansion):

There are, indeed, a few manufactures, in which the necessary rise in the real price of the rude materials will more than compensate all the advantages which improvement can introduce into the *execution* of the work. In carpenters and joiners work, and in the coarser sort of cabinet work, the necessary rise in the real price of barren timber, in consequence of the improvement of land, will more than compensate all

27 *Ibid.*, 712. This latter concession appears, however, to clash with Smith's view that the joint-stock company is only likely to be successful (without an exclusive privilege) when engaged in operations easily reduced to a routine (*ibid.*).

28 Smith was on close terms with James Watt while at Glasgow University; he was also intimate with John Roebuck, of the Carron ironworks, who financed further experimentation upon Watt's basic invention (made at Glasgow in 1765) of the principle of separate condensation. Roebuck's share in the Watt patent was taken over by Boulton of the Soho (Birmingham) hardware works in 1773 upon the former's bankruptcy. The Boulton-Watt partnership was extended to the actual production of steam-engines which commenced in 1775 following a special Parliamentary Act extending patent protection (cf. Lord, *Capital and Steam Power*, 71f., 108f., and Campbell, *Carron Company*, 16–17). We can thus be sure that Smith was thoroughly familiar with the severe problems relating both to the perfection and commercial application of the steam engine.

29 See discussion below, 35.

the advantages which can be derived from the best machinery, the greatest dexterity, and the most proper division and distribution of work.

But in all cases in which the real price of the rude materials either does not rise at all, or does not rise very much, that of the manufactured commodity sinks very considerably (243; author's emphasis).[30]

We have in fact already seen[31] one implication of this relationship, namely that the operative restriction upon increased labour productivity due to technical progress is *not* the previous availability of wages goods but that of raw materials (and simple tools). But the restrictions imposed upon output by the need for materials will apply, needless to say, at *all* times, and not merely during periods of technical advance, although it appears in its most striking form during such periods. To the extent that raw materials constituted in Smith's account the most important non-labour input in the *manufacturing* sector, the fixity of the materials-output ratio takes on particular significance.

Two qualifications must, however, be emphasized. In the first place, the constancy of the materials coefficient was applied to operating and not to maintenance functions. As we shall see, Smith recognized technological improvements which by simplifying fixed capital allowed savings both of maintenance labour and maintenance materials. Secondly, Smith's assumption of constancy in the materials coefficient was applied only to materials of a given kind; he did allow for changes in the *nature* of the raw materials utilized. One of the most celebrated technical developments of the century is Darby's method permitting the use of coal and coke in iron smelting in place of charcoal (which, although invented in 1709, was not generally applied until mid-century).[32] Although Smith does not refer to the invention by name, he was aware of the differences between the smelting process used in North America with its extensive forests, and that adopted in Britain[33] at a period when wood prices were rising secularly as a result of extensions of cultivated areas to wastes.[34] The evidence, provided by Smith himself, allows us to assume that the economic pressures governing the adoption of Darby's technique were appreciated. In fact, substitution in *consumption* between wood and coal is discussed explicitly.[35]

30 Cf. Ricardo's paraphrase of Smith's position in *On the Principles of Political Economy*, in Piero Sraffa, ed., *The Works and Correspondence of David Ricardo*, I (Cambridge, 1951), 93–4. Ricardo accepted that manufacturing prices tended to fall.

31 Above, 153–4.

32 Cf. P. Deane and W.A. Cole, *British Economic Growth 1688–1959: Trends and Structure*, 2nd ed. (Cambridge, 1967), 96; Lord, *Capital and Steam Power*, 24.

33 With regard to the colonies: 'There is no manufacture which occasions so great a consumption of wood as a furnace, or which can contribute so much to the clearing of a country over-grown with it' (*Wealth of Nations*, 547). In Britain: 'In some manufactures, besides, coal is a necessary instrument of trade; as in those of glass, iron, and all other metals' (*ibid.*, 825–6).

34 *Ibid.*, 166

35 *Ibid.*, 165–7.

WAGE-RATE VARIATIONS AS A MOTIVE FOR LABOUR-SAVING PROCESSES?

In many cases the new processes discussed by Smith involve a higher capital-labour ratio, and are usually devoted to reducing unit labour costs. But their introduction is not formally explained in terms of a response to variations in wage rates. It seems rather to be a coincidence that wage rates are rising and labour-saving methods are introduced *pari passu*, the same general cause being responsible for both phenomena. We shall try to show that this is in fact the Smithian position.

Insofar as alternative, already existing, capital-intensive methods are adopted simply as a response to input-price changes there would be no theoretical reason to expect costs per unit of output to fall. Their adoption would indeed prevent costs from rising as far as they would otherwise rise were there no alternative methods, but certainly there would be no net reduction. The effect of technical change, however, is to reduce unit costs so that after all inputs have been accounted for, including fixed capital, unit costs decline. Now in his discussion of the effects of 'improvement' on costs and prices – a process frequently involving the adoption of increasingly capital-intensive methods – Smith makes it clear that the *secular* trend of real prices is downwards. The increasing machinery-labour ratio which is recognized thus reflects 'technical change' – albeit frequently of a non-revolutionary kind and dependent on scale – and not the adoption of capital-intensive processes *in response* to wage increases.

These propositions are illustrated in the following key extracts. It is clear that the effect on prices of the upward trend in real wages characterizing an expanding economy, is outweighed by the reduction in the quantity of labour required per unit of output as a result of new techniques and improved organization, made possible by larger scale plants and by external economies:

The increase in the wages of labour necessarily increases the price of many commodities, by increasing that part of it which resolves itself into wages, and so far tends to diminish their consumption both at home and abroad. The same cause, however, which raises the wages of labour, the increase of stock, tends to increase its productive powers, and to make a smaller quantity of labour produce a greater quantity of work ... There are many commodities, therefore, which, in consequence of these improvements, come to be produced by so much less labour than before, that the increase of its price is more than compensated by the diminution of its quantity (86).

It is the natural effect of improvement, however, to diminish gradually the real price of almost all manufactures. That of the manufacturing workmanship diminishes, perhaps, in all of them without exception. In consequence of better machinery, of greater dexterity, and of a more proper division and distribution of work, all of which are the natural effects of improvement, a much smaller quantity of labour becomes requisite for executing any particular piece of work; and though, in consequence of the flourishing circumstances of the society, the real price of labour should rise very considerably, yet the great diminution of the quantity will generally much more than compensate the greatest rise which can happen in the price (242–3).

It is to be emphasized that Smith simply takes it for granted that the size of the average productive unit will in fact expand as the aggregate capital stock increases. (It is quite likely that he has here confused the aggregate capital stock with that of the firm.) He also takes it for granted that the resultant increase in productivity normally more than balances the increase in wage rates. The entire discussion of rising capital-labour ratios which tend to reduce unit labour costs seems to reflect an introduction of new processes made profitable by larger scale, rather than an effort to 'economize' or to achieve minimum cost by means of substitution. The argument of Smith implies strongly that an increase in the wage rate, if unaccompanied by increased scale of plant (or by external economies), would *not* of itself lead to the generation of labour-saving inventions or the adoption of existing labour-saving processes. But the fact remains that Smith expected labour-saving techniques to be introduced during periods of economic expansion which were envisaged as periods both of rising wage rates and scale of plant.

A few words are in order regarding the actual course of labour-saving technical change during the eighteenth century. In the early decades, the process of *adoption* of new technology remained sluggish: Kay's 'flying shuttle' of 1733 (applicable to both wool and cotton weaving), was only beginning to be widely used in the 'sixties; and Paul's machine of 1738 utilizing the device of spinning by rollers both in wool and cotton, was only introduced in Lancashire after 1760. The search for labour-saving inventions continued culminating in the late 'sixties – at a time when the pressure of growing population upon natural resources was being felt – in the celebrated devices of Hargreaves and Arkwright (and that of Crompton in 1779) which eased a severe labour bottle-neck in the spinning branch of the cotton industry.[36] But an important characteristic of the early machines must be noted. While there is evidence of rising money and real wage rates in industrial centres after 1760,[37] the new devices were not basically substitutes for highly-skilled, relatively well-paid labour; it was not high wages as such, but high labour costs relating to the

36 Deane and Cole, *British Economic Growth*, 97, 183n. Ashton, *The Industrial Revolution*, 33–4, 91. The references are to Hargreaves' 'spinning jenny' (invented c.1764, patented 1770); Arkwright's power spinning by means of the 'water frame' (patented 1769); and Crompton's 'mule' (patented 1779).

37 Available wage-rate data are notoriously difficult to interpret but the evidence for the building trade suggests that daily wage rates of labourers in London and Lancashire and those skilled workers in London, Lancashire, Kent, and Oxfordshire tended upwards during the first third of the century; that thereafter until the 1760s there was little change; while in the last third of the century series for both skilled and unskilled in all areas (apart from London) tended significantly upwards. The most striking advance appears in the Lancashire series 1760–5. Estimates for agriculture suggest that wage rates increased during the second half of the century in much of the North but were relatively stagnant in the South, East, and Midlands. Indications in the coal and iron industries are of little change between 1740–60 and an upward tendency thereafter (Deane and Cole, *British Economic Growth*, 18f.).

poorly-paid spinners and – in the case of Kay's flying shuttle – to the less well paid of the weavers that was the great stimulus for their introduction.[38] Secondly, by the 'sixties and 'seventies the economy was experiencing an upward movement in the costs of raw materials, including cotton, wool, and dyes and – in the late 'seventies and early 'eighties – of credit.[39] On the whole, the adoption of the celebrated labour-saving textile devices was apparently not in direct response to rising wage-rates, and occurred in any event when particularly sharp increases in the price of materials, as well as of labour, were reducing profit margins.[40]

We have seen that Smith regarded both rising wage rates and raw material prices to be characteristic of periods of expansion while new technology tended to be directed *specifically* at the labour, and not the materials input. Yet it was not rising wages as such to which he attributed the bias either at the inventive or innovative stages. It is rather the increase in scale which is emphasized. We conclude that while Smith failed to specify the actual techniques he has in mind, the typical kind of technical improvement of a labour-saving nature described in the *Wealth of Nations* is consistent with the early weaving and later spinning mechanisms, insofar as the relaxing of the labour bottleneck thereby permitted was not related directly to rising wage rates. Moreover, as Smith implied, the effort to apply labour-saving techniques indeed picked up

38 For example, putters-out found it necessary to go further afield to find spinners as the market expanded entailing rising costs of distribution and collection. A prize was offered by the London Society of Arts in 1760 for a spinning machine on the grounds that manufacturers 'find it extremely difficult in the summer season when the spinners are at harvest work to procure a sufficient number of hands' (cited in Charles Wilson, *England's Apprenticeship, 1603–1673* (London, 1965), 371–2). A similar situation existed in coal mining; thus atmospheric or steam engines took the place of unskilled poorly-paid men at the pumps. Cf. Ashton, *An Economic History of England: the 18th Century*, 108–9.

39 Ashton, *The Industrial Revolution*, 91; T.S. Ashton, 'Some Statistics of the Industrial Revolution,' *The Manchester School of Economic and Social Studies*, XVI (1948), reprinted in E.M. Carus-Wilson, ed., *Essays in Economic History*, III (London, 1962), 238; A.H. John, 'Aspects of English Economic Growth in the First Half of the Eighteenth Century,' *Economica*, XXVIII (1961), reprinted in *ibid.*, II, 372–3.

40 The secular decline in interest rates during the century until the mid-fifties, from a range exceeding 8 per cent to about 4 per cent on long-term business loans, may have encouraged the introduction of various projects. To the extent that in manufacturing industry financial resources were derived from reinvested profits the phenomenon would be less significant than for public utilities, chartered companies and the like (Ashton, 'Some Statistics of the Industrial Revolution,' 238). But it has also been suggested that the significance of reinvested profits may have been exaggerated by commentators. (Cf. A.H. John, 'Agricultural Productivity and Economic Growth in England 1700–1760,' *Journal of Economic History*, XXV (1956), reprinted in E.L. Jones, ed., *Agriculture and Economic Growth in England 1650–1815* (London, 1967), 186.) Smith was disconcerted, we have seen, by contemporary bank financing of long-term projects in agriculture, mining, and iron-making, but he by no means limited his discussion of the interest rate to these sectors.

momentum only with the general expansion of activity; most new machines tended to be introduced in good times when employment was rising.[41]

We should further emphasize a second characteristic of the early textile improvements. Both the Kay and the Paul devices were relevant largely to *domestic* rather than factory production. Moreover, the spinning jenny and the mule were both adaptable for use in cottages and the domestic spinning of cotton yarn.[42] Accordingly, it is not too surprising if we find that Smith is not deeply impressed by these developments given his attention to technical progress generated in factory operations. It is, therefore, unjustified – particularly in light of the slow adoption of the various inventions – to consider his references in the case of the woollen industry to a number of ancient labour-saving devices as evidence of his *unawareness* of contemporary developments, or as a reflection of his relevance only to the 'pre-industrial' scene.[43]

In any event it must be recognized that the textual evidence is unclear. It is true that we find a general downplaying of innovations in woollen manufacture in the *Wealth of Nations*: 'In some employments ... the same quantity of industry will always produce the same, or very nearly the same quantity of commodities. In the linen or woollen manufactures, for example, the same number of hands will annually work up very nearly the same quantity of

41 See Deane and Cole, *British Economic Growth*, 96–7; and also E.J. Hobsbawm, 'The Machine Breakers,' in Hobsbawm, *Labouring Men: Studies in the History of of Labour* (London, 1965), 12

42 According to Mantoux (*The Industrial Revolution in the Eighteenth Century*, 263–4): 'The jenny, the simplest of all spinning machines, was used in Yorkshire about 1773, a few years only after its invention, but its use does not seem to have been very general before 1785, that is before the time when in the cotton industry it was already being supplanted by the mule and the water frame.' Labour was fearful of reduced wages but the jenny was welcomed by the West Riding master spinners since 'it enabled them to increase the output of their workshops without making any alterations in their traditional organization. Far from favouring the progress of capitalism, the jenny seemed to have provided the small master with a new weapon with which to safeguard his independence. This was the secret of its success in a country which was, above all others, the home of small-scale industry.'

   See *ibid.*, 250–1 regarding the mule. The mule, which replaced the jenny was, also, adapted for use in the cottages, and its commercial introduction in the mid-eighties further contributed to keep the old system alive.

43 The references are to the exchange of the rock and spindle for the spinning-wheel; the introduction of machines which aid in 'winding of the worsted and woollen yarn, or the proper arrangement of the warp and woof before put into the loom; ... [and] the employment of the fulling mill for thickening cloth in place of treading it in water' (*Wealth of Nations*, 246). None of these labour-saving improvements, as Smith points out, were recent changes.

   Cf. Mark Blaug, *Economic Theory in Retrospect*, 2nd ed. (London, 1968), 39, for the view that Smith failed to deal with the characteristic features of the industrial revolution. Similarly R. Koebner, 'Adam Smith and the Industrial Revolution,' *Economic History Review*, XI (1959), 388–9, who comments that it is remarkable that Smith did not ponder on the effects – 'actual or potential' – of the flying shuttle, the jenny, and the water frame: 'He saw no reason for diverting thought to these and other innovations of his time.'

linen and woollen cloth.'[44] Yet Smith also speaks of 'great improvements in the coarser manufactures of both linen and woollen cloth' which 'furnish the labourers with cheaper and better cloathing.'[45] The context makes it clear that he was largely dealing with eighteenth-century developments. Subsequently he notes particularly rapid growth of the Scottish linen industry especially after 1756, and of the West Riding coarse-woollen industry after 1766.[46]

TECHNOLOGICAL DISPLACEMENT OF LABOUR

Smith paid little attention to the possibility of technological unemployment in his analysis of labour-saving technical change.[47] The question of 'reabsorption' of those men displaced at the original level of output was never investigated formally. In fact the problem was not recognized. It is, simply, taken for granted that there must be an output expansion to allow any unit cost reductions: 'The intention of the fixed capital is to increase the productive powers of labour, or to enable the same number of labourers to perform a much greater quantity of work ... In manufactures the same number of hands, assisted with the best machinery, will work up a much greater quantity of goods than with more imperfect instruments of trade' (271).[48] Implicitly, the entire labour force is required at the new higher level of production (in principle, one might add, in this or some other sector).

We may consider several explanations for the neglect of the issue. First, we recall the close relationship between the use of fixed capital embodying innovative methods and specialization. The introduction of machinery is frequently treated as subsequent to the division of labour: 'as the operations of each workman are gradually reduced to a greater degree of simplicity, a variety of new machines come to be invented for facilitating and abridging these operations.'[49] But if the individual operators are strictly interdependent,

44 *Wealth of Nations*, 116. Cf. also 58.
45 *Ibid.*, 78.   46 *Ibid.*, 84.
47 It should be noted that machine breaking by workers fearful of displacement had already taken place or was currently occurring. Examples are the Spitalfield weavers in 1675; and the Lancashire machine-wreckers of 1778–80. Cf. Hobsbawm, 'The Machine Breakers,' 11n; Mantoux, *The Industrial Revolution*, 264.
48 It has been pointed out that Smith's argument seems to suggest that improvements themselves tend to bring about extensions of the market. Cf. Alexander Gourvitch, *Survey of Economic Theory on Technological Change and Employment* (1940; New York, 1966), 36.
49 *Wealth of Nations*, 260. This may result from the fact that the source of new knowledge is to some extent the floor operators themselves. (Cf. Hollander, 'Some Technological Relationships in the *Wealth of Nations*,' 193.) But it is by no means necessarily so: even specialist inventors may find it easier to invent once on-the-plant operations are simplified.
    Marx has drawn the useful distinction between a process such as is implied by Smith and a 'complex system of machinery' wherein the 'process as a whole is examined objectively, in itself, that is to say, without regard to the question of its execution by human hands, it is analysed into its component phases; and the problem, how to execute each detail process, and bind them all into a whole, is solved by the aid of machines, chemistry, &c.' (*Capital*, 413–15).

it follows that while labour hours may be saved by the new technique, and in principle unit costs reduced at the original output, no individual labourers can be dispensed with. This in itself masks the labour-saving effect of the technical change. And while it should be possible to enjoy the benefit from the cost reduction at the original level of production if the employer could make – and pay for – only partial use of his body of workers, Smith frequently argued as if the individual employee (and, given the interdependence of workers, the work force as a whole) was a fixed cost item to the firm.[50] The joint effect of the technical inability of displacing *individual* operators, and the 'constancy' of labour costs implies that the profitability of new capital-intensive methods lies only in their output-expanding effect. The question of reabsorbing labour – either men or man-hours – displaced at the original output level did not present itself.

A second, and perhaps more significant, explanation lies in the fact that the technical changes were expected largely in times of expansion. They were designed to raise the output obtainable per man *in response* to growing demand. The *practical* issue of displacement simply did not arise in such circumstances. As we have seen, Smith himself is explicit that it is in fact in periods of 'demand pull' that technical improvements can be expected.

50 A number of instances may be given. Specialization is uncommon in agriculture because 'it is impossible that one man should be constantly employed in any one of [the operations required]' (*ibid.*, 6). But unless the farmer were under an obligation to pay each man for more hours than are required of him, there is no reason to avoid the specialized processes since the employer could pay only for the man-hours of labour required. Smith also contrasts the cottar system, wherein cottagers were not fully occupied in one occupation, with more 'recent' systems in which the worker earned most of his wages in a single occupation. The wages of the cottagers were relatively low because household manufacture was not 'the principal business from which any of them derived the greater part of their subsistence' (*ibid.*, 116–17; 246–7). Cottage work is cheaper than 'that which is the principal or sole fund of the workman's subsistence' (*ibid.*, 247). Thus generally actual earnings would not be related to hours of effort exerted: 'A man must always live by his work, and his wages must at least be sufficient to maintain him' (*ibid.*, 67). Furthermore, consider the numerous references to the need for additional 'capital' as a prerequisite for specialization: 'When the work to be done consists of a number of parts, to keep every man *constantly employed* in one way, requires a much greater capital than where every man is occasionally employed in every different part of the work' (*ibid.*, 326; author's emphasis). Such statements imply that the employer *is concerned* in keeping his workers fully employed which would be the case only if the labourer must be treated as a fixed cost item.

In addition to the cottagers, Smith refers to 'independent workmen,' 'journeymen who work by the piece (*ibid.*, 83), and to 'servants who are hired by the month or by the year, and whose wages and maintenance are the same whether they do much or do little' (*ibid.*, 84). Some statements do not fit in well with our interpretation: Smith refers, for example, at one point to 'workmen [who] are paid by the piece; as they generally are in manufactures ...' (*ibid.*, 82). On balance, however, the weight of evidence suggests that Smith regarded specialist operators in the complex processes as constituting a fixed cost item.

Cf. Adolphe Lowe, 'The Classical Theory of Economic Growth,' *Social Research*, XXI (1954), 136 for similar emphasis on output-expanding, as distinct from labour-displacing, technical changes.

CAPITAL-SAVING TECHNICAL CHANGE AND LABOUR DISPLACEMENT

The 'standard' case of technical change in the *Wealth of Nations* involves an increase in the capital-labour ratio. Yet considerable attention is paid to the case where the new technology takes the form of *simplifications in process* which economize on the use of fixed capital:

... all such improvements in mechanics, as enable the same number of workmen to perform an equal quantity of work with cheaper and simpler machinery than had been usual before, are always regarded as advantageous to every society. A certain quantity of materials, and the labour of a certain number of workmen, which had before been employed in supporting a more complex and expensive machinery, can afterwards be applied to augment the quantity of work which that or any other machinery is useful only for performing. The undertaker of some great manufactury who employs a thousand a-year in the maintenance of his machinery, if he can reduce this expence to five hundred, will naturally employ the other five hundred in purchasing an additional quantity of materials to be wrought up by an additional number of workmen. The quantity of that work, therefore, which his machinery was useful only for performing, will naturally be augmented (272).

It is sufficiently obvious ... in what manner every saving in the expence of supporting the fixed capital is an improvement of the neat revenue of the society. The whole capital of the undertaker of every work is necessarily divided between his fixed and his circulating capital. While his whole capital remains the same, the smaller the one part, the greater must necessarily be the other. It is the circulating capital which furnishes the materials and wages of labour, and puts industry into motion. Every saving, therefore, in the expence of maintaining the fixed capital, which does not diminish the productive powers of labour, must increase the fund which puts industry into motion, and consequently the annual produce of land and labour, the real revenue of every society (276).

The operation [of exporting bullion], in some measure, resembles that of the undertaker of some great work, who, in consequence of some improvement in mechanics, takes down his old machinery, and adds the difference between its price and that of the new to his circulating capital, to the fund from which he furnishes materials and wages to his workmen (280).[51]

In the present case maintenance labour is actually *displaced* in the first instance, although it is subsequently reabsorbed into the operating functions. Now there are several problems: Smith does not explain adequately the mechanism by which such re-employment will become profitable. Although he talks of an *increase* of circulating at the expense of fixed capital it should be noted that in fact on his own terms there is no such increase. While there does

---

51 The phenomenon of process simplification is implied in a passage in Smith's *History of Astronomy*, in J.R. Lindgren, ed., *Early Writings of Adam Smith*, 66: 'A machine is a little system, created to perform, as well as to connect together, in reality, those different movements and effects which the artist has occasion for ... The machines that are first invented to perform any particular movement are always the most complex, and succeeding artists generally discover that, with fewer wheels, with fewer principles of motion, than had originally been employed, the same effects may be more easily produced.'

occur a fall in fixed capital, there is simply an alteration in the use to which a *given* circulating capital is put, such that net output can now be increased. It is essentially the fact that circulating capital is released for use by operating personnel which Smith considers as a guarantee of employment without justifying the supposition.[52]

The argument, it is interesting to note, is in line with subsequent nineteenth-century analyses which run in terms of the effect of technical change upon the wages fund. Later economists, however – particularly Ricardo in his chapter 'On Machinery' – allowed that technical change might *reduce* the fund and thereby generate unemployment at the going wage rate.

To rely upon the maintenance of circulating capital to assure re-employment is clearly of itself inadequate. It is necessary to investigate also the technological relationships which must be satisfied between labour and fixed capital. Some attention was in fact paid to the issue insofar as Smith emphasizes that output would be expanded from 'that [the new equipment] or any other machinery.'[53]

Smith, as usual, did not illustrate his category of 'capital saving' technical change. But we can find illustrations with which he may have been familiar. Of particular significance is the possibility of running furnaces in iron manufacture for longer periods as a result of the replacement of charcoal by coke (the Darby process) as at Carron.[54] The *logic* of Smith's argument also applies to several major changes introduced after 1776. In fact, in its improved form, Watt's steam engine permitted not only reduced fuel costs compared with the atmospheric engine and water-wheel but also substantially reduced maintenance costs since the new method did not require the heavy fixed capital investment in hydraulic works.[55]

52 Cf. Cannan, *Wealth of Nations*, 272n.

53 *Ibid.*, 272. Even if Smith assumed fixed technical proportions between machinery and labour, this does not imply that equipment is always 'fully employed' in the sense that it is utilized twenty-four hours per day throughout the year. All the proposition implies is that *when in use* other resources are required in technologically determined ratios with it. Thus the expansion of output from 'other machinery' need not conflict with fixed coefficients. Insofar as it is *new-type* equipment which is involved there is no problem at all, since it may be able to support a larger labour force than the original equipment even when the comparison is made on the basis of *full-capacity* utilization. The nature of the production function is discussed in Chapter 4.

54 H.J. Habakkuk, *American and British Technology in the Nineteenth Century* (Cambridge, 1967), 161.

55 Ashton, *An Economic History of England*, 110–11. Some further examples of capital-saving technical changes (although some of them were after Smith's time) are the replacement by iron of copper and brass in engine parts, of stone and brick in bridges – the first iron bridge was erected in 1779, and of timber in structures – a development of the last years of the century; tools and machines made of wrought iron which were lighter, more efficient, and more durable than those of wood; a variety of means of saving horse power – including the Newcomen engine applied to pumps etc., which saved horses in and near mines; and various new forms of inland transport.

AGRICULTURAL PROGRESS

In attempting to define Smith's account of technical progress in the agricultural sector we are again faced by his tendency to specify inadequately the timing of the changes which he had in mind. Our interpretation must also make allowance for the growing appreciation on the part of economic historians that many of the changes traditionally linked with the 'classical' agricultural revolution of the second half of the eighteenth century in fact were accomplished, or well under way, at a much earlier date.

At the outset of the discussion we may refer back to Smith's fundamental proposition that in the course of economic development the extensions of tillage on the one hand – and consequent reductions in the supply of cattle produced at zero cost on the wilds – and rising demand (related in part to increasing population and real purchasing power) on the other will force up cattle prices ultimately rendering the commercial production of butcher's meat profitable, at which time some land areas – initially prepared for cereals – will be utilized for cattle raising.[56] The crucial level of cattle prices, Smith suggests,[57] had been achieved in the early seventeenth century in the environs of London and subsequently in more remote areas of England although at the time of writing perhaps not quite universally. In Scotland on the other hand it was only since the Union that the commercial raising of cattle had become anywhere profitable.[58]

It is in this context that reference is made to various (land-saving) fodder crops which tended to check the rise of meat prices where commercial cattle raising had become well established:

In the progress of improvement, the period at which every particular sort of animal food is dearest, must naturally be that which immediately precedes the general practice of cultivating land for the sake of raising it. For some time before this practice becomes general, the scarcity must necessarily raise the price. After it has become general, new methods of feeding are commonly fallen upon, which enable the farmer to raise upon the same quantity of ground a much greater quantity of that particular sort of animal food. The plenty not only obliges him to sell cheaper, but in consequence of these improvements he can afford to sell cheaper; for if he could not afford it, the plenty would not be of long continuance. It has been probably in this manner that the introduction of clover, turnips, carrots, cabbages, &c. has contributed to sink the common price of butcher's-meat in the London market somewhat below what it was about the beginning of the last century (225).[59]

56 See especially *Wealth of Nations*, 217f. discussed above, 141. That population increase – in addition to increased real income per head – was partly responsible for such increase in demand is clear (*ibid.*, 220, 235).

57 In equilibrium the price of cattle relative to that of corn will be such as to compensate for a supposed differential productivity disadvantage (*ibid.*, 149).

58 *Ibid.*, 151, 220, 225.

59 That the advantage of artificial grasses, clovers and roots lies not in any labour-saving effect, but rather in their economizing of land is emphasized by Smith elsewhere: 'The use of the artificial grasses, of turnips, carrots, cabbages, and the

As in the approach to manufacturing technical progress the present account of
the adoption of *land-saving* methods reflects a casual view of the generation
of new technology, for it is by no means adequately explained why or how
'new methods of feeding are commonly fallen upon.' We may, however, be
justified in understanding Smith as attempting to express the conception of a
supply function relatively more elastic in the long run than in the short run.
The adoption of the new-type root crops permit a significant output expansion
and assure a reduction in price *compared with the initial short-run level*. But
what is involved, if this view is correct, is not in fact exogeneous technical
change based on hitherto unknown technology – and a downward *shift* of the
supply function – but rather the adoption of hitherto known technology
unprofitable at an initially low level of output, that is a movement along an
elastic long-run supply curve.

Similarly dairy farming, at least in England, had become a profitable undertaking, the prices of milk, butter and cheese having, in general, achieved an
adequate level relative to those of butcher's meat and corn: 'It seems to have
got to this height through the greater part of England, where much good land
is commonly employed in this manner.'[60] The undertaking of additional
expense by the dairy-farmer in response to higher prices is described in the
following detailed account which implies an ultimate limit to rising marginal
costs:

The business of the dairy, like the feeding of hogs and poultry, is originally carried
on as a save-all. The cattle necessarily kept upon the farm, produce more milk than
either the rearing of their own young, or the consumption of the farmer's family
requires ... [and] goes to market, in order to find the best price which is to be had,
and which can scarce be so low as to discourage him from sending thither whatever is
over and above the use of his own family. If it is very low, indeed, he will be likely to
manage his dairy in a very slovenly and dirty manner, and will scarce perhaps think
it worth while to have a particular room or building on purpose for it, but will suffer
the business to be carried on amidst the smoke, filth, and nastiness of his own kitchen;
as was the case of almost all the farmers dairies in Scotland thirty or forty years ago,
and as is the case of many of them still. The same causes which gradually raise the
price of butcher's-meat, the increase of the demand, and, in consequence of the
improvement of the country, the diminution of the quantity which can be fed at little
or no expence, raise, in the same manner, that of the produce of the dairy, of which
the price naturally connects with that of butcher's-meat, or with the expence of
feeding cattle. The increase of price pays for more labour, care, and cleanliness. The
dairy becomes more worthy of the farmer's attention, and the quality of its produce
gradually improves. The price at last gets so high that it becomes worth while to
employ some of the most fertile and best cultivated lands in feeding cattle merely for
the purpose of the dairy; and when it has got to this height, it cannot well go higher.
If it did, more land would soon be turned to this purpose (226–7).

---

other expedients ... have been fallen upon to make *an equal quantity of land* feed a
greater number of cattle than when in natural grass' (*ibid.*, 151; author's emphasis).
60 *Ibid.*, 227.

While the processes whereby cattle came to be raised commercially for butcher's meat had long been completed in England, and for dairy produce more recently, the relatively high prices of poultry and of hogs currently ruling suggested to Smith that commercial production in these cases was not yet fully under way. Yet the particular sharpness of the price increases implied too that the supply of hogs and poultry produced at zero cost must have fallen with 'the diminution of the number of cottagers and other small occupiers of land; an event which has in every part of Europe been the immediate forerunner of improvement and better cultivation.'[61]

We have noted that while Smith emphasized an upward trend in the price of butcher's meat during the course of development he at the same time recognized that, *once commercial cattle raising was established*, production costs would tend downwards from an initially abnormally high level thus reducing the price differential with corn. Yet he did not neglect technical progress in the production of vegetable foods, specifying both the adoption of land-saving innovatory products – specifically potatoes and maize – and scale economies available in field as distinct from garden cultivation:

The extension of improvement and cultivation, as it necessarily raises more or less, in proportion to the price of corn, that of every sort of animal food, so it as necessarily lowers that of, I believe, every sort of vegetable food. It raises the price of animal food; because a great part of the land which produces it, being rendered fit for producing corn, must afford to the landlord and farmer the rent and profit of corn land. It lowers the price of vegetable food; because, by increasing the fertility of the land, it increases its abundance. *The improvements of agriculture too introduce many sorts of vegetable food, which, requiring less land and not more labour than corn, come much cheaper to market.* Such are potatoes and maize, or what is called Indian corn, the two most important improvements which the agriculture of Europe ... has received from the great extension of its commerce and navigation. *Many sorts of vegetable food, besides, which in the rude state of agriculture are confined to the kitchen-garden, and raised only by the spade, come in its improved state to be introduced into common fields, and to be raised by the plough: such as turnips, carrots, cabbages, &c.* (241–2; author's emphasis).[62]

But particular attention must also be paid to the dependency of efficient arable cultivation upon the commercial raising of cattle. Thus the backward state of farming in large areas of Scotland is related precisely to the slow development of a cattle-raising industry. For the full extension of cultivation depended upon adequate supplies of fertilizers,[63] which could only be forthcoming if it were profitable to raise herds of cattle for meat (in which case fertilizer is almost a free good). Prior to the Union the price of meat had been

---

61 *Ibid.*, 226.   62 Cf. *ibid.*, 78.

63 Fertilizer supplies would have to be generated on the farm itself because towns were few and far between. Cattle might be maintained by pasturing directly, or in the stables – using land for feed – and carrying out manure to the fields. If the price of cattle was low the first method would be unprofitable and the second even more so. The bringing in of manure from the wilds would usually be prohibitive.

too low to make it worthwhile for the farmer to keep cattle other than for tillage, and the dung from these cattle was accordingly inadequate for the land which could be ploughed. Consequently, the practice followed was to cultivate only the most fertile parts of the farm or those closest to the farm-house:

In these circumstances [of low cattle prices], therefore, no more cattle can, with profit, be fed in the stable than what are necessary for tillage. But these can never afford manure enough for keeping constantly in good condition, all the lands which they are capable of cultivating. What they afford being insufficient for the whole farm, will naturally be reserved for the lands to which it can be most advantageously or conveniently applied; the most fertile, or those, perhaps, in the neighbourhood of the farm-yard. These, therefore, will be kept constantly in good condition and fit for tillage (221).

Prior to the Union – which opened up a larger market for meat – properly cultivated land did not exceed, we are told, a quarter or a third, and in some cases a fifth or a sixth of the whole farm. At best, the remainder or parts of it were occasionally ploughed and exhausted. In fact, because of the lack of an essential ingredient in farming, even the working animals were not fully used: 'The farm, though much understocked in proportion to what would be necessary for its complete cultivation, being very frequently overstocked in proportion to its actual produce,' so that 'even that part of the lands of Scotland which is capable of good cultivation, could produce but little in comparison to what it may be capable of producing.' This system was still common in certain regions of Scotland despite an upward movement since the Union in cattle prices. Three reasons are given: first, custom and ignorance played a part. Secondly, although higher cattle prices made it profitable to maintain larger cattle stocks, farmers were too poor to afford the necessary initial investment, the higher price of cattle itself making it more difficult to purchase an adequate herd for meat production. Thirdly, even when the herd could be afforded many farmers had not yet 'put their lands in condition to maintain this greater stock properly.'[64] For the necessary preparation of land itself required an initial source of good fertilizer. Thus farmers were caught in a vicious circle and, Smith believed, the problem would not be overcome for many decades: 'These natural obstructions to the establishment of a better system, cannot be removed but by a long course of frugality and industry; and half a century or a century more, perhaps, must pass away before the old system, which is wearing out gradually, can be completely abolished through all the different parts of the country ...' (222).[65]

64 *Wealth of Nations*, 221-3.
65 Moreover, he forecast the adoption of a similar system in North America (where large and accessible supplies of wild animals kept down prices): 'It must be a long time after the first establishment of such colonies, before it can become profitable to feed cattle upon the produce of cultivated land. The same causes, therefore, the want of manure, and the disproportion between the stock employed in cultivation, and the land which it is destined to cultivate, are likely to introduce there a system of husbandry not unlike that which still continues to take place in so many parts of Scotland' (*ibid.*, 223).

Where the old system remained in force the most fertile lands would initially be kept 'constantly in good condition' and any increase in capital would permit an extension of the cultivated area to less fertile or more distant parts of the farm.[66] However great the *technological* possibility may have been for the intensive cultivation of land, farmers would increase output, where possible, at the extensive margin. On the other hand it is implied that a *progressive* system is characterized by a full-fledged interdependence between tillage and pasture.

The movement towards larger units of production is given much attention in the *Wealth of Nations*. The early trend towards consolidation is formally accounted for in terms of a general change in social habits on the part of the great barons, encouraged by the growing availability of fine manufactured goods – produced domestically or imported – rather than as a deliberate response to particular movements in factor prices or the prices of agricultural produce.[67] These objects of consumption provided the great landowners with new outlets for expenditure in place of their traditional support of menials, and encouraged a concern with deriving the maximum rent from the land:

The personal expence of the great proprietors [upon manufactured goods] having in this manner gradually increased, it was impossible that the number of their retainers should not as gradually diminish, till they were at last dismissed altogether. The same cause gradually led them to dismiss the unnecessary part of their tenants. Farms were enlarged, and the occupiers of land, notwithstanding the complaints of depopulation, reduced to the number necessary for cultivating it, according to the imperfect state of cultivation and improvements in those times. By the removal of the unnecessary mouths, and by exacting from the farmer the full value of the farm, a greater surplus, or what is the same thing, the price of a greater surplus, was obtained for the proprietor, which the merchants and manufacturers soon furnished him with a method of spending upon his own person in the same manner as he had done the rest (390).

Evidently the original productive unit was inefficient, and the adoption of the preferable unit represents a move *towards* the production function. In the case of the early movement Smith emphasizes the effect of increased rents per acre upon the tenants' investment decisions. The implication is that tenants responded by attempting to raise yields per acre: 'The same cause [new modes of expenditure] continuing to operate, he [the landlord] was desirous to raise his rents above what his lands in the actual state of their improvement, could afford. His tenants could agree to this upon one condition only, that they should be secured in their possession, for such a term of years as might give

66 Rent in the traditional system was in fact paid for a larger area than could be used; with increasing capital a farmer would tend to extend the area in use. We may also note Smith's awareness in his discussion of Scottish farming that part at least of the farmer's outlying land was – despite the lack of fertilizer – 'regularly cultivated and exhausted.' But output in the latter case is reduced to a bare minimum and there is no continuous flow of produce from such fields.

67 *Wealth of Nations*, 388f.

them time to recover with profit whatever they should lay out in the further improvement of the land.'[68] This too implies a movement towards the frontier.

We have referred above to Smith's account of the continuing displacement during the eighteenth century of 'cottagers and other small occupiers,' in his discussion of rising poultry and hog prices. We may also recall his recognition of the heavy investments involved in 'clearing, draining, enclosing, manuring, and ploughing waste and uncultivated fields, in building farm-houses, with all their necessary appendages of stables, granaries, &c.' in his advice to bankers regarding their discount policies.[69] As far as these contemporary processes of enclosure are concerned Smith does not emphasize any labour-saving effects. It is only in the case of the rare Scottish enclosures that reference is made to labour saving and it should be carefully noted that it is specifically pasture rather than arable cultivation that was involved.[70]

We shall consider the motivation for the eighteenth-century movement from the viewpoint of Smith's attitude towards the 'improving landlords.' It is to be noted first that Smith in a letter to Lord Shelburne of 1759 implies that the landlord is, or rather ought to be, 'socially' motivated undertaking extensive improvements for the social good:

We are no strangers in this country to the very noble and generous work which your Lordship has been employed in in Ireland. We have in Scotland some noblemen whose estates extend from the east to the west sea, who call themselves improvers and are called so by their countrymen when they cultivate two or three hundred acres round their own family seat, while they allow all the rest [of] their country to lie waste, almost uninhabited and entirely unimproved, not worth a shilling the hundred acres, without thinking themselves answerable to God, their country and their Posterity for so shameful as well as so foolish a neglect. Your Lordship, I hear, is not of that opinion, and tho' you are not negligent either of the elegance or magnificence of your country Villas, you do not think that any attention of that kind dispenses with the more noble and important duty of attempting to introduce arts, industry and independency into a miserable country, which has hitherto been a stranger to them all. Nothing, I have often imagined, would give more pleasure to Sir William Petty, your Lordship's ever honoured ancestor, than to see his representative pursuing a Plan so suitable to his own Ideas which are generally wise and public spirited.[71]

Yet it is doubtful whether we would be justified to deduce from this letter that in Smith's view improvements were, or in principle could be expected to become, largely dependent upon public-spirited benefactors.[72] In the *Wealth*

---

68 *Ibid.*, 390.   69 *Ibid.*, 291.

70 'The present high rent of enclosed land in Scotland seems owing to the scarcity of enclosure, and will probably last no longer than that scarcity. The advantage of enclosure is greater for pasture than for corn. It saves the labour of guarding the cattle, which feed better too when they are not liable to be disturbed by their keeper or his dog' (*ibid.*, 150).

71 Letter dated April 4, 1759 in W.R. Scott, *Adam Smith as Student and Professor* (Glasgow, 1937), 245.

72 We should bear in mind the fact that Lord Shelburne had put Smith in charge of

of Nations he refers explicitly to the self-interest of the landlord: 'The proprietor of land is interested for the sake of his own revenue to keep his estate in as good condition as he can, by building and repairing his tenants' houses, by making and maintaining the necessary drains and enclosures, and all those other expensive improvements which it properly belongs to the landlord to make and maintain' (879–80). And accordingly Smith recommended that care be taken to choose those forms of land taxation least likely to effect the profits yielded by improvement. For example, increased land values due to improvements should be exempt from taxation for a fixed term of several years: 'The landlord would certainly be less disposed to improve, when the sovereign, who contributed nothing to the expence, was to share in the profit of the improvement.'[73] In the same context Smith also recognized expense and risk attached to *inventive* activity; it is only the wealthy landlord who can afford to undertake risky experiments relating to land improvement. And it is only he who can afford to adopt capital-intensive processes of cultivation:

his son's education at Glasgow which was a considerable honour not only to Smith but to the University and it is not surprising that Smith would neglect to discuss the profit motive in his correspondence. Cf. Scott, *ibid.*, 239f.

On the other hand, it should be noted that Smith gives no explanation for the continued expenditures by landlords even during periods of depressed grain prices, other than a reference, which might in principle be applicable, to landlords who choose not to extract a full economic rent (*Wealth of Nations*, 144). (See G.E. Mingay, 'The Agricultural Depression, 1730–1750,' *Economic History Review*, VIII, 1956, reprinted in Carus Wilson, ed., *Essays in Economic History*, II, 309–26.)

Corn prices after 1700, Smith observed, were generally below the level obtaining throughout most of the seventeenth century. After 1764 prices rose above the level of the previous century, although the upward movement commenced from approximately 1750. The initial downward trend is said to reflect an increase in the price of silver rather than changes in the agricultural sector itself (*Wealth of Nations*, 198f., 474). Smith was, however, loathe to attribute the subsequent reversal to anything more significant than a series of poor harvests (*ibid.*, 240). In particular, he seems to deny that rising population and real incomes led to increased corn prices.

For a modern account of agricultural price movements, see Deane and Cole, *British Economic Growth*, 92f. Prices began rising slowly after 1743, following a period from about 1717 of general decline; in the 'sixties and 'seventies the price increases were particularly significant. These movements are attributed to rising population and demand in the period 1745–55 and the ensuing decades – and not to any fall in supply – and a series of poor harvests in the late 'sixties and early 'seventies.

73 *Wealth of Nations*, 784. Similarly, the church tythe is condemned because it reduces the motive for investment by both landlords and farmers: 'The tythe ... is always a great discouragement both to the improvements of the landlord and to the cultivation of the farmer. The one cannot venture to make the most important, which are generally the most expensive improvements; nor the other to raise the most valuable, which are generally too the most expensive crops; when the church, which lays out no part of the expence, is to share so very largely in the profit' (*ibid.*, 789). Cf. *ibid.*, 879–80 for further warning against introducing changes in the system of taxation which might threaten the return on landlords' investments.

It is of importance that the landlord should be encouraged to cultivate a part of his own land. His capital is generally greater than that of the tenant, and with less skill he can frequently raise a greater produce. The landlord can afford to try experiments, and is generally disposed to do so. His unsuccessful experiments occasion only a moderate loss to himself. His successful ones contribute to the improvement and better cultivation of the whole country (784).

Yet Smith's attitude to the landlord is, at least on the surface, an ambivalent one. While agreeing that the landlord 'should be encouraged to cultivate a part of his own land' because of the improvements introduced, he nonetheless warned that any encouragement must be 'to a certain degree only,' fearing that otherwise 'the country (instead of sober and industrious tenants, who are bound by their own interest to cultivate as well as their capital and skill will allow them) would be filled with idle and profligate bailiffs, whose abusive management would soon degrade the cultivation.'[74] This ambivalence, however, is more apparent than real. It was the great traditional landowners in whom Smith had little confidence, for their major outlays were 'unproductive.' On the other hand, the new commercial landowners – who were in the main merchants – had all the qualities necessary for successful improvement.[75] In the following passage Smith speaks of them as 'bold undertakers' willing to make large innovatory expenditures:

Merchants are commonly ambitious of becoming country gentlemen, and when they do, they are generally the best of all improvers. A merchant is accustomed to employ his money chiefly in profitable projects; whereas a mere country gentleman is accustomed to employ it chiefly in expence. The one often sees his money go from him and return to him again with a profit: the other when once he parts with it, very seldom expects to see any more of it. These different habits naturally affect their temper and disposition in every sort of business. A merchant is commonly a bold; a country gentleman, a timid undertaker. The one is not afraid to lay out at once a large capital upon the improvement of his land, when he has a probable prospect of raising the value of it in proportion to the expence. The other, if he has any capital, which is not always the case, seldom ventures to employ it in this manner. If he improves at all, it is commonly not with a capital, but with what he can save out of his annual revenue. Whoever has had the fortune to live in a mercantile town situated in an unimproved country, must have frequently observed how much more spirited the operations of merchants were in this way, than those of mere country gentlemen (384-5).

74 *Ibid.*, 784. Specifically, Smith objected to leases which defined the particular method to be followed: 'Some leases prescribe to the tenant a certain mode of cultivation, and a certain succession of crops during the whole continuance of the lease. This condition, which is generally the effect of the landlord's conceit of his own superior knowledge (a conceit in the most cases very ill founded), ought always to be considered as an additional rent, as a rent in service instead of a rent in money' (783).

75 On those grounds he strongly attacked the law of primogeniture and 'perpetuities of various kinds' which prevented the sale of lands in reasonably small parcels. Cf. *Lectures*, 228; *Wealth of Nations*, 364, 392.

How 'accurate' a picture of the events in the agricultural sector did Smith in fact present? The phenomena which we have encountered in the above account include the introduction of (land-saving) fodder crops. The availability of the requisite technology is taken for granted. While the argument is poorly expressed, Smith appears to envisage the adoption of new-type fodder crops as a means of expanding output, in response to particularly high prices of meat and dairy produce relative to those of cereals, rather than as an example of exogenous technical progress. The development of a commercial meat and dairy industry permitted, in turn, increased efficiency of tillage since advantage could be taken of the resultant supply of fertilizer in a rotating system of forage and vegetable crops.

There is no indication that the discussion was limited to the last third of the eighteenth century; on the contrary, Smith clearly had in mind a process underway since the preceding century, related to relative price movements, but requiring also the overcoming of various rigidities due to 'custom and ignorance,' and the generation of adequate capital supplies for the purchase of herds and for the preparation of the grounds. It was largely the landlords – deriving from the merchant class – rather than the tenants who were said to be responsible for much experimentation and for the requisite investments relating not only to clearing, drainage, enclosure, and fertilizing, but also to the repair and construction of their tenants' houses.

The broad lines of Smith's account are consistent with recent researches.[76] In the first place the traditional emphasis upon events in the second half of the eighteenth century – particularly the sharp increase in the rate of enclosure by Act of Parliament, the adoption in newly enclosed areas of the crop rotations of the Norfolk (four-course) system of cultivation involving wheat, turnips, barley and clover, the introduction of drilling, and of new breeds of cattle and sheep – is becoming increasingly suspect. It is rather from the mid- or late seventeenth century that discernible changes in agrarian practice constituting the commencement of continuing advance are dated. These changes relate, in particular, to the cultivation of various artificial grasses (clover, sanfoin, and ryegrass), the use of the turnip as a field (as distinct from a garden) crop and the rotation of cereals with livestock in new systems of mixed farming – all of which are noted by Smith – as well as to the artificial irrigation of fields, and the more systematic breeding of cattle.[77] Impediments

76 See particularly, C. Wilson, *England's Apprenticeship, 1603–1763*, 141f., 243f.; Eric Kerridge, *The Agricultural Revolution* (London, 1967), 15–40; E.L. Jones, 'Agriculture and Economic Growth in England, 1660–1750: Agricultural Change,' *Journal of Economic History*, XXV, 1965, reprinted in E.L. Jones, ed., *Agriculture and Economic Growth in England 1650–1815*, 152f. and 'Introduction,' *ibid.*, 1–17; A.H. John, 'Agricultural Productivity and Economic Growth in England 1700–1760,' *Journal of Economic History*, XXV, 1965, reprinted in *ibid.*, 172f.; John, 'Aspects of English Economic Growth in the First Half of the Eighteenth Century,' 360–73; and John, 'The Course of Agricultural Change 1660–1760,' in L.S. Pressnell, ed., *Studies in the Industrial Revolution* (London, 1960), 125–55.
77 It has been pointed out (John, 'Aspects of English Economic Growth,' 363–64) that

to the diffusion of these developments are related partly to the inappropriate-ness of the heavy clay soils of central England, but as Smith observed also to various social rigidities (especially where the communal system of farming persisted) and to a lack of capital to finance the acquisition of suitable stock. The parliamentary enclosures are seen as the culmination of a long-time process of land reallotment and improved agrarian organization. Of particular importance is the suggestion – corresponding with Smith's position – that the adoption of rotations involving fodder crops during the period of approximately 1650 to 1750 – in some cases long available and indeed long in use in the Low Countries as field crops and, even in English kitchen gardens – was related to an increase in the relative prices of livestock to those of cereals.[78] The expansion of *cereal* production during periods of poor grain prices (1730–50) is partially attributed to a willingness on the port of landlords to 'subsidize agriculture' for a variety of social reasons – a phenomenon also casually alluded to in the *Wealth of Nations* – in effect tending to compete for suitable tenants by various inducements particularly land improvements failing, at least in the immediate run, to exact a full economic rent.[79]

SUMMARY AND CONCLUSION:
SMITH AND THE INDUSTRIAL REVOLUTION

We have demonstrated in our earlier discussion of 'Industry Structure' the complexity of Smith's account of the contemporary British economy, reflecting the fact that Britain was in a transition state. The same complexity is apparent in Smith's analysis of technical change. But the problem of interpretation is rendered particularly difficult by Smith's failure to be explicit about the phenomena he has in mind.

It is sometimes argued that Smith overlooked a technological revolution

the typical form of agricultural innovation – particularly significant in the areas of lighter soils (as in southeast England) – based on the use of clovers, artificial grasses and roots, and associated with enclosure were land saving but capital and labour using. This process was partly balanced by the conversion of the heavier soils to pasture as in the Midlands (and according to Smith in Scotland), where there occurred some release of labour.

Josiah Tucker included among the advantages enjoyed by a wealthy country in agriculture the possession of 'good Enclosures, Drains, Waterings, artificial Grasses, great Stocks, and consequently the greater Plenty of Manures; also a great Variety of Plows, Harrows, &c. suited to the different Soils; and in short of every other superior Method of Husbandry arising from long Experience, various and expensive Trials.' *Four Tracts Together with Two Sermons on Political and Commercial Subjects* (Gloucester, 1774), 22.

78 Jones, 'Agriculture and Economic Growth,' 159.

79 *Ibid.*, 160–1. Declining interest rates after 1720 might also have been a relevant stimulus.

It should be emphasized, however, that while low grain prices during the first half of the century may, perhaps, be partly related to agricultural innovation (John, 'Aspects of Economic Growth,' 365), Smith emphasized rather the effects of new technology on the prices of other foodstuffs and attributed the low grain prices to deflationary increases in the price of silver.

proceeding under his nose.[80] This view has sometimes been qualified on the grounds that while Smith was indeed not the prophet of industrial capitalism his oversights were not very serious. If he failed to discuss the early textile, metallurgical and power inventions, this was not a grave omission because they were very imperfect to begin with and slow to take hold. And he could not be expected to say anything of the subsequent major developments relating to power machinery since they occurred at too late a date.[81] Others argue that he might well be expected to have recognized the earlier technological developments, and believe that in fact he must have done so. Accordingly, they seek an explanation for his failure to discuss them.[82]

The conclusion to which we are led, however, is that Smith did in fact recognize and deal with many of the important technological developments prior to 1776, with the significant exception of those occurring in the cotton industry. A reason for this latter omission must be sought; but for the rest his discussion is remarkably complete.

We have noted in this chapter Smith's recognition of iron-ore smelting with coke instead of charcoal in Britain (in contrast to North America); the early invention of the atmospheric engine and its subsequent improvement; and a warning against rapid easing of import restrictions specifically in the case of silk because of the danger to fixed capital investments therein. The names which might be attached to these specific developments – those of Darby, Newcomen, and Lombe – were unfortunately not given by Smith. It would, however, be a remarkable coincidence if Smith's references were to different developments.

In several analyses of technical progress Smith covers a variety of broad phenomena about which we can be less certain of what specifically he had in mind. But frequently it can be said that the logic of the argument is applicable to certain contemporary events. Thus the analysis of capital-saving technical change might be illustrated by the effects of the Darby process. But the argument is perfectly suited to cover the replacement by Watt's rotary engine of Newcomen's atmospheric machine (or even Watt's own original steam engine) used in combination with the water-wheel. For the invention made it possible ultimately to dispense with costly hydraulic works. The possibility of steam-powered factories freed from dependence upon water is one of the most striking features of the technical revolution. Our point is not, of course, that Smith was aware of this *particular* development (although without doubt he was familiar with Watt's early inventive efforts). Rather we suggest that he recognized – and emphasized – a category of cases into which the development falls.[83]

80 E. Lipson, *The Economic History of England*, III (London, 1947), 54n; W.D. Grampp, 'On the History of Thought and Policy,' *American Economic Review*, LV (May 1965), 130: 'Smith seems not to have been aware of the technology that was emerging in his day.'

81 Eli Ginzberg, *The House of Adam Smith* (New York, 1934), 148f. and 237f.

82 Koebner, 'Adam Smith and the Industrial Revolution,' 381–91.

83 Watt's initial steam engine (based upon the 'separate condenser' principle) was developed at Glasgow and Carron. Commercial production of the engine began at

A second instance relates to Smith's formulation of labour-saving technical change. His concern largely is with output-expanding improvements such as would break the labour 'bottleneck' in circumstances of demand expansion. This category, in principle, would cover the efforts underway after mid-century – by Paul, Kay, Hargreaves, and Crompton – to raise labour productivity particularly in the spinning branch of the textile industry.

We add that the account of land-saving innovations and the general course of eighteenth-century agricultural development in the *Wealth of Nations* is a particularly 'accurate' analysis of events in the agricultural sector.

We have also noted the role attributed to economic pressures in determining the particular direction of technical progress. For example, the adoption of alternative fuels in iron smelting was related to changes in relative fuel prices. On the other hand, the nature of technology imposed certain constraints: rising prices of raw materials could not be overcome by the development or adoption of methods economizing their use. And labour-saving processes in manufacturing were related to scale rather than to rising wage rates, although it is true that increases in wage rates and scale were envisaged as usually occurring together. The empirical fact is, however, that the category of labour 'saved' by the changes in textiles (and in coal mining) was the lower-paid workers; accordingly Smith's analysis was highly relevant to contemporary events.

We have also pointed out in this chapter the slowness with which several of the textile developments – for example those by Kay and Paul (the 'flying shuttle' and spinning by rollers) – were introduced, partly because of initial technical imperfections. These devices were relevant largely for domestic manufacture. This is true also of Hargreaves' 'spinning jenny.' (Even Crompton's 'mule,' invented in 1779, was adaptable to domestic work.) But Smith's emphasis was upon developments taking place in *factories* – at least as far as new technology is concerned – so that we may appreciate a certain downplaying of textile developments (which might also have confirmed his recognition of the *slowness* of technical advance). Although in fact he did not neglect cost-reducing changes in the traditional textile industries, it was the progress underway in the metal-making plants, particularly those at Birmingham, that most impressed him.

It is frequently said that almost the sole factor in economic progress in

Soho in 1775. (An engine was actually erected at Boulton's hardware works to pump water for power.) But essentially the machine merely carried out the same functions as the earlier atmospheric engines. It was applied in pumping at reservoirs, brine works, breweries, distilleries, copper mines and iron works and to drive water wheels. (The Newcomen engine had the advantage at coal mines.) In brief, the engine still was of limited applicability.

Watt's invention of the 'rotary engine' (1781) permitted ultimately the application of steam-power quite generally and independently of water. The commercial production of the new-type engine dates from about 1786. Cf. Lord, *Capital and Steam Power*, 97, 147f., 161f.; Ashton, *The Industrial Revolution*, 68–9.

Smith's view was the division of labour. There is little doubt that much emphasis is indeed placed by Smith upon the contributions to new technology emanating from the specialist user of equipment on the floor of the plant. But it is also clear that this potential was seen to be limited. Furthermore, neither the international transmission of knowledge nor the contributions by specialist inventors and machine makers were neglected. It is formally true that the division of labour is almost the sole source of technological progress; but we must understand the term in this context in the broadest sense. Thus Smith attributed the atmospheric machine and the water-wheel to specialist inventors. There can also be little doubt that he was fully aware of the experimental efforts by Watt at Carron and Glasgow. In fact surprisingly extensive attention was paid to fixed capital not only in terms of 'embodied' technical change but also within the context of capital-saving innovation. We conclude that Smith viewed fixed capital as a crucially strategic phenomenon, particularly in light of its small significance in 'quantitative' terms throughout much of contemporary manufacturing.

It is the case that the 'undertaker' is often seen in the *Wealth of Nations* as one who – in Spengler's words – 'adjusts to circumstances rather than bring them about.' Change is not, on the whole, generated in Smith's system by a minority of creative 'entrepreneurs.' This is not perhaps too surprising, given Smith's characteristic eighteenth-century downplaying of innate differences from person to person. But once again it is a matter of degree only. Smith does on occasion make (approving) reference to the risk-taking innovator and he attempts to isolate the characteristics likely to be most favourable to improvement. (In any event it is appropriate to remark here that the cumulative effect of minor technological changes should not be played down. To this day little empirical work has been done to estimate the relative contributions to productivity of major and minor changes.)

It is of the greatest importance to be clear of the precise contribution by Smith to the discussion of division of labour. He was, it is true, concerned with the splitting up of occupations and the development of specialized crafts. But his true originality lies in the attempt to account for the *sub*-division of labour *in terms of plant size,* and raw material and seasonal characteristics; and the dispersion of processes between plants *in terms of industry size.* In these respects Smith made a significant advance over earlier treatments of the subject. To recognize factory operations alone would itself have been significant; but to analyse the determinants of profitable organization therein is an indication of a sophisticated appreciation of the phenomenon.

But we are certainly not attempting to argue that Smith was aware of the entire process of industrialization. We may refer here to the fact, discussed above, that machinery was largely seen to be *complementary* to labour rather than a substitute for it. And in addition we should emphasize the absence of any discussion of the effects of power-driven equipment upon industry organization.

It may be said that one of the most striking features of industrialization was in fact the *integration* of processes within the large-scale plant to take advantage of a common source of power, rather than its dispersion.[84] There is no evidence of any awareness by Smith of this trend. There were, it is true, few early illustrations (although Smith might have considered the Lombe factory in the case of silk).[85] A striking case prior to the publication of the *Wealth of Nations* was, however, to be found in cotton spinning. We refer to the (water-driven) integrated factory established at Cromford in 1771 by Arkwright which utilized the 'water frame.' Several additional plants were established before 1780 – at Belper (near Derby), Birkacre (in Lancashire), and Manchester – using complex machinery embodying a significantly improved carding device. According to Mantoux 'we see that as early as 1775 textile machinery had developed into a system, the interdependent parts of which were able to perform all the successive operations of the industry, save the last and most difficult, that of weaving.'[86]

It should be emphasized that it was only in 1785 with the cancellation of Arkwright's basic patents (relating to the initial spinning mechanism and the improved carding device) that the spinning factories began to become a *general* phenomenon. Moreover, while Watt's original engine was adopted in 1785 by one or two mills to drive the water wheel, the use in spinning of Watt's *rotary* engine – which released mills completely from dependence upon water-power – occurs only after 1790 when the engine was adopted to drive the 'mules.'[87] Yet in light of Smith's remarkable observational qualities and his skillful use of historical and contemporary data the fact that he did not note even the preliminary steps towards the integrated factory does require some comment.

The reason may lie in the fact that the new development took place in the cotton industry. He simply failed to take into account events in a minor part-time domestic occupation with a miniscule sales value throughout the 1760s. The same establishment as that of Arkwright's Cromford plant in any of the major manufacturing sectors would probably have caught his attention. It is nonetheless surprising that Smith had nothing to say about the growing signifi-

---

84 The rising costs involved in the distribution of materials and the collection of finished goods upon expansion of output also contributes to explain the increasing advantage of centralised operations in factories over the domestic system.

85 As did Josiah Tucker. See above, 67n.

86 Mantoux, *The Industrial Revolution in the Eighteenth Century*, 226. Cf. Ashton, *An Economic History of England*, 116, and A.E. Musson and Eric Robinson, *Science and Technology in the Industrial Revolution* (Toronto, 1969), 427f. We note that Watt's original steam engine was not applied to drive the water-wheels at the early Arkwright plants. The first use of Watt's engine for this purpose in the cotton industry was in 1785. (Mantoux, *The Industrial Revolution in the Eighteenth Century*, 232; Ashton, *The Industrial Revolution*, 73.)

87 Crompton's 'mule' which had features both of the jenny and the water frame, and which came into use after the mid-eighties, was adaptable to cottage use and kept the domestic system alive for a while, as we have seen.

cance not only of Manchester *but also of Glasgow* in the production of cotton and semi-cotton goods.[88]

The attention paid to the traditional branches of activity and the corresponding neglect of cotton may not be due only to a quantitative difference in size. One of Smith's fundamental objectives was to attack contemporary distortions in the pattern of activity; these distortions – manufacturing regulations, guild statutes, Acts of Parliament, and so forth – were relatively insignificant in the new industries so that his attention was not attracted to them.[89] Yet Smith might have referred to attempts by established manufacturers to prevent the production of pure cotton goods – such as the Act of 1721 – and the successful petition to parliament by Arkwright in 1774 which thwarted their opposition.[90] And we have seen that much attention was paid to Birmingham hardware despite the absence of traditional forms of regulation in that city.[91]

We must recognize Smith's failure to appreciate the developments in the cotton industry. And we note – although with important qualifications – an emphasis upon progressive improvement attributable to competitive pressures. But we cannot conclude that he failed to anticipate the industrial revolution. To have paid the degree of attention we find in the *Wealth of Nations* to the determinants of plant and industry organization, to fixed capital and its maintenance, to the differential factor-saving effects of technical change, to the contributions to knowledge of specialist inventors and machine makers, at a time when the changes usually associated with the industrial revolution had not yet occurred, or were only just occurring, shows remarkable insight.

88 Josiah Tucker, it will be recalled (above, 67n.), makes reference to the industry (1757); and the author of *Considerations on the East-India Trade* (1701) was preoccupied with the free importation of relatively cheap printed cottons and calicoes.

89 While insisting that Smith neglects to discuss the innovations of his day, Koebner 'Adam Smith and the Industrial Revolution,' 389f., argues that he did not do so because of unawareness of them. It was rather because he did not see that the contributions of the 'projectors' were very important for economic progress. This evaluation, it is suggested, represented an error of judgment, failing to give the combined contribution of the 'inventive genius' and of the 'business spirit' its proper due. The main reason suggested by Koebner is that Smith's major concern was to attack the merchants and manufacturers for distorting the pattern of activity. On balance, the negative effects of their influence-peddling outweighed their contributions to innovation.

90 Mantoux, *The Industrial Revolution in the Eighteenth Century*, 224–5; Wilson, *England's Apprenticeship*, 293.

91 *Wealth of Nations*, 120–1.

EIGHT

The approach to economic development

We are concerned in this chapter with Adam Smith's attitude towards economic development, defined in terms of rising *per capita* income, bearing in mind the approaches taken both in the *Theory of Moral Sentiments* and the *Wealth of Nations*. We shall also consider the role envisaged by Smith for government in the developmental process including, particularly, the financing of education. We turn finally to alternative policy objectives to development in the fourth section with special reference to national defence. At the outset it is in order to recall Smith's observations regarding the contemporary state of employment and real wages.

THE STATE OF EMPLOYMENT AND REAL WAGES

There are numerous scattered references in the *Wealth of Nations* to indolence, pauperism, and vagrancy.[1] One explanation offered for the phenomenon of unemployment runs in terms of the effect of the statutes of apprenticeship and of corporations in obstructing the free movement of labour between occupations and places. Workmen released by declining trades could not seek employment elsewhere because of the restrictions on movement and consequently had 'no other choice but either to come upon the parish, or to work as common labourers, for which, by their habits, they are much worse qualified than for any sort of manufacture that bears any resemblance to their own. They generally, therefore, chuse to come upon the parish.'[2]

Whereas corporation laws, Smith tells us, were common throughout Europe,

---

1 E.g., Adam Smith, *Wealth of Nations*, 72: here Smith refers to European artificers who wait 'indolently in their workhouses, for the calls of their customers.'

2 *Ibid.*, 135. Although the statute of apprenticeship is said not to apply to linen manufacture, production thereof was too localized geographically to be able to absorb many men: 'It is not much cultivated through the greater part of the country.'

England suffered from an institution peculiar to herself, namely the system of poor laws which further obstructed the movement of labour. Smith gives a rather full account of the growth and effects of these regulations:

The very unequal price of labour which we frequently find in England in places at no great distance from one another, is probably owing to the obstruction which the law of settlements gives to a poor man who would carry his industry from one parish to another without a certificate ... The scarcity of hands in one parish, therefore, cannot always be relieved by their superabundance in another, as it is constantly in Scotland, and, I believe, in all other countries where there is no difficulty of settlement ... ; we never meet with those sudden and unaccountable differences in the wages of neighbouring places which we sometimes find in England, where it is often more difficult for a poor man to pass the artificial boundary of a parish, than an arm of the sea or a ridge of high mountains, natural boundaries which sometimes separate very distinctly different rates of wages in other countries (140).[3]

In his discussion of the efforts of manufacturers to influence governmental intervention in their favour, Smith refers to the extension of exemptions from import duties from raw materials strictly defined, to cover also what in effect should be considered as partly-finished products. The particular case emphasized is that of the free importation of linen yarn, the spinning of which, Smith claims, is a labour-intensive process. These importations displaced domestic spinners or depressed their wages: 'It is the industry which is carried on for the benefit of the rich and the powerful, that is principally encouraged by our mercantile system. That which is carried on for the benefit of the poor and the indigent, is too often, either neglected, or oppressed.'[4] Whether such intervention is regarded as an *important* cause of unemployment is doubtful, but the recognition of a body of indigents by Smith is noted, and it is implied that monopsony-monopoly power may be partly responsible.

Some attention is paid to cyclical variations in employment. In years of poor harvests there is likely to be a reduction in labour demand – on wage-fund grounds – at the same time that the labour supply rises as the means of self-employment tend to fall. In these conditions 'a considerable number of people are thrown out of employment, who bid against one another, in

3 Professor Viner refers to the absence, in the *Wealth of Nations* of any general comment on the problem of poor relief: *Guide to John Rae's Life of Adam Smith* (New York, 1965), 101. But it would be more relevant to raise the question of the absence of any broad discussion of the *role of government* in relief; it is certainly not clear what is implied in Smith's hostility towards the law of settlement about his attitude towards the right to relief. It is clear, however, that he deprecated the high death rate typical in the foundling hospitals and parish institutions (*Wealth of Nations*, 79). A general statement in his *Theory of Moral Sentiments* (1759; New York, 1966) to the effect that 'the peace and order of society is of more importance than even the relief of the poor' (see below, 248) can by no means be taken as a rejection of the right to relief. But in any event there is evidence, we shall presently argue, of a change in Smith's attitude towards labour between 1759 and 1776 which might be reflected also in his approach to relief.
4 *Wealth of Nations*, 609. Discussed below, 303.

order to get it, which sometimes lowers both the real and the money price of labour.'[5] Apparently, the short-run problem is soluble by flexibility of wages.

Despite the references to pauperism and unemployment Smith was optimistic regarding the secular pattern of real wages and employment. It seems to be his view that the contemporary problem of unemployment was a local one only – explicable largely by institutional impediments to mobility – or when more general to be of a short-run nature only.[6] For Smith is careful to note that average real wages exceeded subsistence and were tending to rise.

That real wages were in excess of subsistence is deduced by Smith from indirect evidence:

In Great Britain the wages of labour seem, in the present times, to be evidently more than what is precisely necessary to enable the labourer to bring up a family. In order to satisfy ourselves upon this point it will not be necessary to enter into any tedious or doubtful calculation of what may be the lowest sum upon which it is possible to do this. There are many plain symptoms that the wages of labour are nowhere in this country regulated by this lowest rate which is consistent with common humanity (74).

The common complaint that luxury extends itself even to the lowest ranks of the people, and that the labouring poor will not now be contented with the same food, cloathing and lodging which satisfied them in former times, may convince us that it is not the money price of labour only, but its real recompence, which has augmented (78).

The secular upward trend of average real wages is explained in terms of the increased efficiency of food production in the following passage: 'The real recompence of labour, the real quantity of the necessaries and conveniencies of life which it can procure to the labourer, has, during the course of the present century, increased perhaps in a still greater proportion than its money price. Not only grain has become somewhat cheaper, but many other things, from which the industrious poor derive an agreeable and wholesome variety of food, have become a great deal cheaper' (78).[7] But within the Smithian structure a reduction in the price of wage goods does not, strictly speaking, represent an independent cause of real wage increase, and the operative cause of the upward movement was evidently seen to lie in the secular increase in demand for labour *pari passu* with the expansion of the economy as a whole:

5 *Ibid.*, 86.
6 Smith may also have envisaged unemployment as being, in part, a consequence of government intervention inducing a premature outflow of capital. See the discussion of alternative uses of funds in Chapter 10.
7 The rise in agricultural productivity and the probable effects flowing from the resultant increase in *per capita* real incomes are discussed in E.L. Jones, 'Agriculture and Economic Growth in England, 1660–1750: Agricultural Change,' *Journal of Economic History*, XXV (1965), and A.H. John, 'Agricultural Productivity and Economic Growth in England, 1700–1760,' *Journal of Economic History*, XXV (1965), both reprinted in E.L. Jones, ed., *Agriculture and Economic Growth in England 1650–1815* (London, 1967), 152f and 172f.

The money price of labour in Great Britain has, indeed, risen during the course of the present century. This, however, seems to be the effect, not so much of any diminution in the value of silver in the European market, as of an increase in the demand for labour in Great Britain, arising from the great, and almost universal prosperity of the country ... In Great Britain the real recompence of labour ... has increased considerably during the course of the present century ... owing to the peculiarly happy circumstances of the country (200–1).[8]

The fact that Smith envisaged Great Britain to be enjoying a state of full employment and of growing employment opportunities can also be deduced from the ease whereby the demobilization in 1764 of more than 100,000 servicemen was achieved. In a relatively short period the men were reabsorbed into the work force without any general downward pressure on wages:

By the reduction of the army and navy at the end of the late war, more than a hundred thousand soldiers and seamen, a number equal to what is employed in the greatest manufactures, were all at once thrown out of their ordinary employment; but, though they no doubt suffered some inconveniency, they were not thereby deprived of all employment and subsistence. The greater part of the seamen, it is probable, gradually betook themselves to the merchant-service as they could find occasion, and in the meantime both they and the soldiers were absorbed in the great mass of the people ... Not only no great convulsion but no sensible disorder arose from so great a change in the situation of more than a hundred thousand men, all accustomed to the use of arms, and many of them to rapine and plunder. The number of vagrants was scarce any-where sensibly increased by it, even the wages of labour were not reduced by it in any occupation, so far as I have been able to learn, except in that of seamen in the merchant service (436).

It is common for eighteenth-century writers to assume the existence of a reserve of unemployed or underemployed labour, which might be called into employment upon an increase in demand. But Smith does not emphasize this phenomenon. It is noted only as of historical interest: 'Our ancestors were idle for want of a sufficient encouragement to industry. It is better, says the proverb, to play for nothing than to work for nothing.'[9] Some further indirect evidence for the proposition that Smith did not consider the problem of unemployment to be serious – at least in the absence of artificial impediments to mobility – may also be drawn from his failure to discuss the role of government in poor relief, apart from his call for the abolition of the settlement laws.[10]

8 See the discussion in P. Deane and W.A. Cole, *British Economic Growth 1688–1959*, 2nd ed. (Cambridge, 1967), 21; Peter Mathias, *The First Industrial Nation* (London, 1969), 217–18. Available data indicate an increase in money-wage rates especially in Lancashire and other industrial centres which was adequate to assure real-wage rate increases, until the early 1790s, even after food prices commenced an upward trend in the 1760s. No such trend is discernible in the rural South.

9 *Wealth of Nations*, 319.

10 Professor Coats has emphasized the fact that Josiah Tucker, who also strongly attacked the settlement laws, similarly believed there to be no shortage of employ-

THE DESIRABILITY OF ECONOMIC DEVELOPMENT

The *Theory of Moral Sentiments* contains a formal downplaying of economic development as defined above:

For to what purpose is all the toil and bustle of this world? What is the end of avarice and ambition, of the pursuit of wealth, of power, and pre-eminence? Is it to supply the necessities of nature? The wages of the meanest labourer can supply them. We see that they afford him food and clothing, the comfort of a house, and of a family. If we examine his economy with rigour, we should find that he spends a great part of them upon conveniences, which may be regarded as superfluities, and that, upon extraordinary occasions, he can give something even to vanity and distinction.[11]

Moreover, any surplus income (over some undefined 'minimum') is said to be meaningless to the recipient. Thus the ambitious poor man may exhaust himself in acquiring wealth only to discover that 'wealth and greatness are mere trinkets of frivolous utility, no more adapted for procuring ease of body or tranquility of mind, than the tweezer-cases of the lover of toys.'[12] The inability of high command over goods and services to provide genuine happiness is only recognized when it is too late: 'Power and riches appear then to be, what they are, enormous and operose machines contrived to produce a few trifling conveniences to the body, consisting of springs the most nice and delicate, which must be kept in order with the most anxious attention, and which, in spite of all our care, are ready every moment to burst into pieces, and to crush in their ruins their unfortunate possessor.'[13]

The real costs of acquiring higher income in terms of mental and physical effort thus far exceed the real benefits which are derived therefrom. But mankind tends to be misled, runs the argument, by the apparent 'fitness' of commodities and services to generate well-being: 'If we consider the real satisfaction which all these things are capable of affording, by itself and separated from the beauty of that arrangement which is fitted to promote it, it will always appear in the highest degree contemptible and trifling.'[14]

Yet the error of judgment, Smith continues, has the fortunate effect of stimulating economic activity: 'it is well that nature imposes upon us in this manner. It is this deception which rouses and keeps in continual motion the industry of mankind.' What requires notice is the precise nature of the advantages of growth which here evidently relates in part to *aggregate* rather than average income; for the emphasis is placed upon the large population which can be maintained by a large national product: 'The earth, by these labours of mankind, has been obliged to redouble her natural fertility, and

ment opportunities and no problems of long-run involuntary unemployment in the absence of such intervention ('Economic Thought and Poor Law Policy in the Eighteenth Century,' *Economic History Review*, XIII (1960), 49–50).

11 Adam Smith, *The Theory of Moral Sentiments* (1st ed. 1759; 6th ed. 1790 [last in Smith's lifetime]; ed. used here is new ed. published by H.G. Bohn, New York, 1853, reprinted 1966), 70.

12 *Ibid.*, 261.

13 *Ibid.*, 262.

14 *Ibid.*, 263.

to maintain a greater multitude of inhabitants.'[15] Since it is apparently presumed that total happiness increases along with the increase in total population – at subsistence – the expansion of the total national product is a desirable objective.

We draw attention at this stage to a utilitarian case developed by Smith in favour of the contemporary income distribution. Inequality is essential, runs the argument, to assure the maintenance of order and stability (although it is hinted, less desirable on other grounds) :

After the persons who are recommended to our beneficence, either by their connection with ourselves, by their personal qualities, or by their past services, come those who are pointed out, not indeed to what is called our friendship, but to our benevolent attention and good offices; those who are distinguished by their extraordinary situation – the greatly fortunate and the greatly unfortunate, the rich and the powerful, the poor and the wretched. The distinction of ranks, the peace and order of society, are in a great measure founded upon the respect which we naturally conceive for the former. The relief and consolation of human misery depend altogether upon our compassion for the latter. The peace and order of society is of more importance than even the relief of the miserable. Our respect for the great, accordingly, is most apt to offend by its excess – our fellow-feeling for the miserable, by its defect. Moralists exhort us to charity and compassion. They warn us against the fascination of greatness. This fascination, indeed, is so powerful, that the rich and the great are too often preferred to the wise and the virtuous. Nature has wisely judged that the distinction of ranks, the peace and order of society, would rest more securely upon the plain and palpable difference of birth and fortune, than upon the invisible and often uncertain difference of wisdom and virtue. The undistinguishing eyes of the great mob of mankind can well enough perceive the former: it is with difficulty that the nice discernment of the wise and the virtuous can sometimes distinguish the latter. In the order of all those recommendations, the benevolent wisdom of nature is equally evident.[16]

It should also be kept in mind that *leisure*, as well as security, was elsewhere said by Smith to be an essential precondition for all advanced intellectual endeavour:

But when law has established order and security, and subsistence ceases to be precarious, the curiosity of mankind is increased, and their fears are diminished. The leisure which they then enjoy renders them more attentive to the appearances of nature, more observant of her smallest irregularities, and more desirous to know what is the chain which links them all together ... *Those of liberal fortunes*, whose attention is not much occupied either with business or with pleasure, can fill up the void of

15 *Ibid.*, 264. Some attention is, however, also paid to the greater refinement of life permitted by higher productivity. The 'deception' referred to 'first prompted [mankind] to cultivate the ground, to build houses, to found cities and commonwealths, and to invent and improve all the sciences and arts, which ennoble and embellish human life' (*ibid.*, 263–4).

16 *Ibid.*, 331–2. Added in sixth edition (1790).

their imagination, which is thus disengaged from the ordinary affairs of life, no other way than by attending to that train of events which passes around them.[17]

The case in favour of inequality expressed in the *Theory of Moral Sentiments* must, however, be evaluated in conjunction with the view that the distribution of income – apparently severely unequal – is in actuality more or less egalitarian. For the wealthy landlord can consume scarcely more than the 'meanest peasant' and accordingly distributes the means of subsistence to his servants and others who are 'employed in the economy of greatness; all of whom thus derive from his luxury and caprice that share of the necessaries of life which they would in vain have expected from his humanity or his justice.' In consequence, 'the produce of the soil maintains at all times nearly that number of inhabitants which it is capable of maintaining.'[18]

In addition, as already pointed out, the poor are in any event at least as well equipped psychologically as the rich to attain genuine happiness. It is indeed in this context that the celebrated term 'invisible hand' appears long before its use in the *Wealth of Nations*:

[The rich] are led by an invisible hand to make nearly the same distribution of the necessaries of life which would have been made had the earth been divided into equal proportions among all its inhabitants; and thus, without intending it, without knowing it, advance the interest of the society, *and afford means to the multiplication of the species*. When providence divided the earth among a few lordly masters, it neither forgot nor abandoned those who seemed to have been left out in the partition. These last, too, enjoy their share of all that it produces. In what constitutes the real happiness of human life, they are in no respect inferior to those who would seem so much above them. In ease of body and peace of mind, all the different ranks of life are nearly upon a level, and the beggar, who suns himself by the side of the highway, possesses that security which kings are fighting for.[19]

It is sometimes suggested that Smith's concern in the *Wealth of Nations* was with the 'economic man' devised as a construct of the mind or an abstraction

17 *Principles Which Lead and Direct Philosophical Enquiries, Illustrated by the History of Astronomy,* in J. Ralph Lindgren, ed., *The Early Writings of Adam Smith* (New York, 1967), 49–50 (author's emphasis).
18 *Theory of Moral Sentiments,* 264. Economically, Smith's error lies in failing to recognize that the landlord is enjoying *his* income and the servants their incomes.
   Cf., *ibid.,* a further uncomplimentary reference to the rich: 'The rich only select from the heap what is more precious and agreeable. They consume little more than the poor; and in spite of their natural selfishness and rapacity, though they mean only their own conveniency, though the sole end which they propose from the labours of all the thousands whom they employ be the gratification of their own vain and insatiable desires, they divide with the poor the produce of all their improvements.'
   de Mirabeau in the *Tableau Economique avec ses explications* (1760; tr. 1766) expressed a similar optimism, based on much the same grounds, regarding the inequality of income. Cf. E. Cannan, *A Review of Economic Theory,* 2nd ed. (London, 1964), 294.
19 *Theory of Moral Sentiments,* 264–5 (author's emphasis).

which removes part of his psychological make-up and retains only the economic motive.[20] This interpretation may seem unlikely in light of the trivial nature accorded to the economic end in the *Theory of Moral Sentiments*.[21] An alternative view, which in this regard is less troublesome, is that Smith was concerned in the *Wealth of Nations* with the 'entire man' but in the 'anonymous' market place where there is little scope for the various social sentiments.[22] Whether or not this latter interpretation better reflects Smith's intentions, we must take into account the fact that even in the former work he did *not* recommend an abysmally low standard of living for the poor. Smith's apparently complacent attitude towards the poor was qualified.

We derive support for this view in part from criticism in the *Theory of Moral Sentiments* of Mandeville according to whom, Smith contended, 'every thing ... is luxury which exceeds what is absolutely necessary for the support of human nature, so that there is vice even in the use of a clean shirt, or of a convenient habitation.'[23] Moreover, the legitimate object of government, we are also told, is or should be, 'to promote the happiness of those who live under them' and to assure that the people 'are better lodged, that they are better clothed, that they are better fed.' Smith accordingly approved of subsidies and the like granted to the linen and woollen manufacturers, and of the 'patriot,' that is the individual who exerts himself in the public interest, for example by the repair of high-roads.[24] It would, accordingly, be justified to regard Smith's position in the *Theory of Moral Sentiments* as one in support of economic development as a prerequisite for an increased population at a 'reasonable' level of subsistence, and as a denigration of any surplus income over this (undefined) minimum. Insofar as attention is paid to the material requirements of the poor, Smith diverges from mercantilist doctrine.[25]

20 Cf. H.T. Buckle, *History of Civilization in England* (New York, 1885), II, 351f.
21 Yet it should also be borne in mind that in the *Wealth of Nations* Smith's conception of economic self-interest refers not merely to the accumulation of wealth strictly defined, but to every motive to action – including a desire for leisure, for honour and so forth – except those designed to promote the well-being of others. Cf. Jacob Viner, 'Adam Smith and Laissez Faire,' in J.M. Clark *et al.*, *Adam Smith 1776–1926* (Chicago, 1928), 132–3; and Glenn R. Morrow, *Ethical and Economic Theories of Adam Smith* (1923; New York, 1969), 75–6.
22 Jacob Viner, 'On the Intellectual History of Laissez Faire,' *Journal of Law and Economics*, III (Oct. 1960), 60; Glenn R. Morrow, 'Adam Smith: Moralist and Philosopher,' in Clark, *et al.*, *Adam Smith 1776–1926*, 167; and Morrow, *Ethical and Economic Theories of Adam Smith*, 7–9.
23 *Theory of Moral Sentiments*, 456–7.
24 *Ibid.*, 265–7.
25 Cf. a similar conclusion by Lord Robbins that Smith's argument, according to which the distribution of happiness is less unequal than the distribution of wealth, need not conflict with the view that *ceteris paribus* the beggar would benefit from an increase of real income (*The Theory of Economic Development in the History of Economic Thought* (London, 1968), 164). The admission by Smith, of the necessity for minimum living standards, even in the earlier work, is discussed at some length by James Bonar, *Philosophy and Political Economy*, 3rd ed. (1922; London,

We must also allow for a change in emphasis in Smith's attitude towards economic development in the *Wealth of Nations*. In the first place, of course, the opening paragraphs of the work place the emphasis squarely upon average annual income: 'According, therefore, as this produce, or what is purchased with it, bears a greater or smaller proportion to the number of those who are to consume it, the nation will be better or worse supplied with all the necessaries and conveniencies for which it has occasion.'[26] Equally important, the index was not intended to serve as a mere statistical fiction; capital accumulation was desirable at least in part because it raised the living standards specifically of the *labouring* class. It is true that in consequence, population was expected to respond and – in the absence of further increase in the demand for labour – wages per head to decline; yet the initial upward pressure on wages of itself was regarded as desirable: 'It deserves to be remarked, perhaps, that it is in the progressive state, while the society is advancing to the further acquisition, rather than when it has acquired its full complement of riches, that the condition of the labouring poor, of the great body of the people, seems to be the happiest and the most comfortable. It is hard in the stationary, and miserable in the declining state' (81). The advantages of rising average wages are even more graphically expressed in Smith's laudatory comments upon the observed contemporary upward trend:

Is this improvement in the circumstances of the lower ranks of the people to be regarded as an advantage or as an inconveniency to the society? The answer seems at first sight abundantly plain. Servants, labourers and workmen of different kinds, make up the far greater part of every great political society. But what improves the circumstances of the greater part can never be regarded as an inconveniency to the whole. No society can surely be flourishing and happy, of which the far greater part of the members are poor and miserable. It is but equity, besides, that they who feed, cloath and lodge the whole body of the people, should have such a share of the produce of their own labour as to be themselves tolerably well fed, cloathed and lodged (78–9).

In this regard it will be recalled that seventeenth- and eighteenth-century writers frequently emphasized the national importance of a *large* population at low living standards; despite a concern with pauperism it was assumed typically that the population was too small for the territory. In the *Wealth of Nations*, by contrast, the emphasis is upon the desirability of circumstances generating a *growing* population: 'The most decisive mark of prosperity is

1967), 170f. (Similar views are attributed to Francis Hutcheson and David Hume, *ibid.*, 113.)

A.L. Macfie, 'The Invisible Hand in the "Theory of Moral Sentiments," ' in Macfie, *The Individual in Society: Papers on Adam Smith* (London, 1967), 107, emphasizes that 'the optimistic theism' of the *Theory of Moral Sentiments* conflicts with Smith's grasp in the same work of the 'seamier side of human nature and life.' Thus 'the suffering and injustices that are never reconciled or recompensed here on earth are a constant theme in the *Moral Sentiments*, though Smith's common sense does lead him to recognize that a considerable amount of justice and due reward is achieved.' (See also Macfie, 'The Invisible Hand,' 117.)

26 Adam Smith, *Wealth of Nations*, lvii.

the increase of the number of its inhabitants.'[27] Thus, while China is described 'as one of the richest, that is, the most fertile, best cultivated, most industrious, and *most populous* countries in the world,' living conditions are said to be frightful,[28] providing an illustration of the proposition that it is *not* 'in the richest countries, but in the most thriving, or in those which are growing rich the fastest, that the wages of labour are highest.'[29]

Moreover, although there is no suggestion that private property should in any way be seriously interfered with, Smith did not hesitate to approve of some induced alteration in the pattern of income distribution in favour of labour. We may refer to two instances. In the first place, he recognized approvingly the element of progression inherent in the taxation of house-rents (insofar as the proportion of the budget of the rich devoted to housing exceed that of the poor) : 'A tax upon house-rents, therefore, would in general fall heaviest upon the rich; and in this sort of inequality there would not, perhaps, be any thing very unreasonable. It is not very unreasonable that the rich should contribute to the public expence, not only in proportion to their revenue, but something more than in proportion.'[30] Secondly, Smith recommended higher tolls on the luxury carriages of the rich than upon freight whereby 'the indolence and vanity of the rich is made to contribute in a very easy manner to the relief of the poor, by rendering cheaper the transportation of heavy goods to all the different parts of the country.'[31]

Also indicative of Smith's attitude towards labour in the *Wealth of Nations* is his recommendation, partly on humanitarian grounds, that protective duties and prohibitions should be reduced *gradually* to avoid unemployment:

The case in which it may sometimes be a matter of deliberation, how far, or in what manner, it is proper to restore the free importation of foreign goods, after it has been for some time interrupted, is, when particular manufactures, by means of high duties or prohibitions upon all foreign goods which can come into competition with them, have been so far extended as to employ a great multitude of hands. Humanity may in this case require that the freedom of trade should be restored only by slow gradations, and with a good deal of reserve and circumspection. Were those high duties and prohibitions taken away all at once, cheaper foreign goods of the same kind might be poured so fast into the home market, as to deprive all at once many thousands of our people of their ordinary employment and means of subsistence (435–6).[32]

We should recall too, in the present context, Smith's insistence that in contemporary circumstances rising wages would stimulate workers to greater effort, in contrast to mercantilist notions which implied a backward-bending labour

27 *Ibid.*, 70; author's emphasis. This index was adopted too by Malthus: 'there is not a truer criterion of the happiness and innocence of a people, than the rapidity of their increase.' (*Population: The First Essay*, 1798 (London, 1966), chap. vi, 108.)
28 *Wealth of Nations*, 71–2; author's emphasis.
29 *Ibid.*, 69.
30 *Ibid.*, 794.
31 *Ibid.*, 683.
32 Although partly because of the technological similarity between processes the 'disorder' occasioned would, Smith suggested, 'be less than is commonly imagined.'

supply function;[33] and numerous statements to the effect that landed proprietors as well as capitalists 'love to reap where they have not sown,' that in old-established and slowly expanding or stagnant countries 'rent and profit eat up wages, and the two superior orders of people oppress the inferior one,' and that social inequality gives masters the advantage in bargaining in conditions of economic stagnation. There is no complacency or 'optimism' in these remarks and there can be little doubt that economic development was considered to be a desirable objective as the means of raising the living standards of labour.

We do not, however, intend to suggest that there are no references to the advantages of a large population in the *Wealth of Nations*. The division of labour is related – although infrequently – to population size: 'What takes place among the labourers in a particular workhouse, takes place, for the same reason, among those of a great society. The greater their number, the more they naturally divide themselves into different classes and subdivisions of employment.'[34] But in light of Smith's expressed concern with the serious distributional implications of a 'populous' and 'stationary' economy it is unlikely that great weight could have been placed upon the productivity advantages as such forthcoming therein. It should be emphasized, however, that in a *growing* economy the efficiency advantages might be increasingly assured while at the same time high average wages are maintained.

We note further that the celebrated maxim relating the division of labour to 'the extent of the market' may indeed imply the desirability of a large population.[35] But the preceding observation again applies; it is expansion rather than the dimensions of the economy that assures against a depression of *per capita* wages. It may be added that although a growing population might indeed generate an extension of the market it is not clear to what degree Smith explained contemporary extensions in these terms, and to what degree he ascribed them to rising average incomes since both forces were in fact recognized.[36]

33 See above, 163.
34 *Wealth of Nations*, 86.
35 *Ibid.*, 17f. Although reference is made to population size as a determinant of the market, almost the entire discussion concerns the significance of satisfactory transportation facilities. Cf. also *ibid.*, 147: 'Good roads, canals and navigable rivers ... [are] the greatest of all improvements.'
    We note, however, elsewhere an emphasis upon the magnitude of the domestic *urban* population as a particularly significant determinant of the market for *agricultural* products. This issue is raised in the context of a criticism of contraints imposed upon industry and trade in the supposed interest of agriculture: 'Whatever, besides, tends to diminish in any country the number of artificers and manufacturers, tends to diminish the home market, the most important of all markets for the rude produce of the soil, and thereby still further to discourage agriculture' (*ibid.*, 650). Similarly, 'the greater the number and revenue of the inhabitants of the town, the more extensive is the market which it affords to those of the country.' (*Ibid.*, 356. See also *ibid.*, 476.)
36 A reference to expanding markets in North America in consequence of rapid population expansion casts some light on the issue (*ibid.*, 202): 'as its advances in agriculture, industry, and population, are much more rapid than those of the most thriving countries in Europe, its demand must increase much more rapidly.' The fact is,

Our discussion thus far suggests that Smith regarded as desirable the expansion of national income as a means of assuring adequately high *per capita* wages and at the same time of permitting and stimulating the *growth* of population. The emphasis is upon the advantages of change in, rather than the absolute dimension of, national income. At this point we wish, however, to draw attention to a sense in which the magnitude of the capitalist sector as such – and accordingly growth in the aggregative sense – had in Smith's view certain desirable consequences.

These relate in the first place, to various personal characteristics typical of the capitalist sector. Thus 'whenever commerce is introduced into any country probity and punctuality always accompany it,' in consequence not of 'national character' but of 'self-interest, that general principle which regulates the actions of every man, and which leads men to act in a certain manner from views of advantage.'[37] Similarly, Smith ascribed greater 'security' to the capitalist sector: 'Nothing tends so much to corrupt mankind as dependency, while independency still increases the honesty of the people.'[38] But even in this case the ultimate cause of the differential behaviour pattern relates to the higher *per capita* earnings in the capitalist sector compared with those 'paid out of revenue': 'The establishment of commerce and manufactures, which brings about this independency is the best police for preventing crimes. The common people have better wages in this way than in any other, and in consequence of this the general probity of manners takes place through the whole country.'[39] Secondly, and of fundamental significance in the context of aggregative expansion, is Smith's position that the entire population mechanism is in any event relevant in the *productive* sector, although only to the extent that real *per capita* income increases are not devoted to 'luxury' items.[40]

We conclude that Smith's concern was with rising *per capita* income partly

however, as Smith never tired of emphasizing, that average incomes were rising also with particular rapidity in the colonies.

The account of land-utilization patterns in developing countries also depends upon the increasing demands for various commodities – hitherto free goods – generated by growing population and rising *per capita* income (*ibid.*, 235).

Compare conflicting positions on this matter adopted by Adolph Lowe, 'The Classical Theory of Economic Growth,' *Social Research*, XXI (1954), 136–7; and J.J. Spengler, 'Adam Smith's Theory of Economic Growth – Part II,' *Southern Economic Journal*, XXVI (July 1951), 7–8.

37 Adam Smith, *Lectures on Police, Justice, Revenue and Arms* (1763), ed. E. Cannan (1896; New York, 1964), 253.

38 *Ibid.*, 155. Cf. *Wealth of Nations*, 319. In these terms Smith explained the lower capital-crime rate of Glasgow compared with Edinburgh. (The general position is maintained subject to a minimum level of education, discussed below.)

Cf. a similarly optimistic view expressed by David Hume, 'Of Refinement in the Arts,' in E. Rotwein, ed., *David Hume: Writings on Economics* (London, 1955), 19–32.

39 *Lectures*, 155–6. The poverty of those dependent upon the spending of revenue by the wealthy is similarly emphasized in the *Wealth of Nations*, 319; thus in the various court towns of the Continent 'the inferior ranks of people ... are in general idle, dissolute, and poor.'

40 See above, 161–2.

for its own sake and above all to assure adequate average wages, and partly as a means of encouraging population expansion and consequently the extension of the productive or capitalist sector. Expansion of the productive sector, in turn, was recommended in part because of the productivity advantages of large scale, and in part because of the desirable social and personal characteristics engendered therein. The two-fold objective imposed mutual restrictions. On the one hand, the nature of the real income increase which was considered to be desirable was constrained, for the extensive enjoyment of high average income in certain 'luxury' forms would fail to stimulate population growth. On the other hand, mere magnitude of dimension in terms of capital, population, aggregate output – as distinct from the expansion thereof – did not guarantee high *per capita* incomes for labour despite high productivity.[41]

It is true that Smith in the *Wealth of Nations* adopts upon occasion a denigration of material well-being similar to the *Theory of Moral Sentiments*. We call attention to his discussion of the institutions required to curb 'cowardice' and to develop 'martial' attitudes among the masses. 'Happiness and misery,' runs the contention, 'which reside altogether in the mind, must necessarily depend more upon the healthful or unhealthful, the mutilated or entire state of the mind, than upon that of the body.'[42] Similarly, in a discussion of the desirability of complete freedom of trade in corn – with particular reference to exportation – Smith conceded in an extraordinary comment that some degree of control might be necessary to satisfy an unjustified concern of the public with its material welfare: 'The people feel themselves so much interested in what relates either to their subsistence in this life, or to their happiness in a life to come, that government must yield to their prejudices, and in order to preserve the public tranquillity, establish that system which they approve of.'[43]

41 Our analysis conflicts with a recently expressed view of Smith's position according to which the concern was with aggregate – as distinct from *per capita* wealth – mainly because of the *large* population which might be maintained thereby. See Jacob Viner, 'Adam Smith,' *International Encyclopedia of the Social Sciences*, vol. 14 (1968), 325.

42 *Wealth of Nations*, 739. We may also refer to Smith's enthusiastic endorsement of the division of labour – despite severe inequality of income – on the grounds that the workman 'even of the lowest and poorest order, if he is frugal and industrious, may enjoy a greater share of the necessaries and conveniencies of life than is possible for any savage to acquire' (*ibid.*, lviii), or that the peasant lives better than an African king (*ibid.*, 12). There are even stronger statements to the same effect in the 'Early Draft of the *Wealth of Nations*' (c.1763) in W.R. Scott, *Adam Smith as Student and Professor* (Glasgow, 1937), 325–7. For example: 'If we consider, I say, all those different conveniences and luxuries with which he [the labourer] is accommodated and consider what a variety of labour is employed about each of them, we shall be sensible that without the assistance and co-operation of many thousands, the very meanest person in civilized society could not be provided for, *even in what we very falsely imagine*, the easy and simple manner in which he is commonly accommodated' (*ibid.*, 325; author's emphasis).

43 *Ibid.*, 507. (But he insisted that the price above which restrictions on corn exports are imposed should be at a very high level.) Smith's comments were motivated by a

These comments are apparently in conflict with the general course of the argument in the *Wealth of Nations*. For, as we have seen, Smith applauded the contemporary upward trend in *per capita* wages and deplored the pitiable living standards of labour in those societies which, while possessing great populations, were stagnant. But we may to some degree overcome the disaccord if we once again ascribe to Smith disapproval of *excessively* high average consumption on 'moral' grounds, and because of certain social disadvantages such as the weakening of the nation's 'martial' spirit and, we might add, possibly because of the implied failure of the population mechanism. To take this view of Smith's position, however, suggests that the *desiderata* of policy cannot be defined unambiguously but depend upon the particular circumstances which happen to rule. It also follows that the dif-

bill of 1773 on grain exports. In a later edition, probably the second (1778), Smith added (*ibid.*, 510): 'So far, therefore, this law seems to be inferior to the ancient system. With all its imperfections, however, we may perhaps say of it what was said of the laws of Solon, that, though not the best in itself, it is the best which the interests, prejudices, and temper of the times would admit of. It may perhaps in due time prepare the way for a better.' This addition is sometimes attributed to the influence of Edmund Burke, who was critical of Smith's professional arguments for free commerce, referring to various frictions of interest. (Cf. Jacob Viner, *Guide to John Rae's Life of Adam Smith*, 23f.) But in light of Smith's concession noted in our text, which appeared in the first edition of 1776 (and of other concessions to retaliatory measures discussed below), there seems little reason to believe that any significant change in attitude on his part occurred.

Moreover, the 'characteristic' Smithian principle, from the outset, is that a 'rational' system of duties might be designed, although specifically as a *revenue-raising* as distinct from a *protective* device. Cf. *Wealth of Nations*, 832-3: 'The high duties which have been imposed upon the importation of many different sorts of foreign goods [would] never have been imposed, had not the mercantile system taught us, in many cases, to employ taxation as an instrument, not of revenue, but of monopoly.' And *ibid.*, 836: 'it seems not improbable that a revenue, at least equal to the present neat revenue of the customs, might be drawn from duties upon the importation of only a few sorts of goods of the most general use and consumption; and that the duties of customs might thus be brought to the same degree of simplicity, certainty, and precision, as those of excise.'

Smith recommended accordingly (*ibid.*, 834) the imposition of moderate import duties upon manufactured goods as a means of raising revenue similar to those already imposed upon foreign wines and brandies, and certain colonial and East Indian luxury foods. This extension would replace the system of prohibiting imports of certain manufacturers, and 'our own workmen might still have a considerable advantage in the home market.' Smith also sanctioned a (moderate) *export* tax on wool (such as then existed) as a means of raising revenue (*ibid.*, 618). Although Smith rejected the prohibition of wool exportation he regarded the product on these grounds as a particularly suitable candidate for an export tax. For wool is a joint-product with meat, so that the detrimental effect of interference with exportation upon wool prices had not led to any serious reduction in sheep rearing and wool production. Although there might be some small price increase the woollen manufacturer would nonetheless retain an advantage over his foreign competitor: 'It is scarce possible to devise a tax which could produce any considerable revenue to the sovereign, and at the same time occasion so little inconveniency to any body' (*ibid.*, 619).

ference between Smith's two major works with regard to the desirability of economic development (in terms of rising average income) is one of degree rather than of kind, for the former after all justified a *'comfortable'* standard of subsistence for labour. But the difference is nonetheless sufficient to permit a particular concern with the absolute magnitude of wealth and population in the first work only.

GOVERNMENT INTERVENTION IN ECONOMIC DEVELOPMENT

Throughout the *Wealth of Nations* Smith makes use of a presumptive case in favour of laissez-faire based upon the 'natural right' of individuals not to be interfered with. (Amongst numerous applications, this principle is strikingly utilized in the condemnation of the Settlement Acts – as a 'violation of natural liberty and justice' – and of interference with colonial enterprise, and in defence of the regulation of paper money as the exception which proves the rule.) [44] Whether an extensive program of government intervention *in the interest of economic development* would have to be rejected on the grounds that it conflicted with the principle of natural liberty is a question which Smith rarely raised formally, although the general tenor of his work would suggest a rejection of far-reaching control. It is true that a passage in the *Theory of Moral Sentiments*,[45] already referred to, implies that the government itself represents an arm of the natural order: 'The perfection of police, the extension of trade and manufactures, are noble and magnificent objects. The contemplation of them pleases us, and we are interested in whatever can tend to advance them. They make part of the great system of government, and the wheels of the political machine seem to move with more harmony and ease by means of them.' Yet despite this view of the role of government Smith subsequently formulated his celebrated assault upon the 'man of system,' implying severe disapproval of excessive intervention: 'The man of system ... is apt to be very wise in his own conceit; and is often so enamoured with the supposed beauty of his own ideal plan of government, that he cannot suffer the smallest deviation from any part of it ...; in the great chess-board of human society, every single piece has a principle of motion of its own, altogether different from that which the legislature might choose to impress upon it.'[46]

Further evidence may be drawn from Smith's treatment of the corn trade, already referred to, which established the general rule that completely free trade in corn was in principle desirable to assure that 'the scarcity of any one

---

44 *Wealth of Nations*, 308: 'Such regulations may, no doubt, be considered as in some respect a violation of natural liberty. But those exertions of the natural liberty of a few individuals, which might endanger the security of the whole society, are, and ought to be, restrained by the laws of all governments.'

45 *Theory of Moral Sentiments*, 265.

46 *Ibid.*, 342–3. Cf. *Wealth of Nations*, 423: 'The statesman, who should attempt to direct private people in what manner they ought to employ their capitals, would not only load himself with a most unnecessary attention, but assume an authority which could safely be trusted, not only to no single person, but to no council or senate whatever, and which would nowhere be so dangerous as in the hands of a man who had folly and presumption enough to fancy himself fit to exercise it.'

country' may be 'relieved by the plenty of some other,' and, it will be noted, *to assure the farmer his natural right not to be interfered with*: 'To hinder, besides, the farmer from sending his goods at all times to the best market, is evidently to sacrifice the ordinary laws of justice to an idea of public utility, to a sort of reasons of state.'[47]

Yet intervention in the interest of expansion was not rejected out of hand.[48] Apart from the role which he allowed government in the provision of 'public works' and 'public institutions,'[49] Smith recommended the maintenance of the current maximum rate of interest imposed by the usury laws to prevent 'prodigals and projectors' from cornering the supply of loans: 'Sober people, who will give for the use of money no more than a part of what they are likely to make by the use of it, would not venture into the competition. A great part of the capital of the country would thus be kept out of the hands which were most likely to make a profitable and advantageous use of it, and thrown into those which were most likely to waste and destroy it.'[50] Furthermore, as a means of encouraging agricultural investment and experimentation, Smith recommended tax abatements for those landlards who cultivated part of their own land: 'It is of importance that the landlord should be encouraged to cultivate a part of his own land. His capital is generally greater than that of the tenant, and with less skill he can frequently raise a greater produce. The landlord can afford to try experiments, and is generally disposed to do so.'[51] Thirdly, we note that Smith approved of British colonial practice which had restrained the engrossing of uncultivated land by obliging proprietors to improve and cultivate a certain proportion of their property within a limited time.[52] And as a further instance we recall that Smith suggested the use of excise taxes to alter the pattern of working-class consumption as a device to assure population expansion.

These instances of legitimate intervention, it will be noted, are largely directed at the encouragement of *investment* at the expense of luxury outlays,

---

47 *Ibid.*, 506–7.
48 Even in the case relating to free corn exportation, he conceded that if some countries imposed constraints, others – particularly small states rather than England or France – may legitimately find it prudent to follow suit and limit exportation to assure adequate supplies for the domestic market; and he accepted some slight control in the interest of public order, as we have seen.

Cf. *ibid.*, 434 for a general discussion of the justification of retaliatory protection. On the whole retaliation may be justified 'when there is a probability' that the measures taken 'will procure the repeal of the high duties or prohibitions complained of.'
49 *Ibid.*, 681f. Cf. the discussion in Jacob Viner, 'Adam Smith and Laissez Faire,' 138f.
50 *Wealth of Nations*, 339–40. Whether Smith ultimately accepted the force of Bentham's criticism of his case for a legal maximum, as is sometimes suggested, is an open question. Cf. Jacob Viner, *Guide to John Rae's Life of Adam Smith*, 18–19.
51 *Wealth of Nations*, 784. Conversely, the landlord who charged a fine for the renewal of the lease should be penalized because he 'takes from the tenant so great a part of his capital, and thereby diminishes so much his ability to cultivate the land' (*ibid.*, 783).   52 *Ibid.*, 539.

speculative ventures and the like. This accords with Smith's disapproval of excessive consumption expressed even in the case of labour and *a fortiori* – in light of his consistent assaults – in that of the upper classes.[53] But they should not be exaggerated as evidence of support for an extensive governmental program.[54] Moreover, what requires particular emphasis is Smith's overwhelming rejection of policies designed to stimulate more rapid expansion by altering the allocation of a given capital stock as distinct from intervention concerned with the stimulus of net capital accumulation. It is precisely the attempt to demonstrate on analytical grounds that such forms of intervention can only slacken the rate of growth which represents his fundamental challenge to mercantilist thinking.

GOVERNMENT AND THE LABOUR MARKET

We have commented in an earlier chapter upon Smith's observational qualities and suggested with regard to contemporary technological developments that his awareness was more profound than is usually believed. A similar issue arises with regard to the contemporary state of governmental intervention in the labour market, for it has been frequently remarked that internal regulation of industry in England was in practice undergoing a natural process of rapid decay although the statute books were still full,[55] while Smith showed little awareness of the phenomenon.[56]

53 It is true that Smith contrasted 'parsimony' with 'prodigality' which refers to consumption actually encroaching upon capital (*ibid.*, 322), but the contrast seems to be merely a formal one, for he appears to disapprove of excessive consumption as such, as for example in the dictum (*ibid.*, 489) – in a section added to the third edition of 1784 – that 'in public, as well as in private expences, great wealth may, perhaps, frequently be admitted as an apology for great folly.'

See too Smith's view that excessively high profits are likely to have *a negative* effect upon savings (*ibid.*, 578): 'The high rate of profits seems everywhere to destroy that parsimony which in other circumstances is natural to the character of the merchant. When profits are high, that sober virtue seems to be superfluous, and expensive luxury to suit better the affluence of his situation.'

54 In fact Smith summarized his position regarding policies suitable for agriculture by calling for complete freedom of enterprise (*ibid.*, 785): 'The principal attention of the sovereign ought to be to encourage, by every means in his power, the attention both of the landlord and of the farmer; by allowing both to pursue their own interest in their own way, and according to their own judgment; by giving to both the most perfect security that they shall enjoy the full recompence of their own industry; and by procuring to both the most extensive market for every part of their produce, in consequence of establishing the easiest and safest communications both by land and water, through every part of his own dominions, as well as the most unbounded freedom of exportation to the dominions of all other princes.'

55 Jacob Viner, 'The Economist in History,' *American Economic Review* (Papers and Proceedings), LIII (May 1963), 3: 'In England, at least, it was not until mercantilism as a body of practices was entering into a coma from internal causes that there began to emerge any systematic and general attack on it as doctrine, with David Hume and Adam Smith as the sole prominent leaders of the attack.' Details of the process of 'decay' will be found in E. Heckscher, *Mercantilism*, 2nd ed., I (London, 1955), 221–325.

56 Thus Jacob Viner argued ('Bentham and J.S. Mill: The Utilitarian Back-

Smith's attention was directed at the restrictive privileges of corporations; the statute of apprenticeship; and the laws of settlement. In his discussion of the Elizabethan Statute of Artificers (1563) establishing in England the requirement of a seven-year apprenticeship term, it is made quite clear that the regulation was in practice interpreted to apply only in market towns and to those trades established prior to 1563 and was not extended to any newer trades, such as those of Manchester, Birmingham, and Wolverhampton. By a particular statute (of 1675), Smith noted further, the linen industry – of 'capital' importance although not geographically widespread – was completely freed from regulation. He refers too to modifications in the law (in 1672, 1714, and 1763) which removed all limitations on the geographical or occupational movement of ex-servicemen. In Scotland, with the 'least oppressive' of all European corporation laws, there were no general regulations regarding the duration of apprenticeship; moreover, corporations (each of which might have its individual rules) were usually easy to enter upon payment of a small fine, while weavers of linen and hemp cloth – 'the principal manufactures' – amongst others were free to exercise their trades in any town corporate without fine.[57]

The predominant concern of Smith was, however, with the settlement laws (a peculiarly English institution applying also to unskilled labour), the disadvantageous effects thereof representing, in his view, 'the greatest perhaps of any in the police of England.'[58] In this regard he refers to changes in the law during the seventeenth century and in particular to a system of certification introduced in 1698 and extended in 1714 intended 'to restore in some measure that free circulation of labour which those different statutes had almost entirely taken away.'[59] He doubted that the modification had proven

ground,' *American Economic Review*, **XXXIX** (March 1949); reprinted in Viner, *The Long View and the Short* (Glencoe, Illinois, 1958), 307): 'It is often overlooked that it was with reference to internal as well as to international free trade that Adam Smith made his famous statement that "To expect, indeed, that the freedom of trade should ever be entirely restored in Great Britain, is as absurd as to expect that an Oceana or Utopia should ever be established in it" [*Wealth of Nations*, 437–8], and this although when he wrote, by obsolescence rather than by deliberate repeal, the restrictions on internal freedom of trade had already become largely inoperative.' Cf. W.D. Grampp, 'On the History of Thought and Policy,' *American Economic Review* (Papers and Proceedings), **LV** (May 1965), 131: 'There is a kind of writing that opposes a principle of policy in a way that suggests the writer is opposing the policy of his time. Smith deplored the regulation of trade in a way that has made many believe he was arguing against his age. If he was, he must have had the Elizabethan Statute of Artificers in mind. When enacted it provided for extensive regulation, but after 1660 it was administered in a way that weakened both the principle and the practice of regulation; and by 1700 the courts refused to enforce it. It was not repealed until 1814. Its history illustrates the distinction between enactment, administration and enforcement.'

57 Cf. *Wealth of Nations*, 120–1; 135; 437.

58 *Ibid.*, 135.

59 *Ibid.*, 138. The object was to encourage parishes to accept outsiders whose settlement elsewhere was confirmed by their home parish.

effective; evidence is drawn not merely from the opinion of legal authorities but from the facts – as he observed them – regarding wage-rate differentials in England and Scotland: 'The very inequal price of labour which we frequently find in England in places at no great distance from another, is probably owing to the obstruction which the law of settlements gives to a poor man who would carry his industry from one parish to another without a certificate,' for in Scotland where there were no constraints 'we never meet with those sudden and unaccountable differences.'[60]

Finally, Smith noted that national and county wage regulation was 'in disuse,' although particular acts attempted to deal with individual trades and places, as for example a regulation (of 1768) regarding a legal maximum in the case of London tailors.[61] Similarly, price control was no longer utilized except in the case of bread (1758).[62]

Now it is doubtless true that Smith exaggerated in his condemnation of internal regulation and generalized excessively from particular instances.[63] But the textual evidence, as we have seen, suggests that he was nonetheless aware of some diminution in the degree of internal control of industry, while clearly believing that the problem (particularly the laws of settlement) remained serious, basing his position, in part, upon his reading of the empirical evidence. In any event, it appears unjustified to attribute to Smith the view that free internal trade was an unachievable dream. His remarks in this regard were, in fact, largely directed at the regulation of foreign trade.[64]

Apart from the institutional impediments to the process by which wages in different occupations were kept in line, Smith was confident that the market process could be relied upon to generate appropriate supplies of skilled labour.[65] We may illustrate the extent to which he tended to play down the restraints imposed on mobility by the difficulty of acquiring the necessary skills. For example, in a discussion of the consequences of abolishing trade

60 *Ibid.*, 140.   61 *Ibid.*, 141.   62 *Ibid.*, 144.

63 His assertion that 'there is scarce a poor man in England of forty years of age ... who has not in some part of his life felt himself most cruelly oppressed by this ill-conceived law of settlements' (*ibid.*, 141) was subject to criticism by eighteenth-century observers. See Cannan's references *ibid.*, 141n, and those cited in J.R. Poynter, *Society and Pauperism: English Ideas on Poor Relief, 1795–1834* (London, 1969), 6n. Interestingly enough, one of his critics, John Howlett, based himself on the impressive expansion of Sheffield, Birmingham, and Manchester as evidence of the inconsiderable effect of the act of settlement. In fact, Smith himself referred to Birmingham and Manchester, as we have seen, in his discussion of the limited application of the statute of artificers.

64 For the state of intervention in international trade see R. Davis, 'The Rise of Protection in England, 1689–1786,' *Economic History Review*, XIX (1966), 306–17.

65 The following discussion is drawn in part from S. Hollander, 'The Role of the State in Vocational Training: The Classical Economists' View,' *Southern Economic Journal*, XXXIV (April 1968), 513–25.

barriers, Smith denied that long-term unemployment would result on the grounds that workers may easily transfer from one trade to another: 'Though a great number of people should, by thus restoring the freedom of trade, be thrown all at once out of their ordinary employment and common method of subsistence, it would by no means follow that they would thereby be deprived either of employment or subsistence ... To the greater part of manufactures ... there are other collateral manufactures of so similar a nature, that a worker can easily transfer his industry from one of them to another.'[66] It was in fact precisely upon these grounds that Smith condemned contemporary practices relating to apprenticeship: 'Long apprenticeships are altogether unnecessary. The arts, which are much superior to common trades, such as those of making clocks and watches, contain no such mystery as to require a long course of instruction ... How to apply the instruments and how to construct the machines, cannot well require more than the lessons of a few weeks, perhaps those of a few days might be sufficient. In the common mechanical trades, those of a few days might certainly be sufficient.'[67]

In fact, according to Smith the degree of skill required in manufacturing was less than that in agriculture where the system of apprenticeship was not applied:

The policy of Europe considers the labour of all mechanics, artificers, and manufacturers, as skilled labour; and that of all country labourers as common labour. It seems to suppose that of the former to be of a more nice and delicate nature than that of the latter. It is so perhaps in some cases; but in the greater part it is quite otherwise ... (101).

There is scarce any common mechanic trade ... of which all the operations may not be as completely and distinctly explained in a pamphlet of a very few pages ... Not only the art of the farmer, the general direction of the operations of husbandry, but many inferior branches of country labour, require much more skill and experience than the greater part of mechanic trades. The man who works upon brass and iron, works with instruments and upon materials of which the temper is always the same, or very nearly the same (126–7).

Smith recognized *geographical* immobility apparently unrelated to the laws of the land. In commenting on an observed permanent difference between real wages paid to town and to country labourers he remarked: 'After all that has been said of the levity and inconstancy of human nature, it appears evidently from experience that a man is of all sorts of luggage the most difficult to be transported.'[68] In his highly optimistic treatment of *occupational* mobility

66 *Wealth of Nations*, 436–7. Cf. *ibid.*, 134–5.
67 *Ibid.*, 123. This may have been an error of judgment. It was partly because the Carron ironworks could not supply the skilled artisans whose help was essential that Watt's experiments on the steam engine could not be easily completed. See T.S. Ashton, *The Industrial Revolution, 1760–1830* (London, 1966), 68.
68 *Ibid.*, 75.

Smith apparently believed that this observation was irrelevant.[69] The equalization process whereby money-wage differentials compensate for subjective evaluations of work and other non-monetary characteristics attached to each occupation requires of course the assumption of 'mobility,' or rather *enough* mobility to meet the conditions of net equalization without creating chaos. Some degree of inertia and of attachment to locality relating to the risk and cost of moving must exist. Yet Smith's references to geographical immobility actually imply a degree of inertia in *excess* of this required amount.

Although Smith emphasized the ease with which skills may be acquired by the working class he was, at the same time, acutely aware of the fact that workers could not afford a costly education: 'the common people ... have little time to spare for education. Their parents can scarce afford to maintain them even in infancy. As soon as they are able to work, they must apply to some trade by which they can earn their subsistence.'[70] Smith did not evidently fear that the exclusion of workers from occupations requiring a heavy preliminary 'investment' in education in any way prevented the process of net equalization of returns. He apparently presumed that a sufficient number of relatively wealthy individuals were available to assure that, in the long run, excessive returns in such occupations would be eliminated.[71]

The classical economists, in general, based a case for government intervention in education on grounds of a divergence between social and private returns. So far as *vocational* training is concerned, however, Smith considered that private and social returns coincide so that the market can be relied upon to generate adequate investment. Consider for example Smith's references to an earlier discussion by David Hume to this effect:

'Most of the arts and professions in a state,' says by far the most illustrious philosopher and historian of the present age, 'are of such a nature, that while they promote the interests of the society, they are also useful and agreeable to some individuals; and in that case, the constant rule of the magistrate, except, perhaps, on the first introduction of any art, is, to leave the profession to itself, and trust its encouragement to the individuals who reap the benefit of it. The artizans, finding their profits to rise by the favour of their customers, increase, as much as possible, their skill and industry; and as matters are not disturbed by any injudicious tampering, the commodity is always sure to be at all times, nearly proportional to the demand' (742).[72]

A clearer statement to the effect that normally social and private returns may be presumed to coincide cannot be imagined. Yet the allowance that government aid might be called for 'on the first introduction of any art' should be

69 This problem is mentioned by Francis A. Walker, *The Wages Question* (New York, 1875), 193.
70 *Wealth of Nations*, 737.
71 The Smithian analysis was severely criticized by J.S. Mill. (See above, 132n.)
72 The reference is to the *Discourses on the First Decade of Titus Livius*, Book III, chap. i.

noted carefully, for it is possible that Hume and Smith would have adopted a different attitude in an economy undergoing rapid changes in products and processes.

Some reference may be made at this juncture to Smith's recommendation that a modernized curriculum was desirable for working-class children. Elementary education should be extended to 'geometry and mechanics': 'If in those little schools ... they were instructed in the elementary parts of geometry and mechanics, the literary education of this rank of people would perhaps be as complete as it can be. There is scarce a common trade which does not afford some opportunities of applying to it the principles of geometry and mechanics, and which would not therefore gradually exercise and improve the common people in those principles, the necessary introduction to the most sublime as well as the most useful sciences.'[73] To some extent it may appear that vocational training is implied in the above recommendation and indeed that Smith was implicitly recognizing the impediments to mobility created by limited educational opportunities. Although on balance it would appear that the emphasis is upon elementary education rather than on the training of specific skills, it is nonetheless significant that a relatively ambitious program was recommended in order to raise the productivity of the working force.

It is, moreover, essential to note that in arguing the case for more or less public aid to elementary schooling he paid attention not only to beneficial 'social' effects of a general kind resulting from literacy, but also to specifically economic advantages. In fact, to the extent that many workers were initially receiving no education, or very little education, or education of very low quality, the introduction of adequate elementary training would tend to increase mobility. Indeed, starting from an illiterate base it is difficult to distinguish elementary from vocational training since, frequently, the former is a necessary prerequisite of the latter.

The economic advantages are implied in the elementary-school curriculum recommended by Adam Smith which included, as we have just seen, 'the principles of geometry and mechanics ... the necessary introduction to the most sublime as well as the most useful sciences.' It is also the case that amongst the stultifying effects of specialization – which could be countered by education – Smith included the danger that the industrial worker would find it ultimately impossible to operate 'in any other employment than that to which he has been bred.'[74] We conclude that Smith's optimism regarding the high degree of mobility – upon which was based his confidence in the operation of the free market in the provision of skills – was contingent upon a necessary minimum degree of elementary training, towards which government was advised to contribute.

73 *Wealth of Nations*, 737–8. The government would establish parish schools. But the teacher would be paid only in part from public funds. Fees would be charged to assure against the 'dereliction of his duty.'
74 *Ibid.*, 735.

ALTERNATIVE POLICY OBJECTIVES

A few words are in order regarding alternative and possibly conflicting goals of policy to that of development. Smith recognized the legitimacy of certain instances of governmental interference designed to encourage particular industries, on grounds of 'defence.' Thus the Navigation Acts, introduced in the interest of British shipping – by imposing restrictions on the use of foreign shipping in the British import and coastal trades, and in the colonial trade – although quite illegitimate from the point of view of growth, were justified: 'The act of navigation is not favourable to foreign commerce, or to the growth of that opulence which can arise from it ... As defence, however, is of much more importance than opulence, the act of navigation is, perhaps, the wisest of all the commercial regulations of England.'[75] A similar justification (albeit somewhat half-hearted) is given for the granting of subsidies to particular defence industries: 'If any particular manufacture was necessary, indeed, for the defence of the society, it might not always be prudent to depend upon our neighbours for the supply; and if such manufactures could not otherwise be supported at home, it might not be unreasonable that all the other branches of industry should be taxed in order to support it. The bounties upon the exportation of British-made sail-cloth, and British-made gun-powder, may, perhaps, both be vindicated upon this principle.'[76]

Whether these concessions should be emphasized is, however, another matter. In defining the nature and scope of the investigation undertaken in the *Wealth of Nations* Smith, after all, wrote that 'the riches, and so far as power depends upon riches, the power of every country, must always be in proportion to the value of its annual produce.'[77] It was Smith's objective in this context to show that, at least as a first approximation, the two ends are not in conflict, so that governments concerned with national power do not generally need to interfere with the allocation of capital. For the foundation of national power lay in the taxation capacity of the state which was defined in terms of the rental, profit and wage income in excess of subsistence and which, it was en-

75 *Ibid.*, 431. The emphasis here is upon the economic disadvantage to foreign traders of arriving in British ports without cargo, which causes a reduction in the number of foreign sellers and correspondingly of foreign buyers with the consequence that we 'are thus likely not only to buy foreign goods dearer, but to sell our own cheaper, than if there was a more perfect freedom of trade.'

76 *Ibid.*, 488–9. This precise formulation appeared in the third edition of 1784. In the first two editions the bounty upon the importation of American 'naval stores' was similarly justified. (Cf. Cannan, *ibid.*, 485n.)

77 *Ibid.*, 352. Cf. *ibid.*, 397. 'Political economy, considered as a branch of the science of a statesman or legislator ... proposes to enrich both the people and the sovereign.' A similar position was adopted by David Hume, 'Of Commerce,' in Rotwein, ed., *Writings on Economics*, 5: 'The greatness of a state, and the happiness of its subjects, how independent soever they may be supposed in some respects, are commonly allowed to be inseparable with regard to commerce; and as private men receive greater security, in the possession of their trade and riches, from the power of the public, so the public becomes powerful in proportion to the opulence and extensive commerce of private men.'

visaged, would be maximized in a competitive economy in the absence of intervention.[78] Moreover, Smith in fact recommended that Britain relinquish her monopoly in the colony trade, one of the key features of the Navigation Acts, on the grounds that it 'depresses the industry of all other countries, but chiefly that of the colonies, without in the least increasing, but on the contrary diminishing, that of the country in whose favour it is established.'[79] Indeed he recommended the abandonment of the American colonies entirely if they could not be justified on *economic* grounds:

The rulers of Great Britain have, for more than a century past, amused the people with the imagination that they possessed a great empire on the west side of the Atlantic. This empire, however, has hitherto existed in imagination only. It has hitherto been, not an empire, but the project of an empire; not a gold mine, but the project of a gold mine; a project which has cost, which continues to cost, and which, if pursued in the same way as it has been hitherto, is likely to cost, immense expence, without being likely to bring any profit; for the effects of the monopoly of the colony trade ... are, to the great body of the people, mere loss instead of profit ... If the project cannot be completed, it ought to be given up. If any of the provinces of the British empire cannot be made to contribute towards the support of the whole empire, it is surely time that Great Britain should free herself from the expence of defending these provinces in time of war, and of supporting any part of their civil or military establishments in time of peace, and endeavour to accommodate her future views and designs to the real mediocrity of her circumstances (899–900).[80]

We may discern on Smith's part the objective of goading the government to reform, in order to justify the retention of the colonies. But the emphasis upon the economic criterion is clear. It is, therefore, likely that Smith's approval of the Navigation Acts was severely limited (perhaps to those sections only relating to the British import and coastal trades). And we deduce that the formally straightforward dictum 'defence is of much more importance than opulence' was after all maintained subject to a degree of 'cost control.'[81]

78 More specifically we read: 'In modern war the great expence of fire-arms gives an evident advantage to the nation which can best afford that expence; and consequently, to an opulent and civilized, over a poor and barbarous nation.' *Wealth of Nations*, 669.

79 *Ibid.*, 577.

80 Cf. *ibid.*, 592. For a full discussion of Smith's attitude towards the American colonies and of the alternative open to the British government, see Donald Winch, *Classical Political Economy and Colonies* (London, 1965), 14–24, where it is also noted that both Josiah Tucker and David Hume favoured freedom for the colonies (*ibid.*, 18–19).

81 However, some commentators have discerned a greater element of 'dualism' (that is inconsistency) in Smith insofar as he condemned mercantilist protection while maintaining an 'equivocating' interest in defence and power. Cf. Charles Wilson, ' "Mercantilism": Some Vicissitudes of an Idea,' *Economic History Review*, X (1957), 182–3.

Although the charge of serious 'dualism' is in our view exaggerated, we can find no justification for the view expressed by E. Heckscher that power for Smith 'was only a means to the end' of opulence (*Mercantilism*, II, 17).

It is of relevance for any evaluation of Smith's attitude towards goals of policy to recall his concern with the potentially dehumanizing effects upon the labourer of one of the key requisites for growth, namely specialization. Yet what must be emphasized in this regard is the recommendation that governments should subsidize education as a countervailing measure: 'His dexterity at his own particular trade seems ... to be acquired at the expence of his intellectual, social, and martial virtues. But in every improved and civilized society this is the state into which the labouring poor, that is, the great body of the people, must necessarily fall, unless government takes some pains to prevent it.'[82] There is no suggestion that economic growth should be slackened on these grounds. (At the same time – if our earlier interpretation reflects accurately Smith's intentions – any permanent increase in average income beyond some ill-defined minimum level in fact met with disapproval on moral and social grounds. It may only be surmised that under certain conditions Smith might have recommended an alternative approach.)

There are other costs of economic development implied in the *Wealth of Nations* as far as the growth of towns is a concomitant phenomenon. For the town labourer is said to be in danger of losing the support and control exerted by his neighbours, typical in the small village, and consequently might 'abandon himself to every sort of low profligacy and vice.'[83] Smith accordingly lauded the small religious sects which tended, in his evaluation, to provide the labourer with the necessary social contacts. And the state might contribute by the encouragement of 'public diversions.'[84] Once again, there are solutions to the negative aspects of growth.

SUMMARY AND CONCLUSION

Our discussion of economic development in the *Wealth of Nations* reveals the significance to Smith of various extra-economic objectives. While in contemporary circumstances, rising average income was desired particularly as a

82 *Wealth of Nations*, 735. Indeed Smith insists that even if the state did not benefit from the education of the poor in matters of defence, there would still be an obligation to assure that the poor 'should not go altogether uninstructed' (*ibid.*, 740). In fact the argument has implications for the matter of income inequality. For it is specifically the poor who are the victims of the various disadvantages of specialization.

　　Cf. *Lectures*, 255. In his discussion of the 'inconveniencies arising from a commercial spirit,' Smith refers not merely to the effects of specialization but to the neglect of the education of the young who enter the work force at a very early age. Here too education is recommended for its beneficial social effects.

83 *Ibid.*, 747. Malthus was to make a related though not identical observation: 'The unwholesomeness of towns, to which some persons are necessarily driven, from the nature of their trades, must be considered as a species of misery ...' (*Population: The First Essay*, 108).

84 *Wealth of Nations*, 748. Smith was careful to insist that this 'encouragement' would merely take the form of 'allowing perfect liberty to all those who for their own interest would attempt, without scandal or indecency, to amuse and divert the people.' Yet even this position conflicts with typical mercantilist doctrine.

means of assuring labour an 'adequate' standard of living, Smith at the same time disapproved on 'moral' and 'social' grounds of excessively high consumption, and clearly found undesirable a constant population in the face of significant capital accumulation and a rapidly rising demand for labour. On the other hand, we have noted that the optimism of *The Theory of Moral Sentiments* which served as rationale for the desirability of a large population in that work is severely qualified in the *Wealth of Nations*. Our conclusion, therefore, is that a *large* population was not in itself regarded as a particularly desirable objective. On the contrary, the unfavourable income distribution, from the point of view of labour characteristic of stagnant economies, however large, is much emphasized despite the potential for productivity increase deriving from scale. Scale economies might, however, be obtained in an *expanding* economy while at the same time wages per head are maintained at a satisfactory level.

A central feature of Smith's writings upon the issue of development is the relative weight attached to possibly conflicting goals. Indeed he formally insisted that the fundamental concern of policy should be with national power recognizing a potential conflict in certain cases with development. His preoccupation with the 'martial' spirit of the masses – threatened to some degree both by excessively high consumption itself and by specialization, a fundamental prerequisite of growth – his support for a standing army, his allowance of a case for intervention in favour of British shipping and various other industries, all illustrate the dictum that 'defence is of much more importance than opulence.' But the interpretive problem is less serious than it may appear. In the first place, we have noted Smith's presumption that as a rule the objective of defence would best be served by those same processes of the freely-operating market which generate a maximum net revenue product from the community's resources; intervention in favour of particular industries was recommended in very few cases. What requires emphasis above all is the fact that where a conflict between the objectives of 'defence' and 'opulence' is recognized, the forgone opportunities (that is the alternative costs) in following the former objective are made quite explicit. Finally, it will be recalled that certain of the social disadvantages inherent in the developmental process might be overcome by various forms of government intervention, particularly in the elementary education of the poor, also required to assure the necessary minimum knowledge essential for the operation of the free market in the provision of vocational skills.

NINE

Foreign trade: theory and policy

VENT-FOR-SURPLUS THEORY

On several occasions in the *Wealth of Nations* Smith formally explains the advantages of foreign trade in terms of the 'vent-for-surplus' argument[1] according to which trade absorbs the output of *factors otherwise unemployed*:

When the produce of any particular branch of industry exceeds what the demand of the country requires, the surplus must be sent abroad, and exchanged for something for which there is a demand at home. Without such exportation, a part of the productive labour of the country must cease, and the value of its annual produce diminish. The land and labour of Great Britain produce generally more corn, woollens, and hard ware, than the demand of the home-market requires. The surplus part of them, therefore, must be sent abroad, and exchanged for something for which there is a demand at home. It is only by means of such exportation, that this surplus can acquire a value sufficient to compensate the labour and expence of producing it (353).

In every period, indeed, of every society, the surplus part both of the rude and manufactured produce, or that for which there is no demand at home, must be sent abroad in order to be exchanged for something for which there is some demand at home (359).

A further passage relates to the same phenomenon and, in addition, refers to the advantages of a large market for high efficiency:

Between whatever places foreign trade is carried on, they all of them derive two distinct benefits from it. It carries out that surplus part of the produce of their land and labour for which there is *no demand* among them, and brings back in return for it something else for which there is a demand. It gives a value to their superfluities,

---

1 The term is used by J.S. Mill in his critical account of the Smithian position: J.M. Robson, ed., *Collected Works of John Stuart Mill*, vols. II and III, *Principles of Political Economy* (Toronto, 1965), 591. Cf. also *ibid.*, 574.

by exchanging them for something else, which may satisfy a part of their wants, and increase their enjoyments. By means of it, *the narrowness of the home* market does not hinder the division of labour in any particular branch of art or manufacture from being carried to the highest perfection. By opening a *more extensive market* for whatever part of the produce of their labour may *exceed the home consumption*, it encourages them to improve its productive powers, and to augment its annual produce to the utmost, and thereby to increase the real revenue and wealth of the society (415; author's emphasis).

In fact, the argument is extended to apply to a variety of more complex cases such as re-exportation: 'When the foreign goods which are ... purchased with the surplus produce of domestic industry exceed the demand of the home-market, the surplus part of them must be sent abroad again, and exchanged for something more in demand at home.'[2] An example is the British importation of American tobacco for re-export: in this regard Smith argued that if the possibility of re-export of American tobacco (in excess of domestic needs) should cease, then importation thereof must also cease 'and with it the productive labour of all those inhabitants of Great Britain' engaged in the manufacture of goods for the American market.[3] The argument is parallel to that of the standard case of direct trade.

What justification is offered for the assumption that surplus resources cannot be devoted to production for domestic consumption? The only suggestions, given in the first of the above passages, relate to the existence of a considerable degree of specificity of factors (in the present instance spare British factors are physically capable of producing only woollens, corn, and hardware, and cannot be diverted to the production of any other goods for which there is a demand at home), and to a high degree of domestic demand inelasticity for those products which can be produced.[4]

The essential outcome of the argument is that in the absence of trade there will exist surplus productive capacity. Introducing foreign trade will not, therefore, require any transfer of resources away from domestic production: there is a *net gain*. In sharp contrast in this regard is Ricardian trade theory according to which resources are initially in full employment so that the introduction of trade involves a *reallocation* of activity.

2 Adam Smith, *Wealth of Nations*, 353.
3 *Ibid.*
4 Cannan in an editorial comment (*ibid.*, 353n) suggests that 'it is supposed the country has certain physical characteristics which compel its inhabitants to produce particular commodities.' In principle, the problem might also arise from extreme internal immobility of factors. Cf. Hla Myint, 'The "Classical Theory" of International Trade and the Underdeveloped Countries,' *Economic Journal*, LXVIII (June 1958), 322: 'The concept of a surplus productive capacity above the requirements of domestic consumption implies an inelastic domestic demand for the exportable commodity *and/or* a considerable degree of internal immobility and specificness of resources.' It is here suggested that inelastic domestic demand is not a *necessary* condition. But logically it would seem that *both* inelasticity and factor 'specificness' (or immobility) are required.

It has been argued that the vent-for-surplus theory is highly appropriate as a rationalization of the historical experience of certain underdeveloped economies. Such economies with small technical and capital resources 'operate under conditions nearer to those of fixed technical coefficients than of variable technical coefficients'; and opportunities for reallocation of resources *between* products requiring different factor proportions are limited because of inelastic demand both for domestic goods (largely basic foodstuffs) and export goods (largely industrial raw materials). Such an economy may suffer from an imbalance between its productive and consumption capacities.[5] Unemployment in *sparsely* populated countries may be explained in these terms. For the rationale is not acute land shortage, but the inapplicability of the neo-classical equilibrating mechanisms whereby an initial disproportion between labour and land is corrected to assure full employment of at least the relatively scarce factor. Rapid growth can be accounted for by entry into trade whereby available resources are drawn into productive use.[6]

The Smithian treatment of trade is, however, by no means clear-cut. Alternative and, in key respects, conflicting approaches are to be found in the *Wealth of Nations*. We turn to consider this issue.

THE ANALYSIS OF COLONIAL TRADE POLICY

It is first established in a discussion of colonial trade policy that the relevant criterion for purposes of policy evaluation is the effect upon the *level of employment* presumably of productive labour. In these terms, Smith condemned the monopoly of British capital in colonial trade:

The colony trade, however, it may perhaps be said, is more advantageous to Great Britain than any other; and the monopoly, by forcing into that trade a greater proportion of the capital of Great Britain than what would otherwise have gone to it, has turned that capital into an employment more advantageous to the counry than any other which it could have found.

The most advantageous employment of any capital to the country to which it belongs, is that which maintains there the greatest quantity of productive labour, and increases the most the annual produce of the land and labour of that country. But the quantity of productive labour which any capital employed in the foreign trade of

---

5 *Ibid.*, 326. In Myint's view 'Adam Smith himself thought that the pre-existence of a surplus productive capacity in an isolated economy was such a matter of common observation that he assumed it implicitly without elaborating upon it. But he did give some hints suggesting how the "narrowness of the home market," which causes the surplus capacity, is bound up with the underdeveloped economic organization of an isolated country, particularly the lack of a good internal transport system and of suitable investment opportunities' (*ibid.*, 323). Basically each self-sufficient economic unit cannot find a market to dispose of its potential output so that there is no incentive to produce more than its own subsistence (*ibid.*, 328).

6 It is possible to rationalize expansion of activity whereby land and labour are actually used in fixed ratios although coefficients are not fixed technically: cf. David Simpson, 'Further Technological Relationships in *The Wealth of Nations* and in Ricardo's *Principles*,' *Canadian Journal of Economics and Political Science*, XXXIII (Nov. 1967), 585–90.

consumption can maintain, is exactly in proportion, it has been shown in the second book, to the frequency of its returns ...

But the monopoly of the colony trade, so far as it has operated upon the employment of the capital of Great Britain, has in all cases forced some part of it from a foreign trade of consumption carried on with a neighbouring, to one carried on with a more distant country, and in many cases from a direct foreign trade of consumption to a round-about one (566–7).

The entire analysis of the effects upon the profit rate of the Act of Navigation – designed in part to exclude foreign capital from the colony trade – implies continued full employment of capital,[7] and to this extent seems to contradict the vent-for-surplus theory. The legislation, by reducing *total* mercantile capital dealing with North America, artificially raised the profit rate on *British* capital initially engaged with the colonies, thereby attracting capital from alternative investments.[8] And although the emphasis throughout the discussion is upon the rate of profit upon 'mercantile' capital, Smith recognized a general tendency for the monopoly to attract capital away from – or at least check the rate of investment in – domestic agriculture and industry raising the average profit rate in the economy *as a whole* to the disadvantage of Britain: 'Whatever raises in any country the ordinary rate of profit higher than it otherwise would be, necessarily subjects that country both to an absolute and to a relative disadvantage in every branch of trade of which she has not the monopoly!'[9]

Smith's analysis of the effects of an abandonment of the monopoly implies the possibility of reabsorption in the domestic sector of factors released from the foreign trade sector. A reduction in the large tobacco imports to the level of British domestic requirements, for example, would simply require an increase in export sales to various new foreign markets:

The goods which Great Britain purchases at present for her own consumption with the great surplus of tobacco which she exports to other countries, she would, in this case, probably have purchased with the immediate produce of her own industry, or with some part of her own manufactures. That produce, those manufactures, instead of being almost entirely suited to one great market, as at present would probably have been fitted to a great number of smaller markets.[10]

7 *Wealth of Nations*, 562f. The Act of Navigation is summarized, *ibid.*, 430.
8 High profits on British mercantile capital attracted capital in particular from the European and Mediterranean branches – raising profits elsewhere and lowering somewhat those in the colony trade until a new equilibrium was reached. Smith points out that the contraction in other branches was aggravated by the fact that the colonial economies – and accordingly their trading requirements – were growing at a faster rate than British capital accumulation: 'The mercantile capital of Great Britain, though very great, yet not being infinite; and though greatly increased since the act of navigation, yet not being increased in the same proportion as the colony trade, that trade could not possibly be carried on without withdrawing some part of that capital from other branches of trade, nor consequently without some decay of those other branches' (*ibid.*, 563).
9 *Ibid.*, 565.
10 *Ibid.*, 569.

The argument thus far, does not necessarily require an actual transfer of resources between export industries; but such a transfer is not ruled out, implying a considerable degree of mobility and non-specificity of factors.[11] But the next stage of Smith's argument is particularly revealing. Direct trade had a higher 'frequency of returns' than the roundabout variety. Accordingly, the original import requirement could be satisfied more economically, releasing capital resources which would simply be absorbed in the expansion of production for the domestic market. Any implication that foreign trade absorbs capital otherwise idle is clearly belied, while it is presumably taken for granted that land and labour are, in some sense, 'available' for use:

On account of the frequency of the returns, a part, and probably but a small part; perhaps not above a third or a fourth, of the capital which at present carries on this great roundabout trade, might have been sufficient to carry on all those small direct ones, might have kept in constant employment an equal quantity of British industry, and have equally supported the annual produce of the land and labour of Great Britain. All the purposes of this trade being, in this manner, answered by a much smaller capital, there would have been a large spare capital to apply to other purposes; to improve the lands, to increase the manufactures, and to extend the commerce of Great Britain (570).[12]

But Smith goes further. If the abandonment of the colonial monopoly were to be accompanied by completely free trade with the colonies, then a *net* expansion not only of employment (and land use) but of capital as well could be expected:

The effect of the colony trade in its natural and free state, is to open a great, though distant market for such parts of the produce of British industry as may exceed the demand of the markets nearer home, of those of Europe, and of the countries which lie around the Mediterranean sea. In its natural and free state, the colony trade, without drawing from those markets any part of the produce which had ever been sent to them, encourages Great Britain to increase the surplus continually, by continually presenting new equivalents to be exchanged for it. In its natural and free state, the colony trade tends to increase the quantity of productive labour in Great Britain, but without altering in any respect the direction of that which had been employed there before. In the natural and free state of the colony trade, the competition of all other nations would hinder the rate of profit from rising above the common level either in the new market, or in the new employment. The new market, without drawing any thing from the old one, would create, if one may say so, a new produce for its own supply; and that new produce would constitute a new capital for carrying

11 In fact Smith recognized that the kind of commodities produced depended on the particular market involved.

12 In practical terms, Smith's remarks were of particular relevance for the Glasgow re-export trade in tobacco. Smith was, in effect, calling for a withdrawal of resources from this sector. The actual collapse of the trade in 1776 posed 'a remarkable challenge of adjustment.' See S.G. Checkland, 'Scottish Economic History: Recent Work,' *Economica*, XXXI (Aug. 1964), 304.

on the new employment, which in the same manner would draw nothing from the old one (574).

However, while the colonial *monopoly* had diminished the employment opportunities, Britain still enjoyed a net advantage from the colonial trade since 'the new market and the new employment which are opened by the colony trade, are of much greater extent than that portion of the old market and of the old employment which is lost by the monopoly. The new produce and the new capital which has been created, if one may say so, by the colony trade, maintain in Great Britain a greater quantity of productive labour, than what can have been thrown out of employment by the revulsion of capital from other trades of which the returns are more frequent. If the colony trade, however, even as it is carried on at present, is advantageous to Great Britain, it is not by means of the monopoly, but in spite of the monopoly.'[13]

The criterion used in the evaluation of policy regarding the colony trade is thus defined in terms of employment. The entire argument against the colonial monopoly and in favour of the colony trade in its 'free state,' seems to be based on the implicit assumption that productive labour was available. (Presumably, Smith had in mind either productive labour derived from natural population growth, or from the service sector, since no explicit references are made to unemployment.) It must be carefully noted that the emphasis is at all times upon the *capital* constraint. In particular: the abandonment of the monopoly *of itself* would release capital for investment in agricultural and industrial production apparently for domestic consumption. And free trade with the colonies would generate new capital supplies and permit further expansion, given the apparent assumption of available labour and land. By contrast, in the standard version of the vent-for-surplus theory, unused capacity – as well as available land and labour – is implicitly assumed.

EFFICIENCY ADVANTAGE OF TRADE

The vent-for-surplus theory also conflicts with Smith's alternative treatment according to which the advantage of foreign trade lies in the *more efficient* utilization of resources, rather than the use of resources otherwise idle:

What is prudence in the conduct of every private family, can scarce be folly in that of a great kingdom. If a foreign country can supply us with a commodity cheaper than we ourselves can make it, better buy it of them with some part of the produce of our own industry, employed in a way in which we have some advantage. The general industry of the country, being always in proportion to the capital which employs it, will not thereby be diminished ... but only left to find out the way in which it can be employed with the greatest advantage. It is certainly not employed to the greatest advantage, when it is thus directed towards an object which it can buy cheaper than it can make. The value of its annual produce is certainly more or less diminished, when it is thus turned away from producing commodities evidently of more value than the commodity which it is directed to produce. According to the supposition,

13 *Wealth of Nations*, 575.

that commodity could be purchased from foreign countries cheaper than it can be made at home. It could, therefore, have been purchased with a part only of the commodities, or, what is the same thing, with a part only of the price of the commodities, which the industry employed by an equal capital would have produced at home, had it been left to follow its natural course. The industry of the country, therefore, is thus turned away from a more, to a less advantageous employment, and the exchangeable value of its annual produce, instead of being increased ... must necessarily be diminished by every such regulation ... Whether the advantages which one country has over another, be natural or acquired, is in this respect of no consequence. As long as the one country has those advantages, and the other wants them, it will always be more advantageous for the latter, rather to buy of the former than to make (424–6).[14]

If it could be said that Smith intended the vent-for-surplus argument to apply solely to the case of a hitherto isolated country about to enter into international trade,[15] and the argument involving efficiency to apply to a more advanced country long engaged in trade, but faced with a fluctuating world market, the problem would be in principle solved. It could then be argued, that the absence of an equilibrating mechanism was presumed in the first case only, while the established trading country – enjoying a greater degree of flexibility with regard to both factor and commodity substitution – could maintain full use of capacity in the face of fluctuating trade.

But Smith's formulation of the vent-for-surplus argument is *not* limited to the case of an economy about to enter into trade. It is said to apply 'in every period ... of every society' and 'between whatever places foreign trade is carried on.' We have seen its application to complex cases of trade actually engaged in by Great Britain.[16] We are, therefore, faced with two accounts of the

14 An analogy is made with the specialization by the tailor who buys his shoes from the shoemaker and the farmer who in turn specializes and exchanges: 'All of them find it for their interest to employ their whole industry in a way in which they have some advantage over their neighbours, and to purchase with a part of its produce, or what is the same thing, with the price of a part of it, whatever else they have occasion for' (*ibid.*, 424).

   Advantages are sometimes defined in *qualitative* terms as for example the climate of France which is more suitable for vines than is that of Scotland (*ibid.*, 425) and for silks than is that of England (*ibid.*, 7). However, there is also a recognition of *quantitative* differences in factor endowments – as will be made clear in Chapter 10.

   The emphasis in the extract given in the text is upon the savings in resources permitted by importation of a particular commodity rather than by its domestic production. Statements to this effect are not in conflict with the comparative-cost doctrine. Yet it is clear from the same extract that Smith also retained the condition of absolute advantage, and the strictures by Jacob Viner in this regard (*Studies in the Theory of International Trade* (New York, 1937), 439–40) are not unjustified.

15 Myint, 'The "Classical Theory" of International Trade and the Underdeveloped Countries,' 322 suggests that the vent-for-surplus doctrine was suitable for such a primitive isolated economy.

16 John H. Williams, 'The Theory of International Trade Reconsidered,' *Economic Journal*, XXXIX (1929), reprinted in Williams, *Readings in the Theory of International Trade* (Philadelphia, 1949), 253f., has defended the vent-for-surplus

advantages of foreign trade based on sets of implicit assumptions which are contradictory. This conflict was indeed noted subsequently by Ricardo in his critique of Smithian trade theory.[17]

To place the apparent conflict in perspective, it should first be recalled that the only formal rationalization of the doctrine given by Smith takes the form of a very casual hint that British resources are physically capable of producing a very narrow range of products. Although it is possible to justify the argument further – as Myint has done – Smith himself does not do so. We know, however, that this is not Smith's view of the empirical position. He recognized, for example, that even Scotland is capable of producing wine (albeit at enormous expense): 'By means of glasses, hotbeds, and hotwalls, very good grapes can be raised in Scotland.'[18]

We also know that Smith envisaged a high degree of resource mobility – in the absence of institutional and monopoly impediments – and was accordingly satisfied that changes in trade patterns would *not* create serious dislocations in the British labour market. The effects of free trade would, he argued, not be dangerous, for in the absence of artificial restraints, workers can transfer easily between the manufacturing branches since the technology used is so similar.[19] It is precisely because of the similarity between the processes that Smith is optimistic that there will occur no (permanent) fall in the demand for labour, given the community's capital stock: 'The stock which employed them in a particular manufacture before, will still remain in the country to employ an equal number of people in some other way. The capital of the country remaining the same, the demand for labour will likewise be the same, or very nearly the same.'[20]

Moreover, in the context of the roundabout trade in American tobacco – *formally* explained by the vent-for-surplus theory – Smith gives an alternative and more moderate statement of the theory, which is not inconsistent with the efficiency argument. Here the advantage of international trade is not its effect in reducing excess capacity, but rather its greater profitability in terms of a revenue calculation: 'No goods are sent abroad but those for which the demand is supposed to be greater abroad than at home, and of which the returns consequently, it is expected, will be of more value at home than the commodities exported. If the tobacco which, in England, is worth only a hundred

doctrine as relevant for an *advanced* economy. The fact of international trade leading to specialization means that alternative opportunities for the use of capital and labour tend to disappear since the entire development of industry is directed towards a particular pattern which cannot be easily altered.

It is unlikely, however, that Smith had this sophisticated argument in mind whereby trade is initially explained by the efficiency argument, while once the trade pattern is established the degree of 'inflexibility' rises.

17 David Ricardo, *Principles of Political Economy*, in Piero Sraffa, ed., *The Works and Correspondence of David Ricardo*, I (Cambridge, 1951), 294–5.
18 *Wealth of Nations*, 425.
19 See above, 108.
20 *Wealth of Nations*, 437.

thousand pounds, when sent to France will purchase wine which is, in England, worth a hundred and ten thousand pounds, the exchange will augment the capital of England by ten thousand pounds' (458). There is no suggestion that the cessation of re-exports would generate 'permanent' unemployment in Britain despite the statement to this effect in the formal account of the theory described earlier.

When we take into consideration the formal analysis of the Navigation Acts, discussed above, we recall the assumption of full employment of capital at all times. But of particular significance is the fact that in Smith's treatment of contemporary economic growth in Britain there is little to suggest any dependence upon labour supplies hitherto unutilized as would be expected if the vent theory were relevant. Expansion depended rather upon increasing supplies of labour forthcoming in response to high average wages largely in the form of rising population but also by way of increased effort per man. And even in the colonial case – where conditions, in principle, would presumably most closely correspond to those implicit in the vent theory – there is little evidence that Smith envisaged expansion by way of the absorption of hitherto idle labour. On the contrary, the marked sparseness of population relative to natural resources tended to force wages up so that growth was only possible with natural population increase: 'the disproportion between the great extent of the land and the small number of the people, which commonly takes place in new colonies, makes it difficult for him [the farmer] to get this labour. He does not, therefore, dispute about wages, but is willing to employ labour at any price. The high wages of labour encourage population.'[21]

In a sense, mere lip-service was paid by Smith to the vent-for-surplus doctrine. A comment, which is not specifically related to foreign trade, to the effect that 'the capital of the merchant exchanges the surplus produce of one place for that of another' implies a rather innocuous conception, the implications of which are not to be exaggerated.[22] We shall return to the issue in the following chapter.

21 *Ibid.*, 533; for a discussion of the land-labour ratio in the colonies see also *ibid.*, 92, 358.

It might, however, be argued that the state of full employment – both in North America and Great Britain – was *due* to trade; that it was only becaues of trade that full employment existed. However, Smith's formulation that the disproportion between land and labour in new colonies leads to wage increases is stated as a general rule and it is not evident that this was due to trade. But even in the event that full employment was due to trade this would not imply any *particular* theory of trade. For according to the alternative *efficiency* argument, trade economizes capital and therefore allows a faster increase in the demand for labour as capital is released for additional ventures.

22 *Ibid.*, 342.

TEN

The analysis of investment priorities

Adam Smith gave great weight in the *Wealth of Nations* to differential employment-generating capacities of investment in agriculture, manufacturing, and trade of various kinds.[1] The establishment of a hierarchy of sectors, it has been said, is in sharp conflict with the fundamental argument of the First Book according to which an optimum allocation of resources is achieved when profit rates – subject to risk and non-monetary differentials – are everywhere equalized. For *in terms of employment* there would then be less than the 'optimum' amount of investment in agriculture and manufacturing, and more than the optimum amount in foreign trade.[2] This general view suggests that Smith should have recognized formally that government intervention to divert capital towards the labour-intensive sectors is called for as a means of raising aggregate employment.

Smith's hierarchy of sectors was severely criticized on related grounds by David Ricardo who devoted his chapter 'On Gross and Net Revenue' to counter what he considered the error of recommending a large gross revenue – derived from a large population: 'Provided its net real income, its rent and profits be the same, it is of no importance whether the nation consists of ten or of twelve millions of inhabitants.'[3] Similarly, J.R. McCulloch in his edition of the *Wealth of Nations* took Smith to task for apparently according significance to a large population and gross product: 'the prosperity of a country is to be measured by the rate of profit which her capital yields, or (for it is the same

1 *Wealth of Nations*, Book II, chap. v: 'Of the Different Employment of Capitals,' 341–55.
2 Cf. Hla Myint, *Theories of Welfare Economics* (London, 1948), 78. Also J.J. Spengler, 'Adam Smith's Theory of Economic Growth – Part II,' *Southern Economic Journal*, XXVI (July 1951), 2: 'Smith's treatment of capital allocation [is] at variance with his treatment of self interest.'
3 Piero Sraffa, ed., *The Works and Correspondence of David Ricardo*, vol. I, *Principles of Political Economy* (Cambridge, 1953), 347f.

thing) by her capacity of employing capital and labour to advantage, and not by the actual amount of her capital, or the number of her people.'[4]

It is the object of this chapter to show that these criticisms are largely unfounded. In the first place, it was Smith's position that the pattern of investment which should be adopted at any stage of a country's development depended upon circumstances and was not to be determined *a priori* according to some pre-established schedule of priorities. It is in this context that Smith's rationalization for international trade based on quantitative differentials in factor endowments between countries assumes particular relevance. Of further analytical significance is the treatment of factor endowments as changing from period to period according to the particular stage of development achieved. In brief, Smith's analysis of development, we shall attempt to demonstrate, was based squarely upon the principles of allocation theory.

It is essential to recall at the outset the nature of the labour supply function utilized by Smith. The first critique referred to above implicitly presumes the existence of surplus labour for only then does it make sense to claim that a redirection of activity towards the labour-intensive sectors is required as a means of raising employment. Yet there is little to suggest that the contemporary economy, in Smith's view, was suffering from unemployment. On the contrary, the textual evidence implies that as a rule a state of full employment was presumed to exist in contemporary Britain. Rising labour demand entailed upward pressure on the wage rate; and expansion of national income was expected to occur in large part by way of consequential population growth rather than through the absorption into the labour force of unemployed workers.[5]

The immediate concern of policy was thus not with employment. It was, rather, with the maximization of the ('real') national income derived from a given fully-employed labour force. At this point it will also be recalled that the earnings of *service* labour were regarded by Smith as 'transfer payments' rather than as 'original' incomes; only the earnings generated in the productive sector entered into the calculation of national income.[6] But it was Smith's position, as we shall show, that the maximization of the national income – or more precisely, given population, of national income per head – would not be achieved by any artificial redirection of capital within the productive sector towards particularly labour-intensive branches. Although such intervention might assure some increase in the employment of *productive labour* (at the expense of the service sector), the consequence would be an actual reduction, rather than the intended increase, in national income.

The objective of policy in terms of average income requires close attention. The end was desired partly in order to assure a comfortable average return to *labour* and partly – and of particular interest for the present purpose – to assure as large as possible a 'surplus' available for savings (and therefore future

4 J.R. McCulloch, ed., *Wealth of Nations* (Edinburgh, 1863), 159n.
5 See above, Chapter 5, 160f.
6 See above, Chapter 5, 146–7.

expansion of the productive sector) and for taxation. It is true, as Ricardo and McCulloch maintained, that Smith included wages – or rather the wages of productive labour only – along with profit and rent within the designation 'net revenue' (excluding from the gross produce only the depreciation of fixed capital) ; yet they were mistaken in their further attributions.

Formally, Smith's conception of net revenue was utilized in his treatment of the community's *savings capacity*: 'The capital of all the individuals of a nation is increased in the same manner as that of a single individual, by their continually accumulating and adding to it whatever they save out of their income. It is likely to increase the fastest, therefore, when it is employed in the way that affords the greatest revenue to all the inhabitants of the country, as they will thus be enabled to make the greatest savings. But the revenue of all the inhabitants of the country is necessarily in proportion to the value of the annual produce of their land and labour.'[7] Similarly, *tax capacity* is defined in terms of the total annual revenue: 'The riches, and so far as power depends upon riches, the power of every country, must always be in proportion to the value of its annual produce, the fund from which all taxes must ultimately be paid.'[8] Considered literally the impression from such passages may be that the nation's savings and tax capacity would increase, in Smith's view, in proportion with *aggregate* population and the productive-labour force insofar as total net national income – which includes the wages of productive labour – increased. Yet it was not his intention, as Ricardo believed, to recommend a large population. What he had in mind as the 'source' of future expansion and of taxation was the rental and profit incomes and only that part of wages in excess of subsistence. This was frequently clarified: 'It must always be remembered, however, that it is the luxurious and not the necessary expence of the inferior ranks of people that ought ever to be taxed.'[9] The point to note is that in the case of a given (fully-employed) work force it is *immaterial* whether one speaks of the desirability of maximizing the current net national income or specifically that part only in excess of subsistence wage income; Smith on the whole followed the former practice, without representing a large national income achieved by way of mere expansion of numbers (living at subsistence) as a relevant objective of policy. In effect, the immediate concern was with the maximization of income *given* the population.

It was Smith's position that this latter objective would in fact be achieved in the absence of governmental intervention. This is made clear, for example, during the course of his rejection of the infant-industry case for protection (proposed amongst others by Josiah Tucker and Sir James Steuart). While he conceded that protection might permit the more rapid development of particular industries, capital accumulation – and accordingly the growth of future aggregate activity – would in all likelihood be retarded by a failure to maximize the current national income: 'But the immediate effect of every such regulation is to diminish its revenue, and what diminishes its revenue is certainly not very likely to augment its capital faster than it would have aug-

7 *Ibid.*, 347.   8 *Ibid.*, 352.   9 *Ibid.*, 839.

mented of its own accord, had both capital and industry been left to find out their natural employments.'[10] It may also be noted that despite the emphasis upon the differential employment-generating capacities of alternative investments Smith denied explicitly the ability of government to increase the 'quantity of industry':

The general industry of the society never can exceed what the capital of the society can employ. As the number of workmen that can be kept in employment by any particular person must bear a certain proportion to his capital, so the number of those that can be continually employed by all the members of a great society, must bear a certain proportion to the whole capital of that society, and never can exceed that proportion. No regulation of commerce can increase the quantity of industry in any society beyond what its capital can maintain. It can only divert a part of it into a direction into which it might not otherwise have gone; and it is by no means certain that this artificial direction is likely to be more advantageous to the society than that into which it would have gone of its own accord (421).

He can only have intended to question the ability of government to increase the *national income* – the earnings derived from the productive sector – by any redirection of capital from that pattern achieved in a free market, since it is self-evident that the productive-labour force itself could be increased by intervention. It is implied that any such intervention would only tend to *reduce* the national income (or more specifically national income per head).

In what follows we shall consider in detail the precise analytical arguments designed to demonstrate that the principle of allocation according to profit-rate equalization assured the immediate objective of policy *at every stage of the community's development.*

AGRICULTURE AND MANUFACTURES

Smith expressed the view that, but for institutional distortions, 'the towns could nowhere have increased beyond what the improvement and cultivation of the territory in which they were situated could support; till such time, at least, as the whole of that territory was completely cultivated and improved.'[11] In ordinary circumstances, there would be no attempt made by capitalists to invest in manufactures designed 'for distant sale' as long as agricultural resources remained unused.[12]

One reason given for this 'natural inclination' to prefer agricultural investment – and complementary local industries – over manufactures, is the relatively low risk attached to it: 'Upon equal, or nearly equal profits, most men will chuse to employ their capitals rather in the improvement and cultivation

10 *Ibid.*, 425. For a discussion of subsequent criticism of Smith's approach which places such great emphasis upon the role of savings in the developmental process, particularly by John Rae (1834), and J.S. Mill, see Lord Robbins, *The Theory of Economic Development in the History of Economic Thought* (London, 1968), 113–5.

11 *Ibid.*, 357.   12 *Ibid.*, 359.

of land, than either in manufactures or in foreign trade. The man who employs his capital in land, has it more under his view and command, and his fortune is much less liable to accidents, than that of the trader.' Moreover, 'as to cultivate the ground was the original destination of man, so in every stage of his existence he seems to retain a predilection for this primitive employment'[13]

But what mechanism will assure that until agriculture was 'fully developed' there would be in fact investment therein rather than in any other branch of activity, or, in other words, that the profit rate would exceed that in manufactures, or be no lower than the risk premium? *The only reason given by Smith runs in terms of factor endowments and relative factor prices:*

In our North American colonies, where uncultivated land is still to be had upon easy terms, no manufactures for distant sale have ever yet been established in any of their towns. When an artificer has acquired a little more stock than is necessary for carrying on his own business in supplying the neighbouring country, he does not, in North America, attempt to establish with it a manufacture for more distant sale, but employs it in the purchase and improvement of uncultivated land ...

In countries, on the contrary, where there is either no uncultivated land, or none that can be had upon easy terms, every artificer who has acquired more stock than he can employ in the occasional jobs of the neighbourhood, endeavours to prepare work for more distant sale. The smith erects some sort of iron, the weaver some sort of linen or woollen manufactory (359).

It would, therefore, seem to be the *market process* as reflected in the relative price of land which assures, that whilst land remains cheap, the profit rate in agriculture will exceed that in industry, so that investors will prefer the former[14]

INDUSTRIAL DEVELOPMENT

The role of relative factor prices in determining the allocation of resources between sectors is further confirmed by Smith's treatment of British interferences with her colonies. In this regard, we must first recall the argument in

13 *Ibid.*, 357-8.
14 This mechanism is developed elsewhere in the *Wealth of Nations*. With regard to the particularly rapid development of European colonies, Smith wrote: 'The colony of a civilized nation which takes possession either of a waste country, or of one so thinly inhabited, that the natives easily give place to the new settlers, advances more rapidly to wealth and greatness than any other human society' (*ibid.*, 531-2). This rapid progress is attributed to good agricultural knowledge, and habits of subordination and law. As far as pure economic motives are concerned we read: 'Every colonist gets more land than he can possibly cultivate. He has no rent, and scarce any taxes to pay. No landlord shares with him in its produce, and the share of the sovereign is commonly but a trifle. He has every motive to render as great as possible a produce, which is thus to be almost entirely his own' (*ibid.*, 532). Here we see that the price of land certainly comes into the picture. The profitability of investment in agriculture is enormous since there is no rental payment (and no taxes).

the basic chaptetr 'Of Component Parts of Price' (I.v) according to which the relative importance of rent, compared with profits and wages, declines upon each additional stage in the manufacturing process: 'As any particular commodity comes to be more manufactured, that part of the price which resolves itself into wages and profit, comes to be greater in proportion to that which resolves itself into rent.'[15] Essentially, the 'more refined' the commodity, the greater is the importance of the labour-and-capital, compared with the natural resource content.

Smith pointed to British regulations forbidding the establishment in the colonies of steel furnaces and slit-mills – which involve advanced stages in the manufacture of iron – while encouraging the production of pig and bar iron – that is, the preliminary stages of manufacture – both for domestic use and export.[16] Various other restrictions imposed by Britain on internal transport confined colonial industry 'to such coarse and household manufactures, as a private family commonly makes for its own use, or for that of some of its neighbours in the same province.'[17] These restrictions, it was argued, although unjust, were of little practical relevance, precisely because it was in any event unprofitable to produce 'refined or more advanced' products in the colonies: 'Land is still so cheap, and, consequently, labour so dear among them, that they can import from the mother country, almost all the more refined or more advanced manufactures cheaper than they could make them for themselves. Though they had not, therefore, been prohibited from establishing such manufactures, yet in their present state of improvement, a regard to their own interest would, probably, have prevented them from doing so' (549).[18]

15 *Ibid.*, 51.
16 'The liberality of England ... has been confined chiefly to what concerns the market for their produce, either in its rude state, or in what may be called the very first stage of manufacture' (*ibid.*, 547). 'While Great Britain encourages in America the manufactures of pig and bar iron ... she imposes an absolute prohibition upon the erection of steel furnaces and slit-mills in any of her American plantations. She will not suffer her colonists to work in those more refined manufactures even for their own consumption' (548). T.S. Ashton, *Iron and Steel in the Industrial Revolution*, 3rd ed. (Manchester, 1963), 125, argues that in actuality bar iron *was* a refined product.
17 *Wealth of Nations*, 548–9.
18 Cf. also *ibid.*, 532, 575. In fact it has been shown that steel furnaces and slit-mills were actually supressed and new structures prevented suggesting that Smith was mistaken in his belief that the regulations were ineffectual. (Ashton, *Iron and Steel in the Industrial Revolution*, 124–5.)

The notion that the British restrictions imposed on her colonies were not in the British interest was not uncommon. Benjamin Franklin – in Britain 1757–75, and personally known to Smith – argued that the growth of colonial manufactures would not endanger England's hold on the colonial market. Plentiful, and therefore cheap, land permitted the labourer to earn enough in a short period to purchase sufficient land for himself and a family, so that population doubled itself every twenty-five years. But this rapid increase in population – in sharp contrast to the case in Europe which was seen to be fully settled with 'manufacturers' and 'husbandmen' – did not mean cheap labour; wages would remain high because of great areas of unsettled

Here, it is the high price of labour which renders investment in advanced manufactures uneconomic.[19]

It followed, however, from this mode of argument that even the colonies at some stage in their development would find manufacturing profitable: 'In a more advanced state,' he wrote, the British regulations forbidding large-scale industrial projects 'might be really oppressive and insupportable.'[20] The rate of profit in agriculture would evidently tend to fall relatively to that in manufactures as the growth in population led, on the one hand, to a growing scarcity of land, and a consequent increase in rents, and, on the other, to reduced wages.

SOME IMPLICATIONS OF SMITHIAN INTERNATIONAL TRADE THEORY

It is particularly revealing to consider this line of argument in conjunction with the Smithian treatment of foreign trade which runs in terms of the theory of absolute advantage.[21] The theory is designed to explain how the *value returns* generated by the community's given resources can be maximized by way of foreign trade. It is assumed that the organizers of economic activity will seek out the most advantageous use of resources; the average profit rate on capital will be maximized by concentration on those products in which the community has an absolute advantage, rather than by any other pattern of activity. Now we have just seen that Smith took it for granted that in a new country the peculiar advantage would lie in the production of farm produce, because of the large supply of cheap land available. And that the advantage of Europe lay in manufactured produce, because of the relative cheapness of labour and high cost of land. In effect, his analysis defined each country's

land still available. There was, accordingly, little reason to fear that the colonists would compete with the mother country in labour-intensive trades. *Observations Concerning the Increase of Mankind* (1751), discussed by Joseph Dorfman, *The Economic Mind in American Civilization*, I (1946; New York, 1966), 182.

19 The profit rate in agriculture exceeds that in manufacturing as long as agricultural resources remain relatively plentiful and cheap. As the price of land services rises and that of labour falls relatively, the agricultural profit rate falls *relatively* to that in manufacturing, until investment in the latter sector commences. The function of foreign trade is then to permit continued investment in agriculture beyond the level which would have been achieved in a closed economy.

20 *Ibid.*, 549. There is no obvious relationship between the Smithian analysis of 'investment priorities' and his 'forecast' of a secular downward trend in the average rate of profits in a growing economy. We have argued that the relatively high profit rates available in the agricultural sector, frequently emphasized in the *Wealth of Nations*, simply reflects the extreme cheapness of land which is regarded as typical in an economy at an early stage of development. Economic growth tends to alter the factor endowment such that the agricultural profit rate falls *relatively* to that potentially available in manufacturing. There does not seem to be any necessary implication, in the argument for the profit rate trend since, in principle, increasing labour supplies might counter-balance the effect on profitability of increasing land shortage. Yet, as we have seen in Chapter 5, Smith did envisage a downward secular trend in the profit rate as the economy expands.

21 *Wealth of Nations*, 424–6.

'advantage' in terms of its relative factor endowments.[22] This interpretation is clearly confirmed in the following summary:

It is rather for the manufactured than for the raw produce of Europe, that the colony trade opens a new market. Agriculture is the proper business of all new colonies; a business which the cheapness of land renders more advantageous than any other. They abound, therefore, in the rude produce of land, and instead of importing it from other countries, they have generally a large surplus to export. In new colonies, agriculture either draws hands from all other employments, or keeps them from going to any other employment. There are few hands to spare for the necessary, and none for the ornamental manufactures. The greater part of the manufactures of both kinds, they find it cheaper to purchase of other countries than to make for themselves (575).[23]

The recognition of differences between countries in the relative abundance and relative prices of different factors was by no means limited to the case of land and labour. Smith also noted the significance for the pattern of trade of relative differences in supplies of capital: 'Our merchants frequently complain of the high wages of British labour as the cause of their manufactures being undersold in foreign markets; but they are silent about the high profits

22 International differences are frequently defined by Smith in qualitative, as well as quantitative, terms, it will be recalled.
    B. Ohlin has argued that the significance of differences between countries in the relative abundance and relative prices of different factors – and the resultant tendency towards *low money costs* of those goods which use heavily factors in relative abundance – was neglected in the classical comparative-cost doctrine. He has further claimed that the influence on the course of trade of differences between countries in the relative abundance of the different factors was first touched on in French works. (Cf. Jacob Viner, *Studies in the Theory of International Trade* (New York, 1937), 500f.) Professor Viner denies that the relevance of relative factor endowments was neglected in the early nineteenth-century British literature. He even refers to a passage in the *Wealth of Nations* (p. 565) as an indication of some recognition of the issue by Smith (below, 286). However, he fails to emphasize the crucial and pervasive role played by international differences in the land-labour ratio in Smithian economics.
    (See also a number of suggestive propositions in Josiah Tucker, *Four Tracts Together With Two Sermons on Political and Commercial Subjects* (Gloucester, 1774), esp. 26–8.)
23 This formulation flies in the face of the 'vent-for-surplus' doctrine also discussed by Smith according to which the advantages of trade lie in the market opened up for the products of domestic resources which would apparently otherwise be idle, rather than in the more efficient use of resources.
    The only formal rationalization of the argument, however, amounts to a casual hint that British resources were physically capable of producing a very narrow range of products for which domestic demand was highly inelastic. Although it is possible to justify the argument further Smith himself did not do so. In fact, he does not seem to adopt the view of the British economy implied by the doctrine, and emphasized the similarity of technology between various branches of manufacturing which would assure the maintenance of employment upon the removal of protectionist measures.

of stock ... The high profits of British stock, however, may contribute towards raising the price of British manufactures in many cases as much, and in some perhaps more, than the high wages of British labour.'[24] Accordingly, any increase in capital, or any release of capital due to the abandonment of government interferences in trading patterns, would tend to increase Britain's competitiveness: 'there would have been a large spare capital to apply to other purposes; to improve the lands, to increase the manufactures, and to extend the commerce of Great Britain; to come into competition at least with the other British capitals employed in all those different ways, to reduce the rate of profit in them all, and thereby to give to Great Britain, in all of them, a superiority over other countries still greater than what she at present enjoys.'[25] And, in the course of development, the pattern of trade would tend to alter as changes in factor prices – particularly the downward trend in the profit rate – exerted a differential effect on the production costs of various commodities: 'In countries which are fast advancing to riches, the low rate of profit may, in the price of many commodities, compensate the high wages of labour, and enable those countries to sell as cheap as their less thriving neighbours, among whom the wages of labour may be lower.'[26]

It is necessary, after this analysis, to consider briefly the treatment of capital allocation developed in the *Wealth of Nations*, II.v. According to the formal categories established in that chapter, agriculture is more labour-intensive than manufactures, insofar as a given investment outlay supports a larger work force. Yet it seems, from the discussion of resource allocation which we have just outlined, that agriculture was the most profitable enterprise in North America, with its small labour supply and high wages; and manufacturing the most profitable in Britain, with its relatively large labour supply and lower wages. It would appear, therefore, that manufacturing is the more labour-intensive of the two sectors.

The following suggestions may be offered. In the first place, it should be noted that in Smith's demonstration of a higher labour-capital ratio in agriculture 'labouring cattle' is included within the category 'productive labour.' The demonstration is of little value as far as the relationship between capital and the true work force is concerned. Secondly, much emphasis is placed in the demonstration of the 'advantage' of agricultural investment on the contribution of land, and it is apparent that any analysis of resource allocation which pays attention solely to the capital-labour ratio is incomplete. It is clearly possible for investment in a labour-intensive sector – one with a high labour-capital ratio – to be most profitable if the relative 'disadvantage' of a labour shortage and high wage rates is outweighed by the availability of relatively large land supplies and low rents.[27]

24 *Ibid.*, 565.
25 *Ibid.*, 570.
26 *Ibid.*, 97.
27 The following argument confirms that agriculture was profitable in the colonies

AN AGRICULTURAL BIAS?

The outcome of our analysis suggests that the advantages which Smith attributed to agriculture were not defined independently of the economic circumstances – particularly the factor endowments – which applied. The approach implies that agriculture is not 'preferable' to manufacturing or trade in some absolute sense.

Yet, there are numerous celebrated statements in the *Wealth of Nations* which do suggest that the advantage of agricultural investment over any other lies in its ability to 'reproduce' not only profits and wages, but a rent as well, without reference to the factor endowments which happen to exist. The following passage, for example, suggests that agriculture is in some absolute sense 'advantageous'; it is implied that of two countries, one agriculturual, the other manufacturing, with roughly equal rates of profit on capital the former will be 'better off':

The consideration of his own private profit, is the sole motive which determines the owner of any capital to employ it either in agriculture, in manufactures, or in some particular branch of the wholesale or retail trade. The different quantities of productive labour which it may put into motion, and the different values which it may add to the annual produce of the land and labour of the society ... never enter into his thoughts. In countries, therefore, where agriculture is the most profitable of all employments, and farming and improving the most direct roads to a splendid fortune, the capitals of individuals will naturally be employed in the manner most advantageous to the whole society (355).

But the agricultural emphasis should not be exaggerated. The context of the above passage suggests that Smith's objective was to condemn government interferences of various kinds which had *prematurely* diverted resources away from agriculture. Even in Europe, Smith wrote, 'much good land still remains uncultivated, and the greater part of what is cultivated, is far from being improved to the degree of which it is capable. Agriculture, therefore, is almost every-where capable of absorbing a much greater capital than has ever yet been employed in it.'[28] Clearly, Smith still has in mind the issue of relative profitability determined by factor endowments.[29]

It appears then, that the emphasis given to agricultural investments as the most advantageous to society – on the grounds that rents are thereby generated

---

despite high wages. High wages *in themselves* are irrelevant: 'The cheapness and plenty of good land encourage improvement, and enable the proprietor to pay those high wages. In those wages consists almost the whole price of the land; and though they are high, considered as the wages of labour, they are low, considered as the price of what is so very valuable (*ibid.*, 533).

28 *Ibid.*, 355

29 The argument that government interference had distorted the pattern of activity from that which would best reflect the factor endowment – that is from that which would be achieved in a freely-operating system – is given the greatest attention in the *Wealth of Nations*. For example, European state regulations had prevented

– does not have the damaging effects which might be expected from what is a serious error in logic.[30] In applying his economic analysis, Smith had continually in mind the question of factor endowments which determine the relative profitability of agriculture and manufacturing. (It may also be recalled that Smith believed labour productivity in agriculture to be potentially far less remarkable than that in manufacturing.)[31]

Furthermore, if we consider Smith's formal attitude to Physiocracy, it becomes clear that, despite tribute to the peculiar characteristics of agriculture, he yet maintained a moderate and balanced attitude recognizing that there can be 'too much' agricultural investment as well as too little. We refer to the interdependence between country and town – developed in the chapter on 'Agricultural Systems'[32] – one aspect of which lay in the market constituted by each for the product of the other so that the discouragement of manufacturing would rebound against agriculture:

The trade which is carried on between those two different sets of people, consists ultimately in a certain quantity of rude produce exchanged for a certain quantity of manufactured produce. The dearer the latter, therefore, the cheaper the former; and

the creation of small estates and had accordingly reduced the land offered for sale so that the price of land was extremely high – 'a monopoly price.' If landed property were divided equally between the children of the owner, then upon his death, much of the estate would be put on the market, and the artificial scarcity in Europe somewhat reduced (*ibid.*, 392–3). The problem did not exist in North America where 'uncultivated land' was available 'almost for nothing, or at a price below the value of the natural produce; a thing impossible in Europe, or, indeed, in any country where all lands have long been private property' (393).

A further distortion was introduced by the monopoly granted to British merchants in the colony trade. The effect, in the first instance, was an increase in the rate of profit on *mercantile trade* which rendered investment in domestic land improvement relatively unattractive. Moreover, the increase in the *average* profit rate tended to keep up the interest rate to the detriment of landowners by lowering the price of land relative to the rent yielded: 'The price of land in proportion to the rent which it affords, the number of years purchase which is commonly paid for it, necessarily falls as the rate of interest rises' (*ibid.*, 577).

A similar problem arises in a comparison between the policies towards their colonies of various continental European nations. Here Smith again writes as if agricultural investment had peculiar advantages independently of the pattern of resources because of the rent generated (*ibid.*, 540). But the issue once more involves a condemnation of government interference which renders agricultural investment prematurely unprofitable relative to other investments. In this instance it is the practice of 'engrossing' of land which creates an artificial scarcity.

30 See the criticism by J.S. Mill, in J.M. Robson, ed., *Collected Works of J.S. Mill, Principles of Political Economy*, vol. II (Toronto, 1965), 28–9.
31 *Wealth of Nations*, 6.
32 Cf. *Ibid.*, 267: 'Thus the farmer annually replaces to the manufacturer the provisions which he had consumed and the materials which he had wrought up the year before; and the manufacturer replaces to the farmer the finished work which he had wasted and worn out in the same time. This is the real exchange that is annually made between those two orders of people.'

whatever tends in any country to raise the price of manufactured produce, tends to lower that of the rude produce of the land, and thereby to discourage agriculture ... Whatever, besides, tends to diminish in any country the number of artificers and manufacturers, tends to diminish the home market, the most important of all markets for the rude produce of the land, and thereby still further to discourage agriculture.

Those systems, therefore, which preferring agriculture to all other employments, in order to promote it, impose restraints upon manufactures and foreign trade, act contrary to the very end which they propose, and indirectly discourage that very species of industry which they mean to promote. They are so far, perhaps, more inconsistent than even the mercantile system. That system, by encouraging manufactures and foreign trade more than agriculture, turns a certain portion of the capital of the society from supporting *a more advantageous*, to support *a less advantageous species of industry*. But still it really and in the end encourages that species of industry which it means to promote. Those agricultural systems, on the contrary, really and in the end discourage their own favourite species of industry (650; author's emphasis).

The fact is that Smith did not lose sight of factor endowments and relative prices in dealing with economic development; indeed the Smithian analysis of development can scarcely be appreciated independently of the processes of competitive resource allocation. This conclusion may be illustrated further by reference to the role accorded to agriculture in the process of growth. An analysis similar to that of Steuart according to which an agricultural surplus – exceeding maintenance requirements within the agricultural sector – is essential for the development of a domestic manufacturing sector is outlined in the *Wealth of Nations*. It is technical progress in agriculture which in the first instance allows 'the labour of half the society ... to provide food for the whole' releasing labour for the production of commodities in exchange for agricultural produce, and indeed motivating the production of a surplus over internal needs. It is precisely in this context that Smith utilizes the celebrated conception that while 'the desire of food is limited in every man by the narrow capacity of the human stomach' that for the 'conveniences and ornaments of building, dress, equipage, and household furniture, seems to have no limit or certain boundary,' implying a belief – in contrast with that of Steuart – that there scarcely existed any problem regarding the *creation* of wants. Furthermore, it is by increasing the surplus that a larger non-agricultural population can be supported: 'The number of workmen increases with the increasing quantity of food, or with the growing improvement and cultivation of the lands.'[33] Technical progress in agriculture may thus have either or both of two consequences, namely the *release* of labour to non-agricultural uses with no actual increase in aggregate food supplies; or food supplies might be

33 *Ibid.*, 163–4. (Cf. 634f.) A detailed treatment of the analysis will be found in J.M. Letiche, 'Adam Smith and David Ricardo on Economic Growth,' in B.F. Hoselitz, ed., *Theories of Economic Growth* (New York, 1960), 66–8; Nathan Rosenberg, 'Adam Smith, Consumer Tastes, and Economic Growth,' *Journal of Political Economy*, 76 (May/June 1968), 361f.

increased with no initial release of labour, the increased manufacturing work force being recruited from (induced) natural population growth. In the former case wage-goods capital is, in effect, diverted from agriculture to manufacturing (along with the complementary work force); in the latter there occurs a net increase in aggregate wage-goods capital which is made available for the manufacturing sector, and which will only permit increased output therein *pari passu* with any increase in the labour supply. (This increase in capital, it will be noted, is achieved with no necessary diversion of resources from the consumer-goods or service sector.) In fact, in the Smithian account of contemporary British experience technical and organizational changes in agriculture were generating increased food supplies although not releasing labour to manufacturing so that expansion of the manufacturing sector depended largely upon natural population growth.

What must be understood, however, is that the emphasis upon the agricultural sector from the point of view of growth was not utilized by Smith as an argument for its artificial encouragement. Smith in fact went so far as to emphasize the peculiar advantages enjoyed by an economy suitably endowed to devote its resources largely to manufacturing and foreign commerce:[34]

The one [a manufacturing country] exports what can subsist and accommodate but a very few, and imports the subsistence and accommodation of a great number. The other [an agricultural economy] exports the accommodation and subsistence of a great number, and imports that of a very few only. The inhabitants of the one must always enjoy a much greater quantity of subsistence than what their own lands, in the actual state of their cultivation, can afford. The inhabitants of the other must always enjoy a much smaller quantity (642).[35]

The dependence of expansion upon increased food supplies thus entailed an *essential* role for agriculture in a closed economy or in an open economy whose resource endowment induced specialization in agriculture. It is also clear that even in a mixed economy such as the Britain of his day agricultural efficiency took on a significant function in the generation of the circulating capital re-

34 Cf. the argument by Richard Cantillon, *Essai Sur la Nature du Commerce en Général* (1775), ed. H. Higgs (London, 1931), 225: 'When a State exchanges its Labour for the produce of foreign land it seems to have the advantage, since its inhabitants are fed at the Foreigner's expense.'

35 Since French policy tended to encourage too much industry and foreign trade, the Physiocrats had responded and 'bent the rod too far in the other direction' as a response (*Wealth of Nations*, 629). There can be too *much* investment in agriculture. Thus China – in contrast to contemporary Europe – 'favours agriculture more than all other employments.' It was easy to get land leases, for example. And foreign trade was constrained 'within a much narrower circle than that to which it would naturally extend itself, if more freedom were allowed to it, either in their own ships, or in those of other countries' (*ibid.*, 644).

Smith similarly criticizes the encouragment given by the ancient Egyptians to agriculture. They depended on foreigners to export their surplus produce and therefore confined the markets for manufactures to the disadvantage of the latter (*ibid.*, 647).

quired for the expansion not only of agriculture but also of manufacturing. But international trade divorced the growth process from strict dependence upon the availability of productive *domestic* agricultural resources. Wage-goods capital – as indeed any other capital-goods or consumer-goods – might be acquired more efficiently by indirect than by direct means.

Yet in Smith's view the economy which enjoys extensive agricultural resources does possess a fundamental advantage over the economy which lacks them. Smith's policy position regarding economic development amounts to a recommendation that a 'landed nation' should not attempt to undertake industrialization, by artificial means. The essential precondition for successful growth was the generation of adequate capital supplies, which would be forthcoming more readily by concentration on the production of those commodities for which the resource endowment created a cost advantage.[36] Ultimately when conditions were suitable – in terms of the resource endowment – manufactures would be set up 'naturally' in the agricultural economy *which are able to compete against those of the already well-established manufacturing economy* – initially in the domestic market only, but subsequently even in foreign markets. For any initial disadvantage in skills would be temporary only and, in any event, counterbalanced by the presumed availability of cheap domestic raw materials and food supplies:

The continual increase of the surplus produce of their land, would, in due time, create a greater capital than what could be employed with the ordinary rate of profit in the improvement and cultivation of land; and the surplus part of it would naturally turn itself to the employment of artificers and manufacturers at home. But those artificers and manufacturers, finding at home both the materials of their work and the fund of their subsistence, might immediately, even with much less art and skill, be able to work as cheap as the like artificers and manufacturers of such mercantile states, who had both to bring from a great distance ... The cheapness of the manufactures of those landed nations, in consequence of the gradual improvements of art and skill, would, in due time, extend their sale beyond the home market, and carry them to many foreign markets, from which they would in the same manner gradually jostle out many of the manufactures of such mercantile nations (635).[37]

Thus *all* economies in the 'natural' course of development would initially devote their growing capital and labour resources to agriculture alone, and subsequently introduce and extend manufactures. But the more substantial

---

36 *Ibid.*, 632f. In this context Smith includes England and France in contrast to the mercantile states such as Holland and Hamburg.

An economy suitably endowed to devote its resources largely to agriculture is advised to avoid protective measures against manufactures as a means of stimulating the domestic development thereof because in the last resort an increase in the price of manufactures entails a (relative) decline in that of agricultural produce, and consequently tends to depress agricultural activity and the magnitude of the surplus agricultural produce available for expansion (*ibid.*, 634–5).

37 Cf. *ibid.*, 393 where Britain's bright prospect is related to the 'natural fertility of the soil' as well as the excellent means of transport.

and productive is the agricultural base the sounder will be the ability to proceed ultimately to the successful development of a manufacturing sector.

Smith thus adopted a highly 'optimistic' view of the ability of an agricultural economy to overcome any initial disadvantage in the way of industrialization. Yet his comparisons are between economies with differential agricultural bases. It is not so clear that of two similarly based agricultural economies the latecomer would be in so fortunate a position to proceed successfully. Indeed at various junctures in the *Wealth of Nations* Smith implies that it may be rather difficult for a latecomer to catch up in terms of ability to compete. This after all is implicit in his emphasis upon the productivity advantages of scale which counterbalance any upward movement in wage rates occurring under pressure of capital accumulation. And to the extent that the profit rate tends to decline in consequence of 'increased competition' there is further assurance that the advanced expanding economy would retain its competitive advantage.[38] In this respect Smith was on the side of James Oswald and Josiah Tucker against the position of Hume in his essay 'Of the Balance of Trade' according to which the advanced economy would ultimately lose its initial advantage. We should keep in mind the fact that Britain was, in Smith's view, an 'opulent' economy with a splendid agricultural base and industrial potential and ahead in the race. But it is clearly relevant to inquire how, according to Smith, the recommended policy of non-intervention would be justified from the viewpoint either of an economy with poor natural resources or of one which despite plentiful natural resources had entered the race late compared with other 'landed' nations.[39]

It does not seem quite accurate to say that the issue was reconciled by Smith's 'denying the basic mercantilist axiom that industrialization was a good thing and arguing that agriculture was a more efficient producer of economic welfare.'[40] Smith's recommendation was that industrialization *should* proceed in landed states but in 'due time' and not by artificial means. Free trade, as already explained, would be the expedient for 'filling up in the properest and most advantageous manner that very important void which they felt there.'[41]

---

38 *Ibid.*, 86, 97. (See above, 286.) In the early draft of the work Smith is quite explicit that the 'opulent' economy can retain its competitiveness despite high wages: 'The more opulent, therefore, the society, labour will always be so much the dearer and work so much the cheaper, and if some opulent countries have lost several of their manufactures and some branches of their commerce, by having been undersold in foreign markets by the Traders and artizans of poorer countries, who were contented with less profit and smaller wages, this will rarely be found to have been merely the effect of the opulence of the one country and the poverty of the other. Some other cause, we may be assured, must have concurred. The rich country must have been guilty of some great error of police.' (W.R. Scott, *Adam Smith as Student and Professor* (Glasgow, 1937), 332.)

39 Tucker addressed himself to the issue and concluded that in the case of backward countries protection and other forms of intervention were justified. See above, 78, n. 105

40 J.M. Low, 'An Eighteenth Century Controversy in the Theory of Economic Progress,' *Manchester School of Economic and Social Studies*, XX (Sept. 1952), 327.

41 *Wealth of Nations*, 635.

Only one cloud existed on the horizon from the point of view of the opulent and growing economy, namely the state of stationariness which would set in when the country 'had acquired that full complement of riches which the nature of its soil and climate, and its situation with respect to other countries, allowed it to acquire,' and wherein there was neither motive nor ability for further expansion. Provided a latecomer is fortunate enough to possess adequate domestic agricultural resources it might therefore, presumably, ultimately catch up. Smith unfortunately failed to justify the implicit assumption that technical knowledge would ultimately cease to grow. But in any event the prediction was scarcely of immediate relevance for, Smith pointed out, 'perhaps no country has ever yet arrived at this degree of opulence' when free of faulty laws and institutions.[42]

AGRICULTURAL DEVELOPMENT

We turn next to consider Smith's argument regarding land utilization in a developing economy. The case is of particular relevance for the present issue. The process of agricultural development involves the clearing of forests and wastes for the extension of tillage. During expansion supplies of 'wild' cattle, poultry and game – hitherto almost free goods – are reduced at the same time that demand is rising with increasing wealth. Ultimately the (real) price of such goods rises to the point that it becomes profitable to produce them commercially, that is 'it becomes as profitable to employ the most fertile and best cultivated lands in raising food for them as in raising corn.' Beyond this level, the price cannot rise for 'if it did, more corn land would soon be turned into pasture.'[43]

Smith envisaged cattle (for meat) to be the first of the hitherto wild variety to attract a price making it profitable to cultivate land commercially other than for corn and vegetable food. The reason offered runs in terms of relative profitability. The price of venison in Great Britain at the time, for example, was 'not near sufficient to compensate the expence of a deer park.' The commercial production of poultry and hogs occurs between that of cattle and that of venison. When demand rises adequately for pork it will be produced and the price – in equilibrium – 'becomes proportionately either higher or lower than that of other butcher's-meat, according as the nature of the country, and the state of its agriculture, happen to render the feeding of hogs more or less expensive than that of other cattle.'[44] Clearly the choice of products in a growing economy was based upon a profitability calculation, which in turn involved the relative price-cost pattern from product to product.

The relative price of factors used in the case of each product should in principle be of the greatest relevance, although in his reference to 'the nature of the country, and the state of its agriculture' no details were given as to what precisely he had in mind. However, an earlier treatment of the mechanisms governing the relative use of land for pasture or tillage does clarify somewhat

42 *Ibid.*, 94–5.
43 *Ibid.*, 220; cf. 148f.   44 *Ibid.*, 225.

Smith's position. We are told at one stage that the labour-land ratio is greater in corn than in pasture although the output-labour ratio is extremely high: 'A corn field of moderate fertility produces a much greater quanitity of food for man, than the best pasture of equal extent. Though its cultivation requires much more labour, yet the surplus which remains after replacing the seed and maintaining all that labour, is likewise much greater' (148). The reason for the relatively high productivity of corn land (or labour on corn land) seems to lie in the *higher turnover rate of capital* in this case than in pasture. If it is to be profitable to produce butcher's meat rather than corn it will be necessary, Smith argues, for meat prices to rise sufficiently to compensate for the productivity disadvantage. These propositions appear in the following passage: 'Corn is an annual crop. Butcher's-meat, a crop which requires four or five years to grow. As an acre of land, therefore, will produce a much smaller quantity of the one species of food than of the other, the inferiority of the quantity must be compensated by the superiority of the price. If it was more than compensated, more corn land would be turned into pasture; and if it was not compensated, part of what was in pasture would be brought back into corn' (149). In fact, Smith even points to the relatively high profits already to be earned in planting of forests despite the long gestation period of the product:

The scarcity of wood [due to the extension of tillage and pasture] then raises its price. It affords a good rent, and the landlord sometimes finds that he can scarce employ his best lands more advantageously than in growing barren timber, of which the greatness of the profit often compensates the lateness of the returns. This seems in the present times to be nearly the state of things in several parts of Great Britain, where the profit of planting is found to be equal to that of either corn or pasture (166).

Essentially Smith was taking into account not only the comparative revenue yielded by a given land area devoted to corn, to grazing or to timber but revenue relative to costs in each case. This is a vital step towards recognizing the relevance of the input price structure in contributing to the determination of profitability. (Yet the fact is that no use was made of the recognized difference in the labour-land ratios and the turnover rates of capital between agricultural products in the formal presentation of the theories of value and employment.)

THE TRADING SECTOR

The sectoral hierarchy laid down in II.v distinguishes between the differential employment-generating potentials of capital invested in the 'home trade' (the purchase of commodities and their sale domestically), in the 'foreign trade of consumption' (the purchase abroad for sale at home, or conversely), and in the 'carrying trade' (the exchange between the commodities of foreign countries). Two characteristics are involved. In the first place investment in the home trade, Smith argued, replaced 'two distinct [domestic] capitals,' whereas the foreign trade of consumption replaced only one, and the carrying trade none at all.[45] The second characteristic relates to the more rapid 'turnover rate' in the home trade compared with the foreign trade of consumption.[46]

The classification was utilized in the analysis of the monopoly granted by the Navigation Acts to British capital in the colonial trade. While 'the most advantageous employment of any capital to the country to which it belongs, is that which maintains there the greatest quantity of productive labour, and increases the most the annual produce of the land and labour of that country,'[47] the effect of the monopoly had been to divert British capital from close to distant foreign trade of consumption, from direct to roundabout foreign trades of consumption (and in some cases even from foreign trades of consumption to the carrying trade), that is 'from a direction in which it would have maintained a greater quantity of productive labour, into one, in which it can maintain a much smaller quantity.'[48] And although the colony trade was profitable to individual traders it was not socially advantageous in terms of the employment criterion: 'In a trade of which the returns are very distant, the profit of the merchant may be as great or greater than in one in which they are very frequent and near; but the advantage of the country in which he resides, the quantity of productive labour constantly maintained there, the annual produce of the land and labour must always be much less.'[49]

It is thus the criterion of social advantage in terms of the *employment of productive labour* which is laid down in the treatment of the colonial monopoly. Indeed, it is Smith's analysis of trading patterns in general which received the most determined criticism by his successors.[50] But what requires emphasis

45 With regard to the most extreme case, Smith wrote (*ibid.*, 351): 'That part of the capital of any country which is employed in the carrying trade, is altogether withdrawn from supporting the productive labour of that particular country, to support that of some foreign countries.'

46 *Ibid.*, 348f.

47 *Ibid.*, 566.   48 *Ibid.*, 573.   49 *Ibid.*, 568.

50 In writing of Smith's contention that the volume of employment generated in the home branch of trade exceeds that generated by the same sum in any other since the turnover rate of circulating capital in this case is more rapid, McCulloch condemns the implication that the former branch is 'advantageous': 'This is altogether erroneous. If the returns to the capital employed in the foreign trade of consumption be at longer distances than the returns to capital employed in the home trade, they will, when made, be proportionally larger. Dr Smith has shown that, upon an average, all capitals, in whatever way they may be employed, yield the same nett profit; and, so long as they do this, they must, how much soever they may differ, in many respects, be equally advantageous' (McCulloch, ed., *Wealth of Nations*, 164–5n). Equilibrium will be characterized by an equality of profit rates across the board. The rate in slow and distant trading would in equilibrium be equal to that in any other branch. And since the profit rate was the index of national advantage (in McCulloch's view because most capital accumulation came from profits), and private enterprise can be relied on to seek out the maximum profit rate on its investments, there was an identity between social and private interests. He therefore condemned Smith for apparently seeing other indices of social welfare, such as a high level of employment.

is the fact that while divergencies between private profitability and the social advantage defined in terms of employment are recognized they are said to be the consequence of government intervention.[51] Smith talked once more, in the case of trading, of a 'natural balance,' between the various sectors, which was not to be disturbed: 'The monopoly of the colony trade besides, by forcing towards it a much greater proportion of the capital of Great Britain than what would naturally have gone to it, seems to have broken altogether that natural balance which would otherwise have taken place among all the different branches of British industry.'[52] He called, accordingly, for a relaxation of the monopoly which 'can enable her or even force her to withdraw some part of her capital from this overgrown employment, and to turn it, though with less profit, towards other employments; and which, by gradually diminishing one branch of her industry and gradually increasing all the rest, can by degrees restore all the different branches of it to that natural, healthful, and proper proportion which perfect liberty necessarily establishes, and which perfect liberty can alone preserve.'[53]

51 The *average* profit rate, Smith argued, was artificially raised by the exclusion of foreign mercantile capital from the North American trade, and by reductions in British domestic investment because of the attractive investments available in the colonial trade (*Wealth of Nations*, 573).

The effects of government intervention had thus been the diversion of capital from closer to more distant (colony) trade from which the returns were less frequent and although it was profitable, it was not socially advantageous. But there is a further social disadvantage attached to this trade. Since capital generated in the colonies was scarce, and agriculture extremely profitable, there was reliance on foreign sources of capital to finance agricultural projects. These funds were raised less by direct borrowing than by running up trade deficits (see below, 302). But this meant that there was an even slower turnover rate than was usual in distant trading: 'The whole capital, therefore, which their correspondents advance to them is seldom returned to Britain in less than three, and sometimes not in less than four or five years' (*ibid.*, 568). Now it is quite true that the 'correspondent' earns profit on his capital that makes the procedure worthwhile, but there is a disadvantage to Great Britain which could not be made up: 'But, though he [the American planter] may make up the loss of his correspondent, he cannot make up that of Great Britain. In a trade of which the returns are very distant, the profit of the merchant may be as great or greater than in one in which they are very frequent and near; but the advantage of the country in which he resides, the quantity of productive labour constantly maintained there, the annual produce of the land and labour must always be must less' (*ibid.*, 568).

52 *Ibid.*, 570.

53 *Ibid.*, 572. Cf. 353: 'Each of these different branches of trade, however, is not only advantageous, but necessary and unavoidable, when the course of things, without any contraint or violence, naturally introduces it.'

Smith recognized a legitimate role for the colony trade – in the absence of interference – in an argument actually utilizing the vent-for-surplus concept: 'The effect of the colony trade in its natural and free state, is to open a great, though distant market for such parts of the produce of British industry as may exceed the demand of the markets nearer home ... In its natural and free state, the colony trade,

And it cannot be said that his call for freedom from governmental interference reflected an objection to the *kind* of intervention then practised, and
would not have been made in the event that governments were encouraging
high-employment ventures rather than discouraging them. Smith's appeal to
a 'natural balance' is an honest one. For he made it quite clear that if – in the
absence of government intervention – the profit rate in the carrying trade
should rise sufficiently this is to be taken as a sign that further investment is
socially desirable *despite the fact that a given investment therein supports the
least productive labour*:

But if in any of those distant employments, which in ordinary cases are less advantageous to the country, the profit should happen to rise somewhat higher than what
is sufficient to balance the natural preference which is given to nearer employments,
this superiority of profit will draw stock from those nearer employments, till the
profits of all return to their proper level. This superiority of profit, however, is a proof
that, in the actual circumstances of the society, those distant employments are somewhat under-stocked in proportion to other employments, and that the stock of the
society is not distributed in the properest manner among all the different employments
carried on in it. It is a proof that something is either bought cheaper or sold dearer
than it ought to be ... Though the same capital never will maintain the same quantity
of productive labour in a distant as in a near employment, yet a distant employment
may be as necessary for the welfare of the society as a near one; the goods which the
distant employment deals in being necessary, perhaps, for carrying on many of the
nearer employments. But if the profits of those who deal in such goods are above their
proper level, those goods will be sold dearer than they ought to be, or somewhat above
their natural price, and all those engaged in the nearer employments will be more or
less oppressed by this high price ... In this extraordinary case, the public interest requires that some stock should be withdrawn from those employments which in ordinary cases are more advantageous, and turned towards one which in ordinary cases
is less advantageous to the public; and in this extraordinary case, the natural interests
and inclinations of men coincide as exactly with the public interest as in all other
ordinary cases, and lead them to withdraw stock from the near, and to turn it towards
the distant employment (593–4).

It should be noted too that even in the treatment of British colonial policy,
where the employment criterion was formally adopted, Smith placed much
emphasis on the resultant depressing effect of intervention upon the potential

without drawing from those markets any part of the produce which had ever been
sent to them, encourages Great Britain to increase the surplus continually, by
continually presenting new equivalents to be exchanged for it. In its natural and
free state, the colony trade tends to increase the quantity of productive labour in
Great Britain, but without altering in any respect the direction of that which had
been employed there before. In the natural and free state of the colony trade, the
competition of all other nations would hinder the rate of profit from rising above
the common level either in the new market, or in the new employment' (*ibid.*, 574).

for savings even out of wage income.[54] It seems unlikely that he envisaged the drawing into the labour force of unemployed workers at the *subsistence* wage in consequence of the abandonment of the trading monopoly, for it would then be difficult to envisage any 'surplus' available in the wage income for savings and taxation. It is more likely that he assumed that the larger work force would be drawn from the service sector at the going wage rate bearing in mind that only the earnings of productive workers represent an original income in contrast to those of service labour which constitute transfer payments.

We conclude from the foregoing argument that the employment of productive labour was deliberately not utilized as a criterion of policy in a freely-operating system despite the physical possibility of expanding employment by appropriate intervention: 'Every derangement of the natural distribution of stock is necessarily hurtful ... whether it be by repelling from a particular trade the stock which would otherwise go to it, or by attracting towards a particular trade that which would not otherwise come to it.'[55]

Yet while the profit motive was to be relied upon to determine the allocation

54 *Ibid.*, 577. 'The monopoly hinders the capital of that country, whatever may at any particular time be the extent of that capital, from maintaining so great a quantity of productive labour as it would otherwise maintain, and from affording so great a revenue to the industrious inhabitants as it would otherwise afford. But as capital can be increased only by savings from revenue, the monopoly, by hindering it from affording so great a revenue as it would otherwise afford, necessarily hinders it from increasing so fast as it would otherwise increase, and consequently from maintaining a still greater quantity of productive labour, and affording a still greater revenue to the industrious inhabitants of that country. One great original source of revenue, therefore, the wages of labour, the monopoly must necessarily have rendered at all times less abundant than it otherwise would have been.'

Secondly, the monopoly by raising the profit rate in colonial trade diverted capital from land improvement thereby reducing rental income. Finally, since expansion was checked by the monopoly, it is likely that *total* profits were also somewhat diminished: 'All the original sources of revenue, the wages of labour, the rent of land, and the profits of stock, the monopoly renders much less abundant than they otherwise would be' (*ibid.*, 578).

55 *Ibid.*, 597. Thus Holland, because of government intervention, invested less than it otherwise would in the East India trade and suffered 'a considerable loss by part of its capital being excluded from the employment most convenient for that part.' Conversely, Sweden and Denmark found that more capital was invested in East India trade with social losses since capital was 'drawn into an employment which must be more or less unsuitable to their present circumstances. Better for them, perhaps, in their present circumstances, to buy East India goods of other nations, even though they should pay somewhat dearer, than to turn so great a part of their small capital to so very distant a trade, in which the returns are so very slow, in which that capital can maintain so small a quantity of productive labour at home, where productive labour is so much wanted, where so little is done, and where so much is to do' (*ibid.*, 597). In brief, it is circumstances which determine which branches are the most socially advisable: '... when a nation is ripe for any great branch of trade, some merchants naturally turn their capitals towards the principal, and some towards the subordinate branches of it ... If at any particular time that part of the capital of any country which of its own accord tended and inclined, if I

of trading capital, a link is missing in the supporting argument rendering the foundation thereof dangerously fragile. We have seen that Smith recognized a risk differential between agriculture and manufacturing which assures that on 'equal or near equal profits' capitalists will chose to invest first in agriculture and only subsequently in manufacturing. We have also noted that the 'normal' pattern in a growing economy will be investment first in agriculture and then in manufacturing, since *in fact* the agricultural profit rate is likely to exceed that in manufacturing because of the initial high land endowment relative to that of labour. Now a risk differential was also recognized between manufacturing and trade: 'In seeking for employment to a capital, manufactures are, upon equal or nearly equal profits, naturally preferred to foreign commerce for the same reason that agriculture is naturally preferred to manufactures.' Thus it is that 'according to the natural course of things ... the greater part of the capital of every growing society is, first, directed to agriculture, afterwards to manufactures, and last of all to foreign commerce.'[56] Similarly a risk differential between the various branches of trade was said to exist, so that upon equal profits there will be a preference first for the home trade, secondly for the foreign trade of consumption (which includes the colony trade) and lastly for the carrying trade:

Every individual endeavours to employ his capital as near home as he can, and consequently as much as he can in the support of domestic industry; provided always that he can thereby obtain the ordinary, or not a great deal less than the ordinary profits of stock.

Thus, upon equal or nearly equal profits, every wholesale merchant naturally prefers the home-trade to the foreign trade of consumption, and the foreign trade of consumption to the carrying trade ... Upon equal, or only nearly equal profits, therefore, every individual naturally inclines to employ his capital in the manner in which it is likely to afford the greatest support to domestic industry, and to give revenue and employment to the greatest number of people of his own country (421-2).[57]

However, apart from the risk differential which introduces, as it were, a bias in the 'right' direction, there appears to be no analysis, comparable to that used to rationalize the choice by capitalists in a growing economy of agriculture over manufacturing, to explain the sequence of manufacturing prior to trade and the home trade prior to the other branches. The mechanism involving the influence on profitability exerted by the pattern of resource

may say so, towards the East India trade, was not sufficient for carrying on all those different branches of it, *it would be a proof that, at that particular time, that country was not ripe for that trade,* and that it would do better to buy for some time, even at a higher price, from other European nations, the East India goods it had occasion for, than to import them itself directly from the East Indies. What it might lose by the high price of those goods could seldom be equal to the loss which it would sustain by the distraction of a large portion of its capital from other employments more necessary, or more useful, or more suitable to its circumstances and situation, than a direct trade to the East Indies' (*ibid.*, 598-9; author's emphasis).

56 *Ibid.*, 359-60.
57 See a further amplification of the argument, *ibid.*, 593-7.

endowments is apparently limited to the choice betwen agriculture and manu-facturing.[58]

The reason for this difference in approach seems to lie in the fact that Smith did not envisage the applicability in the trading sector of the 'production function.' Mercantile capital was regarded as a floating sum available for the purchase of inventories for resale. The profit on such capital was earned not by its investment in the maintenance of productive labour but by 'buying cheap and selling dear.' It is true that different uses of mercantile capital would generate more or less employment according to whether two, one or no domestic capitals were replaced, and according to the rapidity of the turn-over rate. But such effects on employment were *indirect*, in the same sense that the purchases of a final consumer have indirect effects on employment by replenishing the outlays of employers. And Smith had in the case of agricul-ture and manufacturing deliberately stated that his concern was solely with the *proximate* employment-generating capacities, and *not* with the indirect. Moreover, Smith clearly distinguished between the farmer and retailer – who are 'confined almost to a precise spot, to the farm, and to the shop' – or the manufacturer – whose capital is invested in his plant – and the wholesale merchant whose capital 'seems to have no fixed or necessary residence any-where, but may wander about from place to place, according as it can either buy cheap or sell dear.'[59] Clearly there is little room here for a production function relationship; and the employment directly offered to transportation workers is, in fact, played down:

Whether the merchant whose capital exports the surplus produce of any society be a native or a foreigner, is of very little importance. If he is a foreigner, the number of their productive labourers is necessarily less than if he had been a native by one man only; and the value of their annual produce, by the profits of that one man. The sailors or carriers whom he employs may still belong indifferently either to his country, or to their country, or to some third country, in the same manner as if he had been a native. The capital of a foreigner gives a value to their surplus produce equally with that of a native, by exchanging it for something for which there is a demand at home.

58 The only argument in the case of the allocation of capital *within* trade runs in terms of 'vent-for-surplus.' In fact the vent-for-surplus theory is formulated in the context of different uses of trading capital: 'Each of those different branches of trade, however, is not only advantageous, but necessary and unavoidable, when the course of things, without any constraint or violence, naturally introduces it ...
     The extent of the home-trade and of the capital which can be employed in it, is necessarily limited by the value of the surplus produce of all those distant places within the country which have occasion to exchange their respective productions with one another. That of the foreign trade of consumption, by the value of the surplus produce of the whole country and of what can be purchased with it. That of the carrying trade, by the value of the surplus produce of all the different countries in the world' (*ibid.*, 353–4). But this argument still does not explain why the order of profit opportunities will assure precisely that sequence of investment expected.

59 *Ibid.*, 345. Similarly: 'The profits of the farmer, of the manufacturer, of the merchant, and retailer, are all drawn from the price of the goods which the two first produce, and the two last buy and sell' (*ibid.*, 343).

It as effectually replaces the capital of the person who produces that surplus, and as effectually enables him to continue his business; the service by which the capital of a wholesale merchant chiefly contributes to support the productive labour, and to augment the value of the annual produce of the society to which he belongs (345–6).[60]

DIRECT FOREIGN INVESTMENT

In principle, full international mobility of productive factors would bring to an end movement of goods between countries insofar as the rationale of trade lies in specialization based upon differing factor endowments between the partners.

In dealing with investment in foreign (colonial) trade, Smith frequently has in mind investment by *merchants* in wholesale commerce rather than direct investment in foreign agricultural or industrial ventures. It should, therefore, be noted that while Smith frequently refers to an excess or a deficiency of investment in foreign or colonial trade – as recorded by the profit rate – he is usually referring simply to the extent of domestic investment in the trading sector itself, rather than in foreign (colonial) manufacturing or agri-

---

60 The limitation of the production function to agriculture and manufactures and its largely irrelevant role in wholesale trade helps to clear up an argument of Edwin Cannan (*Theories of Production and Distribution from 1776 to 1848*, 3rd ed. (London, 1917; New York, 1967), 66) that if the issue of turnover rates had been applied to agriculture and manufactures it would have played havoc with Smith's ordering of investment priorities. Formally, Cannan is justified, but the fact is that the concept was seen as being of relevance largely to *trade*. It did not appear in Smith's general view of the production function. (It is true that empirical differences in the turnover rate were recognized in agriculture; yet Smith did not extend the argument *formally* to apply to the problem of employment.)

Marx was to make much of the distinction between the two broad categories of capital and struggled with its implications. (Cf. *Capital*, I (Moscow, 1965), 156f.; and *Capital*, III (Moscow, 1962), 262f., 318f.) There is little truth to Marx's contention that Smith leaves 'merchant's capital entirely aside and mention[s] it only as a kind of industrial capital' (III, 319); clearly the distinction was of great importance to him. But it is true that he was not entirely consistent. In a preliminary remark on the characteristics of the natural price, for example, the dealer is treated as any other capitalist, and special care is taken to assure the inclusion of his profits: 'The commodity is then sold precisely for what it is worth, or for what it really costs the person who brings it to market; for though in common language what is called the prime cost of any commodity does not comprehend the profit of the person who is to sell it again, yet if he sells it at a price which does not allow him the ordinary rate of profit in his neighbourhood, he is evidently a loser by the trade; since by employing his stock in some other way he might have made that profit. This profit, besides, is his revenue, the proper fund of his subsistence. As, while he is preparing and bringing the goods to market, he advances to his workmen their wages, or their subsistence; so he advances to himself, in the same manner, his own subsistence, which is generally suitable to the profit which he may reasonably expect from the sale of his goods. Unless they yield him this profit, therefore, they do not repay him what they may very properly be said to have really cost him' (*Wealth of Nations*, 55–6). Moreover, Smith was prone to switch from the capitalist-merchant to the capitalist-employer rather too easily.

culture.[61] It is certainly clear from the above passage that as far as trading, narrowly defined, is concerned there was a high degree of international mobility of capital.

It is also true that *direct* foreign investment was to some extent recognized, although it is not apparently what Smith has in mind in treating the allocation of capital between the three broad sectors. There is, for example, discussion in the *Wealth of Nations* of direct European investment in the colonies. Smith refers, in particular, to British investment in North American agriculture partly by way of direct lending but more significantly by the running up of trade surpluses:

New colonies ... are always understocked. Their capital is always much less than what they could employ with great profit and advantage in the improvement and cultivation of their land. They have a constant demand, therefore, for more capital than they have of their own; and, in order to supply the deficiency of their own, they endeavour to borrow as much as they can of the mother country, to whom they are, therefore, always in debt. The most common way in which the colonists contract this debt, is not by borrowing upon bond of the rich people of the mother country, though they sometimes do this too, but by running as much in arrear to their correspondents, who supply them with goods from Europe, as those correspondents will allow them (567–8).

Similarly, Dutch capital was directly invested not only in the East Indies[62] but also in Britain and France 'where the rate of interest is higher than in their own [country].'[63]

Of particular importance in this respect is Smith's argument that a tax on interest will lead to an outflow of capital. He clearly has in mind a generally high degree of capital mobility:

Land is a subject which cannot be removed, whereas stock easily may. The proprietor of land is necessarily a citizen of the particular country in which his estate lies. The proprietor of stock is properly a citizen of the world, and is not necessarily attached

---

61 This should be recalled in evaluating the interpretation of J.H. Williams ('The Theory of International Trade Reconsidered,' *Economic Journal*, XXXIX (1929), reprinted in *Readings in the Theory of International Trade* (Philadelphia, 1949), 268) which emphasizes Smith's recognition of international factor movements in response to profit-rate differentials between countries.

62 'The mercantile capital of Holland is so great that it is, as it were, continually overflowing, sometimes into the public funds of foreign countries, sometimes into loans to private traders and adventurers of foreign countries, sometimes into the most roundabout foreign trade of consumption, and sometimes into the carrying trade. All near employments being completely filled up, all the capital which can be placed in them with any tolerable profit being already placed in them, the capital of Holland necessarily flows towards the more distant employments' (*Wealth of Nations*, 597). There is even some mention of British *controlled* – not merely financed – operation in the colonies, especially in the retail branches of trade (*ibid.*, 347).

63 *Ibid.*, 91–2.

to any particular country. He would be apt to abandon the country in which he was exposed to a vexatious inquisition, in order to be assessed to a burdensome tax, and would remove his stock to some other country where he could either carry on his business, or enjoy his fortune more at his ease (800).

Similarly a differential tax by any one country upon wage goods (or presumably any cost item) would have the same effect: 'When, by different taxes upon the necessaries and conveniences of life, the owners and employers of capital stock find, that whatever revenue they derive from it, will not, in a particular country, purchase the same quantity of those necessaries and conveniences which an equal revenue would in almost any other, they will be disposed to remove to some other' (880).[64]

A 'CASE-STUDY'

We have argued that Smith's concern was with a pattern of investment which reflected the economy's factor endowment and pattern of consumer tastes. It was recognized that the particular commodities which should be produced at any given period in a country's development depend upon the particular conditions which happen to prevail. These conditions will be reflected in the relative profit rates on different investments so that government intervention is uncalled for.

Much light is thrown on the issue if we consider an instance where Smith actually condemns the government for *abandoning* import duties on a particular commodity on the ground that its production is highly labour-intensive. While this analysis seems to conflict with our interpretation it may be suggested that it represents the exception which proves the rule.

In the chapter 'Conclusion of the Mercantile System,' added in the third edition of *Wealth of Nations*, published in 1784, considerable attention is paid to reductions in, or exemptions from, import duties in a variety of cases. These cases represented largely raw materials, rather than equipment, since, Smith argued, manufacturers – whose influence is presumed to be responsible for the relaxation of controls – had not wished to create problems for the domestic machine-building industry. Smith does not condemn the relaxation of controls as such. His objection is to the extension of the relaxation of import controls from materials to *semi-finished goods*: '[The exemptions or reductions in duty] are, however, perfectly just and reasonable, and if, consistently with the necessities of the state, they could be extended to all other materials of manufacture, the public would certainly be a gainer. The avidity of our great manufacturers, however, has in some cases extended these exemptions a good deal beyond what can justly be considered as the rude materials of their work' (608). The particular case Smith has in mind is the free importation of brown linen yarn,

64 To the extent that the burden of increased wage costs are here said to fall partly upon 'the employers of capital,' the conclusion conflicts with Smith's position expressed elsewhere (see above, 179f.) according to which such cost increases can be passed on in the form of higher industrial prices and lower rents.

the spinning of which he defines as a highly labour-intensive operation: 'In the different operations, however, which are necessary for the preparation of linen yarn, a good deal more industry is employed, than in the subsequent operation of preparing linen cloth from linen yarn. To say nothing of the industry of the flax-growers and flax-dressers, three or four spinners, at least, are necessary, in order to keep one weaver in constant employment; and more than four-fifths of the whole quantity of labour, necessary for the preparation of linen cloth, is employed in that of linen yarn ...' (608–9). It would appear that Smith is concerned with the consequences of free imports of a labour-intensive product. Yet according to our interpretation this should be of no concern to him.

The sequel to the passage, however, explains Smith's position. In the first place, it is clear that the free importation of spun yarn is part of a general program by the linen manufacturers to reinforce both their monopoly and monopsony power in home markets. The free importation of spun yarn cannot be seen or judged as an isolated phenomenon, for what is involved in fact is a general break-down of competition:

but our spinners are poor people, women commonly, scattered about in all different parts of the country, without support or protection. It is not by the sale of their work, but by that of the complete work of the weavers, that our great master manufacturers make their profits. As it is their interest to sell the complete manufacture as dear, so it is to buy the materials as cheap as possible. By extorting from the legislature bounties upon the exportation of their own linen, high duties upon the importation of all foreign linen, and a total prohibition of the home consumption of some sorts of French linen, they endeavour to sell their own goods as dear as possible (609).[65]

Secondly, the lobbyists based their formal case for free imports of materials on high domestic employment and output. Smith may simply be answering them on their own grounds, namely that the effect of extending the proposals to semi-finished goods was the very opposite.[66] This need not be exaggerated to represent a general case for intervention in favour of employment and output. This is indeed analogous to all the other ambiguous instances which seem to reflect Smith's opposition to a particular form of intervention.

Thirdly, there is a very strong suggestion that – either as a result of monopsony-monopoly power, or for some other reasons – Smith was presuming a state of unemployment:

65 Spinning in the case of linen was, according to Smith, typically done by women working part time and domestically (*ibid.*, 116–17).
66 A similar example can be found in Smith's condemnation of restrictions on the exportation of raw materials. One argument was that British wool – an essential ingredient in fine wool manufacture – had to be kept from foreign hands. Smith denied that British wool was in fact an essential ingredient (*ibid.*, 616), implying his support of the restriction in the event that it were. Once again, however, it may be that Smith was replying to the lobbyists on their own terms.

[The manufacturers] are as intent to keep down the wages of their own weavers, as the earnings of the poor spinners, and it is by no means for the benefit of the workman, that they endeavour either to raise the price of the complete work, or to lower that of the rude materials. It is the industry which is carried on for the benefit of the rich and powerful, that is principally encouraged by our mercantile system. That which is carried on for the benefit of the poor and the indigent, is too often, either neglected, or oppressed (609).

In these circumstances it is scarcely surprising to find Smith showing a concern for labour-displacing imports. The reader should compare these passages with Smith's optimistic analysis of an 'honest' program of free trade, that is one which is part of a general abandonment of internal as well as external constraints.[67]

CONCLUSION

To appreciate Smith's formal emphasis upon the employment-generating capacities of alternative investments we must bear in mind that his objective was to assure the removal of actual forms of governmental interference – which had prematurely diverted resources from agriculture and from various trading sectors – on the grounds that a reallocation according to the principle of profit-rate equalization would allow the expansion of employment in the productive sector consistently with an increase of national income. Our objective has been to demonstrate that this argument should not be interpreted as a general recommendation for the expansion of the productive labour force by all means. Assuming an initial allocation reflecting the equality of profit rates, an artificially induced reallocation of a given capital stock from less to more labour-intensive sectors would only diminish national income despite any induced increase in the employment of productive labour. Expansion of national income would be assured only by capital accumulation financed at each period from the 'surplus,' or net income in excess of subsistence.

We have noted, however, a serious dichotomy in the course of the analytical argument designed to explain the pattern of investments, at each stage of development, likely to be achieved in a freely-operating system. While in the case of manufacturing and agriculture the allocative mechanism was based firmly upon factor endowments and changes thereof over time, a less convincing set of alternative principles was adopted in the account of the commercial sector. Apart, therefore, from the potential for misunderstanding of Smith's analytical argument introduced by his particular policy objectives, we must recognize a failure on Smith's part to justify adequately his position regarding the pattern of investment in the case of commercial activity, Moreover, Smith's analysis of investment priorities, in terms of the effects upon profitability of alterations in factor endowments, does not accord easily with his insistence elsewhere – to which Ricardo took great exception – that the burden of wage-cost increases may be avoided by capitalists.

67 See for example, above, 275.

CONCLUSION

Professor Schumpeter in his celebrated critique has written that Adam Smith's function was merely that of co-ordinator whose 'mental stature was up to mastering the unwieldy material that flowed from many sources and to subjecting it, with a strong hand, to the rule of a small number of coherent principles'; there was not 'a single *analytic* idea, principle, or method that was entirely new in 1776.'[1] There is much to be said for viewing the *Wealth of Nations* as a 'synthesis'; but in our view the downplaying of the achievement implied by Schumpeter's formulation is seriously misleading. For the strength of the work lies precisely in its comprehensiveness – unparalleled at the time – which, as Sir Alexander Gray has observed, reflects a transition in economic literature from partisan pamphlet to scientific treatise.[2] This characteristic of the *Wealth of Nations* is reflected not merely in the extraordinary range of topics treated, but also in Smith's demonstration of a high degree of interdependence between apparently unrelated variables culminating in his development of a more or less consistent 'model' of value and distribution. That steps in this direction had already been taken by Hume, Cantillon, Steuart and Quesnay – reflected for example in a sensitivity regarding method and a growing appreciation of the interdependencies of the system of production and exchange and the organizational function of the profit motive – detracts in no way from Smith's achievement. Apart from this, the adoption of pure novelty in analytical technique as the criterion of 'quality' places too much weight upon a comparison of particular Smithian theories – formulated mathematically – with earlier versions, and neglects the weightings of the variables utilized. Essentially the Schumpeterian view tends to play down Smith's use of historical and contemporary data for analytical purposes, although his genius lay in an ability to find hypotheses to fit his impressions of what the

1 See above, 12, n. 32.
2 *Adam Smith, 1723–1790* (London, 1948), 19.

facts were or had been, in which exercise qualitative judgments play a central role.

Indicative of a certain lack of perspective which seems to derive from a preoccupation with novelty is Schumpeter's evaluation of pre-Smithian price theory. All that was lacking, runs the argument, in the analysis of the 'Scholastics' including the later ethical jurists and natural law philosophers – from which Smith's own analysis is said to derive – is the technical apparatus of schedules and the notion of the margin. In our opinion this evaluation is questionable. To _list_ some, or even all, of the elements which enter into the determination of competitive price is one thing and, to _combine_ them into a consistent theory of allocation is quite another; the moralists including Smith's teachers – while recognizing relevant objective and subjective factors – failed to fuse them into a system of price determination with particular emphasis upon a general tendency towards 'equilibrium.' It is in this light that Smith's contribution may be better appreciated. A preliminary analytical solution was initially developed (in his lectures) – in a general rather than partial equilibrium context – in terms of the mechanism of adaptation of supply to demand achieved by alterations in the distribution of labour (the only factor allowed for) which assures that, in the long run, market prices will reflect production costs or, in Smith's words, which assures 'a natural balance of industry.' This analysis was extended in the _Wealth of Nations_ to include capital and land in addition to labour as productive factors entering into the equilibrating process.

The _formal_ analysis of 'general equilibrium' in the _Wealth of Nations_, it is true, is given relatively little attention, and is in some respects narrowly constrained. The analysis suggests that factor ratios were technically determined and identical from sector to sector, raising the question of whether Smith was aware of these assumptions and whether he used them consistently. But the fact is that Smith was not so much concerned with giving a formal statement of general equilibrium as he was to analyse readjustments to changes. It would not be surprising, therefore, if the formal account was no more than a first approximation. Our examination of Smith's general treatment of factor interrelationships _with constant technology_ – particularly in the context of the effects of changes in factor prices – confirms that in the manufacturing sector certain key ratios were in fact held to be _data_. Particularly important are the labour-machinery ratio; the materials-labour ratio; and the materials-output ratio. However, when full allowance is made for 'new-type' technology – for the most part adoptable only at large scale – then the possibility of alteration in the machinery-labour ratio is admitted; for an increase in the size of the 'firm' is frequently said to be accompanied by a rising machinery-labour ratio, the capital goods 'embodying' the technology in question. (Even the rigid materials requirement might be overcome by way of new technology permitting reductions in the maintenance of fixed capital.) These new ratios, it is true, are still technically determined and there is no generalized recognition of factor substitutability; in particular, while labour-saving processes involving a higher fixed capital-labour ratio are adopted – according to Smith – at the same time as wage rates are tending upwards, no causal relationship is defined and their adoption is related to increased scale of operation. Nonetheless, the strict condition of constant proportions is in practice relaxed. In the case of agriculture also, the impression is that variation in the intensity of operating given land areas was allowed for although by no means emphasized. Finally, the implicit assumption of identical technical proportions between sectors, which is characteristic of the formal analysis of general equilibrium, is also not consistently maintained.

Smith was thus not bound by the strict assumptions implicit in the formal analysis. His treatment 'of the natural and market price of commodities' was perhaps not a *deliberate* first approximation; he nowhere draws attention to the contrast between the formal analysis and practical applications. But there can be little doubt that the formal statements of this chapter had a well-defined objective – namely the explanation of the broad principles of resource allocation – and in dealing with particular issues Smith drew upon relationships which do not appear available to him if we limit our attention to his 'model-building.' In brief, Smith did not fully specify his formal model of the price mechanism but certain characteristics of it were developed during the treatment of actual problems. Similarly, the role of demand in allocation can only be fully appreciated if attention is paid to particular applications of a theory of choice.

The main purpose of the *Wealth of Nations* was evidently not to provide an analytic framework for its own sake. The object of the work was ultimately to define the necessary conditions for rapid economic development in contemporary circumstances and Smith's treatment of the price mechanism must accordingly, in the final resort, be considered with this end in view. It is, in brief, not merely the elaboration of the mechanisms of resource allocation which requires attention, but also the particular uses to which the analysis was put, and it is in the course of Smith's treatment of the historical sequence of investment priorities according to the principle of profit-rate equalization, that a fundamental equilibrating mechanism is utilized, namely resource allocation governed by the differential pattern of factor endowments between economies. Despite the overwhelming significance of the mechanism, the reader of the *Wealth of Nations* will find no hint thereof in the First Book. It is rather in the 'applied' chapters, dealing with contemporary restraints on importation and with the colonial trade, that full and skillful use is made of the mechanism, casting a new light upon Smith's contribution to both theoretical and applied economics.[3] Smith's fundamental concern in the *Wealth of*

3 The contrast between formal statements and practical applications can be further illustrated. The main sectoral differences which are formally recognized in the Second Book are those between agriculture, manufactures, and trade. Differences within manufacturing in the fixed-circulating capital ratio, and differences within either manufactures, or agriculture in the turnover rate of capital are ruled out. Yet in several practical applications such differences do play a part.

Nations was with economic development defined in terms of (real) national income per head. His objective was to demonstrate that reliance upon the free operation of the competitive mechanisms of resource allocation would assure the maximization at any time of the national income generated by the community's given resources, including the force of 'productive labourers,' that is, of labourers in the capitalist sector; it is indeed precisely the assumption of full employment which assured the key role accorded to the micro-economic problems of resource allocation in the *Wealth of Nations*. But what is of particular relevance is Smith's demonstration that during the course of development the community's factor endowments are likely to alter, thereby generating a differential pattern of optimal allocation, in an international setting, from period to period. Demonstration of the non-chaotic nature of the competitive price mechanism was certainly not new with Smith, but the extension thereof to encompass the effects of differential factor proportions upon the pattern of activity superseded even Hume's contribution, which (like that of Gervaise) hinged upon *qualitative* factor differentials between nations. (Benjamin Franklin and Josiah Tucker may have been closer to Smith in this particular respect.) And the application of the principle to the problem of investment priorities *over time* with specific reference to contemporary policy issues represents a formidable achievement; there is much truth in Gray's observation that there is in the *Wealth of Nations* 'no distinction between economic science and economic art.'[4]

The outcome of our argument thus far is that Smith's analysis cannot be adequately appreciated apart from its precise applications. The conclusion is reinforced by consideration of Smith's approach to government intervention as a means of achieving rapid economic expansion. The maximization in each period of national income (or given population of national income per head) guaranteed the greatest achievable surplus – income over subsistence – available for taxation purposes, for capital accumulation, and for current consumption. (In Smith's view the purchaser of services merely transferred to the worker his own 'right' to consume commodities.) It is, of course, capital accumulation which represents in the *Wealth of Nations* the key element in the growth mechanism. Increased investment was essential both as a means of

A similar interpretation may be suggested for Smith's treatment of the wages-fund theory. The formal analysis suggests that changes in the wage rate cannot exert an influence on the total wage bill, a constraint that is only true if factor proportions are identical everywhere and technologically determined. If these assumptions are taken seriously, then crucial obstacles exist in the way of full employment. But these problems were not necessarily obvious to Smith, and, in fact, it seems from our study to be the case that Smith was unaware of the implicit assumptions of his formal analysis.

See too G.J. Stigler, 'The Classical Economics: An Alternative View,' *Five Lectures on Economic Problems* (London, 1949), 25–36 which distinguishes (in a case study relating to Nassau Senior's analysis in the hand-loom weaver report) between the 'working technique' and the 'formal theory' of classical economists.

4 *Adam Smith*, 20.

raising productivity – the capital-deepening process – and as a necessary condition for the expansion of the capitalist sector – the capital-widening process. Since the latter process allowed the achievement of scale economies, we conclude that the emphasis, in this case too, was largely upon expanding aggregate income as a means of raising *per capita* income.

Expansion of the 'productive' sector – capital widening – required not only an increased capital stock but also an addition to the available work force in that sector. However, Smith's vision of the contemporary British economy was not one of unemployment or of such rapid population growth that it was possible to take for granted in the Ricardian manner, even as a first approximation, the availability of 'infinite' supplies of labour at the subsistence level. The requisite supply would therefore have to be derived either from the service sector, or from natural population growth in response to average wages in excess of subsistence. In this regard it is essential to recall Smith's assumption of a degree of immobility on the part of service labour (preventing the equalization of wage rates between sectors); and also his assumption that the population mechanism – which received particular attention – applied only to workers in the productive sector. These assumptions imply strongly that Smith accorded greater significance to population expansion as the source of the labour supply required to assure an expansion of the productive sector than to any transfer from the service sector although the latter was certainly not ruled out. The relative significance of the service sector would accordingly fall with economic growth even if its absolute size remained unchanged.

What, however, was categorically ruled out by Smith as a means of raising productive employment was any redirection, by governmental intervention, of a *given* capital stock towards relatively labour-intensive branches of the productive sector. Such intervention, it was expected, must be abortive and in fact must reduce national income *even when an increase in the productive labour force was assured*. For the objective was not simply the expansion of employment of productive labour. Expansion by way of distorting the competitive allocation of resources, Smith insisted, must *reduce* the national income and it is the growth of national income, or more specifically, national income per head, that was the relevant objective of policy.

In this respect Smith's position is in sharp contrast with that of his mercantilist predecessors, whose vision was, in the large, one of unemployment or underemployment both voluntary and involuntary. Their concern with the absorption of surplus labour is clear from their repeated proposals for make-work projects and the disciplining of the work force. The national importance of the colonies, of various raw materials, of different forms of trading, of trade with different countries, of different domestic spending patterns, were all evaluated in terms of their effects upon domestic employment. (Hume too, it may be remarked, tended to assume unemployment in his monetary analysis and on grounds of employment was not a free trader.) Now Smith of course also distinguished between sectors on the basis of their employment-generating capacities, but in our view it would be a fundamental misjudgment to regard this discussion as a mercantilist 'residue.' His object was to counter actual forms of governmental interference which had prematurely diverted resources away from the agricultural sector. He pointed in fact to the underutilization of land in Britain and on the continent as evidence of this; conversely, he called for greater investment in the carrying trade – the least 'labour-intensive' category – in the event that the profit rate indicated its desirability. In brief, in contemporary circumstances, the productive labour force might indeed be increased consistently with an increase of national income, but this would result in consequence of the *removal* of impediments to competitive resource allocation. The argument frequently made in the secondary literature that the Smithian logic calls for the redirection of capital to labour-intensive sectors, because the principle of profit-rate equalization generates too little investment in agriculture and too much in manufacturing and trade, in terms of employment, does not apply and the charge of serious inconsistency in the *Wealth of Nations* in this respect is unjustified.

Smith has also frequently been charged with serious inconsistency on the grounds that he condemned mercantilist protection while maintaining an equivocating interest in defence and power. It is indeed sometimes suggested that 'nationalism' was the overriding criterion, so that inconsistency is a misnomer; whatever policy was deemed suitable for the 'national interest' was recommended. Our study suggests that neither interpretation is adequate. It may be accurate to ascribe to Smith an overriding concern with national power; but this in his view would best be achieved by those competitive processes which assured the maximization of the surplus – rather than by intervention in support of particular sectors – whereby the *potential* for national defence at each period is maximized. Of equal significance is the fact that in the few cases where intervention in support of particular industries or branches of commerce was recommended the economic cost involved was defined quite explicitly. In both respects, therefore, Smith's reference is ultimately to the market mechanism.

Moreover, with regard to the extent and nature of legitimate intervention at the ports, Smith after all was recommending the replacement of a set of heavy protective devices by a less severe set designed largely for the raising of revenue; evidently it seemed desirable to keep in mind as far as possible, during any reform, the likely consequences for growth of duties or taxes – in any event necessitated for revenue purposes – and to utilize this intelligence in the choice of commodities upon which they would be levied. Similarly, Smith's occasional references to the maintenance of British superiority in foreign markets need not be considered a 'mercantilist residue.' It was obviously necessary to avoid imposing revenue-raising devices which would place British industry at a *disadvantage* in world markets. Smith's proposals represent a significant relaxation in light of the heavy protective duties then current; and it must always be recalled that the recommended reform, it was expected, would be undertaken unilaterally.

It is in this context that Smith's prudential and practical approach to reform may best be appreciated. We have noted his insistence that protective duties and prohibitions must be relaxed slowly in order to avoid sudden and heavy unemployment; his concession that a degree of control over corn exports would be justified in order to assure 'the public tranquility' and perhaps as a retaliatory device; and his justification of retaliatory duties as a means of forcing the removal of those imposed abroad on domestic products. While he ridiculed the interventionist schemes of the 'man of system' he conceded the need to call upon the services of 'that insidious and crafty animal, vulgarly called a statesman or politician, whose councils are directed by the momentary fluctuations of affairs.'[5] But there is a world of difference between this prudential outlook and typical mercantilist recommendations.

One crucial category of intervention, however, found some favour in Smith's estimation (apart, of course, from 'defence, justice and public works'), namely fiscal devices designed to alter the pattern of expenditure in favour of investment and at the cost of luxury consumption. The argument for some intervention by fiscal means was much strengthened by Smith's ambivalent attitude, held in common with Hume and others, towards 'excessive' consumption (by all classes). At the same time, despite an evident concern with development, Smith's continual references to the 'natural rights' of men not to be disturbed represents a significant, though not absolute, constraint upon the extent to which intervention directed towards patterns of expenditure between investment and consumption might be justified.

It may at this point be worth remarking that our interpretation is not intended to imply a denial of a frequent appeal to what constitutes, at least from the economic point of view, '*a priori*' arguments.[6] We have encountered numerous instances, such as the contention that 'as to cultivate the ground was the original destination of man, so in every state of his existence he seems to retain a predilection for this primitive employment,' or that the ultimate basis for exchange lies in the propensity of mankind 'to truck, barter, and exchange one thing for another.'[7] The point, however, is that on the whole such appeals can be discarded while the analytical structure remains intact.

A fundamental conclusion of this study is that it is as misleading to regard the British economy of Smith's day as basically 'agricultural' as it is to ascribe to it the features of a highly industrialized, capital-intensive economy. The agricultural sector itself was actually one of the most capital-intensive sectors,

5 Adam Smith, *Wealth of Nations*, 435.
6 Moreover, the institutional framework essential for the efficient operation of the price mechanism must be kept in mind throughout. Indispensable accounts are given by N. Rosenberg, 'Some Institutional Aspects of the *Wealth of Nations*,' *Journal of Political Economy*, LXVIII (Dec. 1960) ; and Warren J. Samuels, *The Classical Theory of Economic Policy* (Cleveland, 1966).
7 For some peculiar Smithian *obiter dicta* see Arthur H. Cole, 'Puzzles of the *Wealth of Nations*,' *Canadian Journal of Economics and Political Science*, XXIV (Feb. 1958), 1–8.

and structural change within the manufacturing sector was transforming the nature of the economy. It is clear from Smith's account both of the industry structure and of technological change that he was aware of the beginnings of a transition; and it is the trend which matters. We have attempted to show in fact that Smith recognized and dealt with many of the important technological developments prior to 1776 (with the significant exception of those occurring in the cotton industry) basing his analysis in part upon the economic pressures exerted by changing relative prices. On balance, in light of the attention paid to the determinants of industrial organization, to fixed capital and its maintenance, to the sources of knowledge, and to the differential factor-saving effects of various innovations, we reject the charge that he failed to 'anticipate' the industrial revolution.

Bearing in mind both the role accorded by Smith to the price mechanism in economic development and the analysis of the process of technological progress we may evaluate the relevance of the alleged 'Corn Model' as an accurate representation of Smithian growth theory. In our view the model does not seem appropriate; in fact it would be more suitable for the analysis of the seventeenth-century than the mid-eighteenth-century economy. For it neglects the production function in manufacturing; the significance of raw materials – which in many respects played an even more important role than food in capital as a constraint upon employment – receives no attention; and there is no place for fixed capital and accordingly for almost the entire Smithian process of 'embodied' technical change.[8]

Now we do not intend to deny that Smith frequently accorded particular significance – both quantitative and qualitative – to basic 'necessaries.' We have in mind the unique treatment of price determination in the case of corn; the close relationship defined between corn prices, money wages and commodity prices; the dependence of population growth upon corn supplies; and the wages-fund theory. But Smith was keenly aware of rising working-class living standards in contemporary Britain and of the complications which this entailed. When he utilised corn as *numéraire*, for example, it was because it served better than any alternative but not because it was satisfactory in its own right. The degree of sophistication which characterised working-class budgets rendered quite inadequate any simple set of causal relations. Thus the fact that the real counterpart of money wages could not in practise be

8 The growth rate of the economy – defined algebraically above (18, n. 50) as $k(p/w)$ — 1 – will *in practice* depend upon the relationship between the distribution of the initial stock of wages goods between productive and service labour; the average productivity of labour; and the average wage rate. Unless the order of magnitude of these variables can be given, scarcely anything has been achieved by the mathematical formulation. But it is precisely at this point that the real problems of interpretation arise. For example, while the response of population to wage increases above 'subsistence' was certainly taken into account, much emphasis is placed upon upward pressures on the wage rate, due to scarcity of labour supplies, during a period of expansion. And increased productivity cannot be relied upon to counterbalance exactly increases in wages. We cannot presume that Smith was concerned with a regularly progressive economy and must accordingly examine the precise determinants of productivity and average wages.

reduced to basic necessaries threatened the entire population mechanism and suggested to Smith a possible case for the utilization of excise taxes to induce a change in the pattern of consumption. The reaction of population to high average wages was further complicated by the differential patterns of behaviour on the part of labour in the capitalist and the non-capitalist sectors. It would not, therefore, be legitimate to ascribe to Smith use of models incorporating relatively invariant functional relationships and constant conditions since this abstracts from the very problem which concerned him, namely the 'balance' of forces relevant in particular circumstances.[9] To neglect these complications is to neglect some of the essentials of Smith's economics. Finally, it must be repeated that the special role accorded corn at various stages of the argument positively did not preclude an overwhelming concern with the allocation of resources.

Smith's awareness of contemporary technological and sociological developments, we have concluded, was more profound than is sometimes implied. A few words are in order regarding the state of governmental intervention, for it is frequently suggested that Smith failed to appreciate the contemporary process of rapid decay of internal governmental regulation. Our investigation confirms an exaggeration, on Smith's part, of the severity of regulation, but at the same time indicates some recognition of a diminution in control. Smith's overstatement of the degree of internal regulation may certainly have been simply an error of judgment; the evidence was subject to conflicting interpretation by contemporary authorities. But it may also have been deliberate to some degree. Smith, of course, much feared monopolistic and monopsonistic tendencies, which were, in his view, likely in the last resort to be incurable. From this point of view even occasional cases of legal support were reprehensible in the extreme.[10] Allowance must also be made for his a priori principle in favour of free trade based once again upon the 'natural right' of individuals not to be interfered with. While we do not intend to deny a certain 'empirical' or 'utilitarian' outlook – apparently sufficiently powerful to have led Smith to remain silent on a number of burning social issues of the day – there can be little doubt that the principle of natural liberty played an important role in the present case, implying indeed the belief that an appeal in such terms would not fall upon deaf ears. We have, for example, noted his severe condemnation of British interference with economic activity in the colonies despite a belief that the regulations happened to be ineffectual. And the case against the settlement laws contained a similar appeal: the attempt at regulation of the labour market is 'evidently as impertinent as it is oppressive.'[11]

We have observed that when allowance is made for Smith's overriding concern with contemporary issues it is possible to detect a greater degree of consistency

---

9 For this same view, see J.J. Spengler, 'Adam Smith's Theory of Economic Growth – Part II,' *Southern Economic Journal*, XXVI (July 1951), 5.

10 Cf. *Wealth of Nations*, 128–9; 141–2 in particular.

11 *Ibid.*, 122.

in the *Wealth of Nations* than may be apparent at first sight. Thus the serious charge that the Smithian analysis of profit-rate equalization conflicts with that of differential employment-generating capacities of alternative investments is unjustified, for it neglects to take into account distortions in the pattern of activity the correction of which was Smith's objective. Similarly, there is little justification for a charge of inconsistency regarding the broad issue of priorities in national policy. But there remains an element of truth in the observation that 'consistency was not his shining virtue.'[12] A striking instance is the implication of the existence of unused resources in the 'vent-for-surplus' theory of trade, which contrasts with the assumption of full employment of capital and labour implied in the theory based upon 'absolute advantage.' It is true that Smith was engaged in a critique of policies and proposals formally designed to raise employment; we must keep in mind that he was writing a 'tract for the time,' and could better make his case if he could prove his opponents wrong using *their* criteria of policy. Yet it is difficult to resolve entirely the disaccord in this fashion, and we conclude that the alternative approaches to trade based on differing sets of implicit assumptions are not satisfactorily reconciled. (At the same time, the importance of the vent-for-surplus doctrine should not be exaggerated, for it frequently is utilized simply to explain the function of wholesale traders and, in this context, it may be used together with any theory which accounts for regional specialization.)

It is essential to consider the relation between Smith's theory of vent-for-surplus and the so-called 'Smith-Turgot theorem on savings' with an eye to their compatibility. Smith's eulogy of the advantages of capital accumulation, his correspondingly negative attitude towards luxury consumption, and his insistence that the process of savings involves no leakage from the income stream constitute fundamental divergencies from traditional mercantilist positions, although tentative steps in this direction had already been taken, for example, by Hutcheson. For despite their 'doctrine of thrift' mercantilist writers, on the whole, gave qualified assent to the requirement for luxury consumption as a means of assuring a high level of activity. While the Physiocrats also tended to show a formal concern with hoarding and emphasized the necessity for consumption in the interest of productive activity, their position can only be appreciated within the specific context of the French doctrine. It was Turgot, however, who stated with particular clarity that the process of accumulation did not involve any attempt to add to money hoards.

The 'vent-for-surplus' theory has been described as a 'surviving relic of the Mercantile Theory' by J.S. Mill, for international trade – according to orthodox classical doctrine – permits the more efficient use of capital and labour and does not absorb into productive activity resources otherwise idle. But it must be noted that Smith's theorem on savings merely implies that no attempt is made to add to money balances from sales proceeds thus, in principle,

12 A.L. Macfie, *The Individual in Society: Papers on Adam Smith* (London, 1967), 68. Professor Macfie extends the observation generally to eighteenth-century writers, especially members of the Scottish sociological school (*ibid.*, 126).

precluding 'monetary' causes of unemployment and excess capacity; it does not rule out other possible causes. In fact the rationalization for excess capacity in a closed economy suggested by Smith's discussion relates to a severe degree of specificness attributed to domestic resources and high inelasticity attributed to domestic demand for those *particular* products which can technically be produced. There is, therefore, no necessary conflict between the vent-for-surplus doctrine and the theorem on savings.

Smith's forecast of a downward secular trend in the average profit rate with capital accumulation also requires attention in the present context. We have seen that the argument already referred to by Hume and Massie was formally based upon the notion of 'increasing competition.' But this argument was supplemented by a suggestion that an increasing paucity of investment opportunities lies at the root of the problem (although the only instance given of what he might have had in mind appears in a loose formulation of diminishing returns at the extensive margin in agriculture). An explanation along these lines does not, in principle, conflict with the Smith-Turgot theorem. It is true that the profit-rate decline, in Smith's view, might be checked by the acquisition of 'new markets,' but the argument relates to the diversion of *fully utilized* capital towards more profitable branches of activity thus raising the average rate, rather than to the absorption into use of hitherto *idle* capacity. While in our view the position does not necessarily conflict with the orthodox 'law of markets,' classical writers frequently insisted that it did[13] and Ricardo in particular was unable to accept a view of the economic system which envisaged variations in the secular rate of profit unrelated to inverse variations in the real cost of producing wage goods.[14]

Yet there remains one related phenomenon which appears to be in conflict with the Smith-Turgot theorem. The predicted decline in the rate of profit (and accordingly the natural rate of interest) with increasing accumulation is said ultimately to lead to the stationary state where there occurs no further net investment (and accordingly no new stimulus to an expansion of population). But Smith at the same time much emphasized the tendency, in the normal course of development, for increasing investment to be made in the carrying trade which, it will be recalled, 'is altogether withdrawn from supporting the productive labour of that particular country, to support that of some foreign countries.' Moreover, note is also taken on occasion of direct foreign investment undertaken by various European nations with relatively low rates of interest. If we understand Smith correctly, it would appear to be the case that, at least in an open economy, saving may be undertaken which is not reflected in net domestic investment. Our point is not simply that subsequent effects playing back on the domestic economy are not investigated by Smith, but rather that the existence of a potentially serious conflict with the fundamental proposition regarding the nature of saving is nowhere given formal recognition.

13 Cf. Donald Winch, *Classical Political Economy and Colonies* (London, 1965), 30–1, 42–4, 81–5.
14 *Principles of Political Economy,* 344–6.

Smith's physiocratic contemporaries approached the problem of economic growth in terms similar to those of the *Wealth of Nations*, insofar as the emphasis is upon accumulation of capital envisaged as 'advances' permitting time-consuming activity, and maximization of the community's disposable surplus – by attention to 'efficiency' in allocation – as the source of new capital. Moreover, in both Smithian and physiocratic economics (and earlier, in the work of Cantillon), in sharp contrast with traditional mercantilist doctrine, population size fell away as an immediate objective of policy. The general unconcern with the magnitude of population as such is reflected, in part, by the fact that neither Smith nor the Physiocrats showed any concern for the potential 'loss' of population to the colonies such as was feared by some contemporaries; much more attention was paid, by Smith, to the outward flow of capital. This position was indeed maintained at a time not far removed from the Stuart rebellion when it might have been expected that concern for a large body of yeomen would have preoccupied him.

Smith's possible 'debt' to the Physiocrats has been the subject of considerable debate, although perhaps what is really important is how much Smith accepted of the French analysts, rather than his debt to them. Professor Cannan has suggested, largely on the basis of close examination of the contrasts between the *Lectures* and the *Wealth of Nations*, that while Smith's distinction between productive and unproductive labour, the thesis that productive labour is maintained from capital advances, the distributive scheme, and the concept of annual produce, seem to have been influenced by his contact with and knowledge of the French economists, his analyses of the division of labour, of price, and of the wage structure were developed independently. Of particular significance, the general case for economic liberalism had long been adopted.[15] But even Cannan's limited attributions are probably exaggerated. There is in the *Lectures* perhaps more attention paid to the role of capital in permitting time-consuming processes than Cannan is prepared to concede, and the issue is touched upon, as we have seen, by Hutcheson, Oswald and Tucker. Several of Smith's immediate predecessors, including Cantillon and Steuart, were placing increasing emphasis upon productive capital as distinct from purely commercial capital opening the road towards a view of profits as a class income received not only by merchants but by

15 E. Cannan, 'Editor's Introduction,' *Lectures on Justice, Police, Revenue and Arms* (New York, 1964), xxviii–xxxi; 'Editor's Introduction,' *Wealth of Nations*, xxxviii–xliii, and Cannan, *A Review of Economic Theory* (London, 1929), 291f.

At the outset of the *Wealth of Nations*, in the 'Plan of Work,' Smith stated that the growth of national product depended more upon the *efficiency* with which productive labour is used than the relative proportion of the labour force in the productive and service sectors (*ibid.*, lvii–lviii). Cannan has implied (*Lectures*, xxix; *Wealth of Nations*, xli) that this weighting suggests that the great emphasis upon productive labour of Book II – accorded to physiocratic influence – had not yet been achieved when the plan was formulated. Yet it must be borne in mind that capital accumulation was essential for the embodiment of new technology as well as for the support of additional productive labour.

capitalist-employers generally. While the basic physiocratic theory implies that only capital invested in agriculture is capable of generating a net return it was Smith's position (and that of Turgot) that a net revenue is yielded in *all* spheres of activity (although the source of the return in the mercantile sector, it will be recalled, is explained by Smith in terms of the traditional principle of 'alienation'). There is, moreover, some evidence that Smith may have drawn upon the work of James Oswald in his division of cost-price into the component parts of rent, wages and profits which constitutes the basis for the distribution of the entire national income between aggregate rent, wages and profits, and the natural-price doctrine was discussed by William Temple in 1758.

But whatever the extent and nature of Smith's 'debts' the fact is that the Physiocrats were severely constrained by their characteristic doctrines regarding agriculture as the sole wealth-creating activity. Equally significant, inadequate attention was paid to the mechanism whereby resources would be allocated in a freely-operating system and it is difficult to escape the impression that their support for free trade both internally and externally as a necessary precondition of rapid development was not based securely upon a well-constructed analytical foundation. There is also justification for the view that their policy proposals were designed as a device to counter the contemporary pattern of intervention but would have been much qualified in other circumstances. This is above all true of their recommendation for free trade in corn, which was, it would appear, maintained conditionally in light of France's circumstance as a net corn exporter. The Physiocrats, in brief, made appeal to a 'superior' principle, namely the effect of policy upon the price and quantity of agricultural produce. By contrast, Smith's 'agricultural bias' did not lead to much distortion in his applied economics and his policy proposals in support of free trade were more firmly based upon the allocative processes of the competitive price system. Yet we have shown also that Smith did not do full justice to his case in favour of non-intervention when envisaged from the point of view of a developing country poorly endowed with natural resources or one which, although adequately endowed, has entered belatedly into competition with other, relatively advanced, 'landed' nations.

It is further argued by Cannan that Smith – particularly by his use of a theory of capital and productive labour, and by his appendage of a scheme of distribution to an existing theory of price – 'settled the form of economic treatises for a century at least.'[16] But if this view is considered closely it will be seen to be only partially adequate. Ricardo was not much concerned with the issue of productive and unproductive labour; he diverged markedly in the analyses of price, the 'measure of value,' distribution, and the profit-rate trend; it is not even clear whether some of his discussions – such as that of machinery – were in any way related to micro-economic decision-making units, whether in other words they fall within the 'paradigm' of competitive allocation theory. Even where the Smithian approach accords with that of his successors, it

16 'Introduction,' *Wealth of Nations*, xxxix.

was frequently misunderstood. This is revealed in the charge by McCulloch that the analysis of investment priorities conflicted with the principles of profit-rate equalization; and also in the related, mistaken, belief of Ricardo that Smith championed a large gross revenue. And Smith's recognition of the role of differential factor endowments as a rationale for international trade, and of changes therein over time as an explanation of temporal variations in optimal resource allocation went unnoticed. The impression left upon Smith's successors by the *precise* details of his allocative mechanism, or the *precise* relationship envisaged between the theory of competitive resource allocation and economic development was thus scarcely an extensive one.

Yet there remains an important element of truth in Cannan's proposition. The *general* case in favour of laissez-faire and the *general* workings of the competitive process in assuring a tendency towards the establishment of equilibrium wage-rate and profit-rate structures, and the analysis of the relationship between market and cost prices, represent without question a vital link with the future. Moreover, Smith's early nineteenth-century successors had conveniently available to them what appeared already to be a body of 'received doctrine' upon which they could draw, and of equal importance to which they could direct their critical attention; for without doubt, Smith presented an extensive body of economics in a manner which they found supremely worthwhile. In particular, Ricardo's analytical structure relating to distribution was formulated in direct response to that of Smith. It is, in our view, impossible to appreciate the Ricardian innovations without keeping to the fore Smith's formulation of the problem to be solved – the effect of wage-rate changes upon profits – and Smith's own solution.

In matters of aggregative economic theory a number of precise relationships may also be discerned. The conception of capital as 'advances'; the view of the savings process as proceeding in a 'hitchless' fashion; the minimization of the monetary determination of the interest rate; the specification of the relationship between the rates of growth of capital and population as the key determinant of working-class living standards are matters which come to occupy the centre of the stage. Equally important regarding the fundamental matters of method and of ultimate objective, Hume, Smith, and the nineteenth-century classical writers – as Lord Robbins has emphasized – had in common a critical concern not merely with social reform but with reform based upon a systematic body of scientific knowledge.[17] The precise theoretical structures utilized certainly differ from case to case and may have been more or less soundly constructed, but the mode of operation and the general objective – the improved welfare of the working-class in particular – was shared by all.

Our discussion leads on to the relationship between Smithian and Marxian analysis. The characteristic element of Smith's work which is most attractive to scholars in the Marxian tradition is his extension of physiocratic doctrine to allow for the generation of surplus-value in *all* sectors: 'The special feature

17 *Theory of Economic Policy*, 169f.

of the [Smithian] pattern which marked it off from those put forward by earlier economists was the inclusion of *profit on capital* as a general category of class income which accrued to all who used "stock" in the employment of wage-labour, and which was qualitatively distinct both from the rent of land and from the wages of labour.'[18] More specifically, if we consider Smith's occasional attribution to *labour* of the ability to generate surplus value – at least in industry and trade – together with the classification of Book II, chapter v which distinguished sectors according to their respective 'constant' and 'variable' – as distinct from 'fixed' and 'circulating' – elements in a given capital stock we are even faced, in principle, with the Marxian problem of profit-rate equalization. For if profits are in some sense a deduction from labour's contribution and if labour-capital ratios differ between sectors, Marx's issue makes an appearance. Smith, of course, never recognized the problem but it lurks in the shadows.

But even when – as is usually the case in the *Wealth of Nations* – a value-creating ability is accorded to land and capital, the moral justification of property income is questioned. Smith's recommendations, it must at the same time be emphasized, imply a 'reformist' rather than a 'revolutionary' propensity; there is no call for confiscatory measures or any interference with private property rights, despite explicit statements to the effect that 'the affluence of the few supposes the indigence of the many,'[19] or that 'civil government, so far as it is instituted for the security of property, is in reality instituted for the defence of the rich against the poor, or of those who have some property against those who have none at all.'[20] Without doubt Smith (and Hume too) took a hard-headed approach to any schemes for equality in the distribution of wealth; and in the case at hand one may discern (even within the narrow scope of purely economic issues and apart from certain desirable social characteristics attributed by Smith to capitalism in general, and – to a degree – to inequality in particular) a very practical reason for the failure to draw the 'logical' conclusions from such striking observations. Smith was conscious that Britain could not be viewed as an isolated island; any excessive taxation of income would simply assure the transfer of capital elsewhere. This was certainly the basis for his warning against the taxation of pure interest. On the whole, a case might be made according to which Smith championed the *allocative* function of the price mechanism while at the same time he was dissatisfied with the distributional implications thereof. The dilemma was resolved above all by the absence of any practicable alternative to the process of capital accumulation as then undertaken by the recipients of interest and rent, which process in fact provided the best assurance in the circumstances that the labouring classes too would partake of the benefits of economic development. Thus

18 R.L.Meek, 'Adam Smith and the Classical Theory of Profit,' in Meek, *Economics and Ideology and Other Essays* (London, 1967), 18. The contrast with the *Lectures* is emphasized in 'The Physiocratic Concept of Profit,' *ibid.*, 306.
19 *Wealth of Nations*, 670.
20 *Ibid.*, 674. Cf. *Lectures*, 15.

Smith's allowances for monopsony pressure, which in principle imply a rejection of population restraint as the primary solution for depressed living standards, were of little practical relevance during a period of secular expansion such as Smith envisaged. It is equally essential to take into account Smith's outline of the measures which might legitimately be undertaken by the state to alleviate some of the worst defects of the contemporary system.

APPENDIXES

Eighteenth-century population and national income data

Estimates of eighteenth-century population in three years for England and Wales[1] are: 6,569,000 (1761); 7,052,000 (1771); and 7,531,000 (1781).

Estimates for Scotland are for 1751 and 1791 respectively: 1,250,000 (1751); and 1,500,000 (1791). If we assume that population increased steadily over these decades in Scotland we can estimate total British population as follows:

	England and Wales	Scotland	Britain
1761	6,569,000	c.1,312,000	c.7,881,000
1771	7,052,000	c.1,375,000	c.8,427,000
1781	7,531,000	c.1,437,000	c.8,968,000

According to this rough estimate, British population at the time of the *Lectures* would be some 8 million, rather than 10 million as presumed by Smith.

The estimates of population by Smith's contemporaries Arthur Young (1770) and Joseph Massie (1759) – for England and Wales alone – were 7 million and 6½ million respectively.[2]

It should be noted that Smith himself recognized that his estimate of £10 as the average annual income per head in the early sixties was an *understatement* of the true figure. (The calculations of Joseph Massie for 1759, in the case of England and Wales – when corrected for omissions – imply a total national income of £80–90m relative to a population of 6½ million, that is, an average of £12–13 per head.[3])

Because the calculation of £100m as the total national income (given in the *Lectures*) is based upon an exaggerated population estimate, it is difficult to

---

1 P. Deane and W.A. Cole, *British Economic Growth, 1688–1959*, 2nd ed. (Cambridge, 1967), 6.
2 *Ibid.*, 279.   3 *Ibid.*

reconstruct, on Smith's terms, a figure for the mid-seventies. Nevertheless using Smith's exaggerated 10 million as a population base, and allowing for an approximate 7 per cent increase in population from the early sixties to the mid-seventies,[4] we arrive at a population estimate for Britain of some 10.7 million. Smith was fully aware of rising average incomes during the period after the Seven Years' War; but assuming that average incomes remained unchanged at his estimate for the early sixties of £10 per head, we arrive at an aggregate income for 1775 of £107m. In this case the share of agriculture would amount to 56 per cent. If we allow some increase in income per head, and therefore in aggregate income, the proportion would be closer to 50 per cent. It must be emphasized that these calculations are an attempt to arrive at the implied estimates of Smith.

(Estimates by Arthur Young – corrected for omissions – imply a total income for England and Wales alone of approximately £130m in *circa* 1770, with population at 7 million and an average income of some £19 per head. The enormous disparity between the Massie data and the Young data is, write Deane and Cole, 'a fair measure of their failure to inform on the precise level of money incomes in the period immediately before industrialization began to gather a modern momentum.')[5]

4 *Ibid.*, 288.
5 *Ibid.*, 279.

The national product of England and Wales *c.* 1770
(after Arthur Young)

	£m	% total national product
I *Agriculture*		
1 Arable crops	41.734	
2 Timber and copse wood	4.195	
3 Livestock	26.172	
4 Wool	3.199	
5 Hay sold off farms	3.926	
6 Gross output of agriculture	79.226	
7 Less seed, materials bought from artisans, depreciation of draught cattle, maintenance of farm buildings, tythes and rates	21.056	
8 Net value added in agriculture	58.170	45
II *Manufactures*		
9 Wool	5.000	
10 Leather	4.000	
11 Mineral manufactures	6.000	
12 Flax, hemp, glass, earthenware	2.000	
13 Cotton and silk	2.000	
14 All other, including rural artisans supplying agriculture	7.493	
15 Net value added by manufacture	26.493	21
III *Commerce*		
16 Artisans and shopkeepers	6.500	
17 Foreign commerce and shipping	10.000	
18 Other	0.500	
19 Total value added in commerce	17.000	13
IV *Miscellaneous*		
20 Inland fisheries, parks, mines	1.805	
21 Interest	5.000	
22 Public revenue incomes	5.724	
23 Law, medicine, arts	5.000	
24 Rents of houses	4.000	
25 Clergy	4.624	
26 Total miscellaneous incomes	26.153	20
V *Total National Output*	127.816	

Source: P. Deane, 'The Implications of Early National Income Estimates for the Measurement of Long-Term Economic Growth in the United Kingdom,' *Economic Development and Cultural Change*, IV (1955–6),21.

Some growth rates

Tentative data based on contemporary estimates[1] suggest that the average growth rate of the wool industry was some 8 per cent per decade, 1700–41; and some 13–14 per cent per decade 1741–72. Thereafter, the growth rate fell. A striking feature of Scottish development is the growth of the linen industry in the early part of the eighteenth century; but the growth rate declined after 1763. The larger English linen industry followed a similar pattern (although the growth rate was lower), and the industry may actually have suffered a decline in the last quarter of the eighteenth century. In the case of silk a marked expansion occurred in the period 1740–80 but was then checked. In brief, the traditional branches of the textile industry as a whole reached a crucial turning point in the mid-1740s.

Expansion was checked in the last decades of the century, tending to offset partially the phenomenal growth of the cotton industry after 1775. But the cotton revolution may be said to represent a 'continuation' or a 'restoration' of a growth rate initiated in the 1740s: 'It may be doubted whether the rise was more significant than the earlier upsurge which resulted from less spectacular but more widespread changes which affected all branches of the textile industry in the middle of the century.'[2]

As far as the factual record in the case of mining and metals is concerned, it is to be noted that the really rapid growth of Britain's capital goods' industries (iron and steel) dates from the 1780s. The growth rate from 1757 to 1788 was less than 40 per cent per decade while from 1788–1806 it was 100 per cent per decade. But other branches of mining and metallurgy did expand

---

1 P. Deane and W.A. Cole, *British Economic Growth, 1688–1959*, 2nd ed. (Cambridge, 1967), 52f.
2 *Ibid.*, 55.

significantly earlier. Particularly important are the non-ferrous metals: tin,[3] and copper. In fact, the mining and smelting of copper was Britain's major metal industry during the period 1750–75. A rapid increase in coal production also dates from the 1740s. These data add to the view that 'the beginning of rapid industrial growth must be sought before the last quarter of the century.'[4] The pattern is similar in building where rapid growth is recorded after mid-century.

The above course of events is confirmed by the fact that foreign trade was growing faster than the output of the major export industries in the two decades 1725–45. Most of the increase in wrought iron was then exported; and the home consumption of copper and brass even fell during this period while exports rose. Thereafter, the export growth rate fell and in coal, copper and brass the general expansion outstripped the advance in exports. All these trends imply that home developments were absorbing the metals.

On the whole, while it is possible that the pattern after 1745 reflected cyclical and not secular growth – representing only a general upturn after a downswing during the second quarter of the century – there is strong evidence to support the view of secular growth, since even in the early years of the eighteenth century and the late years of the seventeenth there are signs of expansion.

The evidence thus suggests modest progress in the early eighteenth century (1700–25) which was checked, but then followed by a general and stronger expansion after 1745: 'All this does not mean that there was no acceleration in the rate of growth in the eighties and nineties. But it does mean, as the trade statistics suggest, that the acceleration was at least a two-phase process, and that its origins must be sought in the remarkably pervasive if sometimes unobtrusive stimuli that seem to have influenced practically every sector of the industrial economy in the 1740s.'[5]

In agriculture, output was much greater after than before 1750.[6] In fact, there is evidence that the agricultural population *declined* in the first half of the century and rose in the second (although industrial areas grew even faster). Taking corn as representative, agricultural *productivity* rose by 25 per cent in the century, all achieved *prior* to 1750.

During the whole period ending about 1745, the rate of growth of total output averaged less than 0.3 per cent annually (2.6 per cent per decade). But after 1745 the rate rose to about 1 per cent until 1765, or 10 per cent per decade. Thereafter there appears a slackening of the annual rate (until 1785), although at 0.7 per cent it was still double that prior to 1745. In the 1780s there occurred a further advance until at the close of the century the growth rate reached an annual average of 1.8 per cent.[7]

---

3 Note particularly the use of the Newcomen engine in Cornish tin mines in the 1740s.

4 Deane and Cole, *British Economic Growth*, 57.

5 *Ibid.*, 158.   6 *Ibid.*, 75.   7 *Ibid.*, 79–80.

PRIMARY WORKS

[Anon]. *Considerations on the East-India Trade* (1701). In J.R. McCulloch, ed. *Early English Tracts on Commerce* 1856; Cambridge, 1952, 541–629

Barton, John. *Observations on the Circumstances which Influence the Condition of the Labouring Classes of Society.* London, 1817. In G. Sotiroff, ed. *Economic Writings of John Barton*, I. Regina, 1962, 25–112

Baudeau, Nicolas. 'Explication sur le vrai sens du mot stérile,' *Ephémérides*, VIII (1767). In E. Daire, ed., *Physiocrates.* Paris, 1846, 868–73

von Böhm-Bawerk, E. *Capital and Interest.* London, 1890

Buchanan, David. *Observations on the Subjects Treated in Dr Smith's ... Wealth of Nations* 1817; New York, 1966

Cantillon, Richard. *Essai sur la Nature du Commerce en Général* (1755), ed. H. Higgs. London, 1931

Cassel, Gustav. *Theory of Social Economy.* New York, 1924

Clark, J.B. *Distribution of Wealth.* New York, 1894

Douglas, Paul M. *The Theory of Wages.* New York, 1934

Edgeworth, F.Y. *Papers Relating to Political Economy*, II. London, 1925

Fortrey, Samuel. *England's Interest and Improvement* (1673). In J.R. McCulloch ed. *Early English Tracts on Commerce* 1856; Cambridge, 1954, 211–49

Hicks, J.R. *The Theory of Wages.* London, 1932

Hume, David. *Letters*, ed. J.Y.T. Greig. Oxford, 1932

– *Writings on Economics.* London, 1955

Hutcheson, Francis. *A Short Introduction to Moral Philosophy* (1747). In *Collected Works*, IV. Hildesheim, 1969

– *A System of Moral Philosophy* (1755). In *Collected Works*, VI. Hildesheim, 1969

Jevons, W.S. *The Theory of Political Economy*, 1st ed. London, 1871;
  4th ed. London, 1911
Keynes, J.M. *The General Theory of Unemployment, Interest and Money.*
  London, 1936
Kuhn, T.S. *The Structure of Scientific Revolutions*, 2nd ed. Chicago, 1970
Lauderdale, James Maitland. *An Inquiry Into the Nature and Origin of
  Public Wealth* 1804; New York, 1962
Lee, Joseph. *A Vindication of a Regulated Enclosure* (1656)
Le Trosne, G.F. *De l'intérêt social* (1777). In E. Daire ed. *Physiocrates.*
  Paris, 1846, 885–1023
Locke, John. *Some Considerations of the Consequences of the Lowering of
  Interest, and raising the Value of Money* 1691; New York, 1968
– *Two Treatises of Government* (1698), ed. P. Laslett, Cambridge, 1967
McCulloch, J.R., ed. *Adam Smith's An Inquiry into the Nature and Causes
  of the Wealth of Nations.* Edinburgh and London, 1863
Malthus, T.R. *Population: The First Essay* 1798; London, 1966
– *The Measure of Value* 1823; New York, 1957
– *Principles of Political Economy*, 2nd ed. 1836; New York, 1964
Mandeville, Bernard. *The Fable of the Bees; or Private Vices, Publick
  Benefits.* 1st ed. 1714; 6th ed., ed. F.B. Kaye 1732; Oxford, 1924
Marshall, Alfred. *Principles of Economics*, 9th (variorum) ed., ed. C.W.
  Guillebaud. London, 1961, 1
Marx, Karl. *Theories of Surplus Value*, Part 1. Moscow, n.d.
– *Capital*, 1, mod. lib. ed. New York, 1906
– *Capital.* Chicago, 1919
Massie, Joseph. *An Essay on the Governing Causes of the Natural Rate of
  Interest* (1750), ed. J. Hollander. Baltimore, 1912
Mill, J.S. *Collected Works*, vols. 11, 111. *Principles of Political Economy*,
  ed. J.M. Robson. Toronto 1965
Mun, T. *England's Treasure by Forraign Trade* 1664; (written c. 1630);
  Oxford, 1959
North, Dudley. *Discourses Upon Trade* (1691). In J.R. McCulloch ed.
  Early English Tracts on Commerce 1856; Cambridge, 1954, 505–40
Oswald, James. *Memorials.* Edinburgh, 1825
Petty, William. *Economic Writings*, ed. C.H. Hull. Cambridge, 1899
Petyt, William [?] *Britannia Languens* (1680). In. J.R. McCulloch ed.
  Early English Tracts on Commerce 1856; Cambridge, 1954, 275–504
Pufendorf, Samuel. *On the Law of Nature and of Nations* (1672). *The
  Classics of International Law*, no. 17, vol. 11. Oxford, 1934
Quesnay, François. *François Quesnay et la Physiocratie*, 11, ed. A. Sauvy.
  Paris, 1958
Ricardo, D. *On the Principles of Political Economy*, vol. 1, *Works and
  Correspondence of David Ricardo*, ed. P. Sraffa. Cambridge, 1951
Robbins, L.C. *An Essay on the Nature and Significance of Economic Science.*
  London, 1935

Schumpeter, J.A. *The Theory of Economic Development*. Cambridge, Mass., 1934
Senior, Nassau. *An Outline of the Science of Political Economy*. London, 1836
Smith, Adam. *The Theory of Moral Sentiments* 1759; New York, 1966
– *Lectures on Rhetoric and Belles Lettres* (1762–3), ed. J.M. Lothian.
– *Lectures on Police, Justice, Revenue and Arms* (1763), ed. E. Cannan. New York, 1964
– 'The History of Astronomy,' *Essays on Philosophical Subjects* (London, 1795). In *Early Writings of Adam Smith*, ed. J. Ralph Lindgren. New York, 1967, 53–108
– *An Inquiry Into the Nature and Causes of the Wealth of Nations*, mod. lib. ed., ed. E. Cannan. New York, 1937
Sraffa, Piero. *Production of Commodities by Means of Commodities: Prelude to a Critique of Economic Theory*. Cambridge, 1963
Steuart, James. *An Inquiry into the Principles of Political Economy* (1767), ed. Andrew S. Skinner. Chicago, 1966
Taussig, F.W. *Wages and Capital* 1896; New York, 1968
Tawney, R.H. *Religion and the Rise of Capitalism*. London, 1926
Tucker, Josiah. *Instructions for Travellers* (1757), *A Selection of Tucker's Economic and Political Writings*, ed. R.L. Schuyler. New York, 1931
– *Four Tracts with Two Sermons on Political and Commercial Subjects*. Gloucester, 1774
Turgot, A.R.J. *Reflections on the Formation and Distribution of Riches* 1766; New York, 1963
– 'Observations sur le mémoire de M. de Saint-Péravy' (1767). In E. Daire and H. Dussard, eds., *Œvres de Turgot*. Paris, 1844, I, 418–33
– 'Observations sur le mémoire de M. Graslin' (1767), *ibid.*, 434–44
Veblen, Thorstein. *The Place of Science in Modern Civilization*. New York, 1919
Walker, Francis A. *The Wages Question*. New York, 1875
Walras, Léon. *Elements of Pure Economics*, 1st ed. 1874; 4th ed. 1926; ed. William Jaffé. London, 1954

SECONDARY WORKS (RELATING TO ADAM SMITH)
Bagehot, Walter. 'Adam Smith and our Modern Economy.' *Economic Studies*, ch. III. London, 1911, 125–75
Barkai, H. 'A Formal Outline of Smithian Growth Model.' *Quarterly Journal of Economics*, LXXXIII, Aug. 1969, 396–414
Bladen, V.W. 'Adam Smith on Value.' In H.A. Innis, ed. *Essays in Political Economy in Honor of E.J. Urwick* Toronto, 1938, 27–43
– 'Adam Smith on Productive and Unproductive Labour.' *Canadian Journal of Economics and Political Science*, XXVI, No. 1960, 625–30
Cannan, E. 'Introduction' to *Lectures on Justice, Police, Revenue and Arms* 1896; New York, 1964

– 'Introduction' to *An Inquiry Into the Nature and Causes of Wealth of Nations*, mod. lib. ed. New York, 1937

Coats, A.W. 'Adam Smith: the Modern Re-appraisal.' *Renaissance and Modern Studies*, VI, Nottingham, 1962, 25–48

Cole, Arthur H. 'Puzzles of the *Wealth of Nations.' Canadian Journal of Economics and Political Science*, XXIV, Feb. 1958, 1–8

Douglas, Paul H. 'Adam Smith's Theory of Value and Distribution.' In J.M. Clark *el al., Adam Smith, 1776–1926*. Chicago, 1928, 77–115

Eagly, Robert V. 'Adam Smith and the Specie-Flow Mechanism.' *Scottish Journal of Political Economy*, XVII, 1970, 61–8

Ginzberg, Eli. *The House of Adam Smith*. New York, 1934

Goetz-Girey, M.R. 'Reflexions sur La Théorie du Capital d'Adam Smith.' *Revue d'Histoire Economique et Sociale*, XXIII, 1936–7, 311–32

Groenewegen, P.D. 'Turgot and Adam Smith.' *Scottish Journal of Political Economy*, XVI, Nov. 1969, 271–87

Hamoury, Ronald. 'Adam Smith, Adam Ferguson and the Division of Labour.' *Economica*, XXXV, Aug. 1968, 249–59

Hollander, S. 'Some Technological Relationships in the *Wealth of Nations* and Ricardo's *Principles.' Canadian Journal of Economics and Political Science*, XXXII, May 1966, 184–201

Knight, Frank H. 'The Ricardian Theory of Production and Distribution.' *Canadian Journal of Economics and Political Science*, I, 1935. In F.H. Knight, *On the History and Method of Economics*. Chicago, 1956, 171–96

Koebner, R. 'Adam Smith and the Industrial Revolution.' *Economic History Review*, XI, 1959, 381–91

Letiche, J.M. 'Adam Smith and David Ricardo on Economic Growth.' In B.F. Hoselitz, ed. *Theories of Economic Growth*. New York, 1960, 65–88.

Macfie, A.L. *The Individual in Society: Papers on Adam Smith*. London, 1967

Meek, R.L. 'Adam Smith and the Classical Theory of Profit.' *Scottish Journal of Political Economy*, I, June 1954, 138–53. In *Economics and Ideology and Other Essays*. London, 1967, 18–33.

Morrow, Glen R. *Ethical and Economic Theories of Adam Smith*. 1923; New York, 1969

– 'Adam Smith: Moralist and Philosopher.' In J.M. Clark, *et al., Adam Smith 1776–1926*. Chicago, 1928, 156–79

Petrella, Frank. 'Adam Smith's Rejection of Hume's Price-Specie-Flow Mechanism: A Minor Mystery Resolved.' *Southern Economic Journal*, XXXIV, Jan. 1968, 365–74

Robertson, H.M., and W.L. Taylor. 'Adam Smith's Approach to the Theory of Value.' *Economic Journal*, LXVII, June 1957, 181–98

Rosenberg, Nathan. 'Some Institutional Aspects of the *Wealth of Nations.' Journal of Political Economy*, LXVIII, Dec. 1960, 557–70

– 'Adam Smith on the Division of Labour: Two Views or One?' *Economica*, XXXII, May 1965, 127–39

– 'Adam Smith, Consumer Tastes, and Economic Growth.' *Journal of Political Economy*, LXXVI, May/June 1968, 361–74

Rosenbluth, G. 'A Note on Labour, Wages, and Rent in Smith's Theory of Value.' *Canadian Journal of Economics*, II, May 1969, 308–14

Scott, W.R. *Adam Smith as Student and Professor*. Glasgow, 1937

Simpson, David. 'Further Technological Relationships in *The Wealth of Nations*, and in Ricardo's *Principles*.' *Canadian Journal of Economics and Political Science*, XXXIII, Nov: 1967, 585–90

Skinner, Andrew. 'Introduction,' *Wealth of Nations*. Penguin Books, 1970, 11–97

Spengler, J.J. 'Adam Smith's Theory of Economic Growth.' *Southern Economic Journal*, XXV–XXVI, April/July 1959, 397–415, 1–12

Thomson, Herbert F. 'Adam Smith's Philosophy of Science,' *Quarterly Journal of Economics*, LXXIX, May 1965, 212–33

Thweatt, W.O. 'A Diagrammatic Presentation of Adam Smith's Growth Model.' *Social Research*, XXV, 1957, 227–30

Viner, Jacob. 'Adam Smith and Laissez Faire.' In J.M. Clark *et al.*, *Adam Smith 1776–1926*. Chicago, 1928, 116–55

– *Guide to John Rae's Life of Adam Smith*. New York, 1965

– 'Adam Smith.' *International Encyclopedia of the Social Sciences*, 14, 1968, 322–9

West, E.G. 'Adam Smith's Two Views of the Division of Labour.' *Economica*, XXXI, Feb. 1964, 23–32

SECONDARY WORKS (GENERAL)

Allen, William R. 'The Position of Mercantilism and the Early Development of International Trade Theory.' In R.V. Eagly ed. *Events, Ideology and Economic Theory*. Detroit, 1968, 65–81

– 'Modern Defenders of Mercantilist Theory.' *History of Political Economy*, II, Fall 1970, 381–97

Arkin, Marcus. 'A Neglected Forerunner of Adam Smith.' *South African Journal of Economics*, XXIII, 1955, 299–314

Arrow, Kenneth J. and Gerard Debreu. 'Existence of Equilibrium for a Competitive Economy.' *Econometrica*, XXII, July 1954, 265–90

Barber, William J. *A History of Economic Thought*. London, 1967

Blaug, Mark. *Economic Theory in Retrospect*, 2nd ed. Homewood, 1968

Bloomfield, Arthur I. 'The Foreign-Trade Doctrines of the Physiocrats.' *American Economic Review*, XXVIII, Dec. 1938, 716–35. In J.J. Spengler and W.R. Allen, *Essays in Economic Thought*. Chicago, 1960, 215–33

Bonar, James. *Philosophy and Political Economy*, 3rd ed. 1922; London, 1967

Boulding, K. 'Equilibrium and Wealth.' *Canadian Journal of Economics and Political Science*, V, Feb. 1939, 1–18

Bowley, Marian. *Nassau Senior and Classical Economics*. London, 1937

– 'Some Seventeenth-Century Contributions to the Theory of Value.' *Economica*, XXX, May 1963, 122–39

Brown E.H. Phelps. 'The Marginal Efficacy of a Productive Factor – First Report of the *Econometrica* Committee on Source Materials for Quantitative Production Studies.' *Econometrica*, IV, 1936, 123–37

Buchanan, Daniel H. 'The Historical Approach to Rent and Price Theory.' *Economica*, IX, June 1929. In W. Fellner and B.F. Haley, eds., *Readings in the Theory of Income Distribution*. Philadelphia, 1951, 599–637

Buckle, H.T. *History of Civilization in England.* (New York, 1885)

Cannan, E. *A Review of Economic Theory*, 2nd ed. London, 1964

– *A History of the Theories of Production and Distribution from 1776 to 1848*, 3rd ed. London, 1917; New York, 1967

Chalk, Alfred F. 'Relativist and Absolutist Approaches to the History of Economic Theory.' *Southwestern Social Science Quarterly*, 48, June 1967, 5–12

Coats, A.W. 'Is there a "Structure of Scientific Revolutions" in Economics?' *Kyklos*, XXII, 1969, 289–96

Dempsey, Bernard. *Interest and Usury.* Washington, 1943

Dorfman, Joseph. *The Economic Mind in American Civilization*, I. 1946; New York, 1966

Eagly, R.V. 'A Physiocratic Model of Dynamic Equilibrium.' *Journal of Political Economy*, LXXVII, Jan./Feb. 1969, 66–84

Eckaus, Richard S. 'The Factor Proportions Problem in Underdeveloped Areas.' *American Economic Review*, Sept. 1955, 539–95

Faure, J.F. Soulet. *Economie Politique et Progrès au Siècle des Lumières.* Paris, 1964

Fei, John C.H. and Gustav Ranis. 'Economic Development in Historical Perspective.' *American Economic Review* (Papers and Proceedings), LIX, May 1969, 386–400

Fukuoka, Masao. 'Full Employment and Constant Coefficients of Production.' *Quarterly Journal of Economics*, LXIX, Feb. 1955, 23–44

Furniss, Edgar S. *The Position of the Labourer in a System of Nationalism.* 1920; New York, 1965

Gordon, D.F. 'What was the Labour Theory of Value?' *American Economic Review*, LXIX, May 1959, 462–72

– 'The Role of the History of Economic Thought in the Understanding of Modern Economic Theory.' *Ibid.*, LV, May 1965, 119–27

Gourvitch, Alexander. *Survey of Economic Theory on Technological Change and Employment* 1940; New York, 1966

Grampp, W.D. 'The Liberal Elements in English Mercantilism.' *Quarterly Journal of Economics*, LXVI, Nov. 1952, 465–501

– 'On the History of Thought and Policy.' *American Economic Review*, May 1965, 128–35

– *Economic Liberalism*, I. New York, 1965

Gregory, T.E. 'The Economics of Employment in England, 1660–1713.' *Economica*, I, 1921–2, 37–51

Hicks, John. *Capital and Growth.* Oxford, 1965

Higgs, Henry. 'Life and Work of Richard Cantillon.' In Richard Cantillon, *Essai sur la Nature du Commerce en Général*, ed. H. Higgs. London, 1931, 361–89

Hollander, S. 'Technology and Aggregate Demand in J.S. Mill's Economic System.' *Canadian Journal of Economics and Political Science*, xxx, May 1964, 175–84

– 'On the Interpretation of the Just Price.' *Kyklos*, xviii, 1965, 615–34

– 'The Role of the State in Vocational Training: the Classical Economist's View.' *Southern Economic Journal*, xxxiv, April 1968, 513–25

Hoselitz, B.F. 'The Early History of Entrepreneurial Theory.' *Explorations in Entrepreneurial History*, iii, 1951. In J.J. Spengler and W.R. Allen, *Essays in Economic Thought*. Chicago, 1960, 234–57

Jevons, W.S. 'Richard Cantillon and the Nationality of Political Economy.' *Contemporary Review*, Jan. 1881. Reprinted in W.S. Jevons, *Principles of Economics*, London, 1905, and in R. Cantillon, *Essai sur la Nature du Commerce en General*, ed. H. Higgs, London, 1931, 333–60

Johnson, E.A.J. *Predecessors of Adam Smith*. New York, 1937

Kauder, E. 'Genesis of the Marginal Utility Theory from Aristotle to the End of the Eighteenth Century.' *Economic Journal*, lxiii, Sept. 1953, 638–50

Koolman, G. 'Say's Conception of the Role of the Entrepreneur.' *Economica*, xxxviii, Aug 1971, 269–86

Landry, A. 'Les Idées de Quesnay sur la Population.' In A. Sauvy, ed., *François Quesnay et la Physiocratie*. Paris, 1958, i, 11–49

Letiche, J.M. 'Isaac Gervaise on the International Mechanism of Adjustment.' *Journal of Political Economy*, lx, Feb. 1952, 34–43

Letwin, William. *The Origins of Scientific Economics*. London, 1963

Lewis, W.A. 'Economic Development with Unlimited Supplies of Labour.' *The Manchester School of Economic and Social Studies*, xxii, May 1954, 139–91

Low, J.M. 'An Eighteenth Century Controversy in the Theory of Economic Progress.' *Ibid.*, xx, Sept. 1952, 311–30

– 'The Rate of Interest: British Opinion in the Eighteenth Century.' *Ibid.*, xxii, May 1954, 115–38

Lowe, A. 'The Classical Theory of Economic Growth.' *Social Research*, xxi, 1954, 127–58

Machlup, Fritz. 'On the Meaning of the Marginal Product' (1936). In *Readings in the Theory of Income Distribution*. Philadelphia, 1951, 158–74

– 'Marginal Analysis and Empirical Research.' *American Economic Review*, xxxvi, Sept. 1946, 519–54

McNulty, Paul J. 'A Note on the History of Perfect Competition.' *Journal of Political Economy*, lxxv, Aug. 1967, 395–9

Meek, R.L., 'Economics and Ideology.' *Scottish Journal of Political Economy*, iv, 1957, 1-17. In R.L. Meek, *Economics and Ideology and Other Essays*. London, 1967, 196–224

– *The Economics of Physiocracy*. London, 1962

– 'Ideas, Events and Environment: the Case of the French Physiocrats.' In
R.V. Eagly, ed., *Events, Ideology and Economic Theory*. Detroit, 1968,
44–58

Mitchell, W.C. *Types of Economic Theory*, vol. I. New York, 1967

Myint, Hla. *Theories of Welfare Economics*. London, 1948

– 'The "Classical Theory" of International Trade and the Underdeveloped
Countries.' *Economic Journal*, LXVIII, June 1958, 317–37

Myrdal, Gunnar. *The Political Element in the Development of Economic
Theory*. London, 1953

Nabers, Lawrence. 'The Positive and Genetic Approaches.' In S.R. Krupp,
ed., *The Structure of Economic Science*. Englewood Cliffs, 1966, 68–84

Neisser, Hans. ' "Permanent" Technological Unemployment.' *American
Economic Review*, XXXII, March 1942, 50–71

Pauling, N.G. 'The Employment Poblem in Pre-Classical English Economic
Thought.' *Economic Record*, XXVII, June 1951, 52–65

Reder, M.W. 'A Reconsideration of the Marginal Productivity Theory.'
Journal of Political Economy, LV, Oct. 1947, 450–8

Robbins, L.C. 'On a Certain Ambiguity in the Conception of Stationary
Equilibrium.' *Economic Journal*, XL, June 1930, 194–214

– *Robert Torrens and the Evolution of Classical Economics*. London, 1958

– *The Theory of Economic Policy in English Classical Political Economy*.
London, 1961

– *The Theory of Economic Development in the History of Economic
Thought*. London, 1968

Robertson, D. 'Wage Grumbles' (1931). In *Readings in the Theory of Income
Distribution*. Philadelphia, 1951, 221–36

Robinson, Joan. 'Prelude to a Critique of Economic Theory.' *Oxford
Economic Papers*, Feb. 1961, XIII, 53–8

– *Economic Philosophy*. London, 1962

de Roover, Raymond. 'J.A. Schumpeter and Scholastic Economics.' *Kyklos*,
X, 157, 115–46

– 'The Concept of the Just Price: Theory and Economic Policy.' *Journal
of Economic History*, XVIII, Dec. 1958, 418–34

– 'La Doctrine Scholastic en Matière de Monopole et son Application à la
Politique Economique des Communes Italiennes.' In *Studi in Onore di
Amintore Fanfani*. Milan, 1962, vol. I, 149–80

Rotwein, Eugene. 'Introduction,' *David Hume: Writings on Economics*.
London, 1955, ix-cxi

Samuels, Warren J. *The Classical Theory of Economic Policy*. Cleveland, 1966

Samuelson, P.A. 'Economic Theory and Wages.' In D. McCord Wright, ed.,
The Impact of the Labor Union. 1951; New York, 1966, 312–42

– 'Paradoxes in Capital Theory.' *Quarterly Journal of Economics*, LXXX,
Nov. 1966, 568–83

Schumpeter, J.A. *Economic Doctrine and Method*. 1912; London, 1954

– *History of Economic Analysis*. New York, 1954

Sen, S.R. *The Economics of Sir James Steuart*. London, 1937

Smith, Victor E. 'The Classicists' Use of Demand.' *Journal of Political Economy*, LIX, June 1951, 242–57

Spengler, J.J. 'The Problem of Order in Economic Affairs.' *Southern Economic Journal*, XV, July 1948, 1–29

– 'Richard Cantillon, first of the Moderns.' *Journal of Political Economy*, LXII, Aug.-Oct. 1954, 281–94, 406–24. In J.J. Spengler and W.R. Allen, eds., *Essays in Economic Thought*. Chicago, 1960, 105–40

– 'Quesnay: Philosophe, Empiriste, Economiste.' In A. Sauvy, ed. *Francois Quesnay et la Physiocratie*. Paris, 1958, I, 55–74

– 'Mercantilist and Physiocratic Growth Theory.' In. B.F. Hoselitz, ed., *Theories of Economic Growth*. New York, 1960, 113–54

– 'Exogenous and Endogenous Influences in the Formation of post-1870 Economic Thought.' In R.V. Eagly, ed., *Events, Ideology and Economic Theory*. Detroit, 1968, 159–87

Sraffa, P. 'Introduction' to *Principles of Political Economy, The Works and Correspondence of David Ricardo*, I. Cambridge, 1951, xiii–lxii

Stark, Werner. *History of Economics in its Relation to Social Development*. London, 1944

– 'The Classical Situation in Political Economy.' *Kyklos*, XII, 1959, 57–65

Stigler, George J. *Production and Distribution Theories*. New York, 1941

– 'The Classical Economics: An Alternative View.' *Five Lectures on Economic Problems*. London, 1949, 25–36

– 'The Development of Utility Theory.' *Journal of Political Economy*, LVIII, Aug./Oct., 1950. In G.J. Stigler, *Essays in the History of Economics*. Chicago, 1965, 66–155

– 'Perfect Competition, Historically Considered.' *Journal of Political Economy*, LXV, Feb. 1957. In *ibid.*, 234–67

– 'The Influence of Events and Politics on Economic Theory.' *American Economic Review*, L, May 1960. In *ibid.*, 16–30

– 'Does Economics have a Useful Past?' *History of Political Economy*, I, Fall 1969, 217–30

Taylor, Overton H. *A History of Economic Thought*. New York, 1960

Tucker, G.S.L. *Progress and Profit in British Economic Thought 1650–1850*. Cambridge, 1960

Vickers, Douglas. *Studies in the Theory of Money*. London, 1960

Viner, Jacob. *Studies in the Theory of International Trade*. New York, 1937

– 'Introduction to Bernard Mandeville, *A Letter to Dion* (1732).' In J. Viner, *The Long View and the Short*. Glencoe, 1958, 332–42

– 'Bentham and J.S. Mill: the Utilitarian Background.' *American Economic Review*, XXXIX, March 1949. In *ibid.*, 306–31

– 'On the Intellectual History of Laissez-Faire.' *Journal of Law and Economics*, III, Oct. 1960, 45–69

– 'The Economist in History.' *American Economic Review* (Papers and Proceedings), LIII, May 1963, 1–22

– 'Man's Economic Status.' In James L. Clifford, ed., *Man Versus Society in 18th Century Britain*. Cambridge, 1968, 22–53

Ware, Norman J. 'The Physiocrats: A Study in Economic Rationalization.' *American Economic Review*, XXI, Dec. 1931, 607–19

Williams, John H. 'The Theory of International Trade Reconsidered.' *Economic Journel*, XXXIX, 1929. In *Readings in the Theory of International Trade*. Philadelphia, 1949, 253–71

Winch, Donald. *Classical Political Economy and Colonies*. London, 1965

REFERENCES TO WORKS IN ECONOMIC HISTORY

Ashton, T.S. *Economic Fluctuations in England, 1700–1800*. Oxford, 1959

– 'Some Statistics of the Industrial Revolution.' In *Essays in Economic History*, III, ed. E.M. Carus-Wilson. London, 1962, 237–51

– *Iron and Steel in the Industrial Revolution*, 3rd ed. Manchester, 1963

– *The Industrial Revolution, 1760–1830*. London, 1966

– *An Economic History of England: The 18th Century*. London, 1966

Beales, H.L. *The Industrial Revolution*. London, 1967

Brandenburg, S.J. 'The Place of Agriculture in British National Economy Prior to Adam Smith.' *Journal of Political Economy*, XXXIX, June 1931, 281–320

Campbell, R.H. *Carron Company*. Edinburgh, 1961

Checkland, S.G. 'Scottish Economic History: Recent Work.' *Economica*, XXXI, Aug. 1964, 296–313

Coats, A.W. 'Changing Attitudes to Labour in the Mid-Eighteenth Century.' *Economic History Review*, XI, 1958, 35–51

– 'Economic Thought and Poor Law Policy in the Eighteenth Century.' *Ibid.*, XIII, 1960, 39–51

Coleman, D.C. 'Labour in the English Economy of the Seventeenth Century.' In E.M. Carus-Wilson, ed., *Essays in Economic History*, II. London, 1962, 291–308

– ed. *Revisions in Mercantilism*. London, 1969

Court, W.H.B. *A Concise Economic History of Britain*. Cambridge, 1958

Davis, R. 'The Rise of Protection in England, 1689–1786.' *Economic History Review*, XIX, 1966, 306–17

Deane, Phyllis. 'Implications of Early National Income Estimates for the Measurement of Long-Term Economic Growth in the UK' *Economic Development and Cultural Change*, IV, 1955

– *The First Industrial Revolution*. Cambridge, 1967

Deane, Phyllis and W.A. Cole. *British Economic Growth, 1688–1959, Trends and Structure*, 2nd ed. Cambridge, 1967

Habakkuk, H.J. *American and British Technology in the Nineteenth Century*. Cambridge, 1967

Heckscher, Eli F. *Mercantilism*, 2nd ed. London, 1955

Hobsbawm, E.J. 'The Machine Breakers.' In *Labouring Men: Studies in the History of Labour*. London, 1965, 5–22

John, A.H. 'The Course of Agricultural Change 1660–1760.' In L.S. Pressnell, ed., *Studies in the Industrial Revolution*. London, 1960, 125–55
– 'Aspects of English Economic Growth in the First Half of the Eighteenth Century.' *Economica*, XXVIII, 1965. Reprinted in E.M. Carus-Wilson, ed. *Essays in Economic History*. London, 1962, II, 360–73
– 'Agricultural Productivity and Economic Growth in England, 1700–1760.' *Journal of Economic History*, XXV, 1965. In E.L. Jones, ed. *Agriculture and Economic Growth in England 1650–1815*. London, 1967, 19–34
Jones, E.L. 'Agriculture and Economic Growth in England 1660–1750: Agricultural Change.' *Journal of Economic History*, XXV, 1965, 1–18. In *ibid.*, 152–71
– 'Editor's Introduction.' *Agriculture and Economic Growth in England 1650–1815*. London, 1967, 1–48
Kerridge, Eric. *The Agricultural Revolution*. London, 1967
Lipson, E. *The Economic History of England*. London, 1947
Lord, John. *Capital and Steam Power, 1750–1800*, 2nd ed. London, 1966
Mantoux, P. *The Industrial Revolution in the Eighteenth Century*. London, 1961
Mathias, P. *The First Industrial Nation*. London, 1969
Mingay, G.E. 'The Agricultural Depression, 1730–50.' *Economic History Review*, VIII, 1956. Reprinted in E.M. Carus-Wilson, ed. *Essays in Economic History*, II, London, 1962, 309–26
Musson, A.E. and Eric Robinson. *Science and Technology in the Industrial Revolution*. Toronto, 1969
Pollard, Sidney. 'Fixed Capital in Britain.' *Journal of Economic History*, XXIV, Sept. 1964, 299–314
Poynter, J.R. *Society and Pauperism: English Ideas on Poor Relief, 1795–1834*. London, 1969
Redford, A. *Economic History of England 1760–1860*, 2nd ed. London, 1960
Wilson, Charles. 'Mercantilism: Some Vicissitudes of an Idea.' *Economic History Review*, X, 1957, 181–8
– *England's Apprenticeship 1603–1763*. London, 1965

INDEX

Absolute costs *see* international trade
Accumulation *see* capital
Advances *see* capital
Agriculture: cost conditions in 141–2; data on 95–8, 109; and growth process 68, 98–9, 288–92; and investment priorities 280–1, 286–8; and land utilization 292–3; Steuart on 68; technical progress in 102, 227–36. *See also* land, landowners, Physiocracy, rent
Allen, W.R. 12n, 33n
ALLOCATION
and factor endowments 278, 281, 283–5, 287
and international trade 270, 283–5
and investment priorities, 277–8, 280–8, 302, 314
via price mechanism 114–24, 139–40, 140–1, 171–2, 173n; Cantillon on 41–2; Lee on 36–7; and Mercantilism 33–5, 58–9; North on 36; and Physiocracy 44–7, 48–50; and scholastic economics 28, 31; Steuart on 42–3
and risk 280–1, 298
Smith's contribution summarized 307–8
See also exchange value, investment priorities
Apprenticeship laws 242, 259, 261
Aquinas, St Thomas 27–8, 135
Aristotle 29, 135
Arkin. M. 61n. 77n

Arkwright, R. 220, 240, 241
Arrow, K.J. 10n
Ashton, T.S. 101n, 104n, 107n, 108n, 109n, 112n, 209n, 214n, 220n, 221n, 226n, 238n, 240n, 261n, 282n

Banks: contemporary failures of 216n; and long-term finance 98, 108, 215–16
Barber, W.J. 204n
Barbon, N. 56, 72, 76–7, 34n, 35n
Barkai, H. 155n
Barton, J. 181n
Baudeau, N. 82, 84–5, 81n, 91n
Beales, H.L. 103n, 104n, 112n
Bentham, J. 257n
Birmingham 67n, 100n, 105, 210, 216, 238, 241, 259, 260n
Black, J. 214n
Bladen, V.W. 147n, 159–60n
Blaug, M. 114n, 117n, 120n, 222n
Bloomfield, A.I. 49n
Böhm-Bawerk, E. von 95n
Bonar, J. 249n
Boswell, J. 105n
Boulding, K. 156n
Boulton, M. 105n, 217n
Bowley, M. 20, 31n, 33n, 34n, 155n, 169n, 200n
Buchanan, D.H. 171, 172–3n
Buckle, H.T. 249n
Burke. E. 255n

Campbell, R.H. 109n, 216n, 217n

Cannan, E. 6n, 33n, 38n, 144, 186n, 188n, 193, 195–6n, 197n, 202n, 248n, 269n, 300n, 316–18

Cantillon, R. and allocation *via* price mechanism 38–9, 41–2; and 'balance of labour' 56; on cost price 40, 135; on demand for labour 70; on landlords' spending patterns 70n; his method 39, 41n, 61n, 116; and operation of labour market 69–70; and Physiocracy 44n; on population mechanism 70; and population size 316; on profit 40–1, 72, 317–18; on rate of interest 72; on specie distribution 76; on trade criteria 289n; on wage structure 132n

CAPITAL

accumulation of: data on 112n; and demand for labour 157; role of money in 205–7

as advances 66, 79, 80–1, 116, 151, 152, 316

circulating: analysis of 200–1; as constraint on employment 65, 193, 199n, 225–6; defined 155; in manufacturing 106, 111; materials as 153–4, 218; Steuart on 65

demand for services of 150–6

fixed: in agriculture 98, 112; and capitalist organisation 112n; defined 154–5; depreciation of 145–6, 154, 202–4; destruction of 107n; functions of 154–5, 223; maintenance of 193n; in manufacturing 106–7, 111; in mining and metallurgy 67n, 108, 112; and money 145, 155n; and scale 142n; significance of 239; in silk industry 104, 107n, 111, 237; at Soho works 105n

human 130–1

productivity of 150–6, 170–1

and savings process 188–91

structure 153, 157, 159, 191, 193–4, 196–7, 198; and employment capacity 193–9

supply conditions 167–71

turnover rates of 197–8, 199
See also interest

Capitalistic organization 112n, 122, 150–1, 152; and profit-rate structure 133

Carmichael, G. 134

Carron Company 105, 109, 209, 216n, 217n, 226, 237n, 239, 261n

Cary, J. 60n, 66

Cassel, G. 10n

Chalk, A.F. 17n

Checkland, S.G. 272n

Child, Sir J. 35n, 62n

Clark, J.B. 7

Classical economics 171–4, 314–15, 317–18. *See also* Hume, McCulloch, Malthus, Marx, Mill, J., Mill, J.S., Ricardo, Senior

Coal: consumer choice of 139; industry development 108–9, 112; industry location 109–10; in iron-making 109–10, 218; price determination 166n

Coats, A.W. 13n, 64n, 65, 66n, 95n, 245n

Cole, A.H. 311n

Cole, A.W. and Deane, P. 97n, 98n, 101n, 110n, 111n, 112n, 147n, 161n, 218n, 220n, 222n, 233n, 245n

Coleman, D.C. 58n, 59n

Colonies: industrial development of 281–3; industrial regulation of 282; manufacturing in 99; physiocratic approach to 87–8; and profit rate 184; trade policy regarding 265, 270–3, 295–6n

Comparative costs *see* international trade

Competition: conditions for 125–7; nature of 126, 143; and price determination 119; and profit rate 182–3

Condillac, L'abbé de 81n

Considerations on East-India Trade 61, 67, 77, 240–1

CONSUMPTION

of durables 190

and working-class budget 177

of luxuries 249, 254, 255–6, 267, 311; defined 162n; Hume on 64n; Mandeville on 249; North on 71; in mercantilist literature 57–8

substitution in 109n, 138–9, 218
See also demand

Copyright protection 217

Corn: dealers 139–40; export subsidy 165n, 178; labour productivity in production of 171n; land and rent 171; as measure of value 176n, 177n; price data 175n, 176n, 233n; price

determination 45–6, 171–6; prices and money wages 163, 175n, 176–8; quantitative significance of 98n; trade policy 48–50, 126, 254–5n, 256–7
Corn model of growth 18–19, 113, 191–2, 311–13
Corporation Laws 123n, 259
Cost of living 138
Costs of production *see* value
Court, W.H.B. 104n
Crompton, S. and mule-spinning 220, 238, 240n
Cyclical fluctuations 158–9n, 243

Darby, A. his iron-making process 109, 218, 226, 237
Davenant, C. 35n, 52n, 57, 60n, 61, 62, 77
Deane, P. 104n. *See also* Cole, A.W. and Deane, P.
Debreu, G. 10n
Defence 264, 267
Defoe, D. 57–8, 60, 63n, 65n
Demand 33n, 43n; applied theory of 138–43; elasticity 53n, 115, 118–19, 139; for food 165; for productive factors 149–60; schedule 67, 118, 119; secular expansion of 224, 227, 252; and supply 121. *See also* consumption, exchange value
Demobilisation 98n
Dempsey, B. 29n, 30n
Depreciation *see* capital
Derby 67n
Diminishing returns *see* production function
Distribution: aggregative 118n, 147–8; in mercantilist literature 34; and natural price 117; policy 67, 246–8, 249, 251, 319–20; productivity theory of 170–1; 'pseudo' 144; Ricardian theory of 4–5; in scholastic literature 31; and specialization 67, 254n; and stationary state 171, 184–6, 250–1; as theory of service pricing 3–4, 5, 6, 31, 34; and value 171–9. *See also* profit, rent, wages
Division of Labour *see* specialization
Dorfman, J. 283n
Douglas, P.H. 131, 128n, 133–4, 136n, 148, 151n, 167n
Du Pont de Nemours, P.S. 80n
Duns Scotus 28, 29

Eagly, R.V. 15n, 79n, 206n
Eckaus, R.S. 10n
Economic development: defined 6n; desirability of 246–56; and government intervention 256–8, 308–9; in mercantilist literature 53, 55, 64; and population size 61, 252
Economic growth 246–7, 252, 253; evidence regarding 96–7, 110n; some rates of 324–5; defined 20; in mercantilist literature 59; and net income 204; in physiocratic literature 78–80; and price level 206–7. *See also* corn model, economic development
Economic man *see* profit motive
Economic policy *see* government
Economies of scale *see* scale, production function
Edgeworth, F.Y. 7–8
Edinburgh 253n
Education: and curriculum 263; and charity schools 38, 70n; financing of 262–3; and specialization 215, 266; vocational 262; and wage structure 130–1
Employment *see* labour
Enclosures 231–3
Encyclopédie 105
Entrepreneurship 168, 169, 170
Exchange between town and country 99
Exchange value *see* value, exchange
External economies *see* production function

Factor proportions *see* production function
Faure-Soulet, J.F. 48n
Fei, J.C.H. 96n
Ferguson, A. 58n
Forster, N. 35n
Fortrey, S. 57, 59–60
Franklin, B. 282–3n, 308
Furniss, E.S. 59n, 61n, 63n

Galiani, F. 137n
General equilibrium 3, 6n, 9–10, 13–14, 19–20, 114, 122–4, 306–7
Gervaise, I. 74, 76n, 77, 308
Ginzberg, E. 237n
Glasgow 110n, 237n, 239, 240, 253n, 272n; University of 217, 233n
Goetz-Girey, M.R. 95n
Gordon, D.F. 13n

Gourvitch, A. 223n
Government: and corn trade 254, 254–
5n, 256–7, 311; and defence (and
power) 61n, 264–5, 267, 310; and
economic development 256–8, 308–9,
311; and education 263; extent of
regulation by 313; and income distribution 251, 319; and industrialization 290–2; and investment 257–8;
and labour market 243, 258–64,
294–5, 297, 302–4; and poor relief
243n; and protection 255n, 310–11;
and public works 257; and rate of
interest 257. See also apprenticeship
laws, navigation acts, settlement laws,
taxation
Grampp, W.D. 33n, 237n, 255n
Graslin, M. 51n
Gray, Sir A. 305, 308
Gregory, T.E. 57n, 58n, 61n, 63n
Groenewegen, P.W. 50n, 85n, 118n, 133n

Habakkuk, H.J. 226n
Hales, J. 33n
Hamowy, R. 58n
Hargreaves, J. spinning jenny of 220,
238
Heckscher, E. 34–5, 36n, 258n, 265n
Hicks, J.R. 7n, 9n, 11n, 18, 191n
Higgs, H. 39n
Hobbes, T. 31n
Hobsbawm, E.J. 222n, 223n
Hobson, J.A. 7–8
Hollander, S. 28n, 29n, 196n, 209n,
223n, 260n
Hoselitz, B.F. 79
Howlett, J. 260n
Hume, D. his attitude to labour 64; on
capitalist sector 253n; on Carron
Company 216n; on colonies 265n; on
declining rate of profit 72–3, 183,
315; on distribution 118n, 250n, 319;
on economic growth 77–8, 291; on
interest rate 72–3; on international
specialization 77; on luxury consumption 64n, 311; and method 318; on
national power 264n; on operation of
labour market 44n; on paper money
75n; on protection 76n, 77–8, 309;
on qualitative resource differentials
77, 78, 308; on Smith's cost-price
theory 118n; on specie-flow mechanism

75–6, 205, 206–7; on vocational
training 262; on wage determination
51n
Hutcheson, F. on capital 66, 316; on
declining rate of profit 73n, 183, 315;
on demand 33n; on distribution 250n;
on luxury consumption 58; on price
32–3, 134–5; on real value 130n; and
savings 58, 314

Index numbers 127
Industrialization 290–2. See also investment priorities
Industrial organization (structure) in
domestic and factory units 67, 95n,
103–6, 111, 208–9, 222, 238; and
integration of processes 239–40; and
mercantile economy 112n, 122, 133,
204–5n, 299–300; and structural
change 110–11
Industrial revolution 21–2, 110, 112–13,
222n, 236–41
Innovation see technical change
INTEREST
Cantillon on 40; 'dilemma' of 167; a
disposable surplus 169; and profit
168; Quesnay on 83–4; taxation of
169–70, 301–2, 319
rate of and abstinence 131, 168–9;
Cantillon on 72; control of 257; data
on 221n; Hume on 72; and loanable
funds 73, 168; Locke on 36n, 71; in
mercantilist literature 34, 70–3;
monetary theories of 71; North on 36,
71n, 72; Petty on 71n; Steuart on 44n;
Turgot on 80
See also capital, saving
INTERNATIONAL TRADE
absolute cost theory of 101n
and colonial trade policy 270–3
comparative cost theory of 77, 274n,
284n
and direct foreign investment 300–2
and factor endowment 273–4, 278,
283–5, 314
and market size 268–9
and protection: of corn trade 254,
254–5n, 311; and employment 101–2,
108; Hume on 76n; infant-industry
case for 59, 279–80; retaliatory 257n,
311; for revenue 255n, 310
and specie-flow mechanism 174–6,
205–6, 206–7; Cantillon on 76;

development of 74n; and foreign-exchange rate 34, 75n, 206n; Hume on 75, 206–7
'vent-for-surplus' theory of 268–70, 274–6, 284n, 299n, 314–15
Invention *see* technology
Investment: and demand for loanable-funds 71–2; mercantilist conceptions of 52; Quesnay on financing of 84. *See also* capital, saving
Investment priorities: and agriculture 286–93; between agriculture and manufactures 280–1; and allocation theory 277–8, 280, 287, 302, 314; and declining rate of profit 283n; and industrial development 281–3; and international trade 283–5; and trading sector 293–300

Jaffé, W. 10n
Jevons, W.S. 39n, 137n, 153n
John, A.H. 221n, 235n, 244n
Johnson, E.A.J. 59n
Joint-stock companies 216–17
Jones, E.L. 235n, 244n

Kames, Lord 78n
Kauder, E. 134n
Kay, J. inventor of flying shuttle 220, 221, 238
Kerridge, E. 235n
Keynes, J.M. 64
King, G. 98n
Knight, F.H. 3–4, 5, 12, 14, 20n, 120n, 122, 185n
Koebner, R. 212n, 222n, 237n, 241n
Koolman, G. 170n
Kuhn, T.S. 6n, 11, 12–13, 15

LABOUR
attitude towards 252–4, 267, 319–20; in mid-eighteenth century 64–5; physiocratic 88
deductions from product of 149
demand for 156–60, 176, 180n, 225–6, 243
and distribution of work force 97, 103–4, 224n
disutility of 128–9
employment of: cyclical variations in 158–9n, 243–4; mercantilist approach to 53–7, 64; and policy 270, 273, 278, 309; state of 245; and capital struc-

ture 193–9, 225–6
and government intervention 258–64
measure of value 127–9, 135–6, 176n, 177n
mobility of: and education 263; and wage-rate structure 261–2
monopsony pressure on 185–6, 319–20
productive and unproductive 146–7, 159–60n, 194n, 199n, 253; demographic characteristics of 139; physiocratic conception of 81–2, 90
and self-employment 224n
supply of 160–3, 278; in mercantilist literature 58, 62–3, 251–2
unemployment of 242–4; and Mercantilism 59; and specie-distribution 75–6; and Steuart 72n; technological 223–4; Tucker on 66–7
See also capital, wages
Land: agricultural use of 199; productivity of 149–50; supply conditions 163–7; utilization patterns 171–2, 227, 253. *See also* agriculture, Physiocracy, Quesnay, rent
Landowners: Cantillon on 41n, 70n; commercial 217; 'improving' 164n, 232–4; Quesnay on 84
Lauderdale, Lord 6, 151n, 215n
Law, J. 56n
Lee, J. 36–7
Leisure 247–8
Lessius 30
Letiche, J.M. 74n, 288n
Le Trosne, G.E. 81–2n, 82–3
Letwin, W. 17, 34n, 35n, 36n, 39n, 62n
Lewis, W.A. 147n
Lipson, E. 237n
LOANABLE FUNDS
demand for: Cantillon on 72; Hume on 72; North on 71
supply of: Cantillon on 72; Hume on 72; interest-elasticity of 73; and minimum supply price 168; North on 71
See also capital, interest
Locke, J. 31n, 36n, 67n, 71
Lombe, T. silk-throwing mill of 104n, 237, 240
London Society of Arts 221n
Lord, J. 104n, 105n, 214n, 217n, 218n, 238n
Low, J.M. 71n, 73n, 117n, 205n, 291n
Lowe, A. 18n, 212n, 224n, 253n
Lugo 29–30

McCulloch, J.R. on Smith's analysis of investment priorities 277–8, 294n, 318; on Smith's approach to population size 277–8, 279; on Smith's estimate of population growth 161n

Macfie, A.L. 212n, 250n, 314n

McNulty, P.J. 126n

Machlup, F. 9n, 11n

Malthus, T.R. on desirability of growing population 251n; on Smith's corn measure of value 176n; on Smith's theory of corn-price determination 171, 172n, 173–4; his theory of productive organization 6; on unwholesomeness of towns 266n

Malynes, G. 34n, 55–6, 74n

Manchester 240, 259, 260n

Mandeville, B. on luxury 58, 162n, 249; on profit motive 35n, 37–8; on sumptuary laws 38

Mantoux, P. 103n, 214, 214n, 222n, 223n, 241n

MANUFACTURING
brewing 105n
cost conditions of 142–3
cotton 67n, 100, 110, 240–1; Cromford spinning plant 240; location of 109n; technical change in 220
data on 101, 109–10
'for distant sale' 99, 100
glass-making 105n
and government 106
hardware 100; Boulton's plant 105n; high wages in 105; organization of 104–5; progress of 103, 110–11, 112, 211; technical change in 111
linen 67n, 100, 102; organization of 104; in Scotland 223
location 100
materials requirements in 106
Mun on diversification of 55
organization of 103–6
physiocratic approach to 81
potteries 105n
prices: and costs 177–8; trend of 142–3, 218; factor-price changes and 123, 179–81
silk 100, 101, 102n, 237; and Derby throwing mill 67n; factory organization in 104, 105n; fixed capital in 107
tanned-leather 100
technical progress in 102, 111

technology in 108, 198
textiles: relative decline of 110–11; slow progress of 103, 211
wool 67n, 100; location of 109n, 223; organization of 104; technical change in 220

Marginal analysis see production function

Marshall, A. 7–8, 9

MARX, K.
on capital structure 193–4, 196–7, 198, 205n, 300n
on 'complex system of machinery' 223n
on disposition to save 169
on profit-rate equalization 196n, 319
on Smith: and capital accumulation 189n; and depreciation 146n; and specialization 215n
on unemployment and subsistence wages 186–7

Massie, J. 73n, 183, 315

Materials: and British competitive advantage 103, 111; and materials-output ratio 217–18; prices of 123–4; and quality changes 218

Mathias, P. 107n, 245

Measure of value see corn, labour

Meek, R.L. 16n, 44n, 47n, 79n, 83, 84n, 85, 91n, 112n, 117n, 209n, 318–19

Menger, C. 137n

Mercantilism: and allocative mechanisms 33–7, 58–9; analytical quality of 12n; and attitude to labour 63–4; and economic development 53, 55, 64; and efficiency 86; and employment 55–6, 302–4, 309–10; and foreign-trade surplus 52–3, 55–6, 57, 61–4, 73–4, 79; and Hume 78n; and luxury consumption 57–8; Physiocrats on 48, 79; and population 59–64; and precious metals 52; and productive investment 79; and profit motive 34–7; and savings 70; and wealth 52

Merchant marine 98n

Methodology 11–17, 116, 318; 'absolutist' 4, 6, 12; and Cantillon 39, 41n, 116; and external influences on economics 15–16; and 'progress' in economics 12, 16; and standards of evaluation 15–17; and Steuart 42, 116

Mill, James 123n

MILL, J.S.

on employment capacity 195–6n
on Smith: and agricultural investment
    287n; and international trade 268n,
    314–15; and savings in growth process
    280n; and wage structure 131n,
    132–3n
Mining and metallurgy: fixed capital in
    67n, 108, 112; and colonies 282; and
    iron smelting 105n, 218, 237
Mirabeau, Marquis de 81n, 248n
Mingay, G.E. 233
Misselden, E. 35n
Mitchell, W.C. 215n
Molina 28–9, 135
Money: and fixed capital 145; and
    growth process 205–8; and note issues
    75n, 110n, 205, 206n, 207; and
    Quantity Theory 73–4; and rate of
    interest 71. See also international
    trade
Monopoly price see exchange value
Monopsony 185–6, 319–20
Montesquieu, M. de 67, 75n
Morrow, G.R. 249n
Mun, T. on elasticity of demand 53n;
    on employment 53–5; on foreign
    exchanges 34n; on foreign trade
    policy 35n, 53–5; on Quantity Theory
    74n; on savings 54, 57
Musson, A.E. 240n
Myint, H. 14n, 269n, 270, 274n, 277n
Myrdal, G. 16n

Nabers, L. 17n
National income: accounts 144–7,
    192–3; estimates 97, 109–10, 321–2,
    323; net 145–6, 202–4; per capita
    278–80
Natural price see exchange value
Natural rates of factor returns 117, 120
Natural rights 256, 311, 313
Navigation Acts 264, 265, 271, 276, 294
Neisser, H. 7n, 10n
Newcomen, T. steam engine of 109,
    214, 226n, 237
North, D. as free trader 36, 76n; on
    rate of interest 36, 70–1, 72; on
    sumptuary laws 36; on supply of
    loanable funds 71
North, R. 36n, 60n

Ohlin, B. 284n
Oswald, J. 78n, 117n, 291, 316, 317

Paradox of value see exchange value
Patent protection 217
Paterson, W. 76n
Paul, L. his spinning-by-rollers device
    220, 234
Pauling, N.G. 56, 58n
Petrella, F. 205n
Petty, W. on control of profit motive
    35n; on cost price 135; on economic
    development and population size 61;
    on 'par' between land and labour
    43n; on saving 52n; on subsistence
    wages 63n; on technical progress 61,
    65
Petyt, W. 59, 60, 61, 62
Phelps-Brown, E.H. 9n
Physiocracy: and agriculture as sole
    wealth-creating activity 81; and
    allocation 44–7, 48–50; analytical
    characteristics of 317; and attitude to
    labour 88; and class harmony 148;
    and corn-price determination 45–6;
    and corn trade 46, 48–50, 91–2; and
    consumption 84, 88–90; and effi-
    ciency 86; and fixed capital 81n,
    87n; and government intervention
    48, 86, 90; and net product 82–3, 84,
    91–2; and population size 87; and
    'productive' activity 81–2; and profits
    40, 46–7; Smith's relationship with
    287–8, 316–17; and tableau éco-
    nomique 44, 50, 78–9; and technical
    progress 87. See also Quesnay, Turgot
Pollard, S. 105n, 112n
Population: and corn export subsidy
    165n; estimates of 96n, 160–1, 321–
    2; and food supplies 68–9, 165;
    Hume on 160n; and market size 252,
    267; mercantilist approach to 59–64;
    physiocratic approach to 87; policy
    regarding 250–1, 252–3, 254n, 267,
    277–8, 279, 316; and productive
    sector 161, 254, 309; and subsistence
    wages 185, 187; and working-class
    budget 139, 161, 162–3
Postlethwayte, M. 66
Potter, W. 56
Poynter, J.R. 261n
Price see exchange value
Price level: and specie-flow mechanism,
    174–8; and growth 205–7; and wage-
    rate changes 179–81; and profit-rate
    changes 182n; Ricardo on, 181–2

Price mechanism *see* allocation, exchange value

PRODUCTION FUNCTION
characteristics of 142–3, 306–7
diminishing agricultural returns: at intensive margin 51, 69; at extensive margin 125n, 183–4n, 231
and economies of scale 142–3, 211–12, 219–20
and external economies 219
factor proportions: fixed 8, 122–4, 199n, 226n, 270; between sectors 122
substitution relationships 124, 199n, 218, 238, 306–7
marginal analysis 3–4, 5–6, 7–11, 51, 138
materials coefficient 217–18
and national income 204–5
and similarity of processes in manufacturing 108, 198
and trading sector 299–300
Productive and unproductive labour *see* labour, wages
Profit: and aggregative income shares 148; and cost price 32, 40, 43, 197; as deduction 149, 152n; injustice of 152; motive 34–7, 233, 248–9, 279–80, 307–8, 311; and interest 168; nature of 168, 170; as original income 151, 171; in physiocratic literature 40, 46–7; and productivity of capital goods 155–6; and return to 'inspection and direction' 106; in scholastic analysis 27–8, 29–30; secular trend in rate of 72–3, 179, 182–3, 315; structure of rates of 120–1, 127, 133, 196n, 318; taxation of 169–70; an uncertain income 40; 'upon alienation' 40–1, 42
Protection *see* international trade
Property income 150, 151, 152, 252, 319–20
Psychology: and capitalism 253; and differences in ability 213n, 239; and specialization 215, 266
Pufendorf, S. on price determination 31–2, 134, 135; on prices of services 31n; on profit 32; on real value 130n

Quesnay, F. on agricultural profits 83; on allocation *via* price mechanism 44–5; his attitude to labour 88–9; on capital 79; on capitalistic activity 80; on colonies 88; on finance of investment 84; on foreign trade in corn 46, 91–2; on hoarding 84, 89–90; on intervention in labour market 48; on labour-saving technology 87; on luxury 90–1; on manufacturing earnings 81; on net product 82, 91–2; on population size 87; on price of corn 45–6; on price theory 45–8; on productive activity 81–2; on productive consumption 90; on rent 46–8, 85, 166; on subsistence wages 45n; and *tableau économique* 44

Rae, J. 280n
Ranis, G. 96n
Real value *see* value, real
Redford, A. 11n, 103n, 104n
Rent: and aggregative income shares 147–8; of corn land 171, 179; as cost item 171; as deduction 149; differential 165, 167, 172n; as disposable surplus 169; effect of wage-rate variation on 179–81; estimates of 97n; of food-producing land 164, 179; as 'monopoly' price 163–4; *per* acre 120–1; and physical surplus 164, 172; physiocratic doctrine of 46–8, 84–5, 166; and productivity of land 149, 167; as residual element in price 164, 171, 173–4n; and scarcity of land 167; Smithian and Ricardian theories of, contrasted 166–7; and technical change 167n; and transfer payments 167

RICARDO, D.
on corn prices and money wages 177n
on distribution 3–4, 5–6, 318
his economics as 'detour' 6, 14
on international trade 269
on machinery 226
on net revenue 146
on productive labour 191n
on savings process 191n
on secular trend in manufacturing prices 218n
on rent 164, 167, 171
on Smith: and coal price 166n; and corn price 171, 172n; and declining rate of profit 315; and effects of wage-rate changes 181–2; and international-trade 275; and investment priorities

277, 318; and net national income
204; and price 122n; and rent 166–7
on subsistence wages 186
on wage structure 144n
Risk: compensation for 168; of innova-
tion 170, 216; of invention 233; and
rate of profit 216n, and resource
allocation 280–1, 298; and scholastic
price theory 27
Robbins, Lord 19–20, 20n, 59n, 170n,
184n, 185n, 189n, 249n, 280n, 318
Robertson, D. 7n
Robertson, H.M. 33n, 115, 134
Robinson, E. 240n
Robinson, J. 17n, 121
Roebuck, J. 217n
Roover, R. de 27
Rosenberg, N. 169n, 216n, 288n, 311n
Rosenbluth, G. 159n, 172n, 177n
Rotwein, E. 78n

Saint-Peravy, de 51n
Samuels, W.J. 311n
Samuelson, P.A. 11n, 14, 20n
Savings: and abstinence 131, 168–9;
and disposable surplus 169, 204,
278–80, 308–9, 316; Mercantilism
and 52, 54, 57, 70; process of 188–
91; and psychological disposition
169; Quesnay on 84, 89–90; and rate
of interest 73, 131, 168–9, 258n; and
'Smith-Turgot theorem' 80, 188,
314–15
Say, J.B. 6, 170
Scale: and dispersion of processes 209,
239; and subdivision of labour 104–5,
208–9, 239; and use of fixed capital
142–3n
Scholastic economics 306; and allocation 28, 31; and costs of production
27, 29–31, 135; and just price 27–8,
31; and price theory 27–31; and
profits 27–8, 29–30; and risk 27; and
usury 28n, 70; and utility 29, 135
SCHUMPETER, J.A.
on Barbon 35n
on Cantillon 76n
and 'dilemma' of interest 167
and diminishing returns 51n
his evaluation of Smith 12n, 51n, 305–6
on external influences in economic
thought 16n
on Hales 34n

and innovation 212
on Laical Scholastics 31n
on Mandeville 37n
his methodology 17n
on physiocratic conception of capital
79n
on progress in economics 12n, 16n
on Ricardo's theory of distribution 5–6,
14
on scholastic price theory 27, 30n
on Smith: and circulating capital 200n;
and equalization of factor returns
120n; and interest 169n; and 'paradox of value' 137n; and real value
127n; and rent 167n; and specialization 215n
on specie-flow mechanism 74n
on substitution principle 5–6, 11
on Turgot 51n
Scotland: agricultural organization in
229–30; commercial cattle raising in
227; industrial growth of 110n. See
also Glasgow
Scott, W.R. 117n
Sen, S.R. 42n
Senior, N. on abstinence 169; his hand-
loom weavers report 308n; on materials co-efficient 124n; his theory of
productive organization 6
Settlement laws 64, 243, 245, 259–60
Sheffield 67n, 260n
Shelburne, Lord 105n, 232
Silver 'digression' on 174–5
Simpson, D. 270n
Skinner, A. 42n, 138n
Slavery 211n
SMITH, ADAM
on advances 116, 151–2, 316
on agricultural investment 280–1
his agricultural 'bias' 286–92
on allocation via price mechanism
114–24, 140–1, 171–2, 277–8, 280–8,
302, 307–8, 314
as applied economist 307–8
on banking 98, 108, 215–16
on capitalistic organization 112n, 122,
133, 150–2
and Classical School 171–4, 314–15,
317–18
on colonies 184, 265, 270–3, 281–3,
295–6n
on competition 125–7
his consistency 313–15

SMITH, ADAM (cont.)
and contemporary events 15–16, 21–2, 307–13 *passim*
and contemporary economists 305–17 *passim*
and corn model of growth 113, 191–2, 311–13
on defence (and power) 61n, 264–5, 267, 310
on declining rate of profit 179–87, 315
on demand 115, 118–19, 138–43
on diminishing agricultural returns 125n, 183–4n, 231
and disposable surplus 169, 204, 278–80, 308–9, 316
on economic development 246–58, 308–9
on economic growth 96–7, 205–7, 246–7, 252, 253
on economies of scale 104–5, 142–3, 208–9, 211–12, 219–20, 239
on education 215, 262–3, 266
on employment capacity 193–9, 225–6
on enclosures 231–3
on entrepreneurship 168–70
on equalization of factor returns 114, 116–17, 120–1, 127–8, 130–3, 197n, 261–2, 318
evaluations of 5, 305–6
on factor endowment and international trade 273–4, 278, 283–5, 308, 314
on factor demand 149–60
on factor productivity 148–59, 159–60n, 167
on factor supply 160–71
and formalization of his economics 14, 21, 122, 313
and general-equilibrium paradigm 13–15, 306
and Glasgow 110n, 217, 233n, 253n, 272n
on government regulation 256–66, 308–11, 313
his *History of Astronomy* 213n, 225n
and 'improving' landlords 164n, 232–4
and increasing manufacturing returns 142–3, 218
on industrialization 281–3, 290–2
on industrial organization (structure) 95–113, 208–9, 222, 238–40, 311–12
and industrial revolution 110, 112–13, 222n, 236–41
on interest 168–9, 257

SMITH, ADAM (cont.)
on investment 150–6, 257–8
on investment priorities 277–300, 302, 314
and 'invisible hand' 248
on joint-stock companies 216–17
on labour theory of value 116–17
on land-utilization patterns 171–2, 227, 253, 292–3
his *Lectures on Police, Justice, Revenue and Arms*: on advances 116; on capital accumulation 189; on education 266n; on Hume and 'public opulence' 207n; on industry structure 95–7; on labour supply 163; on law of primogeniture 234n; on market and natural price 114–16, 134–5; on price level and growth 207n; on profit of stock 319n; on specie-flow mechanism 206n; on technological change 212–13n
his *Lectures on Rhetoric and Belles Lettres* 21
on leisure 247–8
on luxury consumption 249, 254–6, 267, 311
on market and natural (cost) price 115–21
and Marx 186–7, 318–19
on materials co-efficient 217–18
and measure of value 127–9, 135–6, 176n, 177n
on mercantile economy 112n, 122, 133, 204–5n, 299–300
and Mercantilism 52, 249, 302–4, 309–10, 314, 316
his method 116, 307–8, 318
on mobility 261–3
on money: and accumulation 205–7; and fixed capital 145–6
on monopoly price 125, 166n
on monopsony 185–6, 319–20
on natural rights 256, 311, 313
on Navigation acts 264, 265, 271, 276, 294
as observer 311–12, 313
on 'paradox of value' 137–8
and Physiocracy 287–8, 316–17
and policy objectives 20–1, 277–80, 307–10
on price level 174–82, 205–7
and problems of interpretation 17–22

SMITH, ADAM (cont.)
on productive and unproductive labour 146–7, 159–60n, 161–2, 199n, 253, 309
on profit motive 233, 248–9, 279–80, 307–8, 311
on property income 150, 151, 152, 251, 319–20
on risk 170, 216, 233, 280–1, 298
and Scotland 110n, 227, 229–31
on silver 174–5
on slavery 211n
and "Smith-Turgot theorem' 188, 314–15
on sources of new technology 210–17, 233
on specie-flow mechanism 174–6, 205–7
on stationary state 171, 184–6, 250–1
on subsistence wages 162n, 174n, 185–7, 309, 319–20
on substitution: in consumption 109n, 138–9, 218; in production 124, 199n, 306–7
his *Theory of Moral Sentiments*: on distribution and economic development 242, 246–9, 250n, 254; on government intervention 256; on poor relief 243n
on value and distribution 117, 171–9, 317
on 'vent-for-surplus' theory 268–70, 274–6, 284n, 299n, 314–15
and *Wealth of Nations* early draft of 117n, 291n
See also capital, corn, distribution, government, international trade, labour, land, manufacturing, national income, population, production function, profit, rent, saving, specialization, taxation, technical change, value, wages
Smith, V.E. 120n
Soho (Birmingham) works 105n, 108n, 111, 217, 238
Specialization: and advances 152; in agriculture 102, 209–10; and dispersion of processes 209, 239; and distribution of income 67, 254n; and education 266; illustrations of 105, 208–9; and innovatory investment 223; and international trade 59, 77,
283; and invention 153; in manufacturing 209; and market size 208–9; and materials 210; Petty on 65n; psychological effects of 215, 266; and scale 105, 208–9, 239; at Soho works 105n; and subdivision of plant labour 104–5, 208–9, 239; Tucker on 66; in watch-making 67–8
See also technical change
Specie-flow mechanism *see* international trade
Spengler, J.J. 14, 15n, 33n, 38n, 39n, 45n, 49n, 56, 70n, 79n, 162n, 169n, 212n, 213n, 239, 253n, 277n
Sraffa, P. 14
Stark, W. 4n, 6n, 95n
Stationary state: distribution in 171, 184–6, 250–1; and monopsony 185–6
Steam engine 109, 214, 217n, 226, 237, 240, 261n
Steuart, J. on agriculture and economic growth 68, 288; on allocation *via* price mechanism 42–3; on 'balance of labour' 57n; on cost price 43, 135; on demand 43n; on diminishing returns 69; on employment capacity 65; on infant-industry case 59, 279; his inter-sectoral analysis 42n; on labour-saving technical change 65; his method 42, 116; on population growth 68–9; on profit 43, 316–17; on rate of interest 71n; on subsistence wages 63, 69; on wage structure 132n; and under-employment assumption 72n
Stigler, G.J. 13n, 15n, 126n, 136, 164n, 308n
Stocks and flows 188n, 192
Subsistence *see* wages
Substitution *see* consumption, production function
Sumptuary laws 36, 38
Supply elasticity 119; schedule 119–20. *See also* exchange value
Supply and Demand *see* exchange value
Surplus: defined 82; disposable 169, 204, 278–80, 308–9, 316; in physiocratic literature 79, 316

Taussig, F.W. 152n, 156n, 199–200n
Tawney, R.H. 36n
Taxation capacity 204n, 279; excise

139, 257; of interest 169–70, 301–2, 319; of profits 180–1n; of rent 169–70; of wage goods 178n, 180; of wages 179–80

Taylor. O.H. 170n

Taylor, W.L. 33n, 115, 134

Technical change: in agriculture 102, 227–36; capital-saving 146, 193n, 202–3, 218, 225–6, 237; demand-induced 224; and foreign-trade balance 66; and innovatory investment 112, 209, 223; and innovatory rewards 170; labour-saving 217–18, 219–20, 220–2, 238; land-saving 214n, 227–9, 238; in manufacturing 102; in mercantilist literature 65–8; in physiocratic literature 87; and raw materials 102–3, 111; risk of 216, 239; and scale 142–3, 211–12, 219–20; in textile industries 221–2. See also specialization

Technology: and invention 211, 233; similarity of in manufacturing processes 108, 261; sources of 210–17

Temple, Sir W. 62–3, 118n

Thweatt, W.O. 18n

Torrens, R. 123n

Towns growth of 266

Trading: and investment priorities 293–300; and production function 299–300

Transportation 103; and market size 252n

Tucker, G.S.L. 169n

Tucker, J. on agricultural technology 236n; on colonies 265n; on cotton industry 240n; on declining rate of profit 73n; on demand 67; on economic growth 78, 291; on factory organization 67; on fixed capital 67; on full employment 245–6n; on infant-industry case 59, 279; on international trade 284n, 308; and Lombe mill 240n; on Settlement acts 245n; on technical change 66–7; on time-consuming nature of advanced technology 66, 316; on unregulated trade 35n

TURGOT

on allocation *via* price mechanism 50–1
on capitalistic activity 80
on disposable surplus and manufacturing profits 85; and rent 85n; and wages 86n
on distribution 118n
on equilibrium 50, 51
on profit-rate structure 50, 133n
on rate of interest 80, 168n
his theorem on savings 80, 314–15
on wealth, 80

Unemployment *see* labour
Unwin, G. 104n
Utility *see* value

VALUE, EXCHANGE

and cost ('natural') price 5, 115, 116n, 117, 120–1, 177–8; Cantillon on 39, 40–1; and corn 171; in physiocratic literature 45–6; Pufendorf on 32; in scholastic literature 27–9, 29–30; Steuart on 42

determination of 115–16, 117–21; and agricultural produce 171–2, 179; and corn 173–6, 179; and manufactures 177–8, 179; and mines and quarries 179n

and distribution 117, 171–9, 317
and labour costs 114, 116–17
labour theory of 116, 128
and monopoly price 125, 163–4, 166n
and 'paradox of value' 33n, 137–8
and secular cost conditions constant 140; decreasing 142–3, 217–18; increasing 141–2
and 'supply and demand' 121
and utility 134, 136–8; Hutcheson on 33n; Pufendorf on 31; in scholastic literature 29, 135
and 'utility and scarcity' 34, 134, 137
See also allocation, demand, profit, rent, supply, wages, investment priorities

Value, real: corn measure of 129n 176n, 177n; defined 127, 128; Hutcheson on 130n; labour measure of 127–9, 135–6, 176n, 177n

Veblen, T. 96n, 170

Vent-for-surplus *see* international trade

Vickers, D. 42n

VINER, J.

on changing attitudes to labour 64n
on charity schools 38n
on classical trade theory 284n

on early free-trade literature 76n, 77n
on government intervention 255n, 257n, 258n
on Mandeville 37n, 38n
on Mercantilism 34–5, 52, 56, 57, 58
on physiocratic doctrine of *laissez-faire* 45n
on profit motive 34–5, 249n
on scholastic economics 31n
on Smith: and international trade 274n; and poor relief 243n; and population size 254n; and specialization 209; and specie-flow mechanism 205n
on specie-flow mechanism 74n, 205n
on Steuart 44n

WAGES
as aggregate income share 148
and economic development 250, 254, 267
and labour productivity 159, 160n
fund 149, 153, 156, 159, 308n; and advance economics 199, 204; Cantillon on 70; and factor proportions 199n; Steuart on 68–9
money: determination of 176–8; and efficiency wages 66n; and food prices 54n, 62n, 63n, 175n, 176–8; and manufacturing cost price 177–8
as net income 145–6, 199, 201–4
of productive and unproductive labour 147

rate of: data on 220n; determination of 157–8; effects of changes in 123, 179–81; and labour-saving technology 219–20; as rationing device 159
structure of 114, 116–17, 120–1, 127, 128, 130–2, 318; Cantillon on 39; and disutility 128–9; and mobility 261–2; Steuart on 44
subsistence 162n, 174n, 186–7, 309, 319–20; Cantillon on 39n; Marx on 186–7; in mercantilist literature 58, 60, 62; and monopsony pressure 185; Mun on 54n, 55; in physiocratic literature 45n; and population 185; Steuart on 44, 63; Turgot on 50–1
Wages fund *see* wages
Walker, F.A. 262n
Walras, L. 6n, 10
Ware, N.J. 49n, 89n
Water-wheel 215n
Watt, J. 105n, 214n, 217n, 226, 237, 240, 261n
West, E.G. 215n
Whatley, G. 35n, 76n
Wicksell, K. 199n
Williams, J.H. 274–5n, 301n
Wilson, C. 97n, 105n, 109n, 221n, 225n, 235n, 241n, 265n
Winch, D. 265n, 315n
Wolverhampton 67n, 259

Young, A. 56, 98n, 101, 108, 110